John Dos Passos

―――

A TWENTIETH CENTURY
ODYSSEY

John Dos Passos

A
TWENTIETH CENTURY
ODYSSEY

Townsend Ludington

CARROLL & GRAF PUBLISHERS, INC.
NEW YORK

Copyright © 1980 by Townsend Ludington

Introduction to the paperback edition copyright © 1998 by Townsend
Ludington

First Carroll & Graf edition 1998

Carroll & Graf Publishers, Inc.
19 West 21st Street
New York, NY 10010

Library of Congress Cataloging-in-Publication Data is available.
ISBN: 0-7867-0527-2

Manufactured in the United States of America

To the memory of CTL and CGCL;

and to JRL and JTP, Jr.

I cannot rest from travel; I will drink
Life to the lees. All times I have enjoy'd
Greatly, have suffered greatly, both with those
That loved me, and alone; . . .
Much have I seen and known,—cities of men
And manners, climates, councils, governments, . . .
ALFRED TENNYSON, "ULYSSES"

The United States themselves are essentially the greatest poem. . . . Here at last is something in the doings of man that corresponds with the broadcast doings of the day and the night. Here is not merely a nation but a teeming nation of nations. Here is action untied from strings necessarily blind to particulars and details magnificently moving in vast masses.

WALT WHITMAN, PREFACE TO THE 1855
EDITION OF *Leaves of Grass*

I say we had best look our times and lands searchingly in the face, like a physician diagnosing some deep disease.

WALT WHITMAN, *Democratic Vistas*

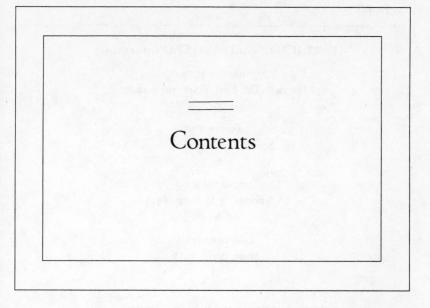

Contents

PART IX: CENTURY'S EBB, 1960–1970

Photographs follow page 110 of text

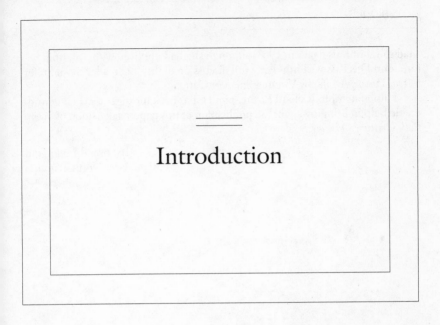

Introduction

Authors welcome the opportunity to revise, clarify, and expand upon their earlier work. I am no exception and appreciate this occasion. But the temptation is to try to do too much: change this infelicitous phrase, correct that assertion, and so forth. *John Dos Passos: A Twentieth Century Odyssey* can stand on its own, needing only a little help now in the form of corrections. It was well received when it was published in 1980, and I am pleased that it is again available to those wishing to acquaint themselves better with a writer who has been, and remains, acknowledged as an important twentieth-century American author.

Dos Passos's most significant works—*Three Soldiers* (1921), *Manhattan Transfer* (1925), and the three volumes which constitute *U.S.A.* (1938), as well as some of his reportage—have proven to be modernist masterpieces which place him high among the writers who came of literary age immediately following World War I. For several reasons, among them that Dos Passos was rarely humorous, some critics have found it hard to accept that he was by intention satirical. Sarcastic, even bitter? Yes, but to those critics simply flat, and nothing is likely to change their opinions. We nevertheless should recognize Dos Passos's repeatedly stated intention to satirize and judge him at least partly on that basis.

When gathering information about Dos Passos's parents and his early childhood, I accepted as fact various family stories as they were passed on to me by relatives, only to discover after *Twentieth Century Odyssey* was published that things had not been quite as I presented them. Dos Passos's father's wife, Mary Dyckman Hays, was not an invalid as I had been told. Lucy Addison Sprigg Madison, Dos Passos's mother, was not a widow as she claimed to be after her affair with his father began. She remained legally married to her first husband, Ryland

Madison, until his death in 1903, although she had not lived with him from before John Dos Passos's birth. For a full discussion of this, the reader should refer to *Dos Passos: A Life,* by Virginia Spencer Carr.

I am grateful to Richard Layman and Charles Schlessiger for their considerable help in bringing about the publication of this paperback edition of *Twentieth Century Odyssey.*

Townsend Ludington
Chapel Hill, North Carolina
November 1997

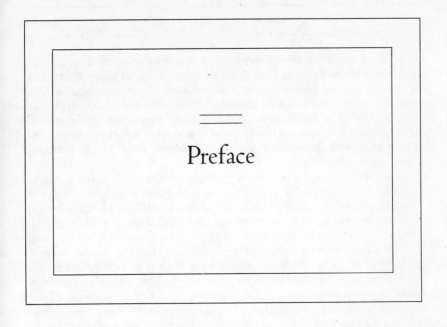

Preface

"I am a writer. I was born in the United States in 1896."

Thus began John Dos Passos as he took stock of himself amid the political swirl of the Cold War and Joseph McCarthy's hunt for Communist subversives. The year was 1953, and his statement was a testament to the patriotism of his close friend, Horsley Gantt. Although Dos Passos's trilogy *U.S.A.* was regarded as a classic of radical literature, the government investigators receiving his statement had no reason to question his own loyalty to America. He had already journeyed far from the political Left.

Dos Passos described his education at Harvard and his involvement in World War I, first as an ambulance driver for the French Army and later as an American soldier. He discussed his interest during the 1920s in the Soviet experiment, an interest which he stated stemmed in large part from "the youthful intellectual's desire for change for the sake of change" as well as the Communists' "humanitarian pretensions." He became, he admitted, one of the chief literary spokesmen for the radical Left in the 1930s, before the traumatic experiences of the Civil War in Spain disillusioned him. "I have paid a certain penalty for my change of attitude," he asserted, outlining his subsequent acceptance of the American system of government. Having embraced the United States, he came in his later years to an absolute certainty about the threat of Communism and the need to nurture a Jeffersonian democracy in his chosen country.

The life of John Dos Passos lends itself more readily than most to the metaphor of the journey. An odyssey both literally and ideologically, it grew out of disparate, sometimes contradictory elements. He was the illegitimate son of a forty-two-year-old Southern gentlewoman and an eminently successful corporate lawyer, a self-made man who was an amalgam of Victorian attitudes. Raised largely abroad, Dos Passos as a child and later as a writer perceived himself to be an outsider, a "man without a country" and a "double foreigner." Yet he was less a social loner than he often cast himself or than he seemed to be to others. He was also less the political activist than his writings made him appear or than many of his readers assumed. An enigma in an often flamboyant era, his very elusiveness makes him an intriguing subject for the biographer.

If he made his Ithaca the United States, he nevertheless took that nation to task. Like one of his heroes, Walt Whitman, Dos Passos thought of America as "essentially the greatest poem." Still, he was rarely uncritical of it; like the Whitman of *Democratic Vistas*, he strove to look his land "searchingly in the face."

Dos Passos spent his life peering out at the world around him and recording what he saw. He traveled, wrote, painted; he witnessed much of the literary life of the first half of the twentieth century and knew many of its principal actors. His novels are important for their innovative expressionistic techniques, but he was more than a literary experimentalist. *U.S.A.* and some of his later works are among the important American political fiction; yet he was not merely a political novelist. And he was more than a *rapporteur:* his chronicle fiction and volumes of reportage add up to a panorama—personal yet wide ranging—of the state of his nation during the twentieth century.

T.L.
Washington, D.C.
May 1980

Special Acknowledgments
and a
Word about the Text

Many people helped with this biography. In a section for acknowledgments following the text, I have tried to mention all those persons to whom I am indebted. Here I should like to express particular appreciation to several persons without whose friendship and aid *John Dos Passos: A Twentieth Century Odyssey* might not have been written.

Elizabeth Dos Passos's courtesy and encouragement have been exceptional. While always ready to help, she permitted me complete freedom. I cannot conceive of a more satisfactory relationship for a biographer to have.

Recollections and insights about the subject are essential to any biographer. I have been privileged to know friends of John Dos Passos whose respect for him and his work made them willing to talk repeatedly with me. I should like here to acknowledge especially Dudley Poore, Horsley Gantt, Rumsey Marvin, C. Dickerman Williams, John Howard Lawson, and Sydney Fairbanks. I am deeply grateful for their friendship.

James T. Patterson, Jr., read and criticized my entire manuscript with a scrutiny that could only come from the closest of friends. The steadfast encouragement of two friends, Charles P. Corn and Jerret Engle, during the vicissitudes of producing a book frequently sustained me, while that of another, Helen Wilson, kept me from straying from the task. I thank them all.

A word about my use of Dos Passos's papers is in order. Where a letter or journal entry has appeared in *The Fourteenth Chronicle: Letters and Diaries of John Dos Passos,* I have cited that as my source. I have, however, in all cases returned to the original documents when quoting from them, so anyone comparing the quotations here with the same ones in *The Fourteenth Chronicle* will note occasional differences in spelling, punctuation, and even wording. An advantage of returning to materials a second time is to be able to correct errors made earlier.

In quoting from Dos Passos's papers, I have corrected misspellings except where such seem of particular interest. I have, however, left the punctuation as he rendered it. Except as in the case of his letters in French to Germaine Lucas-Championnière, I have in quoting included the foreign words and phrases he used and have translated these where it seemed necessary for clarity. Translations of other works are my own.

To give the reader at least some small sense of Dos Passos's artistic eye, each part of the book begins with one of his sketches. Most of these were quickly rendered during his travels. I am indebted to Elizabeth Dos Passos for permission to use them.

T.L.

John Dos Passos

A TWENTIETH CENTURY
ODYSSEY

PART I

═══

A Hotel Childhood,
1896–1912

CHAPTER ONE

Birth and Parentage

In the spring of 1912, the prominent corporation lawyer John Randolph Dos Passos wrote from New York City to his younger cousin Ida L. Pifer, living in Chicago. "I want you," he told her, "if you can secure the time to go & consult the birth register of Chicago—to see if anyone by the name of Dos Passos was dropped there in the month of January 1895–1896–1897—there are not many of us around and I should like to know about the above.

"If you can secure the time," he wrote, but meant to be more insistent, adding, "And let me drive it home by asking you to send me the information at once & before I go to England if I must go." His offhand manner and vague reason for wanting this information hid his true concern. In fact, he wanted to be absolutely certain no one had registered the birth of a Dos Passos during those years, because he was about to take publicly as his stepson the boy whose guardian he had ostensibly been for some years. He found that no record existed of a Dos Passos being born in Chicago during those years because Cook County, Illinois, did not then require all births to be registered.

Thus in 1912 the boy, John Roderigo Madison, took the name of his "guardian," who two years earlier had married the boy's mother, Lucy Addison Sprigg Madison, and the couple could rest more secure, knowing that there was no written record to refute the sham that young John R. Madison was John R. Dos Passos's ward before becoming his stepson.

The boy was, in fact, the illegitimate child of the lawyer and Lucy Madison. He was born on January 14, 1896, in a hotel in Chicago along the shore of Lake Michigan. Lucy, then almost forty-two years old, and John R., fifty-one and nearing the peak of his career, went to Chicago, far from their homes, as inconspicuously as they could, for the occasion. Possibly they registered in their hotel under false names; certainly Lucy was attended by only a few people. John R.'s later worry about the Chicago birth register assuredly stemmed from his fear that Lucy's doctor, despite the parents' desire for secrecy, might have recorded the birth of the child.

The parents were deeply in love; yet they could not marry. John R.'s feelings for Lucy were reflected in a note he wrote Ida Pifer the day after the three of them had met in 1902 in New York. The meeting had been a surprise, but he tried to put the best face on it and told Ida that Lucy now planned to visit her. "You are sure to fall in love with her," he told Ida. "She is gentle, vivacious, full of womanly qualities—and withal a lady—which embraces everything. We have known each other many many years—on my side she has created virtues in me. I have found in her spirit & mind a fountain of good and generous and beautiful sentiments worthy of God's best creation. This is a short note," he added, "but it is meant to contain a great deal." It did; Ida had become a kind of confidante to John R., so while he told her far from everything about his and Lucy's relationship, she understood what lay behind his words.

Lucy was a widow, but John R. had a wife, Mary Dyckman Hays Dos Passos, who was Catholic so religious laws, not to mention conventional mores, militated against divorce. Only in 1910, after the death of his wife, would he and Lucy be able to marry, and not until 1912, after John R. had checked with Ida Pifer, would Jack Madison publicly take the name Dos Passos. In time he would become a major American author, writing about the shock and disillusionment he felt after his experiences in World War I; about the frenetic pace of American life in the twentieth century; and, finally, writing repeatedly about the roots of the American tradition as he struggled to make sense for himself and, he hoped, for his countrymen of their sometimes violent, always complex industrial and technological society.

Lucy's loneliness as she recuperated from the birth of her son in Chicago, far from the East and South she called home, is easy to imagine. Her life could not be what she desired for herself and the baby, at least while Mary Hays Dos Passos lived. Her emotions toward her lover were not shallow, but the stigma of having borne an illegitimate child weighed heavily on her. Although the baby might be said to be the child of her dead husband, this was possible only where she had not been known before. She realized her life was doomed to be remote from familiar surroundings.

Born February 9, 1854, Lucy Sprigg came from a family prominent in Petersburg, Virginia. The Spriggs traced their American ancestry back to Sir Thomas Sprigg, who went to Maryland in 1634 with a land grant from the king of England. Her father, James Cresap Sprigg, was a civil engineer who during the Civil War managed the Confederate railway system in Virginia. The family went through the siege of Petersburg. Their home was destroyed; the children claimed to remember chasing after "mini-balls" which rolled in the streets. They visited wounded soldiers with their mother, and during the worst of the siege they lived for protection in a cave with other women and children. Robert E. Lee was a frequent visitor to their home; Lucy's generation of Spriggs all recalled being swung up on the general's famous white horse, Traveller. After the war the Spriggs moved to Washington. James Sprigg worked on the building of railroads to West Virginia. Before he started, the family took in paying guests to help with expenses, and Lucy, when she was old enough, took a secretarial job with the United States Government.

As a girl, Lucy composed poetry of a conventional sort, such as her poem written in 1869, which began:

> *I dreamt Thee in the shadow,*
> *I saw Thee, in the light,*
> *I heard Thee in the thunder's peal,*
>   *And worshipped in the night.*

Thee was her God. The poem decried being driven from God's presence "by the flaming sword or marriage ring." Despite such adolescent fervor she would marry. She remained religious always, sentimental and dependent. When she met John Randolph Dos Passos in the mid–1880s she was already widowed and living in Washington, D.C., with one son, James, by her first husband R. R. Madison, whom she had married in 1872. A heavy drinker, he had died young, leaving her alone and lonely.

It was easy to fall in love with John R., as her lover liked to be called. He was dapper, assured, and affluent enough to make her life comfortable, while she was attractive, even beautiful. Her sister-in-law was unimpressed and remembered her as "rather conceited and overbearing but witty and gay," someone who "glamorized the men." A niece who knew Lucy and her two sisters, Mary Lamar and Lilly, thought all three impressive. "They carried themselves well," she recalled, "entered a room under full sail, heads high, never unnoticed." Such women would have caught John R.'s eye. He liked beauty and style and was sure he could charm where he wanted to.

The two had met as early as 1885, so that in February of that year Lucy's son James wrote to her in Washington from 18 East Fifty-sixth Street, John R.'s house in New York, where James was visiting Louis Dos Passos, the lawyer's and Mary's son. "My dear Mother," James began, "My valace arrived savely only the handle was broken." He reported that he had been to the "Roalor Skating Rink" and to a museum. Louis, he declared, "is a very nice boy. . . . I am just having a splendid time. . . . Mr. Dos Passos'es house is beautiful. Mrs. Dos Passos is a very nice lady, but a little lame."

How much Lucy and John R. saw of each other from the start is not apparent, but it was probably a substantial amount. He frequently had business that took him to Washington, D.C., and, because Mary Dos Passos traveled little, John R. could quite easily be by himself to see Lucy there. He was considerate of his first wife, with whom he continued to live, but it was Lucy who aroused his passion, so that, by 1892, they were most certainly lovers. In August of that year, doubtless to be near him, she stayed at the Monmouth Hotel in Spring Lake on the New Jersey coast, to which he sent a disconsolate letter from nearby West End, where his family was summering: "I wonder in my heart if you feel as isolated without me today as I do without you my sweet Lucia? If you do I pity you." As he would for the nearly eighteen years more before they were married, he felt torn by doubts and worry: "I thought of [you] all last night—when will this end? And if it does end will it be better? . . . Such vagaries—such a life—for the last few years," he complained. "This constant anxiety—thinking about you—unsettles me and unfits me for mental labor." He had recently dined and talked with James, Lucy's son, probably to advise him about schooling and finances, for John R. until his death looked after him. But assuredly he had not spoken to anyone of his relationship with Lucy, because increasingly hard though it might be, he strove to keep that entirely secret. "I may get desperate & come down this evening," he closed his letter. "If I feel as I do now I certainly shall! God bless you my Sweet Lucia," he ended, leaving this letter, as he did many notes to his mistress, unsigned.

After her second child was born in 1896, Lucy took him abroad and spent much of the time there until 1907. James, nearly twenty-three years older than his half-brother, went his own way, financed at least partly through John R.'s largess. He was enrolled at Phillips Exeter Academy from 1890 to 1892, then attended the Massachusetts Institute of Technology, the University of Virginia, and ultimately received a law degree at George Washington University. Subsequently he studied in Germany and Switzerland before returning to Virginia, where he was provided work on the large farm John R. owned in Westmoreland County.

At least one aspect of life abroad was easier for Lucy: there fewer questions would be asked about her second child's father; and, when John R. could be in Europe on business, as he frequently was, he could travel openly with Lucy and with their son if they chose to take him on their trips. By 1897 Lucy and young Jack, as Dos Passos was called, had settled in Brussels, where she could be near American friends. The two remained in Belgium for the most part until 1901, when they returned to Washington, D.C., and moved into a large, gabled house at 1201 Nineteenth Street, N.W., several blocks away from the White House. Dos Passos went to the Sidwell Friends School for the school year 1901–1902, until he and his mother moved abroad again, this time to London, which would be home for him through the fall of 1906.

Although Lucy spent considerable time in London, she frequently traveled on the Continent to meet John R. on his business trips, or to the United States to be with him when he could escape business and family obligations. During the school years from 1902 to 1906, Dos Passos lived in London with two women whom he called Auntie Kate and Auntie Lou—Mrs. K. A. Gee and Miss Louisa Meakin. They were extremely fond of him, and he of them; yet his and Lucy's lives were hardly idyllic because they were nomads. He longed to go to school in America, and she despised the evasions and outright lies that her situation created, though she felt hemmed around by circumstances.

She felt more than hemmed around, in fact. Life was misery when John R. was absent, bliss when he could be with her. Theirs was always a romantic love. They were together whenever they could be, but propriety and the press of John R.'s business affairs interfered with their seeing each other as frequently as they desired. During the years before she and John R. were finally married, Lucy sometimes felt driven to distraction, which she expressed in letters, scrawled—some in pencil—to John R. What remains of the letters are scraps, incomplete, torn as if they were meant to be thrown away. Perhaps the pieces are rough drafts of letters which Lucy composed, then never sent; perhaps John R. received them and meant to destroy them, but did not entirely, for some reason. They are undated, but clearly written after the birth of their child and before 1909, when Lucy had the first of a series of strokes which severely weakened her and increasingly made her an invalid. Misspelled, crossed out, underlined, her words reveal the intensity of her emotions:

> You cannot love me—I told you in all truth, I could not stand this existance
> another another an other day, God has placed it out of my power—I have
> waited—I have bourne all—you are not fair with me. You say is it so hard to
> claim your son: one can do nothing without courage
> bravery, especially when you know you are honest true and good. I am ready
> to fight the world for my hearts love and win like Hague I will go forth alone.
> Why can't you open your heart to me? I am the best friend you have on earth
> —you need no caution. My deep love can pierce your stoutest armor—tho' that
> is nothing—any woman can do that—and I feel sure your deepest secrets are
> known to Mrs. Dos Passos. She knows, and revels in the Fact—that you are
> dishonouring me now the poor defenseless woman who trusts you—now—
> don't because the thought that she is a dying woman is

The page ends there. One can imagine John R.'s dilemma. He dearly loved Lucy, but the social restraints against doing what she asked of him were strong. He was vain, he liked the acceptance he had gained among the wealthy, and he was ambitious in his work. Publicly acknowledging Lucy and their son would damage his prestige, so he hedged. But she persisted, another time earnestly lecturing him:

> To be true, great, honest, above all else, that alone will take the sting out of
> her venom—when I think of you being the target, for slanderers, and black
> mailers, I would take each one and all by the throat, and place you where you
> deserve to be above and beyond the power of any one to hurt you and there
> is only one way, place yourself on a solid foundation of truth

John R.'s unwillingness to leave his wife especially angered Lucy. In this same letter she continued:

> those
> but even that false statement, will place you and me in a false light no matter
> how good—Oh darling will you be afraid any longer of this woman? Remem-
> ber the years are passing and what matters—Take whatever money I have,

and let us go away
~~if~~ you cannot ~~arrange an alternative~~ let us go away for a time and
<u>think</u> quickly—Take care of yourself

Lucy begged him repeatedly to flee from his wife and New York to be with
her, but he could not satisfy her completely. He saw her when he could, but he would
not admit publicly his relationship to her or to Jack. She was, to her shame, an unwed
mother whose partner was kept secret. Her situation, she penciled in another letter,
had become the "common property of all" because of John R.'s misrepresentation
of the truth. She went on:

God will give me strength, it is for <u>my</u> <u>life</u>, this honor of my darling sweetheart
and the much beloved boy—There could be much happiness, but I dare not
think of that—take passage <u>at</u> <u>once</u>—go abroad—I can arrange in two or three
days—it is imperative for you, for me—I must get away from here—I have
suffered more than I can explain—during your absents—I must act—I cannot
remain quiet any longer—I nearly collapsed twice

The emotional strain grew from the fabric of lies she was forced to weave, and
as long as she remained unmarried to John R., she did not exaggerate when she wrote
about nearly collapsing. Her anxieties created stress that was partly responsible for
the strokes that began in 1909. At the end of June that year, she wrote John R.
minutes after speaking to him on the telephone in New York:

The telephone rang a few moments ago—I felt dead, lifeless—I recognized
your voice—in an instant—my heart beat to suffocation, every artery throbbed,
my whole nature is alive, filled with intense excitement—sleep has left—fled
—I must write—My sweetheart—I love you as intensely as ever in my life, yet
—I must leave you—you cannot make up your mind to leave the woman who
has been the bane of your existence, and I cannot <u>live</u>, and see the decay the
torture of nerve and body, of the one, who has been the sunlight of my life—
God will not let me live, to <u>know</u> you again, will gratify her vanity by living
under the same roof—long years ago—you said, "Lucy if I had to save one or
the other—I would save you"—I <u>know</u> now it can never be—God knows I have
tried, because of my great love, everything on earth to save you—all the nature,
the Great-God has given me has been lavished on you—I have suffered torture,
with a face lighted by the ecstasy of suffering for you—Yes, I loved you so
madly, every pain was bliss—I must go away <u>at</u> <u>once</u>—Jack wrote me, L"

When he was around her, Jack could not have missed his mother's suffering.
He loved her, and she sheltered and coddled him, particularly during the lonely years
when they lived abroad, apart from John R. and apart often from children the boy's
age with whom he might play. While the young Dos Passos admired his father, it
would be strange had he not also resented him. The father caused the boy's mother

to suffer when he was absent, and John R. came between mother and son when he was present.

It was an exceptional man whom the young boy partly resented. An aggressive man, John R. in his fifties was described as "a slim, lithe figure of middle height; always well, even elegantly, dressed; quick in movement, suggesting an athletic habit and love of the outdoor world." The man who described him thus, J.I.C. Clarke, told of being aware of John R.'s "keen dark eyes gazing directly at you" and noted in particular "the sharp compression of the face" which his baldness exaggerated. Clarke was impressed by John R.'s "ivory-surfaced dome of thought," certainly a striking feature, even if somewhat awkwardly described. John R.'s "cavalier moustache," an "arched nose," a "well-shaped mouth and a good chin" combined, Clarke felt, to give the "outer resemblance of an aggressive intellectuality within. His facial play includes many moods, from genial laughter, when his eyes sparkle, to the gravest kind of concentration, when the brows contract, but the quickness of change is more notable than anything else."

Dos Passos remembered his father much the same way, but short, not of middle height, broad shouldered, bald, and with "gray moustaches that bristled like the horns of a fighting bull." His moustaches were truly "cavalier," remarkably long so that he had to wax them frequently to keep their rakish curl. The veins stood out on his forehead, and when he went walking he had a defiant spring in his step as he strode along swinging a cherry cane. He did not belie the impression he gave of immense energy. He "got up at six or earlier and charged into each new day like a bull charging into the arena." When he arose, he first "did a half hour of vigorous setting up exercises. Then he plunged into whatever cold salt water was to be had."

This ebullient man had been born in Philadelphia on July 31, 1844, the fifth of six children of Manoel Joaquim Dos Passos and Lucinda Ann Cattell. According to Dos Passos, his grandfather Manoel emigrated in 1830 from Ponta do Sol, a village on the island of Madeira. He was somehow involved in a stabbing incident, so hastily signed on a ship for America. He landed in Baltimore and there began work as a cobbler and later, a shoemaker. Next he moved to Philadelphia, where he married and had a family.

John R.'s childhood, he told his son, was not easy. Manoel earned little, had a violent temper, and particular culinary tastes. Dos Passos's father told him that if Manoel "didn't like the way a dish was cooked he would raise the window and pitch it out into the street," despite the family's poverty. "The hungry children would sit in their chairs wide-eyed with horror at seeing their dinner disappear." Whether in rebellion against his father or simply because he was himself adventurous and strong-willed, John R. early tried running off to sea, but soon returned and began work in Philadelphia as office boy for a law firm, where his reading in the law and in literature constituted his formal education. With his income he helped support his family until the Civil War began, when he enlisted in the Pennsylvania militia as a drummer and, according to his official biography, "fought at Antietam and later campaigns." But, "So far as I know he never saw combat," wrote his son. John R.

"was sent home from the reserves back of Antietam with a severe case of dysentery."
His next step was to apprentice himself to a lawyer named Price and at the same
time attend law courses at night at the University of Pennsylvania. In 1865 he was
admitted to the Philadelphia bar, then two years later moved to New York City.

When a Frenchman, Emil André, killed his wife in a rage in broad daylight
on a city street and John R. took on the unenviable task of lawyer for the defense,
he first attracted attention to his abilities. Despite the absence of extenuating
circumstances, John R. persuaded the jury to return a verdict of manslaughter
instead of murder. The wealthy Stokes family turned to him when their son, Edward
S. Stokes, was accused of shooting Jim Fisk, a flashy financier whose greatest
notoriety came from having attempted, along with Jay Gould, to corner the gold
market in 1869. Stokes, enamored of Fisk's mistress, shot him in front of witnesses
in the lobby of the Grand Central Hotel. John R. first assisted in Stokes's defense.
When the defendant was convicted, John R. took over the appeals procedure, and
in June 1873 the verdict was overturned, largely due to John R.'s efforts.

Successes like these led to attention in social circles. That December, he
married Mary Dyckman Hays, the daughter of wealthy New York socialites. He
opened an office in the Mills Building near the New York Stock Exchange and
brought in as a partner his brother Benjamin, to form the firm of Dos Passos
Brothers. Increasingly his clientele came from brokerage firms, and he became an
expert on the laws of commercial exchange. With his acute mind and a decided flair
for language, he began to write, in 1882 publishing *A Treatise on the Law of Stock-
brokers and Stock Exchanges.* The book was successful, even to becoming the
standard text on the subject for years.

Brokerage law led to ever-increasing intimacy with a number of brokerage firms
as their confidential adviser, and thence to work in corporation law. Companies
repeatedly sought his expertise about problems of incorporation. When H. O.
Havemeyer wanted to set up the American Sugar Refining Company in 1891, he
called on John R., whose efforts produced a part of the great "Sugar Trust" which,
by the end of the century, controlled 98 percent of the sugar refined in the United
States. John R.'s fee was said to be the largest ever at that time, and he was further
rewarded by becoming counsel for Havemeyer's creation. John R. also played a large
part in reorganizing the Texas and Pacific, the Reading, and the Erie railroads.

Committed as he was to the concept of large corporations and all that they
symbolized at the time—entrepreneurial capitalism, the individual's right to amass
great wealth, the American rags-to-riches myth—he distrusted increasing government intervention into private business. He distrusted the Interstate Commerce Act
that was passed in 1887, because, he declared, it was a move "strongly toward the
direction of centralization of power in the hands of the Federal Government." He
made no explicit value judgments; but a decade later, when the government began
to move actively against the trusts and to invoke the Sherman Anti-Trust Act of
1890, John R. fumed against regulation and interference with business enterprise.
He defended trusts before the Industrial Commission in Washington in December
1899, then revised his argument and published it as a book, *Commercial Trusts: The*

Growth and Rights of Aggregated Capital, in 1901. The Anti-Trust law, he argued, was "an unnecessary, anomalous and dangerous piece of legislation" because, he told the commission, "every law that you make is, as it were, a nail in the coffin of national liberty. The object of government is not to make laws; the object of government is to avoid making laws—the very reverse to-day of a legislator's habits."

John R. sounded like other defenders of wealth and the status quo—known as the Social Darwinists—during the era. The same year that *Commercial Trusts* was published, the Episcopal Bishop of Massachusetts, William Lawrence, defended material wealth by asserting that it was a definite principle that a strong man would conquer the land, develop natural resources, and put them to use. These steps were man's "divine mission." Lawrence, to prove his point, quoted Ralph Waldo Emerson, who had written, "Man is born to be rich. . . . Wealth requires, besides the crust of bread and the roof, the freedom of the city, the freedom of the earth." What is more, continued Bishop Lawrence, it was also a principle that only a moral person would become wealthy, with but a few exceptions. A year later in 1902, the son of John D. Rockefeller, one of the greatest of the era's robber barons, defended the idea of the survival of the fittest and the emergence of ever more effective business organizations—the trusts—by declaring that "the American Beauty Rose can be produced in splendor and fragrance which bring cheer to its beholder only by sacrificing the early buds which grow up around it. This is not an evil tendency in business. It is merely the working-out of a law of nature and a law of God."

The God- and nature-given freedom to accumulate and the rise to the top of the most fit were ideas crucial to many American capitalists in the 1880s and 1890s and wholly embraced by John R. He asserted, "Without the corporations, without the power of combined financial action, we never would have reached the remarkable condition of commercial and physical prosperity which we now enjoy, to the envy of the balance of the world." And, like the younger Rockefeller, he believed that American business bloomed only at some sacrifice. "Individuals do suffer and must suffer from the consequences of the general march of commercial and manufacturing progress. In that war of commercial development, the batteries of science and skill wound and kill their own countrymen and allies."

Any kind of regulation was anathema to him. If there had to be legislation, he pleaded, let it be by the individual states. He espoused states' rights and stood against the developing trend to let the federal government intervene in interstate commerce. As someone who had prospered in the late nineteenth century, he observed how American corporations had succeeded, and he knew how he had personally thrived—by hard work, intelligence, and a superior grasp of the facts which enabled him to dominate situations. To conclude his argument before the Industrial Commission he declared:

> It is a primary object of every well-founded government to encourage the acquisition of individual fortunes, as it is one of its most sacred duties to guard them for its possessors when they have been lawfully and honestly earned. To encourage men to toil and labor in all the fields of human industry, means the

development and prosperity of the nation, it means the opening of new fields of occupation to the poor, needy and unemployed; it encourages men to tremendous and some times superhuman efforts of skill and energy. . . .

The road to fortune is open to us all, and if we have not individually been successful enough to acquire a great amount of property, we should not seek to belittle the men who have been more fortunate, or to seek in any way to deprive them of it, or diminish its importance or enjoyment. . . . Who are the men who occupy the elegant residences on Fifth Avenue, and on other avenues of the great cities of the country? Not men who were born into the world with large means; but men who from their infancy were thrown out upon their own resources, and by hard work, skill and luck, have acquired fortunes. It should be a matter of pride, to point out these men, as types of American citizenship, and as proper incentives to young people of the present age.

Commercial Trusts is as clear a statement as there is of the position American capitalists took when they bristled against government encroachment, and it is an obvious example of what someone like John R.'s son, growing up in an America reacting against that robber-baron mentality, would protest. The young Dos Passos read the muckrakers—Upton Sinclair, Lincoln Steffens, Ray Stannard Baker—who exposed the greed and corruption of business and government. He saw reform legislation passed during the administrations of Theodore Roosevelt, William Howard Taft, and especially that of Woodrow Wilson. He became familiar with the work of Theodore Dreiser, Frank Norris, and Stephen Crane; knew of Carl Sandburg, artists George Bellows and John Sloan, and photographer Alfred Stieglitz—all of whom in their separate ways were grappling with a newly discovered America, one with its share of misery, its urban filth, and its social inequities. When Dos Passos rebelled against his father's economics, it was at least partly because his father stood so thoroughly for what these younger Americans turned against.

John R.'s interests were hardly limited to trusts. He wrote extensively; in addition to books about the law he tried out ideas for fiction and essays on such subjects as "the Gods of the different centuries," while publishing books and pamphlets called *The Anglo-Saxon Century and the Unification of the English-Speaking People* (1903); "The Trend of the Republican Party" (1904); "Gambling and Cognate Vices" (1904); *The American Lawyer: As He Was—As He Is—As He Can Be* (1907); "The Results and Responsibilities of Our Representative Democracy" (undated); "Observations of John R. Dos Passos upon the Question of Direct Primary" (1909); "Some Observations on the Proposition to Elect United States Senators by the People" (1911); "Farm Credits" (1913), and *Commercial Mortmain* (1916).

The Anglo-Saxon Century, like *Commercial Trusts* in its way, reveals how much John R.'s thought was attuned to elite opinions of his era. An exuberant faith in Anglo-Saxon America played an important part in the nation's course after the Civil War. Many Americans believed that they had a mission to lead the world toward a higher civilization, to Christianize it, and—mingled with these ideals—to preserve and strengthen the dominance of the white race. John R. called for a union of English-speaking peoples, while acknowledging that "the suggestion of an Anglo-Saxon union will be looked upon with disfavor by foreign nations." However, he avowed,

> power lodged in the proper hands hurts no one. Mistakes there may be here and there, but the course of this great race cannot be retarded. It must move forward in the mission to spread Christianity and civilization everywhere, and to open up the undeveloped part of the world to the expanding demands of commerce, and of all that commerce, liberally conducted, implies.

The assured, aggressive lawyer hoped that when the twenty-first century dawned, "the successful anglicisation of the world" would be revealed. "May the real spirit of our institutions and laws prevail everywhere," he inveighed, "and become the universal dialect of mankind."

John R.'s capitalist spirit was reflected in the way he treated money. While he earned large fees, he spent heavily. Never could he acquire "the wholehearted devotion to profit necessary to build up a fortune," wrote Dos Passos. "His speculations were picturesque but they often proved unwise or, to say the least, before their time." Plans for railroads in Mexico enthralled him, and he speculated in land around Chapultepec Park in Mexico City. He was part of a syndicate that tried to win the concession to supply natural gas to Paris. Diesel engines interested him, as did a plan to build tunnels under the Hudson River. With his income he felt he could afford several places, so he kept a home in New York, supported one in Washington for Lucy and their son, and from the early 1880s on, bought up what eventually amounted to some 7,000 acres of land in Westmoreland County, Virginia. Besides these holdings he purchased large yachts, first a converted Gloucester schooner, the *Mary Wentworth*, and then in 1907 a handsome steam yacht, the *Gaivota*, one hundred feet long and reputedly the sister ship of the presidential yacht, the *Mayflower*. But almost always he was anxious, his abilities to earn money stretched to or beyond their limits by his family commitments and his imaginative financial ventures. And instead of improving as he grew older, it seems that his position grew ever more precarious. Sometime after 1910 Ida Pifer wrote him to ask if she might borrow funds to help her purchase a house in Chicago. "Dear Ida," he replied, "I am in [a] peck of troubles—mixed troubles—and I am writing now to tell you how uncertain my movements will be for a couple of weeks at least." He told her that Lucy was very ill, constantly watched over by a trained nurse. Business, which regularly took him between Washington and Albany, frustrated him because Lucy was at that moment "absolutely helpless," her memory "very bad—with no visible sign of progress in sight." But that was not the whole of it. "Besides this I have a mountain of other troubles—You see they run up from a peck to a mountain in a few minutes." He told Ida that he could obtain the money she asked for, but would himself have to take a loan for it. She had apparently invested some money along with him in Mexico, and he asked her, "Have you thought of me in connection with Mexico? All of our plans are knocked in the head and we are lying helplessly on the ground with no chance of progressing at present & not the least opportunity of drawing out the large sums of money we have put in the enterprize. It pours upon me now from all quarters, and if I have any hair or anything else when you see me it will be a sort of miracle." If hair were any mark of freedom from financial worry, then money had long since taken its toll.

But for all his concerns, he was, his son thought, "among the gayest of gay entertainers in a period when social life in New York still had a little of the cordiality of the small town." And he was equally the fine host when he was staying at his farm in Westmoreland County, Virginia, near the mouth of the Potomac River. There, of a Christmas holiday, he would invite his neighbors to a "barbeque" or to a fox hunt across his several thousand acres. The parties, for which he would bring down caterers from Washington, might include a steer skewered and roasted in a large pit, along with a plentiful supply of oysters, punch, and beer in kegs brought by boat down the Potomac. Because he was generous to nearly everyone, the people in Westmoreland County appreciated him. But typical of the man was a time when the *Gaivota's* propellers snarled some fishing nets off the shore of his farm at Sandy Point. Instead of apologizing to the fisherman whose nets he had ruined, John R. berated him for putting the nets out, although the man had a perfect right to do so. When he calmed down, John R. later paid for the damage.

Not surprisingly, he was an excellent speaker and loved to sing, breaking at a moment's notice into a song like "Larboard Watch Ahoy," his favorite. He could also sing most of the score of Gilbert and Sullivan's *H.M.S. Pinafore* and *The Mikado,* or Offenbach's light operas *La Belle Hélène* and *Les Cloches de Corneville.* And he loved to recite Shakespeare. Dos Passos could always picture John R. dressing to be presented to King Edward of England, in "a frilled shirt and black silk stockings," while "strutting up and down in front of the rainstreaked windows reciting Othello's address to the Venetian senate."

"Strutting up and down"—he was a cocky man, sure of himself, and with a confidence that enabled him to plunge eagerly into many things. He prided himself on being an independent thinker. He scorned religious orthodoxy, for example, and had little use for the forms of the Catholic Church in which he had been raised. Yet, his niece remembered she had been told that he called for a priest when he was dying. His independence extended to almost every aspect of his style of life. In New York he invariably walked the whole distance from his home at 18 East Fifty-sixth Street to his offices at 20–22 Broad Street. He liked to boast to his family that he never wore an overcoat, but as his niece said, "You should have seen the thick-thick suits he wore! and no doubt layers of wool under them." And he could be fussy about small matters, scarcely aware that his fussiness might irritate, as when he brought his own tea when he visited, although, his niece recalled, her family used Lapsang Suchong, which tasted no different, she thought. To some people John R. seemed conceited and self-centered. He probably rarely stopped to think how he struck others; he bustled, bubbled, and overwhelmed more reticent people with his enthusiasms.

CHAPTER TWO

Early Education,
1898–1911

To the mature author looking back on them, his first lonely years seemed like a hotel childhood. One may wonder whether Dos Passos's imaginative re-creations of his youth exaggerate his being an outsider and a misfit. The evidence suggests not. He was small and frail as a child, although later he grew to be over six feet tall. He was coddled by his adoring mother, and their travels often kept him apart from other children. The voyages never stopped; scenes rushed by full of people, colors, smells, noises, and when he and his mother moved to England in 1902 after leaving Belgium —but touching down in America so that the boy was reminded of his homeland— he felt like "a double foreigner . . . A Man Without a Country," as he described his autobiographical character Jay Pignatelli in the novel *Chosen Country.* Nothing more accurately catches his own acute yearning to belong somewhere and be among friends.

Among Dos Passos's papers at the University of Virginia are typed carbons of two autobiographical essays which make no attempt to fictionalize his childhood memories. Along with several untyped essays, they are perhaps the best sources to give a sense of his earliest childhood. Almost certainly they are his first effort at autobiography, and they are probably the most accurate, having been written not many years after the episodes occurred, nor composed with an eye to presenting something other than autobiography. It is likely that these typed drafts were among some drawn from what he had written for a composition course he took while at Harvard. Although Dos Passos intended them for possible publication in the *Harvard Monthly,* eventually only one appeared there, an essay entitled "Les Lauriers Sont Coupés." In the unpublished essays, he described his first memories, acknowledging the difficulty of capturing "those sudden pictures, from which the mists are withdrawn for so brief a space. Other memories, vaguer, dusky-winged, throng about you, until your early childhood seems a dull chaos of emotions and glimpses of scenes."

His earliest recollection was of "a meadow of tall grass filled with daisies: everything is damp and warm and scented." His nurse and he followed behind his mother, whose dress swished as she walked along. He recalled the moist grass against his unsteady legs, and a green world, "splashed with white of daisies, and palest blue overhead." His body felt warm and damp from the grass, while a "streaming meadow-fragrance" hung about the whole scene.

What followed was a memory of nighttime in the bedroom of a large hotel, where he lay crying because of a pain in his legs while his mother, "soft and fluffy in a peignoir," cared for him by candlelight. A knock came at the door; a harsh voice asked if the child could not be quieted because the woman across the corridor had complained, and his mother snapped back an answer. Then she tried to calm him by telling a story, "an endless rambling story, about an elephant in scarlet trappings and a little Indian prince whose legs hurt, oh so badly." The young Dos Passos was in tears; then the story changed: the prince was well and lay "sleeping among scarlet and gold cushions on the elephant's back, while a beautiful princess fan[ned] him with a pearl-encrusted fan." Later on the hotel stairs Dos Passos and his mother confronted the lady who had complained. Vividly he recollected his mother's flashing eyes and the ominous rustle of her dress as they brushed past the woman, who, he thought, "looked sheepish and apologetic."

Mingled with memories of these scenes was "the deep melancholy of certain songs." While his mother, vaguely silhouetted in the twilight, leaned over his bed, he heard faint footsteps on the street outside. She sang "a sad little song about sheep and wolves and the cold wind of winter, crooned very low," Dos Passos wrote, so that her song covered him "with veil after veil of unspeakable sadness." The melancholy resembled what gripped him during a dream he had at about the same time, a dream in which he found himself sinking in water "that kept closing over my head in slow regular rings like the brown pond-water I had once seen close over a pebble, while I sank and sank." But he had also from those years a vivid picture of a breakfast table, gleaming silver, a white tablecloth, and brilliant sunlight pouring through a window. Ever after the smell of *café au lait* and the sound of crisp toast being eaten took him back to the pleasant scene of himself and his mother seated "at the little carved table by the window, merry in the greenish light of a spring morning."

These earliest memories were from his first years in Brussels until 1901. Belgium was home, but a place from which he frequently traveled even though hardly more than a baby. He recalled nighttime journeys and "the regular clank of train-couplings and the smell of coal smoke," then "cream-colored villas, shrouded in feathery foliage, and the shrilling salt wind at Biarritz," where he and Lucy vacationed—probably more than once—during their summers abroad, there and at Boulogne-sur-Mer, nearer Brussels on the English Channel in the north of France. All he recollected of these trips were the bits and pieces a small child would retain. On the train down to Biarritz he remembered a Spanish woman sobbing hysterically to his mother because her husband had been left behind at one stop with all their money. As the woman rushed through the train shrieking, "Manuelo, Manuelo," Dos Passos had been struck by "the brutality of husbands"—an oblique slap at his own father, who could travel only infrequently with his mistress and their son. At Biarritz there were carriage rides among the steep hills, vivid colors, chill winds, and a heavy surf that sometimes sent foamy water scudding over the terraces along the shore.

The *épiceries* along a muddy street in Boulogne-sur-Mer were memorable for their odors of coffee, spices, fruits and *petits gâteaux* that issued from them, as was the harbor, "full of the reek of shipping and the dank smell of flats exposed by the tide," and the breakwater out beyond the harbor, where a small lighthouse perched, and where he could watch the channel steamer that crossed to Folkstone and Dover. At Boulogne he passed mornings on the beach, playing with new sand pails and trying to build castles before his nurse hurried him away from the best spots in the sand, from which "rough and very tanned little boys" always forbade the likes of him. He rushed to construct his castles before someone trampled down his efforts, or before his mother bustled him off for his swimming lessons. The only time he could recall finishing a castle "properly surmounted by flags, two American, one French and one Belgian," a huge wave pounded ashore and drenched him, his nurse Marie, and two small girls dressed in white who had watched his labors.

The swimming lessons were torturous. When the weather was cloudy, an indoor pool appeared threatening, the corridors around it dark and the matting cold under his feet. While Dos Passos's mother smiled encouragement, the instructor became enraged at the awkwardness of his pupil, whose misery was never assuaged by the glasses of hot milk that he was offered after each session.

Although these episodes were not atypical of upper-class children at the time, Dos Passos's memories often reflected his acute sense that as a child he was intimidated by a threatening world beyond his own intimate one. The boy occasionally plunged into some small adventure, only to be snatched back by his nurse or his mother. His father, moreover, did not appear in the autobiographical episodes, although John R. was almost certainly with him and Lucy at some point during their trips to Biarritz and Boulogne, and he visited them in Brussels. Later, in fictionalized renderings of these same episodes when a father appeared, it was Dos Passos's intention to present him as at least partly a challenge and a threat to his autobiographical characters.

Almost always his childhood, in retrospect, seemed restricted. In Brussels, Dos Passos remembered being "a small boy in a clean little starched suit . . . alone in the dusky *salon*, stretched out on a black shaggy rug before the fireplace." The rug was a forest where a porcelain bear roamed, searching for prey. Then Dos Passos's imagination turned the rug into a stormy sea, and the bear climbed onto a rock, a piece of coal from the coal scuttle. Soon he had another idea and began pretending that he was in a butcher's shop. He piled coal on the hearth and got smeared with black coal dust. At that moment his nurse swept in, shrieking at his dirtiness, followed by his mother, dressed for a reception in a formal lace gown with a long train. Ashamed of himself now, he burst into tears while he was scolded for his imaginative games.

Dos Passos sought fri...idship, but his memory was of being pulled back repeatedly, as when in Brussels he met a boy in a park, and the two began to play with Dos Passos's red fire engine. Silently they toiled at pouring dust and pebbles in and out of the toy truck. They even started to chatter to each other in French until suddenly their nurses intervened and snatched them away. Another time he tried unsuccessfully to reach out to a child while he and his mother were walking along a cobbled street in Holland. They had just bought themselves two large pretzels when they came upon "a pitiably ragged boy with smudged face, through whose torn shirt I remember catching sight of grimy little ribs." Lucy pressed her son to give the boy a pretzel. Dos Passos pushed his toward the other child, and as he did, the boy's hand, "very rough and hard, brushed against mine." Dos Passos shuddered involuntarily. "For days afterwards," he remembered, "I could feel, at times, that rough dirty little hand brush against mine."

Of course his early life did not always seem lonely. In the autobiographical piece, "Les Lauriers Sont Coupés," published when he was a senior at Harvard, he wrote of the things that evoked his sense of "familiarity and respect, even of awe," that he believed anyone felt for the first city he knew. For him, Brussels was that place. It abounded with "delightful genial things, fountains, and parks and cabdrivers; and above all, the little chocolate-district of winding streets, and cake shops —where was a constant clatter of women in furs and ruffles which reminded me of an aviary at the Zoo, and a marvellous, indescribable odor of eclairs and brioches, and of thick hot chocolate." Like any small child, he yearned for the rich candies and cakes displayed temptingly along the counters. The winding streets had their distinctive odors and sights: smells of chocolate, and swarms of milliners and dressmakers who clustered in lace shops where the boy had to sit quietly while his mother or his nurse chattered endlessly about matters of no interest to him.

More exciting were lunches at cafés like Les Trois Suisses, where he could sit, "solemnly sipping my milk and eating my madelaine, while gnomes and old men with beer mugs leered at me from the walls, from behind placid ladies and gentlemen taking their déjeuner." Occasionally, a gilt lion at the other end of the room would roar, and its eyes, electric-lighted, would flash when a fresh barrel of beer was tapped.

The trolley cars, whose tracks led all through the city and out into wooded parks, were equally enthralling. He particularly liked the yellow, open trolleys which ran during the summer through woods "where bandits assuredly lurked," to Terveuren, a park "of pale green trees and still ponds and dim gravelled walks among the woods." The palace of Carlota, briefly the Empress of Mexico, had been here; hers and Maximilian's names sent chills through him. The palace had burned down, and now a child could roam through the museum made from the remains of the buildings, filled with exhibits from the Belgian Congo. One could be served tea at tables on the terrace and listen to a band play. Lucy told her son as they sat there about mad Carlota and about Maximilian, who had been executed in Mexico. When at dusk Lucy and the little boy returned from the park, he quavered as he and his mother rode along "dark, mysterious boulevards" lit by gas lamps whose reflections flared in the shop windows along the way. As soon as they were home he would be hurried into bed, and as he fell asleep he pictured "the Princess Carlota, with streaming hair and a torch in her hand, setting on fire the palace at Terveuren."

Although he feared the Palais de Justice in Brussels, more terrifying was "a quarter near the Porte de Hal, where frightful gypsies lived." His nurse scared him once by showing him the house reputed to have been that of a king of the gypsies. "He was a gigantic man," declared his nurse, *"un homme immense,* who wore a yellow sash and one huge earring and the gendarmes did not dare touch him. His wife killed him by pouring hot lead into his ears as he slept. . . . And they had a huge funeral; all the riffraff of Europe filled the cemetery and the *agents de police* did not dare stop them." Dos Passos asked his nurse if that had been long ago. "Not very long," she responded, while he huddled down in his bed until Lucy came in to sing to him, so that he remembered the feel of her soft silk evening gown as she crooned,

> *Nous n'irons plus aux bois, les lauriers sont coupés*
> *Les amours des bassins . . .*
> *Voice l'herbe qu'on fauche et les lauriers qu'on coupe.*
> *Nous n'irons plus aux bois, les lauriers sont coupés.*

These years seemed a coming and going full of railroads and stations, exciting but unnerving. He felt an "exultant awe and wonder at the swiftness of trains and the hugeness of crowds," and one image especially remained with him from those days. In "Les Lauriers Sont Coupés" he described it; years later he included it in an early Camera Eye of *U.S.A.,* and yet again, in *Chosen Country,* in the fiction fitting the incident to the themes of childhood innocence, fear, and isolation. His memory, he wrote in the essay, was of

lying, barely awake, in a dim railway compartment with my head on my mother's lap. Above, the two little dark green tassels of the bowl-shaped gas lamp swing to and fro with the swaying of the car. I was watching a small beam of light, escaped from the shade, which travelled up and down amid the blackness of the opposite seat; in my ears sounded the confused jolting rumble of the wheels. I must have been sitting up on my mother's knee a little later, for I remember seeing tiny lights shoot across the blackness of the window. All at once I caught sight of something strange and terrifying outside, a burst of red curling flame, that as it passed subsided into a dull glare. Tremendously excited, I pressed my face against the cold window pane, and stared into the moving blackness. We were rushing past rows and rows of low, black chimneys —potteries probably—from the tops of which came a lurid glare that now and then burst into enormous flaming pillars. Somehow they made me feel, as they dimmed in the distance, the speed and madness of the train.

To a sensitive child the speed and madness were threatening, even if they were thrilling. But Dos Passos could never get away from threats, really, because others loomed up and pressed in on his security—crowds of faces, strangers, laborers—vastly different from the people of his parents' world, or "the huge grimy vaults of railway stations," where the smell of coal smoke was choking and a cold wind chilled him even when he tried to press in against his mother's fur coat. As he walked along the railway platform, a locomotive towered over him and seemed to hiss like some evil monster. "The glare of its huge staring eye was terrifying, as were the sooty men who poked about the great still wheels without seeming afraid. Then to look up at the dim cavern filled with smoke, eddying in brown wraiths about the girders, which struck here and there across the gloom, brought a strange fear and wonder, a peculiar catching of the breath."

The threats were constant. In the first Camera Eye sequence Dos Passos described a time when his mother and he were walking in a park. It was during the Boer War; tempers were high; and the Americans were mistaken for English. An angry crowd of Belgians began to follow them, shaking their fists, throwing stones at their feet and shouting after them, "Englander." Lucy walked faster; then they ran and dodged into a postcard shop. "Non nein nicht englander amerikanisch américain," Lucy tried in her broken German and French. The shop owner comprehended: "Hock Amerika Vive l'Amérique." And Lucy laughed in relief. "My dear, they had me right frightened." The little boy had hidden under the counter, but now he could admire the "postcards that shine in the dark pretty hotels and palaces." He felt safe once more, because Lucy had sheltered him from a world which he was too young to comprehend.

Sometimes Dos Passos would travel with his parents when they were together in Europe. A memorable trip was to Madeira, his ancestral home, where the three of them visited after he had undergone a hernia operation. In one of the unpublished essays written at Harvard, Dos Passos described the trip. He thought he had been six; thus it might have occurred in the summer of 1902, after his stint in the United States at the Sidwell Friends School. The trip left him with vivid images of a miserable voyage from Lisbon to Funchal, during which he lay much of the time stretched out in a steamer chair, "while a kind hearted gentleman fed me strawberries of miraculous sweetness" to offset the seasickness induced by the constant rolling of their "wheezy old steamer."

The bay stretching before Funchal was lovely, "hemmed in by lavender-brown cliffs," while at the far end the town "rose in white and red steps up the mountainside." As soon as the steamer anchored, all sorts of boatmen surrounded her, shouting to the people on board. Dos Passos was fascinated by them and awed by the "small boys, olive skins flashing in the sunlight, [who] dove for the pennies we threw them."

Once ashore, he and his mother—in his undergraduate essay he never mentioned his father—climbed into a *carro,* a two-seated sled with a white canvas top from which curtains hung down. After their luggage was piled in front of them, oxen began dragging the sled up the cobbled streets to the hotel. When he wrote about this episode for his composition course at Harvard, Dos Passos rendered it vividly, giving some hint of his descriptive powers. His instructor, Charles Townsend Copeland ("Copey"), thought it excellent and noted in the margin of the theme paper, "The best thing you've done in English 12—A catalogue of odors compiled by D. P. would be worth having." The scene he described was of a barefooted driver walking beside the oxen,

> brushing off the flies with a long horsehair whisp. . . . Every now and then he lets the metal runners pass over an oil soaked rag he keeps hanging over the shaft. The hot oil emits an exotic intoxicating odor which is my most poignant memory of Funchal. It is an odor unlike any other I have ever smelt, hot and choking and heavy, yet mixed with the fragrance of endless gardens and the tang of the South Atlantic. As it jolts glidingly along, white curtains swaying from side to side, the *carro* groans and creaks painfully.

In Reid's hotel, where they stayed for three weeks, Dos Passos was horrified to find red ants in his bureau drawers; that and "a nice oldish gentleman with two large white moustaches—the American consul I think—who used to bring my mother a gigantic bunch of pink and apricot tinted roses every morning" were all he remembered of the hotel where he stayed. The garden outside, however, was striking, "with its gravelled paths, its wealth of flowering shrubs, and its dark green luxuriant foliage, all impregnated with the cloying sweetness of giant honeysuckle." And he had a vivid recollection of clambering "down the face of the cliff on rock cut steps to the rocks at their base, where a small swimming pool was hollowed out of the live rock." Seaweed on the bottom waved in the eddies that swirled between the rocks as Dos Passos tried to catch the tiny black fish darting among the algae. The pool was ideal, but for him it was disagreeable, because there he first tried to swim on his own—presumably the struggles at Boulogne had been complete failures. "How hard I tried to strike out boldly as I saw other people do who bathed in the real ocean beside the pool!"—his father, a strong swimmer, among them, which Dos Passos did not mention. "No use; hardly did my feet leave the bottom before there was a frightened agonized splutter and a great gulp of burning salt water. Then, after tearful coughing, I would be urged to try again with the same miserable results. Until I begged to," Dos Passos began the next sentence in his essay, but crossed it out, realizing that this would lead him into another topic, and in this essay he meant to be describing scenes, not his relationships as a small child with parents eager for him to prove himself.

As slow and creaking as a trip up the mountain by *carro* had been, so the one down was fast and furious:

> There is a brilliant picture in my mind of white walls and vivid trees shooting past us as we dove down towards the blue sea and the red tile roofs of Funchal. The sled rattled over the stone pavement at a tremendous pace, amid the shouts of the steersman, who held on behind to keep the car from coming to grief in

the ditches that lined the narrow lane. It was an experience that took my breath away: the hot odor of the burning oil from the runners, the glimpse of the dazzling azure sea every moment growing nearer, the bright green foliage that melted into pink villas and white, clustered houses as we sped by.

When many years later he wrote his memoir, *The Best Times,* he recalled other scenes from childhood: in England "sitting on the roof of a coach and four being driven with jingle of harness through green lanes," or having "a picnic under a royal oak in a park full of grazing deer" with his parents and some English friends, among whom was a pretty woman he liked until she plied him with too many questions. In his mind he heard the sounds of corks popping off miniature champagne bottles and remembered eating hordes of small cheesecakes—Maids of Honor—that made him feel ill. He recollected salmon fishing on a Scottish lake, and the blue veins on his father's hands showing from the exertion of rowing their boat, half filled with water after a squall hit them.

Dos Passos wrote in his undergraduate essays of his childish confusion about what was acceptable and unacceptable to adults, the incident of rubbing coal on himself being one example. The same scene appears in *Chosen Country* when Jay Pignatelli thinks back over his childhood. Other memories surface for Jay: an Easter morning and his mother bringing him "a fuzzy pink rabbit on a nest of chocolate eggs," the boy "proud because I'd done not only number one but number two in bed, oh but the rumpus and the scolding and screwed up disgustful faces and the pink rabbit taken away and the scrubbing and the shaking and the soap and slapping water." And mingled with these memories are confusing ones about sex—memories of Jay's French nurse who took him into her bed at night, peeled off his nightdress, pulled hers up to her neck, and rubbed his "poor little dingus up and down her bare belly ' faire les petits venventres,' she called it and she was all furry around the place and when I asked her why it was all wet there she said it was because she'd just washed it but it made me feel funny." Jay recalls the wife of one American in Brussels reclining naked on a couch in front of him and laughing shrilly with his mother. Sex and his loneliness and America all swirled together for the child as he looked outside to see "the red and white stripes and the stars of the flag hanging from a pole above the portecochère and Kentucky was a state and all the states were stars and right here in the conservatory it was American soil like Kentucky, like one of the stars, and Kentucky was where the little naked lady lived."

John R. wanted his son's schooling to be English, believing this would be much superior to an American education. He hoped his boy would get an English public school background, then go to Oxford or Cambridge, because the elder Dos Passos's own learning—for the most part gathered from his incessant delving into the classics on his own—was similar to that of his English friends. He thoroughly enjoyed conversing at length and without fear of appearing snobbish about the likes of the Greek philosophers, about Julius Caesar and Lord Bacon, his son wrote in *The Best Times.*

So it was that Dos Passos, after the sojourn in America, really commenced his education at Peterborough Lodge, a school in the suburbs of London. Since his mother traveled with her lover when she could, Dos Passos boarded with two Englishwomen, mentioned earlier, Mrs. K. A. Gee and Miss Louisa Meakin, while he was in school. For a time he was the only American at Peterborough Lodge, but in the fall of 1904, another boy arrived. Dos Passos remembered the time vividly because his father—though never actually a politician—worked hard that year for the Democratic presidential candidate, Judge Alton B. Parker, who had the support of conservative and eastern Democrats, against Teddy Roosevelt, the Republican incumbent. At Peterborough Lodge the new boy strode up to Dos Passos and demanded to know whom he was for. Dos Passos said Parker, so the other boy threatened to punch him in the nose, but Dos Passos failed miserably to stand up to him.

He went to Peterborough Lodge for his education through the first half of 1906 and appears to have been a good student. Among his papers at the University of Virginia is a report card from the school for the term ending July 31 of that year. His courses were Latin, French, English, Arithmetic, Algebra, and Geometry. There were ten students in all but Geometry, where there were twelve. In his classes he stood first, second, sixth, ninth, third, and sixth, respectively. His teachers reported that his work ranged from "fair" in Arithmetic, to "very good" in French and Algebra. For his Latin teacher he worked extremely well, and it was predicted that he "will do well in the future." His English teacher commented only "good."

Although John R. Dos Passos wanted his son to have an English education, young Jack desired otherwise, so for that reason, as well as his parents' wish to be together more, he and his mother boarded ship for America in the fall of 1906. When he arrived "home" at last, they headed for Washington, D.C., where the first relative of Dos Passos's own age he met was his cousin Lois Sprigg, who remembered the meeting well. Dos Passos was a "handsome dark eyed little boy," so excited to find a relative that he clutched onto her hand and held it, thankful to find someone who might be his friend and who, he sensed, would not mock him because of his formal manners and speech that had in it strains of both a French and an English accent. He felt he had outgrown a treasured collection of lead soldiers, so to show his affection for his newfound friend he thrust at her a box full of them—many of them headless, Lois recalled, but a thrill to get from this shy cousin nonetheless.

For the next several years Lucy lived in Washington, on the New Jersey shore, or in New York, and during the summers spent time at Sandy Point on the Virginia side of the Potomac River near its mouth, where John R. had a large farm. In January 1907, because his father believed that the experience of boarding school would benefit his son, Dos Passos began four and a half years at the Choate School in Wallingford, Connecticut, where his youth and his foreignness sometimes made his life hardly bearable.

Choate School, six decades after Dos Passos's time there, is one of the largest and wealthiest of the New England preparatory schools. Its campus spreads out across hundreds of acres, expensively landscaped, the buildings with a variety of architectural styles which all in their ways lend themselves to the land. Its program and the facilities are impressive, a kind of monument to the missionary enthusiasm that inspired many wealthy and near-wealthy Americans during the late nineteenth and early twentieth centuries and were translated into the creation of private secondary schools.

When Dos Passos got to Wallingford in January 1907 the school was a far different place. It was in its eleventh year of operation; its student body and faculty together numbered fewer than sixty. Its buildings were houses—some built long before—scattered along Christian and North Elm streets, elm-lined dirt roads among open fields around the outskirts of Wallingford, a small industrial town of some 7,000 to 10,000 people.

Although the school was young when Dos Passos arrived, it emphasized from the first its deep roots in American history. A school brochure of the 1970s declares "it was here at the time of the *Mayflower* that the war cry 'Mohawk' struck terror in the hearts of the local Indians; here that the small Quinnipiac tribes asked the white man to settle for the Indian's protection; here that John Davenport and others purchased a tract of land in 1638 from the Sachem Montowese to form on the hill in 1670 one of Connecticut's earliest communities. . . ." And, almost of course, "it was to the center of today's Choate that General George Washington came to purchase gun powder for his Revolutionary army from Caleb Atwater. . . ." The school worked to impress its students with its traditions, reminders that were particularly poignant for the shy Jack Madison, not quite eleven years old and just returned to America.

The first year and a half that Dos Passos was at Choate, Mark Pitman was the headmaster. But in the fall of 1908, the person who would head the school for the next forty years, and who in many ways was the personification of Choate, began his tenure as headmaster. George C. St. John was a stern moralist and a hard worker, a man who personified what Dos Passos's father most admired and who exhorted his students with phrases like "go the extra mile," "for every privilege there is a corresponding responsibility," and "I am not laying bricks; I am building a cathedral." St. John had not been an outstanding student in high school, but had persevered and worked his way to Harvard in 1898. There he toiled hard, even getting his poetry accepted (after many revisions) by the *Harvard Advocate* and earning a place on its editorial board. After graduation he taught at several private schools before arriving at Choate. In 1906 he married Clara Seymour, a bright, scholarly woman versed in the classics who was the daughter of a professor who later became president of Yale. With St. John's tenacity, her intelligence, and their style, they made an impressive pair, just the sort to take over the little school and imbue it with the spirit of industry and moral earnestness that would make it prosper. St. John was in his way a remarkable man, an archetype of the preparatory-school headmaster who flourished during the first half of this century. He believed entirely in the Protestant work ethic. He was a builder and, as he pushed himself, he cajoled and pressed his faculty and students. "You don't understand the Choate spirit," he would berate a teacher who he thought was too slack. He was the sort of man who shaved with a straight razor and took pride in doing so, an admirable man who had a great understanding of men and boys—to a point—and whom they could admire, even love. But some could also hate him.

It was this mixture of feelings that Dos Passos harbored about the St. Johns and Choate. He was drawn to Mrs. St. John, who taught him Greek and no doubt sympathized with the young, intellectual boy whose foreign manners and small size made life difficult for him in a school which emphasized manliness and the strenuous life exalted by Teddy Roosevelt. "I hated boardingschool," Dos Passos would recall many years later, "being called Frenchy and Four-eyes and the class grind." He felt his inadequacies keenly, because he was an easy target for what he called "the clean young American Rover Boys" of Choate. In one of the autobiographical Camera Eye sections of *U.S.A.*, published years later, he wrote that when he tried to skate on a pond near the school next to the silver mills of the Simpson, Hall and Miller Company, "there was shine on the ice early black ice that rang like a sawblade just scratched white by the first skaters I couldn't learn to skate and kept falling down." Other Choate boys called out, "look out for muckers . . ."; and he thought to himself, "Bohunk and Polak kids put stones in their snowballs write dirty words up on walls do dirty things up alleys their folks work in the mills." He saw himself cut off from the laborers and their families, but when he tried to be one of the "clean young American Rover Boys" who were "handy with tools Deerslayers played hockey Boy Scouts and cut figure eights on the ice," who were "Achilles Ajax Agamemnon," he was a failure, at least in his own eyes. "Was it the bar sinister or the nearsighted eyes that made him always fumble the ball," he would later ask, and he judged himself to be bad at all sports; while his foreign accent and sense that he lacked roots made him inept in social situations.

At Choate he may have exaggerated to himself the extent to which he was an outsider, since he was somewhat the morbidly sensitive, introspective adolescent who was self-indulgent and thus an easy target. Life, nevertheless, was misery at times. He was forced into fights he abhorred: "you sat on the bed unlacing your shoes Hey Frenchie yelled Tylor in the door you've got to fight the kid——doan wanna fight him——gotto fight him hasn't he got to fight him fellers?" And the other students would compel him to prove he was not a "girlboy." Dos Passos in his pajamas went at the Kid:

> and your mouth tasted bloody and everybody yelled Go to it Kid except Gummer and he yelled Bust his jaw Jack and Frenchie had the Kid down on the bed and everybody pulled him off and they all had Frenchie against the door and he was slamming right an' left and he couldn't see who was hitting and Tylor and Freddy held his arms and told the Kid to come and hit him but the Kid wouldn't and the Kid was crying

Dos Passos recalled "the bloody sweet puky taste" in his mouth, the bell ringing for lights out, boys racing to their rooms, his crawling into bed crying, head pounding, to have his lone ally Gummer tiptoe into his room to say, "You had him licked Jack." But a teacher was stalking around the halls, caught Gummer out of bed, and punished him, a sort of total defeat for the lonely Frenchie. Such scraps might have been normal rough stuff, and certainly they were common enough, but that made them no easier for Dos Passos to endure. He had to suffer other indignities, another painful and frightening sort of hazing that he had to bear was to be hung out a window by his hands, to the amusement of the other boys.

More than seven years later, as he sat in an army camp in Allentown, Pennsylvania, the cold rainy day, the boredom of the army, and the austere barracks made him think back to Choate. "I can see the room now that I had in the upper school," he wrote in his diary, "with mustard colored burlap on the walls—the bed was under a slant in the roof so that the ceiling rose over it like the side of a tent. There only did I feel secure from teasing and harassing and from games. How loath I was to leave its warm protection in the morning."

But boarding-school life was not only the subtle and unsubtle tortures adolescents could devise for one another. Dos Passos had a few friends at Choate: John Walcott, who would also be at Harvard, and an older boy, Franklin Nordhoff, nicknamed "Skinny," who shared Dos Passos's fascination for animals. Together they were allowed to go canoeing on the Quinnipiac River, which runs near Wallingford, using a canoe Dos Passos's father had given him. Occasional weekends they would camp, and they spent long hours catching animals: rodents, garter snakes, hoptoads, and bullfrogs whose legs they would cook over a fire in a secret hideaway they made near the school pond. The two boys ardently studied their catches, skinning the rodents and frogs and observing the habits of their captive toads. In addition, Dos Passos was permitted to keep a raccoon at the school, so he and Nordhoff were able to create a small world of their own apart from their boisterous peers.

By 1908–1909 Dos Passos had made a place for himself, even though he could not compete successfully as an athlete, which he admitted several years later when he wrote a friend, "I once caught a fly in a baseball game—that's the beginning-end of my athletic record." He was one of two assistant business managers of the school publication, the *Brief;* was on the board of the *News;* and participated in dramatics. Further, that year he ranked second on the honor list for the upper school and at the commencement exercises received the prize for excellence in English and honorable mention for excellence in classics. The commencement program reveals much about the atmosphere at Choate. Given Dos Passos's feeling of isolation at the time, one can sense how that atmosphere forced out the boy's awareness of what America was for him as for those at ease with it. The program took place at the end of May, almost always a lovely moment of the late spring in southern New England. Faculty, students, and guests assembled at the Liberty Tree, first to hear "National Airs" by a local drum corps, then a "Cheering Song" and an address to "Our Friends and Alumni," followed by a speech about "What the Liberty Tree Means." There were next a ritual "Placing of the Soil about the Liberty Tree," the singing of "The Blue and Gold Forever," and, finally, the closing song, "America."

The next year, 1909–1910, Dos Passos's activities were much the same: again he was a member of the *Brief* board, an editor of the *News,* and he remained active in drama. That February he played the part of Sheba Jedd in Arthur Pinero's *Dandy Dick;* and the *Brief* reported that "with bright, winning faces, and handsome costumes, Charleton Wilder and Jack Madison as Salome and Sheba proved grand successes. They acted very well together, and did much toward making the play a success."

When Dos Passos was away at Choate, he eagerly anticipated his vacations with his parents, particularly before his mother's illness became so severe as to be a burden to them all. He saw something of his father, joining him for an occasional weekend in New York. Dos Passos stayed at the Murray Hill Hotel on Park Avenue, while he and John R. saw the best theater that New York offered: Shakespeare, Gilbert and Sullivan, and the then legendary Sarah Bernhardt. Such respites made life bearable at Choate, but one can imagine Dos Passos's loneliness even then: alone at a hotel—unless his mother happened to be in the city also, which occurred less and less often as her illness worsened—and overwhelmed by his "guardian," who insisted that his son dress for ornate dinners, often at such restaurants as Delmonico's. These meetings between the son and the man he could not publicly acknowledge as his father were touching because of their affection, yet unease around each other. Together they sat formally over meals that seemed endless to Dos Passos. He reminisced, "There is a time in childhood when you are embarrassed by everything your parents do. I'd huddle in acute misery while he joshed with the waiters or indulged in boastful talk with some friend who would sit down for a moment at his table." Once, Dos Passos recalled, he took the focus of attention away from John R. when someone asked about beavers; and full of firsthand knowledge from his investigations at Choate, Dos Passos held forth to the pride of his father and the astonishment of his friends, unused to hearing the "fearfully shy" boy say anything.

When these weekends came to a close, Dos Passos had a lonely train ride by himself back to Wallingford, often carrying with him some book that John R. had given him. Despite his awareness of his father's difference from himself, Dos Passos was perceptive enough to see that these gifts of books were part of John R.'s program for him. The son was a voracious reader in any case, but the father wanted very much to have the boy learn widely and to acquire the interests he had. So it was that he poured Milton into Dos Passos on Sunday mornings over breakfast—*Paradise Lost* was better for a person than church. John R.'s reading program for his son had commenced years before. When Dos Passos was eight, his father gave him *Mr. Midshipman Easy*, the first book he remembered receiving. Then it was other sea stories, Ballantyne's *The Coral Island*, histories, and the novels of Dickens and Dumas père.

In the years before 1910, Lucy also traveled toward New York to be as close to John R. and her son as she could. In the spring of 1909, she stayed at the Hotel Rudolph in Atlantic City, New Jersey, for example, while there writing Dos Passos informative, even somewhat humorous letters. But she mentioned not being at all well, and it was about this time that her serious illness began. That fall she was back at the Hotel Rudolph, writing Dos Passos in plaintive tones:

I am so thankful to the Great giver of all benefits, to say I am much better today for every day of improvement takes me near my dear sweet-heart and prince. . . . Thank God dearest in your prayer tonight for showing your dear Mother we cannot be thankful enough—He is ever near to guard, and protect us, thank Him darling in your prayer tonight to make us happy and grateful.

She added that she had a plan for the two of them. Probably it concerned her settling in Washington, for after she went to New York at the end of November to make some arrangements with John R., he wrote Dos Passos that "the princess left for Washington on Saturday, perhaps as you have been informed, and she is to reside at a hotel near at hand until the house is in condition for her to occupy. Her health has steadily improved." Then the day before Dos Passos's birthday in January 1910, Lucy wrote him from Washington, sending him candy, love, and God's blessings. But the hoped-for improvement did not last. By the end of January she was so ill that a letter to Dos Passos had to be dictated to a friend, who added a note saying, "Your mother dictated this and did not write herself as she has been sitting up all day—the first time for a week."

The pattern of life for the next years was being formed by Lucy's condition. There would be less travel as she settled into her home at 1201 Nineteenth Street, N.W., in Washington; but there were still frequent trips to Sandy Point, so that Dos Passos's memory of the period was that he spent little time in Washington, because most of his longer vacations from school were at the farm in Virginia. More and more his mother needed to be cared for, as she was often too feeble to manage herself or her household.

Early in the spring of 1910 Jack received some news from Lucy that he hoped would make her life easier and aspects of his less furtive. On March 20, Mary Hays Dos Passos had died. From England where John R. was when he got the news, he wired Lucy in Washington; then on the twenty-eighth wrote her a letter in French, as was often his wont. His excitement was such that his spelling and grammar were even more awry than usual. "C'est Pache," he began, "et j'ai envoyé une cable deja. Nous sommes aufin libre!" ("It is Easter, and I have already sent a cable. Finally we are free.") He went on to say that for the first time since they had met he could do the thing he had wanted to. In the cable he had already proposed that, after a nominal wait, they marry. He was overjoyed that now they might become husband and wife without scandal and without divorce and hoped that being able to propose on Easter Sunday would be a good omen for their future.

It was in some ways but not in others. Life might be more nearly what all three of them had hoped for, but the strokes, coupled with Bright's disease, which would eventually kill Lucy, had already begun. As Dos Passos and his father feared, nothing was going to stay her physical deterioration for long, whatever change of fortunes might occur. But at the moment when Lucy heard from John R., she was ecstatic and she wrote immediately to her son at Choate: "I received a cable from D. D. [one form of hers and Dos Passos's nickname for John R., also spelled Didi, or Dedi] and feel happy—just received another and the tears came, which I enclose." She supposed that "we will be together, and a sweet content will tinge all our days *now.*" Only to her sweet Jack did she feel she could let out her whole heart, for "he is all in the world to me, and D. D." Further on she exhorted Dos Passos to feel as she did, an emotional burden for an adolescent, although he seemed to have an uncommon understanding of and sympathy for his sentimental, ill mother, so he took her urgings to heart. "We both love [John R.] devotedly," she told Dos Passos, "for he is worthy, and it will give us infinite pleasure to do all in our power to make him happy. He is worthy of our love, and God will bless him." She believed that God had let them "come through the fire untinged, for with *His* help, we are pure gold. Always thank Him," she exhorted her son; "in our happiness we must not forget Him, from whom all blessings flow. Oh darling," she concluded, "I would love to kiss you this minute, for your heart, I know, is with me in everything." She never mentioned Mary Hays Dos Passos's death, nor hers and John R.'s forthcoming marriage, so perhaps her letter may have perplexed Dos Passos. But he was a dutiful son and pleased about his mother's happiness.

Although John R. and he tried to be optimistic about Lucy, it was hard. In May Dos Passos heard from his father that she seemed "much improved but still a little weak in her memory—and quite incompetent to manage financial affairs—the money she has disbursed since she arrived in Washington is enormous and I cannot follow where a good deal of it has gone. I have told her she must draw no more checks." John R. treated Lucy gently and with good humor, understanding that she was incapable of running a household. Thus when she seemed to be purchasing everything that the maid and the cook requested, he did not berate her but pleaded instead, "Don't forget that I am not *a bank.*" If she continued her spendthrift ways, he would soon be destitute, he assured her, and she would too.

Increasingly John R. confided in Dos Passos and treated him like an equal. The father remained busy, involved with people and projects, and enjoyed telling his son at Choate about them, as when he wrote Dos Passos after visiting Thomas Edison at his laboratory in Orange, New Jersey, in January 1910. "I know him very well," John R. asserted, then told of a new storage battery Edison had invented. But even more than for his inventions, John R. admired the man because "in this age when money seems to be the 'be all and the end all' of human ambition, he although very rich, relegates wealth to a second rank, and looks upon his work as his first love. . . . He is a man after my own style—I wish you had been along to have met him. . . ."

While the dutiful son was also a dutiful student, he did know failure. Between his junior and senior years at Choate, he went in August with his parents to Annisquam, Massachusetts, where he wrote George St. John that he had just received the report of his examinations. "I am very sorry to say," he reported, "that I failed Greek. I do not know why I did but I did. I do not think I ought to have failed as I certainly was perfectly well prepared for it. I got an 'E' in it." His other grades, he reported, were satisfactory: a *C* in Elementary Latin, a *C* in Advanced French, a *P.P.* in English, a *B* in Algebra, and an *A* in Elementary French.

He was looking ahead as he wrote St. John. Because he did not like boarding school, he wanted to be out, and so he inquired, "Do you think that I can prepare for college in one more year? I think that my guardian wishes me to do it and then perhaps to travel for a year before entering Harvard." He continued by outlining his courses for 1910–1911 and closed, "We have rented a cottage for the rest of the summer and are enjoying it very much although we don't know a soul."

The trip to Annisquam, on Cape Ann facing toward Ipswich Bay, had been a pleasant one for Dos Passos and his parents. They took their cottage for part of August and September. Although he and his parents knew no one where they were staying, for at least a part of the time Lois Sprigg and her family were guests at the large, rambling cottage, which was perched on a bluff overlooking the water. The property had its own sheltered beach and a bountiful vegetable garden, which the families did not often use because they walked to a nearby inn for their meals. For the children it was a wonderful place to play. Once, inspired by the garden, they decided to produce a feast. Lois, her younger brother Mercer, and Dos Passos wrote out formal invitations to their parents, then set about the next morning to prepare the vegetables, which they picked and washed. There was confusion about how to cook what they had picked, so they settled on boiling everything. When late in the day a swim had revived the tired cooks, the patient parents were able to sit down to the meal, which reflected more enthusiasm than culinary talent, but then they had to help clean up the substantial mess the three children had made in the kitchen. Another highlight of the Annisquam visit was building and launching a boat they appropriately named *The White Elephant*. Mercer designed it and did most of the work, but Lois and Dos Passos pitched in enthusiastically. When it was finished, the boat was formally launched in front of their parents. With Mercer aboard, it floated satisfactorily, but when the heavier Dos Passos got on, the "elephant" slowly settled below the surface, and they realized to their chagrin that they had forgotten to caulk some of the seams.

While Dos Passos reveled in such chances to be with friends his own age, the shy, inhibited boy could be put off even by his cousins, as when, several years after 1910, he visited the Spriggs at their cottage in Bay Head, New Jersey. Lois, some of her friends, and other cousins his age were playing a game of "Up Jenkins" one evening around the dining-room table. The idea of the game was to pass a coin from hand to hand under the table until at a given signal all hands had to slap the top of the table. Whoever was "it" then guessed who held the coin. Lois and one of her cousins decided to tease Dos Passos by sitting on both sides of him and holding his hands instead of passing the coin. Soon he heaved back his chair and announced that he did not see much point to this game, and his discomfort reminded his cousins of his shyness.

When he returned to Choate for his final year, "Maddie," as Dos Passos was nicknamed, served again on the *Brief* board, was literary editor of the *News,* and acted in theater. Late in October the seniors successfully staged a circus in the gymnasium for the rest of the school. Jack Madison, as always, played the role of a girl, that of "Princess Eva, the Charioteeress." In February 1911 he and Charleton

Wilder again had women's parts, this time, reported the *News*, being "two girls as pretty as one could desire to meet" in William Gillette's *The Private Secretary*. "Charl[e]ton's slim figure and auburn curls involved him in endless flirtations behind the scenes as well as on the stage." Dos Passos, playing the part of Eva Webster, was reported to be as pretty as he had been in his role as Lucy in Sheridan's *The Rivals*, but it was noted that he had grown a bit. In fact, he was now a slender, rather gangling youth, approaching six feet in height. A yearbook writer intending to be humorous about the graduating students said of Dos Passos, "Little 'Maddie,' the class co-ed, has made a hit in girls' parts for the past three years." Whether he wanted to or not, he was destined there to play the role of "girlboy," and in the atmosphere of Choate, that could not but be a bittersweet part.

During his last year, Dos Passos faced a crucial decision: whether or not to change his name from Madison. Then, too, there were the questions of whom to tell and when. The matter might seem simple enough, but it was a delicate subject of some concern to John R. and a reminder to his son of his illegitimacy. Although it is not clear when the boy was told of his parentage, certainly by 1910 he had been, and in October he received a letter from John R. saying that his and Lucy's marriage the previous June 21 in Wilmington, Delaware, was no longer a secret. He instructed his son that "hereafter your letters must be addressed to L. S. D. P. and the name of Madison forever dropped." They would attend to Dos Passos's name later, he went on, but added, "I think you had better quickly give out the fact to Mr. St. John—if you wish—I leave it with you—but I think yes—." Dos Passos kept the name Madison through his final year at Choate. On the surface, nothing more had taken place than that the boy's mother had married her son's guardian, but John R. was correctly sensitive about this. Several people beyond the family knew of John R.'s true relationship; consequently he wanted the utmost discretion about the whole affair. A poignant reminder of his father's extreme sensitivity about the matter was the fact that across the top of the letter he wrote "Detruissez" ("Destroy"). To have his father reveal his embarrassment and sense of impropriety would be painful for Dos Passos each time it occurred, and he could not but be resentful of the hypocrisy social mores forced upon his parents, who were both very much a part of conventional society, as he knew he also had been taught to be.

When he returned to school in January 1911, he decided to try as he had before with little success to keep a diary as a way of organizing himself and, too, of furthering his literary endeavors. He had high hopes for his efforts, determining to make his diary "as interesting as possible to myself. I wish to make it a greater success than any of my former attempts, and will try to write it up each evening before I go to bed." With a flourish he inaugurated his latest effort:

So hail, thou patron divinity of diaries—whichever of the Muses thou art—look propitiously upon my attempts to keep a diary and instill me with a desire for literary fame—. May this diary be as interesting as that of Pepys, as historical as that of "Everett?," as useful as Franklin's—so once again, "Hail, Muse of diaries, all hail"

The next day after beginning his diary he faithfully recorded something, although he was hardly exuberant. "Suffered with Ennui most of the day," he declared, and bemoaned the small part he had in *The Private Secretary*. "It's the smallest part in the play," he complained, "except that of John & Knox—and I feel very badly about not getting a better one." Perhaps the ennui was too great, because more than a month slipped by before he looked at his diary again, and this time it was to record his cash account, as his father frequently badgered him to do. "Alas! What resolutions have been broken!" he wrote, and promised himself to try to do better. He meant to be dutiful to his father and, too, he was aware that at times he could seem vague and scatterbrained to his elders.

He struggled amusingly with his funds. In January he had recorded at one point petty expenses paid out: $.50 for glasses, $.50 for scissors, and $.20 for candy, while he had received $.05 from his friend Walcott and had found $.02 in his pocket, so his cash account stood at a meager $3.87. By mid-February that had dwindled to $.05, but when he picked up his diary next it was to declare that "My purse has been restored today from a state of almost total bankruptcy. Have received a pound of candy from Mother etc. and feel quite jubilant."

Life was hectic; he was a senior with things to do like the play and editing the *News* and the *Brief,* so he neglected his diary again all the way into April, when he returned from spring vacation. "Alas! Alas! Alas! I have done no better in keeping my diary—will try hard, however this time," he promised. He was having little better luck with his cash account. He was, he noted, "again in a state of bankruptcy." But this had some reward, at least, for "it is only when I am in that condition that I write my diary at all." That day he had reason to write, then, because he recorded that he had on hand exactly $.04, paid $.04 for stamps, leaving a total of "0"—"Bankrupt Again!"

It was early in April, when Wallingford was disagreeable, that Dos Passos made his most revealing entry. The weather was rainy and cold, and he suffered from a sore throat, which made him a bit peevish. He worked at his diary only briefly, but before he gave it up, he wrote a lengthy entry for April 9. There is a touch of the melodramatic about it, but his feelings were genuine enough. He was the lonely outsider; even as a senior in a system which gave prestige to the top class, he felt unimportant. That day George St. John had given a talk on "being better than those about you and on being a sort of fellow that changes the condition of affairs." Dos Passos noted:

I so wish that I could be a fellow like that—it is terrible to be in a school to be anywhere where no one respects you! I do not know why it is but no one ever treats me as if I were one of them. Every one is very nice to me but—that is all I have no friends—there is no one who cares a rap about me. No one ever seems to speak to me unless it is necessary; no one ever comes into my room to talk to me. If I go into anyone else's room, I feel that I am not wanted —How happy I could be if I could only have one true friend who did not treat me like a damned little fool—Is it because I am younger tha[n] most of the fellows I am with that they neither respect me, like me, dislike me, hate me? I should rather be hated by every one in the school than looked upon as a non-entity—Elisha and Boozer's remarks which they do not think of penetrate deeper than they think—Perhaps I am a "hated little stuck up fool" I certainly try not to be—but it does hurt me to feel that if I should die tonight it would no[t] make any lasting impression on any one. No one would miss me! No one cares for me at all. But I do not care what misery I go through now if I can only in the future be great—Be the greatest man th[at] ever lived—Be such a man that they will all treasure the remembrance of me and say with pride —"I went to school with John R. Dos Passos" (if I ever do assume that name) But I suppose that it is morbid foolishness to write all [this] and can do no good to any one. . . . But if I can make myself great—oh if I can—

He again lapsed after several days; not until early May did he make another entry, inspired by John R.'s having sent him $10 for his account. Although that was cheering, not so were his father's letters about his mother: "Didi does not send very encouraging reports from mother, I hate to think of it, but I am afraid that she will never get well. He and I long to have her well and to do the countless things which we have always planned to do." His fears proved correct; Lucy's health worsened; and his life with her would be saddening while he tended to her needs as an invalid. The loneliness he felt at school was never entirely assuaged by his time at home.

His final spring at Choate rushed to a close. At the senior class dinner, a dull time, everyone was embarrassed and stiff. George St. John took the occasion to invite the entire class back a year hence, and Dos Passos mused, "I wonder where I will be a year from tonight!" During the following weeks he worked on the *Fiction Supplement* of the *News*, to which he had submitted a short story, "The City of Burnished Copper," watched Choate's successes in baseball, and reveled in the spring weather—"nearly like summer and the trees etc. are all out in fine shape." It was a time to enjoy Choate, the warm spring air, the beauty of the school grounds and the Quinnipiac River, and the blossoms of the trees in the surrounding fields. He wondered as graduation time approached if he would get a diploma. He did not, because he was not a senior. But he finished up well; at prize day he won the award for English and tied for eighth on the honor list with four other students. His peers voted him the best student as well as the class grind; and the *Brief* reported that Maddie's intended occupation was to be a lawyer, like his father. At Choate, his usual occupation, the yearbook noted, was studying, and his classmates suspected that he probably would end up as a schoolteacher because of his bookishness.

After his efforts, he took satisfaction in seeing his work in print. "The City of Burnished Copper" appeared in the May 1911 *Fiction Supplement.* He sent a copy of it to John R., hoping that it would please him. Dos Passos's tale is one of the more skillfully written ones in the issue. It tells of a Professor Ludlowe, who leads an expedition into the Sahara to find "the city of burnished copper." His caravan, save for himself and one camel, is destroyed by a sandstorm. He proceeds, is captured by Arabs, escapes, finds the fabled city, and eventually makes his way back to civilization, where no one believes his tale. Dos Passos's style is clear and direct, and there is some effective description. Even so, the story is flat and turns mechanically on predictable devices: a competent job, but hardly notable.

With school nearly behind him, he might smile a bit at the slight implied by what was listed in the yearbook as his favorite expression, "How thrilling." But he recoiled to read that his disposition was "Meek." Four and a half years at Choate were past, and a touch nostalgically and more than a little hurt he wrote in his diary on June 17, 1911:

> Today I spent my last hours as a pupil at the Choate School I left for Boston, with Walcott at 10.25 A.M. Mr. St. John said goodbye rather coldly, but I must expect that, as I have lost favor with him greatly, lately. I did not get a diploma, either, which surprised me a good deal; for I really think that I deserved one.

That day he had shipped his baggage home, then bought some bananas for his trip before he and Walcott headed off for Boston. Once they arrived, Dos Passos checked into Young's Hotel, where he stayed while he took the entrance exams for Harvard on June 19, 20, and 21. Passing these was crucial, for it meant that he was through with Choate, diploma or not, and ready to enter college after travel abroad during the next year. He succeeded; life among the Rover Boys was ended and he had already left more of a mark than he would have expected. Because of his own insecurity, he misjudged George St. John. During the years that followed, his former headmaster wrote friendly, interested letters to both him and his father, and Dos Passos came to realize that St. John was proud of his former student, whose literary talents were developing at Harvard.

CHAPTER THREE

Westmoreland, Virginia, and the Grand Tour,

1911–1912

Although during his latter years at Choate Dos Passos had increasingly to care for his mother when he was home from school, the life was not always burdensome. Accustomed to the world of adults, he had a better understanding of his elderly parents than most children might have had. "It's hard for the young to interest themselves in the troubles of the old—their own seem so much more urgent—but I did have inklings of [my father's] money worries, of his daily struggle to raise funds to protect speculations he believed would at any moment bring in the fortune he needed to assure a comfortable retirement," he declared. John R. dreamed of settling at Sandy Point, where he hoped to farm and write about law reform. And he wanted desperately to enjoy his remaining time with Lucy, so when her illness dampened the pleasures of their five years of marriage, Dos Passos wrote that he could understand "the tragic frustration of Mother's illness." The son did not then rebel as he might have at the demands placed upon him. Later he did, but that reaction was only part of a wider rebellion he was expressing against the Establishment as he conceived of it.

And, too, what would have caused him to express discontent when Virginia, Sandy Point, and the home they called the White House were what he liked most? John R.'s holdings in Westmoreland County were sizable. Starting in the early 1880s he bought up about 7,000 acres that stretched along the western bank of the Potomac River for some twelve miles from Ragged Point, around Sandy Point, to Lynch's Point, where the Cintra post office and a steamboat dock then were. When John R. first began cruising to Sandy Point, Mary Hays Dos Passos, though already lame, and their son Louis, traveled with him. Later, when circumstances changed and Mary no longer went, he continued to take Louis down, presumably not when

Lucy was along. Subsequently Louis and his own family returned to the White House for vacations until it and the grounds around it were sold in 1928.

John R.'s energies were reflected in the development of the estate. In the 1880s he, his family, and guests stayed in a prefabricated house they called the Portable, which had been shipped in sections down the Potomac and set up just behind the beach at Sandy Point. Soon he added onto a farmhouse just inland from the Portable, by building another section onto what had already been constructed over the foundations of the colonial home of Colonel George Eskridge. He also added a wide screened porch around two sides. This became the White House, which Dos Passos knew as home, a large, two-story frame building with plenty of fireplaces to provide heat and rooms to take care of the numerous guests John R. sometimes brought down the Potomac with him. The Portable became a grand bathhouse for the whole compound.

The steamboat dock and the post office at Cintra were roughly a mile from Sandy Point. Between his house and Cintra John R. had a path cut for his carriage. The short ride over the sandy soil among the pines and undergrowth full of wildlife was his favorite, and it became his custom to take the path almost every afternoon, inviting guests if there were any. He often asked his driver, Albert Johnson, who was dressed up for the occasion, to stop along the way while he made tea from an ornate copper kettle heated by an alcohol burner on a decorated, wrought-iron stand, the whole affair being kept in his carriage for the purpose. Even after Lucy became ill, she often joined John R. on these jaunts, and frequently they stopped to chat to one of John R.'s favorite people in the area, Miss Mary Taliaferro, who had a house between Sandy Point and the post office.

John R. brought modern comforts to Sandy Point. He had a telephone line built from Templeman's Crossroads to Sandy Point, a distance of some fifteen miles. For this he received shares in the Northern Neck Telephone Company. But the region then was remote, with great swaths of wilderness and abundant wildlife visible among the innumerable cuts and inlets along the shoreline. Although Westmoreland County was utterly rural in the late nineteenth century, it had an abundant history which Dos Passos absorbed thoroughly.

It was from John R., also, with his interests in history generally and in Anglo-Saxon civilization specifically, that Dos Passos learned about the backgrounds and traditions permeating Westmoreland County. Sometimes referred to by its inhabitants as "the Athens of Virginia," the county was the birthplace of, among others, George Washington, James Monroe, and Robert E. Lee. Among John R.'s lands, Sandy Point was where "Mary Ball, George Washington's mother, spent her youth in the home of her guardian, Colonel George Eskridge. Here she married Augustine Washington in March 1731. She is supposed to have named her eldest son, George, for Colonel Eskridge," according to a historic marker that stands back a few hundred yards from Sandy Point. John R. also owned a place named Hominy Hall, which had been the birthplace of Richard Henry Lee's first wife. In a booklet entitled *Westmoreland County, Virginia: 1653–1912*, T. R. B. Wright, a local historian, told proudly of the history of some of the lawyer's acquisitions, praising him along with other "progressive men of today" who represented "the progress and development of the age in which we live" and who "are in truth the founders, makers, and builders of our great Republic along all lines of human endeavor in the social, industrial, commercial, and agricultural development of our Commonwealth." Wright welcomed John R. and the others to Westmoreland, for it was they who he hoped would "build up the old historic places of Westmoreland so they may rival the ancient grandeur of these colonial homes of colonial days." The prestige of owning these lands must have pleased John R.

According to Wright, Hominy Hall during the mid-nineteenth century had been the home of Colonel James Steptoe,

> whose eldest daughter, by his first marriage, became the wife of Philip Ludwell Lee, of Stratford [the Lee manor not far north of Sandy Point], and mother of his daughters—Matilda and Flora—the noted belles of that famous home of the era of the Revolution; also "Water View," home of the Temple family of the last century, and the birthplace of Hon. John Critcher, who made himself famous in his debate with Hon. George F. Hoar, of Massachusetts, in the Congress of the United States when the latter charged the depravity of the Southern slave holder.

Wright listed others of John R.'s purchases also: Bonums and Springfield, off whose shores a United States schooner, the *Asp*, battled against the British in 1813. The county was a land about which people could lyricize both because of its natural beauty and because of its significance to the South. Wright's booklet, a paean to the county and its people, was a potpourri of any praise he could find, including "Some Verses From Our Home Poets," one of whom was Alys B. Baines. Shortly before Wright put his booklet together, she had hailed Westmoreland in a poem published in the *Richmond Times Dispatch*. Her verse included such lines as,

> *O, a fertile land and fair*
> *Is Old Westmoreland,*
> *Hallowed ground and balmy air*
> *Has Old Westmoreland.*

> .   .   .

> *'Tis a land where great men trod*
> *In Old Westmoreland,*
> *Tis a memory-hallowed sod*
> *In Old Westmoreland.*
> *And the gentle shade of Lee,*
> *It always seems to me,*
> *The Patron Saint to be,*
> *Of Old Westmoreland.*

Pride like this which Tidewater Virginians felt and the atmosphere it created were not lost on the Dos Passoses.

When the boy was spending his school vacations in Westmoreland, the county was remote. The roads were sand beds, and the overland trip to Richmond, two hours in the 1970s, took nearly three days. Most of the trips Dos Passos made then to Sandy Point were aboard the *Gaivota*, which John R. kept in the Potomac at Washington. These leisurely trips down the river Dos Passos remembered with pleasure. Transformations aboard ship were immediate. John R. donned a yachting cap to become the Commodore. Lucy's role was the Princess, and Dos Passos, Monsieur Singe—Mr. Monkey. To serve them were two blacks, Tom, a cook, and Old Ben, who was also John R.'s valet ashore. The voyages were merry; Dos Passos played the record machine equipped with the characteristic large horn of the period. Lucy, as Dos Passos later remembered it, "would lie back in a deck chair, weak and vague, but with a sweet lost look of loveliness she never lost," while John R. rendered a quick tap dance to the music. The Potomac was a river of sights: there were boats to be seen, like the presidential yacht or a Civil War monitor, and many others. Below Indian Head on the Maryland side not far from Quantico, Virginia, Dos Passos saw untouched creeks, sandy points jutting out into the river, and abundant wildlife. Underway, the *Gaivota*'s dinghy towed astern was the best spot to fish from, or if the ship was anchored for the night, one could cast off in the dinghy, while all around were birds to watch: gulls swooping close, coots scuttling across the placid water or rising in a flock, an occasional eagle in the trees along the shore, or crows, calling to one another from their perches—laughing at the *Gaivota* and her crew, or so Dos Passos liked to believe.

The life at Sandy Point was active. Conversation was easy, and there was swimming when the weather was warm, horseback riding, reading, and gardening. Dos Passos was responsible for having a goldfish pond built on the river side of the White House, and as an avid gardener, he taught his cousin Lois Sprigg many things about gardens when her family visited in Westmoreland. Once he was old enough, he supervised some of the care of Sandy Point and occasionally wrote his father about the state of things, as when he reached the farm in the late spring of 1913 after his first year at Harvard. He reported that a new boat landing at Sandy Point and a nearly completed carriage house were fine. The vegetable garden, however, was "a dreary waste—a regular Sahara—chiefly weeds & cabbages." What had been done with seeds that had been sent down to the farm he could not imagine, and he blamed the men working around the place. "The gardener Rhode will not do at all," he complained to John R. "He does moderately well when I am over him, but he does not know how to attend to the garden. Moreover he is stupid and unreliable, and I don't think over honest in little things." After recommending that his father start looking for someone else, Dos Passos closed by urging him to take the advice because "the present people are most unsatisfactory."

By the time Dos Passos began to do some supervising, John R. had also set Lucy's older son James Madison at work on the farm as a kind of supervisor. When Dos Passos was away, he corresponded with James about ideas for planting; clearly

Dos Passos took a keen interest in such matters. James was even a companion of sorts for Dos Passos at Sandy Point, but being nearly twenty-three years older than his half-brother, he was scarcely an intimate friend. He caused his mother and step-father some embarrassment. A gentle, unambitious man who had the good fortune to have been aided by John R., he worked around Sandy Point and frequently drank too heavily, going on sprees, only to return, apologetic about having missed work or an appointment.*

Although Dos Passos enjoyed being aboard the *Gaivota* and being active at the farm, these situations reminded him of the distance between him and those less genteel than he or his family who, from his romantic perspective, lived life as he did not. In a Camera Eye passage of *U.S.A.* he described talking to a wanderer little older than he. The waif had "curly hair and wisps of hay in it and through his open shirt you could see his body was burned brown to the waist." While the *Gaivota* was anchored off Crisfield, a town on the Eastern Shore of Maryland across the Chesapeake Bay from the mouth of the Potomac, the two conversed, and the young Dos Passos was fascinated by the strapping, independent boy, who had "bummed all way from Minnesota" on his way south. When Dos Passos told him that he would have to cross the wide Chesapeake to continue on his way, the boy was not surprised. "I guess it's too fur to swim it I'll git a job in a menhaden boat," he responded, while the inhibited Dos Passos envied the other's vitality and freedom.

Or another time he was awed by a towboat captain who lived in Alexandria, Virginia, and worked the Chesapeake Bay region. Dos Passos recalled the man reaching up to pull the whistle in a pilothouse—perhaps aboard the *Gaivota*—and exposing "the red and green bracelet tattooed under the black hairs on his wrist." The captain told of "oysterin" on the Eastern Shore and of oyster pirates who would shanghai boys to work for them during the winters. The only way to escape was to swim ashore, but the water was icy, and the pirates could be cruel. Once, the captain said, some pirates worked a boy until he died and then heaved his body overboard. The captain remembered hauling in a body in an oyster dredge; he called the corpse a "stiff." "What's a stiff?" asked Dos Passos. "A dead man," the captain answered, and this one was naked, the body beaten horribly with a belaying pin or an oar. "Reckon he wouldn't work or was sick or somethin'," the captain said. His murderer "couldn't a been nothin' but an oysterpirate."

Although there was life, sometimes violence, around Dos Passos, he felt shielded from it, not only from the excitement that people like the bumming youth or the captain knew, but even from the life of the natives of Westmoreland County. John R. might be praised for his progressive spirit—T.R.B. Wright even went so

---

*James Madison remained around Sandy Point even after a large portion of John R.'s land was sold in 1928. He derived some small income from working there until he moved to Smithfield, Virginia, to work in a family concern. He later married, remaining in Smithfield until his death. His drinking made him something of a local character at Sandy Point; during Prohibition, neighbors recalled, he had a penchant for lemon and vanilla extract, which he would on occasion down at a great rate. And a habitual rendezvous of his was at one of the docks along the shoreline, where he drank with bootleggers when they brought their liquor ashore.

far as to write John R. that he was "an adopted Son of Westmoreland" in the same letter in which he asked if the lawyer would like to donate "a portrait or a piece of statuary of some great American" to the courtroom at Montross—yet he was not a native. The Dos Passos family were outsiders who had bought in. Appreciation of them by older families was genuine but from a distance. They were not an intimate part of such social occasions as May 3, 1910, the "Big Day at Montross," the Westmoreland County seat, which was reported soon after in the Northern Neck News of Warsaw, Virginia. May 3 had been the occasion for accepting portraits, tablets, and statues given to the county. "Ladies of Westmoreland" had given a luncheon, followed by speeches from various dignitaries. "The flower and chivalry of the county assembled there," it was reported, and "the brave and patriotic manhood and the presence and grace of cultured and lovely womanhood made [the gathering] brilliant." An organist led in singing Southern songs, national anthems, and hymns, assisted by local young women. As much as Dos Passos might have wanted to be a part of these occasions, he could not have brought himself to be familiar with the Misses Atwill, who sang on the Big Day. He might look on, even dress rakishly in a white monogrammed silk shirt, white flannel trousers, and a flowing red sash around his waist, or on occasion he might ride through the neighborhood on Rattler, a frisky horse that threw him more than once. But as a rule he held back.

He had strong adolescent yearnings. Despite craving the freedom to satisfy growing sexual urges, he felt constrained by his upbringing. Although the young bummer from Minnesota might find a girl whenever he wanted and while Dos Passos sensed that he, too, had opportunities to release his sexual drives with some of the girls around him, social pressures firmly bound him, down in the Northern Neck as elsewhere. When he was older, he understood the strength of these urges, writing about them repeatedly in autobiographical fiction. In a short story, "July," published in 1924, Dos Passos set an autobiographical hero, Jimmy Herf, in the Northern Neck during the summer before Herf's first year at Harvard. The youth feels thoroughly out of place among the country people. When the story opens, the mare drawing his buggy has balked, and as he tries desperately to get her to budge, the daughters of Old Man Oatley, who owns the local store, giggle and titter around the buggy. "Woan he go?" they ask, offering some free advice to embarrass Jimmy: "Put sand in his mouf," "Light a fire under his tail," "Git out and lead him." But the horse will not stir, and the girls hail their father, who quickly makes the mare move. As a kind of refrain during much of the story, a romantic image runs through Herf's mind: "And the lovely Kathleen Cranmer was striding by his side . . . went riding by his side," until at last his heroic persona, Eric Stone, and Kathleen Cranmer, having escaped from a band of villains, leap into a barge rowed by a naked crew and soon lie together, rocking "naked in each other's arms in the brocaded love barge among the lotus flowers." Such dreams of passion are far from reality, though, because Herf's greatest adventures are to buy a pack of cigarettes from Oatley's store and sense the bulge of a young girl's breast against his arm when he teaches her to swim. But no further intimacies result, and Herf's anxiety surges up again and again: from the sight of a woman's stomach full with child; or from the intimations of desire of a minister's wife, more a plea for any emotional response than for Herf's in particular. After his encounter with the woman, Herf takes a naked, solitary swim, and when he returns to the house dares as much as to lay a trembling hand for an instant on the door to a servant girl's room. But just then his aunt comes down the hall where he stands and he retreats, mortified, to his room.

Herf's dream of passion is fulfilled when the storekeeper Oatley and the minister's wife run off together. Herf meets the fleeing couple on the road and later sends the pursuing sheriff off in the wrong direction. Soon after he wanders to the shore to relax and swim, and at that moment he sees the two lovers in a small sailboat heading out toward the Maryland Eastern Shore. Back at his house Herf cannot put the incident out of his mind. What terrible things nice people do, he thinks to himself. Yet this was exciting, and amid his family's chatter about the adventure, he blushes violently, nearly breaking out in tears. Serving himself some spinach, he brushes his hand against the servant girl's bare arm and snatches his hand away "as if he had been burned." His food tastes like ashes in his mouth.

Although the facts of "July" are fiction, the spirit was not. Dos Passos's sense of his own longing was well rendered in the story, for it was a feeling about those days that had stayed with him. He even repeated parts of the episode in a Camera Eye. There the minister's wife did nothing as dramatic as run away, but she appealed to the young Dos Passos just as she had to Jimmy Herf. "A tall thin woman who sang little songs at the piano in a spindly lost voice," she seemed to thirst for Life. Dos Passos remembered a moment walking back along the shore when he felt he ought to kiss her. But he lacked the nerve.

Dos Passos recalled that he had been wildly romantic and wanted to run off "to sea and to foreign cities Carcassone Marakesh Isfahan and liked things to be beautiful. . . ." And as much as wishing for adventure, he craved "the nerve to hug and kiss Martha the colored girl they said was half Indian old Emma's daughter and little redheaded Mary I taught how to swim if I only had the nerve breathless nights when the moon was full. . . ." Yet a third time Dos Passos drew from these small adventures in *Chosen Country*, where the autobiographical hero, Jay Pignatelli, dreams of:

> The cook's daughter whom he taught to swim down at the beach. . . . The older people would be sitting under parasols on the shore and he'd say come on Annie I'll give you a swimming lesson. He was fourteen and she was fifteen and she wouldn't say anything but she'd come out almost to the raft where the water was quite deep up to their armpits and he would hold up her chin with his hand and she'd make frogmotions to learn the breaststroke and he'd hold up her middle with the other hand and she must have liked it because she never said anything when his hand slid up towards her little breasts slippery with seawater or down past the bellybutton that's the same in girls as it is in boys. . . .

And once Jay sees her naked as she takes off her suit after a swim. He yearns to burst into where she stands but does not dare. Rushing to his own room, he changes out of his bathing suit and scurries downstairs to entertain his mother. Dos Passos's sexual fantasies as an adolescent remained only dreams. He could never force himself to seize any opportunity for sex; he was, in fact, somewhat of a prude.

One way Dos Passos might become more at ease with the world, John R. thought, would be for his son to travel extensively in Europe and the Near East. So after passing the entrance exams at Harvard in June 1911, Dos Passos spent his summer at Sandy Point preparing for a trip which his parents arranged for him to take under the tutelage of a young man, a Mr. Jones, whom, Dos Passos recollected, they nicknamed "Uncle Virgil." Jones "had some classical attainments and was planning to become a Dominican monk." He was a pleasant man, and by the time the two sailed for England on November 15 aboard the *Baltic*, they were good friends. Their travels took them from England through France and then south toward Italy through Avignon, Marseilles, and Cannes. The latter part of December they spent in Italy—Genoa, Pisa, Rome, Naples and its environs—before crossing the Mediterranean to Egypt. From Cairo, they voyaged up the Nile, then in February crossed back to Athens before heading to Smyrna and sailing to Constantinople, whence they cruised back through the Dardanelles to Piraeus. They spent several days in Athens, then traveled to Delphi and other places in Greece, finally sailing to Corfu and then Trieste along the Dalmatian coast. On March 10 they took a train to Venice from Trieste and, back in Italy once again, visited Rome after sightseeing in other parts of the country. By mid-April they were in Milan, on their way by train to Paris. "The time is very short now before I shall be with the dear Baby," Dos Passos wrote his mother—Baby—on April 14, 1912. "I will stay a very short time in Paris and about five or six days in London." Early in May he and Mr. Jones had returned to the United States.

John R. missed his son and wrote him frequently, often in French, about the goings on at Cintra, about what Dos Passos was seeing, about John R.'s reading, and about Lucy—always expressing the hope that she was improving. In his imperfect French John R. sallied forth confidently and with humor, as when, two weeks after Dos Passos and Mr. Jones had sailed, he wrote on December 1:

Je suis ici à la Maison Blance—avec Dr Sprigg et deux autre ami—pour la chasse. Ils ont eu une jolie chasse tuant une grande quantite des quails et les lapins. Les oiseaux sout bien numbreuse et la chasse extraordinairement bonne. Ils sont dormi à la Maison Blanche et nous avons trouvé beaucoup des mice dedans et un mouse lit en la centre d'un de nos lits! Il sera bien difficile les a chassé dehors mais j'ai donné les directions à Scott bien impressé et il va à faire une essay les à tué. Jusqua maintenant la troisème jour il a fait le temps marveilleux le soleil etant pas le soleil d'hiver mais d'automme et la Maison Blanche etait radieuse avec son lumiere. J'ai voulu que le famille a été la. Nous avons trouvé les choses en le jardin tres bien et une rose en bloom! La dernière fleur d'étè—Comme he broke forth in a song of exceptional beauty. J'attends les nouvelles de vous bientôt maintenant et j'attend d'entendre les details de votre voyage. Votre Oncle Will est ayant l'occassion de sa né. James est bien mais il n'a pas reçu les nouvelles de vous, il a attendu une lettre de le pilot quand vous êtes parti. Dieu tu garde à jamais.

Affectuesement
Dedi

Mes regards à Monsieur Jones.*

When the letter caught up with Dos Passos in Cairo, he must have laughed at his father's French—a kind of free-form style full of errors, but obviously written with gusto and affection.

The invalided Lucy, when she felt strong enough, tried to write also, although her efforts served only to remind Dos Passos of her deteriorating health, as when, at the end of March 1912, she attempted a letter. "My own darling," she began, "how glad I will be to place my arms around your dear neck again once more of course you have had a glorious time, and if God wills I will have the same trip once again, and with my own." Here her writing became illegible and ended after another five lines. The letter was finished by the woman who had just recently taken over as her nurse, Mrs. Mary E. Harris. "Baby grew tired and stopped writing so I will finish it," Mrs. Harris added and then wrote three pages of news about his parents.

Dos Passos knew well his mother's growing feebleness and the difficulties she had in talking or doing anything physical. He was the dutiful son during his trip, writing often to describe the sights and explain the significance of what he was learning. He could sound stuffy, and John R., amused, warned him to "forego dogmatism" when his letters became too priggish and stiff. But they were not always so. Dos Passos was excited to get to Rome on December 14 and immediately scribbled a card to his father: "Nous sommes arrivés ici de Paris, il y à quelques minutes. Nous sommes a la ville Eternelle! Where Caesar ruled, where Cicero thundered against Cataline, where Virgil read the Aeneid to Great Augustus!" And at the same moment he tried to cheer his mother by exclaiming, "Imperial Rome! Conqueror of the world! Enlightener of the ages! We are within thine ancient

---

*I am here at the White House—with Dr. Sprigg and two other friends—for some hunting. They had a fine hunt, killing a large number of quail and rabbits. The birds are very numerous and the hunting extraordinarily good. They have slept in the White House and we found lots of mice inside and a mouse bed in the middle of one of our beds. It will be very difficult to hunt them outside, but I have given firm instructions to Scott and he is going to try to kill them. Up to now, the third day, it has been beautiful weather, the sun being not a winter sun but an autumn sun and the White House was radiant with its light. I wished that the family were there. We have found things in the garden very well and a rose in bloom! The last flower of summer—like "he broke forth in a song of exceptional beauty." I await news of you soon now and I wait to hear the details of your trip. Your Uncle Will is having his birthday. James is well but he has not received news of you. He waited for a letter from the pilot when you left. God watch over you always.

Affectionately,
Dedi

My regards to Mr. Jones.

walls! From the Imperial City to the Royal Princess love and greeting."

The trip was giving him some of the self-assurance he craved. When he wrote *The Best Times*, he flippa..ly described the tour as one where he "quoted Gibbon in the Roman Forum; read Thucydides (from the trot) in Athens and evoked Julius Caesar and Napoleon while brushing off the baksheesh-seekers in front of the Sphinx." A much-traveled man by the time he wrote his memoir, he could play down the trip and lightly mock himself. In 1911–1912, at the age of fifteen and sixteen, however, he was away from adult authority as he had never been before; he was traveling in Europe again; he was seeing parts of the Near and Middle East for the first time; and now he was mature enough to absorb something of the history and cultures of the Continent and to appreciate the magnificence of its sights.

His concern for historical detail was developing, and in his diary he carefully recorded what he saw. The entries have little if any of the interpretive about them —the stuff of which fiction is made—but they show perception and a sharpening observation and sense of history, as when on December 8 he and Mr. Jones were in Avignon. After breakfasting at their hotel, they left their baggage at the railway station, then went out to look about the walled city, as full of history as anywhere in France. "First we went to the ancient Palace of the Popes, which was begun in 1336 and finished in 1364," Dos Passos wrote in his diary. "Jean XXII the second Pope to live there was one of its chief constructors." Dos Passos's history was not quite accurate, but he did better than most visitors in sorting out the complex history of Avignon, the popes, and the antipopes who resided there from 1309 to 1403.

"The style is sombre gothic and the buildings are being restored by the government," he jotted down, "as they were very much mutilated at the time of the revolution, when the Palace was turned into a fort." He noted some of the large frescoes which were in the process of being uncovered and remarked on the prison "in which [the Italian patriot Cola di] Rienzi was confined during the 11 months he was a prisoner of the Popes." Leaving the palace, Dos Passos and Mr. Jones glanced into the adjoining cathedral, Notre-Dame-des-Doms, set next to a magnificent garden overlooking the Rhône River and Pont St. Bénézet—the "pont d'Avignon" of the famous song—beyond the walls of Avignon. Across the river lay the smaller town of Villeneuve-lès-Avignon, historically fascinating with its tower of Phillipe le Bel and Fort St. André in full view from the garden. It would have been difficult not to be enthralled by the city and its environs, whose history of frequent secular and religious struggles stretched back to Roman times.

The two then crossed the Rhône to Villeneuve-lès-Avignon, "one of the *dirtiest* and most picturesque little places I have been in for a long while," Dos Passos thought. He was correct; photos of Villeneuve among his pictures from the trip show just how filthy the place was: dirt streets, blackened walls—in all it had then a run-down look about it which has since been scrubbed away by the French government. But the filth did not disturb him greatly: "The old walls are well preserved all around the city and are especially interesting on this side of the city, the side overlooking the Rhone and facing Avignon." Even more interesting than the cathedral at Avignon was the church at Villeneuve, because "it was originally the chapel to a monastery of Franciscans, and there are the remains of old cloisters near it. In the vestry, we saw a very interesting and well executed statue of the Virgin in ivory."

Although he was not trying to make these notes sparkle, the marks of his later reportage are here. The diary as well as his letters reveal what he was absorbing: a love of travel, a knowledge of Europe, the Near East, and art—and an understanding and sensitivity about them. Repeatedly he discovered a place or a scene that excited him. Three weeks after leaving Avignon he was in Naples, from where he and Mr. Jones traveled along the steep coastline down to Sorrento. They had intended to take a steamer out to the island of Capri, but rough weather discouraged them, so they hired a guide to lead them to the monastery on top of the Monte Deserto behind the town. He wrote that night in his journal that from the roof of the monastery "we got a magnificent view, one of the most beautiful I have ever seen. On one side stretched the bay of Naples, with Ischia in the far distance and Vesuvius towering above the cities clustered about its base. On the other side, we could see the mountains above Sorrento and behind them the beautiful Gulf of Salerno, while, immediately before us, Capri looked so near that one might almost have tried to throw a stone to it." To add to their pleasure, the monk who had taken them up on the roof then ushered them into the monastery where he served them wine and biscuits. Afterward they hiked down the steep Monte Deserto, ate lunch, and took a carriage to Castellammare and, subsequently, a train to Naples.

Nor was the beauty of Delphi lost on him. In late February the two travelers left Corinth for Isthmia, where they took a steamer up the Gulf of Corinth for Itea. They arrived there late in the afternoon, enjoying "a lovely drive up the mountainside to Delphi which we reached by moonlight a little after eight." The next morning, the last day of February, he recorded:

> When I awoke this morning & looked out of my window a most beautiful panorama greeted my eyes. Delphi lies near the top of one of the spurs of Parnassus and below it stretches a deep valley with numerous gorges leading to it. In the distance one could see the bay and beyond a little slip of land, the Corinthian Gulf. The mountains of Achaea, several of them snow-capped, occupied the far horizon. I took a short walk up the road which winds along high above the valley before breakfast which I enjoyed very much.

He described the ruins which they later explored—interesting but not imposing, he thought, because so little remained. More enthralling was the museum and especially the bronze statue of the Charioteer, one of the finest sculptures Dos Passos had seen.

Although too much should not be read into Dos Passos's comments in his diary or the letters to his parents, it is hard not to see in them the sixteen-year-old boy developing into the writer he would become. He had a dry sense of humor; the evening of December 12 he wrote in his diary about a visit to the casino at Monte Carlo where, he noted, "the bank seemed to win at least 60% of the plays. That shows how profitable the casino is to the principality of Monaco." That day he and

Mr. Jones had traveled on to Genoa, and he was delighted by the train ride which threaded between the Maritime Alps and the Mediterranean. He was amused by his accommodations: "Wc put up at a hotel which boasts that it entertained the Roosevelt family! Hail, immortal Theodore! Which is the greater Napoleon at Avignon or Roosevelt at Genoa?"

Seldom did he respond with unrestrained emotion, although powerful emotions and a romantic instinct lay beneath what he wrote. "My dear Mother," he began a letter on March 22 while he and Mr. Jones were staying at the Grand Hotel in Florence, "we went through the Pitti Palace this morning and then crossed by that famous Ponte Vecchio Passage which Baby talks about to the Uffizi, where we walked for some time. This afternoon we went to see Fra Angelico's marvelous frescoes at the convent of St. Marco. There is a lightness and ethereal charm about them that is wonderful." Here was but a hint of what he felt; yet a cultural and intellectual exposure such as few of his contemporaries ever received worked powerfully on him. Shy, awkward, romantic, he channeled his energies toward art and history. The result would eventually be writing that even while it rang with sympathy for the underdog, had a seeming objectivity about it, reflected his knowledge of the arts and their techniques, and showed a broad learning and a fascination with history.

He could not but be excited by the architecture, the art—the overwhelming sense of history—that pervaded Florence. The Grand Hotel de la Ville where he and Mr. Jones stayed is on the Piazza Ognissanti, bordering the Arno River only a short distance from the center of the city. They would have walked along the Arno and crossed over the sixteenth-century Ponte St. Trinita to get to the Pitti Palace, built late in the fifteenth century. Here they took in, among others, paintings by Raphael, Filippo Lippi, Fra Bartolommeo, Andrea del Sarto, Titian, Tintoretto, and Rubens, hung in the Palatine Gallery. They strolled on to the royal apartments and the silver museum, adorned with tapestries and full of sculptures, silverwork, porcelains, and other art. They might have looked out behind the Pitti Palace into the terraced Boboli Gardens, although it was not until two days later that they took the time to stroll through the gardens, which Dos Passos thought a bit "seedy" and unkept. There they laughed at the amusingly profane sculpture of Little Bacchus, a fat, naked dwarf astride a large turtle. Afterward they crossed over the Arno on the Ponte Vecchio, which Dos Passos could recall his mother had described to him and hoped vainly that she might see once more. On both sides of the bridge are gold- and silversmiths' shops dating back to the sixteenth century, while overhead runs a corridor linking the Pitti and Uffizi palaces. Most times of the day the bridge is jammed with people. Dos Passos might have been reminded of how he saw himself —the outsider, fascinated by humanity, staring at a swarm of people who moved past, yet apart from them. "The stream of sensation flows by—I suck it up like a sponge—my reactions are a constant weather vane," he wrote in his diary five years later as he wandered about Paris before heading to ambulance duty around Verdun. Even then, however, he did not feel part of the stream and believed he still held back from a warm spontaneity as he had in his youth, and four months later with the ambulance corps in Italy he wondered, "Have I the faculty for making friends? I wonder—I seem in my life to have made exactly two—which is little for one so greedy as I." "A double foreigner," as he described Jay Pignatelli, must have been time and again his idea of himself while he moved alongside swarms of people wherever he traveled—in Paris, Rome, and Florence—and as he peered into their lives, their histories, and their roots. Even while he enjoyed being the tourist, he thought about his own sense of rootlessness.

Nowhere does Italy's past come more alive than in the Uffizi Palace, where Dos Passos and Mr. Jones turned next to study the tapestries, sculpture, and paintings by Botticelli, da Vinci, Bellini, Dürer, Holbein, Raphael, Michelangelo, Titian, Caravaggio, and Rembrandt. The two Americans lingered at the Uffizi, then walked through the center of the city to see Fra Angelico's frescoes, passing on their way the most famous landmark in Florence, the Cathedral of Santa Maria del Fiore and the baptistry with its doors facing the cathedral. Farther on they found the Monastery of St. Mark, practically a museum of Fra Angelico's works, where his frescoes adorn the walls of numerous rooms. Dos Passos was struck by the paintings' delicacy and calm even with the artists' ability to depict a swarm of activity and color in a fresco like *The Last Supper*.

If Dos Passos's diary entries did not reveal much of the stuff of fiction, his letters did on occasion. During his stay in Florence he wrote his father at length and proceeded to analyze the character of the Greek Alcibiades. "You ask me what I think of Alcibiades," he wrote on March 28. "It seems to me that he must have been in early life a proud, ambitious, but indolent young man about town in Athens. He had a great deal of magnetism and talent but had no principle except the desire for his own happiness." Dos Passos outlined Alcibiades's career in some detail, carefully choosing his words, editing them here and there. "He seems to me to have been one of the most dangerous men possible. If he had been totally bad, he could have done no harm, but it was his great good qualities, which if united with a moral courage and a disinterested patriotism would have made him a great man, that gave him his immense power to do evil."

The previous month he had amused his father by trying his hand at storytelling. In stilted prose he attempted to describe a dream vividly. "We took the trip to the Temple of the Eleusian Mysteries at Eleusis today by carriage along the Sacred Way over which the yearly procession travelled from Athens," Dos Passos wrote on February 19. After a picnic lunch, he said he had entered a cave in the Acropolis of Eleusis, where "I being weary stretched myself out on the stones and lo, in a moment, I slept.

"Of a sudden it seemed to me that I waked," he claimed, then spun a tale about a vision of a white bird of Truth whose veil thickened or lightened in the presence of "the great tragedians," Socrates, Aristotle, Plato, Cicero, and finally Marcus Aurelius. After these Barbarism swept in and the bird fled. "Then, with a start, I awoke, and realized what I had seen," he asserted to John R. "I had seen the results of the Eleusian Mysteries; though the Mysteries themselves are lost in the depths of time they had brought the scholars, philosophers and poets and all the initiated in Greece and Rome nearer the snow-white Bird." His manner of telling was excessive; even Dos Passos did not take his litany seriously. Further, he knew John R. would enjoy his appre ation of mythology and the attempt to weave a story around it.

As their trip drew to a close the end of March, Dos Passos and Mr. Jones took the train south from Florence to Perugia, then traveled on to Rome for another stay before heading north once more in mid-April. Dos Passos wrote his mother that they would leave Italy on April 15, go to Paris, then cross the channel to England for five or six days in London before sailing for the United States on April 24. By May 5 he and Mr. Jones were approaching New York harbor. Aboard ship Dos Passos made a characteristic and revealing gesture of affection toward Lucy, writing her a postcard when they were almost in sight of Sandy Hook. He expected to send a Marconi wire giving the hour of his arrival. He knew, he wrote, that he would probably get to Lucy at the same moment as the card did, but he wanted her to know he was thinking of her. Two or three days later he arrived in Washington, pleased to be home even if it meant facing the tedium of caring for Lucy. In the nearly seven months since he had left Virginia he had seen and learned much that added to his self-confidence as he prepared to enter Harvard in September 1912.

PART II

Harvard and Spain,
1912–1917

CHAPTER FOUR

Harvard: The First Years, 1912–1915

When Dos Passos arrived in Washington to see his parents after his European tour, he found John R. busy with a case he was arguing before the Supreme Court and increasingly involved in the scuffle going on in Baltimore for the Democratic presidential nomination which eventually went to Woodrow Wilson. Dos Passos's first greeting of his mother was poignant; she was now a complete invalid, requiring constant care. For the moment he was put in charge of the household, but once Mrs. Harris returned to look after Lucy, his responsibilities lessened. He and his father came to like Mrs. Harris very much; she was gentle and understanding with Lucy and able to keep the households in Washington and at the farm going when Dos Passos or John R. was not around.

But even Mrs. Harris's presence that summer did not ease Dos Passos's sense of the weight of his responsibilities. Household bills had to be paid, the marketing done, and the help supervised. On one occasion he had to fire the cook, Lizzie, a constant drinker, whose final binge at 1201 Nineteenth Street after Dos Passos had released her left him with the unpleasant task of cleaning up the maids' room, where she had vomited profusely.

The days passed slowly in Washington during the hot, late spring of 1912, and with Lucy being particularly weak, Dos Passos was restricted in his activities. After his months of freedom abroad, home seemed especially confining. He read voraciously to while away the time and rushed through H. G. Wells's *The War of the Worlds* and a string of his tales that had appeared in *The Strand Magazine*. George Eliot's novels did not excite him, but he forged through them anyway as well as through much of Edgar Allan Poe.

John R., as always, kept in close touch while he was about his business in

Washington and Baltimore. When June arrived, the family traveled to Sandy Point, where John R. visited when he could. Once he twitted Lucy about her extravagances as he was on his way back to Washington. She was incapable of keeping household accounts by then, and the expenditures of money annoyed him. Even so, he wrote with some humor that "It was a wise precaution to tell me not to examine the bills until I was 20 miles away from the White House. Neither my voice nor any other weapon that I had within my reach would have enabled me to show my disapprobation or anger—if I had possessed any such feeling." Then his tone mellowed:

> But the distance also prevented me from expressing the only sentiment I had after glancing over the accounts—one of absolute approval and satisfaction. . . . The mere fact that the milk bill showed the purchase of enough of that fluid to bathe in two or three times—(and aren't milk baths recommended?) And that the druggist bill contained sufficient fluids and powders to poison ten regiments of four thousand men each, neither the one nor the other of these facts disturbed my equanimity.

Such a kindly response when he was perturbed was not atypical. His gentleness with Lucy was touching, especially as he seemed to be boastful, egocentric, and a self-styled participant in important schemes. Busy as he was, he wrote Lucy daily when he was away from her—long letters, in which he might talk about the joy of living, the meaning of dreams, his fancies, or his ideas about beauty, intellect, and the soul. He might begin a letter with a stern rebuke, or a self-indulgent interpretation of what interested him at the moment. That August he wrote Lucy a letter in which he continued a discussion he had already begun about psychology. "Psychology as I said yesterday is an interesting—impressive, very wonderful study," he declared. "It shows the mind, heart and soul of one you gaze at without the aid of the tongue. The expression of one of the features of the face or of all of them together indicates love, sympathy or other kindred passions or often vindictive and adverse feelings." All very serious this was, but then he shifted to a humorous discussion of the meaning of gestures and facial features such as the chin. John R. knew that Lucy was entertained by his lengthy discourses, written in a chatty style. Theirs was a closeness that could not help but move Dos Passos.

In July he and his father journeyed to Cambridge to secure a room for the coming year at Harvard. After talking with the dean and the bursar of the college and making whatever arrangements were needed, they traveled out to Marblehead Neck, where before their dinner John R. wrote Lucy about what they had been doing. "Our real happiness dates back about a little more than a year!" he told her. "And here Jack & I are sitting on the porch, drinking our tea & making a retrospect —covering the whole time." John R., not entirely to be amusing, asserted that the day was momentous. "We have made history today," he went on. "The boy has begun his career. Let us hope that his skull will not grow thicker during the summer but that he will enter college fresh, ambitious and determined to make the name he bears—illustrious—not in riches but in learning. Ma chère et bien aimé bon soir."

Fresh, ambitious, and determined were accurate terms to describe Dos Passos. Although his reticence had not left him, a new self-assurance lay beneath his deference. When he was younger, he had wanted to go to the U.S. Naval Academy at Annapolis, a natural desire given his familiarity with the region of the Chesapeake Bay, his love for the water, and his wish to prove his sturdiness. But his eyesight was too poor for him to be accepted, which was probably fortunate, because he most assuredly would have chafed against the academy's authoritarian regime. He later claimed that while he was in college he did not know what sort of career he wanted; yet it is plain that he yearned to succeed in the arts. He worked hard at his writing. His admiration for his father, while distant, was considerable, and he knew John R. approved of his literary efforts. As his writing developed, it became one area where he could compete successfully. Dos Passos would never be the boisterous, outgoing man his father was, and the son had little interest in the law, a career not in keeping with the man he saw himself becoming. Moreover, he had even then a seldom articulated distrust of the genteel society to which he thought lawyers belonged. Reticent, not until much later in his life would he learn to do such public things as giving reasonably effective readings of his work; but always he remained diffident, and when someone doubted him or challenged his ideas, he was more likely to back off out of politeness than he was to argue vehemently. And, too, he stuttered, particularly when he was nervous or agitated. He had an acute sense of what he thought his upper-middle-class peers judged to be his shortcomings. He accepted their judgments, even somewhat believed that these were his father's judgment of him—although they were not—and so he denigrated himself while becoming increasingly critical of bourgeois society.

But his was a sharp, fresh mind as he was about to enter college. He was both inquisitive and well educated. Having been immersed in Western culture, he was ready to be impressed by the cultural ferment of Cambridge, where his four years were crucial to his development. He often expressed reservations about Harvard; yet he was fortunate to end there, where despite his protestations and his later criticism that the students lived life under a bell glass, he was freer than ever he had been before while among persons who shared his interest in the arts.

The excitement of the Harvard Dos Passos was entering was quickly apparent to him. Under the liberal leadership of its previous president, Charles W. Eliot, it had become an undisputed academic leader among American universities. When Dos Passos arrived in Cambridge, A. Lawrence Lowell was entering his third year as president, and though a very different sort of man from Eliot, he worked just as hard as had his predecessor to improve the university's distinction. Harvard had its share of social snobbery; nonetheless, it was a place where one might be exposed to a wide variety of ideas and cultural attitudes. Students enjoyed the lectures by such learned professors as Charles T. Copeland, who taught composition and imbued his students with an eclectic taste for literature. Copey was but one outstanding example of the instruction the Harvard undergraduate could find. An interested student was sure to know of the opinions of Professors Barrett Wendell and Irving Babbitt, who championed the classics and had few kind words for modern literature and culture, particularly American. But even when Professor Babbitt condemned moderns such as the French Symbolists Baudelaire, Rimbaud, and Verlaine, he was introducing them to his students. Dos Passos and his peers, increasingly enthralled by "the new" in the arts, were more apt to turn in fascination to poets like the Symbolists, partly at least because they represented a revolt from what preservers of tradition like Babbitt espoused.

Journals for student writing abounded. The *Advocate*, the *Lampoon*, the *Illustrated Magazine*, and the college newspaper, the *Crimson*, thrived, although the *Illustrated Magazine*, like another journal, the *Harvard Monthly*, would end with World War I. The *Monthly* was important for Dos Passos. He wrote twenty-eight pieces for it while at Harvard and served on its editorial board. It was the most serious of the literary journals, and when he began writing for it, he became part of an organization that dated back to 1885, when George Santayana and others founded it. The *Monthly* had a proud tradition. Among its editors had been Bernard Berenson, Norman Hapgood, William Vaughn Moody, Robert Morss Lovett, and John Hall Wheelock, and before Dos Passos's day it had published the early poetry of writers such as Edwin Arlington Robinson.

Any sense Dos Passos had of being isolated was more of his own than of Harvard's making. John Reed, who later became famous as a left-wing journalist and the author of *Ten Days That Shook the World*—a 1919 account of the Bolshevik Revolution in Russia—recalled the Harvard of his day in a piece published in 1917. Reed was graduated in 1910, and even if one grants a touch of nostalgia, which despite his radical leanings he had for Harvard, his description nevertheless is true enough. The place he described was a vital university whose students enthusiastically quarreled with what to them was stodginess. "All sorts of strange characters, of every race and mind, poets, philosophers, cranks of every twist, were in our class," Reed declared. He continued:

> The very hugeness of it prevented any one man from knowing more than a few of his classmates, though I managed to make the acquaintance of about five hundred of them. . . . What is known as "college spirit" was not very powerful; no odium attached to those who didn't go to football games and cheer. There was talk of the world, and daring thought, and intellectual insurgency; heresy has always been a Harvard and a New England tradition. Students themselves criticized the faculty for not educating them, attacked the sacred institution of intercollegiate athletics, sneered at undergraduate clubs so holy that no one dared mention their names. No matter what you were or what you did—at Harvard you could find your kind.

Reed told of the college political clubs which sprang up during his four years, fertilized by the spirit of the Progressive Era then abroad in the nation. Two influences worked on Reed, he recalled. One was Charles Copeland, whose own enthusiasm moved Reed toward his career as a writer. The other was what Reed termed "the manifestation of the modern spirit." "Some men," he wrote, "notably

Walter Lippmann, had been reading and thinking and talking about politics and economics, not as dry theoretical studies, but as live forces acting on the world, on the University even." Stimulated by the likes of Lippmann, the political clubs burgeoned. A Socialist Club was formed, as were a Harvard Men's League for Women's Suffrage, a Single Tax Club, and an Anarchist group. Students petitioned for a course about Socialism; they asked to hear radical speakers; and they began an open forum "to debate college matters and issues of the day." The result was that they sensed a thrill about what was occurring beyond the walls of Harvard, and they heeded very little "the Oscar Wildean dilettantism that had possessed undergraduate littérateurs for generations."

In the years immediately after Reed left Harvard, more clubs were founded which together served as important social and intellectual outlets for Harvard students during the fervent years before America's entry into the war. But even though Reed could write that students sneered at the hitherto sacred social clubs, these remained tremendously important, and any student, while despising their inherent snobbery, was conscious of their prestige. A particularly apt anecdote is that when Teddy Roosevelt informed Kaiser Wilhelm of his daughter Alice Roosevelt's engagement to Nicholas Longworth, he added as a matter of course that both he and his son-in-law-to-be had belonged to the socially revered Porcellian Club, one of Harvard's most prestigious organizations.

For Dos Passos clubs were to cause a certain anguish. While he did not crave acceptance among the social lions who frequently dominated clubs such as the Porcellian, he had been brought up among people to whom acceptance into clubs mattered, and his years at Choate were spent among boys whose social evolution would involve passing on to club life at Harvard and beyond. So Dos Passos steeled himself—although the matter was far less important to his parents than he imagined —and prepared for whatever gratification or disappointment might come his way.

Writing about Dos Passos, Malcolm Cowley, who came to Harvard several classes behind him, recalled many years later that Dos Passos "was shy, self-conscious, awkward at sports, and a brilliant student" while at Choate, and at college "he was again a lonely figure, standing outside the terribly snobbish social system of those days, not elected to the Institute or the Hasty Pudding, let alone to a final club."*

Cowley's recollection was partly correct. From time to time Dos Passos saw himself as the lonely figure and on occasion, as in 1917, could wonder to himself if he had the faculty to win friends, and self-pity could make him assert with exaggeration that he had won exactly two. Such martyrdom was a pose in part because at Harvard he was rarely an awkward recluse. In fact, it was during his Cambridge years that he formed many of his most enduring friendships.

Harvard began for him on September 22, 1912. Previously, on his way north

*Cowley's reference to the institute is to the social organization called the Institute of 1770, to which each year somewhat less than 20 percent of the sophomores were elected. The Hasty Pudding was a club to which members of the institute were elected in their junior and senior years.

from Virginia, he had visited John R. in New York for two days. One afternoon he spent at the theater seeing what he wrote his mother was a "howling melodrama, —suicides, murders, villains, villainesses, etc., etc.!" On the morning of the twenty-second he and John R. took the train to Boston and had a farewell lunch at Young's Hotel, where they savored John R.'s favorite dishes of codfish tongues and broiled honeycomb tripe. Afterward, Dos Passos headed for Cambridge and 22 Matthews Hall, his address for the freshman year. There he joined the other freshmen in Harvard Yard, where some of them lived their next four college years as "commoners" in one or another of the dormitories, while the "aristocrats" moved out to live along Mount Auburn Street, catercornered across Harvard Square from the Yard.

At Choate he had learned to study hard, and very quickly he began doing that at college. Early in October he wrote his mother that his time was chiefly taken up with Greek, German, and Latin; a month later he wrote John R. that he was fatigued after spending his entire day reading history. Though a diligent student, his life was not all study. In the same letter in which he told Lucy of his travails with languages, he added that he had gone into Boston the previous Sunday to see "the Boston art museum," most likely the Museum of Fine Arts across from the Fenway, where he had spent a part of the afternoon before walking around the park, vivid in its autumn colors. As the next Saturday would be Columbus Day and a holiday, he planned to spend that weekend in New York with John R.

Boston afforded Dos Passos the opportunity to learn about "the new" in the arts; coupled with what Cambridge offered, it was a rich diet. In the spring of 1913, for example, the International Exhibition of Modern Art came to Boston, a show that would have a profound impact on American attitudes toward art. It became known as the Armory Show, exhibiting hundreds of works of painting and sculpture by Cézanne, Van Gogh, Gauguin, Rousseau, Seurat, Toulouse-Lautrec, Matisse, Redon, Rouault, Duchamp, Picasso, Brancusi, and many, many others. Although some of the art was mediocre, numerous works have come to be regarded as masterpieces. But most important, the art was innovative, modern in the sense that Dos Passos and his contemporaries would define the word. The show caused a furor; reaction was immediate and predictable. Traditionalist critics despised the work and bemoaned lost standards of realism and good taste. American critics and artists who were struggling on behalf of modern art defended the show with zeal, some in the process championing distinctly mediocre achievements while disagreeing with other defenders about what were the qualities of good modern art.

Dos Passos might first have seen the show in New York at the 69th Regiment Armory, where it opened before being taken to Chicago and the Chicago Art Institute. In both cities it had included works by Americans like Stuart Davis, John Marin, George Bellows, John Sloan, and William Glackens. But when it came to Boston to be displayed in Copley Hall, where it remained from April 28 to May 19, all the American and some European pieces were left out because of space limitations. Thus what Dos Passos and thousands of others paid to see was a collection of 244 works of modern European art. Under the headline "Art That Merely Amuses," the *Boston Evening Transcript* ran a long review of the show the day it opened. The reviewer attempted to find merit in the show but found little. "Shorn of its mitigations and stripped of most of the sane productions of modern artists," he wrote, the exhibition "appeals to the curiosity and the love of novelty of the crowd here in Boston with a rather more unblushing countenance and with a rather less disguised aspect of charlatanism and insanity combined" than it had in New York. There the traditionalists had been able to feel easier with the paintings of Ingres, Delacroix, Corot, Manet, Whistler, and others whose less radical work had been included.

The traditionalist critic was furious at the Fauvists, whose works were "charlatanry," and who themselves suffered from "a more or less complete self-delusion, the marks of which in pictorial and plastic art are partly comical and partly pathetic." For him the Cubists and the Futurists fared no better. Words like "disgust," "wearisome," "puerile," and "mental aberration" ran through his review. He could excuse Gauguin, Cézanne, and Van Gogh, whose primitivism and post-Impressionism were well intended, if only partly successful. But Picasso, though reputed abroad to have merit, was without talent. Matisse was "unquestionably a mountebank of the first water, and there is not any reason in the world to take him seriously." The only difference the reviewer found between the Cubists and the Futurists was "that one is worse than the other—the one you have seen last." Among the works of these painters were "the novel geometrical and kaleidoscopic incoherencies of these wonderful geniuses, who think they are expressing the emotions of their souls."

Quoting from a preface to the catalog for the exhibition, written by Frederick James Gregg, the reviewer scoffed at Gregg's remarks, but they were significant, expressing exactly the instinct toward the new of the sponsors of the show and sounding the rebellious spirit of a whole generation of artists and writers—Dos Passos among them—who were just then coming of age. "Art is a sign of life," wrote Gregg. "There can be no life without change, as there can be no development without change. To be afraid of what is different is to be afraid of life. And to be afraid of life is to be afraid of truth, and to be a champion of superstition."

The Armory Show generated the kind of intellectual excitement that Jack Reed had felt at Cambridge several years earlier. Dos Passos sensed that excitement and spent far more time sampling "the modern" than he did the pallid atmosphere surrounding a group of students who came to be known as the Harvard Aesthetes. "The Aesthetes," wrote Malcolm Cowley, "were trying to create in Cambridge, Massachusetts, an after-image of Oxford in the 1890s." A favorite of theirs was *The Yellow Book*, the lively English quarterly which had appeared from 1894 to 1897, publishing the work of Max Beerbohm, Henry James, Arthur Symons, Ernest Dowson, John Buchan, H. G. Wells, Aubrey Beardsley, and W. B. Yeats. Casanova's memoirs and *Les Liaisons Dangereuses* intrigued the Aesthetes, Cowley asserted. Dos Passos, who for a while moved on the fringes of the group, remembered Francis Thompson's poem "The Hound of Heaven" and Arthur Machen's "Hill of Dreams" as favorites of theirs. The Aesthetes, Cowley went on, drank, instead of weak punch, seidels of straight gin topped with a maraschino cherry; they discussed the harmonies of Pater, the rhythms of Aubrey Beardsley and, growing louder, the voluptuousness of the Church, the essential virtue of prostitution. They had crucifixes in their bedrooms, and ticket stubs from last Saturday's burlesque show at the Old Howard.

Some Harvardians languished thus, but Dos Passos was rarely among them. He was serious about literature, and while talk of religion, prostitution, or burlesque naturally tittilated him, he downed few seidels of gin and maraschino cherries and by his junior year mocked the group in a story published in the *Monthly*. In "An Aesthete's Nightmare" a frail young man brings home a statuette of Venus to his college room. After drinking a liqueur, he falls into a reverie in which he is astonished to find himself a philistine Northman. In his dream he smashes his statuette, then awakes to find the Venus lying broken on the floor. But what shocks him even more is his recollection of the pleasure of being a vandal, and in a frenzy he smashes the belongings in his room.

As humorous as the twist of the story is, Dos Passos's satire is of the aesthete's affectations. The young man enjoyed sinking back on his divan, as he called the cot he had covered with an Oriental rug. A Buddha dominated the mantel, while a Maxfield Parrish painting adorned the wall, and the affected student thought that "no jarring note broke the artistic unity of the study. [His] thin bosom swelled with pride as he lay there, amid the luxurious artistic atmosphere he had created for himself, and he thought of the ugly tasteless rooms of his friends." Before going into his reverie, he lighted "a little cone of insense in the lotus-shaped burner before the Buddha," then donned a "pale crepe dressing gown" and Turkish slippers and poured himself a "precious liqueur, of exotic name, which was only obtainable at one monastery, and that a small one, in Dalmatia."

Cowley's description of the Aesthetes is oversimplified, although amusing and revealing of one side of the literary ferment of Harvard. If Dos Passos adopted a touch of the Aesthetes' pose for a time, he did not affect it for three years only suddenly to discover the new art that created such a furor. The Armory Show appeared in Boston the spring of his freshman year, and from at least that point on he read such novelists as Tolstoy, Gogol, Dostoevsky, Turgenev, Chekhov, and D. H. Lawrence; and iconoclastic magazines like *Blast: The Review of the Great English Vortex*, which Ezra Pound and Wyndham Lewis edited for a short time in 1914– 1915, and in which T. S. Eliot's poetry was first published. He plunged as well into the poetry of other modernists such as the French Symbolists and Richard Aldington, Hilda Doolittle, and Amy Lowell.

Meanwhile, Dos Passos's months at home during the summer vacations were a bittersweet experience, made more so by the contrast with the excitement of Harvard. During his visits to Washington or summers at Sandy Point, the tone was often saddening. Lucy constantly grew weaker so that sometimes she lacked strength even to talk for long, and as a result instead of being able to talk about literature, art, and politics with her, Dos Passos, Mrs. Harris, and his father (when he was there) had to share the task of nursing her. During the last years of Lucy's life, John R. took to writing what he called "lay sermons," which he or Dos Passos read on Sundays to the confined Lucy and the rest of that small congregation: Mrs. Harris, whichever of the men was not reading, and any guests who might be visiting. If the "sermons" were untraditional, John R. was conscientious about writing them. His wry humor often revealed itself, as in one which began: "Perhaps I can be more independent and fearless in the expression of my views because my congregation is very small—scarcely ever exceeding four and sometimes mustering only two—and in many instances I have preached to one—one solitary member!" He added that "another reason perhaps is that instead of being paid for my services as a preacher I pay my congregation to listen to me. In fact, I occupy a unique position. Instead of my congregation supporting me I support my congregation—Hence I can be bold in the expression of my views." In this "sermon" he dealt with the idea that civilization would be better off "if the creeds of churches were based upon facts and not upon miracles or fancy." Because all denominations intended to do good, John R. believed mankind ought to be charitable in judging them: "We should welcome the Hebrew—the Muhammedan—the Hindoo—the Chinese religion—as we do the Christian." And he even was willing to give credit to "that blatherskite" Billy Sunday, who "altho a hypocrite, unconsciously makes a real convert once and awhile —only once and awhile—for his religion is sensuous and his evidence of conversion purely physical, yet infrequently he strikes water in the rocky bosom of a few who awaken to a better conception of life and its purposes." John R. objected to religions being "based upon false premises—such as the trinity and the supernatural character of Christ." Had Christ been taken to be "a man filled with good and philanthropic impulses—a teacher of truth—the Christian religion would today be a more effective factor in the world." But, he wondered, what could come "from a system that is based upon," and first wrote "a lie," then crossed that out and added "miracles."

John R. penned a great many of these sermons, as much as an example for Dos Passos as anything else. John R. considered them food for thought, models of writing, and vessels of iconoclasm. Lucy might listen and smile feebly at them with little or no response. Dos Passos, while dubious of his father's dogmatic assertions or his stance toward contemporary events, was provoked by his father's iconoclasm and his strong opinions. The important point is that little John R. did was lost on his son. Whether Dos Passos agreed or disagreed, his father's ideas stimulated him, and he could play them off against his own and against the intellectual stances he discovered at Harvard.

John R. slipped the essay about religion into an envelope across which he wrote: "Essays on Civilization as applied to the War raging in Europe *1914*, By the Commodore." Together, he announced to Lucy, the essays would prepare the way "for a new religion—based upon truth." The World War had convinced him that "all religions are failures" and that "the civilization . . . that Christianity has produced is a failure—complete—total . . . a monstrosity." He abhorred the religious myths that people perpetuated each Sunday even though they knew them to be false.

"Give us a new chapter in life," he demanded. "We must begin afresh—for a religion which produces such civilization—is the religion of Sin Satan and Death combined—it has produced a race of monsters." He asked Lucy to save the letters because he planned to expand some of his ideas to make a collection, "and when it is readjusted or gone over the second time—it may be worth reading." On the back of the last sheet he wrote, "Number 1—November 18th 1914," indicating his intention to continue what was, in fact, more a diatribe than a reasoned argument.

John R. was observant enough to know that, during his son's college years, imposing too much of Sandy Point and care for Lucy would only irritate. The law kept John R. busy, even frantic at times, so for him a stay at the farm was a respite. For Dos Passos, an entire summer would wear heavily. So in late August 1913, John R. sent Dos Passos and John Walcott, his friend from Choate and Harvard, on a trip to Canada before they returned to college for their second year. They visited Newfoundland and Quebec and had a fine time, enjoying experiences like a chilly swim in Placentia Bay—"red-letter" swimming, Dos Passos referred to it sometime later and told of "a wonderful bay, without a house or a town on it, that had a wide white beach backed up by pine forests. We were absolutely the only living things about except white cawing sea gulls. The water was pale green, and simply stung when you got in—but it was like a bath in champagne! After it we danced about the beach like Greek fauns or nymphs."

While John R. toiled as ever, he sensed that it was time to put his estate in order. He was aging; moreover Lucy's health was a reminder of his mortality. Thus in June 1914, he wrote out some funeral instructions and turned them over to his secretary, Joe Schmidt. He wanted to be buried in Virginia, in the graveyard of historic Yeocomico Church near the farm. He wanted no one to wear mourning black for him, as he declared that he considered death "but an epoch in a perpetual journey and as I am sure to enter into a better and happier life." Rather he wanted his family "to hail the event with joy and instead of solemnity to celebrate it with hilarity and mirth." Sounding like the elderly Mark Twain, John R. wrote that "Man is the meanest thing on earth, the lowest in the scale of animal or vegetable life. He who dies therefore is bound to find something better in the next life." He desired that a festival be held at Sandy Point, "with beer punch and the eating auxilliaries served," and he concluded by reminding his survivors as they enjoyed the festivities to "remember that I do not envy them—on the contrary I tender them my sympathies."*

John R. labored as hard as ever during his last years. He continued giving speeches such as one entitled "Political Introspection," an address he delivered for Commencement Day at George Washington University in June 1912. Here he called for stiffening the country's naturalization laws. What he desired was "a real American Union, composed of Americans born here, fully imbued with the true American principles, which means citizens who understand, value and respect the

---

*The envelope was not opened until after his funeral, so his instructions were not carried out—unfortunately, since what he asked for seemed entirely in keeping with the man.

absolute rights of individuals—the personal security of life, limb, body and reputation, of holding private property without diminution, and of personal liberty." He advocated naturalization without suffrage for persons who could neither read nor write and criticized the use of the primary election as a form of direct government, which was contrary to the representative sort it was supposed to be.

John R. worked at his last book, *Commercial Mortmain*, published in 1916, and continued his interest in politics, although, as Dos Passos commented in his memoir, John R. felt increasingly lonely, and his loneliness was "of a man who has outlived his generation. More and more he found himself on the unpopular side of political questions." The reforms he opposed were the direct primary, women's suffrage, and laws enforcing the eight-hour day. *Commercial Mortmain* expressed his constant opposition to the Sherman Anti-Trust Act, which he pronounced a failure. To thrive, business had to be able to operate "untrammeled," and laws such as the Sherman Anti-Trust Act, or the Clayton and Trade Commission laws merely hindered the necessary "natural progress of commerce and trade." He urged remedies for the abuses of business. These reforms, he suggested, might be new methods of taxation, or the counterforce of unions. But mostly he expected that the laws of evolution which caused unfit organizations to collapse would alter the ways and forms of business. He remained to the end a Social Darwinist. Nevertheless, during these years while Dos Passos was at college, his father pleaded more popular causes also, offering a plan promoting farm credits and calling in an article in the *New York Times* for reform of the administration of criminal laws in New York State. He spoke out about international matters, too, for example, writing a strongly worded piece that was published in the *New York Herald* on May 11, 1915, condemning the Germans' sinking of the *Lusitania* on May 7. "There must be a limit upon the acts and passions of men and nations," he asserted, "and when they trespass against the laws of humanity, they must be checked—or society is broken in pieces."

While John R.'s assertiveness reminded his son of his own exclusion—as he saw it—from a life of action and passion, Dos Passos exaggerated the extent to which he was an outsider. Although not winning membership in prestigious clubs at Harvard or being elected to Signet, a literary club which his *Monthly* colleagues joined, he had a circle of friends and participated in the cultural life of Cambridge and Boston. For reading, a solitary occupation, he kept to himself, but there were numerous trips to hear the Boston Symphony, or to see plays performed at the university or in the city.

His reaction to these performances reflected his growing literary acumen. In October 1914, his junior year, he noted in his "Literary Diary" that he had attended Henry Bernstein's *The Secret*, which was well produced by David Belasco, "except that some of the company [were] very poor." It was, he decided, "A most unpleasant & rather needless but very interesting play. Is it 'all technique'?" he wondered. In any event it was "not really satisfying, but absorbing & interesting. Over emotional at times?" He did not answer himself, but decided that the play was "lost by translation & its subtlety confused the American audience."

Although he was not oriented toward college activities, he did participate in several organizations: the Cercle Français, the Harvard Poetry Society, which he helped to found in 1915; and, most important, he became deeply involved with the *Monthly*. As early as the July after his freshman year his first contribution, a short story, was published. In his sophomore year another story appeared, then in his third year, book reviews, an essay about Joseph Conrad's *Lord Jim*, and four stories. During his senior year he was one of the *Monthly*'s most frequent contributors.

While feigning a pose of indifference or even distaste for his studies, Dos Passos was involved in them. He did not take every course seriously, to be sure, and dismissed some as a waste of time. But courses in the main stimulated him and introduced him to subject matter that interested him all his life. Fluent in French, in his first year he took a course in French prose and poetry in addition to German, Latin, and Greek. History already fascinated him: he had a survey course in European history from Roman times until the present, and he studied rhetoric and composition. The next year he pursued those basic interests by taking an introductory course in Spanish and one in constitutional government; while working further on composition, examining the history of English literature from Elizabethan times to the present, and studying types of eighteenth- and nineteenth-century fiction under one of Harvard's famous teachers, Bliss Perry. As a junior he ventured into one of his few science courses, botany, but concentrated on literature and the arts. Perry taught him about lyric poetry; he studied Homer, Herodotus, Chaucer, and Browning, the last under Dean LeBaron Briggs. Charles Copeland taught him more composition, and he studied as well about Italian art and culture of the Middle Ages and the Renaissance, and about ancient philosophy. In his final year he continued his philosophical studies, taking courses in the philosophy and religion of the Greek poets and the philosophy of the Hellenistic period. He delved into anthropology, the history of sciences, read Shakespeare under George Lyman Kittredge, and took yet another writing course, this final one under Dean Briggs.

Anyone examining Dos Passos's college curriculum for signs of his development as a writer would inevitably scrutinize his work for Dean Briggs and Professor Copeland. Briggs apparently did not teach him a great deal, although Dos Passos enjoyed the course. For Copeland he worked hard. Copeland recognized that his student had talent when he read Dos Passos's essays describing his childhood in Madeira, Boulogne-sur-Mer, and Brussels; or another about "Trains: Fragments of Memories," which he submitted to Copeland in November 1914. This last became part of "Les Lauriers Sont Coupés" and subsequently the memories were reworked into *U.S.A.* and *Chosen Country*. "Trains" was of a piece with the other autobiographical essays. Dos Passos recalled the "weird little pictures of fright, excitement, of the trembling joy that is akin to terror, [which] flash through my mind when I hear the mournful shriek of a locomotive whistle." Copeland liked the essay; along the margin of one page he scribbled "uncommonly vivid," and he was enough caught up in it that he overlooked some basic misspellings: a "their" for "there," "it's" for "its," and "Juppiter." But Copeland was not much given to marking those kinds of mechanical faults anyway. He praised the piece and handed it back to Dos Passos, who scrawled a large "A" on it and wrote, half in jest:

A sensitive, vivid, uncommonly agreeable retrospect. You deny your power for accomplishing such a task and in the same breath accomplish it triumphantly. Perhaps the best things in the piece are your first realization of a train and your first realization of a station.

Delightful as this little paper is, if it were much longer it would suffer from a monotony of sentence structure which belongs to the childhood you recount.

CTC per D.P.

Copeland's praise was good to have, and Dos Passos was amused by his professor's dry wit when he had observed that, descriptive though the essay was, its simple sentence structure bordered on being childish.

From the day Dos Passos arrived at Harvard in September 1912, he read widely and with a critical, discerning sensibility. He early began keeping a literary diary with detailed notes about form and content. On September 1, 1914, he started a second volume, the first having been lost during the summer. Filling volume two quickly, he began a third, in which he wrote comments about his reading from December 1914, until the middle of November 1916, after he was graduated from Harvard and had traveled to Madrid to study art and architecture. How thoroughly he was absorbed in literature is clear from his entries in these diaries. During the month of September 1914, for instance, he read works by Fielding, Stendhal, Goldsmith, Chekhov, O. Henry, Lafcadio Hearn, Henry James, Robert Louis Stevenson, George Sand, Turgenev, and a biography of William Morris, as well as essays by De Quincey, poetry by Shelley, and assorted other works. A month later he was reading Jack Reed, George Borrow, Ibsen, Thackeray, and more James, Sand, Turgenev, and others, while during the last three weeks of December, a part of which time he was on vacation from college, he read an enormous amount: Andrew Lang's "Essays on the Homeric Hymns" [probably he meant Lang's *Homer and His Age*, or *Homer and the Epic*]; Oscar Wilde's *A Woman of No Importance;* Pierre Loti's *Mon Frère Yves;* Hardy's *Jude the Obscure; The Promised Land,* by Mary Antin; *Clayhanger,* by Arnold Bennett; and Lady Gregory's *Our Irish Theatre.* Even on Christmas Day he did not let up, carefully noting that he had read Mrs. Robert Louis Stevenson's diary, *The Cruise of the Janet Nichol,* and reread "The Eve of St. Agnes" and parts of "Hyperion" and "Endymion" in his new volume of Keats's poetry, perhaps a Christmas present from his father. Before the month was out he had added James's "The Wheel of Time" and "Collaboration"; Shaw's play *Getting Married; Mon Oncle et Mon Curé,* by Jean de la Brête—"the best type of pour les jeunes filles French literature—'Baked custard' but still very pleasant," Dos Passos noted; and *The Letters of Lady M——y W—t—l—y M—nt—gue,* "very amusing to read, if a little catty in places," he added. And along with the *Letters* he read some Stevenson essays and James's "Owen Wingrave" on the last day of 1914.

Sometimes the comments in his literary diary were brief, nothing more than a note that he had "started 'The Enemy of the People'—Ibsen." Other times he wrote a short paragraph or more, trying to capture what it was that he had liked or disliked about a piece. He was impressed, for example, by John Reed's book, *Insurgent Mexico,* which he finished in early October. It was, he wrote, "A most startlingly vivid picture of Mexico & the Mexicans from a broad human point of view." Especially he admired Reed's way of including "an immense amount of interesting personal anecdote & some amazingly fine descriptions. But best of all is the lack of prejudice and humanity of the work. The author is not afraid of raw facts & forces—perhaps at times he is a trifle sensational—but he is saved from Jack Londonism by a keen sense of humor & a certain refinement of touch. There are some marvelously excellent studies of character; and his point of view is sympathetic and comprehensive." Dos Passos thought that even finer work could be expected from Reed if he could get beyond "journalistic habit." If not, "another shining light will be lost to the elect, another sheep will have failed to reach the fold." One should not make too much of the influence of any single book upon a mind as eclectic as Dos Passos's, but *Insurgent Mexico* made a deep impression on him. Reed was a political activist as well as a good writer, and he could report; yet his work went beyond that. He may well have served as a model—one among many—for the young Dos Passos. Certainly some of what the younger writer praised about Reed's book is what he tried to achieve in his own writing.

Of a very different sort from Reed's was the work of Henry James. *The Europeans* he thought "a delightful, entertaining little story" about "a pair of Europeans [who] are transported into the midst of a puritanic Boston family of the '50s. The characterization is wonderfully careful & delicate & the satire exquisite. The strokes of James' portraits are so fine, so miniature, they remind me of the delicacy of Fra Angelico, or better, of some of the more refined Dutch portrait painters."

He balked when he confronted Oscar Wilde. Four months later after Dos Passos finished *The Picture of Dorian Gray,* he could not say enough about his loathing for the book, noting that:

> When I read Dorian Gray, I can understand Oscar Wilde better than before. The book is loathesome—hateful in conception—with a hideously morbid, genuinely immoral atmosphere. I was much surprised to find how weak the style is and how ineffectually he treats a very interesting theme—not however, so unhealthy, so unredeemed by warmth, by vitality, by good physical animalism, as to be utterly immoral from any point of view.

Characterization, particularly within the context of social satire, fascinated him. The day after he finished *The Europeans,* he completed *Daisy Miller* and immediately jotted down his reactions. "An interesting character study," the short novel was "very subtle, almost too subtle," with its "minute description of a certain kind of woman." James's techniques bothered him a bit; he both liked and disliked the delicate sketch, because while subtle and "almost microscopic," Daisy's portrait seemed "hardly very vivid." "Still," Dos Passos concluded, "a most excellent piece of work of its kind," and he went on to admire James's minor characters, the humor which came through in some "chucklesome" phrase or satiric touch, and a knack for dialogue that matched Oscar Wilde's, "although intensely more restrained and realistic."

Dos Passos must have spent a good part of his days reading to accomplish what he did; the time was an apprenticeship that would later become important. As soon as he had finished *Daisy Miller,* for example, he raced through *Vanity Fair,* a book he loved. That he thoroughly admired it is significant, because as he developed his own techniques and themes, like Thackeray he clung to satire and to a style that went at characters from the outside rather than treating them in depth, as Henry James did. It was not that Dos Passos characterized incompletely. Rather his intention was to define by actions and surfaces, not to present psychological studies. And, like Thackeray, he thought of people *en masse* or of that abstraction called society as the focus of his fiction. The subtitle of Vanity Fair is "A Novel Without a Hero." When Dos Passos wrote his best novels—*Manhattan Transfer* and *U.S.A.*—they too lacked conventional heroes, because he portrayed the foibles of society and peopled his books with figures who seem "puppets"—what Thackeray called his characters in a preface to the novel—caught up in a swirl of social and economic forces beyond their control.

He was marking out a kind of fiction that suited him. Early in December he finished *Small Souls,* by the Dutch writer Louis Couperus. The novel, he wrote in his literary diary, gave "a truly marvelous picture of a Dutch family, of people with 'small souls,' " that he thought was "truly epoch making." Couperus's book took the "realism of *Madame Bovary* and *The Old Wives' Tale* [by Arnold Bennett] a step further." Two months later he reviewed *Small Souls* in the *Monthly,* where he wrote that "The scandal-mongering, carpingly-critical women, and the egotistical, preoccupied men are admirably portrayed. They have all small souls, lead petty, trivial lives; there is nothing great about any of them. Without a trace of didacticism, the novel is a tremendous satire, cold and unemotional, on the life of a small European capital." And of *Vanity Fair* he declared, "The more often I read it, the more delightful it seems. It is certainly one of the great books of the world—the inimitable characters, the satire, the wit, the humorous descriptions, the universality of the book is overwhelming!" No sooner had he finished it than he wanted to begin again, but he did not, at least not immediately, for he plunged into more James: "An International Episode" and his essay on Stevenson from *Notes on Novelists,* and finished *An Enemy of the People,* "a play," he remarked, "of good technique & interest & excellent character drawing, notwithstanding lack of finish in minor points, but rather lacking in power, in 'entertainment.' " A person's reaction to it was intellectual, he thought, but still it was well worth reading, as were all of Ibsen's dramas.

The spring of 1915 he read more of the moderns, although it is clear that he did not discover contemporary fiction and art all of an instant, nor did he ever stop reading more venerable works. He read much of Samuel Butler,

Compton Mackenzie, Conrad, de Maupassant, Meredith, and Synge, among others. D. H. Lawrence's *Sons and Lovers* impressed him: "I never remember reading a franker book," he noted on April 20, "in one passage frankness becomes smut pure & simple. It is a tantalizing piece of work." But perhaps more than anything else, the poetry of Emile Verhaeren astonished and delighted him. Verhaeren, a Belgian and a Symbolist, described in his poems the details, the action, and the energy of modern life. His volume, *Les Forces tumultueuses,* struck Dos Passos as "a very wonderful book of poetry—vers libre with rough hewn pounding meter—full of force and verve—very un-French & vital." While he continued other reading he soon returned to more of Verhaeren's work: *Au bord de la route* and *Les Villages illusoires,* about the latter commenting that " 'Les meules qui brulent' ["The burning haystacks"] is a marvelous poem," and he jotted down one stanza:

> *Aux carrefours, des gens hagards*
> *Font des gestes hallucines*
> *Les enfants crient & les viellards*
> *Levent leur bras déracinés*
> *Vers les flames en étandards*
> *—une meule qui brûle!**

Amid this literary apprenticeship, it pleased Dos Passos to be elected secretary of the *Monthly* in the spring of 1915. He had earned the recognition, and the work would keep him busy his senior year. But he was constantly concerned about his mother, whose health was worsening. It was clear that she did not have long to live. Only a day or two before her death he received a letter from Mrs. Harris, telling of Lucy's situation in Washington. She had nurses around the clock, and her doctor came every day and had just brought a specialist with him. Mrs. Harris did not add that there was little hope.

On May 15, 1915, when Dos Passos got a telegram that she was dying, he took a train to Washington as soon as he could. John R. met him at Union Station and told him she was dead. Dos Passos characteristically kept his grief to himself; the tedium of her long illness had drained the tears from him. Soon Lucy's coffin was put aboard the *Gaivota,* and Dos Passos and his father took her body to Cintra, sailing down the Potomac River, whose banks were lush with the color and warmth of late spring. From Cintra the coffin was carried in a hearse to the cemetery next

---

*At the crossroads, some haggard people
*Make distraught gestures
*Children cry out and old men
*Lift their agitated arms
*Toward the flames which rise like banners in the air
—a burning haystack!

to Yeocomico Church, where it was laid in the red clay earth. Later a single low stone was set at the head of the grave:

LUCY ADDISON SPRIGG
FEBRUARY 9, 1854
MAY 15, 1915.

CHAPTER FIVE

===

Senior Year,
1915–1916

As a result of his mother's death, Dos Passos was reluctant to return to college for his last year, but John R. convinced him that he should go back, and to divert his son he sent him on a six-week trip during the summer of 1915. Dos Passos traveled alone to the West Coast to visit some Sprigg cousins in San Diego. From there he went to San Francisco before he headed back across the country, stopping at the Grand Canyon on the way. Always he kept up his reading. He noted in his diary that during the six-week journey he had read:

More "Don Quixote"
"War and Peace"
Meredith's "The Amazing Marriage"
Hardy's "The Woodlanders"
"Childe Harold's Pilgrimage"
"Femmes d'Artiste" Daudet
Paul Verlaine poems
"Aucassin et Nicholette"
"Intentions"—Oscar Wilde
W. B.'s [Witter Bynner] "The New World"
Read in the Pink French Poems
Hauptmann's "Sunken Bell"

The trip was good medicine. It got him away from Sandy Point and on his own. It indulged his love of travel and, most important in this case, during the trip he met Walter Rumsey Marvin, a boy four years younger than he who was traveling out west with his family. The two met aboard the Shasta Limited when both were on their way to San Francisco. They met a second time at the World's Fair there, and yet again at the Grand Canyon. They began a friendship that would continue throughout Dos Passos's life. At the start, at least, Dos Passos assumed something of the role of tutor to the younger man. Dos Passos's attraction to Marvin was immediate, Marvin liked the things his new friend did, and later he became an important confidant, for the most part through letters. Marvin was an intelligent person who had lived abroad, spoke French, and had a love of literature and the arts. When Dos Passos met him, he had completed his first year of preparatory school at St. Paul's School in Concord, New Hampshire, from which he was graduated in 1918.

On August 28 as Dos Passos returned east aboard the Lake Shore Limited, he wrote his first letter to Marvin. Dos Passos had reconciled himself, he told his new friend, to not meeting the Marvins again "because, you know, you never do meet people again that you want to." Yet he hoped that the mails could keep their friendship alive. Self-disparagingly, he asserted that he was an "abominable correspondent. But," he went on, "it's so rarely I meet anyone who's interested in the same things I am, that I don't like to let him slip through my fingers." And he thought that he and Marvin had a lot in common: food, "first & foremost . . . a splendid subject for letters"; literature; and travel—"I think we both have the disease," he declared, and "all lovers of Italy have something in common, and that a good deal, for once you fall in love with Italy, there's no cure."

Dos Passos described to Marvin his journey after leaving the Grand Canyon. He had taken a hot train ride across the desert to Salt Lake City, then found relief in the cool weather of Colorado Springs, where he had hiked some six or seven miles across the mesa to Manitou Springs on a road along which occasionally passed "scornful automobiles packed with the *petite bourgeoisie*, on sightseeing bent." He told Marvin about his reading and with a note of hope closed by saying that if Marvin felt like writing back, his address would be "Cintra P.O., Westmoreland Co. Virginia" for a good while. "I'd really be awfully glad to hear from you, and should try to reply in due time," he ended, and bade Marvin "Au Revoir," signing himself "J. R. Dos Passos Jr.," a touching blend of the formal and the friendly.

One might speculate that there was something of the physical in Dos Passos's attraction for Marvin. Certainly, this early friendship was indicative of the deep affection that characterized his commitments to those he loved. The strong emotional ties he had with those he befriended were a key to the pattern of his life. It is not hard to understand how in letters he could feel at ease pouring out his thoughts, the distance being a kind of shelter from the intimacy of speaking them to another's face. Then, too, it was easier to try out his ideas on a receptive younger person than on the majority of his acquaintances at Harvard.

It was Dos Passos's shyness, together with his associations with the campus "aesthetes," and some of his awkward mannerisms that encouraged charges of effeminacy. One of his friends, for instance, recalled a walk in Boston with the tall

Dos Passos, who with his long legs and arms strode along, gesticulating in a way that made his companion self-conscious. Across the street some toughs hooted, to Dos Passos's apparent total disregard. Such eccentricities opened him to the charge, sometimes articulated, sometimes not, of homosexuality. One reads with interest a novel he began in March 1916 called *Streets of Night*, which is partly about a homoerotic attraction of an aesthetic Harvardian for another student, a muscular young man who exudes the Life from which the young aesthete quails. *Streets of Night* was not published until 1923, in the wake of Dos Passos's success—and notoriety—stemming from *Three Soldiers*, but as a senior at Harvard he had made some of his first notes for what he then termed *Le Grand Roman*, and he labored at it during his last months at college. When he initially conceived of the novel, he jotted down in his notebook:

LE GRAND ROMAN

Atmosphere of streets at night. Supper tables & garish restaurants. Youth in the city.

1. Friendship—the strong unsympathetic character, the weak boy who adores him. Man of white hot burning idealism, of huge power & desire for self expression—the scene in the run-away.

Love—a woman—the strong man has wild passions love affair absolutely subdues character of girl to him. Hideous jealousy on the part of the boy. Life to him turns to dust and ashes.

3. The hero strides on—he progresses—his [lovers] cannot they are too wrapped up in the old man. Might even become evangelist or something of that sort—He grows older—the others are weak & miserable & destroyed but they keep their youth. At last he utterly breaks with them. They drift away into the sea of faces that you pass in the streets at night.

One might conclude that it was Dos Passos's naïveté in 1916 which caused him not to comprehend fully that the story was about homosexuality as much as it was about a search for Life. His conception of a novel in which a weak boy adores a strong, masculine figure had more to do with Dos Passos's sense of his own college life under a protective bell glass than with a desire for male love. Rumsey Marvin asserted after Dos Passos's death—and there is no reason to doubt him—that he never saw any sign of homosexuality in Dos Passos's friendship.

When *Streets of Night* was published, it was apparent Dos Passos had kept close to his first idea for the novel. Fanshaw Macdougan, the weak aesthete, is ardently attracted to David Wendell, who is a handsome youth with a craving for Life; yet Fanshaw never comes near any sexual intimacy with the stronger man. He adores Wendell, even thinks of embracing him, but there always remains something abstract in his conception of David, who for Fanshaw is a symbol of what he lacks rather than a man with whom he desires physical intimacy. Tantalized by Wenny's masculinity, Fanshaw is equally tantalized by a beautiful but sexually timid girl,

Nancibel Taylor, even for a time half planning to marry her. He is scarcely an autobiographical hero, and the book primarily reflects the several intellectual and emotional tugs Dos Passos felt as a college student. Fanshaw is a pastiche drawn from the people the author knew at Harvard—some of whom were homosexual—and from his derogatory image of a part of himself.

Fanshaw struggles with his attraction for Wenny and for Nancibel, as well as for experiences that would immerse him in Life. At the same time, he loves culture and scholarship. He is an art historian specializing in the Italian art of the Renaissance and can never break away from the security of college life. Even after the excitement of war, which he sees while in the Red Cross, he lacks the daring he thoroughly desires. As the novel ends, he knows he will go back to "Massachusetts Avenue and the College Yard, and the museum and tea with professors' wives." His life will become again a going "to and fro to lectures with a notebook under my arm," and the most he will be able to do is now and again to "walk into Boston through terrible throbbing streets and think for a moment I have Nan and Wenny with me, and that we are young, leansouled people out of the Renaissance, ready to divide life like a cake with our strong hands."

Dos Passos's version of the Harvard aesthete would only be able to dream about an active, vital life. His friends would wonder why throughout his life, obviously intellectual and cultured, he often chose to denigrate intellectuals and aesthetes. Probably he saw too much of himself in them. Thinkers tended not to be doers, and devotees of culture seemed to him to miss the core of life—the excitement, the sights, sounds, and smells of a teeming world around them. He stood back from himself and saw a shy, introverted personality who took easily to a life of the intellect and of art. His was a conscious reaction against that, a forcing of himself out into a larger world. With a voracious appetite for travel already developed, he would plunge himself into activism—in politics, in new forms of art, in anything he could find that would keep him from what he thought was a complacent inertness. He possessed a romantic urge to save him from himself. Herein lay a paradox: when he thrust himself into the "real" world, assuming the role of hard-bitten realist and satirist, the act itself was, of course, the fulfillment of a romantic conception of himself.

One might say that at Harvard Dos Passos was trying out various roles, but regardless of what he wrote in his Fanshaw novel during the spring of his senior year, he felt more at ease at Harvard when he returned in September 1915 than he had before. After living outside Harvard Yard his sophomore and junior years, first in Ware Hall, a building one block east of the Harvard Union, and the next year in an apartment house named Ridgely off the Yard toward the Charles River, he moved back into the Yard his senior year. There, his room, 29 Thayer Hall, was on the second floor, its windows facing in toward the center of the Yard. A close friend, Dudley Poore, recalled that Dos Passos's room had little furniture in it: a small cot, a desk and a chair or two, and few decorations except for an Egyptian print over the door. Nevertheless, Poore remembered gathering there often during Dos Passos's last year with other friends who shared their enthusiasm for the arts.

Poore had first met Dos Passos during the spring of 1915, when the latter came up to him in the Yard after one of Professor Copeland's classes and complimented him on a poem which Poore had just had published in the *New Republic*. By November 1915, Dos Passos and he were good friends, and on the sixteenth Poore wrote in his diary, "I go to Dos' for tea for the first time." A sensitive man himself, Poore was struck that evening by a setting that the lamps in the Yard and a yellow sunset created. He had not been in Thayer Hall long before E. E. Cummings and Foster Damon, two other *Monthly* friends, entered. Dos Passos served tea and cakes, and afterward they all went to Cummings's parents' home for dinner. Such evenings, according to Poore, were frequent. The next night he was back at Dos Passos's again for tea. As he arrived on the second floor of Thayer Hall, Dos Passos, Damon, John Walcott, and Cummings inexplicably were carrying a struggling Stewart Mitchell into the shower. After the commotion, they piled into Dos Passos's room to view his bed, wrecked in the melee with Mitchell, who after the shower episode departed sullenly. With that, Poore, Dos Passos, Damon, and Cummings went off for supper at a small Greek restaurant, the Parthenon. Nine days later Poore was back in Thayer again for tea, while Dos Passos proudly displayed a clockwork bug that he had bought at Marblehead on an outing the previous Sunday.

Such parties were typical, moving from room to room. One evening two weeks later Poore arrived at Robert Hillyer's room to find him, Dos Passos, and William Norris—another *Monthly* friend—drinking rum toddy, which they vowed was nothing but tea. Soon the group rushed outside and ran along nearby Mount Auburn Street, where they danced "with bacchic abandon." Then they moved on to Poore's room at 1 Garden Street, there to down apricot liqueur. Hillyer and Norris left, but Dos Passos stayed, and he and Poore talked on until after two the next morning.

On another occasion Dos Passos gave a party in Thayer Hall for all the members of the board. E. E. Cummings lived in Thayer also; the party moved between Dos Passos's and his rooms, and as Hillyer recounted it, "We sat up drinking and reading poetry nearly all night, and—I think it was four or five of us—went to sleep where we were on chairs and couches." The next morning the editors had to scramble when Cummings's father, the Reverend Dr. Cummings, knocked on his son's door.

Poore did not remember Dos Passos as the silent, lonely person the man himself would have had others see, nor did Poore think that Harvard was restrictive. Furthermore, Dos Passos, a lively, inquisitive person whom others with similar interests enjoyed being around, seemed to thrive on college life in his senior year. He had the companionship of the *Monthly* group and of friends like John Walcott. There was the constant attraction of events at Harvard or in Boston. At the university were plays like those performed by George Pierce Baker's "47 Workshop" group, among whom were some of Dos Passos's closest friends, in particular Edward Massey, whose ideas were important for Dos Passos's own efforts in drama. And in Boston there was during his senior year the rejuvenated Boston Opera Company, which with the Russian ballerina Anna Pavlova presented imaginatively staged operas. The company's repertoire was large. Often, when an opera like Puccini's *La Bohême* did not include a ballet, Pavlova would follow it with one, as in November she did the Puccini work with a suite of dances entitled "Chopiniana."

At other times an entire evening's performance would be given to dance. During February 1916, for example, Sergei Diaghilev's Russian ballet came to Boston on the first of two American tours. Combining music of composers such as Debussy, Stravinsky, Rimsky-Korsakov, and Borodin; the avant-garde decors of Futurist artists like Nathalie Gontcharova and Michel Larionov; and the startling choreography of talented creators like Michel Fokine and Leonid Massine, these ballets of Diaghilev became vivid presentations of new forms in art that made a profound impression on Dos Passos. Decor, costumes, movements, and music were blended to make the audience aware of possibilities for artistic expression often radically different from the traditional.

His final year at Harvard was filled with activities like boisterous teas, an occasional meal at the Cock Horse, a tearoom on Brattle Street, or trips into Boston for a meal at Posilipo's, Jake Wirth's, or Young's Hotel, where Dos Passos would ask the chef to prepare John R.'s favorite dishes and punches for himself and his friends. There were occasional pranks like tossing torpedoes out of Walcott's windows at the Saturday crowds returning from football games, and the more serious stuff of meetings of the *Monthly*'s editorial board, reading one's poetry to others of the Poetry Society, or attending the readings of established poets like Amy Lowell, whom the society invited to speak. Such activities had their amusing side. It was probably for the immense Miss Lowell's address on February 28, 1916, that, Poore recalled, some of the editors had literally to push her up the narrow stairs of the Harvard Union to the *Monthly* offices on the third floor. Beer and pretzels had been set out for the reading, and candidates for the *Monthly* and the Poetry Society were invited, so the room was full and the evening festive. Miss Lowell talked about free verse and then read from her own work. A discussion followed, enlivened by one member of the society, Jack Wheelwright, asking, "How do you write, Miss Lowell, when you have nothing to say?" There was a tremendous silence, and no answer. Cummings then asked whether she approved of Gertrude Stein. "Do *you* like her work?" Miss Lowell shot back as she moved to leave. Cummings stammered, "Yes." "I don't," she replied, and heaved herself out of the crowded room and down the stairs.

Dos Passos might look back on these days and recall a stifling time, but only on those occasions when he felt rebellious against what he recognized as a privileged, if stimulating, experience. Although he and many of his peers avoided a lot of the world outside the Yard, the smaller world within was rarely dull. Rather, it was so lively that it took up most of a student's days unless he strove to avoid letting Harvard fill his time entirely. That Dos Passos thought himself a sequestered loner and sometimes acted that role is but evidence of his several sides. He could be gregarious; he could also seem "a lonely figure," as Malcolm Cowley described him. For Dos Passos, as for most thinking people, college life was almost too secure, and if he was to develop into the writer he wanted to be, he needed to protect himself from the complacency, even conformity, that his *Monthly* friendships and the mellow atmosphere of the Yard could produce.*

His need to get away was what he wrote Rumsey Marvin about in early October of his senior year. Dos Passos was delighted to hear from Marvin at St. Paul's where, Dos Passos imagined, he was too busy to do much reading on his own. Still, he wrote,

> there are always times when all the world bores you or irritates you, and you have a "nobody loves me, I'm going into the garden to eat worms" feeling when some book you're fond of acts like magic. It's like diving out of everything bothersome [and] plunging in a new comforting world where you have adventures and drink Canary sack, and live a dozen people's lives instead of your own puny little one. It must be like that to write books, only nicer. How people get along without reading all the glorious things there are to read, I don't see, but most of them seem to be able to exist very comfortably without it. I suppose the fact that most people don't live at all, merely vegetate like cabbages, accounts for it.

*Dudley Poore thought of Dos Passos as a leader among the group of literary-minded friends who saw each other constantly during Dos Passos's final year at Harvard. I am indebted to Mr. Poore for permitting me to quote from an as yet unpublished manuscript of his in which he describes the Dos Passos whom he met in the spring of 1915 and became close to the following fall. About their first meeting Poore recalled that Dos Passos, "standing near one of the gates [of Harvard Yard] leading out to the Square, speaking in his hesitant way, looking at me with brown eyes enlarged by heavy lenses . . . gave me the kind of encouragement I needed by quoting some lines he had liked.

"By the following year," Poore continued, "we were meeting every day either at his room in Thayer Hall or mine at 1 Garden Street. Soon it was clear that versifying was only one of a number of tastes we had in common. Soon too I found that among my friends none was so good natured or such good company. Dos (as we called him and as I shall call him here) did more things in a week with more gusto than any of us; read more, wrote more, cultivated more people belonging to groups that did not mix; yet when he came to see you was never in haste to leave unless, the hour growing late, it were to carry you off with others to a French restaurant called the Bourse or to an Italian one somewhere on Hanover Street. He could rouse the most unlikely people into activity. On weekends he was the instigator of impromptu walks along the coast, walks that never would have occurred but for him. Beginning at some point reachable by train from the North Station, these were long scrambles over wet rocks where the rush of a wave drenched your ankles or a burst of salt spray burned your lips; ending, it might be, at Marblehead where we downed oceans of hot tea and mountains of cinnamon toast; the whole topped off by a late dinner at Young's in Boston. There, if the evening were warm, Dos would mix in a glass pitcher, with frequent pauses to test the blend, a refreshing punch according to an old recipe of his father's; the wrinkled gray-haired waiters meanwhile hovering near, ready to fetch the extra bottle of white wine or the missing ingredient. These were joyous events when the wisdom of the ages, or such parts of it as were accessible to our youth, was explored without solemnity, the flora of a rock pool on Cape Ann or the flavor of a fruit cup holding our attention as long as the doctrine of universals or of necessity.

"That the week of classes following such an excursion cast any shadow on his enjoyment or led to the writing of any fewer stories or verses was never apparent. Professors, however quick to respond on the rare occasions when we sought them out, showed no desire to meddle with our thoughts outside of class, rightly assuming as we did that it was for us to educate ourselves. No one knew better than Dos how to take advantage of this freedom for his own ends. 'When that Aprile . . . ,' my favorite among his early poems, appeared in his notebook during class on a day when we were all weak with spring fever, 'La Dame en Rouge,' some gaily unpretending verses in French, came into being, rhymes and all, while we were dining at the Bourse, provoked by the antics of a flushed lady in a red hat who waved to us insistently over the top of an adjoining booth. Whatever their nature these poems of his always came directly out of the life we were leading, as if seen through clear glass, whereas what the rest of us wrote at that time was too often clouded with a film of literature."

Dos Passos had developed a propensity for mocking what he thought might be convention. "Most people don't live at all," he asserted, and his own life he deemed "puny." But he and his friends were almost constantly doing something interesting. His pose served his own needs. It appeared in his writing, a sometimes mystifying transmutation of the personality his friends thought they knew and of the scenes and characters he observed.

By his senior year Harvard and Cambridge had come to have a powerful effect on him, not only because of the friends and teachers he had, but because of the ambience, the history and traditions that he might pretend to but in fact could not ignore. Everywhere one turned in the Yard or around Harvard Square there were reminders of the Protestant tradition and of that segment of the population—his parents' friends, the rich and powerful of American society—with whom he had an ambivalent relationship. From his window in Thayer he could look across the Yard at Harvard's oldest building, Massachusetts Hall, dating from 1718; at Hollis Hall, dating from 1762; and at Harvard Hall, completed two years later, which had the first classroom in the college. For some of his meals as well as for other occasions he walked out of the Yard across Cambridge Street to Memorial Hall, the grotesque Victorian-Gothic marvel that was designed by the architects Ware and Van Brunt. The immense red-brick hall was built as a memorial to Harvard's Civil War dead. When Dos Passos walked through the building, he would look up at plaques along the walls to see names that were sharp reminders of the Protestant establishment, names like Cabot, Wigglesworth, and Croninshield.

Or when he went to visit Dudley Poore at 1 Garden Street, his route took him across Harvard Square; then on his left was the Old Burying Ground that dated from the earliest colonial times, with headstones marking the graves of the college's first presidents and ministers. The Ground, also called God's acre, was the graveyard as well for numerous colonial settlers, Revolutionary soldiers, and others who played some role in the first years of the Massachusetts settlement. Beyond the graveyard he passed Christ Church, the oldest building of its sort in Cambridge. Erected in 1760, it was used for a period as a shelter for American troops during the British siege of Boston before being restored as a place of worship when George Washington attended services there on New Year's Eve, 1775. Nearby is 1 Garden Street, a large house which in Dos Passos's college days had rooms for rent, although since it has become the rectory for the church. Across Garden Street from the rectory stands the Cambridge Common, a site designated in 1631 for meetings, cattle grazing, and the training of militia. Soldiers drilled there in the first days of the Revolution; by an elm on the Common George Washington is supposed to have taken command of the Continental Army on July 3, 1775; under another elm the evangelist George Whitfield fervently espoused the Great Awakening during his provocative trips to America in the eighteenth century.

Dos Passos appreciated the history of Cambridge and Virginia, but his particular circumstances as a child and then a lonely adolescent had kept him from participating in it. He kept his distance and repeatedly satirized the kinds of people who wallowed complacently in this history, mouthing shallow rhetoric about American virtue. Later in his writing he opposed the economic system of the Establishment; first while still at Harvard he mocked weak personalities such as his fictional character Fanshaw Macdo_gan who were so imbued with the inhibitions of conventional society that they could not break free. During his senior year his stories in the *Monthly*, such as "First Love," which appeared in the October 1915 issue, lightly satirized characters who burn with sentimental ardor, but to no avail. In "First Love" a boy sits in a study hall dreaming of romantic love, and his teacher discovers him writing misty prose to his vision of a "golden-haired girl." In the same issue of the *Monthly* was another of his stories, "Romantic Education," in which an elderly Spanish woman tells a young man, John C. Ricker, of her full life and makes him realize something of the Spaniard's vitality. "Ah, you do not live, you Americans!" Senora d'Alvarina begins. "You are dried up, like—like your machines to write with. You have not souls." That December the *Monthly* published "A Pot of Tulips," a story about a timid young poet, Stanhope Whitcombe, who yearns for Mabel Fisher, whom he meets in the flower shop she runs. While Whitcombe champions the virtues of aestheticism, he is not so pure that he cannot accept money for poems that appeal to the public. His verse is "of a very inflamed, purple order. *Shame* and *flame* always rhymed together in his poems." Mabel, an amusing caricature of an emancipated woman, decides that she can have a love affair with Stanhope, but when she later discovers that he has been buying flowers for himself and not for a friend as he had asserted out of embarrassment, she has no use for him. With total lack of self-awareness she announces, "I have no prejudices."

Apart from his satirical aims, in these slight tales Dos Passos was experimenting with style. He knew well and admired the poems of the Imagist poets whose work was receiving attention. In the May 1916 issue of the *Monthly* he praised Ezra Pound's anthology *Des Imagistes*, which had appeared in 1914. "The Shepherd," another early story in which a sheltered boy learns about life from an older person, illustrates Dos Passos's effort to achieve in fiction the effects of the Imagists through his employment of vivid color imagery that readers as well as Dos Passos himself would later judge to be excessive. The boy on his way up a mountain turns frequently "to look back at the succession of misty green slopes behind him. On the other side of the forest-darkened valley, violet-blue hills hung along the horizon like clouds. Behind them a red sun was setting."

Such excesses notwithstanding, Dos Passos was developing a competent style even before the publication of *Three Soldiers* in 1921. His poetry also showed development. It was during his senior year that he moved from the shame-flame sort of poem like "From Simonides," which appeared in the same issue as "The Shepherd.'" "There's a purple light in the wine cup's heart, / Friend, drink deep with me," the poem began, and closed,

> *And when thought is fled from the flame of desire,*
> *The fervor of youth and youth's tremulous flowers,*
> *Friend, embrace with me.*

He published few poems of this sort, quickly sharpening his sense of language and his power to use imagery effectively while finding new subjects. He lost interest in the purple light at the wine cup's heart. The Symbolists and the Imagists taught him that anything could be the stuff of poems, so he wrote about street scenes, low-life figures—all things that the hothouse characters in his earliest fiction were too inhibited to be any part of.

In the same issue of the *Monthly* in which his classmate, Cuthbert Wright, wrote a rather prissy essay about pagan morals, Dos Passos published his most mature poem to date, "Salvation Army." Wright espoused "the aesthetic attitude," finding it "human and stimulating to lean back on the cushions occasionally, like a spectator at the classic games, and indulge, for once, a purely aesthetic delight in the physiques and agility of the runners in the footrace." Wright was suggesting that one could practice self-perfection to attain something of "the clean, linear quality of classic art, the perfect outline and gracious contour of the antique. The purgation of the senses, the training of the emotions through discipline, the clear eye and healthy insight . . . these will be the dominant notes of such a life."

"Salvation Army" in both form and subject matter contrasted with Wright's piece. Dos Passos created the scene of a Salvation Army band's raucous noise on a city street:

> *A drum pounds out the hymn,*
> *Loud with gaudy angels, tinsel cherubim,*
> *To drown the fanfare of the street.*

Mingled with the music are an

> *endless rumble of carts,*
> *The scrape of feet, the noise of marts*
> *And dinning market stalls, where women shout*
> *Their wares, and meat hangs out—*
> *Grotesque. . . .*

The rude street people are closer to actuality than to an aesthete's ideal. Many more times Dos Passos dreamed of an idealized aesthetic calm, especially when he was plunged into the grotesqueries of World War I, but in his writing he was moving rapidly away from what Wright espoused.

As he was experimenting with new styles and subject matter, Dos Passos praised other work which treated contemporary life. Reviewing two poetry anthologies for the May 1916 *Monthly*, he lauded the poems in *Georgian Poetry, 1913–1915*, because "imperfectly expressed . . . there is a splendid sense of life about this poetry, of love of mere living, of man's blood and bone, and the golden cornfields that are his setting." Of the *Catholic Anthology* he could say little good except about "the sense of satire, of half humorous character-drawing, well represented, in its more sinister side, by Edgar Lee Masters' work." He admired "Hortense Robbins," from

Spoon River Anthology, and "a certain atmosphere of city life" in some other poems, but for the most part the poetry was as bad as "some of the excesses of the Nineties."

In his correspondence with Rumsey Marvin throughout his senior year, fiction, poetry, and the search for subject matter were frequently what he wrote about, often in response to what his young friend announced he was composing. "Your poem worries me," he told Marvin during the fall. While it had "charm and delightful sincerity, and a nice lilt," he believed it needed to be more concrete and have more restraint. Meter can easily "slop over," he cautioned; to be "poetry in the highest sense," ideas or emotions have "usually to be tied up in a picture, a figure of speech or something like that." Marvin had declared that commonplace topics were not fit subjects for poetry, and Dos Passos responded:

> By all the gods of Flaubert, of Homer, of modern realism and the new poetry, I conjure you, Oh Rumsey, to take back them words. Prize-fights are every bit as good a subject for poetry as fine ladies and illicit love affairs. What is the Iliad but a succession of rather sweary & infinitely bombastic prize fights? Admitted that excessive & artificial use of "sweat and swear" to make poems seem manly and modern is abominable and heinous and in every way to be brought up before the tribunals of good taste and good sense—still, I insist that every subject under the sun [which] has anything to do with human beings— man, woman or child—is susceptible of poetic treatment.

He went further, asserting as did the literary rebels of the day that there was no American literature worth the name, because "we as a nation have not that feeling of the infinite beauty and infinite poetry underlying things—love, war, sunsets, tinpans, lawnmowers, etc etc." Dos Passos was adopting the stance of such critics as Van Wyck Brooks, who bemoaned American materialism and the grip genteel society held on the nation's arts and letters. Dos Passos was refining his ideas, trying them out on Marvin. If he was to make a name for himself, he knew he would have to break with literary traditions, so he set out to do just that. He was not merely a follower after new styles, but he was observant, could see the new, and could read it.

He passed on his enthusiasms to Marvin. He wrote about A. E. Housman's poetry, *A Shropshire Lad,* in particular, because it is "so frightfully simple and repressed, and there is so much more in it than the 'outward shows.' It is one of the most Greek things—in spirit—that I have found in English." He knew the work well and told Marvin of specific sections—IV, IX, VX, XXX, XXXVI, XXXVIII, and LXII —that were favorites. Andrew Lang's sonnet about the *Odyssey* pleased him, especially the closing line, "the surge and thunder of the Odyssey"; and he advised Marvin to read lots of John Masefield's poetry about commonplace subjects and also to read the young British poet Rupert Brooke, whose short-lived career would end in the war, and Kipling, who had a poem somewhere that got Dos Passos thinking about spring and travel.

"It is torture not to be on the move," he wrote Marvin. "The sound of locomotive whistles at night has become maddening—Do you know that wonderful distant sound of rumbling that you hear at night near a railway line? Next to a steamer leaving for foreign ports, that gets me." His restlessness stemmed not only from his excitement about new art and about the world beyond Harvard Yard but also from a desire to be on with things, specifically his writing. It is not surprising that at about the time he began to compose poems such as "Salvation Army" he was "indulging in an orgy" of reading the poets Verlaine and Verhaeren. The latter especially continued to excite him; from Verhaeren as much as from any modern poet Dos Passos got his fascination for the quick pulse of contemporary life, for the noise of trains, the clamor of crowds, and the shapes constructed in an industrialized, urban society. To widen his own experience he took to "wandering about Boston streets at night," he told Marvin early in December. On such excursions "you see the most interesting little incidents and types—types enough to keep any painter busy a century. Then there are little Italian restaurants way down town, where you can get spaghetti and orvieto wine and little shiny red herrings."

As Christmas drew near he urged Marvin to try to meet him in New York for lunch, a matinee, and anything else they could squeeze in. But as close as they got was Dos Passos's accidentally sighting Marvin in Brooks Brothers, where Dos Passos was being fitted for a suit. By the time he could get free of the fitter's tape and chalk, Marvin had disappeared. After only a few days in New York and then Christmas in Washington, Dos Passos went by boat to Sandy Point to spend several days looking over the property before he headed back on a cold trip by boat and automobile to Washington. New Year's Day, 1916, he was in New York, then the next day took the train to Boston. The winter was harsh, and later in January he bemoaned in a letter to Marvin the difficulty of getting exercise. He wrote that walking was a favorite pastime of his; in the spring and fall he occasionally rowed on the Charles, but he could not stand organized sports, and he was a bad ice skater, so his choices were limited. He yearned for warm weather and dreamed of a trip abroad, "war or no war." He went on to say that he was hardly idle, spending his time reading poetry of all kinds—Elizabethan, modern, classic—and he had been writing it, "to the accompaniment of much soulful sucking of pencil ends."

Marvin was slow to answer, so Dos Passos tried to tease him into a response with a humorous edict: "If one Rumsey Marvin does not see fit to write, send postal or otherwise communicate within thirty days with, one, J.R.D.P. Jr., said R.M., alias Rummy, shall incur unheard of penalties of all sorts, better imagined than described." He insisted, "Ecrivez, écrivez, ou, foi de gentilhomme, parbleu, sacré tripes, as they say in Dumas, je—like the witches in Macbeth—'I'll do, I'll do, I'll do.' " Marvin's answer was not long in coming; he wrote that he had plunged into poetry, so Dos Passos urged him to send some on, and he would reciprocate. Soon Marvin mailed some of his efforts, and Dos Passos eagerly offered his criticism. "You're in for theory, criticism and other horrors," he warned. "Don't believe it all, but bits may help you." First he quoted some lines from Verlaine's poem, "Art Poétique":

De la musique avant toute chose

Il faut aussi que tu ı. _illes point
Choisir tes mots sans quelque méprise:
Rien de plus cher que la chanson grise
Ou l'indécis au précis se joint. *

He was trying to get at the matter of words. Marvin had experimented with rhyme; "a rimeless sonnet is certainly a novelty, Rummy," wrote Dos Passos, "but I'm the last one to object to that." He thought Marvin used "good solid rhythm," but as gently as he could he criticized the wording, not "too trite, though it has tendencies in that direction." Marvin's line, "Mundane lights appear as blanks," was less than successful. Words like "joys" were trivial, whereas words like "mundane," "puny," and "pretty" were affected, Dos Passos thought, and advised, "Try to run down the simple (not the hackneyed) and colorful words." Description, "not in vague wornout terms but in concrete images," was what Marvin needed. Emotion is expressible better by "a novel *colored* descriptive bit" than by trite phrases like "black despair," he cautioned. Be original, he urged, and do not "moan out poetic palpitations" like those in newspaper poetry. He reminded Marvin to read a lot of verse as a fine way of learning how to write; Tennyson, Kipling, Stevenson, and Browning were always there to learn from.

Late in April Dos Passos returned from his spring vacation to find a letter telling of all Marvin's activities. Dos Passos explained he had not answered earlier because he had been in Virginia "riding, digging in mi garden, among the cabbages, a la Diocletian!" But that was only a part of his activity, as he had been reading at a great rate: Marcus Aurelius, Dostoevsky's *The Brothers Karamazov; Elizabeth and Her German Garden,* by Mary Annette, the Countess von Arnim; the two poetry anthologies he would review for the *Harvard Monthly* in May; and some philosophical textbooks. He wrote the *Monthly* review and in addition worked at some early chapters of *Streets of Night.* He was just back from New York when he wrote, in high spirits from all his activities. Ahead were the last days of college, and after that? He could not say, because it was not clear in his own mind what came next. Then, too, he looked forward to these last months, which were going to be filled with writing projects—he planned to compose a "monumental" essay about the Imagists, Richard Aldington in particular—and with jaunts like a walk out to Nahant, a spit of land which jutted into Massachusetts Bay north of Boston. This he planned to do with a college friend, starting at midnight so they could arrive to see the sun rise over the Atlantic from the cliffs along the shore.

**From music before all else*

It is also necessary that you never
Choose your words without some contempt:
Nothing is dearer than the gray song
Where the imprecise joins the precise.

Five weeks later he was preparing for exams, his last exams, he imagined, unless, as he mused, he might go to Oxford "or somewhere absurd, which is possible." He had begun to think about what he would do after graduation, but the idea of further study was more his father's than his. The intensity of the war and America's reluctant though ever deepening involvement in it made Dos Passos keen to see it firsthand. John R. did not favor the idea and, until Dos Passos was twenty-one, insisted that he have the final say about what his son should do.

About poetry Dos Passos continued to argue with Rumsey Marvin, who rather pompously condemned low-life people as among "life's meaner things." Dos Passos kept insisting that the riffraff to be found in some of John Masefield's poems had a "tragic beauty about them"—he cited in particular a recent narrative, "The Widow in the Bye Street." Bits of that poem "taken by themselves are ugly and disgusting," he admitted, but he insisted that *as a whole,* it seems to me to have a peculiar sort of pathetic beauty—and a marvelous feeling of life." The term "life's meaner things" annoyed him; if there were "meaner" things, they were "stock-brokers and hypocritical clergymen far more often than they [were] women of the streets or prize fighters or any of Masefield's riff-raff." If an idea were to be an idea at all, he warned, then it could not go "according to conventional lines."

Dos Passos had little desire to cling to vestiges of whatever college aestheticism he had indulged in and was working it out of his writing style. When he argued against Marvin's snobbishness toward lower-class life, he was articulating his own changing attitude. Saying that few things "on the breast of the teeming earth" are distasteful, he came back to his point. Marvin's was a narrow point of view, but Dos Passos romanticized his own when he claimed that "You can find a sort of mad splendor in things, the ugliest, the filthiest things if you really look for it—if you don't, as most people do, put up stone walls and bar the gate on it." Hoping to drive the point home about beauty, he quoted to Marvin from Francis Thompson's "queer strangely fascinating" poem, "The Hound of Heaven":

I fled Him down the nights and down the days;
I fled Him down the arches of the years
I fled Him down the labyrinthine ways
Of my own mind . . .

He wrote out several more lines, his point being that, like the narrator in Thompson's poem who fails to escape God, one cannot flee from beauty, which in its diverse forms is everywhere, and one must understand this, or despair, thinking that earth's "harvest-fields / Be dunged with rotten death." In poetry, beauty comes not only from subject matter—which could be almost anything—but from the devices of prosody: rhythm, for one thing. And, Dos Passos concluded, the poetry that was most musical he liked best.

During the exam period at Harvard, Dos Passos was aware that soon he might be undergoing tests of a different sort, though what they might be he was not sure. He restlessly sought new experiences where he could find them, longing "to stretch my legs on a good piece of road and set off, like Gil Blas or Don Quixote and everyone amusing who's ever lived—videre mundum." So he continued his rambling walks, at one point striking out on a long hike through Boston on a Saturday night. It was rainy, and he delighted in the lively orange and yellow color of lights reflected on the wet streets. If he criticized Marvin's attitude, he was being romantic and condescending himself and only partly realized it when he described to Marvin the "wonderful atmosphere of gaiety & a sort of paganism" in the city. "I mean in the cheaper parts of the city—those are the only parts of any city that are ever alive." The vitality of the market near North and Commercial streets excited him: "all the old women, young women, boys, old grizzled men, flashing eyed Italians bringing vegetables and meats—and the reds and greens and yellows were so fresh in the rainy atmosphere." His tone remained that of what he still was, an adolescent discovering a world beyond his own. "It is wonderful what beautiful faces you sometimes see," he commented about the market, "ugly gargoyle-grotesques too, to be sure—still it is all very alive and exciting—when not done up in stays like the life of us cotton-wool plutocrats—because we are plutocrats compared to those people." With a touch of insight he added, "But enough romantic sociology!"

In his market mood he denigrated the "cotton-wool plutocrats," forgetting for an instant that they also could enjoy life in a way that in another mood he found exhilarating. During these last days he had a memorable picnic with others of the Harvard plutocrats. Once they took cold roast chicken, cheeses, jellies, and other picnic items and hiked out into the country, where they had "a most delightful souper sur l'herbe on a hillside that fronted the sunset. I've never known anything so delightful," Dos Passos exclaimed. "It was a wonderful red-orange sunset, fading gradually through rose-purple and violet to a sort of dim lavender with a yellow sheen." In high spirits, he and his friends climbed into a large oak tree to watch the sunset after they had finished their meal—"as if we were Bonnie Prince Charlie being pursued by the King's men"—then they trundled back to Cambridge in the last light of the day. It was characteristic of Dos Passos then to see things in blacks and whites: Harvardians were "done up in stays"; people of the market place were alive and exciting, filled with "gaiety and a sort of paganism." Life at Harvard might seem stultifying yet he and his friends could have a marvelous time enjoying the countryside and be so unconventional as to pile up into a large oak tree to watch a beautiful late-spring sunset. Yet even then he was didactic to the point where in his writing he hesitated to admit that somewhere in between black and white is where most of mankind exist. Not all Harvardians were bound up in stays; not all the people milling around Boston's open-air markets were warm, vital, high-spirited, although Dos Passos for the moment would not admit it.

Once his exams were over, he was free to indulge in some wandering before the graduation ceremonies at Harvard, so he planned a "Conquest of Cape Cod" with two friends. He wrote Marvin that the trip would be a "vagabondy affair," as he had never been on the Cape and planned to take along only a toothbrush, a razor, and a volume of Meredith's poems. Because his friends backed out at the last moment, midweek he started alone, taking a train from Boston's South Station for

Chatham, about halfway out on the south side of the Cape. Although he admitted later that he wished from time to time for a companion to talk to, he was used to being alone, could enjoy the solitude, and became entranced by the slow journey toward Provincetown. The train, stopping frequently, meandered out the Cape. The Cape Codders were special people, Dos Passos decided, with his eye for exotic types, noticing characters like an old woman wearing "an old fashioned East Indian shawl in [the] wonderful looking style of 1840 daguerreotypes," who got off the train on its way to Chatham.

After staying in Chatham for the night, Dos Passos arose early and set out for Orleans the next morning. He had "footed it all the way . . . (8 1/2 miles)" and then lay down on a low hillside overlooking a small bay at Orleans to write more of his letter to Marvin. "The road was delightful with splendid flowers," he exclaimed, "pinks, catchfly, lupine, immense fat buttercups and marguerites of unparalleled whiteness—It is a gray foggy day—From here I can just hear the breakers on the beach a couple of miles off and right in front of me is a wonderful bay with green islands and silvery channels—rather like the background of La Joconde and about the same greenish silver tonality—J'ai faim—I must find an inn—à plus tard."

After some lunch, he walked the last stretch to Wellfleet, some fifteen miles beyond Orleans. The road wound around ponds and marshes, through low pines and oaks, and by dunes where it ran near the shoreline. He may well have walked out to the Marconi wireless station, perched on a high cliff overlooking the Atlantic below South Wellfleet. The station seemed a remote thing, a strange concoction of four large towers strung with countless supporting cables and transmitting wires. When it was operating, its spark-gap transmitter disk made a crashing roar that could be heard miles away, while sparks flew out from the disk.

If little was lost on Dos Passos, he would certainly have had a sense of American history as he stood on the high bluff by the station overlooking the ocean. If he imagined following the forty-second parallel eastward from Truro, but a few miles north of the Marconi station, the next land he would touch would be the coast of Europe at a point just above the border between Spain and Portugal. Dos Passos knew history of a different sort as well: his own ancestry, so the significance of this point and of the Cape was not lost on him. Where Provincetown stands now, the Pilgrims had first touched shore on November 11, 1620, before sailing across Cape Cod Bay to land at Plymouth. At the northern tip of the Cape the Mayflower Compact was signed. From these waters shipping set out from America during all her history as a colony and then a nation; off the shores of the Cape more than 3,000 shipwrecks had occurred. It was easy to sense the grandeur, and more, the immense promise of the country when he stood by the wireless station, whose location and the electrical genius involved in its creation made it a peculiarly apt symbol of the United States.

The walk into Wellfleet from the Marconi station is some five or six miles. The road swings down toward the inland side of the Cape, running close by the coves and rocky beaches that face onto Wellfleet harbor. Dos Passos got to the small fishing village "weary of limb but refreshed of spirit" after the day's vagabonding.

He found "a quaint little inn, very musty smelling with abnormally steep stairs," where he settled in and wrote Marvin more about the colors of the land and the sounds of the breakers along the shore and of the wind in the pines. "Mais je suis mort de fatigue—bon soir—" he closed Thursday's part of his letter.

The next day he walked the fifteen remaining miles to Provincetown, arriving "a little the worse for wear, but still bearing up," he wrote from his lodging in the New Central House. "Good Lord!" he exclaimed, "they have a town crier here— imagine!" As he wrote, the crier went by, ringing his bell while he shouted out some bit of news. Provincetown, fascinating to Dos Passos in its diversity, was strung out along the waterfront, and the mixed population caught his eye: "Yankees with hardlooking hatchet faces and Portuguese & Canary Islanders—dark & marvellously good looking—The contrast is amazing!" He enjoyed poking around the narrow alleys connecting the town's two main streets. There houses crowd together in European fashion, while small shops spill onto Commercial Street, the main thoroughfare nearest the harbor. But while he found a continental air about Provincetown, it was full of reminders that it was a New England fishing port with its old churches and colonial-styled homes. An inquisitive visitor would soon find out that the alleys had once been runways for boats and that the soil in many of the narrow gardens on the street front or between the houses had been ballast long before for sailing ships. Dos Passos was enthralled by the town, but after only a short stay, he took a slow train back to Boston, as the Cape Cod line was not yet operating its ships across Massachusetts Bay for the summer.

In Cambridge a letter from Marvin was waiting for him, including one of Marvin's latest poetic efforts. Dos Passos found the poem among Marvin's best and so could be severe in his criticism without hurting his friend's feelings. Words and phrases that were inexact should be pulled out. "Give never a windy moan" was overdone, a sound that did not actually exist, and inversions like "moon beams bright" and "freshness green" were needless. Look for new and personal ways of expressing emotion, he urged, and do not let devices like rhyme send the poem astray. Read Keats, he advised, "The Eve of St. Agnes," the odes to autumn and to a nightingale. "I Stood Tiptoe upon a Little Hill" impressed him even if parts of it were "wobbly." "Look!" he counseled Marvin, take the first stanza of the "Ode to Autumn." "I defy you to find a word that doesn't both add to the sense—(the picture) and the sound—'Season of mists and mellow fruitfulness,'" he began, and copied out the magnificent first stanza to make his point.

Several days later came the end of his years at Harvard. June 20, 1916, was Class Day, and whatever his eventual thoughts about college, that day he was pensive, more than a little saddened by the ceremony which marked his graduation. He scoffed to Marvin that he had "marched & counter marched in processions—and heard endless orations." Not wanting to make anything of being graduated, he kept John R. from coming to Cambridge for the exercises. Nor did he attend the ceremonies to receive his diploma, claiming that he was interested but aloof about the whole thing. Yet he admitted that the let-down of being finished would "probably end in a shocking attack of the blue devils," and in his last letter to Marvin from

Harvard he kept returning to the evocative setting of the Yard in the evening after the ceremonies of Class Day. "The Yard is hung with Japanese lanterns," he wrote, "lilting with the music of three bands and two fountains—and I have a pink in my buttonhole." Before coming back to his room in Thayer Hall overlooking the scene, he had wandered among the people dancing in the Yard, "listening to their footsteps and feeling a strange half-melancholy." Then he had returned to his room to write Marvin and gaze out at the scene below from his window seat, a "glow of lanterns and ripple of voices above a low grind of footsteps—through it all runs like a gilt thread, the brazen sound of the band—then the occasional militia uniform give it a

> *There was a sound of revelry by night*
> *And Belgium's capital had gathered then*
> *Her beauty & her chivalry, and bright*
> *The lamps shone o'er fair women & brave men*

atmosphere." Soon he got up and wandered outside again. A strong wind came up and set the lanterns bobbing and the women's dresses rustling; the evening was lovely yet melancholy for him.

He was graduated cum laude, which pleased him despite his claim of indifference. In the June *Monthly* appeared three of the last four contributions he made, the fourth being a brief, nonpolitical review of Jack Reed's *The War in Eastern Europe* which appeared in the July issue. As he was leaving Harvard he turned his gaze eastward and thought more and more about United States involvement in the war. He wrote an editorial for the *Monthly* about a conference on foreign relations to be held at Western Reserve University. The nation could not remain apart from the conflict, he asserted, although he did not advocate declaring war. He called for "constructive pacifism," a vague term, and closed his editorial by stating that "it is useless to mumble sleepily 'isolation.' . . . Our old provincial slumbers must give place to an intelligent and unselfish use of our power for good in world-politics."

More important than the editorial was an essay, "A Humble Protest," in the same issue. Dos Passos decried the contemporary worship of science, which he declared was worldwide. Man's two great aims are to create and to fathom. How, he asked, do these "fare under the rule of science and its attendant spirits, Industrialism and Mechanical Civilization?" Not well, was his answer. Man was no freer than before to produce art, nor any closer to knowing himself, although he might know a great many facts about himself. The scientific spirit, in fact, had caused mankind to construct innumerable hindrances to self-knowledge, "a clutter of inessentials" which had the effect of enslaving people within the industrial system. "Millions of men perform labor narrowing and stultifying even under the best conditions, bound in the traces of mechanical industry. . . ." As if this were not horror enough, science brought on the horror of world war. Germany, "the one modern nation which, as well as having developed the industrial system to its highest degree, has a really great living art, has suddenly slipped back into barbarism. The same civilization has produced Wagner and Von Turpitz, the Eroica Symphony and the ruins of Rheims."

Embodied in Dos Passos's protest was an attitude that would find mature expression in work to come: opposition to bigness, organization, conformity, and rampant materialism. But for this time, the essay and a poem, "Philosophy," also in the June *Monthly*, may be read as a kind of declaration of independence from the Harvard bell glass. The poem sets two old men against the activity of life, as much as to say that their philosophic musings are ineffectual. One old man fishes but catches nothing; the other ponders the moves of "the ivory chessmen of his thoughts" and slowly drowses while the lively sunlight plays across his white robe, until at sunset "he sits and stares / Checkmated in the end."

More than a poem about the philosophic gropings of old men, the poem seems Dos Passos's own declaration. His sympathies lay not with the stymied sages, but with the vital natural world downstream from the old fisherman, where "in the glimmering rapids . . . broken blue reflections dance," and "suddenly, / A fish breaks water, / An arc of flashing silver / In the sunlight." They lay, too, with a boy who comes singing "down the white dusty road before the sage" and "kicks up with bare brown feet / The red-tinged dust of the road." As Dos Passos left Cambridge, the haven of the philosophers, he hoped that there was more than a little of the singing boy in him.

CHAPTER SIX

A Summer of Writing, 1916

Before departing Harvard, Dos Passos arranged to visit Marvin at Marvin's home in New Rochelle. They enjoyed a strenuous few days of walks, talk about books, and visits to art museums at the end of June. Soon after, Dos Passos thanked Marvin for everything—"from strawberries to books & Paulo Veronese I enjoyed myself very much." Then, eager to keep up with his friendships, Dos Passos took the train out to Stamford, Connecticut, to visit his college friend, Stewart Mitchell, nicknamed "The Auk." Mitchell lived with his aunt, a marvelous person who played Bach "raptly and with charm," Dos Passos later reported to Dudley Poore. She spoke with a French accent and seemed very much of the old regime—"Chopin, Liszt (?) old age." She was an occultist, a remarkable character, Dos Passos decided, and concluded, "She ought to be a marquise." His loyalty to his college friends was quickly showing itself. He savored their quirks but avoided cruel comment about them and had no intention of letting these friendships lapse either through spite or neglect.

Dos Passos remained in New York several days more before going south to Sandy Point. The early summer heat and the city's bustle caused him to complain of getting no reading or writing done, something he planned to rectify once he settled in Virginia, "car il me faut devenir sérieux maintenant!" he asserted in a letter to Marvin as if to remind himself that college was done. Even in New York, though, he had actually been reading, struggling through some Portuguese poetry that amused him with its Spanish view of Sir Richard Grenville—"Greenfield," the poem called him—and the battle of the *Revenge*.

By Independence Day he arrived in Sandy Point where Lois Sprigg and her family joined him and John R. for the holiday. On July 5 he wrote Dudley Poore rather boastfully that he was in Virginia "ecstasizing—to the surprise & mild shockdom of certain cousins— . . . over poppies, gooseberries, currents immense Shasta Daisies and other glories. . . ."

Dos Passos told Poore that he already missed the "literary jibber-jabber" of Harvard; his letters during this summer in Virginia ring with his literary passion— both for his own attempts to write vividly and for the works he devoured. He described to Poore the scene around the White House: "a wonderful blowy day and the hollyhocks are nodding and bowing like tall ladies at a country dance—the poppies are all a-flutter and the lavender comes in puffs of glorious fragrance through the window." He was about to swim in the Potomac and then settle down to read Anatole France's "Pierre Noziere." "In fact," he exclaimed, "I am foolish—crack-brained with rusticity & divers delights."

Soon he had an ambitious schedule for himself as he set about seriously to become a writer. He was not yet clear in his own mind what he intended to do as a profession, but all the while he wrote with the idea that this was one career he wanted to pursue. He planned to get up at 6:00 A.M., run on the beach for fifteen minutes, breakfast before eight o'clock, work for two hours in the garden, and then write from ten until noon. After that, a swim, lunch, a short nap, and again writing and some reading from two until five. He would end his day with a horseback ride and another swim. The schedule was not unlike the one the young Benjamin Franklin described for himself in *Poor Richard's Almanac,* and the comparison is apt. Behind Dos Passos's reserve was a fierce desire for success, and that, he knew, required discipline. Little would interfere with the work routines he developed for himself, resulting in production, even though he complained that he was acomplishing little.

His letters from Sandy Point that summer were full of enthusiasms—for travel, for literature, and for his friends, from whom he felt cut off, although his occupation with projects and rural life compensated in part for his isolation. He and John R. continued to discuss plans for his immediate future, which for Dos Passos had to include foreign travel. He applied for work in Herbert Hoover's Belgian Relief organization. As an alternative, he would go to Spain to study architecture, a choice that was not displeasing, because it would mean travel abroad first. To himself, he added that architecture would have to take its chance. John R. was sympathetic while insisting that Dos Passos work toward advancement in some sort of a profession. If John R. was aware that architecture would receive only lip service from his son, he was satisfied that this plan gave the young man's wanderlust a direction.

At Sandy Point Dos Passos dived into the multivolume novel *Jean Christophe* by Romain Rolland. By mid-July he complained of a bilious attack, "probably due to an over-dose of Jean Christophe," for by then he had gotten to volume seven of the work. "Sentimental, moralistic, with a minor prophetic hue, dimly Tolstoian," he found it; yet, he wrote Dudley Poore, "I have a horrid fear that the man is sincere & that that strange being Jean Christophe is alive." At the same time, he was immersed in Gorky's *My Childhood* and soon thereafter, Cellini's autobiography. The book "simply shrieks Italy; Italy at her best," he thought, "golden sun, cypresses almost black against the extreme blue of sky, and all the enthusiasm and vigor and wonderful livingness of it." It was, he decided, a tonic for anyone living in the present, which he pronounced with a flourish was a "seagreen, twaddling, ranting little agelet of greedy capitalists and shallow humanitarians!"

These enthusiasms, though involving, could not keep him entirely free from boredom. Experimentation with a sailing canoe he had rigged himself was enjoyable, but he became lonely over the hot months, once blurting out to Poore that a dry wind was parching everything. It was too hot to walk; he was tired of the roads over which he rode horseback; and the Potomac was full of jellyfish which could give a swimmer a vicious sting. So he implored his friends to write and hoped that his flurry of letters might coax them to respond. "This is a clam," he began a note to Poore, with an arrow pointing to a scribbled sketch of a clamshell, and went on,

> A closed clam.
> Like unto a clam
> Is Dudleyosha
> Apropos of poetry;
> For he writes tons of the
> Most delightful things
> But no creature does he allow to see them.
> He's a flim-flam
> a verse-secretina clam
> Damn!
> (Who says form to me?)

And around the same time he sent Marvin a typed copy of his poem "Incarnation," which had appeared in the *Harvard Monthly* the previous May. Dos Passos thought it might amuse him as it was one of his better Imagistic efforts, a serious piece; yet it had appeared in New York and Philadelphia papers, probably, he laughed, "between the work of Willy Minute (age 9) 'I like to see a little fly / Upon a piece of apple pie' etc. and the latest sonnet of political hue—'Up citizen, see the Republican banners unfold.' "

Dos Passos also began a correspondence that summer with another college friend, Arthur McComb. Two years behind Dos Passos at Harvard, McComb became a friendly adversary for Dos Passos as he self-consciously moved leftward politically. He described McComb much later as "cosmopolitan . . . born in Paris a British subject." The son of an Episcopal minister, he had been brought up mostly in Italy. "He was a convinced pacifist," wrote Dos Passos, "a selfproclaimed reactionary who already admired Metternich: I thought of Arthur as a living exemplar of the nineteenth-century civilization I saw bleeding to death in the nomanslands of France and Flanders." McComb had published a response to "A Humble Protest" in the same issue of the *Monthly* in which Dos Passos's essay had appeared, and he argued that art and industry were not necessarily incompatible, as Dos Passos thought them to be. McComb went further, insisting that because industry and commerce meant wealth, and wealth in turn was the basis of "intellectual and social excellence," so they were essential to art. He favored unimpeded capitalism, for in a society where wealth was divided equally and where there was no private property, there would be no standard of luxury that could check population growth among the poor, and humanity would soon outgrow the resources available for sustenance. "The poor must learn," he concluded, "that the only efficient and permanent remedy for their unhappiness consistent with the maintenance of human freedom, lies in the limitation of their numbers on the one hand and in the protection of capital on the other."

It was to McComb's pacifism and to his conservatism that Dos Passos reacted when, in the midst of reading "The Beloved Meredith" he felt impelled to transcribe for McComb a passage from *Beauchamp's Career*: "No one had any desire for war, only we really had (and this was perfectly true) been talking gigantic nonsense of peace, and of the everlastingness of the exchange of fruits for money, with angels wearing raw-groceries of Eden in joy of the commercial picture." Gleefully Dos Passos underlined the last phrase, then demanded, "Voilà—êtes-vous écrasé?" He complained that McComb's sort of pacifist created various cubbyholes into which he stuffed "all the actions of the forces of unreason," actions described in terms like "official brutality," "fanaticism," "imperialist reaction," and the like. Many people agreed with the terms, Dos Passos acknowledged, but it would take more than these to defeat the realities of aggression. McComb's catchwords would have to take upon themselves "arms and legs and brawny muscles and poison gas shells before they [could] rout actuality." And Dos Passos did not think they could bear that weight. Finally, he did not believe that McComb was willing to sacrifice prosperity for peace, a reference no doubt to the need to forgo trade with the warring European nations if the United States wished to remain truly neutral. They bandied their disagreements back and forth during the next years, and it was good for Dos Passos to have as close a friend as McComb with whom he could disagree while trying out his political ideas. His other friends either saw things more nearly as he did or, like Dudley Poore, were basically apolitical. Dos Passos told McComb in the same letter of his projects: a piece against the attention being given to *Jean Christophe* and an article, "Shelley and the Modern Age," which would decry "the strange sanity of American young men, their lack of idealism, and their 'redbloodedness' "—no doubt a version of the essay that was his first nationally published piece when it appeared in the *New Republic* in October 1916, under the title "Against American Literature." "Au Revoir," he concluded to McComb, "you Mancastrian, you Cobdenite."

Chafing at his isolation, he applauded Rumsey Marvin near the end of August for "rubbing shoulders" with other types and conditions of people on Plum Island, off the eastern tip of Long Island—hardly, one supposes, truly a stamping ground for the masses Dos Passos wanted to hold in such high esteem. He declared he had always missed such activity. "At school I was a most unsocial friendless little beast," he recalled, "and it has been hard to shake off the habit of solitude." A touch of Plum Island would have benefited him, he decided, "although there are people who sort of have solitude in their blood, who are just as lonely in a crowd or on a mountain top—I may be one of them; quien sabe?" What made his reticence more annoying to him was that he desired "the extremest sociability," and for that reason, if for little else, he approved of military service—a hint of why he wanted to get into the war raging in Europe in some capacity.

He urged Marvin to plan a walking trip with him in the Catskills in early September. In two days they could cover a lot of ground, and more, could expand their friendship. Dos Passos's proposition was not without a touch of wistfulness. He tried to suppress his loneliness by talk of the immediate future. He was going abroad, he wrote Marvin, "where as yet undecided," and he vowed not to return until he had "come to grips with old lady adventure—sort of a Search for the Holy Grail." Shortly before Dos Passos wrote this letter, Marvin had confessed to his older friend that he was feeling the pangs of love. Though Dos Passos envied him that, his response was a Whitmanesque assertion that if one were properly transcendental —"in tune with earth and sky"—then one was "already in love with every man woman and child in sight." Dos Passos's response was an attempt to dismiss a matter about which he felt ill at ease. He offered scarce comfort to his friend, which must have been self-evident when he concluded, "I'm probably talking rot." The matter of sexual attraction made him nervous, despite his efforts to belittle its importance. With just a touch of the voyeur, he asked Marvin to "describe *her* or them: Fair? Fat? Thin? Dark? Languid? Vivacious? Frank? Piquante? Mysterious? Seductive? Miscellaneous?"—a question amusingly put, but more serious than he would have admitted.

He was exceedingly more comfortable discussing literature or politics. When Dudley Poore sent him the manuscript of a short story he had written, Dos Passos responded in admiration but urged him to point up one of the characters more and strengthen the motive in the tale. Where he liked it, he scribbled "Viva!" in the margins. Poore took the comments to heart, revised the story, and it later appeared in the *Harvard Monthly* as "A Legacy." The same day that Dos Passos wrote Poore, he responded to the conservative McComb, confessing that for the moment he had fallen back into chaos, having no ideas about the war but a desire to "hack and hew, to agitate against the bogies which are being battered by warfume." He exclaimed that he was "darned serious" about "the forces of reason" banding together. "We want a new Enlightenment—new Byrons new Shelleys new Voltaires before whom 19th Century stodginess on the one hand and 20th Century reaction on the other shall vanish and be utterly routed 'like souls from an enchanter fleeing.'"

Near the middle of September 1916, he was in New York City to put some affairs in order before going abroad, even though his plans had not crystallized. His proposed trip into the Catskills with Rumsey Marvin had not worked, and as his friends were not about, he felt as solitary in the city as he had toward the end of his summer at Sandy Point. He told Poore of wandering around New York all day, only to end in "the horrid state (not unknown to me) in which—from pure watching of other people, from trying to pry into their lives as they pass me on the street— I have reached a point where I feel more like a disembodied spirit than a warm-fleshed human."

One matter that did occupy his time in New York during September and October was to arrange for the publication of a collection of poetry from the *Harvard Monthly* to be entitled *Eight Harvard Poets*. The volume included poems by Cummings, Dudley Poore, Stewart Mitchell, Robert Hillyer, and Dos Passos, among others and, partly underwritten by John R., was to be published by Laurence J. Gomme. The arrangements were slow, because Gomme rightly wanted assurance that he would not be left with the major expense for the book. But even with this to keep Dos Passos busy, the days dragged out while he waited to hear whether the Belgian Relief would accept him. He read even more than usual and wrote idly to Marvin about flirtation and falling in love—the former got boring after five minutes; the latter was more desirable, because he believed in the " 'grand manner,' in love as in other things." He thought that when he fell, he fell hard, although so far the objects of his love had soon faded into the commonplace. The falling he spoke of was more abstract than were Marvin's adolescent amours. In another letter Dos Passos claimed he often fell in love "with a face or a glint of light on hair or an intonation of the voice." But he seemed to succeed in keeping his emotions so much in check that he had had little in the way of romances so far. "The idea of marriages and engagements and all the conventional fluffiness of respectable mating doesn't attract me particularly," he wrote Marvin. "It rather spoils things." His hint of contempt for convention, while no doubt sincere, conveniently shielded his shyness. While he may have burned for a grand passion, he saw respectable mating as "spoiling things." Although he could not yet imagine sexual intimacy with a woman out of whatever degree of friendship, the conventions of marriage for Dos Passos changed things all around, "for a friend married is a friend lost," and his friendships with people of either sex seemed to him rare enough that he wanted to hold on to them.

In his mood of ennui and uncertainty he looked back in September 1916 with nostalgic pleasure on his Harvard days. Dudley Poore wrote him about the loveliness of the early fall in Cambridge, urging him to return to Cambridge, where "over a bottle of claret . . . we will talk divine nonsense concerning the relativity of things and pluck a feather from the flying wings of the Absolute." Dos Passos rejoined that Poore could keep silent about these things, and about the beautiful sunsets and the Charles River. "Darn your soul," he exclaimed, "you've started it all up again—of course I've been mad to go back to violet tinted twilights and the smell of tea and lemon and philosophy and dancing by night on Louisburg Square and la donna mobile and clams." The struggle in his soul to break free of Cambridge was as mighty as the battle of Verdun, he asserted, "like trying to break away from a drug or an unfaithful mistress."

A few days later he heard the fateful news from the Belgian Relief Commission that he was too young at age twenty to serve with them. His discouragement was short-lived because it caused him to decide what he would do: study architecture in Spain. His preliminary plan was to live in the student residence of the university in Madrid while he learned Spanish and took courses in architecture as well as various aspects of Spanish culture that would give him background for further work.

Shortly he procured letters of introduction to three Spanish poets as well as to several other persons who would be in a position to help him, all provided by his father's friend Juan Riaño, an instructor at West Point. The study he anticipated would be needed discipline for one who had adopted the self-effacing pose of having a helter-skelter mind. Even as he planned for Spain, he had in the back of his mind the longer-range plan of joining the ambulance service sometime after he became twenty-one in January 1917.

Although he was eager to leave, there were delays; the first ship he could book passage on was the French liner *Espagne,* not sailing until October 14. The excitement of the upcoming trip made him impatient, despite having plenty to do during the next several weeks. He mocked the red tape of getting a passport and completing various forms necessary to travel abroad during the war, thought he had finished the necessary negotiations for *Eight Harvard Poets,* and kept up his correspondence with his friends. Marvin was told about "The Man on the Street," who en masse is "the forces of darkness—but taken one by one" is something else. "You know," Dos Passos blustered, "I rather divide people into those who see, and those who drift. There are people—you and I and Swinburne—who analyze, who observe, who think, and then there are people who merely follow the bandwagon—the people who are free, who are in revolt, and the people who are shackled by all convention." He cautioned that the alert people were not of any one class, nor the deadened either: "a stupid farmer is no lower on the scale than a stupid Harvard graduate." And mostly what deadens is convention, he warned, "that abominable coverer up of things—niceness." It was evident for whom he was speaking when he added, "It is so hard to get away from the lingo, from the little habits of speech and action, from the petty snobberies of one's own class that it takes a distinct effort to see real 'illumination' and appreciate it. . . ." Snobbery, he decided, is the worst trait. He admittedly sensed these traits in himself, and Spain he hoped would purge him of the less attractive habits of his class.

He could not stand not to get back to Cambridge for a few days before sailing and wired Dudley Poore on September 29: APPEARING BACK BAY 1005 GOMME IS THE LUCKY PUBLISHER. His visit was eminently satisfying. Though agreeably cast in the role of elder statesman, he enjoyed seeing his close friends again before he would be on his own more than ever before. The stay was short, and soon he was back in New York to see about last-minute details, taking the time to write McComb that he was sorry they had missed one another in Cambridge, and clucking his tongue about "Tyranny at Home"—a case of a journalist who was denied a passport to England because he had criticized Woodrow Wilson's policies. Dos Passos carped against what he called "the intolerance of broadminded people." "Mr. Pacifist," he addressed McComb in the stern tone he sometimes employed with him, "war is a human phenomenon which you can't argue out of existence. You people are like Christian Scientists with the yellow fever. All your praying and all your ought nots wont change the present fact. They may change the future, but only through the frank and sympathetic understanding of reality—which is not got by closing doors. . . . Look!" he exclaimed, "the most dangerous features of an evil are its virtues.

Discover these; face them by bigger virtues—and the evil will fade like a ghost at cockcrow."

A few days before he sailed, the first publication for which he was paid appeared in the *New Republic*. He was understandably delighted about being paid $30 for "Against American Literature," the short article which he had written in Virginia during the summer, which appeared in the October 14 issue. He could not resist telling McComb and Marvin about his success. He wrote Marvin that he immediately looked upon himself as "an established light of literature." He wanted to tell people on the street what a fine magazine the *New Republic* was. The article, while hardly earthshaking, echoed much of what such established literary figures as Van Wyck Brooks were saying. Perhaps the most significant part of it was Dos Passos's championing of Walt Whitman, a theme of his that would prove to last. Whitman had challenged America to produce a great literature. What was missing in the nation's writing to date was a sense of roots in the land. "The earth feeling," he wrote, "has been cut out from us. We find ourselves floundering without rudder or compass, in the sea of modern life, vaguely lit by the phosphorescent gleam of our traditional optimism." Can we not overcome "the fetters of 'niceness,' of the middle-class outlook," he asked, and produce works with "the color and passion and profound thought of other literature?" His first professional hewing and hacking was almost embarrassingly close to Brooks's diatribe against American literature, "America's Coming of Age," written a year before. Dos Passos's "sea of modern life" was akin to Brooks's "vast Sargasso Sea" that was America, "a prodigious welter of unconscious life." Little matter, for these ideas were in the air, and Dos Passos was staking out a position for himself among the rebels.

Buoyed by the appearance of his article in the issue dated the very day he sailed, Dos Passos, accompanied by John R., boarded the *Espagne* in high spirits on the fourteenth. Once they had found his cabin, he said goodbye to his father, then settled down to write his friends final letters before the ship pulled away from the docks. He tried to impart to Marvin something of the liner's "ropy pitchy smell" and of the "song of the steam-winches that are saying gr-rr gr-rr in a charming monotone of excitement." There had been, he wrote, "an air of mystery and submarines" about the way officials had inspected his passport and baggage. Write, he told Marvin, care of the Banco Hispano Americano, 1 Calle de Sevilla, Madrid. He closed, "Darn it man, I wish you were coming too."

The *Espagne* slipped away from the pier, and John R. from his office on Broad Street watched the ship's red smokestacks as she headed down river. In his excitement Dos Passos had not sensed his father's loneliness. Neither father nor son suspected that they had seen each other for the last time. That evening John R. sat down and wrote Mrs. Harris about his son's departure:

Well! Jack has gone!
I saw him to the ship at two o'clock & left him aboard. The "Espagne" sails at three. I did not care to wait to bid adieu with hands & handkerchief —So we kissed and parted one hour before he started. From my office window

I could see her go down the bay—a noble ship! The air is full of rumors of submarines outside of Sandy Hook. . . . I would have as soon tried to restrain an angry lion from seizing its prey as to have protested against Jack's going. It is his destiny! It is mine. I can do nothing. He had no more fear of going than he had to walk into his garden at Sandy Point. He is callous to all such influences. He is well stocked with all the necessaries—Irwin had Mary Hillis ship a couple of pounds of Washington Candy in his trunk. He goes out into the world! What will be the result? Let us not try to pry into the future. A noble boy—a more completely educated character—a finer scholar—never went forth. He is out of the nest! . . . God bless him. He is his own guide now. And I am alone! Well! What of it? This is living—the branch has broken from the tree & goes to plant itself in a foreign soil.

I am sending you his article in the New Republic "Against American Literature." It was accepted & he earned his first money $30. If he lives he will make many more dollars—and much fame . . .

His conduct was beautiful: he walked out of the door with me as if he were going for a stroll. We had no regrets to express to each other, and no sighs were made. It was simply a kiss & au revoir.

It is all life.

Dieu te garde—Everything and Everybody seem so far away tonight.

CHAPTER SEVEN

Spain, 1916–1917

Settled in his cabin aboard the *Espagne*, Dos Passos discovered a gift of coffee from Rumsey Marvin's mother. In a letter of thanks written later, he assured her it was a great improvement over "the thin mud they give one for the product on ocean liners." Although the shadow of the war loomed over the crossing, it was uneventful and induced a "complete coma" in him, as he told Marvin when he wrote from Bordeaux ten days after leaving New York. And while he had intended to be industrious about reading and writing, he "just lay around and looked at the sea and felt the damp caressing breath of it and sort of melted into it." There had been the possibility of submarine action, but nothing happened: the only sense of war he had came from an aura of caution that hung over the ship. He had encountered a few people who admitted to sleeping in their clothes, and he heard about one man who slept in his life preserver. They saw three cargo ships and some lights during the voyage, but that was all: no periscopes to signal a deadly presence lurking beneath the waves, not even a porpoise. A practical consideration became the only stuff of drama: as a standard precaution the ship ran without lights and with portholes sealed at both ends of the voyage. When finally they sailed up the Gironde at night to Bordeaux, the ship was on full alert, and the captain ordered everyone to remain awake until they had gained the channel entering the port, because of the hazard of floating mines.

If his crossing was a tepid introduction to the Great War, the scene in Bordeaux of wounded soldiers around the crowded hospitals was a gruesome reminder of the reality of battle. Even so, in Bordeaux he was immediately transported by the beauty of France. "I always feel so at home in France," he wrote to Dudley Poore—"so sort of cosy and homelike" was how he put it in a letter to Marvin, and it was a relief, because he was truly alone for the moment, and lonely. Bordeaux for him was a "furiously beautiful city," he exclaimed, then retracted that. "Nothing furious about it," he told Poore; "its the dead quiet beauty of a perfectly bound book—A wonderful tang of the eighteenth century and streets and streets of perfect High Renaissance houses." The city brought back to him sights, sounds, and smells that particularly drew him to France: "the long windows, the donkey carts full of vegetables, the odor of café au lait and fresh-baked bread in the early morning, the nice little écoliers with their bare legs and their black capes, the horse chestnut trees . . . the cobbled streets, with the grass growing bright green in the chinks of the grey stone."

Yet he was quickly reminded of his solitude and wished for someone whom he could "bubble over to." He took to denigrating himself to Marvin, declaring that it was "remarkable how soon, if I let myself, I relapse into a state of complete cabbagism, without thought of any sort, with merely sensual joy in the colors and scents of the world, or unreasoning discomfort in physical—not exactly physical either—rather in emotional disabilities of my own." Although he tried to set himself up to write, he found it "so darn hard to get outside of oneself enough really to see clearly and to follow frankly your ideas to whatever rocky ground or shaky rope ladder they lead you."

After scarcely a day in France, he left Bordeaux on October 25 and crossed the border into Spain: "*España* Wednesday *Oct 25th* 1916" he wrote in his journal. He spent that night in Irún, a small town across the Bidassoa River near the French border city of St. Jean de Luz. The hotel he found "was very bare and chilly and smelt of rancid olive oil," characteristics, he decided, of Spanish hotels in general. But the people struck him favorably, and he wrote that he "was much impressed 1. by the Basque hats 2. by the slender ankles of the men & women who dont affect stockings 3. by the aquiline noses of all the world." Bemused by all this, he made a quick sketch of what he had just scribbled down.

He hurried south to Madrid on the twenty-sixth, took a room at the Hotel de Londres, and immediately began to organize himself and plunge into the life of the city. He took one of his letters of introduction to the poet Juan Ramón Jiménez and went to see Señor Tomás Navarro Tomás at the Centro de Estúdios Históricos. He registered to take two courses in Spanish language—one under Señor Tomás—and a third in Spanish literature for the next three months, as he expected that listening to lectures in Spanish would be the best thing he could do to learn it. On the twenty-ninth, after four days in Spain, he saw a play, "an endless affair in rhymed verse," entitled *Don Juan Tenerio*. Early the next morning he wrote both Poore and Marvin long letters mostly about Spain but with more than a hint of inevitable nostalgia for the life he had left behind. "Yah Dudley," he began to Poore, but before describing Madrid he admitted to a great homesickness "for that absurd Cambridge," where he had known good friends and convivial times. The thought of the Charles River basin nearly made him weep, he confessed. "It's not college exactly but its the wonderful greying purple of those Boston sunsets and those dingy autumnal streets—'Earth has not anything to show more fair'—imagine quoting

Wordsworth—rather shocking, I call it. I'm trying to beat myself into a state of literary production, always a long job with lazy me—Why isnt there some sort of literary twilight sleep?"

In fact, Dos Passos was demanding a lot of himself; newly arrived in Madrid, and entirely on his own, a wave of self-effacement swept over him. Typically, he thought himself lazy not to be writing more, while actually he was absorbing much from his new culture that would be important to his writing. He was immediately taken with Spain and its people and appreciated the fact that despite its proximity, it was a kind of island apart from the Europe he had previously known.

"They have the most divine chocolate I've ever tasted here in Madrid," he wrote Poore. "It comes in the morning with a funny whitish sweet puff and a roll; and I in addition go and guzzle it in cafés in the afternoon. Then there are many charming donkeys and mules with paniers or two wheeled carts"—here he paused to sketch a cart for Poore—"always with the littlest donkey leading the tandem— their harness is jingly and ornamented with brass nails in merry patterns. Moreover in the lower quarters of the city you see in use pottery of the divinest shapes—water bottles braziers etc." The church bells, he thought, made a compelling sound, "a strange droning insistent clang" which he had never heard before, "as if they still smelt the sizzling of bearded Jews and heard the edifying groans of heretics in tall yellow and red hats." He wrote Marvin that there were lots of "little ragamuffins" about such as Goya depicted in his paintings, and to both his friends he exclaimed about the extraordinary views from around the city of the Sierra de Guadarrama range beyond the plain of Castile, stretching out from Madrid. "The country of Castile is brown and rolling with dry arroyos and irrigated patches much like California only the brown of the hills is a pale nankeen instead of the rich sienna of the California slopes." Behind this, looking from Madrid, he could see the mountains, green and snowcapped in contrast to the brown plain below.

In one letter he told Poore about taking a letter of introduction to the poet Jiménez, "a leading poet" he learned later and then became "quite terrified ex post facto." He never liked to present letters of introduction, and this meeting had its particular language problems, although they "talked most animatedly about American literature—and I wanted to tell him about Emily Dickinson—but didn't quite dare—you see he's an awfully eminent poet and he knew much more about American literature than I did . . . one couldn't go into great detail." Dos Passos was being modest, because Jiménez admired most the poetry of the Americans Robinson, Frost, Amy Lowell, Masters, and especially Whitman, which Dos Passos knew well.

He marveled at Spanish customs. The Madrileños seemed fearful of the night air, and he noticed that in the evenings they wrapped long scarves around their faces up to their eyes, some scarves gaily colored ones of "red and green, purple and yellow," the ends of which, he demonstrated in a sketch for Marvin, the Spanish heaved over their shoulders and down their backs. Mealtimes also were an adjustment: "One has déjeuner à la fourchette—almuerzo—at about one or two and then dinner between nine and ten at night. No one seems to get up in the morning and as late as I have ever been up the cafés and things seem to be in full blast.

My Spanish is almost nil & I have the gayest time making myself understood."

As if to illustrate his response to Spanish life by paradox, Dos Passos turned to Emily Dickinson's poetry when he confided to Poore that all this travel and activity "hardly makes up for the 'polar solitude' [th]at Emily D. says, of me. Brrr —I shan't say how—oh damn it—it's always the same anywhere so why make a fuss about it," he broke off that train of thought and turned to other matters before coming back to Emily Dickinson, whose poems had been much on his mind. The poetry of the reclusive Emily suited him just then, but more, he was in the act of discovering his native culture from the perspective of another land. He wrote Poore that for the past three weeks he had read nothing but her poems and urged him to buy at once her volumes *The Single Hound* and *Poems.* Then he announced, "Oyez Oyez Oyez," and copied out her poem,

> *Papa above!*
> *Regard a mouse*
> *O'erpowered by the Cat;*
> *Reserve within thy Kingdom*
> *A "mansion" for the Rat!*

He also discussed with Poore the fiction he had been writing, a short story "to make the last of that set of New York affairs I've told you about." This was a tale of an old spinster and a young boy whom she adored. He went away to school and never saw her again, except when she was taken ill and he came to her. She found that he had been "totally away from her—with the greatest joy she has ever experienced she tells him to go away, she doesn't want him now." Having renounced what she had longed and wept for, she gradually lost consciousness. The story was soon sent to the United States, but was lost in the mails and consequently never published.

Later that day, October 30, he visited Madrid's Museum of Modern Art, then moved from the Hotel de Londres to the Pension Boston, a less expensive arrangement that would be his home for the rest of his stay in Madrid. His room in the Pension Boston amused him, having, as he described it in his journal,

> two beds (pink pillows) one carved chair, one leather chair, one ancient desk, one pseudo-ancient wardrobe, 1 lavender washstand and a checkered tile floor. Below in the street is a frenzy of noises—all the autos in the world, all the prancing horses all the newsboys, all the old women crying "calenti-tas" seem to have collected into one nerve-racking inferno of noises. How long I shall stand it I don't know, as the Puerta de Sol, seems to be always in a state of ruction and my room, like Chaucers Hous of Fame seems to be a collector and clearing house for all the noises on earth.

He embellished his description of the room when he wrote Poore in mid-November. The carved chair, he decided, was "sentimentally carved"; "a religious picture of a chrome-yellow-Virgin on a black background" hung on the wall, and overlooking the square he had "a balcony where I must have geraniums and a goldfinch—for that's the thing to do in Madrid. . . ." The noise outside in the square was terrific, but he was well located for what he wanted, which was to experience the life of the city. His room "hung over the Puerta del Sol, the biggest & noisiest square in the city," he wrote Marvin. "The noises are really fascinating they are so constant and jumbled into long jangling chords, or something of the sort."

It was not long before he began to venture beyond the city. The second Sunday he was there he hiked into the Sierra de Guadarramas with Señor Carlos Posada, a law student whom he had met at the university. The weather was crisp with an occasional snow flurry. The mountains on an early November afternoon had a "golden yellow color," he noted; then later they "took on a remarkable blue black color of velvet softness, behind which was the pale gold plain of Castilla la Vieja." He wrote in his journal that "the whole day of breaking clouds and deep shadows and sudden views and fierce patches of burning blue was marvelously beautiful." The following Sunday he went into the Sierra de Guadarramas with Señor Posada again. "A wonderful sight it is to see all Madrid in alpine costume & knapsack sally forth on the seven o'clock train Sunday mornings," he told Poore. On his trip he, Posada, and his brother-in-law took a morning train for Cercedilla, a mountain village some sixty kilometers from Madrid. At a spot called the "Twenty Club" they had lunch, then at noon under a "burning greenish blue sky" the three of them—Dos Passos in his "beloved palegreen boots," he recalled—hiked the seven kilometers to the Navacerrada Pass and climbed off to the left up a peak, "the first peak of the mountains of the Siete Picos—a long range that waltzes all around you as the train takes its devious course from Madrid through the foothills." They had "a long grind up through pine woods, lovely gnarled pines shaped like appletrees with the younger trunks of a pale brown, creamy color that contrasted wonderfully with the morning, purpling blue sky and the blackgreen needles in tight bunches." From on top of the bare summit they beheld an extraordinary sight: they had a magnificent view of the mountains, of the "warm yellow-reddish" plain of Old Castile and of the "colder tinted" New Castile. They could see La Granja and Segovia to the north; to the south, El Escorial, Madrid, and as far as the mountains of Toledo, which "hung in long stripes above a grey mist." They climbed a second peak, where at the last they had to work their way up a rock chimney. The north side of the peak "was covered with snow frozen & blown into feather shapes by the wind as you scrambled up the snow on the tiers of feathers." At the top they rewarded themselves with oranges, apples, chocolate, and bananas. The whole excursion seemed glorious to Dos Passos, who felt "right up against the blue, with all the world shadowed and misty, streaked with rich siena of broken and black of pinares below us."

Then as they began their descent they saw two boys ascending the south face of the peak. It was hot, so one of them had stripped down to socks, boots, and his drawers. While Dos Passos and the other two men made their way down from the chimney and onto the next peak, the boy was silhouetted, "a marvelous brown figure, against the sky. All of which gave a finishing touch to the beauty of the mountains."

As the three men walked down the north side below the peaks back toward Cercedilla, they were forced to make their way through deep snow, down through a pass
and "into a southward sloping valley full of lovely pines noisy with streams—Beside
a most nymphaic fountain we ate more bread & chocolate and then trundled back
to the train through a beautiful, lucid—Peruginesque—evening. "Whee!" he ended
this account of the trip in his journal when he wrote it up the next day.

All the hiking that Sunday had not tired him to the point that he could not
begin a long letter to Marvin when he returned to the Pension Boston. Dos Passos,
busy and excited by what he was doing, nevertheless took the time to offer suggestions about the poetry Marvin had included; "the best you've done." His advice was
always to choose unpretentious language—"choking" rather than "gasping," "on"
rather than "o'er"—and so forth. He urged Marvin to keep writing and especially
to read Keats and Shelley. There Marvin could learn something about the employment of words. "The thing," Dos Passos went on, "is to write what you see as simply
as possible. No, not exactly, the main thing is to keep the proper average between
the music of the thing, the meter and the words—& don't be afraid of any word
if it seems to fit—sincerely." Don't ever sit down *to write a poem,*" he advised.
Aim rather "to *express a mood,* or a *picture* or anything." Always a writer had to
look out for "worn out words." It is a case of the piano always being out of tune
so that some notes sound dull. "A great poet is a sort of piano tuner—he cleans the
dusty keys, avoids the strings that are worn to a frazzle and plays his tune." Dos
Passos ended his disquisition for that day, exclaiming, "Honestly, I've never been
in such a musical city as Madrid, everything jingles and rings."

Dos Passos was soon pleased when two friends from Harvard, Lowell Downes
and Roland Jackson, turned up in Madrid on a trip they were taking. As usual,
however, his conscience plagued him, and he complained to himself that "the
excitement of finding myself not all alone in the gloaming" seemed to have ended
any reading or writing he was doing. With Downes and Jackson he explored Madrid
and enjoyed its cultural offerings. The evening after his hike in the snowy mountains
he took up his letter to Marvin again but soon quit: "I have so much to tell you that
it brings on a sort of paralysis," he wrote. "Things to be said jostle and tread on each
other's heels—I am sleepy tonight, so I shall put it off till tomorrow when I shall
be, I hope, more intelligent. A Mañana."

But the excitement was too much to let him return to his letter on Tuesday,
November 14. That day he, Downes, and Jackson walked to El Pardo, a small town
eight kilometers north of Madrid. What appealed most to him was their journey on
foot, "a most beautiful morning's walk through a misty river valley with long yellow
slopes dotted with evergreen oaks . . . under a wonderful burning blue sky with the
Guadarrama mountains rising to meet us as we advanced." Lunch was at El Pardo,
"in the village square under yellow autumnal poplar trees, that dropped their leaves
with a little rustling sound through the perfect glowing sun-drugged stillness of the
afternoon." Even their wine added to the richness of the scene: "the Vino de Jerez
cast a wonderful flare of light on the table where the sun shone through it." The
walk back to Madrid provided an afternoon air "full of the tang of leaves being

burned." As they neared Madrid they climbed a hill facing the sunset and saw the city below, sparkling "with its rows of yellow lights in the blue grey dusk and heard a squeaky organ playing and saw people dancing, whirling under a red gas flare, while the organ ground out its jerky little tune. Mon enfant," he exclaimed when he finally finished his letter to Marvin, "it was a day!" The night he returned from El Pardo he made a note in his journal about the vivid colors of the day and "then the dark and music and dancing at an inn among the trees and the pale stars in the sky in which lagged the last sunset tones. 'Beauty thou hast hurt me overmuch,' " he closed his entry.

And so the weeks in Madrid went as he sharpened his writer's—and painter's —eye for details and colors that would become important elements of his literary technique. As he began to feel more at ease in his adopted city, he absorbed Spanish life with pleasure. "I am quite settled in Madrid now, feel as if I'd lived here all my life," he wrote Marvin on November 15. In addition to the three courses in language and literature, he was taking a drawing course "and jabbering at every chance a confused tongue of my own invention which people sometimes understand." He added to this considerable reading and as much theater as he could arrange, the result being that he could "understand spoken Spanish, if not rattled too fast, fairly well."

Little wonder that he was pressed for time, as he complained to Marvin. Amid all he was doing he worried about never completing any one project, particularly his writing. When Marvin wrote that he was trying to record youthful memories, Dos Passos responded that he did it often, and enjoyed "going back and wandering those quaint dark, dimly fragrant rooms." Best of all about one's childhood, he thought, was that "there was so much charm and wonder—and one never had the cold-all alone in the gloaming feeling or the great Boyg—that are my bugbears *today.*" It was a momentary mood when he wrote Marvin of the warmth of his childhood, for it was not an image that often would be repeated. As it happened his pose when he wrote Marvin was of being lonely and lazy, a pose that seems hardly valid. Dos Passos's imposition of a warmth on his childhood at this time revealed a pattern that would distinguish his creative life. He was momentarily nostalgic for childhood because he felt lonely and drifting, the result of overreaching and discovering he could not achieve all that he had set out to. "I have something internal which gnaws like hell when I'm not busy at something," he declared. "So I exhibit a battleground —between the worm of action and the torpor of inertia—It's damned unpleasant. And when the weather's fine I absolutely can do nothing but look at it, and when it rains the same." Self-pity notwithstanding, his next statement was to the point, an accurate self-assessment: "The world's so darned interesting in every conceivable aspect that it's frightfully hard to shut your doors & windows and sit in the dark of your own intelligence & spin in the attic & to gape at the dance on the green and maybe even dance too—but most of all to spin—." At such times his childhood seemed appealing because of its very stasis and may explain in part why the past became for Dos Passos "the best times."

In Spain he gaped at the dance before him and danced a good deal himself.

He became friends with several Madrileños, one of whom was José Giner, whom he described as "a blackbearded little man . . . a nephew of Giner de los Rios the great educator who was the apostle of the Spanish liberals." Giner knew Castile well; he and Dos Passos took numerous walks together out into the countryside to places like El Pardo or on Sundays into the Sierra de Guadarramas. Dos Passos was both amused and bored by a drawing instructor he hired, who set him to work copying a Florentine bust. He met "a budding sociologist who was translating a book by John Dewey" and swapped English lessons for Spanish with him three hours a week. Also he met José Robles, who became not only his closest friend among this group, but would also play a major part in the traumatic break Dos Passos would have from the Communists and his friend Ernest Hemingway in 1937 during the Spanish Civil War.

Robles in 1916 was a student at the university in Madrid when Dos Passos met him on a train returning from Toledo. Robles was eager to learn English, so the two struck up a conversation and were soon friendly. The Spaniard, Dos Passos wrote, "had a sharper tongue than my educationist and liberal acquaintances. He laughed at everything. His talk was more like [the Spanish writer] Pío Baroja's writing." The two traveled together, and Dos Passos found that Robles's "cynical tales were a tonic after the dogoodism of the liberals." Dos Passos later recalled that Robles was at that time of his life an aficionado of bullfights and drew pictures of toreros, pictures scorned by his academic acquaintances.

The dance at the Pension Boston was worth watching. The more he saw, the more he enjoyed it. By the middle of November he had some misgivings about the pension and wrote Arthur McComb to describe the mix of Spaniards and Americans who appeared for meals. An American gentleman got irritated at some of the goings on; three dull Cubans sat at the end of the table and were prone to spitting on the floor. An American vice-consul annoyed him, but not "a delightful Danish gentleman, an architect, who wears the most amazing clothings . . . and a Don José Castillejo," who he told McComb was a man after McComb's "inmost heart." Don José he described as "an old fashioned, eighteenth-century liberal, the leader of part of the Educational Party in Spain, a very brilliant man, and the enemy of all forms of darkness, also a Pacifist of Lowes Dickinson brand, speaks English French & German very well and is thoroughly delightful." What was more, he had "that subtle humanitarian snobbery of all Lovers of Mankind—I mean," Dos Passos added parenthetically, "one has to hate a little to be human."

He told McComb in November that he was writing another essay as a kind of follow-up to the one that had already appeared in the *New Republic* the day he had sailed for Europe. This time he was asserting that Americans, since they were not of a romantic inclination, had no need for art, which was nothing but "the antidote for the disease of romantic discontent." "Every notary," Flaubert asserted, "has in him the ruins of a poet." Within every American, said Dos Passos, are the ruins of a baseball player. The essay, never published, was tongue-in-cheek, since Dos Passos clearly believed in the importance of art. Nevertheless, in what he wrote to McComb there was a hint of a wry appreciation for the American, sports-loving character. To understand Americans, Dos Passos half seriously believed, one needed to recognize that the average citizen was not a failed artist, but a failed athlete. At the same time, Dos Passos seemed to be trying to distance himself from the "romantic discontent" that had been so much a part of him during his years at Harvard.

The cold of December in Madrid made writing difficult. Still, Dos Passos entered into the spirit with which the Spaniards coped with the raw weather. As he huddled in his room, whose walls he had covered with photographs of his favorite Velásquezes and El Grecos, he wrote Marvin that he was at that moment bundled up in a large woolen cloak he had bought. It was the sort the peasant men wore as togas.

"Togas" led to a discussion of Spain and its anachronisms. It was "a sort of temple of anachronisms," he wrote, full of "the strata of civilization—Celt-Iberians, Phoenicians, Greeks, Romans, Moors and French have each in turn passed through Spain and left something there—alive." While the Roman aspects of Italian culture were "a sepulchre, Roman Spain is living—actuality—in the way a peasant wears his manta, in the queer wooden plows they use, in the way they sacrifice to the dead —not consciously of course, but with a thin veil of Catholicism. The pottery you see in the markets is absolutely Greek in shape. The music and the dances are strangely Semitic & Phoenician Moorish—Even the little cakes in the pastry shops are Moorish—oriental—the sort of things odalisques with henna stained fingers eat in the Arabian Nights." The "jumble" that was Spain continued to impress him deeply: "the peaceful Roman world; the sadness of the semitic nations, their mysticism; the grace a little provincialized, a little barbarized, of a Greek colony; the sensuous dream of Moorish Spain; and little yellow French trams and American automobiles and German locomotives—all in a tangle together!"

Perhaps it was this juxtaposition of many pasts within a vital if insular present in Spain that moved him to write poetry. He explained to Marvin about several poetic sketches that they were "part of a running series of things on Spain . . . very wild and irregular," which he had put down as he traveled, then might rework as many as three or four times before he was satisfied. "Green against a livid sky / In their square dun-tinted towers / Hang the bronze bells of Castile," began the first piece. Its ending was evocative:

> Lurks there in your bronze green curves
> In your imperious evocation,
> Stench of burnings; ringing screams,
> Quenched amid the crackling flames!
> The crowd, the pile of faggots in the square,
> The yellow robes . . . Is it that,
> Bells of Castile, that you remember?

A sense of the Spanish landscape, its people, and the jumble of civilization and traditions he had just described to Marvin were what he hoped to capture in these sketches. He next copied down a piece about Aranjuez, "a sort of Spanish Versailles not far from Madrid with a lovely palace of red brick & grey granite and most wonderful gardens. (I mean the outside of the palace—The inside is as usual, a thing of horror)," he described it to Marvin. The town is forty-seven kilometers south of Madrid in the center of the plain of Castile. The palace Dos Passos admired was built in the sixteenth century for Philip II, at the edge of the River Tagus, then enlarged in the eighteenth century by the Bourbon monarchs, who added more gardens to the royal grounds so that the whole is reminiscent of Versailles. Dos Passos was struck by yet another juxtaposition: the contrast between the poor people he described and the now departed pomp and majesty reflected in the Royal Palace and its gardens:

> The Tagus flows with a noise of weirs through Aranjuez.
> The speeding dark-green water mirrors the old red walls,
> And the balustrades and close-barred windows of the palace,
> And on the other bank, three stooping washer women,
> Whose reddish shawls & piles of linen gleam in the green,
> The swift dark green where shimmer the walls of Aranjuez.

> The tang of the smoke, and the scent of the box,
> And the savour of the year's decay
> Are soft in the gardens of Aranjuez,
> Where the fountains fill silently with leaves
> And the moss grows over the statues and busts,
> Clothing the simpering cupids & fawns,
> Whose stone eyes search the empty paths
> For the rustling silk brocaded gowns,
> And the neat silk calves of the halcyon past.

Aranjuez more than any other place for Dos Passos symbolized the disjunction of past and present. He ended the poem by contrasting "the brown silver trunks of the planes and the hedges / Of box, and the spires of cypress and alleys of yellowing elms" that bordered the royal gardens on one edge of the Tagus, with, on the other bank of the river, "three grey mules pulling a cart, / Piled with turnips, driven by a boy in a blue woolen sash, / Who strides along whistling, and does not look toward Aranjuez."

The third piece in an already long letter to Marvin was about the *día de los Difuntos*, All Souls' Day, and was an effort also to capture the mood of a Spanish scene. In a square women sold tuberoses with which people could honor the dead, whose "presence is heavy about us / Like the velvet scent of the flowers." Adding to the atmosphere were the smell of "Incense of pompons interments" and the sounds of the "Patter of monastic feet" and the "Drone of masses drowsily said / For the thronging dead."

Although his time in Spain did not of itself turn him against America or the World War, the moods of Spanish life, its slower pace, its culture and traditions, reinforced by contrast his sense of the vacuity he had denigrated in "Against American Literature" and had playfully mocked in undergraduate stories for the *Monthly* such as "Romantic Education." He was enjoying a life style that had developed over centuries. While he did not admire all aspects of Spanish life, there was a beauty about the country—its art and architecture—and a dignity, even nobility, about its people that Dos Passos admired. The industrialism and pragmatism of the United States, as well as its pace of life and the rawness of its young culture, stood in sharp contrast.

But even Spanish life could not keep his mind off the war for long. Not until he got to the front lines in France the following summer would he realize the full horror of trench warfare; yet in Spain he was aware of the conflict, a distant thunder beyond the mellow atmosphere of Madrid and its environs. In mid-December he complained again to Marvin about his own lack of production. His awareness of the war's magnitude made his own efforts at writing and studying art and architecture seem futile. He recalled the chilling sight of many wounded soldiers in Bordeaux. "There is something frightfully paralyzing to me in the war," he wrote. "Everything I do, everything I write seems so cheap and futile—If Europe is to senselessly destroy itself—It's as if a crevasse had opened and all the fair things, all the mellow, all the things that were to teach us in America how to live, were slipping in—a sort of tidal wave and flood and fire." If his hyperbole was dramatic in the extreme, his sentiments were utterly serious, and these months in Europe played a great part in producing his later attitudes. "Oh those boys in Bordeaux—limping in and out of the hospitals," he exclaimed in his letter to Marvin. "It is the sort of feeling it gave me when I was awfully small and read somewhere of human sacrifices—the senseless grin of the brass idol—the stench and sizzle of the bodies in the flames—the cold, the blackness, the nauseous hideousness of it. I remember how I closed the history book feeling cold and sick all over—Would to God I could close this one. I sort of lose my nerve when I think of it. . . ."

The concern about the war which he expressed in such moments of genuine melancholy added to the sense of futile solitude that bothered him. One night as he was standing on his doorstep waiting to be let in by the night watchman of his pension, a dreary prostitute approached him and said, " 'Oija, estoy muy simpatica Look, I'm awfully congenial!' in the most coaxing tone. Poor woman—to get to the point where she had to be congenial!" he wrote to Marvin, playing on *simpática*, which for the prostitute meant more than congenial. Just as she spoke the watchman arrived to let Dos Passos in. "Afterwards," he added, "I couldn't help thinking how often I, like the Madrid dama, had wanted to go up to people and say 'oija, estoy muy simpatica,' " a remark that reflected his sense of solitude.

His moments of melancholy solitude were deepened by contrast with pleasures such as those he had with his Harvard friends Downes and Jackson. Theirs was diverting, boisterous companionship. One evening in early December the three of them dined at a German café, and after a meal of roast pigeon and a good deal of beer, they went to see the flamenco dancing of Pastora Imperió and had scarcely settled into their seats in the theater when she appeared. A gypsy strummed a guitar, and "with faintest tapping of heels, faintest snapping of the fingers of a brown hand held over her head, erect, wrapped tight in yellow shawl where the embroidered flowers make a splotch of maroon over one breast, a flecking of green and purple over shoulders and thighs, Pastora Imperió [came] across the stage, quietly, unhurriedly." Her movements were sensuous, the rhythm insistent; and the audience was captivated by her presence, "a queen in plumes and brocade." Full of the spirit of flamenco music and the swagger and gestures of Pastora Imperió, the three Americans returned to the café. It was an exhilarating evening. Jackson arose and went off to bed, but Downes and Dos Passos were intent on walking to Toledo, seventy kilometers away. He wrote Marvin later that the two of them "each took a handful of malted milk tablets (God save the mark) and at 3 AM set out from the Puerta de Toledo, crossed the bridge over the Manzanares and were off along the old road to Toledo." They were not alone; along the road were "huge twowheeled carts, each drawn by three or four or sometimes five hulking mules." Their drivers gave the two Americans drinks from their *botas,* leather wine bottles. In his journal Dos Passos described the predawn setting:

> A most wonderful night with dim stars and the long sweeping hillsides of Castile brownish under the cold moon. Cocks crew and dogs barked in the distance and you seemed to hear the rustling of the stars' skirts as they did their ceremonial dance about the heavens. In the lower places there was a mist and everything was blurred brown-silver. At last the moon set like a wrinkled and rotten orange just as the first steely glow started in the east.

It was a merry journey of the absurd by a self-styled Don Quixote and Sancho Panza. Later Dos Passos asked Marvin, "Do you know the wonderful feel of old old roads which have been worn to a sort of velvet softness by the feet of generations and generations and generations?" Such was the feel of the road they were on, and Dos Passos imagined that the dead as well as the living—"the Romans and the Carthaginians and the Moors and the mitred bishops going toward Toledo, and the mule drivers with skins of wine from the south"—were trooping about Downes and him as they walked and at dawn passed through a small village "with a big buttressed church and a tall leaning church tower and everything pearl-blue and purple and lemon yellow."

At Torrejón, about half the distance to Toledo, early the next morning they halted to rest in the train station. Downes's feet were aching, and only now in the sober light of day did Dos Passos remember that he was due at the American Embassy for dinner, so they boarded a train for Madrid after their memorable walk.

Christmas Eve he celebrated by marching in the streets with the Madrileños. At 3:00 A.M. he finally retired to his room in the Pension Boston, although there was still a great racket in the street below. He had "spent the night marching about with a great big tambourine—the which I have beaten and shaken and banged against my knees and elbows until I'm stiff." "Nóche bú-ená / Nóche d'Alegrí-á" went a tune he could remember. How wonderful it was, he raved to Marvin, "to skip down the street beating a drum when everyone else is beating and singing and dancing—it has the emotional pull that I imagine Indian wardances have." Christmas Day he was invited to join a family whom he had met in Madrid, the Sweeneys, for their Christmas party, where, he noted in his journal, they played blindman's bluff.

Soon after Christmas he headed off on a two-week trip to the south and east of Spain. He traveled as far south as Cartagena, then worked his way up the Mediterranean coast to Tarragona, before turning back to Madrid. Just before the New Year he wrote Marvin from the market town of Alcázar de San Juan, in the region of La Mancha, almost due south of Madrid, that he had gratified one of the ambitions of his life: "I possess a cloak—a real bona fide cloak"; and he drew a sketch of himself in a broad-brimmed hat and flowing cloak, with a "Knapsack a l'allemande" at his feet. La Mancha is the land of Don Quixote, he reminded Marvin, who, if he had not read Cervantes's work, should "abandon all else, get chucked from school even—but *read it.*"

He was about to board the *rápido* for Cartagena as he wrote. "Rapido only in contradistinction to the trenes mixtos that go so slowly you sometimes forget the direction you are proceeding," he added. Then he described his trip thus far. He had arrived in Alcázar de San Juan that morning and had immediately been overwhelmed by La Mancha, which was "wonderful . . .—a high tableland, bounded by great eroded mountains, scarred with grey arroyos—the earth is red, varying from Venetian brown to an unbelievable carmine." That afternoon he had walked out from the town to a windmill high up a hill where a magnificent scene spread before him: against the vivid blue sky stood the red plain and the gray mountains on the horizon which were marked by white quartz cliffs. Below him lay a lake of a deep blue color, on the edge of which perched a small village, whose buildings were bright white. To add to his pleasure, he was reading "a volume of old Spanish romances of the Cid," far better, he was reminded, than Corneille's play *Le Cid,* which lost its saltiness, "turned into the silken-breeched French of Louis XIV drawing rooms!" He drew Marvin another sketch, this one of the countryside that enthralled him. "Oh it's so wonderful and strange," he concluded, "the very place for the mad ardors, and pathetic beauty of the Knight of the Doleful Countenance—the red and the blue & the grey—and the windmills perched like rabbits on all the hills and the gnarled olive trees climbing up the slopes—." He was just beginning *Don Quixote* again, he said, this time in Spanish, "for about the 'n'th time," and it was "more joyful than ever."

Five days later and in the New Year he was in Alicante, an ancient port city a little more than one hundred kilometers up the Mediterranean coast from Cartagena. The city, he wrote Arthur McComb, was "a high cream colored mountain with a castle—two churches with dark blue domes, pale blue sky, dark blue sea— that is Alicante—more or less messed up by an Avenue of dusty date palms of which the inhabitants are inordinately proud, a busy harbor with nice lateen-sailed fishing smacks, and a weird-looking row of dingy hotels." He warned that he was "in a black mood" about the war that evening, and after describing Alicante he responded to McComb's most recent letter about peace. "My God man, let us have it," Dos Passos exclaimed, "but how?"

Then he returned to what he had elsewhere written to Marvin about the war. Constantly "the misery, the grinding horror of it" he felt ground into him "until it seems almost blasphemy to propound . . . glib pacifist schemes." He yearned for "a sane point of view" to be presented so that he could judge the situation. He loved "Spain and things Spanish," he declared to McComb. "But I can't get the grotesque sight of the one-legged men in Bordeaux out of my head and the hospitals—everywhere hospitals."

Behind all this lay what preyed on his mind: "the grotesque, sublime silliness of officialdom—the censorships, the patriotic porridge so assiduously stirred, the mummery, and all the while with machine-like promptness, with absurd alacrity, the war seizes on the populations, one after another." The result was that quickly all those things, such as the culture he had found in Europe, which "have made worthwhile the cruel welter of life" had been drowned out by the fanfare of war, "and presto—there they are—blackened, scarred, hating: a stench of dead bodies and stupid rows of little wooden crosses, and widows in black—resigned—and everybody resigned." People's resignation was the worst thing of all, he added, and concluded, "I'm getting to the bomb-throwing stage."

Dos Passos walked much of the distance along the Costa Blancha to Denia, just north of the tip of Cape Nao. As he was about to leave Denia, a fishing town with an ancient fort that overlooks its harbor, he wrote Marvin that he planned to walk part of the thirty kilometers to Gandía and travel the rest by train. He reversed his order, first boarding a train and enjoying the third-class carriage which had "a little imperial like on the Paris trains." He was quickly covered with soot, but the view was worth it, because from the top he could see a Renaissance church and a castle as he approached Oliva, where he paused for lunch. The *fonda* where he stopped he claimed was in a dither because of his arrival. "A sizzle of a smell of olive-oil betokens almuerzo—lunch—It is announced Viva!"; and he set to eating what he later recounted to Marvin:

1. A deep chrome-colored soup
2. A stew like a New England boiled dinner, only eatable.
3. Strange tough & garlicky sausages—cold
4. Little fried cakes of potato & liver
5. Nuts & tangerines

He would have liked to linger in picturesque Oliva, with its castle, the ruins of ancient walls, and "the usual Baroque churches with blue tiled domes," but he chose instead to head off for Gandía, walking the coastal route that winds on top of cliffs overlooking white beaches reached by descending through orange groves. He had hiked half the distance when three peasants in a covered, two-wheeled cart

—he called it a tartan—picked him up. They drove him right to his fonda after stopping at "a road side venta, or 'pub,' " to drink a strong brandy with him. They spoke Valencian, and he replied in his still rudimentary Spanish. They "misunderstood each other beautifully with the greatest good nature." Gandía was "an old town of beetlebrowed white washed houses—with wide lower halls where you can see all the family seated about and a tiled floor and little utensils—all like a Dutch interior—there's a palace of the Borjas here—the *Borjas*, who were dukes of Gandía, it seems, before they found fame and fortune and Papal diadems in Rome." That Dos Passos's enthusiastic recounting of the town's history was slightly erroneous distracts not at all from the excitement about Spain his letter conveyed.

The next morning he boarded a train for Carcagente. The train headed inland "through orange groves so thick that the little train brushed against them as it chugged through and knocked off great fat golden oranges that fell with a plunk onto the red exuberant earth." From among the groves the train struggled up through the dry hills behind the coast, then plunged down into more groves as it neared Carcagente, where Dos Passos spent a few hours wandering about the town. The smell of ripe olives and the "rich—cream-colored" houses, particularly several with Italian-like loggias along the top floor, attracted him. Then he took the train the nineteen kilometers southward to Játiva, where he stayed the night before heading north toward Valencia, Sagunto, and eventually Tarragona.

He was fascinated by his fonda in Játiva—"a regular Don Quixote-Gil Blas fonda," he called it—which was in a "palace-place," perhaps what were the remains of a castle located on the site of the original town. His large room looked out over a patio "where a fountain splashes gaily and will lull me to sleep & to dream of the Alhambra & Moorish princesses & Provence roses." But then he laughed and thought of a more pedestrian dream "of the bathroom at home when somebody left on the tap and it overflowed, i.e. the tub," which reminded him of a time when he was "young & charming (like Buttercup)" in London, and he and a friend "played the taking of Port Arthur with my battleships in the bathtub above a luncheon Mother was giving & in our terrific excitement didn't notice that the floor was awash —the guests below in the dining room did; & part of the ceiling fell—c'était un jour pénible," he concluded.

By January 11, 1917, he was all the way north to Tarragona, having visited historic Valencia where, he later wrote McComb, he withdrew in dismay from what he had just thought was a hotel but turned out to be a whorehouse. From Valencia he traveled to Sagunto and then to the agricultural town of Tortosa, inland on the Río Ebro. As he rested in the Gran Café de Tarragona after roaming through some of the city's streets and gateways, he sat down late in the evening to write Dudley Poore about his travels, while in the background someone was "executing"—he underlined the verb—what he supposed was "Chopin con mucho brio on the piano." He told Poore of his trip; of wandering about in his favorite cloak; of walking and entraining by first, second, and third class; of dining in posadas and Cafés de Paris. Tarragona, dating back to a thousand years before Christ—all of the land, in fact—made him exclaim, "But Dudloysha, I am mad about Spain—the wonderful mellowness of life, the dignity, the layered ages." And he wrote about seeing on the train-station platform that morning "two wonderful old men, crouching in the sun wrapped in red and green blankets, with strange infinitely eager faces and bright eyes like the eyes of mice." He was sure they had been at Troy, "the old men who sat 'chirping like cicadas' above the gate and warmed themselves in the sun and looked at Helen as she walked below them." He paused, then added, "the only trouble is —one does want ones friends about & other bits of household furniture—."

A few days later he was back in Madrid, where he settled into the Residencia de Estudiantes, planning to resume his art and architecture classes. He had vague plans for later in the spring: perhaps he would try to join the Norton-Harjes Ambulance Service or find something else that would keep him in Europe and enable him to see the war. But any plans were destroyed shortly thereafter. Dos Passos was shattered to receive a cable informing him that John R. had died January 27, 1917, in New York.

Lucy Addison Sprigg Madison
(Mrs. Elizabeth Dos Passos).

John Dos Passos as a child in England
(University of Virginia Library).

Cartoon of John R. Dos Passos, artist unknown
(Mrs. Elizabeth Dos Passos).

Dos Passos with his parents at Niagara Falls,
circa 1908 (*Mrs. Elizabeth Dos Passos*).

Dos Passos at Annisquam,
Massachusetts, Summer 19
(*Mrs. Lois Hazell*).

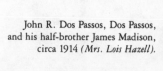

John R. Dos Passos, Dos Passos,
and his half-brother James Madison,
circa 1914 (*Mrs. Lois Hazell*).

Stewart Mitchell, June 1916
(University of Virginia Library).

Dudley Poore, shortly before
sailing for France
in June 1917 *(Dudley Poore)*.

Ceremony formally attaching three American Red Cross Ambulance sections to
the Italian Army, Milan, December 12, 1917. Sydney Fairbanks *(with goatee, third
from left)*, Dos Passos *(fourth from left) (Sydney Fairbanks)*.

Passos in the Ambulance Corps,
1917–1918 (Dudley Poore).

Dos Passos (seated) and Rumsey Marvin in the Auvergne,
Summer 1920 (Mrs. Elizabeth Dos Passos).

Dos Passos (left) at Le Plessis, Easter 1923, at
the home of Germaine Lucas-Championnière (third from left) (Pierre Lostanlen).

Scene from the 1925 Harvard Dramatic Club production of *The Moon Is a Gong*
(later called *The Garbage Man*) *(Billy Rose Theater Collection of the
New York Public Library, Astor, Lenox and Tilden Foundation).*

Dust jacket for the 1926 publication of
The Garbage Man, with a painting by Dos Passos
(Mrs. Elizabeth Dos Passos).

Dos Passos design, probably for a poster,
for John Howard Lawson's play *Processional* (1925)
(Mrs. Elizabeth Dos Passos).

nd Wilson (*Mrs. Elena Wilson*).

John Howard Lawson (*Billy Rose Theater Collection of the New York Public Library, Astor, Lenox and Tilden Foundation*).

assos with Patrick Murphy on *la plage*
aroupe, Antibes, Summer 1925
Philip Barry).

Robert Hillyer (*the Bettmann Archive, Inc.*).

Dos Passos being arrested in front of the Massachusetts State House during
a protest against the Sacco-Vanzetti death sentence in 1927.
(United Press International).

Katy Smith, probably
in the late 1920s
(Mrs. William B. Smith).

Katy, her brother Bill,
and Dos Passos lunching at
home in Provincetown, 1932
(United Press International).

Dos Passos, Theodore Dreiser, and Samuel Ornitz as part of the Dreiser Committee investigating conditions in Harlan County, Kentucky in 1931 *(Associated Press/Wide World)*.

A shot of Hemingway in Spain
taken by Joris Ivens, probably
while shooting *The Spanish Earth*
(the Bettmann Archive, Inc.).

Katy Dos Passos aboard
the Murphy's schooner *Weatherbird*
in Antibes, circa 1932
(Mrs. Honoria Donnelly).

Loyalists remove the wounded from
the University City in Madrid during
heavy fighting in October 1937 *(Wide World).*

Loyalists pushing north in May 1937,
after defeating Franco's troops at Guadalajara *(Wide World).*

(Mrs. Elizabeth Dos Passos)

(Mrs. Elizabeth Dos Passos)

(Mrs. Elizabeth Dos Passos)

(The Bettmann Archive, Inc.)

s. Elizabeth Dos Passos)

John Dos Passos

Dos Passos in his Provincetown living room in the early 1940s *(Wide World)*.

Dos Passos broadcasting in London on BBC with Mrs. Mary Adams in 1941 *(Wide World)*.

Dos Passos as a war correspondent in the Pacific, Spring 1945 *(University of Virginia Library)*.

William Faulkner *(left)*, Malcolm Cowley, and Dos Passos as Dos Passos receives the Gold Medal for Fiction from the American Academy of Arts and Letters in 1957 *(Wide World)*.

Katy and Edith Shay at the time of publication of their jointly written novel, *The Private Adventures of Captain Shaw* (1945) *(University of Virginia Library)*.

Dos Passos with Elizabeth and Lucy at Spence's Point, circa 1957 *(Mrs. Elizabeth Dos Passos)*.

Dos Passos and Lucy on the beach at Spence's Point, August 1964
(Mrs. Elizabeth Dos Passos).

Easter 1966 at Spence's Point. Dos Passos with *(left to right)*
Christopher Holdridge, Lucy, Rumsey Marvin, and Elizabeth *(Rumsey Marvin).*

PART III

The Great War
and After,
1917–1920

CHAPTER EIGHT

===

Home to America,
Spring 1917

Dos Passos had little reason to expect his father's sudden death. During the fall after his son's departure, John R. had frequently written long letters, discussing his own affairs, American politics, life at Sandy Point, or occasional matters of Dos Passos's which John R. had to handle. In retrospect, Dos Passos would find a touch of melancholy in some letters; his father wrote of going to Washington and finding 1201 Nineteenth Street, N.W., "vide et triste." Early in November he wrote from Sandy Point—in French as usual—that he was thinking how far Dos Passos was from the farm, and he felt sad. "You are not only a son to me," he said, "but you are a companion and confidant in whom I have complete confidence. But this feeling of sadness is only temporary, because I would not have you anywhere except in Madrid where I know you will find a great deal for your future. . . ." He joked with his son, suggesting another time that they publish " 'Letters from Madrid' by Monsieur Singe. Deluxe edition, price five dollars. Handsome that. Another book 'Reflections of a Young Man in Madrid' by the same author. Another book: 'An Architect's Impressions of the Buildings of Madrid by a student.' " In Virginia in November, he had reported that he shot quail and that he was in good health, although his letters during the holiday season were those of a lonely man. But his loneliness was not born of self-pity but of a genuine yearning to see his son. Just before Christmas he wrote, "I am your Amanuensis, Secretary and alter ego, for I write all the replies to your letters and take care to see that you are within the rules. In other words we have an association. John R. Dos Passos and Father." On Christmas Day he had turkey by himself because his son Louis was sick; nevertheless, he kept as busy as ever. On January 6 John R. wrote that though the *New Republic* had rejected Dos Passos's essay "Art and Baseball," one Dos Passos had described

to McComb earlier, he should keep writing, and John R. proceeded to tell his son
of the praise and discussion aroused by "Against American Literature."

Early January brought on a sign of gout, but a doctor declared him in satisfactory health. On the fourteenth he wrote Dos Passos in mock seriousness, saluting
him on achieving freedom from his father's "enslavement." By the nineteenth he
was less well, and in what was perhaps his last letter to his son he complained of
not having been able to work all week. He found it difficult to concentrate, despite
having work to do. The next week he would try a little work, he assured Dos Passos.
He went on to tell of British and German ships on the seas, and closed, "Bon pour
ton soir et bonnes reves, Affectuesement, Dedi." Dos Passos learned that soon
thereafter John R. caught pneumonia. The end came quickly: he collapsed in his
home in New York and according to Dos Passos "was found unconscious one
morning on the bathroom floor." Death followed immediately.

Although Dos Passos did not take John R.'s death lightly, in Madrid he was
in a quandary. Should he return to the United States, or as he preferred, remain
abroad? His plans, he wrote Marvin, were "to say the least vague." He thought he
might stay in Spain for a few months more, although he supposed "the conventional
thing to do'ld be to go home." Why? His father was buried; there was no one to
console, and he dreaded the condolences of others and "all the sentimental flutter
that clutters up the great stark events of life."

He told Marvin that "It gives you a queer catching of the breath to find yourself
suddenly alone in the world." While he could be thankful that his father had died
quickly, "without the long sordidness of disease," he suddenly realized that "one
feels as if all one's protection against the knocks and pains of life had been pulled
away—for one hasn't much except the love of others to retire into—It's like a man
who has been walking hours and hours through a blizzard trying to reach a tiny light
that promises warmth and food and rest from the straining exertion—and suddenly
the light has gone."

Even so, in an exchange of letters with his relatives and the people in his
father's office, Dos Passos became convinced that he ought to return to America to
help settle John R.'s estate. Thus, dreading the settlement process and in no mood
to deal with maudlin sentiment, he was in Bordeaux by February 10 arranging for
immediate passage to New York. Slightly less than four months after he had come
to Europe, he was leaving. But it was a crucial four months, because in that time
he had learned a great deal not only about Spain but about himself. His discovery
of Spain had come years before that of others of his generation, and—more important—his was a unique acquaintanceship: he had lived in the country alone, had
shared with Spaniards their daily living, and had not then been immersed in the
romantic mystique about Spain that developed among postwar writers. Dos Passos
would sense his different understanding of Spain, although discretion would ensure
his silence, and his knowledge of the country would account in small part for his
break with Ernest Hemingway in 1937 after they had both traveled to Spain to
observe the Civil War and had left with very different impressions of the situation.

Few ships were sailing from Bordeaux out the Gironde because of the threat of German submarines, so he had to wait until February 18 before boarding the *Touraine*, which remained in the Gironde for two more days before venturing into the Atlantic. She was the first ship to sail for weeks, and the excitement of anticipation during this crossing was electric. At the mouth of the river the ship hove to with all lights out. The next night passengers were not allowed to bed, but were commanded to sit up with their "clothes and life preservers on all ready to take to the boats." The *Touraine* would be sailing in convoy, however, and since a small gale was blowing, Dos Passos imagined that the threat of submarines along the coast would be minimal to the "old slow and rather uncomfortable" *Touraine*. He wrote Marvin that there were a lot of ships crowding the mouth of the Gironde, "waiting . . . to get up to their courage to go out," he supposed. And he was surprised to find his old steamer full of passengers in every class—first, second, and steerage.

Another night on alert followed before the ship was out of danger. In a letter he turned to advising Marvin about college, as he would be going somewhere as a freshman the next fall. Williams College was "the home and original abiding place of the Y.M.C.A. young man," he thought. Chicago had a good reputation, as did Columbia. What was more, neither one had "college" life, an advantage as far as Dos Passos was concerned. Then the University of California and "that other California college"—he could not think of its name—were reputed to be good. Harvard and Yale he considered about equal, although the snobbery at Harvard did not bother him as much as that at Yale, "the sort of thing those sacred 'frats' breed." In closing, he admitted to being a cynic about American colleges.

The voyage took thirteen days. As the *Touraine* passed Fire Island Light his anticipation grew. He had heard a rumor of Germany's suggestion to Mexico of a secret treaty in which Mexico would be deeded "the three southern provinces of the United States," a message which turned out to be the Germans' "Zimmermann Telegram," proposing that Mexico ally itself with Germany if war broke out between Germany and the United States. This was intercepted by the United States. In return, Mexico would receive financial support and would reacquire her former territories in Texas, New Mexico, and Arizona. The idea sounded ridiculous, Dos Passos thought, but this would surely add to the excitement of the war.

When the *Touraine* docked, his father's secretary of many years, Joe Schmidt, met him, and he went first to 18 East Fifty-sixth Street. Then he settled in with his Aunt Mamie—Mrs. James Riely Gordon—at 214 Riverside Drive, while he, as he put it in March, "watched the rapid evaporation of The Estate." At his father's house he found some mail for him; among the letters was a kind note from George St. John of Choate, offering condolences for John R.'s death. "It is less than a month ago that I had a letter from his full of fire and enthusiasm in his pride in your work and the constant happiness that your companionship has brought to him," St. John wrote. But aside from a few letters such as this, there was not much of the veils and tears that Dos Passos claimed he dreaded. There was, however, the tedium and paperwork of settling his father's estate, even though he was not an executor, since Louis, John R.'s nephew Cyril, and Joe Schmidt had been assigned that task.

Despite John R.'s income while he was alive, his estate, surprisingly, was not large. A year before his death he had deeded to Dos Passos "all of the jewelry and precious stones" contained in a strongbox he held and had deeded as well the contents of the Washington house, which had become Dos Passos's after Lucy's death. Six months before John R. died he wrote a will, in which he left small sums of money to various relatives—$2,000 for his niece Annie Kelley, $2,000 for his brother Joseph M. Dos Passos—and to Mrs. Harris, $2,500, and the maid Mary E. Hillis, $500. To his nephew, Cyril F. Dos Passos, he gave "the good will name and business of Dos Passos Brothers—Also my Law Library," while to Dos Passos he left his gold watch, black pearl scarf pin, wearing apparel, and all of his miscellaneous library. Louis was to receive the contents of 18 East Fifty-sixth Street and any jewelry not going to Dos Passos. The rest of John R.'s real estate was to be divided up between Louis and John.

Any income for Dos Passos would be derived from the sale of the Washington house and from the sale or farming of the land in Virginia. In May he went to Washington to dispose of the house there. He told Dudley Poore on May 8 that he had "just sold part of my poor disputed inheritance—Uncles shake their heads and see the beginning of the process of 'running through.' " Because Dos Passos was not interested in finances, during the spring of 1917 he put in trust with his Aunt Mamie his interest in the Virginia land.*

As spring approached he bemoaned the grisliness of how a man after his death became "nothing more than a collection of stocks and bonds and debts and real estate." He wrote Marvin that while waiting for the settlement of the estate he was wasting time that could better be used to write. He hoped soon to find a place for himself where he could put his belongings "and retire into monastic seclusion in order to try and finish that famous novel-thing"—a reference to *Streets of Night.* Although he wondered about how long he could stand New York, it was the right place to find publishers for his writing. Also, he had to deal further with Laurence Gomme about the publication of *Eight Harvard Poets,* a matter which dragged on while Gomme and the eight contributors worked out their last financial arrangements. Correspondence between Dos Passos, Gomme, and the others continued through the spring; Dos Passos even met with Gomme in New York, but it was not until August 1917 that the anthology finally appeared.

On April 7 the United States declared war on the Central Powers. Dos Passos, now more eager than ever to see the conflict for himself, was cursing "barren business details." People, he complained somewhat dramatically, frittered away their lives in trivialities instead of discovering the forces of life—"the great untrivial"— which encompassed them. In fact he had been able to write; the estate matters had not taken all his time, and he had found an apartment for himself, a place he named "the Labyrinth," on the top floor of an apartment building at 15 East Thirty-third Street. After moving into his new place, he occupied himself with efforts to find a

*It might seem that Dos Passos could have been independently wealthy. But because John R. spent almost all of what he earned and because the Gordons turned over to Dos Passos only a small portion of the proceeds from the land, he had little income beyond what he earned from his writing until late in his life.

way of returning to Europe in some military capacity. He hoped that there would be a spot for him either in the mosquito fleet, the ambulance corps, or in some sort of interpreter's position. He asked Marvin not to think him a militarist. Rather, he wanted "to see a little of the war personally—and, then too," he added with a touch of naïve righteousness, "I rather believe that the deeper we Americans go into it, the harder we put our shoulders to the muskets and our breasts to the bayonets, the sooner the butchery will stop."

He could not occupy the Labyrinth until the end of April, when he moved in with a close friend of his from Harvard, Wright McCormick, who was then working for the *New York Times*. The apartment was, he wrote Marvin, a "weird place— the furniture for which has not yet arrived; so we sit on the floor on cushions & stretch out on Turkish rugs."

If Dos Passos sought to live in a "literary" section of New York, he chose well. East Thirty-third Street is at the upper edge of the Gramercy Park section of Manhattan. Farther down in the park had lived literary figures like Washington Irving, Herman Melville, O. Henry, and William Dean Howells. In 1917, while not the heart of artistic New York, it was just north of the areas that were: Greenwich Village and the Lower East Side. Dos Passos was well aware of the intellectual ferment that centered in these two sections, and he was determined to be part of it. Taking the apartment on Thirty-third Street began his edging toward a new and fascinating, somewhat bohemian world of the arts. In 1917 he was an outsider; little more than three years later, he would return from Europe and plunge into Greenwich Village life, by then more confident of himself.

The spirit of Greenwich Village life was infectious, just the sort of thing the inhibited Dos Passos needed. Jack Reed, whose work Dos Passos admired, caught the mood of the Village in a lighthearted poem he wrote in 1913 about Washington Square, the hub of the Village.

> *I would embalm in deathless rhyme*
> *The great souls of our little time:*
> *Inglorious Miltons by the score,—*
> *Mute Wagners,—Rembrandts, ten or more,—*
> *And Rodins, one to every floor.*
> *In short, those unknown men of genius*
> *Who dwell in third-floor-rears gangreneous*
> *Reft of their rightful Heritage*
> *By a commercial, soulless age.*
> *Unwept, I might add,—and unsung,*
> *Insolvent, but entirely young.*
>
> *Twixt Broadway and Sixth Avenue,*
> *And West perhaps a block or two,—*
> *From Third Street up, and Ninth Street down,*
> *Between Fifth Avenue and the Town,—*

Policem[e]n walk as free as air,
With nothing on their minds but hair,
And life is very, very fair,
In Washington Square.

Yet we are free who live in Washington Square,
We dare to think as Uptown wouldn't dare,
Blazing our nights with arguments uproarious;
What care we for a dull old world censorious
When each is sure he'll fashion something glorious?
Blessed art thou, Anarchic Liberty
Who asketh nought but joy of such as we!

The Village had such gathering spots as the Liberal Club above Polly's Restaurant at 137 MacDougal Street. There a person could observe Theodore Dreiser, Upton Sinclair, Vachel Lindsay, Sinclair Lewis, Sherwood Anderson, and Max Eastman; or artists such as Stuart Davis, Marsden Hartley, Boardman Robinson, Art Young, and John Sloan. And the Village was the place where the *Masses* was published, a flamboyant, radical journal that appeared monthly, attacking capitalism and the status quo. It was broadly socialistic, not doctrinaire, while its art, editorials, and essays represented what was most zestful about the Village. The *Masses* was, in fact, a spokesman for the Village's citizenry, coincidentally presenting the work of some of America's best younger artists and writers. It had begun publication in 1912 with Max Eastman as editor, calling itself "A Revolutionary and not a Reform Magazine, a Magazine with a Sense of Humor and no Respect for the Respectable; Frank; Arrogant; Impertinent; Searching for the True Causes . . . A Free Magazine." By the time Dos Passos returned to New York in 1917, the *Masses* was both well known and feared in some quarters. Soon thereafter, because of its editors' opposition to the war—they regularly ran a peace petition—it would be barred from the mails. The resulting loss of subscriptions was a blow, and when in November 1917 Eastman, Reed, the managing editor Floyd Dell, and others were charged by the government with subverting the country's war effort, the *Masses* died.

For Dos Passos in 1917, the magazine had the effect of a magnet. Its artwork caught the spirit of the new that he sought; its ideas were fast becoming his; and its contributors were the people whom he increasingly admired as he learned about their work. The February 1917 issue, for example, had art by Maurice Becker, Boardman Robinson, and George Bellows, among others, and included as always the lively political cartooning of Art Young. A cartoon by Cornelia Barns in the March issue caught the spirit of the magazine. A plutocrat and his wife are being wheeled along a boardwalk, and the caption reads:

"So the men want another raise!"

"Yes, the robbers would take the bread from our mouths." The April issue included a piece by Jack Reed entitled "Whose War?" It ended, as his essays about the war often did, "It is not our war." In that same issue Dos Passos's close friend Robert Hillyer had a poem, "To Congress Concerning the Bill for Universal Military Service," which began:

Ignorant tyrants, reckless and uncouth,
Mad with the fury that foretells your end,
Soldiers and lawmakers and fools, attend
For once the unfamiliar voice of truth.

In the next issue Boardman Robinson entitled a cartoon "Patrons of War" which had an array of caricatures seated or standing behind a table. They were captioned "Fear," "Sentimentalism," "Conservative Press," "Ignorance," "Imperialism," "Endowed Religion," "Americanism," and "Big Business." And in that same issue appeared a piece called "The Real War," by Lieutenant X of the French Army. It was purportedly an article, censored in France, which had been smuggled out by an American. It described what it called an "ignoble war" and told of the conditions for the *poilu,* the French soldier in the trenches who was a "martyr."

The sentiments expressed in the *Masses* played on Dos Passos's mind. He was pleased to find others who thought about the war as he did, and during the spring of 1917 he began seriously to become the critic of government and society who emerged full blown in the late twenties. In a few months his experiences in the war would catalyze the ideas which life in and around Greenwich Village had instilled in him. In April he assailed Marvin for claiming that Americans were independent. "There is nowhere on earth," he declared, "where convention is more hide bound, where the intellectual straight jacket is tighter, where people have less tolerance for the views and actions of others. What we need is to learn to think independently and not to be herded like a lot of sheep with newspapers for watchdogs."

He was near eruption against conventional America as he stewed about what he might do to see the war and as he got deeper and deeper into the Village-*Masses* spirit. Pressing in on his mind was his fear that the war meant the demise of the civilizations that had developed over long centuries in Europe. Now the United States, with hardly a culture of its own when compared to the European nations, would be dragged down too. Then there was the perplexing matter of what form of government to espouse, and what economic philosophy. People were lethargic; how could a person combat that? And what of the masses? It was his romantic instinct to admire them in the abstract. Was that valid, and was he fair to denigrate intellectuals as was his wont? And how could one justify the deaths resulting from the war? Perhaps Germany was guilty and did deserve to be destroyed, but was she the cause of the disease, or just a symptom? The thought of the slaughter revolted him, yet—and this perplexed him—he was desperate to see the action. Early in May he wrote George St. John to thank him for his thoughtful letter about John R.'s death. Some of what preyed on his mind he expressed in a restrained way to St. John:

And we too have entered the dance of death. It was inevitable—I suppose it would have been better had we done so earlier—but I can't quite reconcile myself to the thought yet. The whole condition is so hopeless. It seems as if all our energy—all this complicated civilization the European races have labored and murdered and created for during so many evolving centuries were frittering itself away in this senseless agony of destruction. Germany seems to me rather a symptom than the cause. . . .

Oh, but it is wonderful to live amid the downfall—and perhaps it is the birthpangs too—

He told St. John that in several weeks he expected to sail for France to drive ambulances for the Norton-Harjes unit or work at some other task for the Red Cross. He added, "I have been for a long while very anxious to see things first hand," because, although he did not say so to St. John, he realized that the war was the big event of that time, and if he wanted to be a writer, he should know what it was about.

While in New York he had begun an essay about Spain. In the late spring he submitted it to *Seven Arts*, another of the lively little magazines that emanated from Greenwich Village. In June, two weeks before he sailed for France, Dos Passos received a check for "Young Spain" from Waldo Frank, who along with Van Wyck Brooks was an associate editor of *Seven Arts*. Dos Passos must have been pleased with himself, for he was in excellent literary company. When the essay appeared in August, it was among contributions by the poets Richard Aldington, Babette Deutsch, Vachel Lindsay, and Amy Lowell, and other artists and writers such as Marsden Hartley, H. L. Mencken (defending Dreiser), John Reed, John Butler Yeats, and Randolph Bourne, whose essays against the war were controversial and played no small part in the magazine's demise.

Dos Passos should have been pleased also because the essay was his most mature expression to date, evincing his thorough knowledge of Spain's culture and topography and his empathy for the fiery individualism that characterized her people and that—at this critical time in America's and his own development—was becoming rooted in him. As he considered the languages, art, literature, and politics of the country, he realized "that there are many Spains," a sign as well as a cause of the people's individualistic spirit. "Here lies the strength and the weakness of Spain," he wrote about that spirit. "This intense individualism, born of a history whose fundamentals lie in isolated village communities—pueblos, as the Spaniards call them—over the changeless face of which, like grass over a field, events spring and mature and die, is the basic fact of Spanish life. No revolution has been strong enough to shake it." He was talking about Spain, but he was defining a quality, individualism, that he meant to make basic to his own life. The ideas in "Young Spain" melded with those he was absorbing through magazines like the *Masses* and *Seven Arts* and through life in and around Greenwich Village. To the young man who on the surface appeared conventional enough, the ideal of individualism, of nonconformity, appealed as a way of rebelling. More than he understood, it appealed also because his father had been an individualist, and as Dos Passos grew more self-confident, he came to respect what his father had been more and more.

Sure by late May that he would be in the ambulance service, he trained to drive ambulances at an automobile school on Twelfth Avenue, and learned something of the medical techniques he would need to know, while in his free time he moved on the fringes of radicalism. He wrote Marvin on June 5 that "my only amusement has been going to anarchist and pacifist meetings and riots—Emma Goldman etc. Lots of fun I assure you. I am thinking of becoming a revolutionist!" He and a friend were excited by "a strange little restaurant" on the Lower East Side. The attraction for that section was of a piece with his growing radicalism and its concomitant admiration for "the common man." In the East Side restaurant were "Arabs and Spanish Jews and a weird Arab orchestra and women in ordinary streetwalkers' clothes who dance the most amazing half-Spanish, half-Egyptian dances, while Spanish Jews, Lascars and Turks sit about smoking hookahs and drinking bad beer —It's really too good to be true and reminds one more than anything of bits of the Port Said part of 'The Light that Failed.' " He had decided, he said, "that the only nice and human parts of New York are the East Side and Greenwich Village." He now stood firmly against the Establishment. "Don't believe the *New York Times,* " he implored Marvin, assuring him that he knew whereof he spoke because of Wright McCormick's experience with it. "Believe rather the Call or Masses or the New Republic or the Ladies Home Journal," he instructed and expressed his disdain for the *Times,* which educated, intelligent Americans mistakenly took as "Direct Revelation."

He was a bit giddy during these last weeks before leaving, and excitedly he supposed that after the war he would be "so red, radical and revolutionary" that Marvin would disown him. He had mentioned before the well-known anarchist, Emma Goldman. In this letter he asked if he had told Marvin about sitting next to her table "in the café at the Brevoort sometime ago." The Brevoort, which stood at the corner of Fifth Avenue and Eighth Street, was a landmark in the Village. Its basement café was a favorite of Lincoln Steffens, Eugene O'Neill, Edna St. Vincent Millay, Isadora Duncan, Theodore Dreiser, Walter Lippmann, John Reed, Mabel Dodge, and Max Eastman. The time Dos Passos told Marvin about, he went with friends—perhaps Eastman or some of the *Seven Arts* editors—who knew the people who surrounded Goldman at the Brevoort, "her myrmidons," Dos Passos called them. "We were the outer circle of her glory," he said, describing her as "a Bronxy fattish little old woman who looks like a rather good cook. She has a charmingly munchy fashion of eating sandwiches and pats her myrmidons on the head and kisses them in a motherly fashion." He drew a humorous sketch of the scene, showing Goldman's lover and coanarchist, Alexander Berkman, Goldman, and an "unknown Jewish gentleman," sitting at one table, while perched off to the side were a Sherlock Holmes–like detective and a third table of Dos Passos and his friends, himself in a "strange attitude intended to express excitement."

In an only slightly less lighthearted tone he wrote Arthur McComb about these same goings-on. Not that he was not serious about the issues at stake, but he could not hide his delight at the excitement of political rallies and police raids. He told of going to pacifist meetings such as one in Madison Square Garden where Max Eastman thrilled the audir ce with his antiwar rhetoric, and of being dispersed by the police. He claimed to know now of "the cossack tactics of the New York police force." He had been in a raid and had almost been shoved into a "black maria," a police wagon, when detectives swarmed into a Greenwich Village apartment where Dos Passos and his friends were enjoying an arty dance recital. Only after one member of the party called the district attorney would the law officers depart. "Every day I become more red," he wrote. "My one ambition is to be able to sing the internationale."

Then he turned on his own group, "a pretty milky lot," he thought, with their "tea-table convictions" and "radicalism that keeps so consistently within the bounds of decorum." He praised the "thrust and advance and courage" that now lay entirely "in a few of the East Side Jews and in a few of the isolated 'foreigners' whose opinions so shock the New York Times." He wanted to "annihilate these stupid colleges of ours, and all the nice young men in them, instillers of stodginess in every form, bastard culture, middle class snobbism." In this mood he declared that "Until Widener [Library] is blown up and A. Lawrence Lowell assassinated and the Business School destroyed and its site sowed with salt—no good will come out of Cambridge." Exuberantly he closed his letter, "Sans culottely Dos."

In this mood he prepared to sail for the war as an ambulance driver, which was the role in the war of a remarkable number of Americans who later became significant literary figures—Dos Passos, Cummings, Lawson, Hillyer, and Hemingway were but several. On June 20, "a brazen hot afternoon," Dos Passos boarded the *Chicago* amid a lot of patriotic fanfare; a band playing a hula-hula on the docks and people dancing among the luggage at boatside and singing anti-German songs. He found his stateroom, which he was to share with three other people. The ship was "laden with gear, patriotism and young men in uniform." Settled in his quarters, he wrote McComb, whom he told to take courage despite the domestic oppression that resulted from being at war. He pleaded with him to write often; Dos Passos expected "dark days." For his part, he would report what he could about the chance of revolution, using the code word "Nagel" for it. With Marvin he was more subdued than he had been in some time. He was sure that he would need Marvin to cheer him up, because "you see I dont believe in the 'spiritual good' of war and I expect to have one hell of a time until I get accustomed to taking ambulance loads of pulverized people about."

As he wrote, the *Chicago* began to pull away from her berth at the docks: "Hurrah—the whistle's blowing and the old tub is starting to move." He reminded Marvin to write: "Your letters'll be food and drink and ice cream sodas—to my dusty imagination." Then he peered out at New York harbor and exclaimed, "Gee the river's glorious, pink and grey and pale orange with lights." Despite his bravado of recent weeks, he was awed by what he was sure lay ahead, and, like many another occasion before, his sense of being alone weighed on him even while he was eager to be gone.

CHAPTER NINE

===

The War in France,

1917

Aboard the *Chicago* the Americans were charged with excitement and with expectations of high times in Paris. They kept singing,

God help Kaiser Bill
God help Kaiser Bill
Oh, old Uncle Sam,
He's got the infantry
He's got the cavalry
He's got artillery . . .
Then by God we'll all go to Germany
And God help Kaiser Bill

Like several million other Americans, they thought the war would be, if not exactly a lark, then at least a time for some roistering. Little matter that the war in the trenches had been for the Europeans one characterized by tedium, incredible misery, and staggering numbers of casualties. After the struggle was ended in November 1918, most of these same Americans would see their experiences far differently than they had in June 1917. During the fighting 115,660 Americans died in combat or from disease; 205,690 were wounded; 4,526 were taken prisoner or reported missing. These numbers were large, but minuscule compared even to the hundreds of thousands of men the French and Germans lost in one battle at Verdun. There, although estimates vary, the French put their losses during the ten months of heaviest fighting in 1916 at 377,231. Of these, 162,308 were reported killed or missing. Another account set France's losses at Verdun at 469,000. The Germans estimated their losses at 337,000 and admitted to more than 100,000 dead or missing. The numbers might be even higher, for after the war 150,000 unidentified bodies, or parts of bodies, were gathered from the morass around Verdun and placed in the *ossuaire* that stands as a grim memorial on the battlefield. The knowledge of the slaughter of foreign soldiers at battles like Verdun and the Somme had nearly as much effect on Americans as the casualties to their own countrymen. World War I was the first major conflict most of them had known. Not since the Civil War had such huge numbers been engaged in combat, and not since then had Americans—or anyone else—known such carnage. Although the United States in many ways was no longer a naif by 1917, the war shook the nation profoundly.

For the many Americans who experienced combat, the world afterward appeared different. Their energy and optimism did not seem to be able to cure something malicious about human affairs that the war revealed to them. One could fight to end the conflict, but gassings, maimings, and pointless slaughters caused by asinine orders issued by field-grade officers who had no rendezvous with death made young Americans believe that life had a perversity about it which they had not known before.

When afterward such participants in the war as Hemingway, Cummings, Dos Passos, and others described their initiations in books like *In Our Time, The Sun Also Rises, A Farewell to Arms, The Enormous Room,* and *Three Soldiers,* other Americans understood what these authors were saying about war, government, society, and the individual's relationship to them. Americans began to recognize how different was the twentieth-century world from what they had known before, and their perceptions of themselves and of their country changed.

The real shock of war still lay ahead for Dos Passos during his voyage across on the *Chicago.* The trip was one of the best he had ever made; he lazed about, sleeping a good deal of the time on deck near the bow of the ship, and eating. After he had been aboard for a week, he roused himself enough to write a poem that conveyed his feelings at that moment. It reads in part:

I have no more memories.
Before,
My memories with various strands
Had spun me many misty-colored towns,
Full of gleams of halfheard music,
Full of sudden throbbing scents,
And rustle of unseen passers-by—
Vague streets rainbow glowing
For me to wander in . . .

Today,
As if a gritty stinking sponge
Had smeared the slate of my pale memories,
I stand aghast in a grey world,

Waiting . . .
I have no more memories.
Sea and the grey brooding sky—
Two halves of a flameless opal—
Glow soft and sullenly
In a vast sphere about me
As I, very drowsy, lie
On the deck; by the rise and fall
Of the sound of spumed water
Lulled into dreaminess,
Into a passionless mood
Of utter lassitude,
A dull Nirvana where stir
Negations without stress. . . .

He felt during the voyage as if he were making a break with his past—"I have no more memories," he wrote, and the boisterous Americans aboard ship strengthened his sense of the difference between his past and this moment. Because he had grave doubts about the wisdom of America's entry into the war, he was more thoughtful than most of them; he had not forgotten the scenes at Bordeaux of the casualties of warfare: the wounded and mutilated French soldiers in the streets.

There was only one submarine scare, he told McComb, toward the end of the voyage; what was thought to be a periscope, however, was nothing but a log. Dos Passos took heart in finding five Socialists aboard the *Chicago*. One of them was John Howard Lawson, a political activist and playwright, who became an intimate friend. Lawson was a charismatic man, brilliant, outspoken, and worldly, whom Dos Passos liked immediately. Soon, Dos Passos would be influenced by Lawson's politics as well as his ideas about the drama. More prevalent than Socialists aboard ship were the militarists, whose conversation Dos Passos occasionally caught. The air was filled with the spirit of war, fomented by such as Theodore Roosevelt's son, Archie, whom he heard agree with another officer that by the end of the fighting America would be one of the strongest military powers anywhere, ready to—at which point Dos Passos could not hear what the two said. But he could imagine, and their bellicose spirit disturbed him deeply.

At the very end of June, just over four months after he had sailed out of the Gironde for the United States aboard the *Espagne*, he returned to France, ironically in a happier mood, although he was headed into warfare, than when he had left. But as if to forewarn the Americans that war was not only the boisterous time they were experiencing, at the mouth of the Gironde the *Chicago* steamed through debris from a ship that had been torpedoed shortly before. Her spars stuck up out of the shallow water where she had foundered, and launches were still towing lifeboats to land with survivors aboard.

In Bordeaux, the Americans were warmly greeted by Frenchmen, enthusiastic that the United States had entered the war. As the ambulance section marched

through the streets toward the railway station, an old man rushed out from along
the sidewalk and clapped a hat on one American's head. The gaiety of the moment
did nothing to make the r w volunteers more serious: "Whores—protection etc—
Champagne," Dos Passos scribbled afterward in his journal as his train wound slowly
north toward Paris through a countryside especially colorful in the early summer-
time. Dos Passos, speaking the best French among his group, was the one to leap
down at each train stop to buy wine, *petits pains*, or *flûtes* of the crusty French bread
for the others. The scenes were idyllic, heightening the contrast between that
moment and the war which lay to the north. At Poitiers, about halfway to Paris,
he was so struck by this contrast that he tried to catch what it meant in a poem
beginning:

> *Wide grey-green fields,*
> *Dappled with swaying vermillion,*
> *Everywhere glowing with stains of poppies,—*
> *Poppies sprung from old sad fields*
> *Of a battle long fought out . . .*
> *How many years, oh God,*
> *Before the blood of battles springs up*
> *Into the arrogant glowing youth*
> *Of poppies?*

On July 2 the ambulance drivers reached Paris late in the evening at the Gare
d'Orsay, hailed horse-drawn cabs, and were taken to the Hotel du Palais. The next
morning Dos Passos walked to the headquarters of the Norton-Harjes unit at 7 rue
François Premier, where he discovered Robert Hillyer and another Harvard friend,
Frederick van den Arend. From them he learned that Dudley Poore and E. E.
Cummings were also in France. Dos Passos, Hillyer, and van den Arend spent a day
or two in Paris while they were being outfitted for uniforms and other administrative
matters were being handled. The three wandered along the Seine from the ambulance headquarters to the Île de la Cité, admiring Notre Dame on their way to the
Palais de Justice to see the delicate Sainte Chapelle, sandbagged against air raids,
within the courtyard. Crossing back to the Right Bank by the Pont Neuf, they
wandered through the gardens of the Louvre and, beyond those, the Tuileries. The
puppet shows along the walks and the thin tarts one could buy in the kiosks recalled
for Dos Passos his childhood and his love for the beauty of the city. Then in the
evenings when they strolled the boulevards, they sensed another Paris, one consumed by the war. On July 31, as Dos Passos waited for a slow convoy to head toward
the front, he described it in his journal: "Paris—A strange Paris of whores and
tragically sad widows—The abandon of complete misery—My God—how ridiculous
it all is—I think in gargoyles." Earlier in the month he had written McComb about
Paris, with its grotesques and its "usual Paris American wine woman and song air"
more intense than ever, heavy with a "strange recklessness." In the cafés English
and Canadian officers acted wildly, certain that these were their last flings before

they were to die. "I don't think this is literary straining after mood at all costs," Dos Passos added, "it may be." When he recalled Paris during his trip in convoy, the grotesqueries caused by this misery amidst the city's beauty and culture made him think of the Middle Ages, where men "had the right idea in their rollicking grotesque dance of Death." He wanted "to write a novel called the Dance of Death"; but by the time he got to it, he feared the idea would be much used.

Dos Passos was ordered to a Norton-Harjes training camp at Sandricourt, forty kilometers to the northeast of Paris. The camp was on the grounds of what had been a hunting preserve for a Marquis de Sandricourt. "It's a perfectly ordinary French farmhouse with none of the bats or weirs or mills or other fabled delights of May," he wrote Poore on July 9. It lacked any of "the thrilling sixty foot ratholes of the *Front*—but the country is delightful: rolling hills of wheat and blue corn flowers, wheat and red poppies and great plumed clouds." At that moment he was seated "under a clematis vine at the foot of an old wall, watching the silver and gold sunset," while to the north he heard "a noise as of people moving furniture in the next house"—the rumble of the artillery along the front. Suddenly a grasshopper sprang onto his paper and gave him such a waggish look out of the corners of its "large sly eyes" that he was sure it had read the "twaddle" he was scribbling. "I know his opinion of it," Dos Passos told Poore. "It was fully expressed in the rear view of backward jerking legs he just gave me."

At Sandricourt the new drivers had no cars to practice with, so they drilled and drilled—and learned to swear. "One swears and filthifies largely and joyfully," he wrote McComb. "Military discipline plus greasy soup remove all joy of life—one waits with faint hope for the moment of release." The several weeks at Sandricourt increased his distaste for the monotonous regimentation of the military. Once when he was supposed to be on fatigue duty, he sneaked off through a break in a wall to write Poore. He complained about the drilling, which was endless because the authorities wanted to make a good showing for General John Pershing, who was supposed to inspect the camp soon. "My God what damn rot. . . . The only human thing I've done has been make hay for one delightful afternoon—on a hillside with a lovely view. Of all the damned inanities that have ever enslaved and stultified people, the military humbug is the stupidest—Imagine us drilling and hanging flags about to honor a damn general—when the country is starving and god knows what else." A cynic might have responded that Dos Passos was lucky to get away with but a few short weeks of drilling, because his paramilitary regime was less arduous than what most soldiers went through. That, however, was not his point. The more his individualistic bent was thwarted, the more he rebelled. His opposition would grow fiercer, and the seeds for *Three Soldiers* began to take root.

While at Sandricourt he received a letter from Stewart Mitchell bringing him up short and reminding him that his glib protests did not strike everyone as being keenly perceptive. Mitchell chided him because "you have begun to treat me as you have always treated Mr. [Woodrow] Wilson: demand things with an immense insouciance." Mitchell had little to say about Dos Passos's intellectual stance. Concerning that Dos Passos would have to make his "own peace with reason," but

Mitchell thought that his friend was always precisely where Woodrow Wilson was not; hence Dos Passos's "eruption of socialistic pacificism" was "a perfectly predictable result of [Wilson's] having declared war." At least one friend reminded Dos Passos that his progress to where he now believed he stood politically was not the entirely reasoned process he wanted it to be. Dos Passos was where he was because he opposed authority figures.

When his training was completed near the end of July, Dos Passos returned to Paris, where he joined a section of ambulance drivers to go to the front. He was pleased to be with Hillyer and van den Arend. They were ordered to Châlons-sur-Marne, east of Paris and less than one hundred kilometers from the front. At Châlons, they disembarked and were marched "through grilling hot streets full of powdery dust to a big arid 'park' of automobiles & camions." In their temporary home, a hot barracks, Dos Passos had his first chance to talk at length with the poilus —"the hairy ones," the slang term for the French infantrymen. In his journal he noted that all of them "told the same story of utter boredom—and desolation—Hate of the Germans is rung in now and then, conventionally, without convictions—one is too tired to be anything but bored." While his unit, Section Sanitaire 60, waited at Châlons, the French celebrated the occasion of the commandant's receiving a decoration. Evergreens enlivened the barracks; every table in the mess hall was decorated with wildflowers, and all the troops were served a large meal and extra white wine. Amid laughter, sweat, and general camaraderie, the decorated officer and the general who had made the presentation passed through the mess hall, drinking a toast at each table and giving a quick speech about "bonne santé à toute *la France* une seule grande famille" ("good health to all France, one large family"). That same night the Americans were in their first air raid. A siren sounded; bombs fell in the distance, and the drivers rushed outside to look in the clear nighttime sky for the German planes, but saw none and only imagined they could hear them.

Waiting behind the lines, Hillyer, van den Arend, and Dos Passos had time to sightsee. In Châlons they visited an "unimpressive" cathedral and other less dreary sites. Far more pleasurable was swimming during the hot weather in the Marne, wearing "delightfully abbreviated & striped French tights." Their appearance became increasingly military, for van den Arend and Dos Passos clipped their hair very close, but that, he wrote Poore from the village of St. Martin-les-prés, had not prevented him from getting a flea bite on his left cheek. What he scribbled in his journal he generally wrote his friends: on the same day that he had jotted down his idea about thinking in gargoyles, he wrote Poore, "If I could sculpt—I'd carve grotesques. The medievals had the right idea—Death is a rollicking dance—Pain writhes into gorgeous jigs about the Arch-Satirist's drunken throne. Gall is as intoxicating as sweet wine—The horror is fun—but don't think: Shriek with laughter along with the gods." He felt "caught in the toils of the ridiculous—Reality seems a leering gargoyle." The only remedy was laughter. As he wrote he could hear the cannon "growling like the devil along the north—and ambulances are scooting by along the main road," activity so intense that he believed his section might get into the fight the next day.

The anxiety, excitement, and anticipation that gripped him made him anxious to create new fiction, but he feared that his past methods were inadequate. They disgusted him now, and he was positive he needed fresh techniques to deal with the welter of experiences pouring in on him. "The stream of sensation flows by," he wrote in his journal. "I suck it up like a sponge—my reactions are a constant weathervane—a little whimsical impish—giggling—sneering at tragedy." Then he inscribed yet another diatribe against the time:

> Horror is so piled on horror that there can be no more—Despair gives place to delirious laughter—
>
> How damned ridiculous it all is! The long generations toiling—skimping, lashing themselves screwing higher and higher the tension of their minds, polishing brighter and brighter the mirror of intelligence to end in this—My God what a time—All the cant and hypocrisy, all the damnable survivals, all the vestiges of old truths now putrid and false infect the air, choke you worse than German gas—the ministers from their damn smug pulpits, the business men—the heroics about war—my country right or wrong—Oh infinities of them! Oh the tragic farce of the world. Hardy's Arch satirist is more a bungling clown than an astute and sinister humorist.

Calmer, he described the time in Châlons and observed with some astonishment that he was enjoying himself "vastly," although he worried if he would ever be able to make something of these experiences. He accused himself of being lazy, "lacking in conviction," and was certain only that the direction of all his earlier writing had been wrong. Now he had "cleared the space for the new edifice," where something fresh would begin. He was not sure what methods he would use; yet these notes— or if not the notes, the experiences—marked a fresh beginning. His previous skepticism now took deeper root as he observed the conditions of war. Quickly he conceived that the satire which he had employed lightly at Harvard and had sharpened during his months in Spain was the mode best suited for the commentaries he meant to write about contemporary society, so it remained to perfect a technique with which to shape his satirist's vision.

In St. Martin-les-prés the ambulance section was billeted in the dance hall of what had been an inn. While Dos Passos wrote, a soft rain fell. He sat in the beer garden of the inn trying to imagine how many drinks had been drunk there and how many wedding parties had caroused. The setting and the warm rain made the world seem romantically "soft and warm with the phallic glow!" Behind him in the inn the cooks for the convoy were preparing supper "with an inimitable air of Savarins cooking for Henri Quatre." The entire scene made him think of what was some of the simple good about life: food, the company of women, music, and a beautiful landscape. Young people should govern the world, he decided at that moment, not "the swagbellied old fogies in frock-coats that do" who had made a "God-damned mess" of things. "Better any tyranny than theirs," he scrawled furiously in his journal, "down with the middle aged!"

Despite the activity along the front, Section 60 did not go directly into action at the beginning of August. The ambulances were placed on call behind the lines and for the next few weeks shuttled from one area to another. They operated out of a small village named Erize-la-Petite, on the road which came to be called the Voie Sacrée between Bar-le-Duc and Verdun. August 2 Dos Passos wrote in his journal that Erize-la-Petite was "the damndest godforsakenest hole I ever landed in." It was "a small village straggling along two sides of the main road." Close to Verdun, the village had been repeatedly pounded by shelling, so that many of its buildings were destroyed. Here Dos Passos was finally experiencing the signs of war. The atmosphere around Erize-la-Petite was one of "complete dead quiet." Ambulance sections were coming together there in preparation for a major Allied offensive at Verdun to begin on August 20. In the weeks before the attack, the rain was constant —"rain rain rain" Dos Passos wrote on August 3. "Erize must have been a fairly unattractive town to begin with, but now, with half the houses mere shells full of rubble and muddy manure and the ground all about trampled to soup by crowds of troops and camion drivers—it is unbelievably gloomy—symbol of all the intense brooding boredom of war." That night he and van den Arend walked along the Voie Sacrée and noticed the "utter quiet." It was too quiet, Dos Passos thought. The rolling countryside behind Verdun had "all the stillness of a charnel house, rather than the comfortable stillness of night. It is dark and damp and moldy smelling like a tomb."

As is so often the case in war, before the offensive the troops had days of slack time. August 4 was a Saturday, and that night the French and Americans got drunk together on the powerful red wine nicknamed *pinard*—"bull piss," Dos Passos noted —which the army issued copiously to the soldiers. The rain had produced "a foot of soupy mud round the cars," so to avoid it he had lifted his cot up on one of the stretchers inside his ambulance, where he lay listening to drunken voices outside. That evening he and van den Arend had taken another walk, this time over the hills around the village, "through a harsh violent evening—crudely funereal—with jagged clouds in constant flow overhead," while around them jutted up "wooden crosses" that made each small rise seem a Calvary.

Ideas for the new fiction Dos Passos wanted to write were growing. On August 5 he wrote that "the great war novel is forming gradually in my mind. I have almost a feeling that the Streets of Night will get incorporated—will be part I." He tried an outline but produced only a brief sketch, from which one can deduce little except that already he had in mind a novel about the time prior to the war—the college days that are the subject of *Streets of Night*—and then about the war itself. Even as he was first being initiated into war, he attempted to describe it. Later, he appended an ending to *Streets of Night* to bring the central character, Fanshaw Macdougan, back from the war, yet the novel showed little of the conflict. Fanshaw, in fact, ignored the experiences of battle and retreated into the Cambridge bell glass once again. But at about this time Dos Passos began another novel, the first chapters of which he wrote alternately with Robert Hillyer. They gave the book the title "Seven Times Round the Walls of Jericho," but it was never published, although

Dos Passos completed a draft during the months after Hillyer returned to the United States in September 1917. Its first three parts take the central character, Martin Howe, from his childhood through his college years and some months in New York immediately afterward. A fourth part takes Howe into the war. This section, not integral to the other parts, Dos Passos separated and revised to become *One Man's Initiation: 1917*, his first published novel. But that was later. On August 5 all he could outline about Part II of his "great war novel" was "The war . . . the philosophy of scorn," and then he quoted from Verlaine: *"De trop de delicatesse/J'ai perdu la vie"* ("From too much fastidiousness/I lost my life").

Wandering in the vicinity of Erize-la-Petite he found a brook by which he could sit when the weather was fair. While he wrote in his journal on August 6, an elderly Frenchman came by and struck up a conversation. He was "a delightfully hale elderly gentleman with a sparkle in his eye—who turned out to be a natural philosopher and I am sure a disciple of Jean Jacques." The Frenchman showed Dos Passos and his friends how he fished for trout with "a certain skimming waterfly." The village schoolteacher, he enjoyed the stimulating talk of these intelligent foreigners. Two days later Dos Passos, Hillyer, and van den Arend listened to his tale of how the Germans had vandalized his house in 1914 when they swept across France toward Paris. That evening the three visited him in his small garden along the edge of the Voie Sacrée, and as they sat, through the grille fence they saw the infantry of the first regiment in the forthcoming attack moving toward their assembly point just behind the front lines. The schoolteacher had been describing to the Americans "how the villagers used to dance in the open square in summer—before the war— when the first camion—full of shouting drunken men—powdered with white dust —climbing about and dangling in all positions from the super structure of the camion" passed by. The trucks were "in long convoys filling the village street with rumble and shouting." A short time later the three ambulance drivers were drinking some white wine with the schoolteacher and his wife, when the commandant of the attacking regiment, "a delightful large man with large whiskers and round glasses," came jauntily into the garden "with a little bearded captain with one arm in a sling and ugly long teeth—they were very cordial and pleasant and full of wonderful verve and animation—theirs was the honor of attacking first."

The scene along the Voie Sacrée of the camions advancing impressed Dos Passos profoundly: "the holocaust with slow regular speed—goes past—grind of brakes—slush of wheels," he wrote, "and we, infinitely bored, sit in our ambulances, waiting for orders to bring them back—when the offensive has been pulled off— c'est rigolo." It appeared repeatedly in his fiction, and as if to work free of the horrifying images, he wrote them out in letters to his friends, as he did to Marvin at the end of August, after the offensive was over:

> For some reason nothing I've seen since has affected me nearly as much as the camion loads of dusty men grinding through the white dust clouds of the road to the front. In the dusk always, in convoys of twenty or more escorted by autos full of officers, they would rumble through the one street of the ruined village.

The first night we were sitting in a tiny garden—the sort of miniature garden that a stroke of a sorcerer's wand would transmute into a Versailles without changing any of its main features—talking to the schoolmaster and his wife, who were feeding us white wine & apologizing for the fact that they had no cake. The garden was just beside the road, and through the railing we began to see them pass. For some reason we were all so excited we could hardly speak —Imagine the tumbrils in the Great Revolution—the men were drunk & desperate, shouting, screaming jokes, spilling wine over each other—or else asleep with ghoulish dust-powdered faces. The old schoolmaster kept saying in his precise voice—"Ah, ce n'était pas comme ça en 1916 . . . Il y avait du discipline. Il y avait du discipline—" ["Ah, it was not like that in 1916 . . . There was some discipline. There was some discipline—"].

And his wife—a charming redfaced old lady with a kitten under her arm kept crying out

"Mais que voulez vous? Les pauvres petits, Ils savent qu'ils vont à la mort" —["But what do you want? The poor little ones, they know that they are going to their deaths."]—I shall never forget that "ils savent qu'ils vont à la mort" —You see later, after the "victory," we brought them back in our ambulances, or else saw them piled on little two wheeled carts, tangles of bodies with grey crooked fingers and dirty protruding feet, to be trundled to the cemeteries, where they are always busy making their orderly little grey wooden crosses.

While he was still in Erize-la-Petite, Dos Passos wrote McComb a long letter describing his, Hillyer's, and van den Arend's activities. Dos Passos told McComb that there were "increasing indications" of revolution in France—referring, no doubt, to the recent unrest and mutinies that had plagued the army—and he hoped that revolution might occur in America too, because such was the only thing that could relieve nations from the grip of their present governments. He described to McComb the poignant scene with the elderly French couple in their garden, and then he added in closing, "Arthur I'm in despair about it all."

As Dos Passos waited along the Voie Sacrée for the new offensive against the Germans to begin, he began to sense the real nature of war. Many men wrote about their experiences in the Verdun sector, from which one can sense what that extended battle was like. Even today parts of the area appear ominous, dominated by the *ossuaire* near a fortified position called the Ouvrage de Thiaumont, hard fought for during the battle. Control of the position had changed fifteen times during the fighting of 1916, and each time the cost in lives had been great.

Although parts of the Verdun sector have been seeded with pines and thick brush now covers much of the battle zone, the scars of the war remain, particularly where the fighting was most intense. Rubble and stones remain tossed up from the incessant bombardments that went on, while sections of the area are closed to tourists with the warning that unexploded mines and shells still lie in the fields that roll away from Verdun and the forts which stood beyond it as a major perimeter of defense. Signs along roadways or on the remains of a fort tell that here such and such Germans or Frenchmen fought gallantly before they were killed. Covering one earth-filled trench known as the Tranchée des Baïonnettes is a simple concrete roof, put there as a sort of monument to honor the Frenchmen buried in the trench under the rubble heaved upon them during a German bombardment. Through the intense shelling, the French remained at their positions, and legend has it that the bayonets which still protrude up through the earth mark where the poilus stood ready for hand-to-hand combat until they were buried by the earth.

The Verdun that Dos Passos saw had come to look like the "humid skin of a monstrous toad," as a French pilot put it. To another aviator, an American, out beyond Verdun "there is only that sinister brown belt, a strip of murdered nature. It seems to belong to another world. Every sign of humanity has been swept away. The woods and roads have vanished like chalk wiped from a blackboard; of the villages nothing remains but grey smears. . . . During heavy bombardments and attacks I have seen shells falling like rain."

On the ground the scenes during bombardments were, if anything, worse, because there the most awful forms of death stared a person in the face: a horse, still hitched to a wagon, floundering down in a mud-filled shell crater and after two days no one heeding it; the body of a Frenchman killed by a shell and "laid open from the shoulders to the haunches like a quartered carcass of meat in a butcher's window"; a "torso, without head, without arms, without legs, struck to the trunk of a tree, flattened and opened"; and everywhere in the battle zone, skeletons, hastily made crosses, and the stench of rotting flesh. Whether Dos Passos actually saw such carnage in 1917 is a moot point; he knew of it, and quickly he came to agree with the young French officer who wrote, "Humanity is mad!" in his diary just before he died fighting for control of Fort Douamont. "It must be mad to do what it is doing. What a massacre! What scenes of horror and carnage! I cannot find words to translate my impressions. Hell cannot be so terrible. Men are mad!"

Apprehensive about what lay ahead yet eager to see, the ambulance drivers prepared to move up to the front lines on the eve of the offensive. Dos Passos on August 15 noted in his journal that he had been amusing himself in three ways: "1. Writing a novel in collaboration with Bobs [Hillyer] 2. Eating & drinking omelets & white wine 3. Having wonderful naval fights with fleets of paper boats on the brook—." Then he added, "Tomorrow we go to the Front to a devilish hot section. Don't forget Athos, Porthos & d'Artagnan." That same day he wrote Dudley Poore that "Tomorrow we enter the critical part of the farce—The utter goddamnable ridiculousness of it! Lies, Lies, lies, lies are the supreme fact of life—to combat them with body & soul one's sole duty—But not seriously. By God . . . 'I built my soul an altar-fire of laughter in the face of doom.'

"We're going into a damn hot place. . . . There's an offensive coming off—."

The attack was intended to retake ground lost the previous year to the Germans and to consolidate gains made during the autumn of 1916. It was a major offensive. To prepare the way, the French employed 2,500 artillery pieces in their bombardment of the German positions. Then early on the morning of the twentieth, the poilus swarmed out of their trenches, accompanied overhead by airplanes that strafed and bombed the Germans. That evening, the French recaptured the slope called Mort Homme, and four days later they took Hill 304, both considered strategic strongpoints of the Verdun sector. The fighting continued at a slackened pace into September, when by the eighth the French declared their offensive a victory.

Dos Passos's section was moved into a valley behind a wood called the Bois d'Avocourt. The drivers' task was to carry the wounded from *abris*—shelters—just behind the front lines back to medical centers well to the rear. The *abri,* an underground emergency ward, was supported by beams and protected well enough so that only direct hits could harm it. In a typical abri one "descended a long, inclined stairs, wide enough to admit the stretcher-bearers, to a room big enough for an operating table and medical equipment, and along the walls, the bunks or stretchers on which [the drivers and medical personnel] slept." A doctor was in charge, whose job was to treat the wounded enough so that they could survive the rough and often long ride back to the field hospitals.

Dos Passos's first direct experience in action did not have the dramatic quality about it one might have expected. Then, too, his experiences seeing wounded soldiers in Bordeaux and during the days prior to moving into action had inured him to some of the horrors. Nevertheless, his first action impressed him. Huddled in the abri at Station P2 where he was assigned, Dos Passos had time to describe it. He wrote Marvin about his first night of work, when down in the shelter during a poison-gas attack he and his co-driver, Jim Parshall, lay on their bunks with their masks on, listening to shells explode and shrapnel lash the abri "like somebody flailing about with a whip." Although the French veterans slept through the bombardment and the gas with their masks on, Dos Passos lay awake reciting every poem he could recollect and repeated the Lord's Prayer and "Now I lay me down to sleep" over and over. In the early morning when the all-clear sounded, he and Parshall went aboveground to start their ambulance while wounded were being loaded in it. Shrapnel had torn the body of the Fiat ambulance and had even ripped through Dos Passos's cap, which he had left on the seat, but the engine and tires were not damaged, so the two drivers headed off, one pushing to get the car started out of the thick mud while the other drove and the wounded groaned from being jolted as the ambulance lurched through the mire. Dos Passos remembered seeing wretched horses and mules, still hitched to French 75-mm cannon, standing by the road "heaving and gasping with popping eyes and bloody nostrils." He and Parshall were not badly harmed by wafts of gas, but they had to stop frequently to vomit as they drove to the rear.

He wrote Poore that he and Parshall did all their work from P2, "except for one post we go to at night amid the splendor of starshells and through the heady patter of machine guns." They were gassed every night, which was what bothered him most. His excitement about actual combat was as great as was his repugnance. "It's queer how much happier I am here in the midst of it than in America, where the air was stinking with lies & hypocritical patriotic gibber," he confessed to Marvin after being under fire for three days. At that moment he was sitting in the abri with his gas mask over his shoulder and his helmet on, while aboveground a battery of heavy French cannons, 220-mm's, jarred his concentration with their incessant firing. But while he enjoyed what he was doing, he felt "so deeply bitter" that he could "produce nothing but gall and wormwood." "The war is utter damn nonsense," he declaimed, "a vast cancer fed by lies and self seeking malignity on the part of those who don't do the fighting." Governments deserved less than anything else in the world to be fought for, and "none of the poor devils whose mangled dirty bodies I take to the hospital in my ambulance really give a damn about any of the aims of this ridiculous affair—They fight because they are too cowardly & too unimaginative not to see which way they ought to turn their guns." He warned Marvin, "For God's sake, Rummy boy, put this in your pipe and smoke it— everything said & written & thought in America about the war is lies—God! They choke one like poison gas—."

There was little hatred of the enemy on the front lines, he found. Prisoners and captors laughed and kidded each other a lot, and atrocities were scarcely heard of; they "sort of fade away in reality." He wrote Poore that the ambulance had carried "lots of wounded Huns, delightful people all, and most friendly with the French," who, in turn, were "invincibly charming even to prisoners, whom they reluctantly —to fulfill the convention call sales boches, but without conviction."

En repos on August 24 in the village of Avocourt, slightly behind the front lines, Dos Passos dozed away the afternoon in the garden of the remains of a pink stucco house, where there was a pool with a fountain, no longer filled with water. He and his friends used the pool for shelter whenever German shells came too close. Despite the war, the garden was blooming, "full of such plaisaunce with its white roses and its fat-juiced pears and its white blotches of phlox-flowers among evergreens that it makes one hate still more all the foolishnesses with which men try to disturb the rich ease of life." Why, he asked himself, should death—which ought to be tranquil—instead "comes in the evil shriek of a shell?" To serve governments, was his answer; yet these were "only makeshifts—like patent toothpaste—less important perhaps—and who would die for toothpaste, or kill for it."

Seated in the garden he noticed that the contrast between it and "the gas waves of stupidity" of the war prevented him from concentrating on "any one rhythm or mood." Ideas came to him "in little hesitant showers, like flower petals when a wind blows after rain." Swirling together were his admiration for the camaraderie of the French, a feeling of "utter anathema" toward America and its smug phraseology, a vague unease about his own bitterness, a fascination with the profanity the war produced, and always, his sense of "the utter goddamned ridiculousness of things." Like many other persons who had experienced the military, he had discovered that cursing was the only recourse against the sometimes absurd nature of existence.

During the offensive he tried to record in his journal as much as he could of all that he saw. The nonchalance of the French toward the miserable conditions in the trenches was heroic. At one point he could not get to sleep because of all the "flies & the fleas and the biting & nipping & crawling things" that he had picked up in the abris. He thought then of the doctor in one shelter, who stood outside examining a cheese while German shells fell around him and French stretcher-bearers shouted at him to get under cover. But the doctor, inured to the bombardment, bent over the cheese, remarking in a bemused way, "But there are some little animals in it—look at the little animals—how big they are."

In the other abri that Dos Passos served, the ritual aspects of the meals the French had even during a bombardment fascinated him. They seemed able to ignore the war at these moments; he recalled a doctor and a chaplain drinking from their delicate wineglasses and discussing linguistics even as they were under bombardment and being pelted with a spray of pebbles. Such scenes were the stuff of which he wanted to write. He meant to be catching every scene that rushed by him. "Gosh," he exclaimed, "I want to be able to express, later—all of this—all the tragedy and hideous excitement of it. I have seen so very little. I must experience more of it, & more." Then he reiterated some of what the war was to him:

> The grey crooked fingers of the dead, the dark look of dirty mangled bodies, their groans & joltings in the ambulances, the vast tom tom of the guns, the ripping tear shells make when they explode, the song of shells outgoing, like vast woodcocks—their contented whirr as they near their mark—the twang of fragments like a harp broken in the air—& the rattle of stones & mud on your helmet—
>
> And through everything the vast despair of unavoidable death, of lives wrenched out of their channels—of all the ludicrous tomfoolery of governments.

Three days later, while he sat in the garden of the pink stucco house once again, he described to Marvin more of the scenes of war. This was the same letter in which he told of seeing the camions loaded with French troops going toward the front. He assured Marvin that Jane Addams's assertion—ridiculed in the press—that troops were often drunk when they went into combat, was true. Pinard, strong tobacco, and a mixture of rum and ether, called *agnol,* were what made combat bearable.

The Bois d'Avocourt, he wrote, had become "a fantastic wood"—a "ghoul haunted woodland" that smelled of "poison gas, tangled with broken telephone wires, with ripped pieces of camouflage . . . filled in every hollow with guns that crouch and spit like the poisonous toads of the fairytales." After both sides had shelled each other during the night, it was a strange sensation at dawn to evacuate wounded through "woodland roads, with the guns of the batteries tom-tomming about you & the whistle of departing shell & the occasional rattling snort of an arrivée." Only with great difficulty could the drivers reach the rear, because of "the smashed artillery trains, past piles of splintered camions and commissariat wagons." The wood had become "one vast battery—a constant succession of ranks of guns hidden in foliage, and dugouts, from which people crawl like gnomes when the firing ceases and to which you scoot when you hear a shell that sounds as if it had your calling card on it."

After a few more days of action Dos Passos's ambulance section was pulled out of the line on September 1 and sent for rest to Givry-en-Argonne, a small town near Sainte Menehould. Having been under fire for the past two and a half weeks, his group had "sniffed too much gas—with the result of diarrhea and dysentery and other horrors," he wrote Poore. And five days later he sounded a now-familiar theme: "Curiously enough I adore la vie militaire, apart from my convictions. Its been a long orgy of food & drink with intermittent excitements of shells & assorted horrors."

From Remicourt, another village in the Argonne, he reported to his friends that his Norton-Harjes volunteer ambulance unit was being taken over by the American Red Cross, the purpose being part of a plan to integrate the ambulance groups into the regular army. The drivers' choice, he told Marvin, would soon be whether to enlist in the army or retire. The scene of the transfer of command was an amusing one: punctuated by incoming shells, the ceremony consisted of Richard Norton— the Boston brahmin who had been one of the organizers of the unit—sporting a monocle and shaking hands with each of his drivers, who were lined up in ranks before him. Norton ended his speech to his men by declaring, "As gentlemen volunteers you enlisted in this service and as gentlemen volunteers I bid you farewell." Among them wandered the section's pet, a dog named P2, and each time a shell landed nearby, the ranks of drivers clutched their helmets and crouched down as pebbles and dirt showered them. The jowled officers from the U.S. Army had less restraint. As soon as they could, they ran for shelter, looking nothing like the devil-may-care veterans that the ambulance drivers believed they had become.

CHAPTER TEN

Paris and Italy, 1917–1918

The simplest way for Dos Passos to remain in Europe and see further service was to enlist in the Red Cross, which he hoped to do after his release from the Norton-Harjes unit. In the meantime he and the other drivers remained on duty for another month under the command of the Médecin Divisionaire. Their work was light, so they had the chance to enjoy the early fall around Remicourt. The local cheese, a camembert full of the "ozone of clover and cows and placid contemplation," pleased him. He and van den Arend, when not otherwise occupied, spent their time "sitting under a haystack reading and contemplating and eating the aforementioned cheeses through Elysian September days 'season of mists and mellow fruitfulness.' " In the evenings they walked into a neighboring village to "drink infinities of café-au-lait or white wine with sirop de groseille" and listen to the French soldiers sing, complain, or boast, until at eight-thirty the cafés were closed by military law.

Little action occurred in their sector now that the offensive was over. Dos Passos found the time entertaining, even to "a purely perfunctory daily bombardment and a weekly mine explosion—of which the Germans & French warn each other beforehand." The drivers were evacuating soldiers, he joked, who "hurt themselves opening tins of singe [monkey] or who fall down the entrance of abris or who have pull enough with the doctors to have their tags marked 'commotion' [shock] or 'debilité generale.' " No one had enough to do, so the officers were tightening up the discipline, and Dos Passos at the end of September found himself "confined to the barracks . . . for having gone to dinner at the charming little town near us without having procured permission so to do."

Constantly he reiterated his despair about the futility of the war. "Will always another hydra head rise to spew venom and blindness over our poor attempts to make ourselves at home in the sunny world?" he asked Poore. If only there were hope for escape from the clutches of "a few people in frock coats [who] want to protect their 'interests,' " then he would not feel so like finding an isle of oblivion where he might "forget the stupid world in drunkenness of earth," some place "where the English language and Singer sewing machines are unknown—where there are no croix de guerre or decimated battalions." Even so, he reminded himself, "there is always the miserable teasing need for speaking one's mind the responsibility —the feeling that if someone, in all the abject cowardice of our generation, showed a little courage—just once—there would be a new singing of the carmagnole—an assault on new Bastilles."

While he awaited release from duty in October, he heard the news that Cummings and Williams Slater Brown had been arrested for what the French censors considered treasonous statements. He tried unsuccessfully to contact Cummings, and the incident—Cummings would remain in a concentration camp for eleven weeks, Brown longer—simply fueled his wrath against officialdom.

That wrath partially subsided when he was released from the volunteer unit in mid-October. He returned directly to Paris, where he took a small, inexpensive, and cold room on the rue Descartes on the Left Bank between the Pantheon and the Seine. Once he had arranged for ambulance service in Italy with the American Red Cross, he moved to the Hotel François Premier, where the drivers were quartered and where he and van den Arend shared a luxurious room. His new ambulance section would be departing soon for Italy, but meanwhile Paris had many pleasures to enjoy. When he was first there he wrote Marvin that these consisted of "many concerts, eating many delightful meals in miscellaneous restaurants, snooping about bookshops—and being as unmilitary as possible." Also, he continued working on "Seven Times Round the Walls of Jericho."

In Paris he found himself "eating the lotos—and a delightful lotos" that took his mind off the war. At the concerts, orchestras played the music of César Franck; with "refined gluttony" he savored patisseries; he walked often from his room across to the Luxembourg Gardens to enjoy "the wistfulness of russet fall"; and more than once he took a long walk in the cold autumn twilight up to Montmartre, where near Sacré Coeur he found a small restaurant whose escargots were succulent. Van den Arend often went with him, and seated on the steps below Sacré Coeur after dinner, they watched the German night air raids when the air above Paris was filled with "the undulant rumble of Boche motors, the moonlight sky streaked with searchlights and flickering with little sparks of shrapnel, the red flare and the growl of bursting bombs in the distance." Then too, around Montmartre one could easily find prostitutes. In *The Best Times* Dos Passos implied that during this stay in Paris some of his earlier inhibitions had departed, and he, like his friend, found a *petite femme*. "*Rigajig, coucher avec* (alas the remorseful prophylaxis that followed)," he wrote. For the most part his wanderings, he told Marvin just before leaving for Italy in the middle of November, were "through autumn gardens and down grey misty colonaded streets . . . poring over bookshops and dining at little tables in back streets . . . going to concerts, and riding in squeaky voitures with skeleton horses." But they consisted as well of wanderings "constantly through dimly-seen crowds and peeping in on orgies of drink and women, of vague incomplete adventures," which was as much as he would tell of his own sexual forays. One evening he had left a friend, probably van den Arend, who had himself picked up a woman as they walked the streets around Montmartre. Dos Passos bumped into a small, appealing girl at a Metro station—if his account of the incident in the autobiographical novel *Chosen Country* is close to fact—and after some soup and wine the two went upstairs in the hotel next to the bar where they had eaten. They made love in the chilly room, then fell asleep. The next morning the girl hurried off to her work as a dressmaker, leaving Dos Passos to his morning bowl of café au lait at the bar where they had been the night before.

For Dos Passos there was nothing sordid about the hasty affair. In the novel, Jay Pignatelli walked back to his place "in peace through the early morning streets full of the clatter of iron shutters being pushed up, busy streets that smelt of cheese and fresh vegetables and of soap from the scrubbed floors of fresh-opened bars. . . . The muscles of his legs felt springy under his well-belted uniform. His feet trod lightly on the paving stones. His eyes travelled lovingly over the carving round ancient doorways." The world seemed a fine place that morning, and finally Dos Passos, like his autobiographical character, felt liberated from some of the inhibitions that had plagued him. At the same time he realized the foolishness of the illusion that there was the some sort of grand life out beyond him which he could not attain. Granted he had been hemmed in by his inhibitions, still there was no pantheistic universe to be in harmony with. The war had made him comprehend that, and a little more than two months later, as he thought about "Seven Times Round the Walls of Jericho," he wrote in his journal that as a college sophomore he was "just beginning to be sure that the ingrained taboos were taboos & not fast in the core of things." He was, nevertheless, still "overfull" of "morbidities & fastidious barriers, with that infantile feeling of being cut off from all the world— not being en rapport." Now he felt "much stodgier & sturdier" and realized that "there is no all the world to be in rapport with." He had the war to thank for making him, as he boasted, "a much heartier son of a bitch than I used to be much readier to slap my cock against the rocks of fact."

Dos Passos's lessening inhibitions extended to his talking more about himself and his work with his friends. Dudley Poore, who had been wounded during his ambulance service that summer and fall, was also back in Paris, so the two saw each other constantly. Dos Passos talked a great deal about his own family; Poore was surprised at how much Dos Passos knew about them. And as they walked along the quays bordering the Seine, he spoke of his illegitimacy with feeling, but not, apparently, with great resentment. Poore thought he was one of the first friends to learn about this, because only John Walcott knew while they were students at Harvard that at Choate Dos Passos had been Jack Madison, a fact which by itself would not have aroused suspicion anyway.

"It was a time of sudden friendships," Dos Passos wrote in *The Best Times*. He became good friends with Tom Cope, whom he had first met at Sandricourt the previous July and who like him was back in Paris after the break-up of the Norton-Harjes unit. Cope soon began work with the Friends' War Victims Relief. Another new friend was Sydney Fairbanks, whom Dos Passos met the day they both were assigned to drive an ambulance, Fiat IV, for the Red Cross. Fairbanks had also attended Harvard, but left to join Norton-Harjes in the summer of 1916. And among the drivers being formed into Section 1, Dos Passos found John Howard Lawson once again, "as full of tales as ever," he remembered. With Lawson was an older man, Gouverneur Morris, a war correspondent who was to travel to Italy with the section. Morris was an entertaining person, in turn entertained by the youthful radicalism of Dos Passos and the others.

"In that part of the book of my memory, before which little could be said, may be found a rubrick, reading: Incipit Vita Nova—and so begins Dante's Vita Nuova & my excursion into Italian," Dos Passos wrote Marvin on November 12 from Paris. As a result of the defeat of the Italians by the Austrians around Caporetto at the end of October, more ambulances were needed. Thus he expected to leave in convoy on the fourteenth. There was some delay before the convoy of Fiats and Fords began the trip, but by the twenty-ninth it had progressed by slow stops to Cannes, whence Dos Passos wrote Poore about his travels. "The section is a joke," he reported, "sometimes sidesplitting, more often dull." The cars were "dilapidated hulks," the mechanics, "hulking idiots," while the leader of the section was "an ill-intentioned ass" and his second-in-command, an "amiable" one. From Paris they had driven the short distance to Fontainebleau, where before they set off the next day, motion pictures were taken of them in the square in front of the palace. From there they headed south into the Loire Valley, stopping at Cosne and Nevers, then driving down and across into Burgundy, spending a night at Mâcon, "a delightful town on the Saône where was a Gothic carved wooden house of great delightfulness." Passing through Lyon, they drove along the Rhône to Vienne where, Dos Passos wrote Marvin in early December, they emerged "into the warmth and sunlight of the valley of the Rhône, where the roads were dusty with the white dust of the Midi and where cypresses rise in solemn exclamation marks among the vines." In Montéli-mar, the next stop, "a white town full of plane trees," Dos Passos met "a vague American countess who hadn't been home for eight years" and a young French boy "whose passion was to faire le piano . . . an amazingly vivid and fiery young person." While Dos Passos worked on his ambulance, the boy chattered away; later, they walked about Montélimar and the youth told him many things about the town "with a wonderful contemptuous familiarity."

When the section commander decided to try for a record run to Marseilles, the result, reported Dos Passos, was that "two Fords, a camion and a Fiat were put permanently hors de combat and the section leader ran the staff car up a tree & left it in Avignon." The convoy had to halt in Marseilles long enough to make repairs to the cars before moving on. Dos Passos and Fairbanks had time for a fine meal of bouillabaisse, then they and Lawson went to a vaudeville show, where the acts on stage and the ease with which Lawson and Fairbanks found attractive women reminded him of his own abashedness. Later, a scene at a café at the edge of the harbor amused and amazed him: "The café of the acrobatic waitresses oh god oh Montreal what a *spectacle.*" The women had a talent for lifting their skirts and seizing with their labia majora pennies the customers would put on the corners of their tables. The waitresses were as casual about it as if, like waitresses in a Boston restaurant, they were courteously serving their customers. The performance seemed unshocking somehow; there was an "utter casuality" about it. "Bah," he wrote in his journal to calm his excitement over the bawdy scene, "one has seen it every day of ones life."

The convoy's amusing problems continued: before leaving Marseilles one of the ambulances burned up in a square, and Dos Passos, never a sure driver, struck another car as he tried to back his into line. Once out of Marseilles, the ambulance drivers took a route through the small town of Brignoles, inland from Toulon, then through Cannes and along the Côte d'Azur toward Italy. At the Italian border town of Ventimiglia the section received a warm welcome, because the Italians believed that the appearance of the Americans preceded the large-scale entrance of the U.S. into the war in Italy, something that never occurred. The drive from the border along the Italian Riviera toward Genoa was beautiful, for the road was "wonderfully dangerous . . . winding among brown cliffs and through steep olive gardens and terraced gardens where white pergolas held up the vines arching paths that led to the doors of preposterous pink and mauve and ochre-colored villas with pea-green shutters." For two days the convoy dipped and climbed along this road at the edge of the Mediterranean, then at Genoa turned inland and halted for a night at Pontedecimo, "a cold and miserable village" just north of the city.

That evening Lawson and Dos Passos rode a trolley the fifteen kilometers into Genoa. The city at night was fascinating, particularly since an oil tanker was burning in the harbor, illuminating the tower and façades of the painted houses in the old city above the port with "a pearly pink glow." The scene stayed with Dos Passos. Several days later he tried out a descriptive sentence in his journal: "a pearly rose glow lit up the pedimented façades of the houses on the hill and the square pointed church tower that rose above them, etching them curiously against the dark hills —behind the town where the lights along streets dotted out new constellations to match those in the brilliant night sky." The image of the harbor was powerful; the sentence, he soon decided, was overdone.

He and Lawson were entranced by the teeming life in Genoa. Old, narrow streets down near the water carried one back into the Middle Ages, a time, he imagined, when the streets would have been packed with "shrines and oaths and meaningful whistles and women leaning seductively from high balconies, and foot-steps lost about sudden dark turns." Drunken sailors, bawdy songs, sensuous women, and orchestras playing "wonderfully noisy Offenbach," *strega* and ices, the ornate marblework above doorways, and the sculpted lions before the colored marble façade of the cathedral of San Lorenzo gave Genoa a carnival atmosphere. The two Americans remained until everything had closed down and the trolleys had stopped running; then they walked the distance back to Pontedecimo. Their hotel was barred, so for what remained of the night they huddled together in a doorway along with Gouverneur Morris, who had drunk too much and likewise missed getting into his room.

Despite a clutch in Fiat IV that would not disengage, necessitating that they stall the car whenever they had to stop, Dos Passos and Fairbanks along with the rest of the convoy soon reached Milan, a "ponderously dull city . . . a city of bankers that might be Denver, Colo., for any charm or beauty," Dos Passos decided. The section was scheduled to leave for the front along the Piave by December 13, 1917. In the meantime the drivers were housed in the Hotel Cavour, a luxurious, if cold, hotel off the public gardens. Despite the dreariness of the city and the weather— it snowed shortly after the section arrived in Milan—Dos Passos found that "Italia and the south and the ancient dream" were not totally lost. Hints of Roman culture and of the Renaissance abounded, while even in the coldest weather women sold flowers—"yellow Solferino roses and chrysanthemums and carnations"—reminding him of the warm south.

If in Paris Dos Passos had his sexual adventure, in Milan he balked at going whoring, as he declared his friends were doing. Together they would see a musical, then proceed from there, while Dos Passos, half yearning to join them in their adventures, could not bring himself to participate. The most temporary love affair might have some import, he told himself; still, seeking after prostitutes differed little from seeking "a barrel with a bunghole in it," which was not worth the trouble. So while his friends had their short affairs, Dos Passos hung back. "I've just been dining with Fairbanks & his whore," he wrote one evening in his journal. The girl was in fact no prostitute, and Dos Passos's hauteur, despite his attraction for her that was obvious to Fairbanks when they were in her company, revealed his defensiveness, even jealousy, in such a situation. A moment later, after commenting about one of Lawson's frequent sexual adventures, in this case one where Lawson had meanly evaded sleeping with a girl who liked him, Dos Passos scribbled in his journal, "What marvellously brutal people are the clever & radical young like Jack & Van! I suppose I'm as bad in my supercilious way—Youth is a hideous period—from some aspects —C'est un horrible gâchis [mess], la vie des hommes." Shy, even inept around women except about making conversation, Dos Passos chose to wander the streets of Milan, browsing in bookstores, or reading and working at his writing that centered on the months in France, an intense period which would remain vividly in his mind for the rest of his days, shaping what he became as a writer. During the months in Italy, he had the time to digest his first encounters at Verdun and in wartime Paris and began to write about them, while through conversations with Lawson, Poore —after he joined the section in February 1918—and to a lesser extent, Fairbanks, van den Arend, and some of the others, he worked toward achieving a style suited to what he meant to convey.

He read voraciously among the many volumes he had brought with him. Poore recalled the two of them buying books in Paris for the trip to Italy before Dos Passos's section left in November. Then during his wanderings in Milan he pored over the Italian literature in the bookstalls of the Galleria Vittorio Emanuele adjacent to the cathedral. He grew excited by the writings of the Italian Futurists.

Reading these then was important, as it was a way to bring together his ideas about the war, the new technological age, satire, and the need to be active and protesting. Further, Dos Passos thought constantly about modern painting. The previous fall he had studied art in Spain; while in New York he had become acquainted with American modernists, and now in Italy he had a second chance—his first had been during his grand tour in 1912—to absorb the nation's magnificent and varied culture while he sought a synthesis of the arts that could express his feelings.

Chief among the Italian Futurists was F. T. Marinetti, a Milanese poet, novelist, and essayist whose Futurist Foundation Manifesto in 1909 had been the basis for the movement. Although Futurism began as a literary movement, it had its greatest effect in visual art and was closely linked to Cubism and subsequent movements like Dadaism, Surrealism, Constructivism, and Social Realism. The Futurists were fascinated with contemporary technology: "a racing car," Marinetti asserted, "is more beautiful than the *Victory of Samothrace.*" They were, nevertheless, critical of contemporary culture although they believed that artistic creation should be something as public as a race or a political rally. "Futurism," wrote the art critic Harold Rosenberg, "replaced the artist as bohemian—identified by his guitar, his wine bottle, and his harlequin mask—with the artist as adventurer and cultural agitator; more exactly, with the artist band united by social, philosophical, and aesthetic precepts intended to put them in the van of society as men of the world."

Such a movement attracted Dos Passos. He had a keen interest in contemporary art; he was both drawn to and repelled by burgeoning industrial society; and he sought eagerly to abandon any sort of shallow bohemian aestheticism and to agitate against a complacent culture. Thus while he might want to retire with his guitar and his wine bottle after experiencing what he had called the gas waves of stupidity, he felt impelled to assault the barricades of convention.

When the section left Milan for the front on December 13, 1917, as scheduled, Dos Passos remained behind, because the Fiat still needed repairs, so he waited and waited. Milan had gained no charm during his stay. Three days after the others departed, he lamented his fate to Poore. Stuck in Milan, "a dullness and staleness and a boredom," he was utterly sick of it. The rest of the section were headed to Dolo, a town between Padua and Venice. "I o rage o desespoir am waiting for the Fiat I'm on to have its referendum—I mean its differential mended—I am too bored to read and too bored to write and I am cold and the Cathedral annoys me, Oh God oh Montreal. The picture galleries are closed and the Last Supper is shut up in an abri. . . ."

The days dragged on. Four days later he still waited to leave, passing the time by writing Marvin about his plight "in the worst of verse." His "Bad Ballad of Milan" first recounted the trip down from Paris—"O I have come out of the North countree / On roads that climb from the mist of the Loire"—until he entered "the bankers city desolate." At this point he wrote, "Incipit the Dirge of Milan to be dolefully chanted or keened." The dirge, a lament about waiting in Milan instead of in some more romantic spot, had a refrain that ran,

"Fiat 4, Fiat 4,
Oh mechanician of Milano,
When will she roll my Fiat 4?"
"Piano, signore, va piano."

More delays followed, but by December 30 he had caught up with his section, which still waited for further orders. The life was not hard for the drivers, just slow, because there was little work to do, stationed as far back from the front as they were. Their quarters were a villa on the Venetian side of Dolo. He and others of the section were together in a room that had in it "two beds, three camp cots, piles of blankets and kitbags and miscellaneous confusion."

Dolo was the drivers' base for several weeks, which frustrated them because, friends though they were, too much living together in cold, crowded conditions and too little action became cloying. "The Italian government considers the A.R.C. ornamental but not useful," Dos Passos wrote McComb on December 31. "So here we languish well treated, well fed, gazing sentimentally at the Euganean Hills, and wandering to the border of the lagoon to gaze at Venice—where we are not allowed to go, for some subtle reason. Oh God the ennui of our rather gilded slavery." The most exciting thing that happened was an occasional air raid at night, when exploding bombs lit up the sky, searchlights pierced the night, and shrapnel arched through the air, while in the background one heard the drone of airplane engines.

As 1917 drew to an end, Dos Passos thought back over the year: "The last minutes of the seventeenth abortion of an abortive century are flying and the obstetrics of the New Year are at hand," he wrote in his journal. A year earlier he had been in Cartagena, romantic with its "dark Phoenician streets with latticed bays & big bird cages and shrill whistling of birds—and the ruined castle on the hill where the gypsies lived." Since then much had happened to make sense of: his father's death, "those beastly months in New York—and the Rabelaisian roister of the summer on the fringes of death's dull carmagnole." He still had not sorted out these experiences in his mind and sometimes felt blown in one direction or another like a weathervane, but as he had written to Marvin the day before, it was "curious, but I have to admit—that I never had a more interesting year."

The one constant was his hatred of cant and hypocrisy, which seemed to be centered in governments. When two Red Cross majors reeled drunkenly into the drivers' quarters to wish them a Happy New Year, Dos Passos grew furious at what they said. The section was in Italy more for propaganda than for work, the Italian officials' idea being that this show of support would encourage the Italian soldiers to remain in the trenches. "God," he exploded, "it made you want to vomit to hear it." He would do his job, but privately he found officialdom more and more an anathema, and he thought of himself increasingly like Sinbad in a popular ballad of the time that Fairbanks had quoted to him, to his great delight:

Sinbad was in bad
In Tokyo and Rome

In bad in Trinidad
And twice as bad at home. *

While he waited impatiently for more excitement, he spent two nights early in January at a hospital in nearby Mestre, sitting with another driver, Coles Seeley, who was gravely ill with pneumonia. With time heavy on his hands, he began a long letter to Marvin, first praising his friend's latest poem, the best he had done yet. Still, words like "smooth'st," "azure heavens wide," or "lordly eagle" sounded like "dead Keats & Shelley" language. "Read Masefield Read Chaucer," he implored, to get a sense of language that is alive. Just then the lights in the hospital faded, and the church bells sounded an air raid warning. But nothing appeared in the evening sky, so Dos Passos returned to his letter.

He wrote Marvin that he had been unable to produce much verse, only some fragments, because he lacked conviction. But he might better have said that the last several months, for all their action, had been prosaic rather than poetic and that he was reacting against what he thought to be his earlier romanticism. He had been writing "copious notes of all sorts" and had been working on both a diary and the novel begun with Hillyer. "The first book is finished," he announced, then in detail told Marvin what it was about: The "infancy of Martin Howe—a sensitive child— nicknamed Fibbie from his habit of telling steep & impossible yarns." At school Howe becomes friendly with "a young fellow with a sceptical turn of mind" with whom he has the usual sorts of adventure.

Through the first book "runs the influence of a literary uncle & of a little French girl, Fibbie's nurse's daughter—whom the uncle finally has a liaison with." The uncle dies, but "that doesn't mean anything, any more than bald descriptions of events ever do," Dos Passos hastened to add. What was important was "a general undercurrent of the feeling that instead of Fibbie being the liar—it is Society—& the uncle is the sensitive soul which the world ends by killing." The uncle's influence remains over Suzanne, the French girl, and over Fibbie for the rest of the novel. Dos Passos had not yet decided whether the two should meet again, but in any case they would "buckle against the incomparable asininity of things in general—conventions, social ordinances, the lies of a civilization, living in the shell of a totally different way of life—now dead a hundred years or more." To describe the novel made it sound like rubbish, he feared, but he did not think it was. He knew that what he had written was still "crude & abrupt and jerky," since Lawson, van den Arend, and the others to whom he had read parts kept emphasizing the problem.

**Fairbanks, who admired Dos Passos's intellectual sophistication, took pleasure in reciting humorous verse to his co-driver. On another occasion he likened Dos Passos to the character in a jingle that went:*
  There was an old man of Thermopylae
  Who never did anything properly
  But they said "If you choose
  To boil eggs in your shoes
  You cannot remain in Thermopylae."
Dos Passos was amused by this, and as he increasingly expressed his dislike of officialdom and as his antics infuriated the Red Cross officers, he recognized that the verse pertained to him.

However, "it tries to state my present point of view towards things as vividly and frankly as possible."

As if to bring Dos Passos back into the present, Mestre was bombed later that night in what was the "jolliest" air raid Dos Passos had seen yet. He walked to the balcony of Seeley's room and watched the action: searchlights crisscrossing, antiaircraft guns firing, bombs exploding and shrapnel falling, and machine guns "tap-tapping."

After describing all this to Marvin the next day, he closed by urging Marvin not to join the Flying Corps, which offered money and kudos, and one could *faire la bombe* to the accompaniment of wine, women, and song. But death was a pretty certain thing, and there was "too much interesting on the orb of the world—for any such speeding up of existence to be necessary except for the very jaded." And besides, he mused, "the war is awfully poor sport—in any branch of the service," none of it "like being pursued across the Gobi desert by Tatar horsemen in flamingo-colored coats." Marvin should read Stendhal's *The Charterhouse of Parma*, Dos Passos thought, especially the first part about the romantic youth going to Waterloo. Then, thinking as much about himself as about Marvin, Dos Passos added, "Of course, I'm not saying that [the youth] wasn't glad afterwards that scepticism had followed experience, instead of preceding it."

When the ambulance section left for Bassano on January 6, 1918, Dos Passos and Fairbanks remained behind because, as usual, Fiat IV needed repairs. That was frustrating, but at least three days later while they still waited they had the chance to see Venice. The two of them reached Fusina, whence a steamer crossed the lagoon to Venice. On board the boat they were told that without some sort of permit they could not go ashore in Venice, so they stood in the bow of the steamer, admiring the view of the city as it loomed up before them. The next day in his journal Dos Passos described what they had seen: colors setting one another off, and as the boat approached Venice, the grays of the day and of the city at a distance becoming reds, greens, and oranges. Down canals as the steamer approached shore, Dos Passos caught glimpses of "the intricacy & charm of Venice." He let his mind run for a moment; these brief impressions he saw from aboard the steamer carried him into "the vast company whom Venice had . . . dragged out of the sordidness of life" for an instant. Something of a Coney Island sideshow was evident about the city, where there was "a vast & beautiful & varied vulgarity about it" that he liked. He felt moved to write a poem—one of his best, as it turned out:

> *Doges coming down to the sea*
> *To inspect wharves & cargoes*
> *To sniff with the noses of merchant princes*
> *The quality of peppers & spice bales*
> *That negro slaves are unloading*
> *Marmosets pulling at their velvet gowns*
> *Parrots shrieking on chrome-yellow bales*
> *Heat and a smell of ships*

And the sweat of galley slaves
And the rinds of the fruits of the orient
That drift in the green tide towards the Lido

.   .   .

Venice rises like a dream
Sharpening dull brains to the brilliance
Of the varied color of earth
Out of the sluggish lagoon
Of the popular imagination

This first effort was little more than the idea for the poem. Two days later he tried again, and eventually the language became imagistic and sharp. The second, vague stanza was dropped. Instead he ended with a three-line stanza:

And out on the green tide towards the sea
Drift the rinds of orient fruits
Strange to the lips, bitter and sweet.

Thwarted in his first attempt to see Venice, Dos Passos returned two days later, having on the intervening day hiked the thirty kilometers from Dolo to Padua and back. "Venice achieved," he exclaimed on January 11. He took "the usual gondola ride" amid façades of palaces, then visited the Doges' Palace and the Basilica of St. Mark. Many of the works of art had been removed to Florence because of the threat of invasion, and the weather was dreary and cold, so despite his earlier enthusiasm he now found Venice "totally dead—swathed in sandbags—shops & shutters closed, windows boarded up." Still, he decided, "There was enough life left in it to excite me considerable."

In Dolo after his trip he revised his poem about the Doges, then wrote another that became the title poem for *A Pushcart at the Curb,* his volume of verse published in 1922. Unlike the first poem, this one came easily; later he published it almost exactly as he had first scribbled it out:

My verse is no upholstered chariot,
Gliding oil-smooth on oiled wheels,
No swift and shining modern limousine
But a pushcart, rather . . .

A crazy creaking pushcart, hard to push
Round corners, slung on shaky patchwork wheels,
That jolts & jumbles over the cobblestones
Its very various lading:

A lading of Spanish oranges, Smyrnian figs
Flyspecked apples—perhaps of the Hesperides

Curious fruits of the Indies, pepper-sweet—
Stranger—choose & taste

On his birthday he was allowed to return to Venice to buy condensed milk for the drivers who remained in Dolo, giving him another chance to admire the beauty of the city and its surroundings. Later, though, bored by the lack of action, he asked himself what was the use of absorbing color impressions if he could not "follow it up by any reactive process." He feared he was a sponge, unable to create, while he desired "to plunge head down into the abyss & with huge arms measure off." Here he scratched a long line across his diary. "Damn," he closed, "I'll go to bed!"

On January 16 he and Fairbanks finally left Dolo, spending the night at Cittadella in the quarters of an English officer to whom they had given a ride, before arriving in Bassano the next day. The town, on the banks of the Brenta, is within view of Monte Grappa, where the Italian front had been drawn. Boredom was less of a problem there. The drivers evacuated wounded from the lines above Bassano and often were sent on runs to nearby Asolo. Close to their quarters, batteries fired salvos each morning, so once again Dos Passos was near combat, but not of the intensity of the previous summer.

The ambulance runs could be wild, like one of forty-odd kilometers from Asolo to Cittadella near the end of January. He and van den Arend drove early in the morning to Asolo, picked up wounded, and then headed to Cittadella. During the trip van den Arend ran into some horses, while Dos Passos managed to blow out the ambulance's lights. The exhaust pipe got so hot it glowed red, then broke, so that the flames shot out, menacing the gas lines. When they managed to deliver the wounded, they returned to Asolo for a breakfast of eggs and red wine, after which they climbed above the town, whence they could see around them mountains, foothills, and below, the mist-covered plain, a striking scene that by contrast made all the more poignant the absurdity of the war.

Thoughts like that, however, got people in trouble. At the end of January a driver in Section 1 by the name of Heine Krieger—"a young fellow of German parentage," Dos Passos noted—was forced to leave because Italian censors had found derogatory remarks about the Italians in letters he wrote. The authorities asked the Red Cross to arrest and court-martial him, but eventually he was asked only to resign. The charges against him were that he had divulged military information; that he had been critical of the Allies; and that, according to the American major in charge of the section, he had used "low language," a "low moral tone," in his letters. Dos Passos believed the incident in truth stemmed from Krieger's German ancestry—it was infuriating because it was foolish. He thought of Cummings's and Brown's misadventure and could only be disgusted about the bigotry and the mindless jingoism that produced it. The night before he wrote about the Krieger affair in his journal, he had commented that "the one thing that enslaves people more than any other to the servitude of war is nationalism—the patriotic cant . . . all the noxious influences of the world seem to have thrown their tentacles about it—Its the mask of all the tradegreed & the glory greed."

From America friends occasionally sent him clippings that reminded him of the patriotic cant at home. Stuck in his Bassano journal was a clipping from an issue of the *New Republic*, a letter to the magazine captioned "Is German Infectious?" The piece discussed a purported examination of whether prominent figures thought the teaching of German could harm children. "Perhaps a fourth of the notables interviewed saw no particular danger in continuing the teaching of the German language," the writer, Carl H. P. Thurston, concluded. And at about the same time he received an article taken from the *New York Times* magazine of December 30, 1917, entitled "Pacifism Diagnosed as Disease of the Mind," by Dr. Mary Keyt Isham. Her point was that pacifists have a psychological need to approve any form of subordination, because "deep under the upper crust of their personalities [is] concealed a seething desire to be completely, inevitably, relentlessly, unreservedly overwhelmed by a subjugation from which there [is] no escape." Unknown to themselves, they struggle against this desire. Thus "toward a Government which demands something, but not all, they grow hostile and even anarchists." Ultimately, they are unpatriotic because they refuse to accept responsibility.

Amid attitudes like these, Dos Passos knew that if he continued to write as he already had to his friends he might soon be in trouble. In March rumors passed through the section about persons who might be kicked out of Italy because of inflammatory letters or pro-German sentiment. It would be Lawson, van den Arend, or himself, Dos Passos was sure; "one of us must be [kicked out], as there is a rumor that there are three people in this section whose letters have been taken exception to by the Italian government." The situation was delicate, he noted, and now "the sword of Damocles" hung over him.

In February his difficulties still lay ahead. Meanwhile, the drivers made many runs whenever combat grew more intense. Their most important and frequent trip was to bring wounded soldiers off Monte Grappa, which involved navigating a treacherous, zigzag road that the Italians had constructed, largely by hand, during that same winter. Despite its steepness and sharp turns, the road had no guard rails, causing the drivers to accept readily the story that a camion had disappeared over the road's edge one night and plummeted down the mountains.

But the excitement of Monte Grappa was too rare to keep the drivers entertained. "We get spurts of active duty, long cold night rides," he wrote Marvin in mid-February, "but a great deal of the time you are free." Whenever he could, he took long walks toward the front lines, as when, early in February, he and van den Arend hiked from Bassano along the Brenta toward the mountains and a few days later walked almost ten miles toward the north from the town of Valstagna, close by Bassano. They passed through Italian defenses until a sentry stopped them and led them before a group of officers, who cordially served them Marsala and, later, white wine. While the Italians showed them their defensive positions, Dos Passos learned that he and van den Arend had been climbing for two hours along a road that the Austrians dominated from a nearby ridge. In retrospect their foolhardiness seemed amusing.

Their evenings in Bassano were enlivened by as many as three or four bombings a night. "One stands shivering in the window and watches the *searchlights* & the electric sparkle of machineguns and the great red flare of bombs that explode with a thunderous snarl that rips the horizon—and the shrapnel bullets and cases simply rain about our heads," Dos Passos wrote. A week later, he described going into Bassano to buy food and drink to celebrate the arrival of Dudley Poore and another driver, Fred Bird. While Dos Passos was buying some condensed milk, he noticed the clerk becoming agitated. The town had begun to be shelled, and the clerk scurried to close the storefront shutter. People bustled about the streets; some peddlers tried to pack up their fruits, but spilled them out along an arcade and down some steps onto the town piazza; then several French generals scrambled into a staff car that raced down a side street while they tried to get their caps on; a camion full of soldiers passed through the square and stalled, while a man trying to crank its engine slipped and fell before the engine started. Finally the truck hurried off, leaving the square empty as the shelling stopped, except for Dos Passos and three other ambulance drivers who remained, shrieking with laughter, waving their bottles of wine and devouring chocolate.

With Poore and Bird now among them, Dos Passos and his group were more spirited than ever. Poore was already a good friend of Dos Passos and van den Arend, while Fred Bird was a witty man who soon had the group laughing with droll remarks like those about an Italian woman he had an affair with. "I'll say she was good to me," he told his friends once. "She tucked me in her dead fiancé's pyjamas." While drunk another time he complained to the group, "She calls me Sasha and wants me to be a classical dancer. Hell, I don't want to be a classical dancer, I want to go into the grain business." Their humor extended further, as when in February Poore read about the death of Empress Tai-Tou of Abyssinia, which became the excuse for a mock wake. Constructing a large, black effigy with white eyes, they laid it out on Lawson's cot, cooked one of their many meals of eggs served with wine, and during a bombing recited poems around the effigy. For the occasion Dos Passos composed a "Rondel to our Lady of Abyssinia," which began:

> Our Lady lies on a brave high bed—
> On pillows of gold with gold baboons,
> On red silk deftly embroidered—
> O anger & eggs & candlelight—
> Her gold specked eyes have little sight.

He wrote out three more stanzas; then Poore added some lines, "*subjoineth the attendant and unhallowed Crew*":

> The omelet's done
> The bombing's begun
> O we'll eat five thousand eggs
> Till we can't stand on our legs
> Bombarding's fun

> *If you don't run*
> *But sit in your abris of omelets & wine*
> *While outside the shrapnel-splinters whine*

His lines ended,

> *And you may be sure you'll grow no skinnier*
> *Although there'be mickle grief within yer*
> *For the late deceased empress of free Abyssinia*

Finally, Sydney Fairbanks contributed "A Mackeronick Dirge to the Late Deceased Empress of Abyssinia" that started:

> *L'Impératrice vient de mourir—*
> *Anger and eggs and the candles gleaming—*
> *Once again the planes are here*
> *Hear the sirens screaming.*

Its fifth and last stanza read,

> *L'âme errante dans la nuit—*
> *Seek we cause for laughing, wearily*
> *Dont le vent fait morne bruit*
> *God but the game goes drearily!*

While they awaited calls for service, egg feasts and drinking were frequent. Four days after the wake for Tai-Tou, Dos Passos, too full of what had become the steady diet of the section, grumbled that the drivers had made up for the bad food by having feasts of eggs "fried, boiled, shirred, scrambled, and indeterminate. The egg is," he decided, "undoubtedly the rex and imperator of foods," and he wrote a poem, "Voluptà in Zabaglione," about that rich Italian dessert of eggs, sugar, and wine, "Champagne-colored,/ Deepening to tawniness . . ./ Thick to the lips and velvety/ Scented of rum and vanilla/ Oversweet, oversoft, overstrong," that he had had too much of, along with the heavy, sweet Sicilian wine, Marsala. Such fare induced a deep languor and dreams of Venus until abruptly, "One goes/ And pukes beautifully beneath the moon,/ Champagne-colored."

Several nights later Dos Passos suffered acutely from too much Marsala. Having already drunk a good deal of it on an empty stomach after returning cold and wet from an ambulance run to the village of Carmignano, he began to drink a liter more. After downing it, he dramatically recited poetry for his friends, then started for bed, only to have the room whirl around him. Miserable, he vomited, and a short time later, Fairbanks, also drunk, decided that he would prove he was sober by wriggling on his stomach into the room where Dos Passos, Poore, and Lawson were conversing. Ingloriously Fairbanks crawled through the vomit to everyone's amusement, and "laughter dissolved into sleep with a sensation like going down a shoot the chute," as Dos Passos wrote the next night.

Such cavorting did not impress the Red Cross authorities. The group of friends got a reputation among the other drivers for being, if not troublemakers, then at least eccentrics. Months later Dos Passos got a letter from Ed Massey, saying that he had been talking with someone who was in Section 1 after Dos Passos and his friends had left. Among the section the group was notorious for its antics, which without a doubt did as much to get Dos Passos in trouble as did his letters.

By the middle of March as he prepared for a two-week leave, he was sure the authorities were after him. "The hounds are on the scent," he wrote in his journal. He wondered what his choices were: "Jump into Vesuvius with a case of lacrimae Cristi? Enlist—would to God I thought I could manage it—as a brancardier [stretcher-bearer] in the foreign legion?—Or Spain?—to find peace somewhere where one can write and read and draw and let the damn world go to ruin—." He did not know what to do and had half a sense that he had little choice in the matter. Frustrated, he closed his entry,

     Damn   —   Damn
   Damn   Damn   Damn
   Damn   Damn

The next morning Dos Passos put these concerns out of his mind and with Poore, Lawson, van den Arend, Bird, Fairbanks, and another driver, Fred Bragg, left Bassano. Their first stop was Bologna, where Dos Passos admired the colors and shapes of the buildings, "orange houses and green shutters—great smooth wall places of orange and umber and pale yellow and grey—and brick arcades and carved windows—and in the midst the drunken leaning towers—the red tower of the Asinelli shooting heavenwards with a wonderful soar." As they toured the Cathedral San Pietro, the Palazzo di Rienzo, and the churches of San Petronio and Santo Stefano, they were much taken with an old woman who guided them, keeping up all the while a commentary in an appalling mixture of Italian, French, and English.

Dos Passos recalled having "a rich meal of spaghetti and some kind of little birds washed down with dark dark wine." Since their leave papers listed their destination as Paris, the stationmaster at Bologna directed them to an express for France. But they avoided that and instead boarded a smoky, crowded train for Rome, where they arrived the next morning after a cramped trip. They walked about the old part of the city, then in the afternoon took a carriage out along the Appian Way. On the third day of their leave they strolled about Rome some more, and Dos Passos, Poore, van den Arend, and Lawson planned how they might break away from the other three, whom Dos Passos called the *incubi* at moments when he felt they were clinging too closely.

All of them headed south to Naples on board a train that passed through "shadowy Alban hills and the faint green and tan landscape of Romagna, then through a wide flat valley in the Apennines, the mountains getting rougher and bleaker all the time." In Naples, they saw Vesuvius smoking off to the east and had time to ride a lift up behind the city to look back over the Mediterranean coastline. The next day, while Lawson stayed behind in Naples and Bird, Fairbanks, and Bragg went their own way, van den Arend, Poore, and Dos Passos walked down to the harbor to try to find a boat going to Sorrento, across the Bay of Naples. Finding none, they began the long walk to Pompeii, finishing the journey by catching a train that ran around the base of Vesuvius. They arrived late in the afternoon, so no one else was around, and they were free to "wander delightfully about the ruins in a sparkling wind full of the odor of almond blossoms." While they were preoccupied with the ruins, the gates to the site were locked for the night—but this only added to their excitement. After dark they scaled the fence that bordered Pompeii, then found nearby a trattoria, the Albergo del Sole, where they savored a meal in a small arbor outside the restaurant.

The meal, Dos Passos thought afterward, was his first "lyric" one since Paris, but that was due as much to the beautiful setting and the pleasure of being free as to the food and wine. The next morning before the three began a hike to Castellammare, Dos Passos noted in his journal some of the things he remembered most vividly: among them a statute of Artemis and the house of the Vettii, which displayed, he remarked a bit pompously, the "Puery Roman Taste" because on a vestibule wall was a painting of a "man weighing his penis against a money bag." Days later he recalled "the beauty of incidental decoration and of small bronzes" and asserted that the erotic paintings on the walls of what had been a whorehouse were "the best drawn things in Pompeii."

The distance from there to Castellammare is about five kilometers, which the three friends walked in time for lunch before taking a trolley as far as the small town of Meta, where they debarked to hike across the Sorrentine peninsula to Positano for the night. The afternoon walk was magnificent, "one of the most glorious walks in my life," so good as to be indescribable, Dos Passos wrote. He began a letter to Marvin that evening, still enraptured by the hike, which had taken them "along a road that hung on the cliffs above the sea." Almond blossoms, anemones, and a myriad of other flowers along the way were "too marvellously beautiful" to describe; yet the beauty of Positano was even more striking. Set in a valley that descends to the Mediterranean along what is now called the Amalfi Drive, Positano rises up a steep slope. During the day its houses, some with gaily decorated domes, show brilliantly in the clear sunlight and are marked off by flights of steps which crisscross between the buildings. "I'm overwhelmed and smothered in beauty," he wrote as he sat looking out across the town, "sight and smell and the soft wind off the sea in your ears." All this had made his dinner one of the best ever, a simple meal of "risotto, omelet, cheese & such oranges as the 'apples' of the Hesperides must have been." In this mood he discovered an entire countryside in the light red wine he had drunk, lyricizing to Marvin that it was "full of the brisk hills and the great exhilarating spaces of the sea, and the smell of thyme and gorse and almond blossom and rosemary and basil and lavender from the fields that make little ribbons of velvet among the shaggy rocks."

His pleasure grew even greater as the three hiked the next day to Amalfi, halting only long enough to admire its square, dominated by a historic cathedral. They continued to Ravello, in the hills above Amalfi, then walked down along the coast through Minori and Maiori before stopping in the small seaport of Cetara, set in a cove dominated by a Saracen tower that perched on one point of land. Here they found a house whose occupants, an aged couple, served them dinner: two dozen eggs at least, Poore was sure, and bread and wine. Dos Passos struck up a friendship with the couple that was carried on by postcard for many years. After the meal and tired already, the three walked beyond Cetara to Vietri Sul Mare, which they did not reach until nearly midnight. Here they found a café and, exhausted, began to drink coffee while flirting with some girls. Finally they took a room, but their excitement and the coffee made sleep difficult, particularly as their straw mattresses were hard and the owner's chickens shared their room with them.

Early the following morning they took a train along the coast through Salerno to a spot near Paestum, the site of what had once been Poseidonia, a prosperous Greek colony. The train stopped to let them off close to the site, so they could walk down a trail that led them to the broad, flat beach nearby. They stripped off their clothes and plunged into the clear water, then dressed and walked back to the site of the ancient city, whose ruins from the Greek period are some of the best preserved in the world. No one was around, so just as at Pompeii the place was theirs, except for some sheep grazing on the grass among the temples and broad stone streets which weave through the ruins. They spent the rest of the day at Paestum, Dos Passos "in the state of prostrate worship Greek things always put me into," he later wrote Marvin. Such an emotion there is understandable. Always, but particularly in the early spring, the grass is rich, filled with violets and blossoming bushes that surround the large Greek temples. The bright sun and clear air have preserved the stone, so a remarkable proportion of three major temples still stands, two of them "a glorious burnt orange" and the third a clean whitish-gray.

After hours of roaming through the ruins and basking in the warm meadows around them, the three found a house nearby. An old woman who lived there fed them some spicy cheese, bread, and wine while innocently inquiring if they might know her son, who had emigrated to America and now lived in Brooklyn. Afterward, as they were about to leave Paestum, Lawson drove up in a horse-drawn cab that he had taken the forty kilometers from Salerno. He regaled them with tales of his amours in Naples, while they wandered again among the temples. It began to rain, so the four of them hurried into Lawson's cab and drove back toward Salerno, boarding a train for Naples that same night. From there they headed straight to Rome, then took a train to Florence, where they spent the last part of their leave before returning to Bassano on March 31.

When he got back to the section, Dos Passos had mail from America awaiting him. Cummings, released from La Ferté Macé and back in Cambridge, Massachusetts, had written at the end of January, describing to Dos Passos his misadventures with the French authorities. He wrote about his and Slater Brown's arrest and subsequent internments in concentration camps, his for eleven weeks, Brown's supposedly for the duration of the war. (In fact, by the end of February he too had been released and sent home.) Cummings was ill from the effects of La Ferté Macé but was improving, he as red his friend. He added with a touch of mimicry of official jargon that everyone—which meant mutual friends like Hillyer—said that Dos Passos was a hero, a fearless and exemplary driver who played baseball with the 155-mm artillery. And he closed his letter by telling how much he yearned for "la Ville Immense, la Ville Réale, la Femme Superbe et Subtile qui s'appelle—tu le sais —Paris." In his letter he also asked Dos Passos to send Brown cigarettes or postcards if he could, although of course this would have been useless, as Brown had been freed before Dos Passos received Cummings's letter.

Dos Passos did attempt to help Brown, but had no success. Hearing from Cummings increased his fury against authority, that and knowing he was being watched by the Red Cross. "Of course people have always called out against the servitude of their lives," he wrote in his journal in early April, "but we, today, do seem particularly enslaved. . . . There has never been a time when a person who despised & detested the world's phrases and turpitudes and heroisms was so utterly bound."

The day before he wrote this, he had received a cable from his uncle and aunt, the Gordons, asking him to come home at once to America. The executors may have sensed something awry in the way Dos Passos's Aunt Mamie Gordon was transacting her trusteeship of his share of the estate. Whatever the cause, they refused to renew an agreement that had to do with administering the estate. Dos Passos had no real interest in the matter, however, and could not even remember what the agreement was.

He was of no mind to return to the United States as long as there was more to experience, although he was tired of being ordered from one village to another with little service to perform. His detestation of officialdom grew when he spoke to Italian enlisted men, observed the sometimes cruel, haughty attitudes of the officers, or read books like Alfred de Vigny's *Servitude et Grandeur militaire,* written more than eighty years before, which told of "the Napoleonic sort of wars, where people fought for kudos and for personal devotion and for strange outworn stupidities, but stupidities that had a charm and a halo of belief about them." Men of de Vigny's time, Dos Passos thought, could not have conceived of modern warfare in which everyone was caught up and "in which the trader has dressed himself up in the old outworn armor." Financial greed motivated men's actions, Dos Passos had come to believe, so that behind all the present pomp and rhetoric lurked "the murky factory chimneys that are our world's God." The world had become the victim of petty tyrannies, he concluded the next day after he was ordered down from a steeple in the village of Borgo, where he had found a comfortable perch to write in. Now everywhere there were the equivalents of "little bumptious sergeants [who were] chasing poor devils off the steeples that afford them the only spots in a crowded world where they can think and look at their poor stock of dreams."

Despite his boredom he was working hard on "Seven Times Round the Walls of Jericho." By mid-April he had finished part two and outlined the third part, which was to express ideas like "the slow realization of the oppression of government," "the realization of slavery," and to describe scenes drawn from his own experiences during the past months in the war, "pictures of the war front," "glimpses of Paris," "Pinard —cigarettes," "Night under gas," "the shelled roads," and "Atrocities—the mountain of lies." Ultimately his war experiences became a fourth part and were cast as a separate work that became *One Man's Initiation: 1917*.

Amid his general depression about the war, he occasionally saw a possibility for change, as he did one evening after talking with three other members of Section 1, one of whom, although favoring the war, was basically against militarism. "I suddenly became tremendously hopeful," Dos Passos wrote, because "here were three people—Americans out of totally different environments all absolutely determinedly against the machine that has been crushing us all." He did not know what could encourage the struggle against the machine. "I suppose one should do something conspicious if possible," he wrote, then added, "I hate conspicuousness."*

Dos Passos's dark mood that spring led him deeper into trouble with the authorities. The latter part of April he took a two-day leave to Milan, never his favorite city, and from there he wrote Arthur McComb, who had taken a job with the American diplomatic service in Spain after leaving Harvard. Dos Passos lamented the ugliness of Milan, then told his friend to look up José Giner in Madrid, whom he was writing on McComb's behalf. The letter to Giner was no harsher than others he had written earlier, but it was intercepted by the censors and turned over to Red Cross authorities.

What Dos Passos wrote Giner was that war, no matter where, consisted of boredom, slavery to all sorts of military stupidities, an interesting sort of misery, and the need for warmth, bread, and cleanliness. He assured Giner that there was nothing beautiful about modern warfare. He had seen it for nearly a year, he remarked, and any illusions had vanished. It was no more than an enormous, tragic digression in people's lives which brought death to the intellect, to art, to everything that mattered; and only people like Giner, who worked for revolution, remained to protect the good things of life. Others struggled suicidally because avaricious nations were caught up in a world drunk with commerce. Throughout the Western world, with the exception of Spain and a Russia now in the throes of revolution, Dos Passos saw only slavery to industry, money, and business. Even America, he feared, had

---

*These comments revealed a pattern to his life. Thoroughly committed to speaking out against whatever he saw to be "atrocities—the mountain of lies," he nevertheless hated conspicuousness. And so he would write One Man's Initiation: 1917; Three Soldiers; U.S.A.; The District of Columbia trilogy, Midcentury, and other satiric chronicles, or he would speak out in the New Masses and later, in the National Review. Yet having expressed himself in print, he would seem to disappear suddenly from the scene, would decline to make a speech on behalf of some cause he supported, or would stammer a polite demurrer when challenged face-to-face about a point. His politically committed friends would be puzzled, and his admirers dismayed. He was not a public man. Only with effort, and only through his writing, could he speak out. A part of the reason his satire was so often grim, so seldom funny, was the fact that only through his writing could he express the fury he felt toward injustices as he saw them. Edmund Wilson once asked him in genuine puzzlement how it was that someone who liked people so much and was so warm personally could write such harsh, gray satire. The answer was that he saved his rage for his writing. Thus it sometimes became hyperbole, stinging and provocative, even shrill.

extinguished liberty with its new conscription law. The plutocrats had triumphed.*

Before the issue of this letter came to a head, Dos Passos served out the rest of his enlistment. He cont᠎ ᠎ued to evacuate wounded from villages around Bassano, in weather that in late April was cold and wet, while about the villages hung "a smell of soggy soup and shitten hillsides and miserable soldiers." He grew even more disgusted with some of the Italian officers, who, he learned from Dudley Poore, insulted and abused a peasant girl to the point that Poore thought she was going to be raped. The next morning the officers were incensed when they heard a rumor that the girl had slept with a corporal. Dos Passos abhorred their "swinish uppishness." "God they are a nasty crew," he fumed, "even the rather decent ones have the same disease—their overbearing nastiness to anyone they dont lick the boots of is disgusting."

Such incidents were not isolated; he knew of a Sardinian lieutenant kicking a sergeant around a room, and of a subsequent feud between the lieutenant and his captain, who ordered the junior officer to pick up trash around the quarters of an ambulance section. When the lieutenant refused, he was ordered arrested, but countered by filing complaints against the captain. Amid these squabbles, Dos Passos had some last, interesting conversations with various Italians about what would happen after the war. The people, especially a "pleasant Bourgeois captain"; a lieutenant, "a woozy looking young fellow with a clever aquiline nose"; a "flaccid red lieutenant"; and a "curious ecclesiastic, Dom Pietro," gave him the idea for some of the characters in *One Man's Initiation: 1917* when he began several months later what was first part four of "Seven Times Round the Walls of Jericho."

Years afterward Dos Passos wrote that just before being released from duty when his enlistment was up at the end of May, he crossed paths briefly with Ernest Hemingway, who had just arrived at Schio with Section 4 of the Red Cross ambulance. Sydney Fairbanks and Dos Passos often transported wounded to a hospital nearby, where they would eat with Section 4; and Hemingway and Dos Passos recalled talking on one occasion. Fairbanks remembered the meeting. He felt excluded from the conversation, but noticed that Dos Passos and Hemingway understood each other immediately; the latter, though opinionated, was impressive even then.†

When Dos Passos, Poore, van den Arend, Fairbanks, and perhaps Lawson—although he may have preceded them by a short while—were released at Bassano, they traveled first to Vicenza before heading south. Their ultimate destination was Rome, where they planned to get new assignments with the Red Cross, Dos Passos hoping that he might be sent to Greece. He thought on the other hand he might

*When Dos Passos was later confronted with this "incriminating" letter by Red Cross officials, his first response was, "Gosh, that was a good letter!"

† That this meeting occurred seems doubtful on the basis of evidence presented in Carlos Baker's biography of Hemingway, according to which, by June 6 Hemingway had not yet arrived at Schio, but was temporarily in Milan, while Dos Passos, according to evidence among his papers, was released from Section 1 on May 30 and immediately left for Rome. But since both writers, and Fairbanks as well, remembered the occasion, it appears that someone's recording of dates was inexact.

forgo any service and travel to Spain to see McComb and to escape officialdoms of every sort. At Vicenza, the others left Fairbanks, who returned to Milan while they enjoyed themselves, halting at Bologna, Pistoja, Lucca, Pisa, San Gimignano, Siena, and Orvieto. Each city had something that delighted Dos Passos: in Pistoja an Ospedale del Ceppo and a frieze by della Robbia; in Lucca the churches "wonderfully alive and beautiful"; in Pisa the leaning tower and the Campo Santo; in San Gimignano the towers which added to its medieval appearance. Siena and Orvieto likewise had preserved their medieval tone, causing Dos Passos to plunge himself romantically into Italian art and culture before arriving at Rome, where he would have to deal with the charges of disloyalty that had been brought against him during his last weeks at Bassano.

In Rome, he spent almost two weeks attempting to clear up the imbroglio with the Red Cross. He recalled that the official at the Red Cross headquarters to whom he spoke was Major Guy Lowell, one of the officers who had annoyed him by his drunken New Year's speech back at Dolo. Lowell recommended that Dos Passos return to the United States as quickly as he could. When he asked Lowell the reason, the major was silent, except to show him a copy of the letter to José Giner, and perhaps letters to McComb and others on behalf of Cummings and Slater Brown as well.

Jack Lawson, less seriously implicated in the disloyalty charge than Dos Passos, remained in Rome and took a job doing publicity for the Red Cross. This gave him access to various papers, among which he turned up a copy of the letter to Giner with the comments of an official named Bates on it. Bates had recommended to Lowell that Dos Passos be dishonorably discharged, because, Bates asserted, he belonged to a "group of Pacifists in the section." Despite Bates's "repeated warnings, a general notice on the subject, the example of Heine [Krieger] who was discharged from their section, this man has still endangered the cordial relations existing between us and the Italians." Bates thought it was time for "another object lesson." As for the others—meaning Poore, van den Arend, and Lawson—there was less reason for action, except that due to their pacifism they ought not to be employed again by the Red Cross. In addition to Bates's note to Lowell, Lawson's copy of the letter had comments written in the margin. One that "the writer seems to possess some education but in his long letters uses expressions not in conformity with it," amusing as it is, suggests that Dos Passos, like Krieger before him, was found guilty of a low moral tone.

When Dos Passos reached Rome, he first thought his group was "managing to prove [their] innocence to the Red Cross officials," he told McComb. The others did, but he could not, so he and Major Lowell agreed that he ought to go to Paris to try to settle his affair with the Red Cross officials. After days during which he made excursions like long walks along the Appian Way and had evenings of good operas—Bellini's *Norma*, Donizetti's *L'Elisir d'Amore*, and Verdi's *Aïda*—he hated to leave the "almost unbelievable mellowness of Rome," where there was a "feeling of endless age, a mellowness of disillusion in which all crude bright things have burned themselves away in a wonderful selfpossession of pale eternity." He wired his Aunt Mamie Gordon that he had been "falsely accused" and pleaded with her to help him find a new enlistment through her contacts in Washington, as enlistment began to appear to ' e the only way he could clear his name and remain in Europe. Then the night of June 20 he said goodbye to his friends before boarding a train alone for Paris, stopping along the way in Turin, where he enjoyed the opera *Tosca.*

In Paris, he went immediately to the restaurant named the Rendezvous des Mariniers along the Quai d'Anjou on the Île St. Louis. He had met the owners, a family named Lecomte, the previous fall and had become a close friend. Now he took a room above their restaurant. It was an excellent spot to be, historic and scenic, overlooking the Seine and Pont Marie, and while the threat of a dishonorable discharge was distracting, the Quai d'Anjou and the rest of Paris were so pleasant that Dos Passos was able to work hard. His mind was on writing once more. When Marvin made what Dos Passos considered some "fatheaded" remarks about free verse, he told him they were just that and asked, "What the devil does it matter what one calls it?—I'm perfectly willing to have it called syncopated prose of hypersulfate magnesium. I break it into lines because I want the pauses to come in certain places and ordinary punctuation will not quite do—That is virtually why 'regular' poetry is broken up into lines." Even in most of the "regular" poetry since the Elizabethan era, he realized, line breaks meant nothing, and he added, "You'll find that Milton is written in paragraphs." Swinburne was "one of the few poets I know who keeps the value of the break at the end of the line." To demonstrate what he was saying, he wrote out for Marvin two of his own poems, one describing a scene in Tivoli, the other, the church Saint Germain in Paris.

The city sometimes seemed empty and sad to him, but there was activity and excitement nonetheless. The Germans conducted air raids against Paris almost nightly and shelled it by day with a long-range gun located near Laon, 130 kilometers away. The shells took five minutes to arrive, so in Paris criers would shout out a warning as soon as word came in by telephone that the gun, often referred to as Big Bertha, had been fired. Parisians died, but, Dos Passos wrote, the French "insisted on treating Bertha as a joke. They laughed cynically when little President Poincaré turned up promptly after each explosion to congratulate the survivors." Dos Passos recalled watching a shell explode in the Seine while he was browsing among the bookstalls along the quays. Immediately fishermen pushed out into the river in their boats and netted the scores of stunned fish that floated to the surface. "I'm in the path, I'm in the path of the big cannon," the French sang defiantly in their nightclubs.

During this time one of Dos Passos's companions was Kate Drain, a handsome, lively woman who had come to Paris the previous summer to work as a nurse's aide in the American Volunteer Hospital. Before Section 1 had departed for Italy the previous fall, Dos Passos had met her, and now he passed many hours at her apartment on the top floor of a building along the Champs Elysées. Dos Passos had regaled her with his tale of how on ambulance runs he would always stall his car at a certain crossroads near Chemin des Dames, a ridge line between Soissons and

Reims, and how all he could do was get out and laugh. In the summer of 1918, he again gathered with Kate Drain's friends at her apartment, where, she recalled, the others listened to him while he sat on the floor eating camembert cheeses as he read from "Seven Times Round the Walls of Jericho." After the friends remained one night until the early morning hours, she apologized to the concierge, who responded only, "But why didn't they stay the whole night?" Dos Passos was one who might have liked to, for he was strongly attracted to Kate Drain. But his reserve, if nothing else, stood in the way, and their friendship remained platonic.*

Dos Passos took time to lecture Marvin about "the Temptations of St. Anthony" and to try to counter "the Y.M.C.A. idea of the period of storm and stress in a young man's life when etc. etc." He reminded Marvin that life is a sweaty, semeny business and . . . one shouldn't be shocked by its commonplace mechanisms any more than by the digestive juices." The "leering hints of filth" that accompanied discussions of sex irritated him, for both "the muddiest monster and the most cream and white damosel" were human and fit company, if one but saw them right and knew the facts about matters like venereal disease.

There was time, also, to plan another book—something he then referred to as "The Letters of an Embusqué"—and to read. The projected book that was taking form in his mind came closest to being realized in *Three Soldiers* and *One Man's Initiation: 1917*, which were protests against conformity, repression, and war. Although in July he still did not realize that part four of "Seven Times" would be better if separate, his ideas for another book were what shaped that part and distinguished it from the earlier three. Something of what became his first collection of essays, *Rosinante to the Road Again*, may have been on his mind also, but he seemed to be thinking more of a polemic against "the system" than a study— granted partly political—of the character of Spain. At the same time he was reading James Joyce's *A Portrait of the Artist as a Young Man*, which, he noted on July 21, he had just finished for the second time. "Pray God I shant start imitating it off the face of the earth," he added. "I admire it hugely—It is so wonderfully succinct and follows such curious byways of expression—old abandoned roads that are overgrown but where the air is cleaner than in the modern dusty thoroughfares— constantly churned by people's footsteps."

Dos Passos's last days in Paris were exciting because, along with the air raids and shelling—which relented during July—the Germans mounted what turned out to be their last great offensive, a strike at the French lines from Château-Thierry to the south and the Argonne forest to the north. Between July 15 and 18 the Germans forged ahead, but at Château-Thierry French and American troops held them, and on the eighteenth the Allies counterattacked, driving the Germans back and essentially marking the end for them. The combat occurred only forty miles

---

*Kate Drain soon fell in love with Jack Lawson, and the issue of marriage arose in 1919 after she became pregnant. Lawson was not eager to take the step; before he eventually did, according to Dudley Poore, Dos Passos volunteered to marry her. The gesture suggests both Dos Passos's strong physical attraction to the beautiful woman and his romantic nature. The attraction was mutual. Late in her life, Kate Drain Lawson remarked that, while she had loved Lawson, Dos Passos was one man she would have married.

from Paris, so the wounded were transported there, where American authorities pleaded for persons on leave or off duty to aid. Dos Passos volunteered and served as a stretcher-bearer. He particularly remembered a night when his task was to "carry off buckets full of amputated arms and hands and legs from an operating room." Writing Marvin a short time later, he avoided any lurid details, but he admitted that it had exhilarated him; "doing 'unskilled' labor must make one lay hold on the elementary facts of existence in a wonderful way," was how he put it.

Before leaving Paris he had no success with the Red Cross authorities, who notified him that if he attempted to travel to Spain or Switzerland he would be arrested, and gave him the alternative of returning voluntarily to America to settle his case or being deported, so his hopes of enlisting in the army ambulance service and of a new assignment to Greece, Palestine, or somewhere else were thwarted. In August he traveled to Bordeaux, where on the eleventh he wrote Lawson from "a most gorgeous café with large painted ladies in green and gold and the sunlight scrumptiously hot and white outside." He lamented that "my bitching, my twilight, my soucis proceed." Nothing had availed, so "followed by a cortege of curses" he was sailing for America to throw himself "at the feet of Washington," hoping that he would "arise whiter and more patriotic than the lily and with the same attributes as to toiling and spinning." He was sailing on the *Espagne,* and he told Lawson to imagine him posing like Napoleon in the stern, poised to strike against his enemies, while dirges were chanted where "dismal will rhyme with abysmal, and howl with Lowell and hates with Bates and fetter with letter."

Aboard the *Espagne* he relaxed for a quiet voyage. Apparently he had adequate funds from his Red Cross wages and his small personal income, so he traveled first class for once, and there were few passengers aboard. The weather was good— "heavy moist gulfstream weather" he wrote Lawson from shipboard. He read a lot; *The Duchess of Malfi, The White Devil,* and the *Confessions* of Jean Jacques Rousseau were some of his fare. And he wrote furiously. "I have all but finished part four and last of the Roman Comique," he declared. The rest of "Seven Times" he had left behind with Dudley Poore in Paris, since he did not want to risk losing the entire manuscript were something to happen to the *Espagne.* How precisely he meant to draw upon his experiences is clear from his notes for chapter six of the fourth part, indicating that he intended to include scenes about troops passing on the Voie Sacrée, his sense of boredom, a road under bombardment, mules along a road struggling the morning after being gassed, barrages, a gas attack, and a priest and a doctor dining during a shelling.

But the languid atmosphere caused his pace to slacken, so eventually he set his narrative aside before finishing it. Amused by some of the people and events aboard ship, he struck up a brief friendship with a major general, an American, and was intrigued by a Y.M.C.A. man who explained to a Greek priest something about the origins of the organization. Most amusing, perhaps, was his friendship with an Episcopal chaplain, which resulted one Sunday in Dos Passos attending a church service and enduring "the hymn-droning and the brutal energy-worshipping sermon and the badly played Largo and all, and the prayer for the Allies and the thanking

of God for his efforts in deflecting submarines from the good ship *Espagne.*"
"Hurrah for the unapt," he began this entry in his journal. To cap the episode off,
he wrote, he even passed the plate.

While Dos Passos was returning to America on the *Espagne,* his former
headmaster at Choate, George St. John, sat down and, ignorant of the fact that his
former student was coming home, wrote him a letter. It was sent to Paris, so Dos
Passos did not receive it for several months. Well intentioned though St. John was,
his words reflected an idealism and a patriotism that Dos Passos now distrusted
profoundly. St. John told his erstwhile student that he had found some lines from
Richard II, spoken by John of Gaunt, the Duke of Lancaster, whose spirit corresponded with Dos Passos's and every other American's:

> *God in thy good cause make thee prosperous!*
> *Be swift like lightning in the execution,*
> *And let thy blows, doubly redoubled,*
> *Fall like amazing thunder on the casque*
> *Of thy adverse pernicious enemy.*
> *Rouse up thy youthful blood; be valiant and live.*

St. John went on to say that men like himself might soon join younger Americans;
he fervently wished he could. The place for older Americans seemed to be beside
the young like Dos Passos. St. John added another quotation which he thought
would have suited had the United States remained "blind and 'neutral.' " The gist
of the quotation was that had the nation not fought, it would have perished in its
security. He was utterly sincere in what he said; yet there is an irony that he wrote
just as Dos Passos, skeptical, even scornful of American attitudes, was returning
home under threat of a dishonorable discharge after a year of the boredom, horror,
and fear engendered by war.

CHAPTER ELEVEN

America and France Again, 1918–1919

As soon as he could after landing in New York in August 1918 Dos Passos took a train to Bay Head, New Jersey, to visit his cousins the Spriggs for several days. The incongruity between Bay Head, with its "little square houses in rows, the drugstores, the board walk, the gawky angular smiling existence of an American summerresort," and his life during the last year was appalling; there was a remarkable innocence and an opulence about American life. "Still," he reminded himself, "I love America— oh but the Hun-gabbling."

Along the beach he found a quiet spot to write in an old boat resting high and dry near the boardwalk. He was anxious to work on his novel, and at the same time he mulled over ideas that were to become part of a play that one of the characters in "Seven Times" would write. But it was hard to concentrate; the sound of the waves and the wind and the salt air and a box of chocolates beside him were distracting. His mind wandered back to his voyage home, and to a Swiss man whose charming wife had died during the trip. "It was so unnecessary to have her die, to extinguish so wantonly such a harmless existence," he wrote. "Landing in New York with his wife's body—What a hell."

What appalled him the next day as he wrote in his journal and what he wanted to work into his writing were "the grotesques, the farce-like quality of American life" as well as his now familiar theme of the need to tear down old systems, conventional governments, and begin anew. Sitting on the beach, he looked back up at the houses behind the boardwalk and sketched a scene of homes crowded together, telephone wires crisscrossing above them, and a large billboard protruding out alongside. "Cannot we let the old gods die? / Cannot we/ Huge striding men naked shining strong untrammeled with loud voice cry," he scribbled out next before halting.

Two days later he returned to New York to visit a few days with his Aunt Mamie Gordon and her family. "New York—in the Gordons' apartment," he complained on August 27. "O the querulous malaise that New York and the stuffy comfort of American Homes always throws me into." The blandness of the Gordons' place drove him to work again on the poem that he had a first inkling of at Bay Head, so he next wrote out a fuller version of the final product, that would begin, "In a hall on Olympus we held carouse." He dreamed of the evenings in Bassano, when the young radicals talked of revolution and the deaths of the old gods. "O who will take a drum and pound out the new tune? / O who in a new song will drown the priests' nasal tune?" he ended his first attempt. Then he crossed those lines out and wrote, "And where are the songs that should slay the old lies / Where is the dawn that should burn through hid skies." Those lines were closer to the frustration he felt about the possibility of change. But they were too didactic, and before he published the poem he altered it to end:

> In a hall on Olympus we held carouse,
> In our talk as banners waving names,
> Songs, phrases of the garlanded dead.
>
> Yesterday I went back to that house . . .
> Guttered candles where were flames,
> Shattered dust-grey glasses instead
> Of the fiery crocus-colored wine,
> Silence, cobwebs and a mouse
> Nibbling nibbling the moulded bread
> Those spring nights dipped in vintage divine
> In the dawnward chanting of our last carouse.

He hoped that the Gordons would help him clear his name with the Red Cross so he could enlist in some branch of the military to return to Europe as quickly as he could. His Aunt Mamie knew James Brown Scott, president of the Carnegie Peace Foundation in Washington and during the war a major in the Judge Advocate Corps. By the thirtieth Dos Passos was in Washington and had talked to Scott, who apparently helped him clear his record so that he could return to New York to enlist.

Scott, Dos Passos recalled, was a kindly man who grimaced as he heard the explanation of how the trouble with the Red Cross had occurred. At that moment Scott seemed a part of the oligarchy that Dos Passos was intent on breaking down. After talking with him, Dos Passos wrote in his journal that "the idea of individual liberty does not exist anywhere." He believed that in all of his lengthy conversations with the major, "not a ripple of it broke the calm of his oligarchic way of looking at things." Some real sense of individual liberty had to be developed in any new social contract, he believed. "The balance sheet between the powers over the individual of a national government and the good to the individual of a national government must be drawn," he went on. He was thinking about his own work as he declared, "Something must come out explaining in terms that the simplest person will understand that all the rights so many centuries have bled or struggled for, the rights of the governed against the governors—at the present day are so non-existent as to leave no inkling in the mind of anyone." Man's fight to free himself from the systems he had created is an "unended and unending battle."

At this point Dos Passos stopped his disquisition about personal liberty to make some notes for section seven of part four of "Seven Times." The incidents he listed for that section:

The man who danced Spanish fashion
The curé and the captain dine
The sentimental little man who killed a German
The fireworks of war
The men who would die
The casting of the dice

were precisely in the order in which they would appear in *One Man's Initiation: 1917*. He was very nearly finished—there would be only four more short sections totaling twenty-four pages—and he was trying to bring his ideas about war, liberty, and government together. He struggled, not entirely successfully, to translate what he put in essay form in his journal into fiction. His problem was that he was so intent upon explanation that his novel lacked the vitality of good fiction. Section seven of *One Man's Initiation: 1917* contains some vivid description, but what Dos Passos in the next weeks attempted to write as fiction reads like the polemics he had written in his journal shortly before.

After Labor Day, September 2, Dos Passos's attempts to complete his novel were slowed as back in New York he pressured his draft board to waive the eyesight requirements for enlistment. He was able to complete section seven and a page and a half of section eight. Then, probably while the draft board awaited approval from medical authorities of his waiver request he left New York, and he and Rumsey Marvin set out from Stamford, Connecticut, on a hiking trip to Danbury and along the Housatonic River north to the Massachusetts border. Marvin recalled that in Danbury, Dos Passos at first had trouble getting a room for the night because he wore a beret and spoke with what sounded to the locals like a foreign accent.

A short time later, Dos Passos took the train to Boston, where he spent four days with Edward Massey in Cambridge, seeing friends and enjoying the Harvard environs. On September 17 he noted that he was "at Eddie's most blissfully—moving about Cambridge, o the familiar smell of the Cambridge mist, the leisurely dinginess of Cambridge—the smell of it, the smell of it." He had always resented partly being inside the bell glass of Harvard; yet he recognized that college had been a fine time, home as much as anywhere he had lived. "How few places I have really been intimate with Cambridge Virginia London, Brussels," he went on. "And it seems the most loved of all, loved and hated [is] Cambridge." He recalled "all the smells of the Cambridge streets, of the fruit stores, Rumbos and Gomatos, of the lecture halls, of the meals, of my rooms, of Bobby's [Hillyer] room, of the Auk's [Stewart Mitchell] room and Katy's [John Walcott] room and Dudley's room and Eddie's room. Vale vale vale—" he wrote, turning his mind to a play he wanted to begin. This evolved from what he had first intended to include in "Seven Times." Now, back at Cambridge with his friend Massey, a dramatist, Dos Passos thought more seriously about the play. "An idea has come to me for a *Fantasy* with music first act to be set with sunflowers at back and then a yellow drop with purple and lavender buildings of New York—a garden—Greenwich Village—a boy and a girl." While the girl walked in the garden, the boy was to climb up a skyscraper and hit the moon with a sunflower stalk. There would be a blackout, and the next scene would take them into "the land of lost desires." Vegetables in the garden would tell about how they had been prosperous, living in the country, but now were poor in the dirty city. Unpromising though the idea might sound, Dos Passos kept at it. Eventually he finished a play, less fantastic than his first conception, in the expressionistic mode. When it was produced in 1925 by the Harvard Dramatic Club, it was entitled *The Moon Is a Gong,* and a year later was staged at the Cherry Lane Playhouse in Greenwich Village. In 1926, the play was published by Harper and Brothers, New York, under a new title, *The Garbage Man.*

While he was in Cambridge, he worked on the last lengthy section of "Seven Times," what would become chapter nine of *One Man's Initiation: 1917.* This was to be "the great discussion" to take place between Jean Chénier, a Jesuit, André Dubois, a revolutionary, Sully, an anarchist, Merrier, a Socialist, and two Americans, Martin Howe (Fibbie) and Tom Randolph. Dos Passos first summarized for himself what "Seven Times" had been to this point:

> The first part was Fibbie's getting of freedom—from the family—its religion —its way of looking at things its success-worship—*its sex ideas*
> Then New York and freedom and the gradual feeling of being caught up in the net of the nations. Flags—the world—Governments must go in.

Here Dos Passos wrote out the discussion between the characters, carrying it through for eight pages before ending on a despairing note. "O the lies the lies they kill us with," the revolutionist Dubois laments. "All society is a structure of lies— of lies for self interest by those in power who work on the cowardice of men. O if men were not cowards if men trusted themselves instead of their lying governors there would be none of this supreme asininity of war. . . . *Nous sommes tous des poires,*" he concludes. Dos Passos ended the discussion by quoting the last lines of Shelley's long political poem "Hellas":

> *Cease! drain not to its dregs the urn*
> *Of bitter prophecy.*
> *The world is weary of its past,*
> *Oh, might it die or rest at last!*

In the published novel the lines remained, not spoken by Dubois, but thought by Howe as a kind of refrain to the conversation.

Dos Passos did not have long to enjoy Cambridge life, because within two weeks he was inducted into the Medical Corps in New York City, where his examiner let him memorize the eye chart. The draft board promised him his waiver, and after a few lyrical phrases about the excitement of war from the man who made out Dos Passos's papers, the new recruit was directed to Allentown, Pennsylvania, to Camp Crane, a dismal spot in what had been a fairgrounds, where the buildings still had signs on them: POULTRY AND PIGEONS, LONG HORNED CATTLE EXHIBIT, SOFT DRINKS, BAR. To the soldiers, the place was known as Syphilis Valley.

As soon as he reached Camp Crane, he spent a day going through a physical examination in which he failed his eye tests. No waiver had arrived yet, so he telegraphed Major Scott, through whose efforts one would be produced several weeks later. In the meantime he was assigned to a casuals company, a group, he asserted, made up from the unwanted of the Medical Corps, which itself consisted largely of the unwanted from other army units. He was amused—and a bit horrified—during his physical to observe a clerk typist struggle to copy the account of a man recently discharged for imbecility.

The routine of the casuals company bored him immensely. To add to the tedium, the camp was quarantined because of influenza, so the soldiers could not leave the base. Dos Passos felt like a prisoner, hemmed in by the green paling fence and the three strands of barbed wire that surrounded the camp. Queen Ennui seized him, he told Rumsey Marvin, after being there only a few days. She was "the most powerful of all goddesses. She wraps her sleepy shawls round one and dangles before my eyes her toys and jumping jacks, her teasings and itchings, desires that die before they are born, yearnings after music and wandering and work, after unknown cities and friends and desert isles and sun mottled rivers to bathe away all restraints in."

Despite his boredom, he was learning about another side of life, reading a great deal, and writing. For the first time, Dos Passos was really thrown in with the American common man as he never had been before. Even in the ambulance corps he was among Frenchmen and, for the most part, persons like himself, young men out of college who had volunteered for the service because of their idealism or a desire for adventure. Now he was among men who came from segments of society he had never known, many of whom had no desire to travel, had no political interests, and little if any knowledge of the arts. The first Sunday Dos Passos was at Camp Crane he thought he caught the mood of these people as he watched the camp band perform. While the musical instruments glittered in the sunlight, men and women milled about near the soldiers, creating patterns that shifted "like the bits of a picture puzzle cut into scraps by the alternation of sun and shade—shifting and forming into pictures—purple and black, drab yellow and lilac against a background of khaki." He saw in the faces of the young women their quest for men, while the men with their faces of brown reddish healthy youth returned the glances, and behind the looks was a picture of "skirts lifted and clothes undone—of white legs and hair between them and the necessity of junction of body strain to body."

"You can't imagine the good nature and blundering willingness of the American privates," he wrote Jack Lawson. "It gives an idyllic low comedy quality to things." He found himself amid the routines of nightly movies, Sunday prayer meetings in the Y.M.C.A. building, shoveling coal, sweeping floors, and washing innumerable windows—"Hast ever washed windows," he asked Rumsey Marvin. "It's a merry sport." He claimed that he had washed 7,898,976,432,148,264,312,800 and a few more of them that day while observing his fellow soldiers. He had wanted to be among these people, he reminded himself; now he was drowning in them. His sometime feeling of desperation stemmed from his eagerness to get back to Europe, yet in the meantime he was absorbing materials for his writing.

"Organization kills," he told himself as he struggled to create amid the menial tasks that some soldiers had to do, while the more favored could lounge about, working sporadically at easy typing jobs. "The Gospel of the army is cunning," he thought. "The wisdom of the snake under the meekness of the sheep is what wins out." He wrote out three commandments for survival: "never let them get anything on you"; "graft—get privileges others haven't got—worm yourself into confidence"; and "seem neat and prosperous—as if you had money in the bank." He wrote Arthur McComb that he repeated the phrase "organization is death" over and over as he swept floors and washed windows. Although he grumbled, he was not unhappy to be in the service, because he had always wanted to divest himself of class and the monied background. The army might be the best way to do that. From there, he might be able to "see clear."

Before reporting to Camp Crane, he had finished "Seven Times," leaving the manuscript in New York to be worked on later. Now the novel lay in two parts, one with friends in France, the other in America. Soon he arranged to have a copy of the second half sent to Ed Massey in Cambridge, asking him to forward it to Arthur McComb in Spain. Massey balked because he was sure that censors would object to the radical ending.

But Dos Passos was not particularly worried about "Seven Times." He had begun to imagine another novel about his war experiences, especially about his ever-increasing hatred of organizations and conformity. He thought it might be entitled "The Sack of Corinth"; eventually it was published as *Three Soldiers*. It grew out of the excruciating tedium of Camp Crane. Every letter to his friends told of his ennui, and he even wrote poems to Queen Ennui, "iron goddess, cobweb-clothed / goddess of all useless things," whom he asked to blind his eyes to the clouds, the sky, and the wind that reminded him of all the places he would like to be, romantically pursuing the horizon.

Bemoaning his bad fortune in being stuck at the camp, quarantined and awaiting a waiver for his eyesight, he was nevertheless absorbing impressions that became the basis for *Three Soldiers* and would remain with him long after he had completed it. "How about having it start in a camp like this with different fellows telling each other their life history," he wondered as he struggled to begin. The characters for the fiction were before him. Christfield, one of the three soldiers, was drawn from Christenbury, a man from Indiana who like his fictional counterpart hated another soldier in his section. After the second man was made a corporal, Christenbury at one point had drawn a knife on him, swearing to anyone who would listen that he was going to push the corporal overboard on the voyage to Europe.

A "little raucous-voiced Californian named Fuselli" became the Fuselli of the novel, testimony to how closely Dos Passos intended it to be a realistic description of military life. The real Fuselli was full of tales about his family and girl friends, from a "tough street corner lounging crap shooting past" that impressed the still overly fastidious Dos Passos, who felt easier about mocking the propaganda films shown to the troops than he did talking freely about sex. One Sunday night early in October the soldiers saw what Dos Passos considered a "particularly inept" movie, which showed Americans rescuing girls and old women from the brutalities of the Germans. Bad as the film was, Dos Passos was sure he could sense "a wave of hatred go through the men," whose shouts of "goddamned bastards" and "cocksuckers" were sincere. They seemed imbued with the spirit of war; the soldier next to Dos Passos during the show had the idea that in Europe he would be "snatching halfraped Belgian women from the bloody claws of Huns." Enraged, another man blurted out that he did not fuck women, "but I'm going to—God—I'd give anything to rape some of those German women. I hate them—men women children and unborn children—They're either jackasses or full of the lust for power just like their rulers are—to let themselves be ruled by a bunch of warlords like that. . . . Indeed indeed," concluded Dos Passos, "the country is warmad."

The previous January he had declared that he had become "a much heartier son of a bitch" than he used to be; yet amid the boredom of Camp Crane and the earthiness of the soldiers he decided that, while he might have gotten a better grip on *"things"* since the days at Choate or Harvard, he was much as he had been. He still was a loner, still could not mix easily with other people, still sought the solace of his own room, or bunk, or whatever his private shelter at the moment might be. Amid these soldiers he was an outsider, a fastidious, gangling, nearsighted college graduate peering in at barracks life, fascinated by a situation where, as he wrote, "everyone wears a phallus on his sleeve." Dos Passos was then an intellectually mature young man who struggled in the face of the social conventions he had learned to understand the emotions he felt and heard expressed around him. Behind his attempt at objectivity about sexual matters lay a prudishness that he only partly admitted to himself.

"They are sane about sex in the army, aren't they?" he commented to Rumsey Marvin. It was, he thought, "a comfort not to have the sacred phallus surrounded by an aura of mystery and cant"; yet "the piece of tail attitude" of Americans offended him. Sexual relations ought to involve "a human relation," not be only a matter of a casual piece of tail. If he could not admire the soldiers' promiscuousness, it is hard to see how he could truly admire their sexual attitudes. Yet sex was a subject that interested him hugely, he told Marvin, quickly adding, "almost in a scientific way. . . . One has no data to go on, as the moralizers have falsified everything; so one has to find out for oneself—and it is so shrouded in the mists of conflicting conventions that research is fascinatingly difficult." Despite Dos Passos's one or two brief affairs in Europe, he had little to go on because he was still thoroughly constrained.

After more than three weeks of such amateur sociological observations, Dos Passos got his waiver, enabling him to join Ambulance Section 541 which was being formed to leave for France. The top sergeant of the section was an amusing man named O'Reilly, another veteran of the volunteer ambulance group. He appointed Dos Passos to be the acting quartermaster sergeant, so by the end of October Dos Passos's spirits were up. He had something to do, amid rumors that the section was leaving momentarily for France. Finally they marched out of Camp Crane on October 31, the acting quartermaster sergeant fussing at his troops for badly arranged packs. A train ride to their next destination, Camp Merritt, New Jersey, was slow and tiring. At Camp Merritt, because of tight security, Dos Passos had to keep the troops from wandering outside. The confinement went on for eleven days before the section was embarked aboard the *Cedric.* But the anticipation of sailing made the days seem more lively. Dos Passos enjoyed Sergeant O'Reilly, "a delight: a regular New York Irish politician always ready to do a friend a good turn and play a mean trick on an enemy." And the other men in the section were equally entertaining. One had been a taxi driver, Dos Passos reported to Rumsey Marvin; another had driven a hearse, and others were "cowpunchers and railroad men and farmers and bakers and butchers and candlestick makers," just the sort of people Dos Passos the egalitarian wanted to be among.

Early on the morning of November 11, the day of the Armistice, Section 541 left Camp Merritt to board ship. Rumors were rampant that the war was ended, but the soldiers were not sure. The worried men grumbled about going overseas to "clean up shit" if the war was actually over; others, however, were excited about the chance to get abroad. But before they could enjoy France, they had to endure the voyage across the Atlantic in convoy.

Jammed aboard the *Cedric,* Dos Passos and his section were assigned to the mess detail. While the ship rolled along, his outfit had to serve nine sittings a day far below decks, which entailed his coercing his men—themselves half ill—into doling out food to the other troops, equally sick, in the hot, rancid atmosphere of the messroom. For a week Dos Passos headed the mess detail; the experience, though miserable, had in its way as much effect on him as had Camp Crane or, perhaps, even his experiences around Verdun or Bassano. He observed with keen interest the hierarchy of command: officers looking for trouble among the troops, sergeants enjoying the powers of command, and the troops, made sheeplike by the army routine. He was not sure about his own reactions to the authority being an acting sergeant had given him. After several days of mess duty, he commented to himself that "ordering people about—habitually—as a daily occupation—is the most remarkable experience I ever had. It is so curious bawling people out." He was not good at it, and he did not like it, finally, but he was enough fascinated by the urge for power and recognition that he transferred his sense of that urge to Fuselli in *Three Soldiers.* The antimilitary author disliked the bureaucratic details of the sergeant's job; the shy, aloof college graduate understood the appeal of authority.

Whatever excitement had been generated by embarkation on the *Cedric* was dulled during the long passage, which lasted the better part of two weeks. By the end of the voyage few men were still enthusiastic; most were "a seasick homesick rather blue bunch of troops." The atmosphere, Dos Passos thought, was caught in a conversation he had standing on deck in an utterly dark, rainy night. He felt "the terror of submarines and loneliness and strange unaccustomed things." "Sea cold, sea dark," he noted, and "the little comfortable soul torn out of its groove and shivering in the great shaggy world." As he wrote in his journal in that mood, his mind wandered back to the experience of Verdun. Without commenting on its significance, he hurriedly jotted down his vivid memory of a lurid image he had dreamed, of the sun which "was filmed over like a bloodshot eye and began to sway and wabble in the sky as a spent top sways and wabbles, and whirling rolled into the seas vermillion ways so that pitchblackness covered me." The darkness of the night on the Atlantic brought back this memory of another sort of darkness. He did not dwell on Verdun, but—like countless others—he had his own nightmare vision of its horror.

The *Cedric* docked at Southampton, from where, struck with influenza, Dos Passos's section was sent briefly to Camp Winnal Downs, near Winchester. He caught the flu also, for four days struggling against the disease that produced, he felt, symptoms of every illness known to man: "pneumonia, T.B., diphtheria, diarrhea, dyspepsia, sore throat, whooping cough, scarlet fever and beri-beri." Later he declared that he was determined not to go to a hospital because so many soldiers who did never reappeared, apparently dead from the epidemic. His cure, he claimed, had been "a bottle of rum [bought] from a grubby Englishman who was pimping for some women he said he had in a sandpit just outside the camp."

Miserable with the flu, Dos Passos saw nothing of Winchester save a few red gables and the large square belfrey of the cathedral during the several days he spent at the camp before the section was shipped from Southampton across the channel to Le Havre. Finally returned to France, Dos Passos hoped for better things for what he called "O'Reilly's Travelling Circus," which was assigned to an American base camp in Ferrières-en-Gâtinais, some eighty kilometers south of Paris in the Loire region.

In France, Dos Passos's spirits could not remain utterly down for long, even though the "monotonous army routine" seldom changed. Ferrières was a charming town, where he quickly discovered the Hotel du Cheval Blanc, in which he could eat leisurely dinners and watch the goings-on of his fellow soldiers with fascination and amusement. The site of the base camp at Ferrières was an ancient abbey. From among "crumbling cusps," he wrote Jack Lawson, stove pipes stuck out, while "the click of typewriters reeling up red tape echoe[d] in the gothic vaulting and disturb[ed] the rooks in the mossgreened trees." The local bread was delicious; beer and wine were cheap and good, and he even managed meals at the Cheval Blanc despite having no money. He complained about the high military collar constantly galling him, and he objected to the American soldiers drunkenly sneering at the French, but these complaints had become almost routine. He welcomed work, which occasionally became heavy, as on one Sunday when he had to write seemingly endless reports, typed "with two fingers on a lame Corona." Having work made him no less critical, however; after a day of writing these reports he noted in his journal, "The all pervading red tape of the army is something stupendous."

Material for *Three Soldiers* continually accumulated. Amid the idle conversations at the base camp Dos Passos heard snatches of "the farce and the deformed enormities of war" such as talk of a "mad house where they choked the noisy insane man," a tale "of the man under sentence of court martial—of the wild ride from St. Nazaire to Paris with a drunken convoy Wanderings behind the front of an unattached soldier." And always, the men were "Drunk, Drunk, Drunk." At the local cafés the Americans hung around the French barmaids like "dogs round a back door where they half expect to be fed." The men yearned for the prostitutes who frequented the Cheval Blanc and another café Dos Passos often visited. Amid such goings on there were serious conversations, such as one about death, a sergeant asserting that it was but a little thing to die. "In the generations a man is nothing. Tout est bien fait dans la nature," he declared. "Dans la mort il n'y a rien de terrible." Man, thought Dos Passos then, truly was nothing in the military, but he did not agree with the rest of the sergeant's sentiment. To him man amounted to something, and death in war was often horrible.

Dos Passos claimed that the end of his brief career as acting quartermaster sergeant occurred when he attempted to drill his section before a visiting colonel. At Ferrières he had been in the habit, whenever ordered to drill the men, of marching them out to an apple orchard, where behind a high wall they would smoke cheap tobacco and tell stories. Thus prepared, he and they made a shambles of their drill inspection. The rout was completed when Dos Passos marched the troops into a stone wall and they broke out in laughter. The story is too familiar to ring quite true, but Dos Passos no doubt fumbled at his commands, and the incident convinced his superiors that the nearsighted, stuttering man lacked the necessary military bearing.

The demotion did not demoralize him for long. With little work to do at the base camp, he obtained frequent passes and traveled to spots near Ferrières: Fontainebleau, from where he hiked the short distance through beautiful woods to Barbizon; Sens, "a delightful holy little town where the dank streets drip holy water and the rain sprinkles like a hyssop out of a benitier"; and Montargis, a town but several kilometers south of Ferrières. Sens particularly attracted him. He liked its architecture and described to Dudley Poore its atmosphere of the Middle Ages, contrasted to a "yearning for the modern and for speed" that was expressed in "an exquisitely ugly Hotel de Ville built right under the wrinkled aged nose of the cathedral, tweaking it, pour ainsi dire." Sens, because of its mellow atmosphere, set his imagination to work, so that the gargoyles on the cathedral "dripped as they ought," while the moss on the house roofs was as "vivid as emeralds" and his face had the "pleasant flushed feeling of having been rained on all day."

Despite his claim of being overwhelmed by lethargy, Dos Passos by the end of the year was in fact busy with projects. Having heard that the army would permit qualified soldiers to study in Europe, he had written the Army Overseas Educational Commission in Paris applying to study anthropology. And to Rumsey Marvin he lightheartedly outlined nine reasons why—besides having little money—he could not accept Marvin's proposal of travel to Latin America. As soon as he could get free of the military, he declared, he intended to rewrite "Seven Times Round the Walls of Jericho" and find a publisher; write the "Sack of Corinth," "a monumental work on America Militant"; write the play that had been on his mind; put together a collection of essays; study the anthropology of religions; learn to paint; paint; and, finally, visit Abyssinia.

Before he was free to pursue these projects, however, he was assigned as part of another section, 523, to Alsace, where acting as an interpreter he was stationed at Saussheim "in the land of sauerkraut and wiener schnitzels," he wrote Rumsey Marvin in mid-January. Here, too, his duties were not onerous, so he traveled about the region, enjoying Strasbourg in particular, with its elaborate cathedral and "old carved wooden houses that hang story after ornamental story over the street."

The Army Overseas Educational Commission accepted his application for study; thus early in March he was released from duty to return to Paris, where he was to study anthropology at the Sorbonne. Such was his official purpose for being there. In fact, as soon as he arrived and had taken a room on La Montagne St. Geneviève, close by the Pantheon and only several streets over from the Sorbonne, he sat at his typewriter "from morning till night with intervals for food—delicious sizzly Paris food and concerts," while he reworked the manuscript of "Seven Times."

Dos Passos would have to serve two more weeks of military duty later in the year, but at least, as he wrote Marvin in March, he was provisionally free. "Libertad libertad!" he exulted, sensing that he could now begin in earnest to work on his several writing projects. He was correct; during the next glorious months he could write without interruption for the first time, while living the sort of life that became the ideal of many expatriates. He even enjoyed occasional lectures about the religion of Greece and Rome and about Mayan culture, but his great pleasures were going to art shows, concerts, and operas, sketching in an art class, and being free to see friends such as Robert Hillyer—returned to Europe as a lieutenant in the army—Tom Cope, Kate Drain, and soon, Jack Lawson.

Paris that spring, he would reminisce, was a city "already in the disintegration of victory," a place where the rigors of wartime were being replaced by permissiveness. But that was important, because the atmosphere furthered what he termed the "creative tidal wave" which had begun during the last years of the nineteenth and the first years of the twentieth century. Paris in 1919, he was sure, "was the capital of Europe." Modern painting—the work of the Cubists, the Fauvists, Modigliani, Gris, and Picasso—was pouring out fresh and startling. "This too," he added, "was the Paris of new schools of music. Satie presided over Les Six. There was Poulenc, and Milhaud. Stravinsky was beginning to be heard. The Diaghilev ballet was promoting a synthesis of all the arts."

The techniques of the new were to become the means to express "the feelings of savage joy and bitter hatred" of Dos Passos and his companions that spring. Theirs was a bittersweet mood; they were in Paris at the most beautiful time of year, but they had served in the war, and now as outsiders they watched the progress, or lack of it, of the Peace Conference. Dos Passos and his friends had learned to be cynics: "we were convinced that life in the militarized industrialized nations had become a chamber of horrors and we believed that plain men, the underdogs we rubbed shoulders with, were not such a bad lot as they might be." While they imbibed the life of the city, they had ever-increasing hopes that a social revolution would erupt to tear down the structures they now despised. And this seemed a real possibility because Paris was in turmoil. In a Camera Eye section of *Nineteen Nineteen* Dos Passos described a scene from the time around May 1919. A general strike was in effect; no buses, taxicabs, or metro lines were running. The city was emblazoned with red flags and signs protesting the war and the Peace Conference. Government guards rode on horseback through milling crowds and hit at the Parisians with the flats of their swords. From among the sounds of the angry crowd came voices singing the "Internationale." Soon the protest grew in violence; an old woman was shot; the crowd began to retreat before advancing troops, who were now firing to kill. Dos Passos and a friend, running with the crowd, dodged into a café just as the proprietor slammed down his iron shutters. Later, they looked out in the rain at the street, empty but for a few signs of the turmoil. Most revealing of the futility of the attempt at revolution was a torn handbill that read *L'Union des Travailleurs Fera*, but the rest was gone.

Although the political situation in Europe was unsteady during the months after the Armistice, and although the first of May was supposed to mark an uprising against the entrenched governments, no general revolution occurred. What did happen was that the atmosphere of ferment and political unrest spurred an outpouring from young artists such as Dos Passos. He was entering upon a decade in which in Europe as in the United States social conditions combined to draw forth important literature. He was maturing intellectually; he was eager to write; a sense of the new was in the air; and it seemed possible that great changes might occur. Yet— and this was an important ingredient as a kind of irritant—traditional social and political systems continued and frequently oppressed the common man. When Rumsey Marvin dared to write him about "the machinery of government," Dos Passos rebuked him by saying that the "simile of government is all very well but it is no time for similes when someone is sitting on your necks. A false idea, a false system, and a set of tyrants, conscious or unconscious," he lectured Marvin, "is sitting on the world's neck at present and has so far succeeded in destroying a good half of the worthwhile things in the world. Do you realize what it means to have half a continent in ashes and starving," he asked. This was "a time to save what we can of the things worthwhile and to decide damn quick what things are worthwhile and what are not." To emphasize that a government was not an abstraction or a thing apart, he reminded Marvin that "the machinery of government means a set of people, individuals, with individual greeds and stupidities."

The most important thing he could do was to work as rapidly as he could on his manuscripts, since he was convinced that they were his best means of speaking out. He tried out his work on his friends each day. Jack Lawson had taken a room at 45 Quai de la Tournelle, on the Left Bank directly across from the Île de la Cité, the site of the Lecomte's *Rendezvous des Mariniers* on the Quai d'Anjou. After writing and revising, Dos Passos walked to Lawson's rooms to read from the revisions for "Seven Times" to him, often to Kate Drain, and to others, the group taking time for dinners, usually on the Quai d'Anjou. A friend of Lawson's who joined them and whose opinion Dos Passos valued was Griffin Barry, "a very delightful man, a friend ... of Compton Mackenzie, who has spent the year in Russia necessary to enlightenment, it seems," Dos Passos confided to Poore early in April. Barry, a political radical who was then working for the United Press, was the one who gathered together around Lawson and Dos Passos other radicals and near-radicals. In 1919 Dos Passos was impressed by Barry. Much later, he remembered him as a literary arriviste, "the insider incarnate" who claimed to have slept with every woman a person might mention. He was, Dos Passos recalled, "full of the lingo of Mabel Dodge's salon in New York. Love must be free. Everything must be frank; talk, talk, talk. He was the future Greenwich Village encapsulated." Barry was excited to find Dos Passos and the others, whose political radicalism Barry fired with his own fervor. Intrigued with them, he soon brought into the group Robert Minor, among others. Minor, an active radical, had drawn excellent political cartoons for the *Masses* before it died in 1917, and he would continue to play a role in left-wing politics. To several of the gatherings he brought Mary Heaton Vorse, an American author whose writing about social problems influenced Dos Passos. She and he met then in Paris; they became good friends interested in many of the same causes.

Lawson and Barry suggested changes in the second part of "Seven Times" when Dos Passos read it to them. Most of April he worked to revise and cut it, only at the end of the month feeling confident enough about the section to write Dudley Poore that "Part Two of Fibbie saw uttermost completion today. Now only Part Three remains." By then he realized that the last section of the novel did not belong with the first three parts. "Part Four of Fibbie has been amputated and has become something else," he continued three weeks later, writing Poore to explain that "the fourth part of Fibbie was never part of him at all. I merely pretended that it was, and as soon as it was read aloud my pretense collapsed. That's all. I'm going to enlarge it and put in steam heat and enameled bath tubs and call it France 1917 or something of the sort and try to publish it that way. Really it's rather fun suddenly having two children instead of one."

He had not pulled all the sections of "Seven Times" together at that point, but hoped to find a publisher on the basis of what was complete. When Robert Hillyer left Paris at the end of April, he took half of the manuscript with him to the United States. He was to give it to Lawson, who had departed for America two weeks earlier, agreeing to try to find a publisher for the novel. As soon as Lawson received the partial manuscript, he turned it over to the literary agency of Brandt and Kirkpatrick. Although Dos Passos had hoped to be finished with part three by June, not until the following October 1 did Brandt and Kirkpatrick receive it, at which time A. C. Brandt wrote Dos Passos that he was discussing it with Alfred Knopf, who had expressed interest in the first half.

The fate of the book, like politics, was important to Dos Passos, but neither consumed his life. The beauty of springtime in Paris lay before him, especially after he moved into Lawson's rooms on the Quai de la Tournelle when Lawson left in mid-April. From there he overlooked the Seine and Notre Dame on his left. He made frequent short forays into the countryside, to clear his mind of the intensities of Lawson, Minor, and his other literary-activist friends. Often these trips were instigated by Hillyer, who had little interest in politics. On one rainy morning in mid-April, he and Hillyer started out along the river from St. Germain, a town a short distance to the northwest of Paris. He wrote Rumsey Marvin from a café in the village of Conflans-Ste. Honorine that the Seine was "green and brown and shining, crowded with barges with blunt prows, painted in yellow and red." The gray day was "soft as the breast of a dove," a mellow day as they walked through a forest to the village of Herblay, across the Seine from the muddy path along which they scrambled. They called to a boatman, "a very ancient creaking man," who ferried them to the other side where they found lodging in Herblay. Earlier the same morning that Dos Passos wrote Marvin, he and Hillyer had listened to a mass "sung for Palm Sunday in a beautiful little old sandstone church—full of fighting children."

Excursions like this meant as much to Dos Passos as anything he did. He felt momentarily free of the concerns his conscience pressed upon him; all that was romantic in him responded to the spring, the soft rain, the Seine, and the quiet beauty of the French villages. He felt, he wrote Marvin, full of the spirit of the songs of the thirteenth-century minstrel Colin Muset. "De toute joie m'est bel," began one from which he took a refrain to make a verse of his own. "I've forgotten all my woes," he wrote, closing:

> Tribondainné, Tribondel
> O I'm full of soft delight
> Tribondainné, Tribondel
> From my eyelids to my toes.

Many of Dos Passos's friends could not fully comprehend the side of his personality that caused him to—as they saw it—dodge their company on occasion. He could tolerate only a limited amount of the constant presence of anyone before he felt the need to retreat. So he continued his excursions through the spring, later in April traveling by himself to Rouen to enjoy its sixteenth-century atmosphere and to imagine Emma Bovary and Leon in this setting as Flaubert described them. Several days later he visited Chartres and spent the better part of two days admiring the sculpture of the cathedral and strolling through streets that rose among gardens up from the river Eure. The town was quiet, "full of nuns and seminarists and flatfooted red faced priests," he wrote Marvin. "In the cathedral multitudes of little old women in black shawls adore a very ancient black virgin. I can hear them now," he asserted, "wailing importunate at every pause in the mumbled Latin of the priest.

Vièrge toute puissante, mere de dieu, prier pour nous, maintenant et à l'heure de notre mort. Down what long ages have those little old women kneeled and abased themselves before their goddess."

Despite the seeming freedom his status as a student gave him, Dos Passos felt constrained by the army. He could not move about as he pleased; he had to wear a uniform, and he had to be careful about being seen with officer friends. Dos Passos craved his discharge, planning to travel to Spain once he was out of the army, despite having been accepted as a candidate for a doctorate at the Sorbonne and halfheartedly thinking that he might follow the academic path. During the spring he repeatedly urged Dudley Poore, who was studying in England, to seek his discharge in France so that he could stay there if he chose to. Since Dos Passos became sure as the spring wore on that he would not continue to study at the Sorbonne once free of the army, he also tried to convince Rumsey Marvin to voyage to Spain so the two of them could hike there.

Although Dos Passos had not completed the revisions to "Seven Times" and was still fussing with what had been its fourth part, which he was now recasting as a separate novel, in May he began writing "The Sack of Corinth," later to become *Three Soldiers*. "Have written three chapters of the *Sack of Corinth,*" he wrote Dudley Poore on May 21. When he began the novel, he had in mind something structured like "Seven Times," a *Bildungsroman* which took Martin Howe from childhood through college and to the verge of his experiences as an ambulance driver in the World War. Dos Passos from the beginning conceived of the idea of portraying what happens to several men in the army, but he originally intended first to show at least one of them, the most nearly autobiographical character, John Andrews, in his childhood discarding some toy soldiers exactly as, in the army, he would be discarded and his freedom destroyed by the organization. In what Dos Passos later labeled as "Ex prologue of Three Soldiers" he depicted a young child playing with and mutilating some of his toy soldiers. The piece concludes as the child, finished with the game, furtively puts the soldiers who are still whole in rows where they are most conspicuous. The broken ones he hides, thinking that he might fix them later:

> He collected carefully the bits of the soldiers he had pulled to pieces and dropped them down a crack in the floor in the corner of the room. Then he washed his hands very clean, cleaner than usual, and brushed his hair, and went down to sit beside Mother on the back porch.
>
> And the soldiers stood there, while the dusty twilight gathered about them, identical, in rows, khaki rows, blue rows, all in the same attitude, all cast in the same mould, and the dust settled about them through the evening as they stood motionless.

As symbolic action the episode was well rendered, if heavy-handed. But it was unnecessary, and Dos Passos abandoned it, beginning *Three Soldiers* at a training camp and having the men themselves fulfill the roles of the toy soldiers. Andrews, Fuselli, and Chrisfield—the three soldiers—are molded by the military regime;

subsequently each in a different way is broken, hidden, and then discarded by a force that cares nothing about them except as integers in a system. The idea that systems molded humans obsessed him, so while the three soldiers in his fiction were entrapped, he felt that personally he must struggle harder than ever to avoid such pitfalls.

Around the time Dos Passos was writing the first chapters of *Three Soldiers*, Rumsey Marvin seemed too complacent about the United States, and Dos Passos reacted passionately, warning him that the two of them were "too lively" and had "too much curiosity, too many desperate desires for unimaginable things to let ourselves be driven down into the mud of common life." Dos Passos was positive that "it is so much harder than it has ever been before to lead a good life, to dominate life instead of being driven in the herd." Only in the worst of feudal times did intelligence and vigor have to struggle as hard to survive. An "all-pervading spirit of commerce," a "new religion of steel and stamped paper" dominated modern life, to which one's response should be "to think clearly and piteously, to love without stint, to feel in one's veins the throbbing of all the life of all the world." Weren't these better than success—at college making Phi Beta Kappa, being tapped for a senior society, and later growing "a paunch on the income from slave-labor," he asked Marvin. "Forgive much rot," he closed, but added that there might be a bit of sense in what he wrote. His style was hyperbolic; yet he was entirely serious about what he said.

Something of what he was striving to achieve in his writing was appearing in the music then being performed in Paris. Debussy's opera *Pelleas et Mélisande*, for example, which had caused a riot when it was first presented in 1902, fascinated Dos Passos. The opera's avant-garde techniques were unlike almost anything he had experienced, but they appealed to his own modernist sensibilities, and like Debussy, he sought to combine several mediums of expression. The blending of music, language, poetry, and setting drew Dos Passos back repeatedly to the opera. "I've been for the second time to *Pelleas and Mélisande*. I can still feel my blood tingle with it. It is as great as anything," he wrote Dudley Poore in the latter part of May. Almost immediately he went again to the Opéra Comique, where it was being performed: "Pelleas for the third time was as delightful as ever, more so. It's ridiculous but I think I'll go again," he wrote Poore soon thereafter.

Pelleas and Mélisande was hardly the only music that interested him. Alone, or often with Tom Cope, he attended concerts as frequently as he could. One evening in June when they were at the Gaveau, a concert hall where the Russian singer Kubitsky was performing, Cope recognized a friend their age he had met the previous year at Brains, a village south of Nantes. Her name was Germaine Lucas-Championnière, and when Cope introduced her to Dos Passos, he realized that she was the sister of a doctor whom he had met two years earlier while he was driving ambulances at the front near Verdun. Dos Passos was taken with her; she was attractive, shared his interest in music, and knew much more about it than he. Immediately they began going to musical performances together, returning again and again to *Pelleas et Mélisande*—she was, she recalled, *fou de musique* and eventually saw *Pelleas et Mélisande* more than sixty times. He frequently visited her family at 52 Rue de Clichy, becoming almost a part of the family. While she played the music of Stravinsky, Poulenc, or Auric at the piano, he had tea and conversed with Madame Bibi, as he called Germaine's mother. The compositions of the young French composer Darius Milhaud intrigued them as well. After hearing a concert of his music in mid-June, Dos Passos wrote Germaine Lucas-Championnière in French, "Mademoiselle, please, who is Darius Milhaud? . . . I would very much like to know who this man is whose name I have never heard of. Americans, as you well know, are barbarians, Thracians, Hyperboreans. Isn't it so, O Athenian?"

He was a little in love with her, and she was attracted to this tall, intellectual American who spoke fluent French, but she showed no signs of responding to his few attempts to ask her out. He thought to declare his love to her before the rest of her family at their apartment, but could not bring himself to, and after some time their relationship became a friendship rather than an incipient romance.

As long as Dos Passos's classes continued at the Sorbonne, he could lead this idyllic life, but once they ended, the special detachment was dissolved. While he waited for his army discharge to be processed, he was put in a casuals company and shipped at the end of June to Gièvres, where, in a kind of limbo, he lifted scrap iron back and forth across some railroad tracks. The army had difficulty locating his service record, which he needed for his release, so he lingered on at Gièvres, sinking into "a state of despair such as I've never suffered before," he wrote Marvin. Desperate after ten days, Dos Passos took an unauthorized absence and, carefully avoiding the military police, found army headquarters at Tours, where a master sergeant retrieved his records and wrote out discharge orders for him. He hurried back to Gièvres in time for roll call the next day, presented his orders to his astonished commanding officer, and was discharged on July 11.

Free at last, he returned to Tours, where he bought civilian clothes: a silk shirt, a gray-blue necktie, bright blue socks, and a "large and pompous brown felt hat" —"emblems of freedom," he thought. He went to a public bath, relaxed long "in a huge brass tub fed by swans-head spiggots," got dressed in his newly purchased clothes and a gray suit borrowed from Tom Cope, stuffed his uniform under some wet towels piled in the corridor of the bath, and emerged a civilian. In a light mood he headed back to Paris, enjoying the towns of Blois and Vendôme along the way before arriving in Paris on July 14, Bastille Day.

CHAPTER TWELVE

Literary Wanderings in Europe, 1919–1920

With the future seemingly open before him, Dos Passos intended to remain in Paris only long enough to put what few affairs he had in order. Several days later he traveled toward Brest, where he hoped to aid Dudley Poore, who he thought was still awaiting discharge there. Poore, it turned out, had already been released and was on his way to Gièvres, planning to meet Dos Passos. It was not until several weeks later that they accomplished a rendezvous in Biarritz.

Dos Passos's ultimate goal was London, where he expected to accomplish two things. In Paris the previous spring Griffin Barry had introduced him to "Trilby" Ewer, an Englishman who was to become a foreign editor of the British labor newspaper, the *Daily Herald*. Ewer had suggested that Dos Passos might serve as a correspondent for the *Daily Herald* in Spain once he had left the army. In London Dos Passos hoped to confirm the job and also to place the manuscript for *One Man's Initiation: 1917*.

After the first excitement of being out of the army had passed, Dos Passos's mood turned contemplative. He talked about himself more candidly to Marvin, whom he urged not to do anything—in the American way—for a few months. Moon about New York, read hugely, and wander down the "stinking canyons of the streets" searching for some adventure that might never come, he advised. Above all, Marvin should not become unenterprising. "I have so suffered all my life from strange brakes that clamp on suddenly whenever my body starts following the erratic parts of my mind," Dos Passos mused. The fault, he decided, lay with his "timid solitary childhood" that left him with "a curious deadening stoicism." He wondered if he might be getting over it, "but it seems to be much easier to acquire than to lose, and it cuts one off so from the acute joys and the acute pains of life. . . . What is more deadly to the soul than armor?" he asked, especially when "every atom of vividness" was needed in the present "barbarous, bloody, tumultuous age." Hardly the hearty son of a bitch he wanted to think he was in Italy in early 1918, he recognized that inhibitions still bound him about, and he thought he must will himself to work free of them, while protesting against them in his writing.

He was in a pensive mood as he traveled along the northern coast of France from Brest to Boulogne, where he would take the ferry to Folkstone. The trip took several days, for he stopped at St. Malo and Mont-St-Michel on the way. "My desires have a-hunting gone. / They circle through the fields and sniff along the ridges," he began a poem as he sat on a train to Mont-St-Michel. The coast of Normandy was familiar to him from childhood, and Boulogne particularly was full of memories: "The famous castles one used to build on the broad trampled sands and the terrifying delight of trying to learn how to swim, and the gorgeousness of the casino with its awnings and banks, and the old barelegged women who fished for shrimps along the shore." He had not meant the trip to be nostalgic, but it became so as he returned to some of the places he and his mother had visited. Did he understand himself? he could wonder. Why satirize his background and his own family in stories and the novels he was trying to complete when in fact he had deeply loved his father and mother? It was partly self-mockery as he attempted to get a grip on himself and to break free of the "deadening stoicism" he had complained of to Rumsey Marvin. But that rebellion was a willed thing; his childhood was more dear to him, he had to admit, than one side of him wanted it to be.

In England he visited the ladies, Mrs. Gee and Miss Meakin, who had cared for him as a child, completed through Trilby Ewer the arrangements to be a correspondent in Spain, and, with Ewer's help, contacted the publishing house of Allen and Unwin about *One Man's Initiation: 1917.* London seemed a "smoky chaos" where he had little desire to remain long, although an atmosphere of "impending doom" about the city made it more interesting than he had known it to be before. But he was eager to reach Spain. The idea obsessed him that modern man was in danger of being "swallowed and ground under the heel of the forces that would make us cogs in the machine," and he was certain that he would find the less industrialized, highly individualistic culture of Spain compatible with his views. Reminded of the alien forces of modernity by the din and smoke of London, he asserted to Rumsey Marvin that he found himself going back ever more frequently to "those restless gods of the Renaissance. They threw off one servitude," he declared, "we will throw off another." At this point he would have been shocked had anyone accused him of championing the past at the expense of the present, as he would some twenty years later. Yet the seeds of such a choice were already planted, as his offhand remarks about the Renaissance might suggest.

His contemplative mood remained when, back in Paris by August 2, he told Marvin that he was wandering the boulevards feeling isolated, "utterly left out of the gaudy stream of life that throbs and thunders about my ears with a sound of kisses and fighting, a tenseness of muscles taut with love and hate." Why did this feeling so often seize him? He supposed it came "of expecting too much of life, of wanting to live more than ever man lived before." He sensed "such an endless welter of experience to untangle" that there was no time to waste on trivialities, or on conventionality. Nevertheless it remained strange how, despite his furious desires, he was "forever rigid in the straightjacket of [his] inhibitions," sick and tired of them, as he exclaimed.

Travel was a palliative; Dos Passos tried to mask his inhibitions by traveling— or probably it was that he hoped to overcome them. Certainly he was less inhibited than he thought himself to be in his moments of loneliness. If he was sexually inhibited, if he found himself being conventionally "nice" when he yearned to shock, nevertheless he was adventurous about traveling, as in the case of the trip he began down through Spain shortly after returning from England.

He and Dudley Poore, intending to cross the border into Spain almost immediately, met in Paris and headed to Biarritz before the middle of August. Poore, however, could not get a visa because the Spanish government had closed the border in reaction against labor strife. As Dos Passos recounted the episode, the two of them set out from the small port of St. Jean de Luz, Dos Passos with a visa he had obtained in Paris crossing legally into Spain, but Poore having to evade the authorities by wading across the Bidassoa River, which separated the countries. They celebrated their tiny invasion with a lunch of small eels at a restaurant near Fuenterrabía. At a nearby town, he and Poore went their separate ways, agreeing to meet further along the northern coast of Spain. Traveling by narrow-gauge railroad from San Sebastian on to Bilbao, then Santander, Dos Passos found Arthur McComb and the Sweeneys, his friends from his first visit to Spain in 1916. After traveling on to San Vincente, then returning to Santander, McComb and Dos Passos met Poore, who with Dos Passos intended to climb the Picos de Europa, mountains which lie between Santander and Oviedo to the west, before rejoining McComb in Oviedo.*

Years later when Dos Passos wrote about this time, he declared that "as the correspondent for a labor paper I wasn't much of a success. Though I was thoroughly interested in syndicalism and socialism and trade union matters, I was continually distracted by scenery and painting and architecture and the *canto hondo* and the grave rhythms of flamenco dancing." Even more, he was fascinated by the great variety of people. His assessment of himself was exactly true, revealing both the strength and weakness of his style of reportage. Readers expecting essays of resounding political analysis and cries for change are disappointed. What they find is sensitive writing that conveys a vivid feeling for the setting and the people. Dos Passos then and later painted backdrops and tried to capture moods—contexts from which, of course, political analysis might emerge.

But during the trip through the Picos de Europa he had few thoughts about politics. The countryside was too impressive, and what filled his mind were scenes like the primitive wall paintings in the Cuevo del Rinal, between Unquera and

---

*Dudley Poore's unpublished piece about his and Dos Passos's trip in Spain tells a different account of their entry. Poore remained behind in Biarritz for several days after Dos Passos went ahead to Santander and only then did he cross the river illegally and eventually catch up with Dos Passos and McComb.

Columbres, and the joggling coach ride from Unquera to Panes, where he and Poore disembarked, lunched, and then walked the twelve kilometers to La Hermida, spending the night there. A journey the next day toward Potes led them through gray gorges out into "wide tawny valleys" full of dark poplars shivering in the bright sun. Ancient churches and a tower in Potes, "like manuscript illustrations," intrigued the Americans, as did the natives like the old woman they met on the road who asked them to give her love to her son Justo, should they meet him.

After a night in Espinama, they hiked the next day along a mountain path toward the small village of Caín and met two Portuguese men, cynical laborers who claimed to have left their country to avoid the draft. Although the workers were vague about the political situation in Portugal, Dos Passos pressed them for their sentiments, which were simple enough: the government had been bad, was bad now, and probably would be bad in the future. "What about foreign influences?" he asked, remembering his role as correspondent. Foreign businessmen were the worst of all, was the response. It was a great shame that there was but one Socialist deputy in the national parliament, the Portugese said, because Socialists at least were not thieves. Politics in Portugal were very backward, they declared, and they hoped for better things in Arenas, a small town in Spain below the mountains toward the Atlantic Ocean.

At Caín Dos Passos and Poore had a relaxed evening, drinking wine with the townspeople while squatting on the ground against a tiny shack that served as the village *taberna*. Afterward, they slept in the house of a local man, one of whose sons was to guide them through the mountains to Covadonga on an arduous walk that began at dawn the next day. "We were a sight despicable before God," wrote Dos Passos in his journal, "a crawling and lumbering up rocky ledges, a groaning and moaning and puffing on grassy slopes, a desperate clinging to gorse bushes, a dripping a streaming a roaring river of sweat. We must have left many sins behind us on the gorse bushes." At the top of their climb they paused for rest in a shepherd's hut, heaving themselves on a bed while an old woman fed them some goat's milk to the amusement of some shepherd boys who stared at them. The milk, some cheese, and cornmeal bread revived them, so they could begin the long descent through country that had about it "a chaotic, meaningless desolation, full of grassy bottoms full of herds, of valleys that wound round stubby cliffs and stopped suddenly." They lost their way and only after much more hiking did they find Covadonga, a "dull, priest-infested town, where as I knew they would from the holiness of the place, the man in the fonda overcharged us," Dos Passos complained. The next day he and Poore walked to Oviedo, where they met Arthur McComb. Dos Passos then took a short trip to Avilés before the three of them traveled by train to Madrid, halting along the way in León and Valladolid.

Despite the pleasures of the trip down through Spain, Dos Passos let himself be nagged by the fact that he was not working at his novel while he traveled. "To lose the habit of writing is the worst thing on earth that can befall one," he declared with unnecessary self-deprecation to Rumsey Marvin. He had not lost the habit of writing, but so intent was he about his work—and so disciplined about doing it—

that he felt frustrated whenever traveling hindered him. In his quiet way he was intensely ambitious, and all his life he would quickly become restless if circumstances kept him from writing for any length of time. He complained that he had produced hardly anything new for a year. Acknowledging that he had rewritten a good deal of work, he found it "intensely difficult to get into the creative way of thinking." *Three Soldiers* weighed on his mind. He wrote Marvin that he had begun it the previous winter in Alsace, and now, although "the story's all ready to be written," it would not come. He wanted the novel to express his "utter," he wrote, then paused. "It's not exactly that though. The feeling of revolt against army affairs has long crystallized itself into the stories of three people." The characters and the plot were clear in his mind: "The first part is at training camp in America, the second part at the front, the third in that strange underground world of deserters and AWOL's, the underside of the pomp of war. There is going to be rather a lot of murder and sudden death in it." Naturally he could not work on it while climbing the Picos de Europa, but he would soon be at the novel once he had settled for the winter in Granada, where he journeyed from Madrid.

The three travelers remained in Madrid for a few weeks, sightseeing and attending to their own affairs. Dos Passos awaited money from America; he also found a letter from Mrs. Gee, who had been in contact with Allen and Unwin about the publication of *One Man's Initiation: 1917*. Early in August the publishers' reader had read Dos Passos's manuscript and liked what he found. The main character, Martin Howe, he told the publishers, was chiefly "a peg on which to hang impressionistic pictures of the war," and by putting him through a series of episodes, Dos Passos was able to render a good deal of "the insanity & sordid horror of war." The technique, the reader thought, was fine, the method "powerful, economical, brutally sincere." The single passage that he found weak was the lengthy conversation near the end between three French soldiers and Howe. Yet, he added, if this was actually the way men talked, then it was as valid as the rest. Buy the book, he recommended; "it is good." On the basis of this recommendation Allen and Unwin told Mrs. Gee that they would publish the novel if Dos Passos would underwrite part of the cost. Much as he wanted to see the book in print, he telegraphed the publishers that he did not think he could afford that expense; hence he asked them to accept any offer to publish it that would not cost him money. Soon, however, he changed his mind and accepted Allen and Unwin's proposal.

While in Madrid he revisited the places he had known from his stay there as a student nearly three years earlier. One was the café Oro del Rhin, where he, Lowell Downes, and Roland Jackson had sat one evening talking about the war. Now Jackson was dead, killed soon after he reached the front. Drinking a beer in memory of Jackson, Dos Passos wrote a poem about him while he sat at the same table they had before. It concluded:

> *I wonder in what mood you died,*
> *out there in that great muddy butcher-shop,*
> *on that meaningless dicing table of death.*

Did you laugh aloud at the futility . . .
Or had the darkness drowned you?

But Madrid was too exciting to dwell on the past or on political bitterness for long. Dos Passos renewed his friendship with José Giner, with whom the three Americans took several hikes and met the poet Antonio Machado, whose work he was attempting to translate into English. They talked at length about a variety of subjects, the young American admiring the "large shambling" poet who was developing a new method similar to that of the Symbolists and the Imagists. The two men traveled northward through the mountains to Segovia, where Machado taught, and there they strolled about the ancient city while the Spaniard fascinated the other with his talk.

No stay in Madrid would have been complete without a trip to the bullfights, which intrigued him. To Germaine Lucas-Championnière he wrote a long letter, in which he described the moment in the life of a Spanish city when the entire population, pushing and shoving, streams in one direction. Such was the hour of the bullfights. Entering the arena, as in the last act of *Carmen,* he wrote with amusement, a person takes his seat, recalling the struggles of the Roman gladiators. Scornfully one looks at the blood-red sand in the arena, at the red and yellow wooden barricades which protect the spectators, and at the barred door from which the Christian—no, the bull—is going to enter. Dos Passos described the entire performance at length, the sounds of the trumpets, the colors, the movements of the picadors, the matadors, and the teams of mules that hauled each dead bull away. The fight, he thought, was not a battle, but rather a ritual, a sacrifice that must be like those when hundreds of bulls were sacrificed to the great gods at Knossos or Mycenae, or slaughtered before the high walls of Troy. "It is stupid, it is ugly, it is magnificent. It is like a jumping contest or the Ballet Russe," he concluded. "But the nerves of the twentieth century, as accustomed as they are to streams of blood spilling on the ground, cause the entire ceremony to be an interesting but disagreeable sensation."

Not that he had inhibitions about bullfights, he simply watched them dispassionately without seeing them as the primal struggle they were for a writer such as Ernest Hemingway. Dos Passos watched a fight, described it in detail, understood its archetypal elements, yet thought that twentieth-century man had become too accustomed to bloodletting to respond to the ritual. Furthermore, a restrained man in contrast to Hemingway, he did not seek some sort of symbolic action to justify bluster and bravado. Hemingway, or the other hand, seeking ways to demonstrate his courage and expertise, watched a fight, described it in detail, and thought that the ritual expressed man's continuing struggle with violent death in a world that remained inimical, if not malignant, once the war had ended.

All of Dos Passos's inhibitions had not disappeared, however. Early one evening in Madrid, he and Dudley Poore heard music near their fonda. They hurried to where the sounds were coming from, to discover that the place was a brothel. There the prostitutes, eight or nine of them, were young and quite beautiful, Poore thought. As it was early in the evening, no other men had arrived, and he would have liked to stay to talk with the women, but Dos Passos became extremely agitated about remaining and insisted that they leave at once, which they did.

Several days later the restless Dos Passos left Madrid, planning to end his journey down through Spain in Granada. Poore remained behind, while Arthur McComb headed off to Granda by another route. On his way south Dos Passos visited Jaén, a town that he found especially beautiful, "a town white and amber and saffron, dust colored with roofs of ochre and saffron that climbs part way up the flank of huge rocky hills, where the burnt grass is a shining yellow-ochre, joined to the yellow towers of the castle on the crest by long sprawling ruined walls," he wrote in his journal. The ornate cathedral, the chapel of San Andrés, and the cool, narrow streets from which one looked up at a deep blue sky, the dress of the men —wide-brimmed felt hats, tunics, and tight-fitting, light-colored trousers—and children flying vividly colored kites on the hillsides made Jaén memorable. "Why I left Jaén I really dont know," he wrote later, so taken had he been with it.

A slow, uncomfortable train carried him from Jaén to Málaga on the Mediterranean shore. He hiked along the coastline between the sea and the Sierra Nevada range behind it, basking in the hot sun among "superb burnt hills and irrigated valleys full of banana trees and sugar cane and of the sounds of water running through irrigation ditches." In the province of Málaga, he wrote Rumsey Marvin, "the people in the towns hire a fig tree for the summer and go out under it with their pigs and goats and cats and chickens and eat the figs and enjoy the shade. Life has no problems under those conditions."

In Granada, Arthur McComb met him and they rented rooms in a pension called the Carmen de Matamoros, owned by an elderly woman named Mrs. Wood and operated by her Scottish friend, Miss Laird. Dudley Poore arrived from Madrid, so the three Americans moved into a summer house belonging to the pension. Set behind a garden, the house looked out over Granada. Dos Passos's quarters were "a little bit of Old England," he thought. To his relief, he was able immediately to settle down to writing. His routine was to work most of the day, seated in his room "while a great noise of bellringing and toodling of bugles and braying of donkeys comes up from Granada," before he took a walk through the city's "frivolous courts" and the halls of the Alhambra, "the pastry palace the Moors built among the superb red towers of their fortress on the hill." He declared the summer house a success because the first part of *Three Soldiers* was soon finished. But meals at the pension both amused and irritated him. Mrs. Wood, who was "the redeeming feature of Miss Laird's awesome meals" because of her constant reminiscences about the past, never spoke of a time more recent than fifty years ago and would regale anyone present with "delightfully racy accounts of mid-Victorian traveling that sounded like the European parts of a Meredith novel." Dos Passos enjoyed her genteel bigotry. Having once lived in India, she spoke of the need to keep a foot on the necks of the Indians, for example. But Miss Laird's arch-conservatism and a "sinister American woman" at the pension infuriated him, so to the amusement of the less politicized McComb and Poore he ranted against the ladies' diatribes about the Bolsheviks, although he was not wholly sympathetic with the Russian revolutionaries.

When late in September Dos Passos heard of a farmers' strike in progress against the great landowne   in the region of Córdoba and of an impending revolution against the government in Portugal, he traveled to Lisbon after first stopping in Córdoba, where he talked with several natives from the region, persons who understood the plight of the farm laborers and who supported the strike. A bookseller, his helper, and a carpenter eagerly described to Dos Passos an earlier strike; then they visited an architect, a local official who sided with the strikers. He introduced Dos Passos to the editor of a regional weekly paper, *Andalusia,* who with the architect explained in depth the setting for the present unrest which remained unresolved. Dos Passos saw some hope for change, but when he later wrote about Córdoba, he knew enough about Spain to recognize that "until there grows up a much stronger community of interest than now exists between the peasants and the industrial workers, the struggle for the land and the struggle for the control of industry will be, in Spain, as I think everywhere, parallel rather than unified." The individualism he admired militated against organizing to oppose capitalism and the remains of the feudal system.

He remained in Córdoba long enough to obtain information about the farmers' strike, then traveled west through Mérida to the Spanish border town of Badajoz, thence across the border into Portugal. In Elvas the Portuguese doubted his U.S. passport, because Dos Passos was a Portuguese name and the authorities suspected him of being a subversive. Unable to speak the language, he could not present his case, so they insisted that a *policia* accompany him to Lisbon, for which they charged him $10. Before his escort would leave him, Dos Passos had to cross his palm considerably, the policeman vanishing abruptly when the two confronted the American consul.

Dos Passos soon tired of what he considered the loquacious evasiveness of the Portuguese. After much searching that led him from one person to another, he found a man named Emilio Costa, who was to help him find the information he sought about the incipient revolution. Costa provided him with four letters of introduction, then disappeared. Dos Passos imagined he had scared Costa away by his talk of the suspected monarchist revolution against the republican government, prompting Dos Passos to remark that "the scariness and talk of frankness of the Portuguese is detestable. You might be in France. You feel that everyone has got their damned little irons in the fire and is much too busy feeding slyly little bits of wood to the flame to be interested in anything else." His attempts to gather information were largely unsuccessful, while the Portuguese language frustrated him —he told Stewart Mitchell it was the main vice of the country. "How can you stay in a country where they call your name Dsh Pass-sh?" he asked. "The other day in a trolley-car I sneezed violently into my handkerchief. The man opposite answered in Portuguese." After a week's stay at the Hotel International, he departed Lisbon aboard a train back to Elvas, writing fretfully in his journal that he had spent more time fussing over *Three Soldiers*—"The damned army and the merde colored garments and that wretched Fuselli"—than thinking about Portugal. Glancing around his train compartment full of "elderly, musty funny shaped little men," he concluded that "the Portuguese have an irresistible tendency to benevolence: they are a good people, somewhat dirty, somewhat thievish in a small way, humble god fearing, without swagger and the possessors of a mild ambient gaiety. They are a good sweet little people but at the present moment I dont like them—no not so strong as that—but I dont find them sympatico. Yet the syndicalists and people I've talked to have been most excellent people." Nevertheless, what he would remember would be towns like Sintra, near Lisbon, and Portuguese painting.

His bad temper quite possibly resulted from the fact that he was ill. The long, cold train ride back to Granada from Lisbon was fatiguing; several days later he came down with what was eventually diagnosed as rheumatic fever, a serious illness that disrupted his plans. For several weeks he was weak and feverish and lay in bed, so sick that during the worst stages Dudley Poore and a nurse from the naval hospital in Gibraltar whom Poore had requested by wire cared for him around the clock. A planned trip along the coast to Cádiz to see the autumn grape harvesting was canceled and little writing could be accomplished. But, lying in bed, Dos Passos read a great deal and, once improved, worked some at *Three Soldiers*, all the while grumbling increasingly about Miss Laird's pension.

He also thought about American life. In mid-October, just as he became ill, he wrote a long, revealing letter to Rumsey Marvin about his attitudes toward work and business. Letters from Marvin and other friends in America had depressed him because of the "lack of energy" and the "drifting into boredom" he read in them. Marvin had too much spirit to get caught up entirely in "the regular balderdash of the average sheep"; yet Dos Passos could not understand why his friend should want to go into business, as Marvin then intended to do after finishing college. The "tragic fundamental fallacy" for Americans, Dos Passos believed, though not only for Americans, was that they confused means and ends. Business should be a means to something else; yet look at the faces of businessmen, he admonished Marvin. Their sense of values was inverted, and they became "mules in the tread mill in order that their wives may spend thousands boring themselves elaborately in 'society.'" A person became what he did, Dos Passos insisted, so Marvin should not ever want to become an exploiter of others. Thus, if he were to go into business, at least he should go into the scientific end of it. Be a brain that creates, Dos Passos inveighed, "not a parasite living off other people's brains, off other people's work," sounding a central theme in his writing.

His own father, he thought, was a "tragic example" of a fine brain caught up in the business of making a fortune, so that "when he wanted to start being a person instead of a business man," he could not. John R. could live creatively—"use his brains (not his wits)"—only sporadically. In the nineteenth century there was perhaps more reason to strive for wealth; in 1920 to do so was merely shabby and sordid. Although oversimplified, even trite, this typing of the businessman and of his own father defined Dos Passos's stance as he was on the verge of publishing his first important work. He was committed to writing, to creativity; hence he opposed business America to whatever degree it exploited mankind, although he did not know of any social systems that were truly effective panaceas for the evils of capitalism. When Marvin criticized Marxian Socialism, for example, Dos Passos responded that theoretically Marvin is correct and that he too was intensely suspicious of it. But any system that could improve the lot of the average person he favored. "It's a question of *existence not of theories,"* he reminded Marvin. Two and a half months later, after Marvin had continued his argument against the Communists, Dos Passos wrote back, "about Bolshevism: one has to remember that *all* that is published in the press is propaganda, that the Bolsheviki are the moderate social revolutionaries, a political party, and the Soviets are a system of government based on the idea of 'pure democracy' (so called in the textbooks on gov't.) that every man shall take direct part in the government of the country." He believed that a similar system could exist in America, with geographical instead of Russia's industrial units, if Alexander Hamilton had used "the New England town meeting as the unit of government instead of importing Montesquieu's ideas." He recognized that it was foolish to idealize the Russian situation, but it was "criminal to condemn them unheard. Anyway," he chastized Marvin, "the attitude of condemning everything one does not understand is porcine." Although he was in rebellion against the excesses of capitalism, he had a wait-and-see attitude about Socialism.

After the rheumatic fever subsided, a month passed before Dos Passos could move about. He ventured outside into the crisp autumn air of Granada for the first time on November 16 and two days later managed to walk from the pension into town with Dudley Poore for a coffee. But now thoroughly bored by his inactivity and irritated by Mrs. Wood as well as Miss Laird and the American woman who resided in the pension, Dos Passos returned to Madrid with Poore, traveling first class for once, because he was still very weak. They set themselves up in "a rather sepulchral little chamber," and he soon was working intensely on *Three Soldiers,* writing in the Ateneo, a club for literary and scientific people to which José Giner had given him access. Often in the evening he and Poore attended concerts; "Some music exists outside of Paris," he assured Germaine Lucas-Championnière in mid-December, writing her that he had seen opera—Strauss's *Salomé*—and that each Friday there was a concert where one might hear the music of Borodin, Stravinsky, and, almost always, Franck.

Arthur McComb had returned to Madrid also, so the three friends were together constantly after Dos Passos had finished each day's writing, when they would have tea while he read to them from *Three Soldiers.* He and McComb argued frequently about politics, Dos Passos accusing McComb of taking "stride after stride to the right" while lamenting "the good old times before the war," embracing extreme conservatism, and washing his hands of America. Dos Passos overreacted to McComb, partly because the latter refused to be awed by him and stood his ground. McComb admired Dos Passos but did not think him a great intellect or an astute political mind. He saw things in blacks and whites, McComb surmised, and reacted emotionally.

Dos Passos was not sure where he stood politically in late 1919. Although he might castigate American business or be intrigued by the promise of Socialism, he could—at least when taunted by McComb's conservative reaction against a populist democracy—insist to Stewart Mitchell that, like Walt Whitman, he could still cry "Allons Democracy, I have not deserted you ma femme—up camerados!" Despite absurdities in America like the Red Scare, the Communist witchhunt then in progress masterminded by Attorney General A. Mitchell Palmer, America was intriguing. Besides, he wondered, was there any place better at the moment? Only Italy, perhaps, and Spain.

Lying sick in Granada, he had worried increasingly about publishing his work. Two manuscripts were complete and with publishers; a third, *Three Soldiers*, was well along, and he had much of a volume of essays and one of poems written, while the idea for a play was roughed out. Yet nothing was appearing. So before leaving Granada he wrote Allen and Unwin, reminding them that the previous August they had been willing to publish *One Man's Initiation: 1917* if he would pay part of the cost. Since he had heard nothing from them, he assumed that no American publisher had turned up for it. Now he thought he should go ahead and pay whatever was necessary, because, as he told Stewart Mitchell, although the book was "fairly rotten" and he expected few people to read it, having it in his background might help him later. Allen and Unwin told him that his contribution would have to be £75. He arranged for his executors to send the money from America, and by early January 1920, the manuscript had been cast off by the printers. Allen and Unwin were concerned that the book made only 128 pages, perhaps too short to tempt booksellers.

Publication plans proceeded, however. When Allen and Unwin asked Dos Passos for a descriptive paragraph about himself, he was not quite sure what they desired, but thought that the advertising should emphasize that the book had been written from notes he had made while "an ambulance driver attached to the French army in the summer of 1917" and that he had tried to portray "the state of mind of an American in his first contact with the war as well as the general moral atmosphere of the war at that moment." He had scribbled the notes in dugouts and hospitals, then put them into book form in the fall of 1918, "thinly disguised under a novelistic form." The printers, however—who in England are held responsible for what is published—objected to Dos Passos's portrayal of the moral atmosphere. They feared that they risked libel if certain passages remained. The page proofs he received in April were marked up with suggestions about where he might cut, and where paraphrase. He deleted one offending passage, altered a second that made reference to prostitution, but hesitated about a third, which was, he thought, harmless. Referring to Christ as "old boy" might annoy readers; yet he could not believe that it was seriously offensive. If the printers insisted, however, "You" might be substituted. Allen and Unwin immediately responded that they believed the passage was offensive. They understood that the author desired to show that the hero of the novel "was contemptuous of the behaviour of followers of Christianity in the War"; nevertheless, Dos Passos did not need to make cheap gibes at Christ. Dos Passos told the publishers to omit the offending sentences. Besides, he added, "the incident of the soldiers kicking the prop out from the under the Cross will carry the idea." Somewhat exasperated, he told Allen and Unwin that if they did not want to print that passage, then they were to delete the entire scene: "I am willing to have almost anything omit .d, but I cannot consent to paraphrases." Still the matter dragged on. The printers objected again, and while the publishers did not like dictums from printers, the manuscript had been cast off, so taking it elsewhere would add to everyone's costs; thus Dos Passos was urged to acquiesce. He did, and the slightly censored book was finally published in October 1920.

What the printers had censored made scant difference to the purposes of the book as Dos Passos described them. Martin Howe, the central character, was disillusioned by what he found after he got into action, just as Dos Passos had been, although the book conveyed little of the exhilaration the author had also felt. Its best features were his impressionistic sketches of scenes before and during battle— many of them scenes directly from his own experiences—as well as his straightforward, rather naïve expression of confusion and distress about the gruesome horrors of a war for which he could find no justification. *One Man's Initiation: 1917* was very much a first novel, but what was most significant for Dos Passos was that it was published.

While he dealt with Allen and Unwin in early 1920 he continued the daily routine of writing at the Ateneo, which bored him, despite his love for Spanish life, "delectable, preposterous, decorative, everything." What bothered him was *Three Soldiers,* which he wanted to finish but which dragged on. Typically, he was impatient, for in fact he was writing during the morning and early afternoon of each day and had nearly finished a long handwritten manuscript before leaving Madrid for Barcelona in early March.

Partly because of his impatience, but more, because of what he was trying to accomplish in his own work, he was peevish after reading the January 1920 issue of the magazine the *Dial,* the first to be edited by Stewart Mitchell. The *Dial* had for many years represented conservative views, but in 1918 it had been moved from Chicago to New York, where it had become a journal for radical opinion; and among its contributing editors were Conrad Aiken, Harold Stearns, Randolph Bourne, and Van Wyck Brooks. The January issue, however, seemed anything but radical to Dos Passos, who, discouraged, wrote Mitchell that what had interested readers in the *Dial* of the past year had been "a distinct intellectual trend, that of the Chicago economic-social crowd, of John Dewey and Thorstein Veblen and the rest." If these readers were not to lose their interest, the magazine must give them "something vigorous and definite" to catch their imaginations. Mitchell, Dos Passos assumed, wanted to make the *Dial* literary. As it was, the issue was bland, not "a lion to devour and a banner to lead the assault" that Dos Passos wanted.

The time was ripe, he believed, for fresh minds to impress themselves on "chaotic unleavened America." Now was the moment to shape molds which might ensure that civilization, not barbarism, would rule the country and the world. A writer, in fact, could not avoid the turmoil around him. "There never has been great art that did not beat with every beat of the life around it," Dos Passos declared. The present moment was "on the brink of things" where the world's checks and balances were askew, so that in a decade men might be battling each other for food "amid the stinking ruins of our cities," or they might be subjugated, swarming like ants, "in some utterly systematized world where the individual will be utterly crushed that the mob (or the princes) may live." Melodramatically, he declared, "Every written word should be thought of as possibly the last that humanity will ever write, every gesture of freedom the last before the shackles close definitively." His advice to Mitchell reads like a statement of his own intentions, which were to speak out against "La Servitude Militaire," as he told Germaine Lucas-Championnière a month later. Was that protest? He hoped not, realizing that literature which was only protest was less than art. But since he detested everything military, he suspected that *Three Soldiers* had much of the protest novel about it.

Despite his desire to keep writing, he looked forward to the trip to Barcelona, where he hoped to meet Jack Lawson and his wife Kate Drain, as well as their son Alan, and Jack's sister Adelaide, who became a lifelong friend. But Lawson had become ill, so Dos Passos and the other three sailed the end of March to Mallorca, where they spent several days before the others continued on to Alicante.

Dos Passos returned to Barcelona to collect his few belongings and traveled north over the French border to Carcassonne to meet Lawson, who had traveled by himself from Paris, "at the topmost tower of the city wall" as close to high noon on April 14 as they could arrange it. From Carcassonne they traveled slowly along the Mediterranean coast and hiked the short distance to Nîmes, Arles, and the ruins of the fortified town of Les Baux, before arriving in Marseilles near the end of April. The life of that city continually exhilarated Dos Passos, who described to Marvin the throngs of people moving about the waterfront. It was a gateway to the east, he wrote, and nowhere could one find a more "epic" city, bawdy, farcical, jolly, wild —"talk about a barrel of monkeys!" he concluded.

He and Lawson returned by May 1 to Paris, where he intended to finish *Three Soldiers* and try to place it with a publisher. Dudley Poore, back from Madrid shortly thereafter, took a small apartment on the Left Bank where they prepared Dos Passos's manuscript so that in June he could take it to England, hoping to interest Allen and Unwin in it or in "Seven Times Round the Walls of Jericho." Since hearing in March from A. C. Brandt that the American publishers Boni and Liveright were interested in his writing but that they believed "Seven Times" needed much cutting and rearranging, he had revised it while completing *Three Soldiers*. He first presented Allen and Unwin with the newer novel, about which their reader reported quickly. He thought *Three Soldiers* a powerful book, "a conscientiously realistic account of life in the American army" which effectively portrayed not the action of warfare—of which few Americans saw a lot—but "the filth, the monotony, the feeling that one is a degraded slave, a number, mere cannonfodder." The novel was "a fine piece of realism and a powerful anti-militarist document" containing well-wrought sketches of minor characters even if it was monotonous at times because monotony was what the author sought to portray. Words like "friggin'," "bugger," and "certain sordid scenes with French whores" were offensive but could be revised. The major problem from the publishers' point of view, however, was that the novel would be expensive to produce, yet would not appeal to a large audience, who had little stomach at that moment for antimilitary sentiments or portraits of war. The reader feared that the publishers would decide against publication. Regrettably, they would probably be right, he added, although the book's propaganda value could be important.

While Dos Passos remained in England, where as usual he stayed with his elderly friends Mrs. Gee and Miss Meakin, Allen and Unwin discussed their reader's report with him, debated a short while about publishing *Three Soldiers,* and then told him that they had decided against it. Before returning to Paris, he left "Seven Times Round the Walls of Jericho" with them, and their efficient reader, now thoroughly familiar with Dos Passos's work, soon reported back. "Seven Times" was essentially introductory to *Three Soldiers,* he noted, adding that John Andrews of the latter novel made his appearance about halfway through this one, which had, he thought, more color and variety than its successor, because "Seven Times" dealt with "childhood and boyhood, and the vague yet almost uncontrollably intense impulses of sensitive youth." Although *Three Soldiers* was a more mature work, it was less varied, "a fine picture of the revolt against brutalizing discipline and unmeaning work." "Seven Times," about the youth and college years of Martin Howe, was "a picture of revolt against an old man's—and old lady's—civilization." Although it was "inconclusive, aimless, almost chaotic," the reader liked its "vitality without vulgarity." He hoped it would be published and thought that if enough copies were sold to repay expenses, then Allen and Unwin might consider publishing *Three Soldiers.* Dos Passos impressed the reader, who compared him to the English novelist Basil Hall Chamberlain. Dos Passos was not yet as accomplished as Chamberlain, but more earnest and unlike other young American writers, who seemed to the reader to be more reporters than novelists. Dos Passos was still in the making; nevertheless, he already had genuine powers of emotion and expression.

Despite their reader's enthusiasms, Allen and Unwin decided against "Seven Times" as well, suggesting to Dos Passos that because of parts such as those set at Harvard, the book would not attract English readers. Try American publishers, they advised, assuring him that they were interested in his writing and wanted to see more of it—preferably nonwar fiction, they made a point of adding. As a result of their rejections, they were to publish only *One Man's Initiation: 1917,* a choice that was unfortunate financially: in its first six months after publication sixty-three copies were sold.

Although these rejections were a severe disappointment, Dos Passos was consoled by knowing that other of his writing would appear in print. The *Dial* accepted and in June published his essay about Antonio Machado. He had mailed two more essays to Stewart Mitchell and was already working on other pieces as well as the novel he had begun at Harvard, *Streets of Night.* Further, he wanted to commence serious work on a play he had discussed with Jack Lawson during their recent trip.

Staying with Mrs. Gee and Miss Meakin, he lapsed into the melancholy mood that seized him when he felt lonely and nostalgic. "Rainy day—leaden sky," he wrote to Germaine Lucas-Championnière the afternoon he thought she would be leaving Paris for La Baule on the Atlantic Coast. Half-enamored of the intelligent French girl, he assumed a romantic literary pose quite seriously as he sat in Kew Green, the suburb of London where he had lived as a child. He might have been thinking of Wordsworth's "The world is too much with us" or Eliot's grim images of a gray London and timorous Alfred Prufrock. "I would like to rush out into the countryside somewhere," he wrote. He declared that he lived too much in the city and had forgotten the songs of the birds at dawn, the solitary nights when one could walk in the woods in that murmuring silence where green things grew and small animals could go about their business under the great protective shawl of night.

London was too much with him. It was a little like a cold piece of beef, solid but unattractive, he exclaimed, detesting what he described as the pale, bleached evening light in the suburbs, where every day ended in a small eternity of boredom, without color—deserted streets without life, little red houses whose small roofs stood out against the gray sky with a crushing sameness. England was boring, made by machines, but without the fantastic, macabre atmosphere of the United States.

Sitting in one of those houses, he felt the same despairing boredom that had oppressed him years before during the long, pale afternoons when he craved to run outside and was overwhelmed by mad tingling desires to read or play. Then he dreamed of a vivid life he would live one day. "And now that I find myself in the promised land, is it worthy of yesterday's mad desires?" he wondered, continuing:

> Sometimes I think that I have in me one of those little gray rooms, furnished in the best taste, from which the real things of life—the sun and love and sweat and good, hard work which overwhelms the arms—from which these things, undigested, are excluded and can only enter ordered and shaped through literature. Life has to put on its formal hat and wipe its feet well before it can sit down in the little gray salon of the bourgeoisie.
>
> And sometimes this small gray room seems destroyed, always, at important moments, I find myself shut in there, and I look out through its windows at the large ponderous processions which pass by and disappear along the highway. God, if only one could kill off his grandparents.

"Kill off his entire upbringing," he meant, complaining against the inner conflict between his background and his desire to be unfettered that paradoxically motivated some of his best writing.

Dos Passos felt better after he had returned to France, where Rumsey Marvin joined him in early July 1920, when they headed south from Paris for a walking trip in the Auvergne region. From there Marvin continued on to Italy, Dos Passos returning to Paris, where he remained until leaving for St. Nazaire to board a ship for Cuba on August 7. He craved to be back in the United States for numerous reasons, among them that he wanted to find a publisher for his novels. More important was his sense that he had stayed long enough in France. Life there no longer provided the astonishments he sought; it was too civilized for him, he wrote Germaine Lucas-Championnière just before leaving Paris at the end of July. "The unforeseen doesn't exist," he wrote. "French life is a beautiful ceremony in which every movement is made according to a ritual established generations ago. Everything—for us other barbarians, men from an unfinished ritual—is indescribably gentle—a person is like one of the lotus eaters. Elsewhere life, brutal and cruel, plunges toward new forms of organization." Existence was at that moment "a death struggle against the vast mechanisms which are the slavery of tomorrow." The struggle would never stop; hence a person might pause to enjoy the tranquil rhythms of ancient ways, but the time always came when he could no longer resist the urge to go toward the struggle, which he believed to be intense in America. Although the next morning Dos Passos reread what he had written and decided it was pretty foolish, he meant what he said, less the hyperbole, and mailed the letter.

On his trip toward St. Nazaire, he hiked some, visited Angers and Saumur along the Loire River, and Rochefort to the south, then spent a few days with Germaine and her family at La Baule. Soon he boarded the *Espagne,* which cruised along the north coast of Spain, stopped at Santander and Coruña, then made a twelve-day voyage to Havana. He was amused by the petty shipboard intrigues among the passengers, although as usual kept his distance and worked on a play even while spending most of his time writing what he termed his "Dionysius novel"—*Streets of Night*—which he thought might be called *Quest of the Core.* By the end of August he was in New York, staying briefly at his Aunt Mamie's apartment while he looked for a place of his own. He soon found one, a large room decorated in a heavy Victorian style, at 213 East Fifteenth Street off Stuyvesant Square, just above Greenwich Village.

PART IV

===

The Jazz Age,
1920–1929

CHAPTER THIRTEEN

—————

New York, Europe, and the Near East,

1920–1922

From the moment his ship docked in Brooklyn and Prohibition agents swarmed aboard, "square jawed men with clubs" who snooped around a good deal, Dos Passos was fascinated by New York, he told Jack Lawson. The city, he observed, seemed amusing, "like a badly drawn cartoon," a kind of "Babylon gone mad," where he quickly decided "everybody looks and dresses like the Arrow-collar man." His was a love-hate relationship with New York. He mocked it; yet it excited him and inspired his next major works: the play and, several years after, the novel *Manhattan Transfer*. As much as anything, New York—to him a symbol of 1920s America, the land of the big money—solidified his instincts to be a chronicler and a satirist even before he became the overt political rebel he was by the late 1920s. "This is what industrial America is," he meant to be saying as he wrote about the city in the play and the novel, rendering the effect he believed it had on people by juxtaposing details about the city with satiric portraits of characters, many of them sapped of some part of their humanity by the frenetic pace of life.

"New York—after all—is magnificent," he told Germaine Lucas-Championnière after he had been back a month. It was "a city of cavedwellers, with a frightful, brutal ugliness about it, full of thunderous voices of metal grinding on metal and of an eternal sound of wheels which turn, turn on heavy stones. People swarm meekly like ants along designated routes, crushed by the disdainful and pitiless things around them." The city reminded him of:

Nineveh and Babylon, of Ur of the Chaldees, of the immense cities which loom like basilisks behind the horizon in ancient Jewish tales, where the temples rose as high as mountains and people ran trembling through dirty little alleys to the constant noise of whips with hilts of gold. O for the sound of a brazen trumpet which, like the voice of the Baptist in the desert, will sing again about the immensity of man in this nothingness of iron, steel, marble, and rock. Night time especially is both marvellous and appalling, seen from the height of a Roof Garden, where women with raucous voices dance in an amber light, the blue-gray bulk of the city cut up by the enormous arabesques of electric billboards, when the streets where automobiles scurry about like cockroaches are lost is a golden dust, and when a pathetic little moon, pale and dazzled, looks at you across a leaden sky.

A critic could not ask for a better statement of what Dos Passos intended to portray in *Manhattan Transfer*.

Little had changed about the city, he thought, since he had lived there three years before. Again, as he had in London, he complained to Germaine that he was disoriented and out of step with the rest of the world, "more wandering in the dusty paths of the valley of indecisions than three years earlier." His friends, it seemed to him, were forging ahead in good American fashion; only he remained wandering and lost. His gloom, he might have added, resulted in large part from the continued rejections by American publishers of his two novel manuscripts. Alfred Knopf had looked at them both and decided against them, and at one point Boni and Liveright appeared ready to sign a contract for "Seven Times Round the Walls of Jericho," but nothing came of that either. Someday, he told his French friend in disgust, he would tell her about the great melodrama of the deceits of editors and the machinations of literary agencies, adding melancholy, comical, historical, and philosophic reflections about the Great American Bluff.

Despite such grousing, he was enjoying himself immensely. He saw plays, some of them popular, showy affairs that he scoffed at in letters to Jack Lawson. One such theater experience was *Mecca*, "a dull pompous spectacle" that he was amused by because of its "fornicational goings on that were allowed on the stairs in a rather delightful badly costumed ballet by Fokine." He delighted in the "vast quantities of skinny undressed chorus men" and a menagerie on stage that included two camels, a donkey, goats, monkeys, and a comedy Chinaman and his wife. It reminded him of *Scheherazade;* in fact, he thought several times it was. The Follies in Greenwich Village were entertaining, if too arty, but were relieved by the raw humor of a female impersonator named Savoy. November 1 he went with Lawson's sister Adelaide to see Eugene O'Neill's *The Emperor Jones,* staged at the Province-town Theatre on MacDougal Street. This was a significant play for him to see, because its avant-garde techniques and expressionistic elements were what he was attempting to employ in his own play. The part of Brutus Jones, played by Charles Sidney Gilpin, was superb, and Dos Passos's only complaint was about the lengthy breaks between the many scenes, which destroyed the continuity important to the play.

To add to his pleasure he participated in Adelaide Lawson's sketching classes, and enjoyed seeing exhibitions of new art with her and moving partly in the world of the Art Students' League. His was a thoroughly serious interest in art. He had by this time studied it and had practiced sketching and painting at least since his months in Spain in 1916, and now, although he worked hardest at his writing, he toyed with the idea of being a painter. The thought was probably more a fancy than anything; yet he worked constantly at painting. He knew it enhanced his creativity, as his poetry did, and was part of making him the man of the arts he desired to be.

Another man of the arts whom he saw frequently was E. E. Cummings, who was living in Greenwich Village. Together they might eat lunch—laban and a dish Cummings liked, consisting of raw eggplants squashed in oil of sesame—at a Syrian restaurant on Washington Street; then they would stroll through the flower and vegetable stalls in the Washington Market or walk down to the Aquarium in Battery Park where Cummings, Dos Passos recalled, drew pictures of the sea lions again and again. Both men would jot down words or make quick sketches as they went, because both were as much interested in sights as they were in sounds. "Ball bearings bolts & hinges bought steel bolts, hinges bolts"; "Nickel-copper Nickel-chrome Iron"; "Express service meets the demands of spring" were the sorts of detail that Dos Passos noted down and that later went into *Manhattan Transfer.* He was interested in rendering the staccato rhythms of the city and also, through words, in conveying the visual images that were part of its chaotic life.

The two friends often visited the offices of the *Dial,* which were in a comfortable, three-story brick house at 152 West Thirteenth Street. There they could find friends from Harvard: Stewart Mitchell, Edward Nagel—whose stepfather, the sculptor Gaston Lachaise, had a studio nearby—Scofield Thayer and Sibley Watson, who had been the ones to purchase the *Dial* and transform it into the important literary journal it was becoming. Dos Passos especially liked visits to the *Dial;* he felt relaxed around its offices "with paradise bushes in the back yard . . . a lovely dark stenog named Sophia and some beautiful tall ice-tea glasses." He claimed that the editors spoke only French during office hours, a genteel custom, but delightful.

Late in the afternoon he and Cummings frequently met for tea at the Washington Square apartment of Elaine Orr, a beautiful, elegant woman who had recently divorced Scofield Thayer and to whom Cummings would be briefly married in 1924. Other friends like Nagel, Slater Brown—Cummings's fellow American incarcerated at La Ferté Macé—and Mitchell would gather. After tea they would have supper at one of the numerous Italian speakeasies in the Village—in retrospect they all seemed to Dos Passos to have been named Maria's. Or on Saturday nights they often ate at Moscowitz's Rumanian Broilings, a restaurant near Second Avenue on the Lower East Side where the owner played gypsy music in a basement room painted with scenes of Rumania. Cummings would entertain the whole group, teasing one or another of his friends and reciting from his latest work, or at Moscowitz's they might talk about the Russian Revolution with Yiddish writers who knew a great deal about it.

Alcohol was plentiful. "There's no escaping drinks," Dos Passos wrote Jack Lawson early in November. Prohibition was going to give the entire population of New York the D.T.'s if it continued long enough. "You go into a restaurant and innocently order clam bouillon and before you know it you are guzzling vitriolic cocktails out of a soup tureen. . . . The smallest wayside inn to which one wanders in New Jersey becomes before you've sat down, fountains and cataracts and Niagaras of Canadian whiskey." Hunting for alcohol, he told Germaine Lucas-Championnière, was one of life's great excitements in mad New York. Because it was illegal, everyone drank enormous amounts of every sort of detestable liquor. People were often poisoned, he assured her. If a person had the right connections, he could even buy very fine whiskey from the police.

The country is marvelous, he exclaimed, aroused by New York's preposterous aspects. Although he voted for the Socialist candidate Eugene Debs in November, Warren Harding's election did not surprise him, nor did it particularly disturb him. American politics in 1920 appeared foolish rather than malignant and besides, his interests were in his play, in essays he was completing about Spain, and in *Three Soldiers*, which the publisher George H. Doran accepted after thirteen other publishers, Dos Passos later claimed, had turned it down.

Although the *Dial* had published his essay about Antonio Machado, little else of Dos Passos's work appeared there—a sketch, a few poems and a few reviews—before it ceased publication in 1929. But the *Freeman*, edited by Van Wyck Brooks and Albert Jay Nock—the latter especially a man whose belief in individualism appealed to Dos Passos—was interested in his work and in October 1920, published the first of ten pieces of reportage about Spain that would make up a good part of *Rosinante to the Road Again*. He was asked to do some reviewing as well. The editors gave him a copy of Robert Hillyer's *Alchemy—A Symphonic Poem*, newly published. Dos Passos obliged by reviewing it as kindly as he could. He wrote Hillyer that he had reviewed it, sending him a copy of the typescript. The touchy Hillyer was bothered by Dos Passos's criticism that the long poem was too facile and wrote his friend about it. Fortunately for their friendship, the review was not published, Dos Passos apologizing for any offense. "Why should you hold it unfriendliness on my part that our tastes in poetry differ?" he asked Hillyer, reminding him that "one has to take one's friends bag and baggage—and if they are lumbering oafs like myself put up with many a dainty corn stepped on without malice, with much delicate dinnerware smashed in unseemly gesturing." Hillyer should know, his friend wrote, that in spite of any offending criticism Dos Passos admired him.

Dos Passos valued these friendships. When later he had fallings out with Hemingway and Lawson, it was extremely painful for him. He worked harder than most people at maintaining friendships, backing away from confrontations to the point sometimes where others became annoyed by what seemed his evasiveness. "Stand up like a man and be counted," Ernest Hemingway might demand. "Yes, but . . ." Dos Passos would respond, only speaking out in his writing, except on occasion with longtime friends like Arthur McComb or Dudley Poore, with whom he felt less reticent. Not only was he shy by nature, he had been taught to be polite, a characteristic that continually irked him. But it pleased Elaine Orr, who was fond of Dos Passos because during the sometimes raucous evenings in New York in the 1920s, he could be counted on to be considerate. She remembered that more than once Dos Passos came to her when a party was turning into bedlam and offered to escort her home. The chaos made him uneasy, and he recognized that she felt the same.

His ingrained politeness galled him when he felt he could not step outside it. He blamed his family for it and held up their lives as examples of what annoyed him most about the bourgeoisie. "I have just finished a splendid day by having dinner with my relatives," he wrote Germaine Lucas-Championnière in early December. "They are pleasant, but I detest them. They stupidly hate so many people here. They hate the Jews, the Irish, the Bolsheviks, the Catholics, the Negroes, the Italians, the Poles—everyone who is not as stupid as them. They fear everything—and after all, isn't that the lowest of the low?"

The Frenchwoman became the one to whom over and over he voiced his rebellion against his family. Three weeks later he complained to her about a Christmas Day he had spent with the Spriggs in Washington. He decried the boredom of such family gatherings with the melancholy banter of uncles, the malicious gossip of aunts, and the generally unhealthy affection of "honest folks" for their own kind. Their oppressive and shut-in lives infuriated him. Was it for these that humanity has struggled so hard and endured so much, he wondered. A dislike for sanctimonious propriety overwhelmed him each time he returned to Washington, where he had spent many boring days as a child, and where, he added significantly, his mother died. The result was that the desires he had stifled in his childhood had "forever poisoned for me the childish pleasantries of Christmas. I find it a painful season, full of sniveling memories of poor little agonies long past, so foolish yet so tender —but I detest all that—all that sensibility for the Lotus—one must live vividly in the sun, and shout, march, shout, love—without blanching."

He felt easy about confiding these emotions to the intelligent Germaine Lucas-Championnière because she was far away, not one of the Greenwich Village crowd who would have been astonished by such personal remarks from the reserved man. He had enough sense when he wrote his friend to realize that this was self-criticism as much as condemnation of his relatives. He scorned the bourgeois in himself, but distrusted even more his own sentimentality. Yet why should he not be emotional about his childhood with his mother? There was no reason, except that he still felt too attached to the memories. More than he would have them be, they were a part of him, and this disturbed him, because he was not sure of himself.

Apparently relatives and New York began to loom too large, and once more he felt restless. In addition, he was annoyed by the fact that Doran, after accepting *Three Soldiers*, was insisting that it be altered in several places that might offend readers. Eugene Saxton, his editor, pleaded with him not to be too thin-skinned about the changes. Dos Passos insisted on retaining some of the rough language in his manuscript, some "Jesuses" and "sonsofbitches" in particular. He would even agree to "Jesus" becoming "Jez," but the language must not be cut out because that was the way men spoke in the army. "Freedom of the press," he wrote Saxton, "does not mean compromise. It means publishing what Tom Dick or Harry damn please and letting people lump it if they don't like it."

With Doran scheduled to publish *Three Soldiers* in the spring and *Rosinante to the Road Again* in the fall, Dos Passos craved to return to Europe, whence he planned to travel into Persia. Having arranged to write articles for the *New York Tribune* and *Metropolitan Magazine,* he felt secure to depart New York's *vie littéraire,* so he and Cummings booked passage on an old Portuguese freighter, the *Mormugão,* sailing mid-March from New Bedford, Massachusetts.

They had a relaxed passage that lasted three weeks aboard the ship, which they quickly nicknamed the Holy Roller because of her propensity to roll scuppers-under in a heavy sea, especially when—as was the case almost immediately after leaving port—her engines died. But they soon became accustomed to the *Mormugão's* unsteadiness, got over their seasickness so that they could down the eight courses of oily Portuguese dinner set before them each day, and became good friends with the ship's crew.

After stopovers in the Azores and Madeira, the voyage ended in Lisbon, where, Dos Passos claimed, he tried to interest Cummings in great Portuguese art, but the poet wanted to move on toward France, especially after a tooth became painfully infected. The two Americans first traveled into Spain, visiting Salamanca, Plasencia —full of storks, Cummings noted—Carcares, and finally arriving in Seville, where, with Dos Passos acting as interpreter, a Spanish dentist lanced Cummings's abscess. Much relieved from pain, he joined Dos Passos in marveling at the city's fair. "Such wearing of white mantillas, such driving about in carriages—such dancing of Sevillanos with a solemn air in booths—and bullfights and ballerinas at the café-concert places in the evening," Dos Passos wrote to Rumsey Marvin.

Cummings, also enthusiastic now that he was no longer suffering, described their stay in Seville to his mother in much greater detail. He and Dos Passos had watched two bullfights, and he wrote his mother about his fascination with the gory yet enthralling ritual of each fight. The famous matador Belmonte had been injured the day they had arrived in Seville, so in his place fought Rafael Yallo, an older man who still could perform with great finesse. As exciting to Cummings was the fair itself, with its colors, dancing, beautiful girls, and a merry-go-round that Dos Passos suggested they ride on, "so we sat our pigs (wonderful pigs, with a triple sea-sick motion) in the light of the lanterns and the laughter of thousands of people," Cummings closed his letter to his mother.

Not to his mother but to Edmund Wilson, Cummings related another anecdote about the trip. As they journeyed, he enjoyed the culture and the scenery, but he would occasionally seek a prostitute. When he and Dos Passos arrived in a town, he would want to wander around looking for a woman to pick up, but he could never entice Dos Passos to venture out with him. "I'll just stay here in the hotel, I think," Dos Passos would say. Cummings, bemused, finally asked his companion if he ever thought about women or dreamed about sex. No, was the response, but at night Dos Passos would wake Cummings up by groaning and thrashing in his sleep. "What's the matter, Dos?" Cummings would ask, and Dos Passos would answer that he had been dreaming of wild swans flying overhead. After repeated awakenings, Cummings one day said to him, "You know, sometimes sex appears in dreams in very much disguised forms. You may be dreaming about sex without knowing it. Tell me one of your dreams—what did you dream about last night, for example?" As Cummings, who enjoyed imitating his friend's slight lisp, told it, Dos Passos answered, "Why I dweamed I had a bunch of aspawagus and I was twying to give it to you." Cummings was floored.

Dos Passos preferred to spend his energies hiking and climbing, so they entrained for France and the Pyrenees and met Jack Lawson in St. Jean de Luz before traveling to Oloron, where Lawson left by himself for Toulouse. They, meanwhile, proceeded to the small village of Aidioux high in the mountains. From there they ascended sheep and mule paths into snow and hoped to cross the mountains through the pass Cummings thought was named the Col de Siesta. Fog and deep snow hindered them, but eventually they reached a precipitous dropoff, down which they slid and tumbled until at last they came to a river. Following this through rain and fog, they forded it, descended through meadows thick with furze, then woods, and a steep alpine meadow before wading across a second river, finally to reach a farmhouse. Soaked and exhausted, they pushed on, walking another fifteen kilometers to the town of Biel.

The remainder of the trip to Paris was interesting, but nothing could equal the excitement of the odyssey over the Pyrenees. Once in Paris, Dos Passos stayed in Lawson's rooms at 37 Quai d'Anjou while he finished the last chapters of *Rosinante to the Road Again.* In May he mailed off the last two chapters of that collection of essays, which he hoped were not "too g.d. rotten," asking John Farrar, an editor at Doran, if the publishers would omit italics except in the case of songs and quotations. He did not want Spanish or other foreign words to be overemphasized. Also, he wanted to omit apostrophes in words like "dont," and use dashes instead of quotation marks, his point being that he was trying to create a less formal, perhaps reportorial, style. But he did not feel strongly about these matters and readily accepted Farrar's judgment that readers might be put off by these novelties among an otherwise familiar style.

He accepted as well Doran's decision to wait until the early fall to publish *Three Soldiers,* a rescheduling which they thought would enable them to get more attention for the novel. Dos Passos was too eager to be on with his travels to object strenuously. He hiked in the region of Touraine with Stewart Mitchell early in June, then journeyed to London for several days to visit Miss Meakin and Mrs. Gee and to discuss *One Man's Initiation: 1917* with Allen and Unwin. The sale of only sixty-three copies was most disappointing, even more so because Dos Passos could account for twenty-three of the sales himself. But with *Three Soldiers* and *Rosinante* scheduled to be published, Doran would consider issuing the first novel in the United States under their own imprint. After *Three Soldiers* appeared, Doran bought Allen and Unwin's unbound sheets for *One Man's Initiation: 1917* and bound five hundred copies.

In Paris that spring of 1921 Dos Passos found Paxton Hibben, an American he had met in New York the previous winter, who was in Europe working for the Near East Relief, an organization established by the Red Cross the year before.

Hibben was part of a committee that was to investigate conditions in the Caucasus, now under the control of the Bolsheviks and suffering from repression and famine. He assured Dos Passos that if he could get to Constantinople, there would be a place in the N.E.R. which could enable Dos Passos to travel in Persia.

Adelaide Lawson was in Venice with enough private income to travel, so Dos Passos, planning to travel eastward on the Orient Express, stopped there for several days in early July. It was a "fine jolly place—like Coney Island and a fancy novelty shop on Fifth Avenue mixed with a goodly proportion of Puccini and seasoned with a whiff of sea and salt marshes." Adelaide had paid for room and board in a small pension; he took a room in a hotel overlooking the Grand Canal and wanted her to eat meals with him. She was prepared to move to a room near his in the hotel, but he said no, so after some difficulty she arranged to take one meal a day away from her boardinghouse. Together they remained busy seeing art and each afternoon swimming at the Lido. Never one to stop working, he had brought the manuscript of "Seven Times Round the Walls of Jericho" with him to revise a third time. If *Three Soldiers* sold well, he told Robert Hillyer, then it should be possible to market "Seven Times." If not, then he did not know what to do, and uncertain as he felt about his work, he wondered if he would have the heart to go through the trouble of looking again for a publisher.

Soon he boarded the Orient Express for the long journey to Constantinople. Before he left Venice his anticipation had been aroused by signs scratched on walls proclaiming VV LENIN or M LENIN. An uneasy atmosphere reminded him of the political struggles to the east. It was a suitable forewarning, because the first thing that he saw when he walked into the Pera Palace Hotel in Constantinople was the blood of an assassinated diplomat pooled in a plush chair and on the tiled floor in the lobby. The city was chaotic; White Russian refugees who had fled the Bolsheviks packed in everywhere, most of them impoverished and anguished, but some with enough money that they could jam into the expensive hotels. People were fearful of Bolshevik spies who were rumored to be everywhere; supposedly the assassin of the diplomat in the Pera Palace Hotel was one.

Dos Passos told Jack Lawson that he found himself "in enormous spy infested state in a room overlooking the Golden Horn and the suburb of Kassius Pasha, and the sacred dome of El Ayouli where the mantle of the prophet and the sword of Osman are kept." Every bit as much as in Marseilles or New York—the cities Dos Passos found the most hectic—life was a swirl as the Allies tried jointly to administer the city. The result was disorder. Shortly before he had arrived, the British had raided the important hotels, attempting to round up suspected Bolsheviks, including, so the story went, one woman who was nude and refused to dress, so the soldiers wrapped her in a blanket and hauled her away. Rumors about victories, defeats, and massacres were rife, amid constant noise and jostling. "Talk about whores bawds, concubines and others!" Dos Passos exclaimed, "the streets of Pera beat everything."

When the American naval commander in Constantinople arranged for correspondents to take a voyage to see the nature of the fighting between the Greeks and the Turks, Dos Passos went along. Aboard a destroyer, the correspondents cruised part of the coast of the Sea of Marmara, pausing in several small ports where the devastation of war was apparent. In one port, Greeks, desperate for relief from the Turks who had pillaged their town, crowded the shorelines. In another, Turks surged toward the destroyer; Greeks had attacked them, and they feared further brutalities. No refugees could be taken aboard, so Dos Passos remembered the correspondents sitting morosely in the ship's wardroom during the return to Constantinople.

N.E.R. officials refused Paxton Hibben's request to include Dos Passos in the Red Cross group that was to investigate conditions in the Caucasus. Hibben nevertheless got him on aboard the Italian steamer *Aventino* with them as they sailed for Batum. The trip frustrated Dos Passos, who was not permitted ashore at any of the ports—Inebolu, Samsun, Urdu, Giresun, and Trebizond—along the way. August 7 he sat aboard the *Aventino* awaiting permission from the Soviets to land. The next day a Russian officer issued him the necessary passport, and he was ashore, where, "by the grace of the people's commissars of the Soviet Republic of Georgia temporarily occupied by the Red Army," he wrote Rumsey Marvin, he would commence a voyage inland to Tiflis, then on to Erevan, Tabriz, and Teheran.

The trip to Tiflis was an adventure in itself. The train consisted of a locomotive, three antiquated sleeping cars, and a caboose. In Batum, some 7,000 people swarmed around it, hoping to cling somewhere. Dos Passos ran back and forth along the platform, finally getting an assist through a window into a compartment already filled with people. Several soldiers were thrown out to make room for him, and after considerable delay and rumors about destroyed track, cholera, and an invaded Tiflis, the train headed inland toward the Caucasus Mountains. When he tried to sleep in his upper berth, he was attacked by bedbugs which paid no heed to insect powder he sprinkled around. He finally climbed into the baggage rack above the berth and fell asleep to the sound of people stirring on the car roof just over him.

Once he had arrived in Teheran in October, Dos Passos offhandedly described to Robert Hillyer the next stages of his journey. He had, he said, traveled on various boxcars through

Armenia where everyone was dying of cholera and typhus and starvation, and Adjerbeidjan to the Persian border. Then in an insane fourhorse cab known as a phaeton across deserts and mountains and the fresh trails of nomad raiders, in the company of a Persian doctor who was a great judge of melons, to Teheran, where I recline in somewhat exhausted state at this funny little French hotel.

He did not write of what he had seen: at Tiflis the N.E.R. party invited him into their quarters, where they lived in real comfort, with vodka and wine at their meals, while outside as he later described it, "twenty people a day die of cholera, forty people a day die of typhus, not counting those who die where nobody finds them," and starving soldiers literally collapsed in the streets. Wealthy Russian refugees, members of the old regime, heaped their belongings on the N.E.R. people in return for food. The sight disgusted Dos Passos, who scorned equally the fearful Russian aristocracy, pathetic remnants of a shattered world; the young opportunists who seized on the dilemma of the refugees; and the members of the N.E.R. who were willing to traffic in stolen goods.

He despised such goings-on and hoped that the Communist regime foretold a purging of man's grotesque craving for Things. When Dos Passos spoke about the incidents in *Orient Express*, he voiced just such a hope, but even then as he neared his most left-wing political stance—the book was published early in 1927—he refused to predict the results of the wind that had "blown Russia clear, so that the Things held divine a few years ago are smouldering rubbish in odd corners." Speaking of 1921, he wrote that the moment was "the lull after the fight"; cholera and famine were the gods' and devils' revenge on the Soviet victors. "Will the result be the same old piling up of miseries again, or a faith and a lot of words like Islam or Christianity, or will it be something impossible, new, unthought of, a life bare and vigorous without being savage, a life naked and godless where goods and institutions will be broken to fit men, instead of men being ground down fine and sifted in the service of Things?" He did not know and could only brace himself against the "scaring wind."

Before he left Tiflis, Paxton Hibben invited him to a dinner with the Soviet command. The food was superb; everyone was in good spirits; the nearsighted Dos Passos was led into a narrow room, one wall of which turned out to be a stage curtain which rose suddenly, leaving him facing a large, excited audience. The event was a proletarian poetry festival; Hibben introduced him as an American poet who would recite something. Overwhelmed, Dos Passos managed to blurt out Blake's poem "Ah Sunflower, weary of time," when it came his turn to talk. The crowd supposed the poem was a paean to the Revolution and cheered; Hibben sat in the audience trying to hold in his laughter. The event was a welcome relief from reality, which, Dos Passos recalled, returned even as he and Hibben walked with the cheerful crowd back to the N.E.R. quarters, passing the Cheka, the jail packed with suspected enemies of the new Soviet state.

The N.E.R. would give him nothing to do, so with a Persian doctor, Hassan Tabataba, he boarded a freight car assigned to them, empty but for some bundles of *Pravda* and *Izvestiya*, which accompanied them to Nakhichevan near the Persian border. The sights along the way were depressing: "cholera people dying of typhus on mats along the edge of the railroad track—an endless process of ruined villages, troops, armored trains," he wrote Arthur McComb. At the border the engineer had the two travelers carry their gear into the locomotive cab; the freight cars were uncoupled from behind them, and the locomotive steamed across the Araks River into Persia, where the men debarked in the border town of Dzhulfa. From there the two travelers took a train to Tabriz.

Dr. Tabataba procured their "phaeton"—"a dilapidated vehicle drawn by four ill-favored white horses," was how Dos Passos described it in *The Best Times*. He was much taken with the doctor, whose continual speeches about progress and social democracy and whose medical feats—lancing boils, slitting ulcers, and bandaging broken bones—enlivened the thirteen-day journey in the rickety carriage through the mountains to Teheran. That city, he found, was "a delightful town full of watercourses and huge trees and funny little pastry porticoes and great mud gates plastered with pictures of battles and Shahs in tilework of a rather evil yellow and green hue, overlooked by pink and yellow mountains and by the snow-ribbed peak of Damavand, where the Dirvs crouch in the rocky hollows and cast malice out of the world."

Dos Passos had just settled into his room in the Hotel de France when he became ill with malaria, which was cured only after a good many doses of quinine as well as some nursing from the Polish wife of a Russian engineer and from a vast woman named Shekher, a chambermaid in the hotel. Once his high fever subsided, he was able to wander about Teheran in what he described to Hillyer as "a flabby costume of pink silk, with a nose burned red like an over boiled beet and about my waist a great purple and green sash (to prevent diarrhea)." The Mideast had its exotic aspects: men whose beards were dyed with henna; large, domed felt hats; brightly colored robes; travel by camel; rich red-brown wine; a drink called arak that burned as it went down; and ceremonial processions at that time of year mourning the death of Hosein, the last grandson of the prophet Mahomet. Men dressed in black trudged through the streets of Teheran, casting ashes on themselves and beating their breasts, while others, dressed in white and draped in chains, each clung to the man in front with his left hand and with his right, slashed at his shaven head with the flat of a sword—"rather terrific in the dust and in the lashing sunlight, the reek of blood and the broken sound of trumpets and the hoarse groaning cry of Hosein Hosein," he wrote Tom Cope.

Dos Passos was glad he had traveled into Persia, he reminded himself when he was not miserable with malaria, but he had discovered that he was not a journalist at heart. When he was about to start the trek from Teheran to Baghdad he admitted as much to Rumsey Marvin, while he sat in the Hotel de France waiting for a money order to arrive. He was, he decided, no Richard Harding Davis. Journalism was not his forte, and the sooner he got home and settled down to writing, the better. Impatient thus to be on, he arranged with an Armenian man to be transported to the Iraqi frontier in the man's Model-T Ford. They had an easy journey to the border town of Kasr Shirin; there he was escorted to the railhead in Iraq, eventually finding his way aboard a train, despite the misgivings of the local stationmaster, who insisted that Dos Passos's papers were not in order and his Persian money was no good.

An overnight train ride joggled him to Baghdad, where he checked into the Hotel Maude, a dismal spot that the British used as a junior officers' mess. To add to his discomfort, he became feverish from malaria again, and while he lay on his cot in his bare, unfurnished room at the hotel, he was bitten on the lip by one of the rats that infested the place. His intention in Baghdad was to find a caravan crossing the desert to Damascus, since steamships from Basra near the head of the Persian Gulf around to Marseilles cost too much, and he foresaw little excitement in an airplane trip. The American consul in Baghdad put him in touch with

Gertrude Bell, a remarkably knowledgeable woman then in charge of British intelligence for that entire region. One of her subordinates arranged with two Arabs for Dos Passos's transportation. His mentor would be one of the two, Jassem-er-Rawwaf, who agreed that Dos Passos would be provided a camel and a tent and would be delivered safely to the Hotel Victoria in Damascus. He should pay twenty Turkish pounds, let his beard grow, wear Arab dress, and bring enough supplies for two weeks.

After more than three weeks in Baghdad during which Dos Passos took a trip to Babylon, worked on articles about Persian politics and yet another draft of "Seven Times Round the Walls of Jericho," Jassem and the leaders of the caravan seemed to be arranging for their security during the desert crossing. Finally, Dos Passos, Jassem, and several others were loaded aboard a veteran Model-T Ford and driven the distance to Romadi, a town in the desert on the west bank of the Euphrates River, where the caravan was being staged. After further waiting, Dos Passos packed his belongings in two large saddlebags and was aided up onto a camel whose name he eventually learned was Rima. The trek to Damascus from the time he left Baghdad for Romadi took thirty-nine days, he wrote his friends shortly after it had ended; in *Orient Express* he detailed thirty-seven. No matter, the journey was a miniature odyssey for him that involved long days of travel mounted on Rima, whose rolling gait was comfortable once he got used to it; ten days of raw cold weather; sparse rations; and repeated incidents—including one in which the caravan was fired upon—warding off nomadic tribesmen who demanded protection money. The final hurdle for the caravan was to circumvent the French customs officers who patroled the Syrian border, because Jassem and the others did not want to pay duty on the tobacco, camels, and other goods they intended to sell. The French were evaded, and the last night before entering Damascus Dos Passos fell asleep to the clink of money as it changed hands. The next morning half the camels had disappeared, as well as most of the bales of tobacco, rugs and, he supposed, opium that had been transported. When he thought back to the desert voyage, he was sure it was the best thing he had ever done. "The desert's gorgeous," he wrote Tom Cope, "the people in it are so damn fine. I didn't know the world contained such people—It's an excellent little pippin after all, the world is—When I got to Damascus even the year was new."

Even so, the last bit of the trip into Damascus was excruciating. From where the goods had been sold Dos Passos painfully rode a stallion with a stirrupless saddle until the caravan leader noticed his misery and let him ride on a camel. In Damascus, the leader insisted that Dos Passos visit his relatives: old men in one of the bazaars, a tailor, a café proprietor, and others. Then a drunken French officer tried to take over the carriage in which the caravan leader and Dos Passos had made the final moments of the trip into Damascus. The officer had to be placated, and nothing would do but that the American drink with him, which Dos Passos obligingly did, only then making his way to the Hotel Victoria and several hot baths. His troubles were not over. The next day the French wanted to arrest him for having entered Syria without a passport, which turned up hours later at the American consulate.

Now a legal visitor, Dos Passos became something of a celebrity because of his feat of crossing the desert. The French were suspicious, while the British were bemused. Meanwhile, the Americans fitted him out in an oversized set of tails and took him to a party, where his pinned-in trousers had a way of letting go, to the amusement of the consul and his wife.

The last Dos Passos saw of his Arabian friends was when, clean-shaven and dressed in a suit, he found Jassem in a mosque. He approached the Arab, who was astounded and hurt at Dos Passos's transformation back into a Westerner. Jassem made a formal gesture of farewell, then abruptly turned away and departed, leaving the American genuinely saddened.

CHAPTER FOURTEEN

The Literary Life:
New York and Paris,
· 1922–1924

Amid the excitement of his arrival in Damascus, Dos Passos found a packet of mail addressed to him at the American consulate. Letters from friends congratulated him on the success of *Three Soldiers,* published late in September 1921. As he relaxed in a hot bath at his hotel, he thrived on the news that the novel, provoking controversy among the critics, was selling well. "You are as famous as Wrigley's," wrote Jack Lawson, who assured Dos Passos that the novel had created a "grandiose rumpus" and was "talked about noisily in subways and churches"; but what distressed Lawson was that people's comments in favor of *Three Soldiers* were about as "evil" as those against it. Yet the great thing was that the novel's notoriety gave Dos Passos a magnificent chance to "raise more and concentrated Hell" in America, "this carnival of bêtises." Eugene Saxton had clipped and mailed to Damascus copies of book reviews. Most praised the novel, the reviewer for the December *Atlantic's Bookshelf* calling it "aesthetically honest and quite fearless." Heywood Broun of the *Bookman* declared, "Nothing which has come out of the school of American realists has seemed to us so entirely honest. . . . It represents deep convictions and impressions eloquently expressed."

Less laudatory was the front-page review in the *New York Times Book Review* for October 2, 1921. There Coningsby Dawson attacked *Three Soldiers* as a failure "because of its unmanly intemperance both in language and in plot." He deplored the lack of any "voice of righteousness," hearing in the novel only the "voice of complaint and petty recrimination." Conservative opinion such as Dawson's would continue as, for example, when there appeared in the March 13, 1922, *Chicago Tribune* a diatribe against *Three Soldiers* under the headline: THREE SOLDIERS BRANDED AS TEXTBOOK AND BIBLE FOR SLACKERS AND COWARDS. The author, who remained anonymous but listed himself as "a member of the First Division, a Legionnaire, a father, and a citizen," sensed correctly that the novel was a "blow at Americanism." "Dos Passos," he concluded, "has become the Knight Errant of all that America does not stand for."

Outraged responses like Dawson's and that in the *Tribune* gratified Dos Passos, whose novel about the tedium, injustices, and occasional horrors experienced by three young Americans reflected some of his own travails in the war. The novel now seems contrived and the style a curious pastiche of realism and impressionistically rendered scenes, but his attack against war and organization was already raising the "concentrated Hell" that Lawson wished it would stir up. Dos Passos could rest assured that the book was good because of reviews like Heywood Broun's, or that of Henry Seidel Canby, whose remarks in the *Literary Review* for October 8, 1921, can still stand as a judgment of the novel's importance. "This is by no means a perfect book," Canby wrote, "but it is a very engrossing one, a firsthand study, finely imagined and powerfully created. Its philosophy we may dismiss as incomplete; its conception of the free soul tortured, deadened, diseased by the circumstances of war, we cannot dismiss."

Pleased and rested after several easy days in Damascus, Dos Passos traveled to Beirut, where he remained for more than a week while he relaxed, caught up with his correspondence, and sought passage west. Seated in the luxurious Hotel Bassoul, he acknowledged the packet of clippings Eugene Saxton had mailed him and praised Doran's publicity work. He thanked literary notables like Sherwood Anderson, whom he had met in Paris the previous summer. "Let me blurt out," he wrote Anderson, "that there's nobody in the country such a note means so much from as from you." To his close friends he wrote at length, describing briefly the last stages of his journey across the desert while declaring that he was ready to return to the United States, having, as he told Robert Hillyer, "destroyed the illusion of geography." He had at the moment no more inclination for exotic tours. When civilization finally disgusted him for good, he might "retire to the Nejd and have a great quantity of giggling wives in pink nighties." But until then he would remember three truths: "There's as bad wine to be drunk in Tiflis as on Eleventh Street, the phonographs squawk as loud in Baghdad as they do in Sioux City, and politics are no more comic in Teheran than in Washington, D.C." He assured Hillyer that he was on his way home—"(curious word 'home': I wonder why I used it)," he thought to himself, since he tended to dissociate himself from America so much of the time.

Despite his eagerness to reach the United States, he journeyed in late January to Paris before sailing in mid-February aboard the *Aquitania*. He saw much of Cummings, Slater Brown, and Stewart Mitchell and regaled them with his experiences: "attacks by Bedouins, wildwest style, shooting at Dos with rifles from pony-back, etc. While the fat merchants prayed and the camels kneeled down in sympathy," Cummings recounted to his mother. The four Americans had "several really remarkable parties" in Paris at which Dos Passos enjoyed himself so much that he paid lavishly and eventually had to borrow 800 francs from Cummings for the voyage to America. Before he left he and Cummings discussed *The Enormous Room*, due to be published in the spring. Cummings feared that his editors would bowdlerize it; Dos Passos could not be reassuring, because he recalled Doran's insistence on deleting portions of *Three Soldiers*.

As he departed Paris he promised Cummings that he would try to prevent that sort of editing, and after a rough trip across the Atlantic—"I've never had such seasickness," he wrote Germaine Lucas-Championnière—he immediately visited Boni and Liveright, Cummings's publishers, once he had arrived in New York at the end of February. The publishers wired Cummings for permission to let Dos Passos inspect the proofs of *The Enormous Room*. Cummings agreed, and Dos Passos did his utmost to protect the manuscript from the editors. A month later Cummings thanked Dos Passos, having heard from Elaine Orr about Dos Passos's efforts to do not only "everything possible for the Enormous Room Or La Crise De Logement By Eskling Clueminks Jr.," but "doing the to be brief Impossible! Which kindness, which phalanxforming . . . nocuous indesuetude on thy or your part, I can nor adequately remercier nor worthily immortalize by mere words. . . ."

Dos Passos's efforts, however, did not suffice, and when later in the spring Cummings had the chance to read an advance copy of his book, he exploded. He furiously typed out a statement: TO WHOM IT MAY CONCERN, which he mailed to Dos Passos with the instruction that he confront Boni and Liveright with it. "I desire," wrote Cummings, "that one of two things happen to 'The Enormous Room': either

A)   it be immediately suppressed, thrown in a shitoir

B)   each and all of the below-noted errors be *immediately and completely* rectified without loss of time, fear of money, or anything-damned-else—"

Cummings then listed four character portraits that had been omitted, "for which there is no reason and no excuse," and remarked that, not having the manuscript at hand, he could not tell if other characters had been left out, further harming the sense of the book. "If the portraits omitted were in any way inferior," he wrote, "there might be some (damned little by Jesus) excuse. They are NOT below, and are—in fact—considerably ABOVE, the average in the mutilated book-as-it-stands." He complained bitterly about other omissions, misprints, and the translation of French phrases, which confused the reader who needed to understand when a character was speaking in French. "AS IT STANDS," he added in a postscript, "The book is not merely an eye-sore but an insult." Dos Passos, either consciously or unconsciously, neglected to convey the diatribe to Boni and Liveright; only years later as he was sorting out his papers did he discover it.

When Dos Passos returned to New York in late February, he remained in the city only long enough to plead Cummings's cause and to visit briefly with his Aunt Mamie Gordon and her family. Then he escaped to Cambridge, where he could avoid the publicity stints that his publishers were trying to arrange for him in the wake of the success of *Three Soldiers* and in advance of the publication of *Rosinante to the Road Again* in March, and of an American edition of *One Man's Initiation: 1917* in June—Doran hoping to capitalize on the success of *Three Soldiers* with the five hundred sets of unbound sheets purchased from Allen and Unwin. In addition, they planned to bring out his volume of verse, *A Pushcart at the Curb,* in October 1922. "New York too hectic," he wrote Rumsey Marvin in mid-March, and when shortly thereafter Marvin invited him down from Cambridge to New Haven to give a speech, Dos Passos declined. He had made a policy of not "shoot[ing] my face on any account," and besides, he was no good at it, he declared. When he had tried to give a talk at a "beastly dinner in New York," he had "made a hideous mess of it." Resenting Doran's attempts to turn him into a "prize cow," he had sought out a small back room in an apartment house in Cambridge, where the seclusion enabled him to work on *Streets of Night.*

He was not as much the recluse as he liked to pretend. He constantly visited his close friends Robert Hillyer and Stewart Mitchell in Cambridge, and despite working diligently at his writing, he took the time for pleasant dinners and evenings with them and other friends. He remained away from New York into April, then briefly took a third floor room at 45 Barrow Street before Elaine Orr agreed in May to rent him the rear apartment on the first floor of her studio building behind 3 Washington Square. Dos Passos continued to visit his friends frequently in Boston, sometimes stopping off in New Haven to see Rumsey Marvin at Yale and in certain moods thinking back on his earlier life at Choate nearby. "We are passing by New Haven," he wrote Germaine Lucas-Championnière from the train in early May, "an absurd city, near which I lost some very good years of my youth in a boarding school. It always brings back a little of my old distaste when I see the station where I got off the train bringing me back from New York so much against my will. What one suffers when one is small!"

Such melancholy thoughts occupied him little, however. He quickly settled into life in Greenwich Village and began immediately to enjoy "La Vie Littéraire," as he termed it in *The Best Times.* Several wartime friends were living in the city, and before long he met Edmund Wilson, whom the poet John Peale Bishop introduced him to that spring. Dos Passos waited outside the office of *Vanity Fair* where Wilson worked while Bishop—as Dos Passos remembered it—went in. Soon Wilson, "a slight sandyheaded young man with a handsome clear profile," appeared, and as the three men waited for the elevator, Wilson with an absolute poker face turned a somersault. He and Dos Passos were immediately fast friends; by late in May Wilson wrote Scott Fitzgerald that he had been seeing a lot of Dos Passos, who, Wilson thought, was "extremely nice." He added that Dos Passos was in the midst of a novel "about the devitalized gentility of modern Boston"—*Streets of Night*—which Dos Passos described to Wilson as "a tragedy of impotence."

Elaine Orr's studio apartment seemed thoroughly satisfactory—"je suis très bien," Dos Passos wrote Germaine in May. He was again painting as he had with Adelaide Lawson in 1920. The studio, thus, was lined with stacks of paintings along the walls, but contained little else except a *buhl*—an eighteenth-century Louis XV inlaid cabinet from his family—and a cot. Dudley Poore recalled that Dos Passos had ripped the telephone away from its moorings, a reaction, Poore concluded, against "the system" as Dos Passos discerned it.

For him life in Greenwich Village was excitingly bohemian and, in that sense, rebellious. Trying to write in his studio with a window flung open to catch the spring air, Dos Passos would find himself distracted by the life outside such as "a heavenly hurdy-gurdy man" who one morning strolled underneath his window opening onto the mews. Dos Passos was "utterly disrupted" by the man's playing "The Wearing of the Green," so he stopped trying to work on his novel and wrote Marvin a rambling letter about "Crimes of American Colleges," which included:

A. Inculcate snobbery, social climbing and a system of ideals, catchwords, morals for which I have no sympathy . . .

B. The scholarly type: sycophants time servers, people who juggle the classics because they cant do anything else and secretly wish all the time they were insurance agents

As he warmed to his subject, he revealed a good deal about his stance then, one which he would continue to hold and which explains his rebellion against genteel America. He liked people "simple," he told Marvin, "moderately direct in their emotions, moderately honest in their thoughts, moderately wide eyed and naive," and these qualities he found far more often in "uncollegiate" Americans than in "your goddamned nickel plated rubberized finished theory-fed socially climbing college grad." To him the college graduate represented genteel respectability. Equally noxious, when he felt like a tough-spoken social critic, were intellectual aesthetes. "As for the intellectual class," he exploded, "it can go f—— itself. Its merely less picturesque and less warmhearted than the hoi polloi and a damn sight eagerer to climb on the band wagon in time of need." The intellectuals ought to be segregated, he went on, "in large well padded asylums"; and the only way one could be released would be "to commit an act—a grimey fleshly bedrock act." The result would be the reappearance of very few intellectuals, he declared.

He did protest too much, still reacting against what he saw to be his own shortcomings while he reveled in Village life and, in a curiously innocent fashion, abandoned his reserve on occasion, as once when Robert Hillyer was visiting from Cambridge. After an evening of drinking he and Hillyer shed most of their clothes; then, while Dos Passos sat on the floor of the sparsely furnished studio, Hillyer pranced and twirled in the moonlight that poured through the windows. There was more of a sexual thrill about this than Dos Passos would have liked to admit; yet the whole thing was essentially naïve, an act that paid homage to the spirit of Baudelaire or Rimbaud.

With other friends he did interesting, if less exotic, things, that spring taking a hike from Bryn Mawr to Lancaster in the heart of the Pennsylvania Dutch country. His companions were Marvin, Poore, and F. O. Mathiessen, an acquaintance from

Harvard who later became a famous literary critic. Marvin delighted in Dos Passos's amusement at the names of some of the villages they passed through: Blue Balls, Love Mound, Paradise, and Intercourse, where as he leaned against the town's wooden signpost, he remarked that Intercourse, near Bird-in-Hand, must also have been called Two-in-the-Bush.

In June he, Marvin, and C. D. Williams, Marvin's friend from Yale, took a night boat up the Hudson to Saugerties, from where they hiked in the Catskills before Dos Passos hurried back to New York to attend John Peale Bishop's marriage on June 17. The wedding, at least as Edmund Wilson described it to his and Bishop's close friend, Scott Fitzgerald, was itself a touch of the twenties, or as Wilson put it, a "most amusing piece of buffoonery." That Wilson was not attracted to Bishop's bride partly explains his jaundiced view of the episode, where Bishop seemed to him "scared into stupefaction" so that he stood awkwardly on his bride's train at the end of the ceremony. Members of both families acted less than pleased about the match and said so once they had drunk some champagne. The bride's father, a bit boozy, made grossly amorous advances toward Wilson's Village friends Elinor Wylie and Hazel Rascoe. Amid this, as the reception wore on, "the young intellectuals formed a ring and danced round and round in the middle of the room to the jazz orchestra."

Despite the friendships and the amicable atmosphere of the Village, Dos Passos was reserved in his relationships with others. His friend Wilson, later characterizing him in his novel *I Thought of Daisy*, wrote that Dos Passos—Hugo Bamman in the novel—"was really on close terms with no one." Dos Passos would sample a conversation to catch "the social flavor of a household or a group"; then he would catalog the sample, placing his latest specimen where he thought it belonged in the economic system. Wilson continued:

> He distrusted his family and his early associates, because he believed that they had sold their souls to capitalist institutions; but though he chose to live exclusively with outlaws, in whom he was always discovering qualities heroic and picturesque to the point of allegory, he never managed really to be one of them and perhaps never trusted them, either. So tough remained the insulation between himself and the rest of humanity—the insulation of his Puritan temperament and his genteel breeding, reinforced by his artist's detachment and his special situation.

To Wilson, Bamman-Dos Passos seemed as he walked among his peers "like a human penance for the shortcomings of a whole class and culture." And, feeling so uneasy with others, he would often lurch abruptly away from any gathering, always first courteously expressing his "stooped, stuttered and bubbled good nights," though in fact he remained "detached and remote."

Later in the twenties Wilson noted that Dos Passos had about him a "too-softness . . . set off, or rather, retrieved, by an intransigent, too insistently asserted independence." Elinor Wylie, Wilson wrote, had once commented that there was about Dos Passos "something . . . that was soft that ought to be hard." An innate sensitivity, a genteel upbringing as a mother's boy, an initial unsureness brought about by the simple fact of extreme nearsightedness, and a self-consciousness about a stammer and a slight lis all contributed to that "something" Elinor Wylie observed. It is little wonder that Wilson was struck by what seemed a forced independence when Dos Passos would sound off, would suddenly depart on a daring voyage, or would dress the role of intellectual bohemian, clutching a "flat limp old hat" in his hand, a "musette bag, with a rolled-up painting in it," slung over his shoulder.

If the sensitive Wilson was accurate about his friend's "too-softness," he overreacted to Dos Passos's reserve because, liking him immensely and respecting him as a writer, Wilson was irritated to know that Dos Passos had several sides to his life that Wilson did not share. Dos Passos was not quite so detached and remote as his friend suggested; he could enjoy the circle of friends they had in common; and he was amused by their small eccentricities, such as that of one beautiful woman, the dancer Bernice Dewey, who kept a pet alligator in her bathtub and hypnotized it so much that Dos Passos confided to Wilson that the poor reptile had become rather limp.

Yet, if Wilson overreacted, it was true that Dos Passos remained reserved, particularly around women. To him in 1922 the women in the Village seemed overpowering and sometimes a touch foolish, if also charming. He was not the only person who was conscious of the aggressive New Women who had congregated in the Village. To the critic and biographer Matthew Josephson many of them were "key figures" in the various circles that formed there. He recalled them "as big-bodied and dressed in masculine clothes; sometimes, at social gatherings, they affected 'exotic' costumes of loosely flowing and shapeless robes; generally they cut their hair short, used neither rouge nor powder, and smoked cigarettes constantly. . . ."

Such a person was Esther Andrews, whom Dos Passos described in *The Best Times* as "one of many attractive young women who pour into New York from the Middle West, learn diction at a drama school and yearn for the illdefined glamor of a stage career." She was unable to find an acting job, so worked for *Women's Wear Daily,* all the while scorning the fashion business. She lived with a man, but "children, family, matrimony were oldfashioned notions." According to Dos Passos, she repudiated marriage and celebrated Freedom. He was humorously critical of her when he wrote his memoirs, as he had been during the 1920s when he visited—which he frequently did—Melancholy Villa, as he dubbed her apartment. She was one of the "outlaws" Edmund Wilson referred to whom Dos Passos liked to mingle with—she; her lover Canby Chambers; and others like the witty novelist Dawn Powell; Dos Passos's acquaintance Griffin Barry from the days in Paris after the Armistice; Jack and Adelaide Lawson; and even Whittaker Chambers, who was then a shadowy courier for the Communists.

Like Wilson's character Hugo Bamman, Dos Passos "was rather afraid of women," whom he thought "the most dangerous representatives of those forces of conservatism and inertia against which his whole life was a protest." Yet, wrote Wilson, Bamman "cherished, in his heart, the most romantic expectations" and "was always hoping for some straight, dark, spare realistic girl revolutionist, who would be to him a comrade and a partner." This may be no more than to say that the young writer, pulled in two directions by his genteel and his rebellious instincts, constantly drew back to shield his romanticism. Dos Passos felt ambivalent about his "outlaw" friends and typically, when their world was too much with him, would dart away on one of his trips; or when in New York, he would frequently hasten uptown to ride either a motorboat from Dobbs Ferry or a ferry from Yonkers across the Hudson, the latter leaving him a five-mile walk along the west bank of the river north to his destination, Snedens Landing. There he visited four Chicago women whose acquaintance he had made, the Dudley sisters and Susan Smith. In his typically secretive way he told Greenwich Village friends like Adelaide Lawson that he was visiting a "Little Lady in Green" who lived up the Hudson, and his Village friends assumed that he was beginning to have affairs. In fact, his visits to Susan Smith and the Dudleys were discreet and chaste. The women had created at Snedens Landing a style of life that appealed to Dos Passos. The little town, he wrote, owned at that time by one person, was meant "to be an enclave of nineteenth-century elegance," and he found its life "a *déjeuner sur l'herb* painted by Renoir on the banks of the Seine." As was his wont, he could there indulge his taste for elegance, yet not mix that with what Greenwich Village life meant to him.*

By July 1922, he was tried of the city, so joined Dudley Poore at his parents' home in Skaneateles near Syracuse, New York. From there the two traveled to Maine, where Dos Passos left Poore in Ogunquit while he took a train to Thomaston before embarking on a small steamer for Monhegan Island off the coast, where after a short visit he passed back through Ogunquit, then voyaged to Nantucket Island off Cape Cod before returning to New York by the end of August in order to read the proof sheets for the volume of verse, *A Pushcart at the Curb*, which would be published in October.

Dos Passos was saddened at the end of August to receive word that his close friend from Harvard, Wright McCormick, had been killed August 27, 1922, in a mountain-climbing accident near Contreas, Mexico. But McCormick's death resulted in consolation as well, for a short time later, during a gathering of McCormick's friends at the Lafayette Hotel after his funeral in New York, Dos Passos met Crystal Ross, who had traveled down from Vermont for the service. Their mutual friendship with McCormick was a bond, and she was a bright, lively woman whose interests coincided with Dos Passos's. They quickly took to one another; and subsequently, while she was studying for a doctorate in comparative literature in France at the University of Strasbourg, she and Dos Passos became engaged. But in the

---

*This is not to say that Dos Passos had no affairs during the early twenties. He was attractive to women, who appreciated his kindness and modesty and were impressed with his literary fame. One of the Dudley sisters, Caroline, was for a time in love with him, and, according to someone who knew them both, she tried to make a "literary lion" of Dos Passos. He was flattered by her attention, perhaps even returned her love, but theirs was hardly a torrid affair, and it seems certain they never lived together.

Another woman who had been part of the Greenwich Village scene once remarked that she had been to bed with Dos Passos, but the comment came long after the 1920s and should, it seems, be taken with several grains of salt.

early fall of 1922, their relationship was first a friendship, warm but discreet.

Not long thereafter, in late September or early October, he had a striking encounter with Scott and ˹elda Fitzgerald. He had met them before, but now they invited him to luncheon at the Plaza Hotel, where they were living in high style while they looked for a suitable home in Great Neck, Long Island. Also at their suite at the Plaza that noontime was Sherwood Anderson, with whom Dos Passos enjoyed talking about writing—partly, at least, as a way of avoiding the constant barrage of often embarrassing questions from Scott and Zelda. "Their gambit," Dos Passos wrote, "was to put you in the wrong. You were backward in your ideas. You were inhibited about sex." Such probings made Dos Passos uneasy, but, as he acknowledged, even then he could not become mad at Scott or Zelda; "There was a golden innocence about them and they were both so hopelessly goodlooking."

The luncheon was ornate: Bronx cocktails, champagne, and then something off the beam like lobster croquettes, among other dishes. Fitzgerald, Dos Passos reflected, could never quite manage a fine menu. After luncheon Anderson departed, and the Fitzgeralds invited Dos Passos to ride with them to Great Neck. On the way out to Long Island, Scott talked about writing. It was only then, Dos Passos thought, that Fitzgerald left behind his "preposterous notions about most things," and his mind "became clear and hard as a diamond." The remainder of the trip was a series of awkward scenes. Picking up a real-estate salesman, the Fitzgeralds mocked his patter, mortifying Dos Passos. After leaving the salesman at his office, the three drove to Ring Lardner's place, a large house with a depressingly dark interior. Lardner, "a tall sallow mournful man with a higharched nose," was stone drunk, to the point that he could not speak. Dos Passos and the Fitzgeralds had a drink with Lardner's wife, then departed, Scott repeating to Dos Passos's dismay that everyone "had to have his private drunkard," and Lardner was his.

But the Fitzgeralds had not finished yet. When they passed a carnival as they were driving back to the city, Zelda and Dos Passos insisted on stopping so that they could enjoy some of the rides. While Scott drank from a whiskey bottle he had stored beneath the car seat, the other two climbed aboard the Ferris wheel, but then the disenchantment set in. Dos Passos and Zelda talked at each other, but neither understood what the other meant. He never could explain exactly why; looking back at the episode, he wrote that he believed he "had come up against that basic fissure in her mental processes that was to have such tragic consequences. Though she was so very lovely I had come upon something that frightened and repelled me, even physically."

Unfortunately, she was adamant about riding the Ferris wheel again. They did, and Dos Passos felt even more depressed and puzzled. Afterward, she brooded as they drove the rest of the way into the city. Scott by then had become "sulky drunk," so when Dos Passos was finally able to leave them in front of the Plaza, it was with a great feeling of relief. He continued to like them, he wrote, but their "Sunday supplement" celebrity status grated on his nerves.

Because of such goings-on, it was with some sense of relief that he escaped New York in October, although the primary reason was to give his eyes a rest. Too much

writing and proofreading had affected them badly and had produced severe headaches, so he had them examined by Dr. W. D. Bates, whose controversial method
was to prescribe a series of exercises to strengthen them. Afterward, Dos Passos
traveled to Hickory Nut Gap in the mountains of North Carolina not far from
Hendersonville, where he stayed until the end of the month with the family of
Frederick van den Arend. His eyes had given him quite a scare, he later wrote Robert
Hillyer. Before arriving in North Carolina, he had not been able to work on *Streets
of Night*, and his eyes, he informed Germaine Lucas-Championnière, were like two
large stones which would not function, while his brain swirled with ideas. Although
his illnesses were not entirely over, he recuperated sufficiently in North Carolina to
continue on *Streets of Night*, the only pleasure he derived from the novel occurring
when he had finished it once and for all. Ever since his experiences around Verdun,
his interests had veered away from the style and the subject matter of the manuscript
he had begun at Harvard. Now he intended to publish it to capitalize on the
attention *Three Soldiers* had received and possibly to fulfill the terms of a contract
with George Doran.

But the writing was painful, not simply because of the condition of his eyes.
"There is a very ancient thing that used to be called Streets of Night on which I
am at present working most laboriously," he had written Arthur McComb the
previous spring. "Talk about stale flat and unprofitable—its a very garbage pail of
wilted aspirations—and largely concerned with that futilitarianism I rejoice to see
you abandoning more and more."

This attitude toward the novel continued, making doubly annoying the hiatus
in his work occasioned by his headaches and eye trouble. Finally on October 23,
1922, while still in North Carolina, he could write McComb that he had that
morning finished with "that tiresome bitch Miss Nan Taylor," a reference to one
of the book's main characters. Now he was happy to leave her "to her own courses
toward oblivion." Never, he asserted, had he tried to write something "more an-
tipatico and I fear less successful."

As 1922 drew to a close, Dos Passos was back in New York in his studio
apartment, his spirits good because he could undertake projects more interesting
than *Streets of Night;* because his eyes, he wrote Hillyer, were once more "moderately luminous"; and because he felt otherwise healthy for the moment. In addition,
Dudley Poore was occupying a front apartment next to Dos Passos's, while the
pleasantly hectic pace of life in the Village added further to his enjoyment.

He had been painting with regularity, and early in 1923 he and Adelaide
Lawson had an exhibition of their works and Ruben Nakian, of his sculptures, at
the Whitney Studio Club on West Fourth Street. Inviting the Fitzgeralds to a
reception for the artists on January 5, Dos Passos in his typical fashion mocked the
arty gathering. "Lost articles such as happy phrases, critical conundrums et al will
be confiscated by the management," he scribbled on the invitation card. Rules for
the "desperate tea fight," as he termed the reception, were that "any contestant
looking at the pictures or mentioning the syllable art will be declared to have fouled
and will be removed from the floor. Come and bring a lot of drunks," he advised.

Self-deprecation aside, Dos Passos took his painting seriously; his artwork had a profound effect upon his writing. Influenced by such movements as Expressionism, Futurism, and Cubism, h· tried to reflect these in his own work. If one combines these influences with a contemporary fascination for the city, he has much of the basic stuff of which Dos Passos's mature novels like *Manhattan Transfer* and *U.S.A.* were made. A glance at paintings from the 1920s by American artists as different as Georgia O'Keeffe, Hugh Ferriss, Joseph Stella, or Louis Lozowick, for example, reveals that the city loomed large for artists then. Repeatedly they painted urban scenes, intrigued as they were by the city's immensity, its shapes, its industrial imagery, and its ominous belittlement of individuals, but also its vitality and multiple frenetic rhythms. Which is not to say that Dos Passos or any other artist or writer was wholly conscious of studying his or her predecessors' and peers' work with the idea of copying subject matter and style. "At certain times styles and methods are in the air," Dos Passos wrote much later, and such was the case in the 1920s. He was part of an artistic generation plunged into a renaissance, so that in both New York and Paris he was constantly among people who were rendering their sense of the twentieth century through techniques and styles such as those he had absorbed.

As well as painting, experimental drama intrigued him early in 1923. He had continued intermittently to work at the play he had first conceived during the war. Now he was completing it; in the spring he could write Arthur McComb that he had finished the play that was to be published as *The Garbage Man.* Both these interests emerged in the foreword he wrote to Jack Lawson's expressionist drama, *Roger Bloomer,* published that year—a play, Dos Passos declared, about "the commonest American theme—a boy running away from home to go to the big city." His foreword was a statement not only of what Lawson, but of what he meant to be saying in his work—his paintings and *The Garbage Man* in addition to his fiction. In fact, so closely did Dos Passos's intentions parallel Lawson's that the latter, after he read the manuscript for *The Garbage Man,* told his friend that it had many effects drawn from *Roger Bloomer.* The result was that Dos Passos agreed not to publish his play until Lawson's was out, although he was surprised at Lawson's assertion.

Dos Passos's foreword was less about *Roger Bloomer* in particular than about the need for a national theater, which "the continuously increasing pressure in the grinding machine of industrial life" was going to force into being. A national theater, he wrote, "is the most direct organ of group consciousness" and would be "inevitable" as an expression of mass sentiment as the cities were welded "into living organisms out of the junk heaps of boxes and predatory individuals they are at present." But, he wondered, could the cities spring to life? They had to, or they would "be filled with robots instead of men." Whatever were the ideas for a national theater to express, so far no theatrical production had approached being "a lasting monument to any aspect of New York." The problem was gigantic, "given the unprecedented fever and inhumaneness and mechanical complexity of American life." Even burlesque shows and movies had come closer, although Eugene O'Neill's plays, particularly *The Hairy Ape*, and Lawson's *Roger Bloomer* were beginnings.

The stage was set for *Manhattan Transfer*, which far more than *The Garbage Man* would be his lasting monument to New York. The themes and techniques that he would employ were clear in his mind, and his several years of life in the United States, particularly in New York, had matured his views as a social critic. He was not yet a specifically political critic; that would come a few years hence as a result of labor strife and the Sacco-Vanzetti case. Now he was a satiric observer. "As soon as everything is sufficiently blotted out," he wrote Arthur McComb, "I shall start knocking together a long dull and arduous novel about New York and go-getters and God knows what besides."

In March 1923, with the play completed, Dos Passos sailed for Europe, where he planned to spend most of the summer in France before visiting Spain and returning to the United States. The money for his constant travel he sometimes had to borrow from friends such as Cummings, but he was single, his expenses were few, and he prided himself on living a kind of hand-to-mouth existence that appeared bohemian and adventurous. He had practically no obligations, so during the 1920s the income from his publications and from what his Aunt Mamie Gordon turned over to him as executor of his inheritance was usually sufficient for his needs.

Dos Passos's transatlantic voyage ended in Hamburg, Germany, from where he traveled by train to Paris, remaining there only long enough to see friends, among them the humorist, Donald Ogden Stewart, whom he had met previously in New York. Stewart then or soon afterward took him to meet Gerald and Sara Murphy, an American couple whose elegant style and warmth had deeply impressed Stewart. Dos Passos soon became an intimate friend of theirs, but at their first encounter he was put off by Gerald, who "seemed cold and brisk and preoccupied. He was a dandified dresser," which irritated Dos Passos then, and he was relieved to return to his own modest rooms elsewhere.

Shortly he traveled by train from Paris to Nantes with the intention of paying an Easter visit to Germaine Lucas-Championnière and her family at their summer home, Plessis, near Brains. He hiked the fifteen or twenty kilometers from Nantes, his belongings in his musette bag on his back. As the Lucas-Championnières were finishing their lunch, he appeared at their doorstep, and his first request once seated at the table was for some muscatel. His quick visit was lively; the family and he rowed on the Acheneau River nearby while Dos Passos trailed his jacket in the water behind him because it was somehow soiled with cow dung. Afterward, the friends returned to Plessis, where they organized a sack race, and a photograph taken by one of the family shows Dos Passos in a white shirt, tie and coat, grinning as he waits to leap off in his sack against four other contestants. Later, he did a sketch of the sunset. Then after dinner the family urged him to talk about his trip in the desert of two years before. "Were the women there as pretty as they were supposed to be?" he was asked. "Yes," he responded with a non sequitur, "but you don't see them." After a sound night's sleep in the tiny room above the stables, which he referred to as his beautiful apartment, he departed the next day, catching a boat on the Loire, five kilometers distant from Plessis.

From Nantes he headed south, and during April he journeyed to Florence and on to Rome, perhaps going farther down the boot of Italy before returning in May or early June to Paris. Th re he spent the next few months, which were as much filled with whatever created a mystique about Paris in the 1920s as any moment would be. For one thing, Dos Passos saw more of Gerald Murphy, and his impression was very different from what it had been when Donald Stewart had introduced them. The second time they met Dos Passos and Murphy had lunch with the French painter Fernand Léger, then strolled along the quays by the Seine, with their painters' eyes noticing shapes and colors around them—Murphy had become an accomplished artist, having studied with Léger and the Russian painter, Nathalie Gontcharova. "Gerald's perceptions," wrote Dos Passos, "were rational, discriminating, with a tendency to a mathematical elegance." Murphy's "cool originality" impressed his new friend, for whom a lifelong friendship with both Gerald and Sara began that afternoon.

"I'm not sure whether someone of this generation who has not lived abroad can fully understand what those times were like," Gerald Murphy wrote Dos Passos in December 1959, concerned as Murphy was about the efforts of the young author Calvin Tomkins to write a brief biography of the Murphys which eventually was published under the title *Living Well Is the Best Revenge.* The early twenties in Paris, Gerald continued, "came at the end of an era when most of one's values were those of a classic education and nothing planet-shaking had happened to the arts." He was worried that Tomkins did not have enough understanding "to write about the forces that were loose in the arts at that time of which we felt the import at close range: les Six, Diaghilieff, les Independents, les Dadaists, Picasso, Stravinsky, Brancusi, et cetera, above all life on the Rive Gauche which seems like the Age of Innocence now."

Life on the Rive Gauche: that was what excited Dos Passos for the very reasons Murphy mentioned. Almost immediately after returning to Paris, Dos Passos joined Murphy and others to help paint sets for the Ballet Russe's presentation of Stravinsky's *Les Noces.* The premiere was to be an extravagant affair; Diaghilev persuaded the composers François Poulenc, Georges Auric, Vittorio Rieti, and "the leading interpreter of the new music," Marcelle Meyer, to perform the ballet's four piano parts. George Balanchine, the choreographer, even traveled from Moscow especially to see the premiere. The preparations were frantic, but to Dos Passos's astonishment everything came together at the last instant, and the premiere was a thorough success. So exciting was the whole affair that the Murphys thought there ought to be a celebration. "We decided to have a party for everyone directly connected with the ballet as well as for those friends of ours who were following its genesis," Gerald Murphy remembered much later. He and Sara searched for a suitable place, and when the manager of the Cirque Médrano turned them down with the terse comment that *"Le Cirque Médrano n'est pas encore une colonie américaine,"* they turned next to a barge restaurant situated on the Seine. The party took place June 17, a Sunday, and began at 7:00 P.M. The guests, as Calvin Tomkins wrote, "constituted a kind of summit meeting of the modern movement in Paris."

These included Picasso, Darius Milhaud, Jean Cocteau, the conductor of *Les Noces,* Ernest Ansermet, Marcelle Meyer, Diaghilev, Nathalie Gontcharova, along with her artist husband Michel Larionov, the poets Tristan Tzara and Blaise Cendrars; and Scofield Thayer, the wealthy American who was one of the editors of the *Dial.* After cocktails, a lengthy champagne banquet was superb amid a decor of toys arranged along the dining table; the dinner was further enlivened by piano music and the dancing of the several ballerinas from *Les Noces* who had been invited. Cocteau, terrified of seasickness, wandered about the decks in a captain's dress uniform he had found, announcing into portholes that the barge was sinking; Stravinsky at one point leaped through a large wreath, and the entire affair became a legend.

It was the sort of spectacle that Dos Passos had little taste for then, although he soon regretted having avoided it. "I was shy," he wrote, "and I hated small talk and I didn't like having to answer questions about my writing. I cultivated the pose of sidewalk proletarian to whom riches were vanity." What he did enjoy was visits with the Murphys at their home when they were with their three children, Honoria, Baoth, and Patrick. There they discussed art and ballet as he did with Greenwich Village friends such as Jack Lawson. The talks had a similar influence on his work. That spring, in fact, Gerald Murphy had been commissioned by Rolf de Maré, a Swedish impresario then in Paris with the Ballets Suédois, to create an "American ballet," which would be the curtain raiser for what was to follow, the ballet *La Création du Monde,* by Milhaud. Murphy engaged Cole Porter, living in Venice at the time, to do the score, so later in the summer of 1923 the two created the ballet, entitled *Within the Quota,* about which Dos Passos talked with Murphy at length.

It was, in a general way, the subject of *Manhattan Transfer* put to music, a ballet recording the impressions of a Swedish immigrant freshly arrived in America. In *Manhattan Transfer,* Dos Passos brought not a single immigrant but a number of different types to New York; yet, like the Swede, several are naïfs. The impressions they get of the stresses and frantic rhythms of the city are like those conveyed in the ballet, which employed a movie-piano solo counterpointed against an orchestra playing a "jazz base" score that included such diverse strains as "a Salvation Army chorale, a fox trot, a Swedish waltz, and an allusion to New York taxi horns." The cover of the souvenir program for the ballet was Expressionistic and faintly Cubist, showing a kind of Everyman immigrant figure superimposed on a collage of skyscrapers, trolley cars, trains, steamship funnels, harbor fronts, and scattered dots of people —images of the city and of industrial society. But the most striking part of Murphy's contribution to the ballet was the backdrop he painted, a parody of the front page of a tabloid. On one side of the backdrop was the steamship *Paris* on end next to the Woolworth Building; then over the rest were sensational but—as it was a parody —nonsense headlines like: GEM ROBBERS FOIL $210,000 SWINDLE; EX-WIFE'S HEART-BALM LOVE-TANGLE; RUM RAID LIQUOR BAN; and in the boldest print of all, UNKNOWN BANKER BUYS ATLANTIC. The similarity of this to the italicized portions that begin each section of *Manhattan Transfer* or more, to the Newsreels of *U.S.A.,* is obvious.

Dos Passos was a constant companion of the Murphys during the summer of

1923, saw Crystal Ross when she could get away from her studies at Strasbourg, and saw other friends as well, Cummings among them. He even tried to bring his poet friend together with the Murphys and dragged him to the theater where the sets for *Les Noces* were being prepared. Cummings, however, would have none of what he feared were merely glamorous socialites, so he sat in the back row of the theater, avoiding the Murphys. "I can understand that," Dos Passos told them, "I've spent most of my life keeping my friends apart." Cummings, of course, was not always so reticent. Rather, he liked to socialize with friends he already knew, and one night that summer a dinner at the Café de la Paix with Dos Passos and their mutual friend from Harvard, the writer and editor Gilbert Seldes, produced a memorable occasion that became another one of the minor legends of the era.

Sometime in early July the three companions, having had what Dos Passos described as "one of our long bibulous and conversational dinners," were walking well after midnight toward a club Cummings referred to as "the Calvador Joint of rue Gît le Coeur." Opposite the club Cummings paused to urinate and, as Dos Passos told Cummings's biographer, Charles Norman, "a whole phalanx of gendarmes" set upon him, carrying him off to the *poste de police* at rue des Grands Augustins, while Dos Passos and Seldes followed behind, protesting noisily. Dos Passos entered the police station only to be pushed back. When he entered a second time, he was literally thrown out. Seldes shoved inside as well, but received the same treatment. Before he was forced outside, however, he overheard a fragment of the discussion between an officer on duty and one of the gendarmes who had arrested Cummings:

"Un Américain qui pisse," announced the gendarme.

"Quoi—encore un pisseur Américain?" responded the other.

While Seldes and Dos Passos waited nervously outside, what went on within according to Cummings was that the officer asked him if he would urinate on the sidewalk in his own country. When Cummings responded, "Yes," the officer shouted, "Liar." Cummings asked him why he said that. "Because I know about America—I have a relative there," was the reply. "Where?" asked Cummings. "In Brooklyn."

Despite their distaste for the Americans, after the gendarmes had verified with Seldes and Dos Passos that Cummings did in fact live in the United States, he was allowed to leave, but ordered to report back the next morning. Thinking of Cummings's problems with the French during the World War, the three Americans grew serious, and in the morning Seldes telephoned the French writer Paul Morand, who had a government position at the Quai d'Orsay. Morand arranged to have the charges dropped, so when Cummings returned to Seldes's apartment on the Île St. Louis, he found posters drawn up with the greeting "Reprieve Pisseur Américain!" Shortly thereafter Seldes received a note from Morand, promising that "C. will have no ennui." Several days later, Cummings and Dos Passos visited Malcolm Cowley in Giverny, where they celebrated the episode by throwing a party. "The tale," observed Dos Passos, "lost nothing in the retelling."

Before leaving Paris in August, Dos Passos read the page proofs for *Streets of*

Night, which Eugene Saxton had mailed him, and Dos Passos promised to send back a final chapter that presumably was later in reaching the proof stage because he had added it only after completing the rest of the novel in October 1922. He was due to sail for the United States from Bordeaux on August 30, but first he traveled south down the length of Spain to Nerja, on the Mediterranean coast near Málaga, where he spent a week. The small town, he wrote Saxton, was "one of the sideshows they forgot to close up when the Eden Amusement Company boarded up its door for an indefinite closure." He asked Saxton to mail Scott Fitzgerald an advance copy of the novel when it was ready, a mistake of a sort—although Fitzgerald would no doubt have read it anyway—because as a result he "lost faith in [Dos Passos's] work" and would not regain it until *Manhattan Transfer* was published two years later.

Once Dos Passos arrived in New York, he went almost immediately for the fall to Far Rockaway on Long Island to avoid social life so he could work undisturbed on *Manhattan Transfer,* "a novel," he wrote Germaine Lucas-Championnière, "that I hope will be utterly fantastic and New Yorkish." At Far Rockaway he was able to live quietly; he took a room in a Yiddish boardinghouse facing toward a beach abandoned for the winter. As eyesight and constant headaches had continued to plague him during the summer Dos Passos resumed his eye exercises with new vigor and wrote Germaine in October that he was practicing "the comical system of Doctor Bates for the eyes." Foolish as it seemed, he was sure that he was seeing "better and better." No longer did he have headaches from eyestrain, and he was able to read and write as much as he wished. He might have thought he could see better, but his friends were more amused than convinced when he practiced Bates's methods, one of which involved trying to read small print, for which purpose Dos Passos carried around a miniature Bible, which periodically he would pull out of his pocket and, squinting hard without his glasses, hold up close to his nose and try to read. Less amusing because more alarming was his practice of walking without glasses in an effort to strengthen his eyes. Friends feared for his safety when he would careen blindly along a street.

Dos Passos remained secluded at Far Rockaway through much of the fall, corresponding with or seeing friends less than usual. He returned to the city around Christmastime, celebrated Christmas Day with the Fitzgeralds in Great Neck along with Edmund Wilson, Gilbert Seldes, and others, and stayed briefly at his Aunt Mamie's before taking up residence in Brooklyn at 106–110 Columbia Heights, a building where Hart Crane also lived, facing on the East River and the Brooklyn Bridge. It was a good spot to work; he could look out over the harbor at the city he was writing about, and yet it was enough removed that he could avoid the excitement of the Village when he wanted to, which was most of the time, because he was involved with the complexities of *Manhattan Transfer,* so deeply involved that he even stopped his normal, frequent contributions to periodicals. For over a year—from April 1923 to July 1924—he contributed nothing, and when he did again, it was no more than a poem in *Vanity Fair,* followed two months later in the *transatlantic review* by the short story "July," a piece from an early part of the manuscript for *Manhattan Transfer* which he did not include in the published novel.

Only after it was completed did his work again appear frequently in periodicals.

The early notes for *Manhattan Transfer* from which he worked read somewhat like Gerald Murphy's backdrop for *Within the Quota*. Dos Passos had jotted down observations, slogans, bits of information, and snatches of dialogue on scraps of paper, from which he began to piece together the several narratives that would make up the novel. The ideas seem to have been a swirl when he started, increasing the difficulty of sorting them out and properly relating various themes to the narratives. "O I'm sick of this proletariat movement why don't you do something instead of talk," was a bit of dialogue he thought of having one of the major figures, Ellen Thatcher, say to another, Jimmy Herf. Then his mind had turned to a scene that would set the stage for the narrative of a character returned from the war: "Throwing the prophylaxis kit overboard going into New York Harbor"; then to the general drift of the novel: "Building up to climax of the metropolis motif." He thought of symbols of city life, "Elevated Street Car Ferry boat Elevator Man," as well as of short vignettes and scenes that might capture the sense of the city: "Rabbi Shaving off his whiskers"; "Why not a Biltmore scene—piano playing pink tights . . . social-artistic climbing," and "Fashionable minister scattering ashes of Mrs. Fitzsimmons Clough on the Long Island Speedway." Since his stay in the city in the fall of 1920, when the urban theme was solidifying in his mind, he had been collecting slogans and advertising signs. The notebooks in which he wrote his first tentative drafts of the novel indicate that early on he had the idea of breaking up the various narratives about characters into episodes and interlarding them with the other materials he had gathered, but before weaving the narratives together, he seems to have written them out separately. The more he wrote, the more the work became a "collective" novel about the city, where individuals were less the central concern than the city itself, which overwhelmed and sometimes killed them—as it did the vagabond Bud Korpenning and the playboy Stan Emery—sometimes turned them into stiff, porcelain figures like Ellen Thatcher, or sometimes drove them out, as Dos Passos had planned from the start it would Jimmy Herf: "Jimmy Herf goes away," he closed an early set of notes, "Manhattan Manhattan Manhattan The flight of [Jimmy] and the deaths of old m[an and] child."

As he concentrated his efforts on *Manhattan Transfer,* his finances were in a precarious position early in 1924. He had made little money from the publication of *Streets of Night* in 1923 and apparently had spent most of his income on his travels. "Jesus I am broke. Haven't had a five dollar bill in two months," he complained to Rumsey Marvin just after New Year's. He tried to alleviate the situation by sending Edmund Wilson an article about the Swedish Ballet in the hopes that either Wilson would take it for the *New Republic* or try to place it elsewhere. But Wilson was not interested, and Dos Passos backed off. Peeved at the journals, he facetiously asked his friend if he would like to conspire "to blow up the liberal weeklies," which Dos Passos periodically condemned for their blandness. "We could go disguised as Inflated Dragons of the K.K.K. and nobody would dare to object," he wrote. "Can't you see the headlines 'Burning Cross on Vesey Street. Patrolman Snuffs Fuse Saves Freeman.'"

Although he enjoyed his room at Columbia Heights, he soon felt the need for a change. He liked the idea of a warmer climate, and he was sure he could work faster if he were totally uninterrupted by social demands. So in February he departed New York, visited briefly in Baltimore, then spent several days in Washington, D.C., seeing relatives before sailing on the eighth for Savannah, where he traveled on to New Orleans. Rumsey Marvin, now located in North Carolina, tried but failed to coordinate a walk along Cape Hatteras with Dos Passos, who responded from New Orleans that finances and his writing prohibited him for the moment; he did not think it wise to move at all until the first part of *Manhattan Transfer* was completed. While Dos Passos remained in New Orleans—which he had chosen as a place away from his New York friends and perhaps had chosen also because of the presence of Sherwood Anderson—Marvin repeatedly tried to fit a walk into their future plans. These, however, continued to be vague, since Dos Passos thought he might be voyaging to Russia that summer at the invitation of the Kamerny Theater in Moscow to help them plan an American tour. If that occurred, he did not want anything else to interfere with it. But if the Russian trip did not materialize, he was toying with the idea of a trip to Mexico; furthermore, later in the spring the Murphys invited him to join them in France for a sail in the Mediterranean to begin June 1.

New Orleans served his purposes well during February and early March. He took a room at 510 Esplanade Avenue, owned, he wrote Marvin, by "a little Central American woman with glasses." His room was colorful if seedy, a bed "painted cobalt blue," walls a "peeling apricot," and a ceiling "the color of raspberry ice." He was able to work like a Trojan, he assured his friend, and the only problem other than money was having no one to talk to when he first arrived. Soon, however, he remedied that by introducing himself to Marvin's friend William McComb, who had worked with Marvin on the Pittsburgh *Gazette* and now was employed by the *Item*, a newspaper in New Orleans. McComb and Dos Passos ate together almost every evening, then often moved on to what Dos Passos described as a "regular Frankie and Johnny café called the Original Tripoli, full of vice niggermusic and rotten booze." Dos Passos also saw something of Sherwood Anderson and the author Lyle Saxon and may have even been introduced by one of them to William Faulkner, who was also living there.

The city had the same kind of charm he found in European towns; it suited him to a T., he wrote Marvin early in March. His artist's eye was intrigued by "streets and streets of scaling crumbling houses with broad wrought iron verandahs painted in Caribbean blues and greens," by its squares and wharves, ships and smells of molasses that emanated from the sugar refineries. The levees along the Mississippi were good for hiking amid intriguing vegetation; and everywhere in the city were exotic characters, "inconceivable old geezers in decrepit frockcoats, . . . tall negresses with green and magenta bandanas on their heads, . . . [and] whores and racingmen and South Americans and Central Americans of all colors and shapes."

Only after he had completed a substantial portion of *Manhattan Transfer* did Dos Passos leave New Orleans in mid-March, perhaps stopping briefly at Perdido Bay, between Mobile, Alabama, and Pensacola, Florida, before proceeding down through the middle of Florida on a seven-day walking trip that ended on the west coast at Venice, near Sarasota. From there he caught a ride on a freight train that brought him near Lake Okeechobee, which he crossed in a motor boat. He made his way north to Sebring and there, waiting for a train to West Palm Beach on April 3, he wrote Germaine Lucas-Championnière on a piece of the Sebring Development Company's stationery, bordered with a design of oranges, green leaves, and white flowers. "N'est ce pas que c'est chic ce papier?" he began his letter, then described his trip of the previous week. Now he waited to travel to Palm Beach, "wintering place of senators and millionaires," and thence to Key West, where he felt driven to go by his chronic "islomania."

Florida, in 1924 in the middle of its first great land development, was the land of the big money, a product of 1920s boom time. He marveled about it to his French friend. The state was "fabulous and movie-like," a place where whole cities were built in three months. Ten years ago only the crocodiles knew the interior; now the poor crocodiles were penned in Alligator Farms, and it was necessary to pay twenty-five cents to see them. The entire population expected to be rich in five years, except for those who failed, but no one spoke of that. "One arrives on foot, works a year, buys an orange grove from his wages, then in five years travels in a limosine, in ten years is the founder of a city, is a millionaire or a senator—it's the American Eden," he mocked, "an Eden without the serpent, where the fruit is forbidden to no one, except those who cannot buy it, and it conveys no dangerous wisdom to those who taste of it. But," he added, "how bored these poor Eves and Adams are without any serpent to tease them."

Changing the subject, he told Germaine that when not writing his novel he was spending his free time reading the Bible, a book that he found disagreeable, if devilishly well written, for the most part. "But the church is right," he declared. "This is not a book to put in the hands of Christians. The ferocious tragedy of the Jews' mad egotism will always stand against civilization and happiness." Just then the train for West Palm Beach was due, so he stopped his half-serious disquisition to board it. Subsequently, he enjoyed the train ride down through the keys to Key West, where he remained until the last part of April, writing, and as he wrote Germaine on April 23, savoring the fresh seafood and swimming in the clear, bright sea.

After returning to New York, he did not remain long that spring. The trip to Russia fell through, but not surprisingly Dos Passos craved to return to Europe to enjoy more of the life of the previous summer. He was eager to see the Murphys again, and—although he told few people about her—he was anxious to be with Crystal Ross once more. She was continuing her studies at Strasbourg, but could travel south, and he could visit her in the north of France.

Soon after he reached Paris in June, she joined him. She often stayed, as she did then, at the University Women's Club at 4 rue de Chevreuse, near the Hemingways' flat on rue Notre Dame des Champs. The four saw each other almost daily, while Dos Passos and Ernest met as well to talk about their writing at the nearby café La Closerie des Lilas, Hemingway's favorite. At the time they were both reading the Old Testament and would quote passages to each other. If they had been at the café during an afternoon, Dos Passos would frequently walk back with his friend to the flat on Notre Dame des Champs and there enjoy helping Ernest's wife Hadley give their child Bumby a bath in their cramped quarters, where the wallpaper would swell out from the walls when Hadley heated the water.

Dos Passos that spring enjoyed Hemingway's enthusiasms, which were contagious. Together they watched the six-day bicycle races at the Velo d'Hiver, about which Hemingway became so excited that he got himself a bicycle outfit and cycled along the city boulevards, to the amusement of his friends. "In those days," remarked Dos Passos, "Hem submitted to a certain amount of kidding." Another enthusiasm of the younger writer was horse racing. It may well have been in the spring of 1924 that Hemingway, assuring Dos Passos that he was winning steadily, enticed him to the races at Longchamps and Anteuil. Having been given a tip by the expatriate American writer Harold Stearns, the two collected as much money as they could to bet on a long shot in a steeplechase. The horse looked good, but they lost their money when it balked at a water jump, threw its jockey, and headed in the wrong direction around the track.

Hemingway's great enthusiasm, of course, was bullfighting. The previous summer in Spain he had his first taste of it, finding especially exciting the Fiesta of San Fermín held in early July in Pamplona. In 1924 he hoped to repeat the pleasure, so urged his Paris friends to join him and Hadley there, which several of them did. This was the year before the gathering in Pamplona that would provide the material for *The Sun Also Rises;* still, the episode was memorable, although the atmosphere was fortunately less charged. In 1924 the group consisted of Crystal Ross and Dos Passos; the Hemingways; Donald Ogden Stewart; the writer and publisher Robert McAlmon; a young friend, George O'Neil; William and Sally Bird; and a British captain, "Chink" Smith, whom Hemingway had known during the war.

Dos Passos and Crystal Ross took a train from Paris south to St. Jean Pied de Port, near the Spanish border. They took separate rooms in an inn for that night, and she recalled that their accommodations were attractive despite what seemed an almost standard infestation of bedbugs. During the evening they heard cheering, so came down into the street to applaud some bicycle racers whose tour passed by there. The next morning they began a hike through the pass of Roncesvalles. Dos Passos had no trouble, but Crystal found it difficult to keep up with his long strides. New shoes did not help her, and before long she was fatigued and thankful for the chance to ride a donkey the last part of the more than thirty kilometers to a small Spanish inn near Burguete. There a thick, savory soup of garlic and potatoes with eggs broken into it revived them both. The next day the Hemingways met them at the inn, and together the four traveled on to Pamplona to the Hotel de la Perla, where they had rooms along with the rest of their group, who were boisterous and soon filled with drink and the spirit of the festival. Hemingway had reserved a double room for Dos Passos and Crystal Ross, but she took Donald Ogden Stewart's single room, and he moved in with Dos Passos, to the astonishment of Chink Smith, who was puzzled by Crystal and Dos Passos's chaste relationship.

"I found myself I dont know how at a lot of bullfights in Pamplona at a ferocious fiesta with a lot of fake bohemians," Dos Passos remarked curtly to Jack Lawson after the festival ended. Although he enjoyed himself, he felt restrained and often rather embarrassed by the exhibitionist antics of his friends, particularly Stewart and Hemingway, who seemed compelled to prove their courage by engaging in the amateur bullfights that took place in the ring each morning before the afternoon *corridas*. To the delight of some of the Spaniards, the two Americans performed feats of daring, Hemingway trying to heave a calf to the turf by its horns, and Stewart, determined to prove his mettle to Hemingway, taking the direct charge of a steer, which tossed him. Stewart assured his friends he had not been hurt, but later he realized that he had fractured a rib and the next day left for Paris after more drinking and dancing in the streets. And even Dos Passos, despite his lack of interest in demonstrating his heroism, ventured once into the bullring with the others. When to avoid a steer he cleared the barricade around the ring, he found himself facing the beast in the passage between the *barrera* and the stands, into which he quickly leaped, to his consternation and his friends' amusement.

"It was fun and we ate well and drank well but there were too many exhibition-istic personalities in the group to suit me," he wrote in *The Best Times*. So despite participating in some of the festivities, he and Crystal Ross did things by themselves a good deal of the time, such as taking a train excursion up to San Sebastian on the northern coast. While others danced in the streets, he told her she ought not to, because the Spanish women did not. "We built ourselves a sort of private box," Dos Passos wrote, "from which we looked out at all these goings on, in them but not of them."*

As the festival neared its end, McAlmon and the Birds rode a bus north to Burguete; Crystal Ross had departed from Pamplona with Donald Stewart to return to Strasbourg via Paris, taking with her some film, dirty laundry, and library books to return for the others who planned to stay longer in Spain. The Hemingways joined the three already at Burguete on July 14; then a few days later Dos Passos, George O'Neil, and Chink Smith also joined them, planning a two-week hike from there through the Spanish Pyrenees to Andorra, a distance of nearly three hundred kilometers.

The walk took thirteen days. McAlmon decided to go with the other three, and as they started, Hemingway walked along for several kilometers before turning back to rejoin Hadley. The pace of the hike was brisk; the first day the four covered thirty-five kilometers, which took them well into the Pyrenees. The next day it was forty kilometers, and another, sixty-five. McAlmon stayed with them for six days, but his feet, improperly clad in canvas slippers—*alpargatas*—soon ached, and tennis sneakers could not help much. When they reached Biescas, a town in the mountains from where a bus traveled over the border into France, he halted to return to Paris.

*Exactly how private they were—and how involved the others were with their own participation—is suggested by the fact that none of the several accounts of the 1924 festival in Pamplona mentions Crystal Ross.

The others marched ahead, tired but enjoying the rugged paths that led through primitive villages where they were sometimes taken to be smugglers, nevertheless fed a diet of goat cheese, black bread, honey, and plentiful tortillas. During the trip they drank *agua gigante*, a strong liquor that continually picked them up. Utterly fatigued after the journey, late one night they finally slipped and slid down a mountainside in torrential rains into Andorra la Vella, the capital of the tiny republic. Finding an inn still open, they took three beds and threw themselves on them, only, Dos Passos claimed, to find them swarming with bedbugs.

From Andorra Dos Passos in August journeyed on to Antibes to join the Murphys, who were residing in the Hôtel du Cap while the renovations continued on Villa America, as they decided to name the small villa they had purchased that stood just downhill from the Antibes lighthouse. Friends regularly visited the Murphys and stayed at the Hôtel, as did Dos Passos, who wrote Jack Lawson that he was "working in a red plush room at the Murphys' place at Antibes where I'm being 'entertained' as the New York Herald would say with great elegance and a great deal of gin fizz." Before he left Antibes the Murphys may have been able to move to Villa America, where Dos Passos's room when he visited was almost always the small guest house they called the Bastide. There, as at the Hôtel, Dos Passos could work during the mornings before joining his hosts and any other guests—at that moment Don Stewart was also visiting, as perhaps were Archibald and Ada MacLeish and the Fitzgeralds, who would have come over from St.-Raphaël. The Murphys and their guests would gather for sunbathing, a swim, then sherry and hors d'oeuvres at a small beach called la Garoupe. Afterward they could walk back to the terrace of Villa America for lunch and in the afternoon would explore the region around Antibes. That summer the Fitzgeralds had had marital difficulties; Zelda had fallen in love with a French naval officer, precipitating a crisis between them. Whether any of the pall this created still hung over the scene when Dos Passos was there is not clear; with his usual reticence he said nothing about it, commenting in a guarded way to Lawson that "the Riviera in summer is a strange and rather exciting place. The people are very bastard and peculiar and the landscape is obstructed by villas full of artificial countesses under the influence of opium or spirits or spaniels. Has to be seen to be believed." Shortly before he wrote, he had been struck by "a curious fête at Cannes where the fishermen danced barefoot round the bandstand to the strains of Orpheus in Hades in a curiously hardboiled oversexed way."

Rested but uneasy with too much of this life, Dos Passos left Antibes toward the end of August, traveling north to visit Crystal Ross for a week at Strasbourg, where he enjoyed the German atmosphere and the cool weather after the heat of Spain and the Riviera. They had become engaged; now he pressed her to marry him soon, but she demurred, not sure enough of her own feelings to agree and also wanting to complete her studies out of interest as well as a strong feeling of loyalty to her father, who was supporting her.

From Strasbourg Dos Passos returned to Paris, then traveled north to Belgium to meet Crystal once more in Brugge. From there they crossed the channel in September to England, where in London she stayed at the Russell House, and one of their excursions was for her to meet Dos Passos's elderly friends Miss Meakin and Mrs. Gee. During their stay in London Dos Passos continued to urge Crystal to marry him; yet she stuck to her plans, making their separation when she had to return to Strasbourg especially difficult. But nothing could alter that. By the last day of September he was in Le Havre to embark aboard a ship for New York, where he would reside for the fall at 11 Bank Street in Greenwich Village before returning to Columbia Heights early in 1925.

CHAPTER FIFTEEN

Literary Experimentalism,
Travel as Always,
and Politics, 1924–1926

After the stress of his uncertain relationship with Crystal Ross, the fall of 1924 was quiet, and Dos Passos was occupied almost entirely with his work on *Manhattan Transfer*—"I'm living in extreme calm after various storms," he wrote Marvin, "am very broke, and vaguely comatose." Another storm, albeit a small one, was the painful task of serving as Kate Drain Lawson's witness in December at her divorce from Jack Lawson, who had arranged that Dos Passos appear—painful, because their separation had been depressing to him since he liked them both. The proceedings had their humorous side when Kate's lawyer, seeing the thin Dos Passos, asked her if she could not have found a sturdier witness. Dos Passos's role was to testify that he had a key to Jack Lawson's apartment, that he had gone there unexpectedly, and that he had discovered Lawson in bed with another woman. He so testified, whereupon the judge, to the mystification of everyone, asked, "Did he have his shoes on?"

Dos Passos was particularly close to Jack Lawson during the mid-1920s because of their mutual interest in the drama. His own play, influenced by Lawson's ideas, was produced as *The Moon Is a Gong* by the Harvard Dramatic Club in May 1925, with Ed Massey directing it. Earlier, in January, the Theatre Guild staged Lawson's play *Processional: A Jazz Symphony of American Life in Four Acts,* which was an intriguing experiment similar to Dos Passos's own concepts. About it Lawson wrote in his preface to the published version that he had "endeavored to create a method which shall express the American scene in native idiom, a method as far removed from the older realism as from the facile mood of Expressionism." He saw all about him "the grotesque of the American environment, the colorful exaggeration of the American language." Fashioning these into a drama set in a West Virginia coal mining town during a strike, he hoped to express something of "the reality of

America spiritually and materially," because at the moment its inner meaning had not been discovered. Hidden beneath "the hokum of advertisements, headlines, radio speeches" was some "inner necessity, a sense of direction." What the key to finding this was, he did not know. He could have been speaking of Dos Passos's themes in *Moon*, where, as the reviewer for the *Boston Traveler* of May 13, 1925, observed, "The central theme is the conflict between the individual and society, between the 'society misfit' who wants to lead his own life, and organized society, forcing him to fit into its groove." Dos Passos's expressionistic drama was well received in Boston. The "futuristic settings" he designed for the production were effective, and the play seemed amusing and spirited, although the reviewer for the *Boston Evening Transcript* objected to an overuse of jazz accompaniment and too great a likeness to the techniques Lawson had employed in *Processional.*

Dos Passos's enthusiasm for *Processional* and other experimental dramas led him to speculate that realistic theater was outmoded. For *Vanity Fair* that spring he wrote a piece entitled "Is the 'Realistic' Theatre Obsolete?" He believed it was, reasoning that if the theater were to survive, it would have to find a new function for itself beyond what movies and photography could do better: portray the real. The theater, on the other hand, Dos Passos argued, was more capable of welding "into a sentient whole the rigid honeycomb of our pigeonholed lives"; it could be "the focus of mass emotion." To understand themselves in the context of modern life, Dos Passos was saying, people needed to break away from their traditionally literary approaches to the drama and to appreciate the rhythms and staccato action in plays like O'Neill's *The Emperor Jones, The Hairy Ape,* or most particularly, *Processional,* which was "a very unsophisticated attempt to invade the audience's feelings by the most direct and simple means that come to hand."

His enthusiasm extended beyond drama to new art in general; he was likely to respond favorably to anything that might further its cause. Early in 1925 the artist Maurice Becker wrote him about an attempt to revive the *Masses,* the radical journal suppressed by Woodrow Wilson's administration in 1918. The revived magazine became the *New Masses,* every bit as lively and irreverent as had been its predecessor. Dos Passos's interest in the *New Masses* stemmed from a concern for what he termed in *The Best Times* a "native American radicalism," a broad radicalism that extended beyond politics—certainly beyond specific political creeds —to independently radical expression of all sorts. "Just received your announcement without the *pronunciamento* that somehow got left out," he answered Becker. "From the list of names I gather you are trying to start something like the old MASSES. If that's so I'm absolutely with you and would gladly do anything to help. The MASSES was the only magazine I even had any use for. Let me know more about it. You can use my name anyway if it's any good to you." His offer was accepted, and when the first issue appeared in May 1926 Dos Passos was listed on the executive board along with Becker, Joseph Freeman, Mike Gold, Paxton Hibben, Louis Lozowick, John Sloan, Rex Stout, and Egmont Arends, among others.

Because he was committed to artistic innovation, he took time away from writing the new novel that spring to review an exhibition of Adelaide Lawson's painting at a small gallery on West Fourth Street in New York. He was enthusiastic about a New York where at the same moment could hang collections of paintings by Georgia O'Keeffe, John Marin, and Lawson, whose work in particular he admired because of the color and force with which it presented people and things. Like her brother Jack's plays, Adelaide's paintings appealed to Dos Passos—his friendship with her aside—for their similarity to what he was attempting to render in his art. Her paintings, he wrote, were "the work of a woman whose universe is so vigorously individual that she has had no need to set it down in terms more abstract than things, faces, clouds, boats, houses." He admired her "unexpected combinations of things, moods of color, aspects of human character," which became a kind of "painting of the solitary" that had great appeal to individuals who balked at letting the "sausagemachine" of American life grind them up.

Interested as he was in art and its ways of expressing the themes weighing on his mind as he neared artistic maturity at the age of twenty-nine, painting was nevertheless a diversion from his main effort to complete the manuscript for *Manhattan Transfer*. During the early months of 1925 he labored at it, bemoaning to Rumsey Marvin the fact that he still had "an incredible amount of work yet to do" before May, when he had promised a final version for his new publisher, Harper and Brothers. Although he was still writing late in March, he took a busman's holiday to Provincetown for a change of milieu, probably visiting in Cambridge on the way to see something of Ed Massey and his plans for the production of *The Moon Is a Gong*. In Provincetown Dos Passos secluded himself in a small house to work uninterrupted and cheaply, accompanied, he wrote Marvin, only by "a volume of Casanova, an oil stove named Jiminy, and a big toastburner named Gog and Magog." Despite the press of his publisher's deadline, he felt renewed after several days of work interspersed by long walks and a seafood diet. A week of this, and he returned to New York, still working hard to complete *Manhattan Transfer* so that he could leave for France.

In May he was able to present the manuscript to Eugene Saxton, but soon thereafter, partly due to his fatigue, he was struck by the rheumatic fever which had plagued him several years before in Spain. He was admitted to the Midtown Hospital on East Fifty-seventh Street, where he returned on and off until mid-July, only to return once more at the end of July to have his infected tonsils removed because the doctors believed these were related to his other maladies. When he could, he rested at Columbia Heights, but he was stiff and sore, and to Hart Crane he appeared so thoroughly drained of strength that Crane wrote Waldo Frank that the bout had almost finished Dos Passos. He and Crane had become good friends; they would have occasional dinners together, and Dos Passos would try to calm the poet when he was in one of his emotional, often alcoholic, frenzies. When both had been out late, Dos Passos if he met up with Crane might urge him to go home to bed instead of roaming, as Crane frequently did. He would return to Columbia Heights, but then hide in the entry way and dart back out after Dos Passos had gone to his own rooms.

While he was still sick, Crystal Ross returned to the United States after completing her studies. She arrived aboard the new French liner, the *De Grasse*, in June, to be met at the docks by her father, her brother, and Dos Passos. Although Dos Passos was ill, she remained in New York for some time, staying at the Lafayette Hotel and attending the theater with him when he felt well enough. They discussed marriage once more, Dos Passos pressing her to go ahead. She, however, was still uncertain because she felt somewhat unsure of herself among Dos Passos's circle of friends, and more, because she believed she must return to her home in Texas. His dismay deepened, but she could not be dissuaded.

Their romance had cooled despite a deep affection for each other. It may have been that the frequent, lengthy separations had turned their minds to other people; perhaps they realized that they were not likely partners. Dos Passos, at any rate, sought a romantic relationship; yet, without being entirely aware of it, he also sought a woman who could organize and look after him, and Crystal did not seem to be that. Their engagement had not been successful, and Dos Passos in 1925 might have had more than an inkling that they would never marry. Hence he may not have been entirely surprised—although he felt frustrated by his helplessness to do anything about it—when early in the spring of 1926 she wrote to tell him that she was engaged to marry Lewis Dabney, a Texan. "I never understood exactly why people get engaged—the only time I ever did the most disastrous things happened," he confided to Rumsey Marvin after she had written, and he hinted that part of his own error had been to let the engagement drag on.

Dos Passos's frustration about his engagement in 1925 was lessened some by his desire to return to Europe. In early May he had heard from Hemingway. Dos Passos, enthusiastic about his friend's writing, had praised it to the publisher Horace Liveright, who in March contracted with Hemingway for the publication of *In Our Time*. Hemingway, claiming to be drunk, wrote in an amusing fashion to thank Dos Passos for his help, to complain about editorial changes the publishers wanted to make, and alternately to brag and complain about the money he was or was not making. Boni and Liveright wanted to drop the story "Indian Camp" and also to cut the short interchapters, he reported, and in addition they had forced him to delete his "Up in Michigan" story because of its explicit description of sexual intercourse. He did not mind this last change, because the story he had substituted, "The Battler," was better anyway, but he felt torn apart by the other proposed cuts because the collection as it stood had a tightness and hardness that would be destroyed. Boisterously he gossiped about Donald Ogden Stewart, who he claimed had boasted to have outdrunk Dos Passos back in America. Hemingway could not believe this, remembering how Stewart had vomited during the drinking bouts in Pamplona the summer before. Urging Dos Passos to get to Europe so they could drink together, Hemingway sent love from his wife Hadley and himself, begging in a final line that Dos Passos try to prevent Boni and Liveright from cutting *In Our Time*.

Dos Passos, perhaps ill by the time he received Hemingway's letter in May, was hardly in a position to do much about editorial decisions, but Hemingway's tough-guy exuberance no doubt amused him and added to his anticipation of the months abroad. As soon as he could after leaving the Midtown Hospital at the end of July or early in August, he organized his affairs, which included discussions about *Manhattan Transfer* with the Harpers. The publishers objected to some of the frank language in the novel. Dos Passos was disgusted by their expressed conviction that "Kerist!" was not blasphemous, but "Christ!" was, and by their naïve belief that the term "three a day" meant having intercourse with three men a day, or that "fanny" meant "penis." Yet, "after the battle with the gelding shears," the book was not entirely castrated, Dos Passos wrote Hillyer from aboard the *Paris*. "Perhaps," he granted, "half a testicle remained on the left side." With the final version of *Manhattan Transfer* complete, he was delighted in late summer to leave New York behind, where life had seemed "like being rolled naked in metal chips." He relaxed aboard the *Paris*, an easy voyage helping him recuperate from the last vestiges of his recent illnesses.

A European trip would not have been complete for Dos Passos without a sojourn at Villa America. This visit he stayed some length of time, relaxing in the Bastide and hoping that the warm weather would improve his health. With the Murphys he enjoyed the routine of picnics, swimming, and afternoon trips into the hills behind Antibes. The Murphys had acquired an aged racing yacht, the *Picaflor*, shortly before Dos Passos arrived. Accompanied by Vladimir Orloff, a Russian émigré who had designed sets for Diaghilev until settling in Antibes with the Murphys, Gerald and Dos Passos commenced a cruise in the Mediterranean. They were good sailors, Orloff, expert, but when a squall hit them during a night voyage toward Genoa, they found themselves in serious trouble. They were flying a large balloon jib which they did not want to cut free; their halyards jammed, and they bore helplessly on, coming dangerously close to capsizing in the high seas. They decided to try for the harbor at Savona, only to discover that they had missed the channel in the dark. As the storm drove them toward a rock barrier outside the harbor, Orloff managed to drop their two anchors, and they were able to bring the ship into the wind within forty yards of the rocks, barely avoiding disaster. After some hours, a tug pulled them safely into the harbor, where the sailors docked the *Picaflor* alongside a wharf. But before the adventure ended, the tug, backing toward the yacht, swerved to avoid her and tore away her bowsprit.

Later, sailing back along the Italian Riviera aboard the repaired *Picaflor*, Dos Passos wrote Jack Lawson about their "ignominious" arrival in the harbor, then changed the subject to Italian Fascism, which had rendered Savona dead, he thought, a stark contrast to what he remembered from the time he and Lawson had passed through it in 1917. Now it was "the most fantastically sinister place" he had ever been in. The restaurants, the streets, and the harbor had no life about them, except for one café where a small group of paunchy thugs drank glasses of crème de menthe and a few sallow-faced boys sat playing chess and drinking tea. It was depressing.

Before going south to Antibes, Dos Passos talked to Hemingway in Paris about taking a trip into the Rif country in northern Morocco, where Abd el Krim was leading the Berber tribesmen in resistance against the French. Back in Paris in

October, Dos Passos talked further about the idea, but when he went in December, it would be without Hemingway, who stayed behind to finish *The Torrents of Spring,* his mean-spirited parody of Sherwood Anderson's novel *Dark Laughter.* With that mailed to the United States on December 7, the Hemingways left for Schruns in the Austrian Alps.

Before leaving for Morocco, Dos Passos had seen Ernest frequently. He was present when Hemingway purchased a painting for Hadley entitled "The Farm," by Joan Miró. Ernest did not have enough money, so Dos Passos helped him raise the necessary 5,000 francs after he had won the right to buy the painting by rolling dice with his friend Evan Shipman, who also coveted it. That transaction was conducted in a friendly spirit, but Hemingway was less amicable about *The Torrents of Spring,* which he began after he had finished the first draft of *The Sun Also Rises* on September 21, 1925. Soon, he had written enough so that he read from his manuscript to Dos Passos as they sat in the Closerie des Lilas. Parts of the parody made Dos Passos laugh, and he readily agreed that Anderson's *Dark Laughter* was "sentimental and silly," but he urged Hemingway not to go through with publishing the piece, because Anderson, one of Hemingway's early benefactors, did not deserve such treatment. Moreover, *The Torrents of Spring,* Dos Passos thought, was not excellent, and Hemingway should follow *In Our Time* with another first-rate piece of work.

Dos Passos believed he had convinced his friend against publishing *The Torrents,* but Ernest's less admirable side dominated his decision in this case. He did not like to be beholden to anyone, and this was his way of breaking with Anderson, with whom he was then being compared. Moreover, Liveright had an option on his next two books, but Hemingway was certain the publisher would not want to bring out the parody, since Anderson was also published by Liveright. Thus, Ernest could break his agreement, something he was eager to do because he hoped to sign a better contract for *The Sun Also Rises* with Alfred Harcourt, Alfred Knopf, or Scribner's, whom Scott Fitzgerald had alerted to Hemingway's talent. The upshot was exactly as Hemingway desired; Liveright refused *The Torrents;* Maxwell Perkins at Scribner's, anxious to get *The Sun,* accepted the parody, and Hemingway was free of a contract he did not want.

Dos Passos's literary fortunes were less tumultuous at that moment. *Manhattan Transfer* was published on November 12. It had become his custom to avoid the publicity surrounding the publication of a book; this occasion was no different. In Paris, he was utterly away from it and may not even have had word of how the novel was received before he traveled south to Morocco in December. *Manhattan Transfer* perplexed some critics and was an outright offense to upholders of the genteel tradition like Paul Elmer More, who would soon term it "an explosion in a cess pool." But others found it superior. "Wasn't Dos Passos' book astonishly good?" Scott Fitzgerald asked Max Perkins late in December. The reviewer for the *New York Times,* H. L. Stuart, called the novel "a powerful and sustained piece of work," despite what he termed Dos Passos's "exasperated sense of the unpleasant." He correctly linked the author with impressionist and "super-naturalist" writers, the latter term being akin to what the reviewer for the *Literary Review*, Herschel Brickell, called "Neo-Realism," which stressed "the ugly and sordid." "One must grant it a rough vigor and something of the vitality of our island," Brickell wrote, "much, too, of its commonness and sheer vulgarity." For him, as for many readers, however, the book was interesting primarily as "a literary experiment."

But most pleasing of all to Dos Passos whenever it was that he read the reviews clipped and mailed him by Harper and Brothers was that of Sinclair Lewis, who in the *Saturday Review of Literature* declared *Manhattan Transfer* to be "a novel of the very first importance" which could be "the foundation of a whole new school of novel-writing." Lewis speculated that Dos Passos might be the originator of "humanized and living fiction" more nearly than were already renowned American novelists like Dreiser, Cather, or Sherwood Anderson. "I regard *Manhattan Transfer*," Lewis wrote, "as more important in every way than anything by Gertrude Stein or Marcel Proust or even the great white boar, Mr. Joyce's *Ulysses.*"

With *Manhattan Transfer* Dos Passos achieved artistic maturity. The novel, which included the expressionistic techniques he had developed during the previous several years, was a montage about New York that presented a wide variety of characters who passed through the pages of the novel to demonstrate the author's themes of materialism, conformity, political corruption, and lack of communication. The book was a satire, in places harsh and bitter, but also amusing because of Dos Passos's use of burlesque as well as the ludicrousness of the lives of some of the characters, who dashed helter-skelter about a city that loomed larger throughout the book than any of the individual figures. If he had not achieved the "humanized and living fiction" which Sinclair Lewis claimed *Manhattan Transfer* was, he had caricatured New York and members of its population effectively—had succeeded brilliantly in achieving what he had set out to do.

Satisfied that *Manhattan Transfer* was the blend of technique and theme he desired, Dos Passos in December voyaged to Morocco by himself and on Christmas Day was in "a little halfdeserted town on the edge of the Sahara," he told Eugene Saxton. He was semi-ill with an incipient case of rheumatic fever. That, loneliness, and the fact that the revolt of the Rif was not materializing—thus providing him with a subject for his reportage—demoralized him. As was not infrequently his wont during one of his solitary treks, he wrote a friend—this time Arthur McComb— about the miseries of solitude. Shortly before New Year's, 1926, he complained of his "melancholy reflections on the falling of hair, the loss of friends, the disappearance of ocean greyhounds. . . . It is a ridiculous and repulsive spectacle that one offers, I fear, continuously scuttling about the world from place to place like a cockroach running away from a light. I am assailed by wise adages and knowing saws. The trouble is they are all quite true—rolling stones gather neither moss nor information."

When his illness subsided, he traveled during January and February to Marrakesh, Magador, and Rif before settling later in February in Tangier, where he hoped to discover more about Abd el Krim's revolt. Little came of the revolt, however, and he was ready to leave Morocco even before a cable from Jack Lawson arrived, asking him to become a director of the New Playwrights Theatre, which Lawson, Mike Gold, Francis Faragoh, and Em Jo Basshe were organizing in New York with the backing of the financier Otto Kahn. Dos Passos liked the idea. Besides, Lawson had been instrumental in arranging for *The Moon Is a Gong* to be produced, it was to open March 12 at the Cherry Lane Playhouse in Greenwich Village, and Dos Passos wanted to see it performed. As soon as he could, he caught a mailplane from Tangier and was bounced to Cette, with stopovers in Alicante, Valencia, and Barcelona. But before leaving France in December, he had agreed to meet the Hemingways in Schruns upon his return. This he did after traveling up through France on the train in early March. The Murphys joined them for what Dos Passos recollected was "the last unalloyed good time" he had with Ernest and Hadley. During the week he spent with them, they all skied—Gerald and Ernest well, Dos Passos horribly, so that he ended coming down the slopes sitting on the backs of his skis. The food, drink, and general festival atmosphere kept the group lively, while Hemingway pleased them by reading from *The Sun Also Rises.*

Then for Dos Passos it was time to return to the United States. He arrived at the end of March, soon enough to see one of the last performances of *The Moon Is a Gong.* The play was not a success in New York and ran for only eighteen performances. It was interesting, however, as an experimental drama. The events of the play suggest the frantic pace of twenties life; American society is seen to be disintegrating—an urban wasteland—and the two Everyman figures of the play, Tom and Jane, are finally claimed by Death, presented throughout in various roles but at the last as the Garbage Man. Dos Passos's intention was to produce a "show"; as a result the drama lacked a story and some depth of characterization, qualities audiences expected when the author clearly had a serious intent also. Vaudeville and social protest, in other words, did not mix well, or at least they did not in the experimental mode Dos Passos employed. Stark Young, as sympathetic a reviewer as there was, could only offer lukewarm praise while comparing the play to Lawson's *Processional.* He thought *The Moon Is a Gong* "more interesting theatre than most of the season, but it falls far below *Processional;* its jazz element is not integrated with the body of the drama; it lacks the powerful emotional gift, the dramatic compulsion, the rough tragic vigor and, most of all, the extraordinary sense of the theatre that *Processional* showed."

Dos Passos was disappointed by his play's reception although ready to explain it away as resulting from the public's lack of understanding of his intentions and innovative techniques. The lack of success did not dampen his enthusiasm. Rather, it increased his belief that Americans needed to understand what artistic innovation was trying to convey in order to begin to comprehend the new social and political forces at work in industrial society. Thus, in the spring of 1926 at the age of thirty, Dos Passos commenced the period of his greatest political activism. His involvement with experimental drama and with the New Playwrights Theatre in particular kept him in close touch with radicals like Mike Gold, for whom politics was a way of life. In addition to the drama there was the *New Masses,* which began publication in May, 1926.

The *New Masses* group was pleased to have the author of *Manhattan Transfer* among its regular contributors. Dos Passos, in turn, appreciated the chance to publish frequently in a journal sympathetic to his beliefs. "The idea as I remember was to revive the pacifist 'radical' tendency on the old Masses," Dos Passos wrote Daniel Aaron many years afterward, noting that it was not until later that a strict Communist Party ideology took hold of the *New Masses*.

For the June issue, he wrote a piece describing the *New Masses* he would like to see, responding in part to Mike Gold, who had earlier referred to him, Dos Passos asserted, as a "bourgeois intellectual." The most interesting aspect of Dos Passos's essay is that he took an independent, questioning stance and that, to the annoyance of committed Communists like Gold, he maintained that stance during the next six years when he was thought to be a convinced fellow-traveler, or by many, a Communist in fact as well as in spirit. He was more in agreement, however, with the anarchistic spirit of the Spanish writer Pío Baroja, whom he had admired for many years; with the Jeffersonian social theories of Albert Jay Nock, who edited the *Freeman* from 1920 to 1924 and for whom the enemy was the state; and with the economic theories of Thorstein Veblen, who in *The Theory of the Leisure Class* attacked that class's materialistic values, while in *The Engineers and the Price System* he described how engineers and technicians, properly organized, could effect a revolution in the leadership of production. Veblen, in fact, had as much influence on Dos Passos's thought as anyone ever did. Many years later, responding to John P. Diggins, who had written an article about Veblen and Dos Passos, he wrote that he had been extremely interested in the "technocrats" during the twenties and "was certainly much influenced by my enthusiastic reading of Veblen."

"As mechanical power grows in America," wrote Dos Passos in 1926, "general ideals tend to restrict themselves more and more to Karl Marx, the first chapter of Genesis and the hazy scientific mysticism of the Sunday supplements." The present was no time for "spellbinders" to lay down hard and fast laws about anything. "Particularly," he emphasized, "I don't think there should be any more phrases, badges, opinions, banners, imported from Russia or anywhere else." From the days of Columbus, in fact, the American continent had been cursed by "imported systems"; what was needed now was not another import, but a native brand of political thought.

The *New Masses* he wanted was something that would be "a highly flexible receiving station that will find out what's in the air in the country. . . . Being clear-sighted" at a time "when the pressure is rising and rising in the boiler of the great imperial steamroller of American finance" that was always trying to grind down contemporary civilization was a matter of life and death. Introspection and doubt were what the *New Masses* needed, not any set of instructions, be they from Moscow or the steel mills of America.

Understandably, Mike Gold, who as a committed Communist made a habit of trying to goad bourgeois intellectuals leftward, was peeved. In the same issue as the one in which Dos Passos's statement appeared, he responded, crying out "Let It Be Really New!" which was an attack on the "vague esthetic creed" of writers like Dos

Passos and Jack Lawson as much as on any plan for action they might have. Gold's thrust at Dos Passos came early; it is remarkable how consistent it is with the complaints the radical Left lodged against him all during the years he was their literary almost-darling. The trouble with writers like Dos Passos and Lawson, asserted Gold, was that they "hug chaos to their bosoms, and all the heroes of their fiction wind up in chaos and failure." This "pessimism, defeatism, and despair," nevertheless, was not the only possible path for writers opposed to the status quo. Younger ones had discovered a new path, that of "the world of revolutionary labor" —a vague, if noble route, one might observe.

As if to reaffirm what he had written, Gold's review of *Manhattan Transfer* appeared two months later. Calling the novel "a barbaric poem of New York," he observed that Dos Passos's work reflected "bewilderment." The central protagonist, Jimmy Herf, "is tortured by American commercialism and always seeks some escape." Dos Passos, however, did not understand how to help Herf, who at the conclusion of the book tries to escape the chaos of Manhattan only by plodding along a highway out of the city looking for a lift. "How fur ye goin?" asks the driver of a truck. "I dunno," answers Jimmy, "pretty far"—a response which, Gold was correct, is an affirmation of nothing except the negative effects of urban life.

The answer to Dos Passos's problem, according to Gold, was to "read History, psychology, and economics" and to become active in the labor movement. Dos Passos, instead of standing aloof, needed to "ally himself definitely with the radical army, for in this struggle is the only true escape from middleclass bewilderment today." More acutely than perhaps he was aware, Gold ended by observing, "Dos Passos suffers with nostalgia for a clean, fair, joyous and socialized America," by which Gold meant the egalitarian democracy of individuals that had been the ideal before the young nation one hundred years earlier. Such a democracy, Dos Passos would come increasingly to realize, was what he could commit himself to, but it would be another eleven years and a number of literary and political battles before he would declare once and for all that the United States was his chosen country, and a Jeffersonian form of democracy, his political creed.

As if to show that he partly agreed with Gold, Dos Passos, in the June issue of the *New Masses* in which appeared their exchange, wrote an impressionistic piece about a visit he had made with a large group of intellectuals to Passaic, New Jersey, where the United Front Textile Committee headed a strike against textile mills in the area. Workers had been striking for several months by the time Dos Passos arrived; violence had occurred, and strike supporters had been banned from speaking. Dos Passos's point was that, for all their good liberal intentions, the intellectuals were helpless. Seated inside "a row of taxicabs, shining sedans of various makes, nicely upholstered," the liberals talked about "outrages and the Bill of Rights, we, descendants of the Pilgrim Fathers, The Bunker Hill Monument, Gettysburg, the Boston Teaparty . . . Know all men by their presents . . ." while outside stood "groups of yellowish grey people," the impoverished strikers, staring blankly as the intellectuals got briefly out of their sedans in Passaic, only to be politely herded back in by sheriffs' deputies cradling "shiny new riot guns." The irony of the scene was not lost on Dos Passos, the irony of democratic ideals, contradicting capitalist realities, liberal ineptness, and the intellectuals' unwitting collaboration with a system that exploited the workers while denying them the right to protest.

The themes and the style of the piece foreshadowed those Dos Passos would employ in the Camera Eyes of *U.S.A.* several years hence, especially in those dealing with labor strife in the 1920s, and most particularly, with the case of Sacco and Vanzetti, to which he turned his attention during the spring of 1926 after his sympathies for the laboring man had been aroused once he had viewed the miserable conditions at Passaic. Nicola Sacco and Bartolomeo Vanzetti, two Italian anarchists, had been arrested in May 1920, suspected of being accomplices in a robbery-murder in South Braintree, Massachusetts, on April 15. On the basis of circumstantial, often conflicting evidence, they had been found guilty in July 1923, a finding which still stood in 1926 despite repeated motions for a new trial and worldwide attention to the case.

Dos Passos traveled to Boston in June to gather information about Sacco and Vanzetti. He met Aldino Felicani, an Italian printer, the chief organizer of the committee formed to defend the anarchists and the person who asked him to report about efforts for a new trial. Dos Passos was impressed with his honesty. Then he visited Vanzetti in the Charleston penitentiary, Sacco at the Dedham jail, and various defense witnesses, and came away in each instance more firmly convinced than before of the pair's innocence, hence more firmly committed to defending them from the forces that worked against them: "the blind hatred of thousands of wellmeaning citizens" whose prejudices, fanned by the frenzy of the Red scare of 1919–1920, had played a large part in the Italians' conviction; "the superhuman involved stealthy soulless mechanism of the law," dubiously represented by a narrow-minded judge, Webster Thayer; ambitious, less-than-scrupulous prosecutors; as well as an antiquated legal procedure in Massachusetts that forbade the introduction of new evidence once a conviction had been rendered. Dos Passos's first presentation of the facts as he found them appeared that August in the *New Masses.* Because he had by then agreed to put together a pamphlet for the Defense Committee, the material became part of *Facing the Chair: Story of the Americanization of Two Foreignborn Workmen,* which appeared in the spring of 1927 after he had returned to Massachusetts during the fall of 1926 to gather more data.

Having written the piece for the *New Masses,* Dos Passos wanted to leave New York for a rest. He and Rumsey Marvin had finally been able to coordinate a walk along North Carolina's Outer Banks, so in late June they gathered—along with C. D. Williams, then an Assistant U.S. District Attorney in New York, and Hugh Lemy, associate editor of *Collier's*—at the home of Walter Williamson in Wrightsville Beach, near Wilmington, North Carolina. Their host sent them on their way with a half-gallon glass jug of corn liquor, which they cautiously sneaked aboard a bus for Beaufort, up the coast. Stopping in Morehead City, they deposited the jug in the men's room of a hotel, Lemy being the only one who thought it worthwhile to pour some of the "corn" into his canteen. From Beaufort they crossed Bogue Sound to Cape Lookout and slept that night on the floor of the Coast Guard station there.

The next day they walked along the shore of Core Bank, occasionally stripping off their clothes and plunging into the surf to cool themselves down. They spent that night at the Core Bank Coast Guard station; then with the help of the Coast Guard, who ferried them across various inlets, they hiked the third day to Ocracoke, where, exhausted, they bedded down comfortably at Captain Bill Gaskill's hotel. The summer sun had been debilitating, so they decided that they would walk the next distance to Cape Hatteras at night. The evening they left Ocracoke they had a lively time square dancing with several pretty girls and drinking Captain Gaskill's concoction of Grape-Ola mixed with orange extract. Because the heavyset, fair-complexioned Lemy had suffered during the long daylight walks, he decided to remain at Ocracoke when the others left about midnight to walk along the shoreline in the light of a full moon. C. D. Williams recalled wild ponies galloping over the banks and rotting hulks of wrecked ships which cast grotesque shadows on the sand. Eventually they reached Manteo, just short of their goal of Kitty Hawk, and took a ferry across Albermarle Sound to Elizabeth City, there catching a train to Norfolk, Virginia, then to Richmond, where they explored Civil War memorials and gave a lighthearted interview to one of Marvin's friends, a reporter for the *Richmond News Leader*. The next year, they announced, they were planning a voyage to Asia. Dos Passos avowed that they had discovered more beautiful girls in Buxton, North Carolina, on the Outer Banks than anywhere else in America. Marvin and Williams readily agreed.

It had been an enlivening trip and a welcome respite for Dos Passos from the seriousness of Sacco and Vanzetti's case, which he again turned to as soon as he was back in New York. Much of the next several months was involved with collecting additional information and materials for *Facing the Chair*. In July, he moved out to Mount Sinai, near Port Jefferson, Long Island, where he could work in quiet, there sharing a house with Jack Lawson and his second wife, Sue. After a morning's writing he could swim, canoe, or sail in a small boat named *Earnest Endeavor*, he told Germaine Lucas-Championnière. But the task at hand as well as his own inclinations kept him on the move; late in August he was in Westport, Connecticut, conferring with an editor of the *New Masses*, no doubt about Sacco and Vanzetti. Soon thereafter he was in Boston, continuing his search for information, and in October he journeyed from Cape Cod to Provincetown after having completed some phase of the work for *Facing the Chair*.

Provincetown appealed to him more and more. He had known it since his college days; now he enjoyed a stay because an increasing number of literary friends either lived there or visited from New York as he did. One person he met this time who became a lifelong friend was Eben Given, who lived at the edge of the harbor on Commercial Street. Given recalled meeting Dos Passos in 1926 during a party at the home of the writer Susan Glaspell. Dos Passos, in his usual rumpled suit but sporting a bright orange, knitted tie, talked about Sacco and Vanzetti, but what Given remembered particularly was Dos Passos's enthusiasm for Ernest Hemingway's new novel, *The Sun Also Rises*, published that October.

It is no wonder that Given was struck by Dos Passos's interest in *The Sun Also*

Rises. This was the book Dos Passos had hoped would follow *In Our Time* rather than *The Torrents of Spring.* But more, the subject matter fascinated him. He knew firsthand the festival at Pamplona, as well as most of the people who served as Hemingway's models. Further, about the time he talked with Given, he wrote a review of the novel for the *New Masses.* "A Lost Generation," Dos Passos titled it, and in the radical spirit of the *New Masses* he disapproved of the decadence of the characters. If this generation of intellectuals was not going to lose itself, he complained, "for God's sake let it show more fight. . . ." He praised Hemingway's style of writing but claimed not to understand the novel. Yet, he did, of course, because Hemingway's point was to satirize the romantic self-indulgence of his characters. With a satiric thrust that Dos Passos's readers for the most part would not have caught—one might even suppose it a private gesture to his friend Hemingway—he wrote that the novel struck him "as being a cock and bull story about a lot of summer tourists getting drunk and making fools of themselves at a picturesque Iberian folk-festival. . . . It's heartbreaking." That was the kind of proletarian statement Mike Gold could approve of. One can also read into it Dos Passos's disapproval of the exhibitionism he had witnessed at Pamplona in 1924. On another level, the story was not malarkey, but truly a "cock and bull" story, a tale about sex, sexual frustration, and bullfights. Dos Passos was more praising and insightful than he seemed to be.

But late in 1926 politics preoccupied—and frustrated—him. Referring to the months before the execution of Sacco and Vanzetti, Dos Passos wrote much later: "In Boston the work of the Defense Committee was hampered by continual patient efforts of the American C.P. to take charge of the agitation." His assertion in *The Best Times* was at least partly hindsight, sounding the theme that he harped on unrelentingly once he had broken for good with the Communists in 1937. In the fall of 1926, any manipulation by the party was less apparent. Nevertheless, the emotional controversies and political infighting that surrounded the case were not something he could stand for long, added to which were arguments, sometimes political but mostly aesthetic, among the directors of the New Playwrights Theatre group which that fall was preparing for its first season. Further, he meant to visit Crystal Ross in Texas. "Harried heckled and harassed by various trains of events" was how he described himself to Rumsey Marvin. Thus he felt impelled to leave New York, planning a trip south and west that would take him by mid-December to Mexico City, where his friend Susan Smith was then living, and where he hoped to learn about the art inspired by the recent revolution.

He traveled first to Virginia to visit his half-brother James Madison at what remained of John R.'s estate; then he turned west to Staunton in the Blue Ridge Mountains, from there taking "a long solitary walk" for three days in "superb Indian summer weather." He covered nearly twenty-five miles a day, the second afternoon hiking through a snowstorm into Warm Springs, where after a swim in the sulfur baths, he relaxed that night in the inn that had been made from the town's courthouse. The next day he walked to Covington, from where he caught a train for Louisville, Kentucky.

For all his traveling, Dos Passos had not seen that much of mid-America by 1926. This trip was important for him, because he was beginning to form an idea of a proletarian novel that would attempt to chronicle, to paint a panorama of the nation during a turbulent era in its history, rather as *Manhattan Transfer* had a city. Hence he was eager as he traveled west to absorb all he could of places less glamorous than Paris or even New York like Louisville—"a grey sprawling redbrick dingy kind of place, full of darkies and jews. The Ohio flows tawny between the bridges under the sleety wind, the water looks dense and solider than the misty banks and the smudged blocks of buildings"—or St. Louis, where he next went, describing it soon thereafter to Edmund Wilson as "the most sooty Dante-dismal sprawl of a red brick town in process of demolition I ever saw in my life. Hoboken times Cambridgeport times Redhook and with a continual smell like a chimney on fire." But he had enjoyed himself there, getting a flavor of the city and meeting an acquaintance of Wilson, Harry Turner, who filled him with talk about St. Louis. He traveled next to Dallas, where he visited Crystal Ross, expressing his dismay that there had been so little chance to talk with her about her decision and wondering if she had not been impetuous. He changed nothing, however, and they departed friends, but nothing more.

CHAPTER SIXTEEN

Arrival at
the Political Left,
1926–1928

Dos Passos's dismay at the ending of his engagement to Crystal Ross was lessened by his anticipation of an enlivening stay in Mexico. From Dallas he traveled to San Antonio, then in mid-December took a train from Laredo south to Mexico City, where after renting a room he contacted Susan Smith, perhaps through her learning that the American writer Carleton Beals was living in her apartment building. Beals, whom he had met at one of the organizational meetings for the *New Masses* the year before, was in Mexico City and knew the country well. So Dos Passos asked him for help in straightening himself out in order that he could, as he put it in a note to Beals, "dig up dope about various things." Also, there were several people to whom he hoped Beals could introduce him.

Dos Passos soon felt at ease, especially because he could speak Spanish fluently. "Mexico City is superb," he wrote on a postcard to Stewart Mitchell dated December 15. "Sunshine and beer and cigarettes and flowers and indians—marvellous looking people—I'm having a tremendous time." He met Howard Phillips, another American knowledgeable about Mexico who was soon to start the magazine *Mexican Life*. Through him Dos Passos was able to meet other Americans and numerous Mexican writers, journalists, and painters, many of whom had exactly the stories and lore he wanted to hear. For several weeks he was content to move in and around Mexico City, because, as he wrote Germaine Lucas-Championnière just before New Year's, "One eats spicy meals and drinks excellent beer and everyone lingers to tell stories." He'd had no idea the country was so interesting. The following Sunday he would be attending a bullfight, and he was seeing a lot of painting. What impressed him especially were the murals on public buildings, like the Secretaria of Education. There was, he exclaimed, a small renaissance, with the work of such artists as Orozco,

Rivera, and Montenegro making Mexico City somewhat like Renaissance Florence.

It was typical of Dos Passos's interest in radicalism that what drew him to the revolution as much as the political struggle was the art emanating from it. The "dope" he told Beals he wanted to gather was about painting, aside from the characters and tales that he would make note of for his fiction to come. The huge murals of Diego Rivera, he soon wrote for the *New Masses*, gave "a dramatic sequence" to the "welling up of life" that the artists had attempted to encompass. "Some of it's pretty hasty," he added, "some of it's garlanded tropical bombast, but by God, it's painting." Most impressive, however, was that the art had evolved from the necessity to explain the revolution to the common people, many of whom could not read. "It wasn't a case of ideas," insisted Dos Passos, "of a lot of propaganda-fed people deciding that a little revolutionary art would be a good thing, it was a case of organic necessity." And so a number of painters and sculptors had formed a union, agreeing to equal wages and to a fundamental aesthetic aim "rooted in the socialization of art, tending towards the absolute disappearance of individualism, characteristic of bourgeois epochs, thus approaching the great collective art of antiquity," he quoted from the artists' manifesto. The similarities between the aims of the union and those of the *New Masses* or New Playwrights groups were not lost on him, although he understood the disparity between the social conditions in Mexico and the United States.

One of the painters in the union, Xavier Guerrero, a stocky man of Indian extraction, became a good friend of Dos Passos. Guerrero, who had studied the methods of ancient painters at Teotihuacán, was a committed Communist interested in proselytizing villagers outside of Mexico City. Most of Dos Passos's other city acquaintances were not enthusiastic about traveling far, so with Guerrero he explored among the villages in the mountains behind Toluca. While the Mexican artist preached Communism, Dos Passos sketched and observed, his admiration growing for the Indian peasants.

An American whose tales particularly amused him was Gladwin Bland, a tall, well-built person somewhat older than he, who for years had been a member of the revolutionary union, Industrial Workers of the World (I.W.W.), and an itinerant worker. But that life had been hard, he told Dos Passos, and he had eventually settled in Mexico, married a Mexican woman, and was now selling used furniture, among other business enterprises. He was full of stories about the left-wing movement, Dos Passos recalled, telling them with a satiric skepticism that appealed to Dos Passos's own sense of irony. When he began writing *The 42nd Parallel* a year or so later, Bland's tales loomed large in Dos Passos's mind, and the retired Wobbly (as I.W.W. members were nicknamed) became the model for Fenian McCreary, the most nearly central character in the first volume of the *U.S.A.* trilogy. Mac's story paralleled Bland's so closely that, after his wife had read *The 42nd Parallel*, Bland wrote Dos Passos in mock indignation, declaring, "I can well forgive you for having given me a dose of clapp but for the incident of the cat [a cat nursing its kittens on the family bed of a woman Mac sleeps with], never. 'Mi vida del doctor Jekyll y Mister Hyde' in Mexico was about laid bare in the book."

During this stay in Mexico, Dos Passos often saw Carleton Beals, who came to like him. Dos Passos would frequently seek Beals out at his apartment, and if he was away, Dos Passos would sit down on the front steps to wait, eating an orange, reading a newspaper, and enjoying the sun. When they were together, he refrained from talking about his own work and politics but quizzed Beals about Mexico. Dos Passos got Beals to hike with him out to Ixtapalapa, Tenayuca, and one day to Atzcapotzalco and on to Tacuba, where after a beer, Dos Passos wanted to continue up into the hills to Los Remedios, ten miles beyond. To his disappointment, his friend demurred. Beals on these hikes was puzzled about how Dos Passos, suffering from bad eyesight, could see all the imagery that he poured into his writing as he strode along, head back, eyes squinting. The question was answered when, on top of the Hill of the Star, Dos Passos "pulled out a pair of opera glasses and studied the landscape minutely on all sides and asked many detailed questions."

Beals was sometimes amused by Dos Passos's seriousness, even naïveté, as when, on the trip to Tenayuca in the company of two American college girls who had been introduced to Beals, Dos Passos kept asking him what seemed to Beals foolish questions about why Mexicans did certain things one way or another. Beals gave kidding answers, which Dos Passos appeared to accept as true, although the girls recognized that Beals was teasing, which made one of them extremely irritated. There was an otherworldliness about Dos Passos, Beals thought. He seemed in Mexico never to wear anything other than "loose woven never pressed brown tweeds and heavy walking shoes." Although usually overserious as far as Beals could tell, Dos Passos often appeared secretly amused, frequently laughing in a breathless way while thrusting his head forward when he talked, "shoveling out his mouth" at his listener. "About all he did in Mexico was enjoy himself," Beals recollected. "He was eager to see things and talk with people. He was always the writer and though he undoubtedly had deep feelings about political ideas, they were never the essential part of him. His loyalties were largely emotional, and in many ways he seemed naive about politics."

Clearly Dos Passos enjoyed himself throughout the months he remained in Mexico. "Everything," he wrote Rumsey Marvin, "is exciting and comical and full of drunkenness and fornication." Before he returned to the United States he traveled to Veracruz and Jalapa, which were, if anything, even more picturesque than Mexico City, with a touch of the Wild West, where "everybody carries a gun and people shoot each other if they dont like the way somebody balances a toothpick." Yet life was pleasant and calm, and the people, amiable. It was a land where bears were still shot with bows and arrows and where, he claimed, the boa constrictors were so tame they served as watchdogs while rocking babies' cradles with their tails.

Although Dos Passos usually kept his specific political sensitivities to himself in Mexico, he observed as keenly as Beals believed he did. After trips in February and March into the small state of Morelos, south of Mexico City, he settled down, first in Yautepec and then in the capital city of Cuernavaca, to write about the dead hero of the agrarian revolt, Emiliano Zapata, and about the unrest he noted throughout Morelos. "When the Carranzistas killed Zapata they thought the agrarian movement was dead; his ghost walks uneasily and until it is laid Mexican politics will be perpetually unstable," Dos Passos closed his piece in Cuernavaca.

His sympathies, as always, were against those who exploited the poor and with the "Ten million Mexican peasants and workmen, disunited, confused by political rows, sleeping on a straw mat on the floor, eating off a few tortillas a day and a speck of chile to take away the raw taste of the corn. . . ." Against them were arrayed the power of the Catholic Church, the power of international petroleum interests, and the power of the United States, whose wealth permeated Mexican economics. "Which side are you on," he asked his readers in the *New Masses*, "on the side of the dollar, omnipotent god, or on the side of the silent dark man (he has lice, he drinks too much *pulque* when he can get it, he has spasms of sudden ferocious cruelty), Juan Sin Tierra, with his eyes on the ground?"

While his own answer to the question was clear, his solution to the problem of how to alleviate Juan Sin Tierra's condition was not. In fact, he was no closer to an answer than he had been when writing *Manhattan Transfer*, and the reason was that it seemed inescapably true that man's nature led toward conflict to achieve power, and that power came from organizations which he came to distrust, be they leftist or rightist. He could repeatedly join political groups, sign petitions, or lend his name to organizations like the National Executive Committee of the Moscow-based Proletarian Artists and Writers league—acts that many people took to mark a firm commitment, but they did not because he remained a skeptic.

Dos Passos was so prolific a reader that it is difficult to attribute his ideas to any particular source; yet when a book that an author has read reinforces an idea apparent in his work, the book may clarify the author's beliefs. Such is the case with the provocative study *Man Is War*, by John Carter, published in 1926, which Carleton Beals remembered Dos Passos talking about with great enthusiasm in Mexico that winter.

"The cardinal impulse of the typical human society is toward war," wrote Carter, "and the nemesis of the typical social unit is its inability to escape from the destiny of its own character. All social institutions carry within them the seeds of violence and of death, and all suffer from the profound malaise engendered by the consciousness of this limitation." Given what Dos Passos had seen in the war and his already ingrained belief that "organization is death," it is little wonder that he accepted Carter's somber assertion. What Carter termed "the industrial technique of the great Atlantic system of states" was at that moment conquering the world and was a technique whose ideology took various forms, capitalism and Marxism chief among them, but whose cardinal instincts were always the same: "self-preservation, self-perpetuation, self-aggrandizement," all of them, particularly the last, being a form of conflict. War, "inherent in the Atlantic way of life," Carter defined as "the organized violence of social groups seeking to impose their will by force." Atlantic civilization, he believed, was epitomized at the time he wrote by Britain and the United States, whose Anglo-Saxon civilization had created a distinctive economic form, industrial capitalism, which was to be distinguished from the Catholic economic form of the peasant state—no less warlike—simply surpassed by the other. And, lest anyone deem a Socialist form of economy superior, Carter noted that the alternative to capitalistic individualism was "proletarchy," which represented "the aspiration of those who toil to obtain an equal share in the rewards of all toil." Its aim, "to eliminate war by ending the economic exploitation of weaker people," was admirable; yet its results had been "bloodshed, famine and suffering on a scale which dwarfed the known horrors of recent war. Proletarchy," concluded Carter, "is to-day one of the greatest threats to orderly government and social repose in every country of the world." If Dos Passos accepted these assertions, it is understandable that he was nonplused by the call of a Mike Gold for a workers' revolution, or that, sympathetic with the plight of Juan Sin Tierra, nevertheless he hesitated to offer any panacea.

Man Is War was intriguing. At some points Carter sounded like a conservative, opposing the League of Nations as well as the Communists. But he opposed equally capitalism and industrial bureaucracy. He was the seeker, the skeptic, and finally, the enemy of nationalism, statism, of *isms* in general, because each was but an extension of man's aggressive nature, and wars, he believed, would continue "until the end of time or the creation of a uniform breed of men, speaking one language, holding one faith, solving economic life by labor-saving machinery and by the practice of birth control under rigid state supervision. . . . The world will escape the blight of war when man has ceased to be human," Carter closed his treatise. "The world will find peace when man is extinct. For man is war."

Dos Passos did not accept Carter's every idea, but in the main he admired the book. He was, and would remain, searching for alternatives, and like Carter he distrusted systems and bureaucracies. Thus, while he eventually accepted the form of government in the United States as the best possible alternative to "proletarchy," he remained a harsh critic of capitalist democracy and a satirist of mankind. To him it seemed as though, despite partial or temporary solutions to the problems of society, the world would be at peace only when man had ceased being human—and he was skeptical about that possibility.

Amid the trips and the stimulation of people like Guerrero and Beals, Dos Passos tried to work on his second play, *Airways, Inc.*, which was to be produced by the New Playwrights. But Mexico diverted him, so when he wrote Jack Lawson to find out about the plans of the New Playwrights, he grumbled that *Airways* was not finished; yet he could not write in his "great state of mental and moral decay." When he complained of the same thing to Hemingway, Ernest answered in mid-February from Switzerland that Dos Passos ought to stop for a while, because, just like sexual intercourse, too much writing dried up one's juices. Dos Passos was stale after publishing six books that Ernest could recall. If he felt "all shot to hell," well, that was because people got that way. Some recovered, some did not; and Hemingway had decided that it was an idiotic stroke of fate more than people's characters that gypped them if they never recovered. He went on to boast about the sales of *The Sun Also Rises,* claiming it was outselling the work of Louis Bromfield and Scott Fitzgerald. Hemingway was now receiving constant requests for stories and articles, but he would do only what he felt like doing. At that moment he claimed to regret having published anything, because he felt morose about hurting people by what he wrote. Such regrets stemmed from his depression about his break with Hadley, and he fished for assurance from Dos Passos to assuage his guilt.

After Dos Passos returned in March to New York, where he took his apartment again at Columbia Heights, he obliged Hemingway by writing to assure him that publishing was "the honestest and easiest method of getting rid of bum writing." If a person did not publish, his stuff just festered, while he became pistol-shy. Dos Passos believed in writing and publishing, but still the writer needed someone to flag the bad work, which might turn out to be nothing but "a talented and daintily scented turd." But even turning out poor writing was better than getting "all full of romance and ingrown literature" like Ezra Pound. Besides, *In Our Time* had been "a goddamn good thing to publish," as had been *The Sun Also Rises.*

In the same letter Dos Passos described self-deprecatingly something of his involvement with the New Playwrights. "I'm in deeper and deeper in the drahma every moment," he wrote Hemingway and told him that he was one of five directors of "a little Otto Kahn-undernourished playhouse" which at that moment was the Fifty-second Street Theatre at 306 West Fifty-second. There the group had staged its first two productions, Lawson's *Loud Speaker* and Em Jo Basshe's *Earth,* neither of them successes. The next fall the group would move to the Cherry Lane Playhouse at 40 Commerce Street. Initially Dos Passos enjoyed his association with the New Playwrights: "I do a lot of (against union rules) carrying about and painting of scenery and switching on and off of lights which is very entertaining," he described his chores for *Loud Speaker* to Hemingway. Such tasks he acknowledged would not be his life work; they kept him from writing or worrying, however, and he felt "merry as a cricket" for the moment.

Dos Passos could belittle the "drahma," hinting to Robert Hillyer that he expected its early demise—going "belly up." Friends were dubious about the group's effort: Hemingway had not completely understood why Dos Passos should become involved with drama; Cummings, who was amused by his friend's liberal guilt, was scornful of the entire New Playwrights enterprise—"Isn't it dweadful of me to lie here in this luxurious warm bath while human welations are being violated all over the countwy," he mimicked Dos Passos for Edmund Wilson's benefit. Cummings entertained Wilson with his parody of the group's plays: "Two men sitting around: 'When does the strike begin?' Then the other says in a high falsetto voice, 'Mother's over at the house sewing her eyes out!' "

Hemingway and Cummings, at least during the twenties, were dubious about any venture that linked politics and art, but Dos Passos's doubts about the New Playwrights were for reasons such as artistic squabbles, and he threw himself into the effort for the next year and a half, designing and painting sets, planning future productions, and helping with publicity, which last he did in part by defending the New Playwrights' experimentation in articles for the *New Masses.* In April 1927, he wrote Upton Sinclair to ask if the group might produce his play *Singing Jailbirds,* permission for which was granted; ultimately it was staged by the New Playwrights in 1929 as the next-to-last production before the Playwrights ceased. When Dos Passos first wrote Sinclair, he explained that the New Playwrights wanted to open their second season with his drama. "We are planning a bang-up revolutionary season," he wrote, "revolutionary in social import, in direction, acting and scenery." He proceeded to explain the "considerable rearrangement of scenes" he desired to make, his intention being to sustain the movement, hence the mood, of the drama about labor strife and injustice.

Dos Passos's designing included sets for Paul Sifton's *The Belt*, which opened at 40 Commerce Street on October 19, 1927; and for Lawson's *International*, opening on January 12, 1928. In addition he handled other tasks which he, like the rest of the group, had to accomplish to stretch their inadequate budget as far as they could while coping with the theater's limitations. These he described as a "tunnel-shaped auditorium, gloomy at best, sloping down to a low proscenium, containing two hundred and forty uncomfortable seats, and some of them busted. . . ." Their other facilities were meager; outside the theater was a yard "stacked with the debris of last season's sets which are to be rebuilt into this season's sets, upstairs is a work bench where the props are made . . . and a series of cramped dressing rooms, [while] in the basement there are some offices where the white-collar slaves work on promotion and publicity. . . ."

Differences in taste and politics aside, it was hard to remain enthusiastic about the venture with facilities like these and in the face of generally adverse criticism; yet Dos Passos continued during the life of the theater group to defend its efforts, expressing his belief that knowledgeable people had been stimulated by the experimental productions. Even after the last staging—his own play, *Airways, Inc.*—ended in 1929, he argued for the merits of what the New Playwrights had attempted, although conceding that they had failed. That, however, was in 1929; in the spring of 1927 the theatrical experience was fresh, if fatiguing; often Dos Passos would finish at the theater so late he would have to walk back to Columbia Heights across the Brooklyn Bridge, not arriving at his apartment until three in the morning. But for a while he could tolerate such inconveniences, and he was occupied with enough else that the combative New Playwrights could not by themselves make him despondent.

On his mind was a volume which would be a "series of reportages of the time," not a novel, but a series covering a lengthy period, "in which characters appeared and re-appeared." He recollected that he "was trying to get different facets of my subject and trying to get something a little more accurate than fiction, at the same time to work these pieces into the fictional picture." Despite incorporating nonfiction, his ultimate aim "was always to produce fiction," and he thought himself "sort of on the edge between them, moving from one field to the other very rapidly." The series of reportages was to be "a contemporary commentary on history's changes, always as seen by some individual's ears, felt through some individual's nerves and tissues. These were the *U.S.A.* books."

Although he may not have decided when he began *The 42nd Parallel* that he would write a trilogy, he had clearly in mind what his intentions were, and these remarks were not simply hindsight. From the moment he began the book in 1927 he envisioned what a decade later he described *U.S.A.* as being: "a long narrative which deals with the more or less entangled lives of a number of Americans during the first three decades of the present century." He went on in an introductory note to *The 42nd Parallel* to explain that:

> In an effort to take in as much as possible of the broad field of the lives of these times, three separate sequences have been threaded in and out among the stories. Of these *The Camera Eye* aims to indicate the position of the observer and *Newsreel* to give an inkling of the common mind of the epoch. Portraits of a number of real people are interlarded in the pauses in the narrative because their lives seem to embody so well the quality of the soil in which Americans of these generations grew.

Dos Passos understood that the kind of blend of history and fiction he was writing would confuse readers, and in 1928 he wrote a "Statement of Belief" that effectively summarized his concept of fiction. "The only excuse for a novelist," he wrote, "aside from the entertainment and vicarious living his books give the people who read them, is as a sort of second-class historian of the age he lives in." Dos Passos may have denigrated the value of fiction—fiction often treats matters of more lasting import than does narrative history—yet his intent to bridge the gap between history and the writer's imaginative re-creation of his own experiences was apparent. "The best kind of narrative," he asserted, would combine fiction and history, which was precisely what he had set out to do.

His task as he began to plan his innovative work was difficult because he intended to intertwine a series of narratives—some of them, such as that about Mac, drawn from the stories he had heard in Mexico. But more difficult, or at least more exacting, was the matter of what to select and how to organize the materials that would constitute the Camera Eyes, the short biographies of significant figures, and the Newsreels. He recognized that "the narrative must carry a very large load. Everything must go in. Songs and slogans, political aspirations and prejudices, ideals, hopes, delusions, frauds, crackpot notions out of the daily newspapers."

As he set about the task, he jotted down historical items in notebooks. What is perhaps the first page of all begins:

Newsreel   Monday Jan 1 1900
Boer War . . .

From the start he knew that he would chronicle the twentieth century; apparently he first thought that mention of the Boer War in the opening Newsreel should date the beginning. Eventually he decided to focus more on the United States by commencing the first Newsreel with a song that grew out of the Philippine insurrection, while the Boer War was referred to in the first Camera Eye. It was a wise choice. American imperialism thus immediately became a topic, and by referring to the Boer War in the Camera Eye, he could date the first episode of impressionistic autobiography, where his point was his infantile incomprehension of the world beyond his childish imagination and his mother's skirts.

His inclusion of Newsreels was not random; in the same notebook he remarked:

Need six more		
3 society	Titanic	1910
3 big business	Lusitania	1912
	World War	1914
		1916
		1917

Then in another notebook he gathered characters and incidents for the chronicle. Eventually several of these became the material for *1919*, the second volume of *U.S.A.*, but when he wrote these notes, he was simply listing possibilities:

War Section

The Red Cross in Paris
The trip to Italy of Section 1
Mr. Menglebrook
Doc and John Henry—appleyard
YMCA Secretaries on the rampage . . .
Bill Biggs from Fall River
    Merchant Marine
    killed in a fight in a
    bar in St. Nazaire
    on Armistice night
This is all in the career of Amory Savage,
The man who climbed to fame and
fortune via the Red Cross

Graft, love, air raids
Ritz, freedom,
intelligence department
English tea room,
hotel Quai Voltaire,
cake shops, whorehouses
Henry's Bar

Then the career of the man who didn't make
good by the same method. Ideas kept breaking in.

Another page reads:

The guys who do the work
Doc—Florida cracker
Bill Biggs—Fall River
Fen McCreary—Willimantic
Ed   Chicago
The American waitress who went and

married a Mexican
Ivy Edwards   Wiscasset
Katy (afterward Kathleen) Jones and her
elopement to Mexico.
        job in the follies and [final] setting up
        with a Hawaiian travelling band
The east side factory girl who gets a
job in a museum

And at the same time he wrote a number of pages about the career of Ward Morrison, who would become J. Ward Moorehouse, the figure whose career reaches through all three volumes of *U.S.A.* Dos Passos outlined his intention for Moorehouse thus:

Ward Morrison on the Street
Ward Morrison in Big Business
Ward Morrison in the Great War
Ward Morrison in Reconstruction
Ward Morrison and the Soviets
Ward Morrison and the miners strike
Ward Morrison and the great expansion
Ward Morrison's death and transfiguration*

Among these lists are several of the major characters—Bill Biggs became Joe Williams; Fen McCreary is Mac; Amory Savage is Richard Ellsworth Savage; and from among the ideas for various women may have emerged Margo Dowling, a major figure in *The Big Money.* But more significant about these notes is their factual basis. Dos Passos clearly intended to set the narratives in the history he knew: "The Red Cross in Paris, The trip to Italy of Section 1," and so forth.

And as he gathered his characters and events, he also contemplated the Camera Eye concept, scribbling down several versions of a sort of prose poem in which he attempted to express the function of the Camera Eye. "Camera Eye," he began:

The upside down image in the retina,
piece by piece immediately out of color
                                shape
remembered bright and dark rebuilds the city
[Sunday] sunlight on the downtown streets
[Stained uneven] pavements—Truck cluttered
streets—Terrible dead city on the make—

*Dos Passos may well have made these notes during or directly after his trip to Russia in 1928, where an acquaintance in Moscow with the American publicist Ivy Lee served to catalyze the character of Moorehouse in his mind.

Then he tried again:

> Camera Eye—the careful clipping out of
> paper figures the old photographs   the
> newspaper cartoons shall I make this
> one up—Newspaper photographs of old
> photographs in a trunk the pathetic
> enthusiasm— . . .
>
>   how could you warp the paper figures
> to simulate growth—twist cut out a
> pack and [tickle] whittle it up to eighty
> —shove him through the terribly various
> velocities of time. Imagine paper boats
> that will indicate the swirls and
> eddies of the stream.

These rough efforts were far from what the *Camera Eye* would become; yet the basic idea was there: by rendering impressionistic autobiography in the *Camera Eye* he would chart the growth of the narrator during the era chronicled as well as by the other narrative devices. He would shove the narrator "through the terribly various velocities of time."

While he worked out the subject matter and the organization of *The 42nd Parallel, Orient Express,* his first volume of reportage since *Rosinante to the Road Again* was published in early March. The book contained his pieces about the 1921–1922 odyssey to the Near East and into Russia and included reproductions of his own paintings. The volume was handsome and well received, although the first and only printing was but 2,500 copies. Such friendly reviewers as Paxton Hibben—who had been with Dos Passos during part of the journey—praised it highly, Hibben going so far as to state that "not since Matthew Arnold has one so marshalled English words to paint pictures—nor has the turbid ebb and flow of human misery made such sharp erosions in the copperplate of an artist's mind." Hibben's was one of the reviews most lavish in its praise, but there were others that approached it. *Orient Express* was more important than had been *Rosinante* to solidify Dos Passos's reputation as a writer of nonfiction. Although he was known to the public primarily as a novelist, numerous readers admired him equally for his reportage.

While the appearance of *Orient Express* was pleasing, the pressures from the drama and—more so in the spring of 1927—from his growing dismay at the dismal state of the Sacco and Vanzetti case depressed Dos Passos after he had been back in New York for two months. From Mount Sinai, where he was again sharing a house part of the time with Jack and Sue Lawson, he wrote Germaine Lucas-Championnière in May that he felt very sad at that moment. Partly just a mood, his sadness was more, because he had worked hard on *Facing the Chair,* which appeared that spring, but neither that nor anything else seemed to be budging "the system" which had condemned the two Italians.

When he could, he broke free of New York, going to Mount Sinai, Long Island, or, as at the time of Charles Lindbergh's landing in Paris on May 21, hiking with friends. This time he, Rumsey Marvin, and C. D. Williams took a train to Dover Plains, New York, from where they walked through the Catskills to Danbury, Connecticut, stopping nearby at the sculptor Gaston Lachaise's home where they enjoyed a game of croquet with Hart Crane, Lachaise's guest. Then in June Dos Passos made a brief voyage to the West Indies but returned by the beginning of July because he expected to devote much of his time to doing what he could to aid in the the final defense of Sacco and Vanzetti, whose cause was increasingly desperate.

On April 9, 1927, after numerous legal maneuvers on the part of the defense lawyers, Judge Webster Thayer sentenced the Italians to death. In June, Massachusetts Governor Alvan T. Fuller appointed an advisory committee which included the President of Harvard, A. Lawrence Lowell, to review the case. The committee did and, despite irregularities and important new evidence, announced in early August that they had found no cause for another trial. Dos Passos, like hundreds of other liberals and leftist radicals who were protesting the sentence, was shocked. He immediately wrote "An Open Letter to President Lowell," which was published in part in the *New York Times* on August 8, as well as in other papers. The full letter appeared soon after in the *Nation*. The advisory committee's report was an "infamous document," he charged Lowell, whom he accused of being "a party to a judicial murder" which covered not only Governor Fuller's bias, but the "dirty business" of the Italians' arrests amid the Red scare and "their subsequent slow torture by the spiteful and soulless mechanism of the law." The case, he continued, "has become part of the world struggle between the capitalist class and the working class, between those who have power and those who are struggling to get it. . . . Are you," he demanded to know of Lowell, "going to prove by a bloody reprisal that the radical contention that a man holding unpopular ideas cannot get a free trial in our courts is true?"

In the final weeks before the anarchists' scheduled executions on August 23, protestors gathered on the Boston Common across Beacon Street from the State House to march. Mike Gold recounted how he had been one of forty people to picket on August 10. The marchers were diverse, including a group of Italian workers, five young Finnish working girls, Communists from Chicago and New York, as well as the writer Dorothy Parker and Dos Passos.

As the twenty-third neared, the protests grew larger and more frantic. Dos Passos worked to swell the numbers, telegraphing friends to come to Boston for the final days. Jack Lawson arrived, among others, but Edmund Wilson did not, and he offended Dos Passos by his seeming indifference to the situation when he invited Dos Passos out to Provincetown for a party while the last protests were occurring. "You cant imagine how queerly your wire [the invitation] jangled my nerves—Jesus X Columbus—man didn't you realize we were all virtually mad up in Boston—You try battering your head against a stone wall sometime," he wrote Wilson a month later.

To Dos Passos, despite the growing sense of futility, there was something inspiring about the protestors who gathered in Boston during the final days; "it was," he told Wilson later, "as if, by some fairy-tale spell, all the different kinds of Americans, eminent and obscure, had suddenly, in a short burst of intensified life, been compelled to reveal their true characters in a heightened exaggerated form." Among them were many different kinds of writers and artists; Katherine Anne Porter recalled seeing Dos Passos, Lola Ridge, Paxton Hibben, Mike Gold, Helen O'Lochlain Crowe, James Rorty, Edna St. Vincent Millay, William Gropper, and Grace Lumpkin in the picket line on August 21, the first day she marched. The picketers were booed and hooted at by onlookers and occasionally pelted with stones. It became a sort of honor badge to be in the line, and arrest gave the act added luster. The Boston police would permit the marchers a brief stay; then they would move in and make arrests, herding their catches to the nearby Joy Street station for booking.

Dos Passos was among those arrested; in *The Best Times* he laughed it off, recounting how he had been swept up along with Edna St. Vincent Millay, although he was accredited as a reporter for the *Daily Worker* and thus supposedly immune. Within hours her husband, Eugene Boissevain, had paid their bail, and they were free. Many years later, Dos Passos could downplay the incident; at the time he took satisfaction in the mistaken arrest, and one can suppose that he, like the others, invited it.

The Italians were put to death at midnight on August 23 at Charleston prison. Outside hundreds of protestors had stood the deathwatch, waiting for the light in the prison tower to dim, the sign that an electric charge was passing through Sacco and Vanzetti. "It was a moment of strange heartbreak," Katherine Anne Porter thought. At the sad farce of a trial afterward of those who had been arrested— Porter, Millay, Hibben, and Dos Passos among them—Porter remembered Dos Passos in the jammed, dirty courtroom, sitting with her and holding a newspaper above her head while she tried to smoke, although it was prohibited. A policeman yelled at them, but Dos Passos remained unperturbed. He had about him, she recalled, "a wonderful, gentle composure of manner, and I have never forgotten his expression of amiable distance from the whole grubby scene as I put out the cigarette and he folded his newspaper, while the greasy, sweating man in the blue suit stood above us and went on glaring and bawling a little longer, just in case we had not heard him the first time." The defendants were charged with loitering and obstructing traffic; Dos Passos was acquitted because of his status as a reporter, while the others were found guilty and fined five dollars each.

"Well it's all over now and gone down in History—as far down as the public press can push it and hundreds of aviators have thrown themselves into the sea and everybody feels fine.... What about this goddamn human race anyway?" Dos Passos asked Hemingway ruefully a short time afterward. Not as resigned was the piece he wrote for the *New Masses:*

This isn't a poem
This is two men in grey prison clothes

began his lyric tribute to the Italians.

They are dead now
The black automatons have won.
They are burned up utterly
their flesh has passed into the air of Massachusetts
their dreams have passed into the wind.

Yet, while the automatons—the governor, the Superior Court judges, the college presidents—breathed sighs of relief, Sacco's and Vanzetti's deaths had given the wind new speed:

Their fire has burned out the wind
the stale smell of Boston

and had united in protest "millions of men marching in order."

At that moment of writing Dos Passos had moved as far to the Left as he ever would. "America our nation has been beaten by strangers who have turned our language inside out," he wrote eight years later to describe his emotion at the time. "We are two nations," he continued, "we stand defeated America." In the fall of 1927 he saw his task more urgently than ever as working to change the industrial capitalist system which had denied justice for two admirable, common men. Toward this end he turned his attention to the new volume that was forming in his mind; thinking about it as well as seeking some respite after the exhausting weeks of protest in Boston, he journeyed out Cape Cod to Provincetown in September.

Anyone examining a map of the United States can see at a glance that the forty-second parallel of north latitude cuts across the nation somewhat above its middle. From the East Coast, the parallel first passes through Truro on Cape Cod within several miles of Provincetown, where the Pilgrims first set foot on American soil in November 1620. The line next passes almost exactly through Plymouth, Massachusetts, where the Pilgrims landed a short time after to begin their settlement of the North American continent, and where three hundred years later, Bartolomeo Vanzetti had been peddling his fish before his arrest. The parallel runs south of Boston, then west below Detroit, which became the hub of the automobile industry in the twentieth century. Next the line cuts through the northern suburbs of Chicago and eventually passes out into the Pacific Ocean along the northern boundary of California. If a person had to pick any degree of latitude to follow which went near or through places significant to the nation, past and present, he might very possibly choose the forty-second parallel. Such a thought was on Dos Passos's mind while he was on Cape Cod in the wake of the Sacco-Vanzetti episode, beginning to work on the book that would grow into a trilogy. Eventually he entitled the first volume *The 42nd Parallel* to suggest the geographical sweep of his ambitious chronicle.

Provincetown in September was at its best and a pleasant interlude before he returned to New York to help with Paul Sifton's *The Belt,* the New Playwrights' first offering of that fall. Dos Passos designed the sets for the play, which opened on October 19 for a run of twenty-nine performances. The drama suited his interests; it was an expressionistically rendered satire on Henry Ford's assembly-line techniques which produced standardization and human misery. The idea of using a large conveyor belt on stage was intriguing, but the stage was small and the acting unpolished—at least according to Brooks Atkinson—so once again the New Playwrights suffered from the critics' barbs. *The Belt* was "vigorous and febrile," allowed Atkinson, but it was "humorless, hackneyed in the expression of ideas and clumsy in workmanship—more racket than drama." Attempting to express the stifling effect of machinery, the group had stifled their production with too much equipment.

The New Playwrights and the first chapter of *The 42nd Parallel* kept Dos Passos hard at work in New York into April 1928, his only breaks being short visits such as one to Wilmington, Delaware, in early October for a weekend party at the Fitzgeralds'. He designed the sets for Lawson's *International,* the Playwrights' first production of 1928, which opened on January 12 and ran for twenty-seven performances. During the 1927–1928 season he continued to defend in print experimental drama, arguing for the New Playwrights offerings and in April, lecturing the drama editor of the *New York Times* about how to understand E. E. Cummings's play *Him,* which had been poorly received. *Him* seemed to Dos Passos good, innovative theater that was "a very direct and vivid presentation of the tangle of one man's consciousness in relation to his love for his girl." Cummings's approach, noted Dos Passos, was not to string out a series of events that created a conventional plot, but to give the audience something more like the "Freudian analysis of a dream."

Still bitter about the Sacco and Vanzetti episode, Dos Passos lamented American writers' and artists' "indifference to politics," which he considered "sinister," because, as he told Edmund Wilson, "it was merely the first step in a process which subsequently involved the discarding of almost every other sort of interest, too, so that there was nothing left except a nonsensical Algonquin joke or an arid poem." Intent on avoiding indifference, he worked to defend a young poet, David Gordon, who had been tried and convicted for publishing an "obscene" poem in the *Daily Worker.* To friends such as Hemingway, Fitzgerald, Marvin, Hillyer, and Stewart Mitchell, Dos Passos sent a letter and copies of the judges' remarks at the time of Gordon's sentencing, as well as copies of the offending poem. Quite clearly the judges were prejudiced against the defendant. The poem, a protest that began:

America is a land of censored opportunity.
Lick spit; eat dirt.
There's your opportunity . . .

was not high art, but did not merit the sentence Gordon received of up to three years in the city reformatory. "The boy's real crime," Dos Passos declared, "was that he was writing for a communist publication and that he was a Russian Jew." He asked his friends to write the city parole board, urging clemency. What mattered at that moment were not the abstract issues, but Gordon's freedom.

Such episodes made him eager to travel to Russia in May. Given the great interest in the Russian experiment—every issue of the *New Masses*, for example, had articles about the U.S.S.R. and advertised lectures and books about it as well as trips to the country—it would have been astonishing had a sympathetic observer like Dos Passos not planned the voyage. He wanted to see firsthand the country's social and political situations while also studying Russian drama. He attempted to obtain free passage and thought he might have it by arranging to feed and care for muskrats that were being shipped to Leningrad. But that did not materialize, so he had to raise the money for the trip, probably by his usual device of borrowing from friends, contracting for articles, and taking an advance on his next book.

By mid-April he was exhausted, driven about to distraction, he told Hillyer. "The past year has been very busy for me," he wrote Germaine Lucas-Championnière. "I have been in prison (a short while), director of a theatre, a gardener [at Mount Sinai], I have designed and made sets and I have written a great many polemical pieces about the theatre and politics and I have finished a play [*Airways, Inc.*]. . . . I am in the process of undertaking a very long and very difficult novel and I am preparing for a voyage to Russia." Tired by these various pressures, he traveled to Key West to visit Hemingway and, he hoped, to clear his mind before leaving for Russia in May.

It was during this short visit that he first took serious notice of Katharine Smith, whether or not he might have met her earlier in the 1920s in Provincetown, where she and her brother Bill, Hemingway's close friends from childhood days in Michigan, occupied a house at 571 Commercial Street along with her friends Edith Foley and Stella Roof. Katy's oldest brother, Y.K., had also been a friend of Ernest's, and she had known as well Hadley Hemingway and Pauline, Ernest's second wife, for many years. Katy, in fact, may have even been engaged briefly to Hemingway; at least she once confided as much to Edmund Wilson's daughter, Rosalind, although one suspects Katy of slightly flippant storytelling, as was her wont, since, born on October 26, 1894, she was almost six years older than Ernest and was known to treat him more like a younger brother than a peer. Perhaps they had carried on a short affair. Ernest wrote about it, but if he exaggerated, it was not the only time he had.*

When Dos Passos arrived in Key West, Katy was visiting the Hemingways on her return from a trip to Mexico. Quickly their mutual friendships as well as their common interest in places like Provincetown and Greenwich Village drew them together. Further, Katy wrote for magazines and subsequently was the coauthor of

---

Hemingway wrote a Nick Adams story entitled "Summer People," in which Nick (Ernest) has sexual intercourse with Kate. But Katharine's brother asserted that she never had an affair with Hemingway. Most likely the intercourse was in Hemingway's mind, as had been that in Milan with his nurse, Agnes von Kurowsky, after his wounding during World War I.

two books with her longtime friend Edith Foley, who married Frank Shay, owner of bookstores in the Village and later in Provincetown. Katy was not the "girl revolutionist" that Edmund Wilson declared Hugo Bamman, his fictional model for Dos Passos, had craved but she was pretty, lively, small of stature, with yellow-gray eyes—some thought them green—that caught one's attention, as did her style. She had wit and could turn a phrase in response to others' comments that could either charm them or put them in their places.*

Her closest friends felt that she could dominate a situation if she chose to, but Dos Passos dominated her—by her choice, apparently, for she adored him. They seemed to others like young, romantic lovers with their private intimate jokes and their special names for each other like "Kingfish," "Possum," or "ape," with a prefix of some sort by which he would make joking allusion to his present endeavor or mood —when later he traveled to gather materials for a series of articles during World War II, he signed himself "investigape" or, lonely because he had been away too long, he was "desolape." She was not especially political and tended to follow Dos Passos's lead. To his leftist friends like Jack Lawson, she appeared conservative; to moderate, apolitical friends like Dudley Poore, she seemed radical, one of the forces pulling Dos Passos leftward in the late twenties and early thirties. Whatever, she and he were deeply attracted to one another in 1928 and, one supposes, had Dos Passos not made definite plans to leave shortly for Russia, they might have married soon, instead of, as they did, in August 1929. Once Dos Passos had left Key West, Katy returned to Provincetown from where she sent him a postcard in June via E. E. Cummings, who would forward Dos Passos's mail to Europe. "Pleased to have met you," she jotted on the card, signing it "Home Girl." She had a way of understating things, but he understood perfectly well her sentiments.

---

*Her wit was apparently inherited. Her father, William Benjamin Smith (1850–1934), was a brilliant man who taught mathematics at the University of Missouri and subsequently mathematics and then philosophy at Tulane. He was a prolific writer and a forceful, opinionated man. The archetypal scholar, he let nothing interfere with his work. A tale about him goes that one summer in Michigan, Y.K., another boy, and two girls went sailing on the lake which their farm fronted. When a storm came up and they did not reappear, the Smith children's aunt ran to their father's study and told him in a frantic voice that Y.K. was gone. Professor Smith pulled himself to his feet, trudged to the edge of the lake, and called out, "Oh, Lord, give up Thy dead," whereupon he went back to his work. When eventually Y.K. and the others returned, Professor Smith greeted his son as if nothing had occurred.

CHAPTER SEVENTEEN

===

Russia and Marriage, 1928–1929

Determined to see Russia for himself despite doubts about leaving Katy, Dos Passos before the middle of May boarded a Scandinavian liner in Hoboken for a voyage to Copenhagen. From there, after a few days of sightseeing, he traveled to London and Paris, remaining long enough to visit friends but also to become dismayed by the tourism: "Jeezus its a rotten dump after Copenhagen—all thick with the Freudian dreams of Iowa schoolteachers at the menopause," he wrote Hemingway in Piggot, Arkansas. From Paris he journeyed south to Antibes to visit the Murphys at Villa America until late July, when he departed toward Helsingfors (Helsinki), stopping over briefly in Berlin to visit Frederik van den Arend. They saw the city's night life, Dos Passos recalled, but it seemed nearly as harsh as the grotesque renderings of it that the German satirist Georg Grosz painted. Dos Passos traveled north to Stettin at the mouth of the Oder River, where he boarded ship for the trip to Helsingfors. There, he waited impatiently during a chilly weekend for his Russian visa and in the meanwhile was bored by the Finnish city which he found dull and antiseptic. When finally his papers were prepared, he entrained for Leningrad as quickly as possible, traveling with an American he met named Kittin, who had been born in Russia.

In Leningrad Dos Passos took a room in the Europskaya Hotel, and for the next few weeks he journeyed out into the city and its environs where, with the help of the Russian-speaking Kittin, he talked with a variety of people and visited places such as the Hermitage, the Smolny Institute, and the Fortress of Saints Peter and Paul. Dos Passos was attracted to the common people with whom he came in contact, such as a young man they met at the Hermitage from the mountainous republic of Kirgiz in the south of Russia. The man, in Leningrad a year, earning his living as an unskilled metal worker, was enthusiastic and fascinated Dos Passos with tales about his people and talk about revolution. He was a voracious reader, at the present devouring Gorky's work. For him, life under the Communists was freer than it had been under the harsh conditions of the Steppes of Kirgiz. There, marriage, for example, was determined by the elders. In Leningrad, a man and woman could live together if they chose to, and, should they desire, could register their marriage if they decided this was what they wanted or if the woman were pregnant.

Two young students whom Kittin and Dos Passos met outside the "huge austerely-proportioned colonnaded" Smolny Institute engaged them in a fervent discussion about Communism and capitalism. "Why," they kept asking the Americans, "why can't [Americans] understand what we are trying to do, why can't the workers in America understand that we are building socialism, why can't the workers in England realize that we are working for them as much as for ourselves?" It was a question that Dos Passos asked himself, or rather, he wondered, "Are the Russians building socialism as they think they are?" He admired their enthusiasms and social fervor, but his instinct for individual liberties dampened his ardor for Communism. He preferred the outspoken independence of Russians such as Valentine Stenich, an older man who had translated some of Dos Passos's work into Russian. Stenich, though the son of a wealthy man, had joined the Red Guards and had commanded a division of the Red Army during the civil war. But apparently his independence had led to trouble, the result being expulsion from the party and a year in prison. During one of the late evening walks on which Stenich and his friends took Dos Passos, they paused before a large statue of Peter the Great on horseback. There, announced Stenich to the others' surprise, was his favorite Russian. Peter had brought order to the nation; he was "the first Bolshevik."*

While in Leningrad Dos Passos met Dr. Horsley Gantt, an American who had come to Russia as a member of the American Relief Administration in 1922. He had visited Pavlov's laboratory, become enthralled with the Russian's work, and since 1924 had been studying with Pavlov. Dos Passos and Gantt met in the lobby of the Europskaya Hotel when the latter heard Dos Passos asking a question in English at the desk. Gantt introduced himself, and another of Dos Passos's lifelong friendships began. The next morning he ate a fine breakfast of strawberries with Gantt, who invited him to visit Pavlov's laboratory.

Dos Passos declined to meet Pavlov, to his later regret, but he did visit the laboratory. Soon thereafter he wrote Cummings about the experience and about Pavlov's opposition to the Communists: "Saw Pavlov's dogs in Leningrad. Incidentally all his work has been on gland secretions other than the sexual and most of his work on the physiology of the brain has been via the saliva glands of a dog where he can measure the secretions." Dos Passos mentioned Horsley Gantt's translation

---

*In The Best Times, Dos Passos recalled that Stenich was "the most vivid of the Russians I met in Leningrad. Poor fellow, he did not have long to live. He was rubbed out early in Stalin's purge of Leningrad writers."

of Pavlov's work, which was to be out that year, adding that the book was expected to create a sensation. Pavlov, he wrote, hated the Soviet government and would roar against it when lecturing; yet it supported his work. "I imagine he really is a great man," he concluded, "nearly eighty with bushy whiskers and never missed a day in his laboratory all through the war and the revolution."

Before leaving in early August, Dos Passos made plans to meet Gantt at Vladykavkaz in September to hike through the Caucasus Mountains. Then he boarded a night train for Moscow, feeling lonely after the friendships of Leningrad, a feeling not lessened by the steady rain that fell all during the trip, or by the heavy mist that shrouded the countryside the next morning.

From the Moscow station he was led to the Moscow Hotel by a young woman official from Voks. No sooner had he settled into his large room than he met the American publicist, Ivy Lee, whose reasons for being in Russia Dos Passos never understood clearly. Dos Passos disapproved of public relations in general, believing the business to be parasitic rather than genuinely creative; yet he admired Lee's commitment to his work and found him entertaining and a relief to be with after struggling with Russian. Their brief friendship contributed more; Dos Passos had written the first chapters of *The 42nd Parallel* by then; and the character who would become as much the central personage as there was in the whole *U.S.A.* trilogy, J. Ward Moorehouse, was beginning to develop. Dos Passos's recollections of Lee, who talked a good deal about himself during their conversations in Moscow, contributed heavily to the portrait of Moorehouse, the idealistic, if shallow, public-relations magnate.

While Dos Passos was in Moscow in August, one of his friends in America wrote him about an editorial in the *New York World* for July 4 which told of Dos Passos speaking on July 3 at an "anti-imperialist" demonstration on Wall Street. Bemused, he wrote the *World*, asking for a copy of the editorial and a retraction. "I don't know whether to be angry or grateful," he wrote. "There are many ways of getting arrested that I would not have been ashamed of," he declared, "and many ways of being editorially roasted that would cause me more amusement than alarm." The editor obliged Dos Passos by mailing him what he had requested. The incident was not important, except that it somehow typified Dos Passos's situation. He was thought to be leading protests—in this case jumping up on the rear bumper of an automobile before being suppressed by police to speak against U.S. imperialism in Latin America. In fact, he was traveling alone on another continent, observing the life of another nation and studying its film and drama.

In Moscow, he quickly established a routine for himself: study Russian in the mornings, tour in the afternoons, see theater each night. This first stay in Moscow —he would return for three more months after a voyage down the Volga and the hike in the Caucasus with Horsley Gantt—he saw films primarily, and drama, although the only play that especially stuck in his mind was V. E. Meyerhold's *Roar China*. Its staging was magnificent, he wrote Germaine Lucas-Championnière soon afterward. The "most interesting and lively people" he had met so far were the film directors, he told Cummings, mentioning in particular Sergei Eisenstein and Meyerhold. Although he did not name him to Cummings, V. I. Pudovkin also impressed him. The film directors asserted that theater was dying; Dos Passos doubted that, observing the vitality of what he saw. What most impressed him was the broad learning of these men. With Eisenstein he talked about the technique of montage, much on his mind then as he struggled to incorporate it into his new novel. Eisenstein, recalled Dos Passos, "had one of the most brilliantly synthesizing minds" he had ever encountered.

The films that he admired were those about the revolution, directed by people who, he wrote Germaine Lucas-Championnière, "adore the camera as if it were a god, but they are full of energy and imagination." He added that, while films had been what he had seen most of, he admired the popular theaters, located in workers' clubs and unions. There the workers themselves half-improvised short plays, calling them Living Newspapers. The acting was always good, and the plays were intriguing, even those that propagandized for hygiene and so forth. It is easy to imagine that the Living Newspaper influenced the spontaneous, topical style of his Newsreels in *U.S.A.*

He wrote his French friend in mid-August from aboard a steamer that was carrying him on a five-day trip down the Volga to Astrakhan, at the edge of the Caspian Sea. Because of Dos Passos's prominence as a writer, the commissar for education, Anatoli V. Lunacharski, had arranged in Moscow for him to meet at Grozny an expedition of Russians and several foreigners who were to explore some of the remoter areas of Daghestan, which Dos Passos could do on his way to the Caucasus. "I have a very small cabin aboard a large boat sailing down the Volga. It is magnificent," he declared to Germaine. His cabin was filled with the scent of apples he had bought in a riverside village, while outside was the scent of the forests they cruised by, and a little scent of the passengers, he added. He was studying Russian, trying it out on other passengers, then returning to study more after meeting with few successes. "Truly Russia is magnificent," he wrote. There were great open spaces everywhere; the rivers were immense as were even the ancient buildings, and all of them had façades that seemed kilometers long. About everything there was an air of an American boomtown. People ate a great deal, drank a great deal, then had to fast a great deal. Things came in large quantities, he observed —people, conversations, even fleas. Here the natives treated foreigners better than anywhere else. Although no Russians had money, their hospitality was extraordinary. Germaine might not believe it, but everywhere there was a feeling of liberty and of a remarkable energy. As he sat writing on the ship's bridge, he was breakfasting on great quantities of tea, caviar, butter, and bread. He described large rafts which floated downriver with the current, and he told of swimming each day in the brown, gentle water. "It is the most enjoyable trip I've taken in a long while," he declared. "I feel happy, and my last mistake, a foolish one, is behind me." He had set afire a box of matches while trying to light his cigarette, he recounted, and had burned his nose and eyelashes. Luckily he had not harmed his eyes; "I see as badly as ever," he commented.

In Astrakhan he had to pass a day before he could board the rusty steamer that was to take him along the western coast of the Caspian Sea to Makhachkala. The trip was unpleasant; the ship wallowed in rough seas so that most of the passengers were sick for the entire voyage. Dos Passos shared a cabin with two other men who lay in their bunks groaning throughout the night, while the watermelons they had brought with them rolled continuously back and forth in the cabin. With great relief he disembarked the next day in Makhachkala, where he bought a train ticket for Grozny to the west in the foothills of the Caucasus Mountains. The expedition he was to join had already left Grozny when he arrived, so it was another day before he caught up with them in the mountains. The group, whose task was to pick sites for new schools in the remote mountain areas, seemed chaotic; Dos Passos claimed he never did find out who was in charge. In the group were a woman schoolteacher, several middle-aged men, a younger man, and Anna Louise Strong, a "big busty selfcentered spinster" from the United States. Nine years older than Dos Passos and a journalist, she was enthusiastic about Communism and an admirable if annoying person to be on the trip, Dos Passos soon decided, because it fell to him to help her along—which meant searching for special things she desired, like canned apricots—since the Russians paid her no particular heed. "Heaven protect us from Anna Louise and all other women with three barreled names," Dos Passos jotted in his notebook on August 28 after he had been traveling with the group awhile.

He remained with them for two weeks, riding horseback through terrain as varied as any he had ever seen. From a town called Botlich, where the expedition remained for two days while the Russians dickered for fresh horses, he wrote Hemingway, describing the land: "The towns are little stone age villages and the country between is wild as hell—In fact I'm having a swell time in Russia." He assured Hemingway that the country was not at all as people described it. "In the first place it's easy to travel and rather cheap. Then there's a great deal of food—beer, vodka, wine and general gaiety—Some people you meet are as optimistic as down town real estate agents—others are still Russian in the Dostoyevski sense, but —things are certainly jollier and more varied than in the States though not so hectic."

Early in September Dos Passos and the others arrived in Tiflis after leading their horses through a high snow-covered pass, then descending dangerously washed-out trails and finally riding a bus the last way into the city. There he parted company with the expedition and journeyed by bus back across the Caucasus to meet Horsley Gantt at Vladykavkaz. They decided that more mountain climbing was in order, so started on foot to Kazbek, through which Dos Passos had just passed. Gantt, to his friend's amazement, walked half the distance barefoot. They climbed Mount Kazbek the next day, then the following day headed on with a guide toward a village called Zaramag. But to find it was harder than anyone had counted on, and they spent the night in a house along the way. Contrary to what he had told Hemingway earlier, food in this region was scarce; they could locate practically nothing to eat. The next day they came upon Zaramag, but all they were able to turn up were five eggs and some old candied crackers, which they had with their tea. As they continued on their trek, their spirits flagged while their hunger grew. That afternoon at the top of a mountain pass, they had a far-reaching view of the valleys of Georgia. Gantt was despondent as a result of his hunger, but Dos Passos, Gantt recalled, became buoyant as he talked about the food that awaited them when they arrived at Batum. It was a small incident that deeply endeared Dos Passos to Gantt.

Fortunately for them both, they soon came upon a resthouse for carters and muleteers. The old man who kept it fed them a thick mutton soup with barley. Revived, they continued to a village, on the way discussing their opinions about Communism. Gantt, an apolitical man, had little interest in the regime and declared for science. Dos Passos claimed that his chief sympathy for the Soviets was their policy then of international pacifism. The two men's political interests lessened, however, when hunger set in once more that evening because there was nothing for them to eat in the village. Aching and famished, they took a ride the next morning in a cart toward the town of Oni, from where they planned to catch a bus to Kutais, in the direction of Batum. Oni had a hotel and restaurant which they frequented for two days as they waited for the next bus. The Hôtel de France where they stayed, once in Kutais, was comfortable except for the strong smell from a watercloset in the center of the building. Dos Passos remained a last night by himself, having decided to head east to Baku, thence back to Moscow, while Gantt left ahead of him for Batum.

That evening Dos Passos ate in a restaurant in Kutais. He was, he wrote later, at last full of food, but overly full of conflicting questions:

> Was the poverty and the desolation the ground being cleared for future build-ing, or was it just the results of oldfashioned ignorant centralized oppression? Were the Georgians inveterate small proprietors or was it just the two or three innkeepers I'd carried on painfully inadequate conversations with? . . . Was this waiter with a dirty apron happier now than under the Czar?

He wondered how he could answer, knowing as little as he did. And so, when later that evening he fell into conversation about these matters with a Russian, the two of them lapsed after a while into slogans about the U.S.S.R. and the United States. Returning afterward to his hotel room, he reminded himself that some things were facts, like the smell from the watercloset. "But," he wondered, "who made the stink? The Soviets or the old inveterate Adam?" He was no closer to an answer about the rightness and wrongness of political systems than he had been months earlier. Maybe the answers would be easier to find in the city of Baku, more like "home," because newer. Still, he asked himself, "how much do you know about home?"

Baku afforded him no answers. When he left Russia in December 1928, he was as full of doubts as ever, despite two months more of life in a Moscow brimming with plays, opera, and film. He had stayed in the apartment of Aleksandr Fadeev and his wife once he returned in October. Fadeev, a successful writer enthusiastic about Communism, later joined the Union of Soviet Writers and was its secretary for a number of years from 1938 on. His wife, Valia Gerasimova, had an important position in the Soviet secret service, the GPU. As their large apartment was close to an army barracks, Dos Passos heard the soldiers singing each morning as they marched to drill. This, long, volatile discussions with the Fadeevs and their friends, and the energies of other Communist acquaintances made him appreciate the "enthusiasm, selfeffacement . . . and that fervid curiosity and breadth of interest that is the magnificent earmark of the Russian mind." Yet he felt he could not get hold of "The Moscow of now, The Moscow of today, The Moscow of the new order" of which all these things were a part.

The theater was more able to be comprehended, he decided, and to it he gave much of his attention. "Now I am established for two months in Moscow," he wrote Germaine Lucas-Championnière on October 9, telling her that he went to the theaters every night with his eyes wide open. Although everything he saw—the Russian life as well as the plays—was so striking that he was getting little writing done, he felt in fine form, had cured himself of New York, and was *fou de théâtre et d'opéra*. Each night was a new spectacle, while in addition there was a plethora of concerts. "Do you know there is an opera by Moussorgsky called "Sorochin-Okaya Yarmak?" he asked, spelling the title as best he could. "Every night I spend an hour deciding where to go," he asserted, finding it "a difficult decision because I want to see and hear everything all at once." Add to theater and opera the cinema and, he declared, one needed to be divided into four parts to do everything. Subtract the hyperbole he enjoyed using with Germaine, and still he was obviously enjoying himself, not at all regretting the fact that he would miss the presidential election in the United States in early November. "Will it be prejudice or popery?" he asked Stewart Mitchell, referring to the two major candidates Herbert Hoover and Al Smith.

When Dos Passos wrote "The New Theater in Russia" for the *New Republic* in 1930, he conveyed many of the same enthusiasms he had in letters to his friends, although in the article he concentrated on Russian drama. He sounded a familiar tune, that American theater was dying, while the Russian was commencing "enormous growth." One of the things that gave Russian theater its strength, he noted, was that each theater had a permanent nucleus of staff; further—and one can hear echoes of Dos Passos's expressed concerns for the New Playwrights Theatre—in Russia there was ample opportunity to experiment in the satellite studios that grew up around the major theaters. Because the studios were small, had a basis in something larger, and were subsidized, they were independent of the public, and that, he had decided, was how things should be if theater were to be vital as well as innovative. "The Russian theatre has never been a business," he concluded. "Now more than ever it is thought of as a public service."

Pleased as he was by Russian arts and the people's hospitality, he had glimpses of the fear the government engendered in the populace. An Englishman and his Russian wife invited him to their apartment one evening. About their place, he noted, was "an air of hurry and dread." The husband wanted to talk; the wife did not want him to, but finally the man poured out his fears. He had believed in the Communists, had, in fact, come to Russia to work for them. Now he would leave if he could, but they would never permit his wife out of the country, and for fear of arrest he did not dare to ask about leaving. Since she was one of the pre-Communist intelligentsia, nothing she could do could ingratiate her with the new wave. After the revolution it had first been the nobility and the "middle-class social revolutionaries" who had been purged; now it was the Trotskyites, the very people who had worked alongside the Bolsheviks. He was most disturbed by the Communists' brutal suppression of the Kronstadt rebellion in 1921, using members of the Cheka. Many among the Communist Cheka were sadists of the worst sort, and the punishments meted out to the Kronstadt prisoners had been cruel beyond description.

Dos Passos felt dazed by the man's talk. "It was terror I'd seen in the man's eyes," he wrote, "in the huddle of the oldfashioned furniture moved into this choked apartment, in the woman's nervous step." He tried to argue that the Cheka were gone now, most of them shot. But the Englishman would have none of it, responding that the fear would never be over for him and his wife until they either died or escaped; and he despaired of being able to do the latter. "We are doomed," he ended. "You know they always come at night. No arrests are ever seen. No one who sees them ever dares tell anyone. Nothing is ever known."

Too much else of interest had been going on for Dos Passos to feel overwhelmed by this reminder of the terror, but as he concluded his stay in Moscow during the first few days of December, he remained unsure, his doubts only half answered, his questions half understood. At the train station as he waited to board for his trip to Warsaw, he was greeted by an actress friend and the company of young people whom she directed at the Sanitary Propaganda Theater. They had all come to say goodbye and wanted to know, she said, where Dos Passos stood politically. He should show his face. Was he with them?

Amid the noise and steam of the departing train, he tried to respond but, he wrote in 1934, "the iron crown tightens on the head, throbbing with too many men, too many women, too many youngsters seen, talked to, asked questions of, too many hands shaken, too many foreign languages badly understood." He tried to explain his complex and contradictory feelings. The train, however, began to move; he had to run for it, and he swung aboard, the Russians' question unanswered.

He arrived in Warsaw on December 4, then journeyed almost directly on to Germany. From Leipzig he wrote Germaine on the eighth, enthusiastic once more about his four months in Russia, which had been like a university. He told her again that he felt revitalized in a "bath of energy." In the U.S.S.R. things were both so good and so bad, the people so fine and so mean, that one got an exaggerated idea of the destiny of the rest of mankind.

Dos Passos was not fabricating his sense of doubt retrospectively in 1934 as he wrote about his evening alone in Kutais or his departure from Moscow. He had remained the doubter, and his hosts the Fadeevs had felt this while he was with them. In late February 1929 Valia Gerasimova wrote him a friendly letter discussing the latest theater in Moscow, especially the plays of Mayakovsky in Meyerhold's theater. Mayakovsky's *The Bourgeois* she found "awfully schematic" when the "petty bourgeois" bought a bright necktie and the "boy member of the Young

Communist League read Engels." But she touched as well on Dos Passos's elusiveness. "It is rather difficult for me to write you," she commented, "because you seem to me not quite real, & your staying with us reminded me a little of a chapter from a sentimental novel. What were you thinking about?" she asked. "What a man are you [sic]? What was funny & what seemed sad to you? You being 'tongueless' made it so difficult to understand you." Although she was commenting partly on his difficulty with the language, there was more than that. He had not made a commitment, and she wanted to know where he stood.

Dos Passos arrived around Christmas in New York, where he took an apartment at 61 Washington Square South and began work immediately to help prepare his second play, *Airways, Inc.*, for its opening in February 1929. He became embroiled in arguments about its staging with Em Jo Basshe, who had taken over much of the running of the New Playwrights to the dismay of the other directors. Basshe fired Ed Massey, who was directing *Airways*, which exacerbated Dos Passos's growing irritation with the entire operation. When he could, he pressed ahead on the manuscript for *The 42nd Parallel*, and as the irritations with Basshe grew, he yearned to leave them behind, but hung on to see his play through to production. He wanted to see Katy Smith again and hoped it would be possible in Key West, from where Hemingway urged him to come south, tantalizing him with stories of excellent fishing and snipe hunting, and Jack Lawson half tempted him to travel to Hollywood with tales of the excesses that one experienced daily among the executives and writers in the film industry. It was crazy but not all bad, he assured Dos Passos; Hollywood was the land of the big money, and every once in a while someone like the young tycoon Irving Thalberg made a decision to produce a worthwhile film with some degree of social significance to it.

Dos Passos was justifiably concerned about his second play. The New Playwrights had an almost unbroken record of nonsuccess, if not outright failure. Their finances were precarious, their organization rent by disagreements. "Dont you ever write any plays," he advised Robert Hillyer before *Airways* opened. "Believe me there's nutten in it, kid—except worry and the loss of hair and hours and wishes causing dispepsia after midnight." He sensed that the production lacked polish and was not merely being modest when he wrote Hillyer that the play would open February 19 but that he could not recommend it. Still, if the Hillyers were in New York, he would get two tickets for them and they could help comfort him.

Airways, Inc. ran for four weeks, playing to many empty seats. It was another drama of the sort that people had come to expect of the New Playwrights; its techniques were expressionistic, its themes anticapitalistic. The play portrayed the effect a money-worshipping society has on human values and had moments of power, but the dialogues seemed stilted and the figures merely caricatures. The run was not a success; Dos Passos put up $900 of his own money to keep it going for the last two weeks but when it closed, he had had enough of the drama even though during the following summer he could write that "in spite of much adverse criticism, from my own point of view the production was very successful: the best acting we ever had and a method of setting and direction that made the audience accept the elimination of the proscenium arch and curtain without batting an eyelash."

He published this after the heat of the struggle was behind him; nevertheless this was not merely an attempt at an upbeat ending to the theater experiment. Less than a month after the play had closed, he wrote Germaine about it. "The battle," he assured her, "went well, except that the critics guillotined me every day and the great public to whom we offer our works made no sign of life." Perhaps, he mused, there was no public for this sort of play, because "the play had been well staged, with excellent actors and stage managers." He personally had worked hard on the sets since the production was staged without funds and with great difficulty. "It was like a great surgical success: the operation went admirably but the patient died," he remarked ruefully, adding that he was "mixed up with a great many people," always a dangerous thing. It was good to be out of the theater, to have some quiet undisturbed by talk or intrigues, and without the necessity to spend one's nights painting sets. "I love to paint sets," he declared, "but in our theatre that was always done after the show between midnight and five a.m., and the third season, I began to be tired."

His experience with the New Playwrights was not without its redeeming features, but when *Airways* closed, he was rankled by Basshe and frustrated by the public's seeming unwillingness to accept new theater. (He could never quite admit that much of what he himself offered was mediocre, even bad.) In March, he resigned as a director, sending a copy of his resignation to the other directors. To Francis Faragoh and Jack Lawson he sent one copy, as it was his last, he explained, adding that he had sent the same thing "to all the directors of the N. Peetoodle of odorous memory."

> I'm hereby resigning as a director of The New Playwrights Theatre and feel that perhaps its worthwhile to sketch out my reasons. First I want to say that the only reason for stopping the theatre now will be the lack of interest or lack of gumption of its directors. Except for the matter of money and organization the theatre is in a better position than it ever has been. For the first time it has a reputation that would mean money and audiences if properly exploited.

One might question his assessment about reputation and wonder what could possibly be more important than money and organization. Dos Passos was sure that the New Playwrights' difficulty from the start had been that they were not "sure of their aims or honest about them. Half the time we have been trying to found an institution and the rest of the time trying to put over ourselves or each other, and occasionally trying to knife each other in the back." No one person was at fault, he believed; rather, all suffered from "a typically New York confusion of aims." If another attempt at staging "new, unpopular, radical, revolutionary or even 'good' plays" were to be made, it would require the realization that "cooperation is not an empty phrase, but a sane and businesslike method of attaining a certain fifty percent of common aims."

When Lawson received the resignation letter in Hollywood, he reacted predict-ably. "Dos," he wrote back, "this is *not* a letter of resignation." He told Dos Passos that everyone should share equally the cost of producing *Airways, Inc.* and included $300 in the letter, expressing the hope that he could pass on $300 more at a later date. As to Dos Passos's other complaints, Lawson thought that the only directors guilty of lack of cooperation were Basshe and Mike Gold. Further, the New Play-wrights Theatre might be in a fine position except for "money and good spirits," but, realistically little else counted. What he and Francis Faragoh intended to do, and what he believed Dos Passos should have cooperated about, was "to write Em Jo saying that we wish him luck and hope he will get money and organize for next season, but that as members of the N.P.T. we gravely object to the use of its name, as well as of our names in connection with the enterprise." Lawson's ideas made good sense, but in fact they were too late. Dos Passos had resigned, and by the end of April, Basshe—the last of the five directors to remain active—had resigned also.

Dos Passos and Lawson remained close friends. Yet, Lawson later believed, the whole New Playwrights Theatre episode had put a strain on their relationship that he never sensed at the time. Lawson came to think that he had been naïve about pushing Dos Passos into drama by producing *The Moon Is a Gong.* At the time it did not occur to Lawson that his friend did not savor being forced to work with a group like the directors, or that he did not really appreciate being committed to left-wing theater. Partly the idea titillated him; as Francis Faragoh commented, Dos Passos saw the experience as "a sort of slumming." He willed his commitment, and the same part of him that enjoyed talking tough with Ernest Hemingway enjoyed the brashness of Mike Gold or the late-night set painting in cramped, proletarian quarters. But the experience chafed also against his discomfort about arguments, his taste for other forms of culture, and his fundamental desire to work alone as a writer. Within five years the issue would become exacerbated, although not apparently or precisely because of any rancor stemming from the New Playwrights. Ten years later, his friendship with Lawson would break off.

With the drama behind him, Dos Passos in March boarded a ship for Key West to visit the Hemingways. Ernest and several other friends of his met Dos Passos at the dock, took him immediately to the Over Sea Hotel to deposit his bag and change clothes, and then led him aboard the boat of Charles Thompson, a local business-man, to go fishing for tarpon. The next days were filled with more such activity; it was the sort of life Dos Passos craved as a relief from New York, and he wrote Edmund Wilson from Key West that he was there "licking my wounds, fishing, eating wild herons and turtle steak, drinking Spanish wine and Cuban rum and generally remaking the inner man," after being "somewhat shattered" by his en-counter with the drama. Key West had lost none of the charm it had had for him in 1924, when he had taken the train down from Palm Beach after his hike through the middle of Florida. "Its a swell little jumping off place—the one spot in America desperately unprosperous," he told Wilson. Its industries were minimal, and the place remained isolated, so that life there was "agreeable calm and gently colored with Bacardi." Swimming, fishing, and eating constituted his entire routine.

Katy Smith was there as he had hoped she might be. Together they enjoyed the things Hemingway planned, for he was a fine host when his mood was right, and this was one of those occasions. It may have been during this stay in Key West that she and Dos Passos quietly decided to marry, agreeing that first he would finish work on *The 42nd Parallel,* while she put her affairs in order. Whether or not they decided then is unimportant; they were in love, and a few months of separation during the spring and summer made them sure about marriage.

In early April Dos Passos returned to New York, stopping in Virginia along the way. But he did not remain in the city for long, soon moving to Erwinna, Pennsylvania, to the home of the writer Josephine Herbst and her husband, John Herrmann, where he could work in absolute quiet. "Now living all alone with a small brindled kitten at Erwinna, Pa.," he wrote Rumsey Marvin at the end of April. "Great walking round here and working like a blue streak." During the rest of the spring he passed in and out of New York, on the first of May being Cummings's best man at his marriage to Anne Barton. The wedding, Edmund Wilson noted in his journal, was a besotten affair. Cummings, at least, had been drinking steadily for several days beforehand—often across the river at Hoboken, New Jersey. The marriage took place at what Dos Passos and Cummings called "the church of the Holy Zebra," All Souls Church at Twentieth Street and Fourth Avenue, but before Cummings could go through with it, he had to sober up by taking several baths. There was a kind of twenties decadence about the whole affair: a pathetic German oompah band tried to play the wedding march afterward at a bar where friends gathered, while the talk was drunkenly foolish. Later, Dos Passos, to everyone's amusement, sang an operatic aria from the bathroom in the Cummings's apartment. Was he ill? Cummings asked. "Oh, no: just singing from sheer lightness of heart."

During this spring of constant travel Dos Passos saw a good bit of Wilson, with whom he discussed his "gigantic novel," which, Wilson wrote John Peale Bishop that summer, was to deal "with the Americanization of the Western world and to appear in three parts, laid respectively in Mexico City, Paris and New York." Dos Passos often saw Dudley Poore, who was living at the Lafayette Hotel, and with him planned a trip to Otisco Lake, Poore's family's summer home near Syracuse. After visiting Katy in Provincetown in June and returning to New York, he left for Otisco Lake the last of the month, intending to remain at the Poores' cottage overlooking the lake for several weeks. There he continued writing *The 42nd Parallel* each morning, afterward working in his host's garden, or walking. Once, living up to his reputation with Poore as a great walker, he hiked the entire distance of twenty to twenty-five miles around the lake. Toward the end of July he traveled west to Chicago to do some of the last research for the novel. From there he wrote Poore to thank him for the visit, reporting that he was sweltering "among the old newspaper files in the library." He was finishing the Newsreels, checking them for accuracy, and filling in where he wanted to achieve an ironic counterpointing of historical facts with bits and pieces from popular culture.

Katy kept in close touch with him after he left Provincetown in June. Her intention was to drive to her family's farm in Michigan with her brother Bill and Edith Foley and then to join Dos Passos in Chicago. From Provincetown on June 28 she wrote him at Otisco Lake that she thought they could set off in a few days. She hoped Dos Passos would not mind if she wrote him often, "because Love must have its say. . . . Do write me, darling," she closed,

and tell me you miss your girl
goil
gerl
gurl
gal
gurrl
Katy

The three had an arduous trip west, arriving at the farm in Horton Bay only after their automobile underwent engine repairs in Ludington, Michigan. They found the farm "an insupportable shock." Trespassers had vandalized the orchard and the house, which was "stripped and gutted"; even the wallpaper was gone. After two weeks of trying to clean up the place, she wrote Dos Passos in Chicago that she expected to be able to join him there at the very end of July. "You are the only guy I could ever talk to at all and I aint able to do that," she told him. "I am afraid lonely and at the same time have tremendous spurts of confidence." But she could not get away from Horton Bay as intended, so suggested that he take a boat or train to nearby Petoskey. They could talk, presumably about plans to marry, and then all of them depart for Provincetown via Canada early in August. This seems to have been what Katy, Bill, Edith, and Dos Passos did, heading north through Mackinaw City, then into Ontario and east through Quebec and down into Maine.

In what was apparently about as quick a ceremony as was possible, Katy, almost thirty-five, and Dos Passos, thirty-three, were married in Ellsworth, Maine. Late in August he wrote Dudley Poore that they had found themselves "taking out a license for one dollar in Ellsworth, Maine and submitting to the ministrations of a slightly used Unitarian minister." Allowing for Dos Passos's downplaying the event, still it must have been simple and brief, though with some gaiety about it. "Nobody seems much the worse for it," he assured Poore, "though at the time it seemed as if the consequences would be fatal. Fortunately there appeared a splendid man with gold teeth all across his face named Mr. Mazurbie who fished a great quantity of Clear River Bourbon (and real Bourbon whiskey) out of his lobster pots and everything had seemed much better since." To add to the gaiety, Dos Passos just before the ceremony ripped the seam in the seat of his pants, so he borrowed a raincoat which he wore while he was married.

By the time Dos Passos wrote Poore, he and Katy had settled down for a month in a small red house that overlooked the Sheepscot River, near Wiscasset. It was an ideal, quiet spot for them—"apple trees, swimming . . . not far off and a sickly kitten," he told Poore. Here he could continue to work at *The 42nd Parallel,* which he had promised his publisher by October. He asked for help, saying that he was still searching for a climaturgical study that mentioned the forty-second parallel and also Medicine Hat, along the fiftieth parallel in Alberta, Canada. What he wanted, no doubt, was some quotation that might describe the changing weather patterns that swept along the parallels, to suggest the changing, tumultuous atmosphere of twentieth-century America. He was also trying to find the words to popular songs such as "Cheyenne on My Pony," "Bury Me Not on the Lone Prairie," "Down on the Wabash," and "There's a Broken Heart for Every Light on Broadway." These would be woven into the Newsreels as part of the backdrop to the other narrative devices. He told Poore in closing that he had enjoyed Chicago, a vital place where people bathed on the lakeshore and changed clothes on the beaches without being arrested. The Black Belt was fine, "much younger and less Jewish than New York," which, he declared with a certain scorn that reflected his recent bout with the theater, was "after all . . . just a stuffy ghetto on a gigantic scale with all the hothouse interest of a ghetto—but after all there's a limit to that sort of thing."

Dos Passos and Katy remained in the house near Wiscasset through September. While there they received lively letters of congratulations from their friends, among them Lawson—who spent most of a three-page letter humorously grousing about the ill state of southern California—and Hemingway, who by then had returned to Spain. He was genuinely pleased that "you men" had married and looked forward to seeing them later in the year in Europe. He was sure Dos Passos's first volume would be excellent. "Trilogies are undoubtedly the thing," he wrote. "Look at the Father, Son and Holy Ghost—Nothing's gone much bigger than that." He'd like to go on a trip to Mexico with Dos, he confided. They could live on what they shot or fished for. Then he closed with more advice for Katy and Dos Passos, and gossip. Do not get too wealthy or involved with the rich, he advised. Donald Ogden Stewart had done that by signing a contract for $25,000 and by becoming friends with the Whitneys. "Sign nothing," he insisted, and "shoot as soon as you see the whites of a Whitney's eye." John Peale Bishop had been ruined by wealth as well. "Keep money away from Katy," was his advice. The Fitzgeralds, meanwhile, had been ruined by "eternal youth," so he advised his friend to "get old" and to "age up Kate." Finally, Dos Passos should keep guns away from her father; "Old Hem" had been ruined by his father's suicide.

In October Dos Passos and Katy returned to Provincetown, staying at 571 Commercial Street, which she owned, while they arranged in nearby South Truro to buy a small house. Hidden from the main road that ran along the Cape, it was quite isolated, "in a lonely and rather somber little hollow where the occasional booming of bitterns is the only sound to be heard," was how Edmund Wilson described the place to Scott Fitzgerald the next year. Here they sometimes lived during succeeding summers, but mostly they farmed the land around it and resided at Commercial Street. Dos Passos and Katy spent the fall of 1929 organizing themselves for their life-to-be on the Cape, while he put the final touches on the novel manuscript, then the galleys and page proofs before he and she were to sail for Europe in December.

For the biographies in the new novel he had done substantial research. Two of the sketches were of Thomas Edison and Charles Proteus Steinmetz, the electrical genius whose inventions enabled the General Electric Company to become a giant in its field. Dos Passos reviewed three books about the men for the *New Republic* during the fall. He did not think any of the three good and complained that they typified the poor quality of the literature about the last fifty years of American industry. What most irritated him was that the literature revealed no more insight than had the subjects themselves into the effects industrialization had on human beings. "Reading [about Edison's] life, you feel that he never for a moment allowed himself to envisage the importance of the changes in the organization of human life that his inventions were to bring about," wrote Dos Passos. Edison, he believed, "would have resented it if anyone had suggested to him that his work would destroy homes, wreck morals, and help end the individual toiler's world he was brought up in." An industrialist such as Henry Ford, "less the mechanic and more the organizer," appeared to be just as unconcerned, Dos Passos added. Steinmetz, he thought, was permitted by General Electric to play the eccentric and Socialist, but to no social benefit. The industrial picture as Dos Passos saw it was dismal, and it was this vision that he meant to convey in his novel. Mechanical geniuses, ignoring human needs, had created machines that were displacing human beings, and twentieth-century society, as Henry Adams had feared when he wrote *The Education of Henry Adams*, was coming to be symbolized by a blindly whirring dynamo instead of by the symbol of human love and unity, the Virgin Mary.

The other significant piece he wrote during the fall of 1929 was a review of Hemingway's new novel, *A Farewell to Arms*, which he termed "the best written book that has seen the light in America for many a long day." His praise was more than that of one friend for another; Hemingway's style was what he sought for himself, one that was "terse and economical, in which every sentence and each phrase bears its maximum load of meaning, sense impressions, emotion." It was, finally, the craft of Hemingway's fiction that he most admired, the more so in an age that tended to minimize craftsmanship, be it artistic or technical. Dos Passos's profound hope as the decade was about to end amid the financial crisis that soon would be identified as the Great Depression was that his own craftsmanship in *The 42nd Parallel* would help Americans to understand what had gone wrong with their industrialized society.

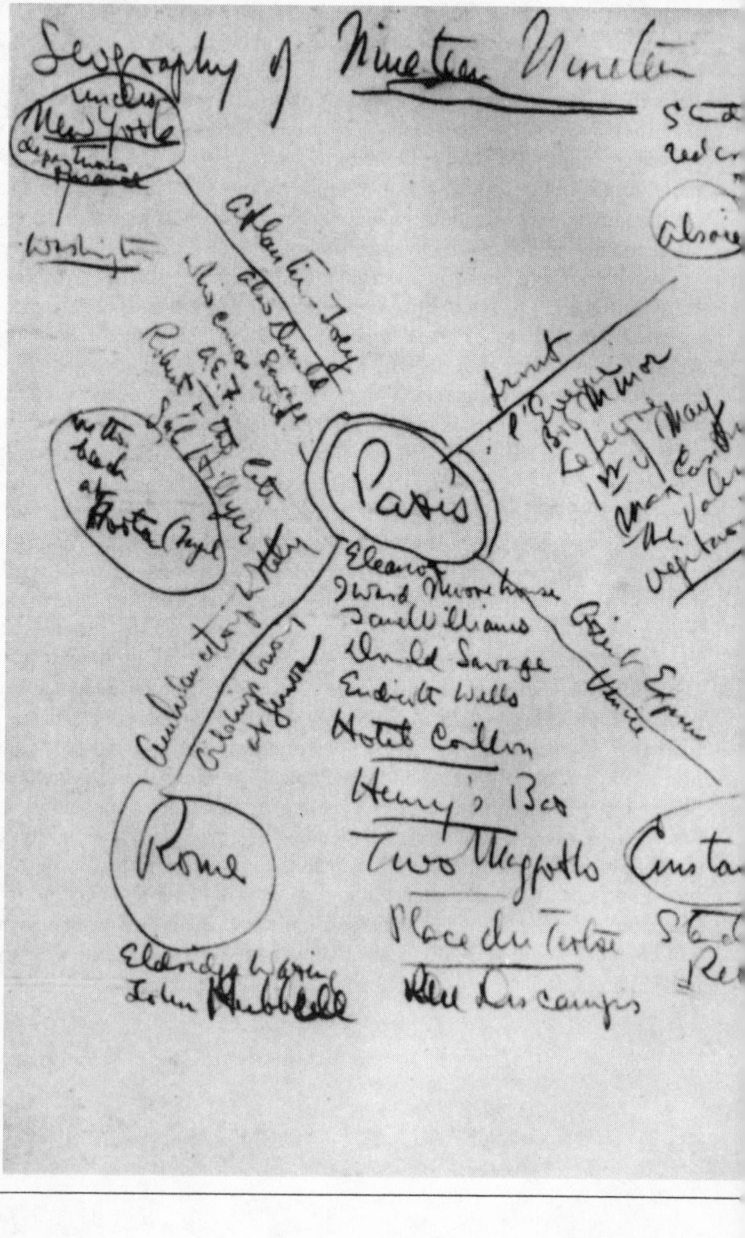

Geography of Nineteen Nineteen

New York

Washington

Paris

Rome

Eleanor
J Ward Moorehouse
Janet Williams
Dick Savage
Endicott Wells
Hotel Crillon
Henry's Bar
Two Magpots
Place du Tertre
Rue des champs

Eldridge Waring
John Hubbell

PART V

===

The
Great Depression,
1930–1936

CHAPTER EIGHTEEN

America's Leading
Proletarian Writer,
1930–1931

With *The 42nd Parallel* in press, Katy and Dos Passos were eager to sail for Europe. They stayed briefly in New York, then boarded the *Roussillon* for the voyage to Bordeaux. It might seem odd that they could leave for an extended trip abroad just after the stock market had begun its collapse. But, Dos Passos wrote later, the Depression "didn't affect me very much personally. Katy owned the Provincetown house where we made our headquarters, and I scraped up what money I could for trips. I used to tell people I had been just as broke before the stockmarket crash as after it. My books could hardly have sold less anyway." Though seeming flippant, his comment was essentially accurate. He and Katy got by during their lives together because between them they owned two houses—until they sold the farm at Truro in 1943—and for a while, a third next to 571 Commercial Street. They managed on the incomes from renting one or more of these, from what each wrote, and from whatever Dos Passos received from the trust held for him by his Aunt Mamie Gordon. After Katy's father died in 1934, she received a small inheritance, but they never were what anyone could define as rich. "I've always lived successfully from hand to mouth without the slightest worry," Dos Passos observed to Katy in 1939, and that was about how they existed, although they by no means suffered. They spent what they earned and sometimes more, which they borrowed from friends or from a bank. They were inveterate travelers, so a substantial amount of their money went for that, but they traveled economically, and often they stayed with friends when away from Provincetown, so their expenses were not as great as one might imagine.

On the Cape their life style was simple. Entertainment was usually a gathering of close friends for drinks and dinner, and although Dos Passos was a gourmet, he ate economically. Neither was a stylish dresser, Dos Passos in particular preferring simple clothes which he wore for a long time. Further, they rarely indulged themselves in other luxuries. Their cars were inexpensive, sometimes bought secondhand, and when Dos Passos had a sailboat at Provincetown, it was a dinghy, never anything larger.

Unworried about their funds, especially because they hoped for some financial success with *The 42nd Parallel,* Katy and Dos Passos in early December 1929 were able to relax aboard the *Roussillon* while he worked on *1919.* The ocean voyage brought to mind his journey in 1917 aboard the *Chicago.* *

As he began to write, he scribbled notes for the Camera Eye sections to set the narrator's own point of view during the tumultuous years just before and after America's involvement in World War I. "Camera Eye," he headed a page:

A Convoy Day—the Rosy & the rainbow and the zone—and the zebrastriped freighters

The sand carts in Madrid the morning before the general strike

— — —

The grove of pines against the clouds above Remicourt where we talked about anarchy—the flies the grey fiats lined up in the valley—

The grenadine guards

———————————

The abandoned beergarden at Châlons-sur-Marne—Down with the swag-bellied middleaged—

———————————

Erize la petite—wooden crosses on the hills
de trop de delicatesse
j'ai perdu la vie

—————

Even after more than twelve years the images of his initiation into war were precise in his mind. These various scenes became embedded in several Camera Eyes as well as in the narrative of Richard Ellsworth Savage, the young, idealistic American whose story became the most nearly central thread running through *1919,* which used the techniques of *The 42nd Parallel* to portray the swirl of life during the years 1916–1919.

**For the first edition, the title of the second volume of the trilogy was written as* 1919, *although Dos Passos preferred* Nineteen Nineteen, *as it appeared when it was published in 1938 as the second volume of* U.S.A.

But, whereas Mac, the central figure in *The 42nd Parallel*, merely tired of radicalism as a member of the I.W.W. and settled in Mexico, Savage—his eye on the main chance—soon compromised his idealism once he had been abroad, worked for J. Ward Moorehouse, and sensed the possibilities for the big money in public relations. *The 42nd Parallel* was thematically open-ended because Dos Passos meant to show a country poised to plunge in a new direction during the first years of the twentieth century. In *1919*, because he was aware of all that had not been achieved by Woodrow Wilson's "war to end all wars" and was becoming aware of the significance of the market crash in 1929, he turned his satirist's pen to the years surrounding the conflict. With *1919*, the trilogy took on a clearer thematic direction. The second volume, he told Malcolm Cowley when it was about to be published in 1932, showed "a certain crystallization (call it monopoly capitalism?) of society that didn't exist in the early part of 42nd Parallel (call it competitive capitalism?)" and he added, "but as for the note of hope—gosh who knows?" In 1932, he was not yet sure if the third volume would contain a note of hope—such would depend on his growing sense of the 1920s from his perspective in the Depression thirties.

In December 1929, Dos Passos thought less about the ultimate mood of *U.S.A.* than about showing Katy the Europe he loved. As soon as they had arrived in Bordeaux, they traveled to Paris, where they were constantly with the Hemingways and the Fitzgeralds. They met Scottie, the Fitzgeralds' daughter, for the first time and liked her, but felt sorry for Scott, who was drinking heavily, and for Zelda, who, Dos Passos recalled, "was far from being in her right mind," obsessed as she was by the notion that she could become a dancer with the Ballet Russe. Four months later, his assessment proved sadly true. In April 1930, she had a nervous breakdown.

Other friends, however, were in a better way. Before Dos Passos and Katy arrived, Hemingway had had his sour moments early in December when word of unpleasant rumors challenging his masculinity and boxing skills got back to him. Then he heard of the suicide in New York of the American poet Harry Crosby, but by the time the Dos Passoses reached Paris he was cheerful again. Fernand Léger and his beautiful wife Jeanne invited Dos Passos and Katy to a fine dinner, and while still in Paris before Christmas they enjoyed the company of Blaise Cendrars, the French avant-garde poet whose work entranced Dos Passos and whom he had met at the Murphys during an earlier visit to France. With Cendrars they toured the Paris cafés, the Dos Passoses amused by his "white samoyed" dog which went everywhere with him.

While still in the United States Katy and Dos Passos had heard from Gerald and Sara Murphy that their son Patrick had tuberculosis, so in Paris they made plans with the Hemingways to meet the Murphys in Switzerland for Christmas. Joined by Pauline's sister Virginia, the five Americans crossed the border into Switzerland on December 21, meeting the Murphys and Dorothy Parker at Montana-Vermala for the holiday. It was a glorious time, Dos Passos remembered. There were skiing and evenings of cheese fondue and white wine, and conversation spiced with

Parker's wit. After Christmas the Hemingways returned to Paris, because they were to sail for the United States and Key West on January 10.

Katy and Dos Passos, in January 1930, headed for Schruns, Austria, where he wrote to Hemingway in Paris that they had had a "swell trip from Sierre—Berne —Zurich Buchs—stopped in Feldkirch & Bludenz due to bad connections but worth it—wish to hell you were along." From Schruns they returned to France, where they joined Cendrars for a week in Montpazier, a walled town in the Massif Central. "Swellest country I ever saw in France and jesus the eats—wild duck, hare truffles pâté de foie—swell wine à volonté and prix du repas ƒ12," Dos Passos wrote Ernest. "Cendrars," he added, "is a hell of a good guy." He was, as well, a spirited one. With only a left hand—his right having been lost in the World War— Cendrars drove his guests at a rapid speed through the mountains around Montpazier. He shifted gears with the hook on his right arm and, asserted Dos Passos, he "took every curve on two wheels" of his sporty Alfa-Romeo.

Dos Passos had intended to head south into Spain after visiting Cendrars, but from his English agents, A. M. Heath and Company, Ltd., he heard in late January that the British publisher Constable wanted to omit the Newsreel and Camera Eye sections in their edition of *The 42nd Parallel.* By the end of the month he had traveled to London to settle the matter, so that a Heath agent could assure the Brandt agency in New York that "all is peace and joy." The sections would be retained.

Returning to the Continent, the Dos Passoses journeyed leisurely through Spain, where in March they arrived in Cádiz for a slow trip via the Canary Islands to Havana aboard a small ship, the *Antonio Lopez.* They lived in comfort and enjoyed the company of an elderly American, a Mr. Loomis, who entertained them with tales about Africa. To their amusement he had taken two staterooms, because as he asked them, he had to have some place to keep his shoes, didn't he?

Dos Passos was not idle during the voyage. He painted watercolors and worked at a translation of Blaise Cendrars's volume, *Le Panama et Mes Sept Oncles.* The watercolors were those which Dos Passos used to illustrate the translation when it was published in January 1931. Reading *Panama or The Adventures of My Seven Uncles,* one can immediately understand Dos Passos's fascination with Cendrars. Not only was the French poet a lively person, his poetry conveyed his vitality and an excitement about the modern era. Cendrars had traveled widely, writing about rivers as distant as the Mississippi and the Bahr-el-Zeraf in the Sudan. His flat documentary style appealed to Dos Passos, as did his desire to be inclusive. A part of one long narrative entitled "Prosody of the Transiberian and of Little Jeanne of France" as Dos Passos translated it reads:

> *I've seen the silent trains the black trains coming*
>   *back from the Far East that passed like haunts*
> *And my eye like the red light on the rear car still*
>   *speeds behind those trains.*
> *At Talga 100,000 wounded dying for lack of care;*

I went through all the hospitals of Krasnoyarsk
And at Khilok we passed a long hospital train full
      of soldiers that had gone mad. . . .

Cendrars's poetry had a special kind of harsh beauty and unflinching imagery from
the contemporary world which were exactly what Dos Passos wanted to convey. The
French poet, Dos Passos asserted in his foreword, was a part of the modernist
movement that, he hardly needed to add, had heavily influenced him:

> The poetry of Blaise Cendrars was part of the creative tidal wave that
> spread over the world from the Paris of before the last European war. Under
> various tags: futurism, cubism, vorticism, modernism, most of the best work in
> the arts in our time has been the direct product of this explosion, that had an
> influence in its sphere comparable with that of the October revolution in social
> organization and politics and the Einstein formula in physics. Cendrars and
> Apollinaire, poets, were on the first cubist barricades with the group that
> included Picasso, Modigliani, Marinetti, Chagall; that profoundly influenced
> Maiakovsky, Meyerhold, Eisenstein; whose ideas carom through Joyce, Ger-
> trude Stein, T. S. Eliot (first published in Wyndon Lewis's "Blast"). The music
> of Stravinski and Prokofieff and Diageleff's Ballet hail from this same Paris
> already in the disintegration of victory, as do the windows of Saks Fifth Avenue,
> skyscraper furniture, the Lenin Memorial in Moscow, the paintings of Diego
> Rivera in Mexico City and the newritz styles of advertizing in American
> magazines.

When Dos Passos and Katy reached Havana in early April, he still needed to
work on the translation, but in Cuba there was much to see before wiring Hemingway that they would probably be arriving in Key West on Friday, April 11. They
found Hemingway in a benevolent mood, thus a fine host, ready to entertain them
as only he could. The news of Sidney Franklin, the American bullfighter, having
been gored in Madrid in March disturbed Ernest, but he worried less about that
when they fished constantly. He, Pauline, and Dos Passos took a boat trip at the
end of April as far as the Tortugas, westward from Key West. Hemingway amused
his guests with new drinks he concocted, his favorite being six to eight ounces of
gin poured into a fresh coconut and sipped through a straw. Before they left, Dos
Passos and Katy may have been around to observe Hemingway, drunk on absinthe,
hurling knives at Pauline's piano.
    Such a display was not amusing, but a letter from Cummings was, praising Dos
Passos's article "New Theater in Russia" which appeared in the April 16 *New
Republic.* "Pleasant weather, Columbus!" Cummings wished his much-traveled
friend; " 'twas even more than a pleasure to read the NR # p. 239 sixth 1 from top
quotes THE MECHANISM OF THE THEATER . . . the mechanism of the circus is masked
close quotes welwellwelll perhaps Not lasciate ogni speranza Afterallll!" Continuing
in his best form, Cummings reported on their mutual friend Morris Werner, who

had departed for Europe: "Ye Wear—ne'er hath paxvobiscumbed elsewhereishly viz parry an burlin en root to the amen soviet yeastcake; he wanted i to go but $, if not sens, forebad. Am almost thru eheuing & reddy to sing "Whan that Ap Reely' we hope to see yousesboths verysoon, Mudumunmushoo!" And to Madam and Monsieur Dos Passos he appended a postscript:

Q; Whence the phrase "virgin forest"?
A; Only G-d can make a tree
                    Anon. (20th C American)

Obviously he was in high spirits, for he did not stop at that but added further:

HATS OFF to thea orthodox flea,
who attempted to bugger a bee
But eamerged from thea fray
in a familea way . . .
which is why wea do things so fee-blea

The poem, he noted in the margin, was "From the Sanscrit."

Before leaving Key West, Dos Passos was pleased to learn about the reception of *The 42nd Parallel,* which had been published on February 19. The book did not sell spectacularly, but perceptive reviewers understood Dos Passos's intentions and admired them. In one of the earliest reviews, Mary Ross in *Books* for February 23 wrote that the volume neglected "the ordinary structures of fiction for a form as intricate as that of a symphony. . . . Its main theme would seem to be nothing less than life in America . . . with a range from coast to coast, from top to bottom of the economic scale, from the sublime to the ridiculous in emotions." She noted that *The 42nd Parallel* was twice as rich in texture as *Manhattan Transfer,* and she admired Dos Passos's "stimulating courage that essays a synthesis of time, class, geography and social theory." Henry Hazlitt, commenting in the *Nation,* had some reservations about Dos Passos's "kaleidoscopic" techniques, but still found the Newsreels to achieve "some brilliant effects." Edmund Wilson, granted his intimate friendship, offered high praise when he wrote that the author had "been able to immerse himself in the minds and lives of his middle-class characters, to identify himself with them." In earlier works, Wilson observed, Dos Passos had not been able to do that, and in a novel like *Manhattan Transfer,* "the characters are seen from the outside and, in consequence, seem sometimes scarcely human." Dos Passos, ever since his first efforts to write fiction, had been striving to achieve the sounds of American voices, so he was particularly gratified by Wilson's comment that "he is perhaps the first really important writer to have succeeded in using colloquial American for a novel of the highest artistic seriousness." He was "not without his characteristic moments of allowing his people to lapse into two-dimensional caricatures of qualities or forces which he hates," Wilson recognized, but that scarcely diminished Dos Passos's achievement. Wilson thought *The 42nd Parallel* was the first of a longer work that when complete could well be "the most important novel which any American of Dos Passos's generation has written."

One of the most perceptive reviews was John Chamberlain's, appearing in the *New York Times* on March 2, 1930. He saw clearly that the book was "a satire on the tremendous haphazardness of life in the expansionist America we all have known, the America which came into birth with the defeat of Jefferson's dream of an agricultural democracy. . . . It is an America 'on the make' that Mr. Dos Passos satirizes, an America filled with people with vague hopes of success—no matter what success." Chamberlain's praise was qualified; he noted the unfinished quality of the work, had doubts about what he called the "trick stuff"—the Camera Eyes and Newsreels—and he did not see any apparent indication of Dos Passos's own philosophy. Yet what was satisfying to Dos Passos was that reviewers like Chamberlain comprehended his intentions. He could be confident that the trilogy would eventually achieve some finished quality, especially as his own attitudes became more clearly defined and when in the volumes subsequent to *The 42nd Parallel* the "trick stuff" blended better by appearing less obtrusive while more related to the fictional narratives and the biographical sketches. The Camera Eyes, for example, were fewer and less about the murky private world of a child becoming an adolescent.

Buoyed by the critical reception of *The 42nd Parallel,* if not by its modest sales, Dos Passos wanted to be on with *1919,* at which he worked steadily for the next year in Provincetown. But before returning there, he and Katy left Key West in May, returned to Cuba, and from there crossed the Gulf of Mexico to Vera Cruz. In early June they left Mexico, to the relief of his English publishers among others, and finally settled down in Provincetown. Constable had become impatient with him because he had insisted that he correct proofs for the British edition of *The 42nd Parallel;* yet on June 6 neither of two sets of proofs had been returned to England. "Frankly," noted Patience Ross of A. M. Heath, "Mr. Dos Passos has been just a bit tiresome over his English publication." Soon, however, that matter was rectified, and Dos Passos and Katy turned to the quiet of the house in South Truro. During the summer he assured Eugene Saxton that he was "working like mad on 1919," which he was able to do with few interruptions on the Cape, and he seemed sedate enough that Edmund Wilson clucked his tongue about it in letters to other friends. "Dos Passos is up here," he wrote Allen Tate from Provincetown late in July. "He has married, bought a little farm in Truro, and decided he is a 'middle-class liberal.' " Wilson remarked that the two of them had been attempting to decide on the precise meaning of that term. Dos Passos, he added, had "finally come to the conclusion that, since the Communist Party with its pedantic Marxism is impossible, the thing to do is to persuade some radical millionaire to hire an Ed Bernays or Ivy Lee to use American publicity methods to convert the Americans to Communism. It is interesting," Wilson added wryly, "to contemplate the kind of Communism this would produce." Soon thereafter, he told Scott Fitzgerald that Dos Passos was "becoming more and more of a respectable householder every day and has decided that he is 'a middle-class liberal.' "

Wilson was amused at Dos Passos's easy conversion to domesticity, but it should not have startled him, since he could have seen for himself that Dos Passos for several years had wanted to settle down. And as for the stance of "middle-class liberal," that should not have been surprising either. Perhaps the term was misleading, but what Dos Passos meant—as Wilson well knew from their discussions that summer—was the person "who isn't forced by his position in the economic structure of society to be pro-worker or anti-worker." In a piece in the *New Republic* that obviously provoked Wilson's comments, Dos Passos declared that middle-class liberals, among whom he placed the technicians in an industrial society, "are the only class to which neutrality is possible in any phase of the struggle." As a writer, Dos Passos believed himself to be one of this class, whether he liked it or not. "Even neutrality," however, "would "be difficult, and to many even the coolest neutrality is going to look like Red radicalism." Liberals, he wrote a month and a half later, needed an Ivy Lee to represent them to the public. Reflecting his interest in the ideas of Thorstein Veblen and in the acute sociological study of middle America, *Middletown: A Study in Modern American Culture* by Robert and Helen Lynd, Dos Passos believed that the middle class was "the class that has the least stake in the game and the most stake in preserving the civilization without which it's too disorganized to live at all." This "section of the business class" held jobs "necessary under any system of organization of industrial society. Engineers, scientists, independent manual craftsmen, artists, actors, writers, experts of one kind or another," they occupied "very much the same position in Russia today under rigorous state socialism as they do in the United States under capitalism."

His stance of supposedly neutral observer was vintage Dos Passos, as anyone who had followed his public statements could recognize. It was hardly different from what he had written in 1926 about the *New Masses* he would like to see. He did not want spellbinders from any side laying down laws. The magazine, he had hoped then, would be a vehicle of expression for the middle-class liberals he described in 1930. His cry to the Left in 1926 had been: let us try to be open to and observant about what effects "the boiler of the great imperial steamroller of American finance" was creating. Let us try to remain balanced and humane in the class struggle while working for change on our terms, was his plea in 1930. While working for change might seem contradictory to a neutral stance, Dos Passos did not see it as such. What he meant to be saying was that the "middle-class liberals," the technicians in any industrial order, needed to stand clear of the violent struggles engendered by capitalism between laborers and employers. The technicians' task was to educate about capitalism those bound into it. The result of new understanding would be change, not to more capitalism, but not to European Communism either. The change would be peculiarly American, stemming neither from the Kremlin nor from the nation's steel mills. He distrusted dogmas and, as he told Wilson at the beginning of 1931, "the first problem is to find a new phraseology that we'll be at home with to organize mentally what is really happening now." His trouble, he acknowledged, was that he could not make up his mind "to swallow political methods." Mostly he favored the I.W.W. aim of building "a new society in the shell of the old," but he thought that about all that the Wobblies' movement had produced were jailings.

While unsure of where he stood and adamantly opposed to doctrines, he believed a person should nevertheless act, and his form of activism was writing. In the same piece in the *New Republic* where he defined middle-class liberalism, he described the work of International Labor Defense. The next month he wrote to the editor of the *New Republic* asking readers to support the Emergency Committee for Southern Political Prisoners, a part of International Labor Defense. The particular incident he cited was the jailing in Georgia of six people who were union organizers accused of advocating insurrection. And in the spring of 1931 he described in an article about the American theater what he thought was needed. "Is the Whole Show on the Skids?" he wondered. His answer was yes, as the theater stood then. What was needed was public theater of the sort he had seen in Russia, "a theatre that will be a social force." The time, he reminded his audience, was one "of sudden and dangerous transition. Industrial life is turning a corner and is either going to make the curve or smash up in the ditch." At such a moment the theater, always "a mass art," could serve as an "organ of contact" between the mass and "the individual members of the crowd," by which he meant that the theater, intelligently used by his "technicians," could educate the masses about themselves and their society. "Through the theatre," he declared, "socially constructive ideas could reach the wider field of the talkies. By socially creative ideas I don't mean little bedtime readings from Marx and Engels; I mean the new myth that's got to be created to replace the imperialist prosperity myth if the machinery of American life is ever to be gotten under social control."

Dos Passos's activism during the summer and fall of 1930 was restricted to calls for financial help and to the articles appearing in the *New Republic*. He remained in Provincetown until October, when he and Katy traveled west, she to visit relatives, he to visit Hemingway, who was hunting in Montana. Although Dos Passos was too nearsighted to be a good shot, he bought a hunting license and followed along after Hemingway while they hunted for a week in the high country. Once he actually got close enough to an elk for a shot, but the firing mechanism on Hemingway's rifle, which Dos Passos was carrying, confused him, and the elk bounded away unharmed. One suspects that he was relieved, as killing big game was no special thrill for him, even if he was fascinated by Ernest's performances.

With Floyd Allington, another of Hemingway's friends, they hunted and feasted until October 31, when the three packed into Hemingway's Ford roadster and started for Billings, the first leg of what was to be a trip to the East Coast. That night they camped in Yellowstone Park, then drove all the next day toward Billings. At dusk Ernest, who was driving, was blinded by the lights of an oncoming car. He swerved, and the roadster plunged into a deep ditch alongside the road. The Ford flipped over, but Allington and Dos Passos were able to extract themselves unharmed. Hemingway, however, was pinned inside, and when they pulled him out, they discovered his right arm was broken. Passing motorists drove the three men to the hospital in Billings, from where Dos Passos wired Pauline Hemingway in Piggott, Arkansas. Later he coaxed the roadster to Columbus, Montana, for repairs, then waited to meet Pauline when she arrived by train. He left only after he determined that Hemingway seemed to be in some comfort.

Christmas 1930, and the first month and a half of 1931, Dos Passos and Katy spent on Cape Cod as he worked at *1919* and contemplated where he stood politically in what was clearly a crisis for American capitalism. While objecting that he could not "swallow political methods," he told Wilson that "if you wait until you've cleared up your vocabulary you'll never say anything and just remain stuttering on the pons asinorum." Yet his doubts about his stance, while perhaps frustrating to him, were a stimulus as he tried to convey his sense of the American scene in his novel. In late January, he told Eugene Saxton that he could not say for certain when the manuscript for *1919* would be completed. Perhaps he would have a manuscript by May 1, but the fall was more certain. "I keep piling up written typewritten pencil-written every kind of written sheets and have a great deal of cutting to do," he told Saxton. Whether just then or later, the cutting he did was to delete great slabs of prose that tended to drift away from the main thrust of the narrative. For instance, early in the narrative about Eveline Hutchins, who is a major figure in *1919*, she meets a wealthy young man, Dirk McArthur. In his manuscript Dos Passos wrote:

> Back in Chicago she saw a lot of Dirk McArthur. Old Man McArthur was president of a bank and on the board of directors of the Northern Pacific. Dirk lived with his mother at Lake Geneva but he had [a] big Pierce Arrow and was always over in Chicago.

In the published edition, only the first sentence remained, for while the rest added flavor, it rambled and did not move the narrative forward.

After getting well along with the manuscript Dos Passos and Katy left Cape Cod for a vacation in February. They first visited New York, where they saw Scott Fitzgerald, who had returned from Europe for his father's funeral. Fitzgerald discussed Zelda's condition with them, describing it as schizophrenia. Most of the time she was quite well, but would periodically lapse into her schizoid state. She was under constant care, however, and Scott hoped now that she realized she was ill, she could be at least partially cured. Dos Passos wrote Wilson that Scott "seemed . . . to have much less nonsense about him than other times I'd seen him. He's fundamentally a pretty solid proposition."

At the moment Dos Passos was writing Wilson, he and Katy were aboard a ship steaming south from New York to Jacksonville, Florida, where they were to disembark, buy a Model-A Ford roadster, and drive to Mexico City. Undoubtedly because of the press to complete *1919*, they did not remain in Mexico for long, but saw friends like Carleton Beals and Howard Phillips while they stayed in Mexico City for only several days. Beals recalled their visit. Katy he thought "a pretty, quick girl with a fine sense of humor and much originality." He first thought that Dos Passos "had a sublime indifference to her; for his legs were so long, his head full of so many things, he was forever marching off so rapidly, that it must have taxed Katy at times to keep up." But Beals soon recognized that "just when Dos seemed striding off to grab a star, he would unexpectedly show Katy bluff tenderness and concern," and Beals came to think that the couple "understood each other uncommonly well."

He recalled an incident that occurred as Dos Passos and Katy arrived in front of their hotel. Katy, who had been driving, walked into the lobby to see about rooms, and while she was gone, a policeman told Dos Passos to move the Ford. In the dusk and heavy traffic, Dos Passos pulled away from the curb, then at the first intersection he plowed into the box from which another policeman was directing traffic. But instead of arresting Dos Passos, the policeman leaped to his feet, smiled, and saluted the American. Stunned but relieved, Dos Passos made his way with the roadster back to the hotel, where Katy had begun to worry about her husband's disappearance.

Perhaps it was during the trip back to Provincetown in March that he and Katy stopped at the Arlington National Cemetery across the Potomac from Washington. Because he intended to make a statement about the idiotic butchery of wars waged by the people who did not do the fighting, he needed to view the Tomb of the Unknown Soldier of the World War, which had been dedicated with great pomp and ceremony in 1921 and—from the moment of the interment of an unknown soldier's remains—had been guarded by a sentry parading before the tomb. The scene at the cemetery was moving, but brought home the ultimate irony of governments causing the deaths of the governed. The piece Dos Passos wrote to conclude *1919*, entitled "The Body of an American," became one of his finest. Filled with his anger, nevertheless the prose poem avoided didacticism as it took the bored voice of a clerk reading the Congressional resolution creating the tomb; the nauseated feelings and the bigotry of the men who were assigned to exhume four unidentified bodies, one of which would be selected to return to the United States and be reburied at Arlington; and the rhetorical puffery of vacuous politicans like Warren G. Harding and played them off against the biography of a very average American soldier who, lost from his outfit, was killed by a stray shell. Drawing from actual accounts of the dedication ceremony on Armistice Day, 1921, Dos Passos gave his piece the ring of fact; yet he condensed, abbreviated, and imagined what he needed to create his effect.

"Whereasthe Congressoftheunitedstates byaconcurrentresolutionadoptedon the4thdayofmarch," he began the piece and joined together words to suggest the uninterested singsong of some clerk. Then after a bit more of the resolution Dos Passos began the narrative about the "John Doe" soldier:

> In the tarpaper morgue at Châlons-sur-Marne in the reek of
> chloride of lime and the dead, they picked out the pine box that held
> all that was left of
>> enie menie minie moe plenty other pine boxes stacked up there
> containing what they'd scraped up of Richard Roe
>> and other person or persons unknown. Only one can go.
> How did they pick John Doe?
>> Make sure he ain't a dinge, boys.
>> make sure he ain't a guinea or a kike,
>> how can you tell a guy's a hunredpercent when all you've got's

> a gunnysack full of bones, bronze buttons stamped with the screaming
> eagle and a pair of roll puttees?
>   . . . and the gagging chloride and the puky dirtstench of the
> yearold dead . . .

Dos Passos did not render the matter of the selection of the casket exactly as
it had occurred; yet what he did was close to fact and far more effective than if he
had been less the novelist and more the reporter. In fact, caskets containing the
bodies of four unidentified Americans had been exhumed from the Romagne Military Cemetery in France and placed in a room of the city hall at Châlons-sur-Marne.
Another American soldier had been selected to pick one of the caskets, which was
returned to the United States aboard the *Olympia,* Admiral Dewey's flagship at
Manila Bay.

The terrible last moments of this John Doe's short existence Dos Passos
rendered impressionistically by reporting the soldier's plea for help to find his outfit
—*"Say feller tell me how I can get back to my outfit"*—while suggesting his very
typical life in the army: "drilled, hiked, manual of arms, ate slum, learned to salute,
to soldier, to loaf in the latrines, forbidden to smoke on deck, overseas guard duty,
forty men and eight horses, shortarm inspection and the ping of shrapnel and the
shrill bullets combing the air and the soreheaded woodpeckers the machineguns
mud cooties gasmasks and the itch." And then, identification tags lost, he lay down
to rest, and an enemy shell killed him. The remains of the body were taken to
Châlons-sur-Marne, then eventually to Arlington, where Old Glory was draped over
the casket, a bugler played taps,

> and Mr. Harding prayed to God and the diplomats and the generals
> and the admirals and the brasshats and the politicians and the handsomely
> dressed ladies out of the society column of the *Washington Post* stood up
> solemn
>   and thought how beautiful sad Old Glory God's Country it was to
> have the bugler play taps and the three volleys made their ears ring.

Dignitaries from all the Allied nations presented military decorations; wreaths and
even an American Indian headdress were laid by the grave. "All the Washingtonians
brought flowers," Dos Passos concluded the sketch, adding finally to show his scorn
for the man he considered the architect of the war: "Woodrow Wilson brought a
bouquet of poppies." So went an episode that epitomized the antiwar and antigov-
ernment sentiments which were at the core of Dos Passos's thinking.

An episode that reflected the grip business had on American life and government, Dos Passos believed, was the career of the financier J. P. Morgan, of whom
he wrote a derogatory profile as one of the biographies in *1919.* The profile for
complex reasons became the subject of a controversy with Harper's, who eventually
declined to publish *1919,* and as a result it came out in March 1932 over the imprint
of Harcourt, Brace and Company. "How extraordinary to have that last minute
change of publishers," Patience Ross wrote the Brandt agency late in December

1931, after she had learned about the move. It was. What had occurred was that Dos Passos had completed the manuscript during the summer and forwarded it to his publishers, where production proceeded until November, when Harper's decided against publication because Dos Passos refused to delete the portrait of Morgan. After the decision was made, Dos Passos wrote Eugene Saxton, "This certainly is a lousy break all round—but its no use worrying any more about it." He told Saxton he had telegraphed the Brandts about getting another publisher, and his main concern was speed, because he had "a hunch there's something fairly timely about the volume and that it ought to come out as soon as possible."

Harper's had no wish to attack Morgan. A number of years earlier, the company had been reorganized, and at that time its president, Thomas B. Wells, also the editor of *Harper's Magazine,* had refinanced the operation through Morgan. Later, when Harper's finances were poor, the loan had been extended. By 1931, the loan had been retired, but Harper's did not think Morgan deserved an insult. Eugene Saxton, as Dos Passos's editor, was caught between the author and the firm. After the incident was over and Dos Passos was with Harcourt, Brace, Thomas Wells— retired from Harper's but still a stockholder and adviser to the firm—wrote Saxton in December 1931 about the matter. Clearly Wells had used his influence against the manuscript:

Dear Gene: While I am not posted as to what course you fellows have taken in the Dos Passos matter, I can imagine how you cursed me when my cable was received at the office. Sorry, I could not have taken any other position. It is difficult to be a business man and a gentleman at the same time as you have often heard me argue. But when the opportunity comes to be both, I think one ought to grasp it. If you have let the book go, we have probably sacrificed a good deal. Just how much I don't know. But we have played the game decently and have nothing to be ashamed of—and we have kept a good friend. If I had cabled "Splendid by all means publish," I could never have forgiven myself for that would have been "mucker ball" of the sort I don't want to learn how to play. As to the business man end of the argument, I think it is damn sound business to keep on terms of easy friendship with the world's strongest private banking house whose influence extends far more widely than any other among the banks of New York.

I am all for freedom of speech and uncontrolled publishing policy. Never in a single instance did Morgan try to control or influence us. He was far too wise for that and when he was bedevilled by our creditors he merely growled and told Lamont to see if something couldn't be done with the business. He could have called his loans any day (they were all demand notes) and then followed Morrow's advice & handed it over to Doubleday. His son could have done the same thing—and told me that unless I could do something—and quickly—that was what he *would* do. But he was too damn decent to force us & twice (I think) extended my option. And that's that. I know you hate the rich—like hell. I have an ardent dislike for almost all mankind. Don't get savage about this episode. That spoils your insides and reduces your liquor capacity. So cheer up & forgive me.

No doubt Harper's resistance annoyed Dos Passos, but his agents had quickly moved his contract to Harcourt, Brace, so he knew late in 1931 that the book would appear without undue delay.

Once the manuscript had been completed, he turned his attention to the causes that earlier he had discussed in the *New Republic* and acted on his belief that a person should do something despite private doubts he might harbor. In August, as chairman of the National Committee to Aid Striking Miners Fighting Starvation, he had written "An Appeal for Aid" that was published in the *New Republic*. Increasingly involved in the attempt to raise money to support the coal miners on strike in Harlan County, Kentucky, he stepped forward when Theodore Dreiser in October called a meeting of the Communist-dominated National Committee for the Defense of Political Prisoners to ask for volunteers to investigate the situation in Harlan County. In addition to Dos Passos, Lester Cohen, Samuel Ornitz, Bruce Crawford, Melvin P. Levy, and Charles and Adelaide Walker agreed to join Dreiser. The trip would not be without its dangers, because feelings ran strong between the miners and the union organizers on one side and the coal operators on the other. There had been during the previous year substantial violence—threats, bombings, beatings, and killings. Harlan County was, as Dos Passos later reported, a "war zone." In addition, the Dreiser committee was viewed, not unexpectedly, as a group of outside agitators and thus treated by local authorities with suspicion.

The group proceeded by train to Pineville, Kentucky, in early November 1931. Dos Passos recalled that he joined Dreiser aboard the train in the company of "a most attractive young woman," whom Dreiser introduced to the others as Marie Pergain, a name that may have been fictitious. Dos Passos, like the others, was surprised that on a trip like this Dreiser would bring along a woman companion, an act that was almost sure to create some scandal and thus lessen the credibility of the committee's findings in the eyes of the public.

In Pineville on November 5 some miners and their wives greeted the writers, who were then ushered to the Continental Hotel, where Dreiser told reporters that the purpose of his committee was "to let the American people know just what conditions are." To this end the committee, which had no firm plans, decided to hold public hearings at which Dreiser would be the moderator, questioning miners, townspeople, and officials like the local sheriff, the district attorney, and newspaper editors. As the committee talked over their plans in a room off the hotel lobby, they began to hear of the wretched conditions in Harlan County from the miners, who testified that shootings and beatings were common, as were raids by local authorities.

The next day the Dreiser committee traveled to the nearby town of Harlan and there set up their hearings in the Llewellyn Hotel. Many of the miners who testified were in the National Miners' Union, controlled by the Communists, who made it obvious that their lives were miserable. The miners were impoverished, controlled almost completely by the financial maneuverings of the coal companies while they lived under the constant threat of harassment. That afternoon Dreiser interviewed the Harlan sheriff, who evinced the expected hatred of the unions, declared publications like the *Daily Worker* illegal, admitted that the majority of his deputies were mine guards in the pay of the coal operators, and ended by serving a suit of $50,000 for slander against committee member Bruce Crawford.

The following morning, November 7, the committee interviewed other local officials in Pineville before journeying to Straight Creek in Bell County to hold more hearings. The writers were invited to attend a meeting of the NMU local to be held at the Glendon Baptist Church. Before that began, they visited the miners' homes. There was, Dos Passos noted, an "utter lack of sanitation"; in another appeal letter written in January 1932, he stated that "the miners, their wives and children live in crumbling shacks, many of them clapboard, through whose cracks pour the lashing mountain winds, rain and snow. 'We're not afraid of the wind,'" he quoted a mother of five children as saying, " 'it's the loose boards in the walls.'"

Perhaps the star witness at Straight Creek was Aunt Molly Jackson, the midwife for the settlement. She told Dreiser of children dying regularly, sometimes "from four to seven a week" up and down the length of the creek during the summer months. Aunt Molly was articulate, militant, and also a fine ballad singer. Dos Passos especially appreciated her lyrics.

> *This minin town I live in*
> * is a sad an a lonely place,*
> *This minin town I live in*
> * is a sad an a lonely place,*
> *For pity and starvation*
> * is pictured on every face . . .*
> *Listen my friends and comrades*
> * please take a friend's advice,*
> *Don't put out no more of your labor*
> * till you get a livin price*

went one of the songs he transcribed. Her singing and the Elizabethan sound of the people's dialect struck Dos Passos as most appealing. They were the sort of hardy people he admired and wanted to help. He and others transcribed the miners' testimonies, which he told of in the *New Republic* and later compiled for a pro-miner volume he edited, of which he much later remarked, "All we accomplished was a volume for the record called *Harlan Miners Speak,*" and he asserted that "the Communist effort disintegrated. A number of the leaders ended up in jail." He may not have been willing later to give enough credit to the Dreiser committee's efforts, for the publicity surrounding it at least called attention to the Harlan situation.

Whatever the ultimate effect of the investigation, Dos Passos worked hard gathering information during the meetings and typing it up. In addition to taking interviews, he collected documents that reflected the plight of the miners, such as receipts from the Pittsburgh Terminal Coal Corporation for Steve and Joe Busa for labor during the half-months ended July 15, August 31, and September 15, 1931. During the half-month ending July 15, for example, Steve Busa had received a credit of $17.32, but he had been charged exactly that amount at the company store for such items as "assignments, doctor, explosives, miner's lamps, Insurance," and so forth. Thus, not only was he paid slave wages, he was in thrall to the company because his entire earnings were turned back into company operated functions. The two receipts for Joe Busa ran the same way.

The Dreiser committee held one further meeting, at Wallins Creek, then by November 9 was on board a train bound for New York. But this was not the end of the episode; the publicity, in fact, was only beginning to grow. The entire committee was soon indicted by Kentucky authorities for "criminal syndicalism," and in the meanwhile Dreiser and Marie Pergain were indicted for adultery, a charge that drew national attention. What had happened was that, trying to pin something on Dreiser, some local authorities stacked toothpicks against the door of his room in the Continental Hotel when they saw Pergain enter it at 11:00 P.M. on November 7. The toothpicks had not fallen over several hours later, so adultery was assumed to have occurred. Dreiser, when questioned by reporters, asserted that, as he was impotent, nothing adulterous could have happened. He was furious about the matter but, because adultery was only a misdemeanor, he had little worry about extradition on that account.

The "criminal syndicalism" charge which was brought against the committee on November 16 was potentially a more serious matter. The penalty for each person could be as great as twenty-one years in prison and a $10,000 fine. Dreiser sent a lawyer to Kentucky to look into the matter and was relieved to hear from him that the matter would probably be dropped if there were no further agitation. The others, like Dreiser, had no intention of standing trial, but did not intend to remain silent, either. Dos Passos, nevertheless, was asked by Earl Browder, then the head of the Communist Central Committee, to return to Kentucky for trial as a gesture against the authorities. Despite sympathizing with the miners, Dos Passos refused. Browder's "sneering tone," he later wrote, disturbed him. More important, he had been furious with the Communists about the way they neglected miners already in jail in Harlan. To Dos Passos it seemed that the miners and he himself were for the Communists only "pawns in the game," and his doubts about the efficacy of the Communists' tactics grew, although he continued to sympathize with their aim of helping the cause of the laboring man.

While he refused Browder's suggestion, he did not withdraw entirely to Provincetown. In December he tried to speak at a rally for the miners in Webster Hall in Greenwich Village. Shy and disheveled, he stood up to speak, only to begin with "Gosh, I don't know what to say." He mumbled a few words and sat down. He also traveled to Washington to report "Red Day on Capitol Hill," as he entitled his piece in the *New Republic* about a march protesting the poverty of the Depression. The piece was pure reportage, lacking didacticism. He described the march, and while he sympathized with the cause, he meant to convey the mood created by the scene of protestors marching on Congress. It was a vignette that said a great deal about the Depression thirties—as he concluded, "Anyway, the jazz age is dead."

CHAPTER NINETEEN

Political Ambivalence,

1932

Tired from his political jaunts during the fall of 1931 but eager to travel again, Dos Passos made plans with Katy during January 1932 for a trip to Key West, Mexico, and the West Coast, using the funds he had received after completing the manuscript for *1919*. From Provincetown they corresponded with Hemingway, who was anxious to see them although complaining about the effort that he had put into *Death in the Afternoon*. The descriptive glossary he had prepared had taken more work than anything else and was packed with new information. Yet, he feared, everyone would assume he had copied it from another book. When Dos Passos wrote that he expected to be seasick during most of a voyage on a trawler he was about to take for a story about the North Atlantic fishing fleet, Hemingway answered in tough-guy style that enough vomiting would put him in excellent condition; anyone who vomited often enough could live forever.

The sea voyage of a little over a week Dos Passos found instructive, and he wrote about it first as a short essay in *In All Countries*, then three years later as part of a lengthy piece in *Fortune* about the Atlantic fishing industry. But at the end of January his main concern was to put the final touches on the volume about the Harlan miners—he worried over the dust jacket design—and on the proofs for *1919*, in which he found small errors. With these matters completed, he and Katy left Provincetown early in February for New York, where they boarded ship to Havana. From there on February 13 they took a ferry to Key West for a four-day visit, three days of which Dos Passos spent fishing with Hemingway in the Gulf Stream. As they fished from the boat belonging to Ernest's friend, "Bra" Saunders, Dos Passos read the manuscript of *Death in the Afternoon*. Soon after he and Katy had departed Key West and were about to land at El Progreso, Mexico, he wrote Hemingway, generally praising the book. On the whole Dos Passos thought it so "hellishly good" and the language "so magnificently used" that as he read it aboard Saunders's boat he had felt that he was reading a classic of its sort. "That's a hell of a good way to feel about a book not even published yet," he added. Since it was that good, "it would be a shame to leave in any unnecessary tripe. . . . After all, a book ought to be judged by the author according to the excellence of the stuff cut out." What he was doubtful about, he told Hemingway during the fishing trip and repeated in his letter, were those places where "old Hem straps on the longwhite whiskers and gives the boys the lowdown," the portions where Hemingway scolded Waldo Frank for his book, *Virgin Spain,* although Frank deserved deflating, and where Hemingway attempted to give "the lowdown about writing and why you like to live in Key West etc." The advice was good, Ernest later assured Dos Passos.

After landing in El Progreso Dos Passos and Katy enjoyed traveling through Guatemala, then visiting Tehuantepec and Veracruz as they moved slowly north-ward to Mexico City, where, he told Eugene Saxton, they had "arrived in fine shape somewhat groggy with scenery, bad roads architecture and chile." Mexico, he wrote Hemingway, was "pretty swell and damn disunited." He raved about the wildlife that Ernest might hunt and concluded, "its a damned extraordinary country anyway and the landscape and sculpture (precolumbian) 'll knock your eye out."

They traveled north to El Paso and then on by train to Tucson, where they bought an old Chrysler roadster and headed west to Santa Monica to visit Jack Lawson. Their return trip east took them across the middle of the continent. By April 27 they were in Baltimore, where they visited Horsley Gantt, now returned from Russia, before driving the next day to New Haven. For Dos Passos and Katy the trip was not merely pleasure, although they were in good spirits and enjoyed such light touches as making up limericks to send to Edmund Wilson.

But the trip was also instructive; Dos Passos had an excellent chance to see the country in which he was taking a great interest. He loved travel for its own sake, but he needed also to get a feel for the United States, whose mood during the throes of the Depression greatly influenced his fiction and was the subject of an increasing amount of his reportage.

By the last of April he and Katy had returned to Provincetown to find the house at 571 Commercial Street in good shape, having been looked after by Bill Smith. A stack of mail awaited Dos Passos, among it reviews of *1919,* which had been published on March 10 during his and Katy's trip to Mexico. The reviews were generally excellent; Dos Passos could take pleasure in knowing that his critics for the most part understood his motives while thinking that his work was becoming better and better. Malcolm Cowley, having clarified for himself Dos Passos's inten-tion to chart the move in twentieth-century America from competitive to monopoly capitalism, declared in the *New Republic* that *1919,* "in which Dos Passos's political ideas have given shape to his emotions and only the Camera Eye remains as a vestige of his earlier attitude," was "not only the best of all his novels; it is, I believe, a landmark in American fiction." And Henry Hazlitt, who had liked *The 42nd Parallel* but had had reservations, was more effusive this time. He could find "no one who is [Dos Passos's] superior in range of awareness of American life." His tone, thought Hazlitt, was akin to Hemingway's, but his "range of sympathy" was greater. The "social implications" of *1919* were similar to those of the work of Dreiser, Lewis, and Sinclair, but whereas the characters of Sinclair, at least, were "wax dummies," those of Dos Passos were "alive and convincing."

Cowley's and Hazlitt's remarks were high praise indeed, but justified. The Depression—along with the events of the Sacco-Vanzetti case in particular—had sharpened Dos Passos's awareness of the conditions of American life and had impelled him to clarify his political thinking, although not in the direction of full acceptance of the Communist Party line, as many people assumed. Social conditions had matured him so that he could combine his technical skills with his artistic sensibility and write a book that placed him on a rarely achieved literary plateau, where he remained at least through the creation of *The Big Money*, the third volume of *U.S.A.*

Most pleasing of all the words of praise he received might well have been a letter from Hemingway that arrived only after Katy and Dos Passos had been back in Provincetown for some time. Hemingway had mailed it in March to his friend in Mexico City, but the letter had not arrived in time to catch the Dos Passoses. In April Hemingway wrote again, mentioning the earlier letter, and Dos Passos wrote back that he was eager to see it. He was not disappointed when it arrived because the letter was one of the most generous Hemingway wrote; it was Ernest at his best, appreciating fine literature and also giving good-spirited advice. He declared *1919* magnificent, four times better than *The 42nd Parallel*, which had been excellent. Dos Passos was writing so well that Hemingway feared something might happen to him. Look out for your food, he jokingly warned. Then he urged Dos Passos in the next volume to avoid one thing, which was to try to create perfect characters. In other words, he meant, do not try to carry the message through the figures. Before Dos Passos rendered an idealized Communist, he should remember that the fellow was probably a fierce masturbator and a physical wreck. Characters should remain people, never become symbols, which was a danger for Dos Passos if he let the Communist or any other line sway his sense of what humanity was. Show, do not tell, Hemingway implored his friend. In *1919* Dos Passos had done just that through the four perspectives of the Camera Eyes, the Newsreels, the biographies, and the narratives. Now, with the chance to do good by showing life as it was, he should not relax, but write as if his life depended on it.

So splendid did Hemingway think *1919*, and so appreciative was he of Dos Passos's advice about *Death in the Afternoon*, that he continued in subsequent letters to assure Dos Passos of the quality of his new book. He should not worry about Malcolm Cowley's doubts about the Camera Eye, Hemingway wrote on May 30. He should have confidence that he knew the world whereof he wrote, and he should be a Communist if he chose to, although Hemingway could never himself be one, despising tyranny—in fact, any government—as he did.

Dos Passos was much buoyed up by Ernest's enthusiasms. He immediately responded to the May 30 letter, acknowledging that he felt uneasy to know that

Hemingway had cut *Death in the Afternoon*—which he mentioned he had done—on Dos Passos's advice. After all, he might be wrong, and he was especially doubtful about the value of his advice when he found himself drawing from Hemingway's remarks as he, Dos Passos, wrote a preface to the Modern Library edition of *Three Soldiers*. Maybe Hemingway ought to use the material as a preface, suggested Dos Passos. In any event, what he had read was "the goddamnedest best piece of writing that's seen the light for many a day on this continent," and he stood ready to crown any unkind critics. He avoided any mention of the political issue, partly because he sensed that there was little point in discussing the matter with Hemingway, who was then basically apolitical, partly also because he knew that Ernest was sensitive about politics as the Depression wore on and more and more writers were taking political stands. Little more than a month after Hemingway wrote Dos Passos, he corresponded with the publisher Paul Romaine, who had included a poem of Ernest's in a volume of William Faulkner's work. "I do not follow the fashion in politics, letters, religion, etc.," Hemingway declared. "If the boys swing left in literature you may make a small bet the next swing will be to the right and some of the yellow bastards will swing both ways. . . . Dos Passos doesn't swing. He's always been the same. To hell with your swingers." His comments in 1932 about writing and about political shifts suggest a part of the reason for the force of his break with Dos Passos only five years later when it seemed to him that Dos Passos was bent on telling rather than showing in his writing. Even more, Dos Passos was swinging from Left to Right, and—never mind his rationale—that seemed somehow immoral, if not "yellow," to Hemingway.

Amid such considerations of politics, Dos Passos knew where he wanted to go with *The Big Money*. Nevertheless he found it difficult to move ahead. He had numerous narrative threads and themes which he meant to keep going simultaneously. What made the last volume more difficult to write than the first two was that postwar life in the United States seemed more varied and more complex even than what he had portrayed earlier, events and the lives of a variety of Americans during the first two decades of the twentieth century. He now wanted to show the era of the big money and its effects, and to do that, he had somehow to widen his panorama of America, while also demonstrating how the nation was splitting apart as the gaps between the economic exploiters, the exploited, and his "liberal" technicians widened. His notes for *The Big Money* indicate his problems. One scanty page reflects how he meant to incorporate his concerns through characters. It reads:

CHARLEY ANDERSON	motors and then
TAYLOR	planes
QUEENIE RIGGS	farm & city lowlife
Thorstein Veblen	
J. WARD MOOREHOUSE	finance
INSULL	
ALICE	The Wright Brothers
Henry Ford	John D.
An Oil Worker	

On yet another page he scrawled:

> Characters for Last Volume
> Doc Bingham
>   Emmanuel R. Bingham
> Ike Hall—was 18 in 1907
> might tell about kid he'd known
> when he was a kid
> Mac—Fen McGreary
> Fred Hoff—IWW organizer
> Ben Evans—automobile mechanic is
> from Louisville Ky in gold field strike
> Maisie's brother Bill Spencer 1912
>   getting rich in Real Estate

And while he began to plan which characters he would use in narratives, he considered which biographical figures should intersperse the other elements of the book, so he jotted down another list of names:

> Frederick W. Taylor
> Henry Ford
> ~~Zapata?~~   Wm. Randolph
>   Hearst
> John D. Rockefeller
>
> Charlie Chaplin
> Babe Ruth ?
> Bert Savoy
>
> The Wright Bros
> Sacco and Vanzetti
> Hall Mills
> Isdo   Jay Insul
> Al Capone
> Big Bill Thompson

As these notes suggest, Dos Passos was striving to achieve a mix that would convey the tumultuous pace of twenties America. Charley Anderson, the narrative figure who was the most nearly central in *The Big Money*, was to represent "motors and then planes," that is, industrial America, while Queenie Riggs, someone who never appeared in the published volume, was to represent "farm & city lowlife." Soon Dos Passos probably decided that Margo Dowling, a tough, beautiful woman whose path crosses Charley's and who becomes a movie actress in Hollywood, sufficed for what he intended Queenie to reflect. J. Ward

Moorehouse, a character in all three volumes, would represent "finance," the dominant factor in the trilogy. No figure named Alice became major, nor would there be "An Oil Worker," but other characters like Ike Hall, Fred Hoff, who had appeared in the Mac narrative of *The 42nd Parallel*, and Ben Evans were melded into Mary French and Ben Compton, labor organizers whose tales reflected Dos Passos's growing misgivings about the value of left-wing organizations. And Doc Bingham, an amusing, two-bit con man in the Mac narrative of *The 42nd Parallel*, reappears briefly in *The Big Money* as a wealthy producer of patent medicines. Richard Savage, by the 1920s thoroughly corrupted as a public relations executive, remains with Moorehouse's firm and bribes a U.S. Senator to work against a pure food and drug bill which would jeopardize Bingham Products, as Doc's large company is called. This incident, like Charley Anderson's death which resulted from his drunken attempt to beat a train through a railroad crossing, symbolized as much as anything for Dos Passos the moral decay created by the big money.

Interspersing the narratives were to be biographies to convey the various stances Americans took during the era. Frederick W. Taylor, the efficiency expert, would reflect one aspect of industrial life, the drive to increase production while—at least in Dos Passos's opinion—neglecting the welfare of the assembly-line workers. Henry Ford stood for something similar, and Samuel Insull, a wealthy financier who late in his life was tried for but found not guilty of financial manipulation and swindling, was to Dos Passos the epitome of "superpower," the force of monopoly capitalism which subverted the likes of Ben Compton, Sacco and Vanzetti, and even people like Charley Anderson and Richard Savage, despite their belief that they were manipulating the capitalist system to their own advantage. Their error, as Dos Passos saw it because of his reading of Thorstein Veblen, was that they had exchanged productive work for money.

The twenties was a time during which the likes of Taylor, Ford, and Insull seemed to emerge at the height of their influence in the United States, and it was a time, too, that created figures like the racketeer Al Capone; that produced sensational incidents like the much publicized Hall-Mills murder trial in 1922; and which spawned vaguely confused, finally pathetic, even if sometimes flashy careers like that of the modern dancer Isadora Duncan—"Isdo" in Dos Passos's notes—who died in 1927, strangled when her long scarf became entwined in the wheel of a moving car. To Dos Passos she represented Art, but in an era like that of the big money, Art became sensationalized and cheapened, while its end was pathetic, if not tragic.

In such a climate true creativity and morality were hidden under surface glitter and facile manipulations. Dos Passos's heroes, aside from the anarchists Sacco and Vanzetti, were brilliant technicians and inventors like the Wright brothers, Thorstein Veblen, and Frank Lloyd Wright. Each in his own way contributed the new ideas that represented America at its best as Dos Passos saw it. He studied each figure carefully: although he already knew Veblen's work, in the course of writing his biographic sketch, for example, Dos Passos read the economist's books, *Absentee*

Ownership and Business Enterprise in Recent Times and *The Engineers and the Price System*, which, with its concepts of creating a revolution through the impetus of engineers and technicians who could then lead the nation's production, was clearly an important influence on Dos Passos's thinking.

Just as Veblen's ideas appealed to Dos Passos, so did the genius but also the simple honesty of the Wright brothers. Dos Passos wrote that, despite the attention paid them in the years after their feat at Kitty Hawk, "they remained practical mechanics / and insisted on doing all their own work themselves, / even to filling the gasolinetank." As for the architect Frank Lloyd Wright, his vision of an America whose buildings expressed the spirit of its people was an ideal for Dos Passos. "Frank Lloyd Wright, / patriarch of the new building, / not without honor except in his own country," was the conclusion to the published version of Dos Passos's biographical sketch. The statement indicates his belief about the nation's attitudes in the 1920s toward one of its true geniuses. In a draft of the biography, Dos Passos was even more explicit, concluding with some of Wright's own words:

> . . . it is easy to realize how the complexity of crude utilitarian construction in the mechanical infancy of our growth, like the crude scaffolding for some noble building, did violence to the landscape. . . . The crude purpose of pioneering days has been accomplished. The scaffolding may be taken down and the true work, the culture of a civilization, may appear . . .

These remained in the published version, but were placed elsewhere. In the draft, Dos Passos added:

> but will the building be fit for free men to live in America if oppression and monopoly are the scaffold.

In addition to selecting figures for the narratives and the biographies who would reflect the culture of the twenties, Dos Passos continued to gather material for the Newsreels, where his intention was to suggest the increasingly frenetic and ultimately chaotic swirl of American life. And so he collected headlines, songs, and items like snippets of jargon-filled advertising for Florida real estate, whose sales he had observed during the land boom of the 1920s. "The climate breeds optimism and it is hard for pessimism to survive the bright sunshine and balmy breezes that blow from the Gulf and the Atlantic," ran one excerpt he included in Newsreel 62. He emphasized the irony of life, and more, the essential lie of the real estate blurbs in the Newsreel by following the quotation with a line from a popular song, "Oh it ain't gonna rain no more," and then two headlines: HURRICANE SWEEPS SOUTH FLORIDA, and SOUTH FLORIDA DEVASTATED ONE THOUSAND DEAD, THIRTY-EIGHT THOUSAND DESTITUTE.

In order to maintain this ironic tone and to show the direction in which the country was headed, Dos Passos faced not only the difficulty of selection, but also the difficulty of organization, a problem that he fretted about well before the manuscript for *The Big Money* was complete. Among his papers are numerous sheets that list the tentative organization of the various sections for the book, an organization substantially different from what was published in 1936.

A revealing page is headed:

THE BIG MONEY
Lives   Headliners   Camera Eye   Newsreel

followed by what he noted in the margin was a "prelude," a segment of the Charley Anderson narrative. Next came a section that Dos Passos indicated dealt with "production." "The American Plan," the biography of Frederick W. Taylor, commenced it, and it included Newsreels, a segment of the Margo Dowling narrative as well as more of Anderson's, and the Isadora Duncan, Henry Ford, and Wright brothers biographies. A brief section followed that Dos Passos indicated was about the "doldrums," including two Newsreels and single Dowling and Anderson segments. Then came the major section of the book, what he noted in the margin was "the bright lights." It was to begin with a biography that eventually did not appear, entitled NORMALCY, undoubtedly about Warren G. Harding. In this section were to be, in addition to Newsreels, portions of the narratives about Dowling, Anderson, Mary French, Ike Hall, and J. Ward Moorehouse, as well as biographies of Veblen, an OIL KING, probably John D. Rockefeller, which never appeared, and a closing one about William Randolph Hearst, POOR LITTLE RICH BOY. The final section of the book was to be about "Down under the boom," Dos Passos indicated. It was to include two segments of the French narrative, and two of Ike Hall's; Newsreels; and biographies about Frank Lloyd Wright and Huey Long, KINGFISH THE FIRST, governor of Louisiana. Dos Passos deleted the Long biography, because he decided correctly that the governor was more properly a subject of the 1930s. He filed Long away in his memory for another book, which would be entitled *Number One* when it appeared in 1943. Other lists of possible ways of organizing the material differed from this one, but always, it is clear, Dos Passos strove to mirror "production," "the bright lights," and "Down under the boom" in his presentation of the 1920s.

His and Katy's travels during the spring of 1931 and 1932 as well as his political conscience had sharpened his perception of the United States. While he planned *The Big Money,* he continued to travel, as in June 1932, when he reported for the *New Republic* about the bonus army of war veterans camped on the Anacostia Flats in the outskirts of Washington, D.C., before General Douglas MacArthur with a reckless excess of force drove them away. Dos Passos's piece, "The Veterans Come Home to Roost," was a sketch of the scene at Anacostia Flats. With sympathy he conveyed the truculence of the veterans. "We got the food, we got the clothing, we got the manpower, we got the brains," he quoted a Washington mail carrier who felt for the bonus army as saying, "there must be some remedy."

Understanding the mood of these people, Dos Passos ventured to Chicago in

June to observe the Republican and Democratic presidential conventions. As he wrote Katy, despite missing her he found the Republican Convention interesting if not always exciting. Sitting after it was over in his gloomy room in Hull House, he told her that the show's liveliest moments were when Herbert Hoover was renominated and when a foolish man attempted to nominate Calvin Coolidge, which so incensed Senator Simeon Fess that he attacked the other man. Now as Dos Passos sat in his room wondering how to write about the convention, he glanced up from his letter to Katy and stared at "the long shadows of a summer afternoon creep[ing] unutterably sadly across S. Halstead Street and down the long shell-raked side street opposite." He thought he would walk out onto the municipal pier jutting into Lake Michigan nearby to sit and think.

Although he soon felt less lonely because he made several trips away from Chicago to investigate politics and working conditions, he could not help but wish he were in Provincetown with Katy. Still, he wrote her just before the Democratic Convention, "This is all very instructive and instruction is our aim. Chicago is certainly the place to hear the great heart of America beat—and it sure is beating out something." He added, however, that nobody knew the code as yet. Others anticipated an exciting convention, but he thought it was clinched for Roosevelt. Maybe not, though, he allowed, because Al Smith had energy and money behind him. Roosevelt, of course, did receive the nomination after several days of hoopla that amused Dos Passos, whose verdict at the time was that from the average out-of-work laborer's point of view, "Hoover or Roosevelt, it'll be the same cops" who would hassle him in the name of the government's laws.

In 1932, Dos Passos was skeptical that the Democrats would be any more able to alleviate the condition of the country than had been the Republicans. He continued through the summer and fall to follow the campaigns of the candidates and observed rallies that the Republicans, Democrats, Socialists, and Communists held in New York City. He eventually voted for the Communist candidates, William Z. Foster and James W. Ford but, at least from the retrospective of 1956, he considered that nothing more than a protest vote, stemming from his "plague on both your houses attitude toward the two conflicting systems" of capitalism and Communism. After Franklin Roosevelt's landslide victory in November, Dos Passos wrote about the rallies he had attended and noted how often audiences booed. He wondered what it might mean, whether it was a purely negative expression or the voice of the forgotten man beginning to be heard in a new way. "Is the great boo of 1932 the death rattle of rugged individualism or is it the first syllable of a new word? Is the forgotten man trying to remember?" he ended his piece about the campaign rallies.

When he wrote this essay for the first issue of the journal, *Common Sense,* he had grave doubts about Roosevelt's capabilities, but the new President's immediate activism after taking office caught Dos Passos's attention. By March 1933 he was describing one of Roosevelt's fireside chats with a hint of enthusiasm. Imagining the President seated in the Blue Room of the White House, Dos Passos wrote:

He is leaning cordially toward youandme, across his desk there in Washington, telling in carefully chosen words how the machinations of chisellers are to be foiled for youandme, and how the many cylindered motor of recovery is being primed with billions for youandme, and youandme understand, we belong to billions, billions belong to us, we are going to have good jobs, good pay, protected bank deposits, we edge our chairs closer to the radio, we are flattered and pleased, we feel we are right there in the White House.

When the cordial explaining voice stops, we want to say: Thank you, Frank. . . .

When Dos Passos wrote the piece for *Common Sense*, he concluded it with a statement, "No wonder they all go to bed happy," and a question: "But what about it when they wake up and find the wagecut, the bank foreclosing just the same, prices going up on groceries at the chain stores, and the coal dealers bill . . . and that it's still raining?" Yet when the piece was published several months later in *In All Countries*, Dos Passos deleted both the statement and the question.

He dropped the irony when the essay was published the second time because, while he maintained a wait-and-see attitude, he was beginning to like what he saw. His assertion in 1956 that his vote for Foster and Ford was only a protest, was not a case of an elderly right-winger excusing youthful errors. As he had been during all of his association with the Left, he remained in 1932 skeptical of the Communist Party. Significantly, just when many observers assumed he was most deeply involved with radicalism, he was if anything drawing back, a claim that is supported by the fact that he began publishing in the independent journal *Common Sense* immediately upon its appearance. After his first essay there, he published only three more pieces in the *New Masses*, by 1932 distinctly a Communist Party organ, and none of his three contributions was a polemic for Communism. One was a restrained bit of reportage about Spain in 1933; a second was an account of a meeting of unemployed workers in Washington that occurred in February 1934; and a third, the most significant of the three, was an essay appearing in the December 15, 1936, *New Masses*, a special issue celebrating the twenty-fifth year of publishing the *Masses*, *Liberator*, and *New Masses*. Dos Passos, no longer listed as an editor, contributed an essay extolling the old *Masses*, which had been "the mouthpiece of the writers and artists of the Village." The *Masses*, he recalled, had been an integral part of "what we used to call The Movement, that upsurge of revolt against the ruling business men of which Bryan was the first messiah in the West and which took in the I.W.W., the Non-Partisan League, Progressivism, the huge growth of Eugene V. Debs's following, and the small town revolt against convention, Sunday-school teachers, and the rusty corseting of conduct left over from the Victorian era." Such "waves of popular insurgence," he continued, had from the beginning of the nation kept it a democracy. In the twenties, he recounted, an effort had been made to create a *Masses* on the same basis as before, but the time was different, and the *New Masses* had soon become "a sort of literary supplement to the *Daily Worker* . . . and [had] done a great deal to educate the country in Marxian thinking. . . ."

But in 1936 the nation was "on the upward surge of a new democratic wave," and Dos Passos, in his last words to appear in the *New Masses*, asserted that he hoped it could become attuned to that wave after breaking out of its "narrow sectarian channel." As much as being a criticism of the direction toward Communism the *New Masses* had taken, his last piece was a paean to the libertarian spirit he had consistently espoused.

While he withdrew from the *New Masses*, he continued to publish in *Common Sense*, to which other writers, leftward leaning but independent of the Communists, contributed. Among the contributors were Archibald MacLeish, Upton Sinclair, Norman Thomas, Louis Adamic, John Dewey, A. J. Muste, and Max Eastman. *Common Sense* began its existence critical of the Roosevelt administration, but its support of the New Deal grew, and as that happened, its differences with the Communist Party became more pronounced. At its inception, one of its editors, Alfred Bingham, attacked capitalism in his editorials. He called consistently for a new economic system and did not sympathize with preachments about revitalizing the one that had led to the Depression. Yet Bingham, who, as the historian Frank A. Warren has written, "was suspicious of what he considered the European dogma of the Marxist parties," did not analyze capitalism in Communist terms. He hoped for a middle-class revolt while downplaying the need for a class struggle and doubting the efficacy of violence. The stance of *Common Sense* suited Dos Passos, who from the first issue was listed for more than ten years as a contributor. Its "platform," carefully laid out on page two of the first issue, declared that it was "an independent publication devoted to the interests of the American people"; that it was "not connected with any political party"; that "a system based on competition for private profit can no longer serve the general welfare"; and that, among other matters, "the job before America is to insure a high standard of living for all by a just distribution of work and wealth." *Common Sense* espoused "the American ideals of liberty, democracy, and equality of opportunity," and it sought "a constitutional convention to adapt the principles of the American Revolution of 1776 to modern needs." Anyone seeking to understand where Dos Passos stood in the depths of the Depression should examine the attitudes expressed in Bingham's young journal.

No more willing in 1932 to throw his wholehearted support to the Communist Party than he had been earlier, yet thoroughly suspicious of capitalism, Dos Passos developed a dialogue with Edmund Wilson, who also sought political solutions. Their discussion continued into the late 1930s and, along with correspondence Dos Passos had with Jack Lawson, was even more revealing of Dos Passos's thinking than what he published. He and Wilson had discussed politics in the spring of 1930 when Dos Passos began to define himself as a middle-class liberal. In 1932, as the Depression worsened, it seemed that drastic steps needed to be taken, and a logical direction for many intellectuals was to espouse more frankly Communist ideology. Wilson, writing in the *New Republic* in February, castigated writers like Stuart Chase, Walter Lippmann, and Charles Beard for continuing to believe that capitalism could reform. "Who today in any camp on the left can have the optimism to believe that capitalism is capable of reforming itself?" Wilson demanded. "And who today can look forward with confidence to any outcome from the present chaos short of the establishment of a socialistic society. . . . Yet," he asserted about those he was berating, "these liberals, who presumably aim at socialism, still apparently pin great hopes on the capitalists." He was edging toward a stance that, although not Communist, seemed hardly different. In April he sent a draft of a manifesto to Dos Passos with a note saying that Wilson, Waldo Frank, and Lewis Mumford had shared authorship of it and were also sending it to Theodore Dreiser, Sherwood Anderson, Robert Frost, Paul Green, Van Wyck Brooks, Evelyn Scott, and Edna St. Vincent Millay. The manifesto, referring to "the present crisis of the world—and specifically of the United States—" pronounced "the imperative need for new social forms, new values, a new human order." It declared that the signers believed several "lines of action" to be essential:

a.   The ruling castes, hopelessly corrupted by the very conditions of their emergence, must be expelled from their present position.

b.   A temporary dictatorship of the class-conscious workers must be set up as the necessary instrument for abolishing all classes based on material wealth.

c.   A new order must be established, as swiftly as can be, in which economic rivalry and private profit are barred; and in which competition will be lifted from the animal plane of acquisition to the human plane of cultural creation.

As writers, the signers declared themselves "supporters of the social-economic revolution," they identified their interests "with those of the workers and farmers of the nation," and they called on other writers, artists, academics, and technicians to do likewise.

When Dos Passos received a copy of the manifesto in Provincetown in May, he suggested some changes: "abolishing all classes based on material wealth" he altered to read, "The producers [he meant workers] must get control of the machinery of production, as the necessary instrument for abolishing the power of money." And in his response to Wilson he said that the manifesto smelled "too strong of Thirteenth Street for my taste," by which he meant it sounded as if it emanated from Communist Party headquarters. He agreed to sign it, but he did not believe it would have much impact. No bankers would commit suicide, and he wondered what Wilson intended to do with it: "post it up on billboards?" It might be printed "on toilet paper like ex-lax advertizing," he teased his friend, or perhaps someone could present it to Herbert Hoover at his breakfast. Dos Passos did not like using party jargon, because, he added in all seriousness to Wilson, "the only useful function people like us can perform anyway is introduce a more native lingo into the business—and, Goddamn it, I havent enough confidence in the C.P. to give it a blanket endorsement." Unless all traces of Thirteenth Street language were eliminated, the effect of the manifesto would be to stigmatize the signers, who wished to remain independent.

Wilson took Dos Passos's words to heart. The two debated further, and in mid-June Wilson wrote Waldo Frank to explain Dos Passos's reservations. The Communist formulas, Dos Passos had asserted, did not include American white-collar workers, a large portion of the population without whom no revolution could succeed. "One ought to emphasize the identity of interests of the petty bourgeois with the proletariat rather than the possible class dictatorship of the proletariat over the bourgeoisie," Wilson noted. He added that Dos Passos thought words familiar to Americans, terms like "plutocracy," "money-power," and "democracy," were important, and he thought the manifesto ought to be entitled "An Appeal to Desk Workers."

Wilson, Dos Passos, and the others could never agree on a version of the manifesto, so it was never published. Several of them made individual statements, however, as did Dos Passos that summer of 1932 in the *Modern Quarterly*, where he responded to a questionnaire entitled "Whither the American Writers?" by asserting that American capitalism had failed, but the system had not yet col-lapsed, and he expected changes rather than its complete destruction. A writer could not avoid participating in the present social crisis, but whether or not he should follow the Communist Party line in his writing was "his own goddam business." Dos Passos did not himself see how "under present conditions" a novel-ist or historian could be a party member, because the party line restricted a writer's freedom. On the other hand, he did not think joining a less radical group like the Socialists would have any more effect on a person than "drinking a bottle of near-beer." For him proletarian literature should be—and he quoted Stalin's phrase—"national in form, proletarian in content." But the problem with the word "proletarian" was that it had come to mean "a band playing the Interna-tionale," when in fact good proletarian literature was not necessarily Marxist or revolutionary. Dreiser, Sherwood Anderson, Jack London, and Walt Whitman were all proletarian writers, he asserted, some of the world's best, in fact. "Marxi-ans who attempt to junk the American tradition, that I admit is full of dryrot as well as sap," he declared, "are just cutting themselves off from the continent. Somebody's got to have the size to Marxianize the American tradition before you can sell the American worker on the social revolution. Or else Americanize Marx." Later, when his remark about the Socialist Party was quoted in a magazine, he wrote the editor to correct what he thought was a misrepresentation that tended to make him more scornful of the Left than he was. He should be presented, he believed as "only hear[ing] thunder on the extreme left." While he and others might "cavil at the Communists," he was convinced that they were "fighting for socialism, i.e. the cooperative commonwealth."

His position, thus, was quite clear as the nation elected a new President, Franklin Roosevelt, and began an era under the New Deal. Dos Passos had doubts that capitalism merited survival; certainly it did not in the form it had taken prior to 1932. He espoused Veblen's ideas about the need for economic restructuring and the eventual leadership of a class of technicians, and he sympathized with the general aims of the Communist Party, although he was not a Communist. A fellow-traveler, perhaps, but even that might be a bit strong. He was less committed than others would have him be; yet he believed he should speak out, even though he doubted that writers could have an important, direct impact on politics. But he could take solace in that he had been consistent about what he had been saying and in that he had been involved as a writer in political causes for longer than those he saw around him who, trying to respond to the economic crisis, were now eager to take their stands.

CHAPTER TWENTY

A Spanish Summer,

1933

Despite the excitement of politics, Dos Passos's chief concern was to get on with *The Big Money.* He and Katy spent most of the fall of 1932 and early spring of 1933 on Cape Cod. In September they traveled to Percé, Quebec, on the tip of the Gaspé Peninsula, enjoying the quiet of the picturesque fishing community, and they took short trips, several to New York, and one early in 1933 to visit the Gantts in Baltimore, where on January 30 Dos Passos's Spanish friend José Robles, teaching at Johns Hopkins, joined them for dinner.

Trips away from Provincetown that winter were short not only because Dos Passos was writing, but because he and Katy were less solvent than usual. He hoped to bring in money by publishing shorter pieces such as one about the Scottsboro boys for which *Esquire* paid him a $200 advance. If he could raise the funds, he had in mind a trip to Spain during the summer because of his intense interest in the country he had not visited for nearly three years. Hemingway had repeatedly described the turbulent political situation there, and Dos Passos had high hopes for the success of the young Republic, created in 1932. Also, Hemingway during the spring of 1933 wrote him from Key West, pressing him and Katy to journey south, where they could relax and make plans for a film about Spain which was being urged on Ernest by the film director Lewis Milestone, who had been inspired by *Death in the Afternoon.* In fact, Hemingway urged, Dos Passos and Katy could join him in Key West, or better, in Cuba, where he planned to go in mid-April, and there they could work out specific plans about places and shots for the movie, then could travel together to Spain in August. He was generous, sending Dos Passos $100 and assuring him that there was more, if necessary. Further, Hemingway felt he could finance most of what would be needed to do the film about Spain.

But Dos Passos's writing and traveling plans were thrown awry when, in Baltimore early in April to be with Katy while she had a tonsillectomy, he became ill once more with rheumatic fever and had to be taken to the Johns Hopkins Hospital. The attack was severe; for a time his limbs swelled so that he was in too much pain to walk or even to write. Katy, slowly recovering from her operation, wrote Edmund Wilson a disconsolate letter. Dos Passos's case bewildered the doctors, she reported, and no one seemed to know how long a cure would take. He was thoroughly depressed despite Horsley Gantt's personal attention and assurances that the medical costs would be kept at a minimum. As late as April 24, Dos Passos still could not write, so dictated to Katy a letter for Hemingway, who immediately responded that he would send on $1,000 to help defray the expenses and pay for the trip to Spain. Dos Passos, able to write by May 3, demurred, assuring Ernest that Harcourt, Brace had promised him a thousand-dollar advance for the Spanish trip. Besides, Horsley Gantt was making the hospitalization so cheap that Dos Passos joked that he was saving money by being there. Four days later he wrote again to report that because the doctors told him he would have to remain absolutely quiet for a month or more, he did not think he and Katy could get to Havana. He mentioned that Gerald and Sara Murphy had invited them to sail to Antibes with them. Dos Passos would not be able to do that, but he did plan to stay at Villa America with them when he arrived in France somewhat later.

Despite Dos Passos's assurances that he did not need the money, Hemingway sent the $1,000, telling his friend that it was off the record and explaining that the money came from a sum Pauline's wealthy uncle had given him for a trip to Africa. The amount was not so much that Dos Passos could relax, but it could make life easier. With a fine thoughtfulness Hemingway hoped that he had not been intrusive. He had, however, been genuinely worried about Dos Passos, who conceded that the money was "an enormous convenience" because the illness was preventing him from doing the groundwork he needed for some of the articles he had planned. "I didnt want to cut into your African trip like that," he wrote Hemingway, then added in the flip, tough-guy tone he sometimes assumed with Ernest, "Jesus that means fifty less jiggs on the safari," a racial slur and an exaggeration he meant to amuse Hemingway, although other friends found the pose strained and atypical.

Dos Passos's friends were loyal during his convalescence. Scott Fitzgerald, in Baltimore to be with Zelda, who was undergoing psychiatric care, visited every few days and seemed in pretty good shape, Dos Passos told Hemingway. The Murphys sent two tickets for the trip abroad—"the wily portuguesee shakes down his friends," Dos Passos commented to Ernest. José Robles visited frequently, and Edmund Wilson was solicitous of Dos Passos's health. Wilson recommended the works of Proust to pass the time. Dos Passos followed the advice, but was not sure it was the proper remedy. After reading for a week or more, he complained to Wilson that although he had "applied hot and cold Proustian complexes to my extraverted limbs and joints," he had gotten hardly any relief. His complaint was that "the phrases are so long and iridescent and the sentences hang out of the poultice in long slightly writhing threads." Ideas ran on for hours, while "individual words and phrases are quite lifeless and have little or no therapeutic value. The sentences escape me like strands of undercooked spaghetti." But six days later he wrote Wilson again, thanking him for books he had sent and confessing that Proust had grown on him to the point that he was impatient to get to another volume. "In fact," he admitted, "I can feel a delicate mould of libido growing all through me, producing a pale fluorescence of tiny incests, tangled inferiorities, a light fuzz of thwarted desires, like you find when you open a rotten peach." He told Wilson that he had also enjoyed the early stages of Nathanael West's *Miss Lonelyhearts* but finished it "as dogeyed as if I'd been reading the New Yorker." And turning briefly to politics, Dos Passos remarked that Roosevelt continued to be "a fascinating performer . . . a sleek wire artist," whose handling of a sales tax bill had been adroit. The upshot would be "that you and me and The Forgotten Man are going to get fucked plenty," but that was almost a pleasure at the hands of Roosevelt who, "if he had false teeth and his eyes were a little further apart he'd be the spitting image of George Washington."

Obviously he was feeling better when he wrote Wilson during the middle of May. Despite Katy's being away in Provincetown to prepare Commercial Street for summer renters and despite a setback from his illness, he was cheerful because of the prospect of the trip to Europe. He knew he would have to remain quiet for a month at the Murphys, but that would be a pleasure, as would the travel subsequently through Spain. He told Hemingway that he and Katy expected to travel south through Barcelona, "mill around," and eventually leave from Vigo or Coruña in order to visit Santiago de Compostela in the northwest of Spain. They planned to rent a small car.

A week later aboard the Italian liner *Contedi Savoia* he extolled the comfort of the transatlantic voyage. He and Katy had been sleeping "twenty hours a day" and eating well. He was buoyed up by the rest and by the fact that, just before he had sailed, he signed a contract with Harcourt, Brace to do a book about the Second Republic in Spain. The volume, he joked, would be "burned by Hitler, pissed on in the Kremlin, used for toilet paper by the anarchist syndicalists, deplored by the Nation, branded by the New York Times, derided by the Daily Worker and left unread by the Great American Public." Further, to aid his expenses Arnold Gingrich of *Esquire* had sent back to him $200 which Dos Passos had returned when he knew he would not be able to write a piece about the Scottsboro boys. Gingrich wanted whatever Dos Passos chose to send him and had added $75 more for some drawings to accompany the piece.

Once in Europe in the spring of 1933, he and Katy stayed at Villa America in Antibes through June. They took short trips to spots along the French coast like Toulon and Marseilles, always one of Dos Passos's favorite places, before they traveled in July into Spain for a stay they enjoyed even if, as he later told "Cap" Pearce, his editor at Harcourt, Brace, "things in Spain politically are not as interesting as I'd thought." For the trip they bought a small, second-hand Fiat they nicknamed the "Cockroach," in which they traveled as far south as Seville, then north through Segovia to Pontevedra on the Atlantic coast, where Dos Passos recalled watching "astonishing fireworks" at the annual fiesta. The townspeople set them off with no apparent regard for safety: "the red, purple and yellow decorations —the colors of the republic—festooned around the crowded plaza went off in a delirium of flowerpost and pinwheels."

They drove west along the north coast of Spain and stopped in late July in Santander, where he and Katy witnessed a scene he took even at the time to be a portent.

There was a Socialist Party rally in the city's bullring. From all over the north of Spain people had come and crowded into the arena, where the main speaker was to be Fernando de los Rios, a cousin of José Giner Pantoja, Dos Passos's friend since his months in Spain in 1916–1917. The day was a hot Sunday in July, so the audience became somewhat wilted as the program wore on; yet its enthusiasm continued during what seemed to Dos Passos some extremely vague, idealistic speeches. But what impressed him were the two white pigeons, symbols of peace, which were to be released after the singing of the "Internationale" to open the rally. When the pigeons were freed, they could not fly and "fluttered groggily over the heads of the crowd, and crashed against the wall of the bullring." After a time one of them did manage to fly off, but the other floundered around and finally halted in the center of the bullring directly in front of the speaker's podium. During Don Fernando's speech the pathetic pigeon continued to droop before the stand, an ominous symbol of the prospects for peace, Dos Passos imagined.

"A sign and portent that was certainly not imaginary," Dos Passos wrote in *The Best Times,* was the hatred in the eyes of people who sat in the cafés watching the Socialists straggle back through the town after the rally. "Gachupines," the café watchers were called in Mexico, "people with gimlet eyes and greedy predatory lines on their faces, jerkwater importers and exporters, small brokers, loan sharks, commissionmerchants, pawnbrokers, men who knew how to make two duros grow where one had grown before." These were the people who had been scorned by the hierarchy during the Spanish monarchy. Now that had been dismantled by the Republic, and these *gachupines* felt they had achieved a new respectability. To them the Socialists were a threat. "The silent hatred of the people at the café tables was embarrassing," Dos Passos wrote as he recollected the scene in Madrid in August, 1933. "Socialists innocent as a flock of sheep in the wolf country," he scribbled in the notes he took at Santander.

When he wrote about the incident in *The Best Times,* it became a part of the sequence of episodes which ended his memoir. The absurdities he observed in Spain in 1933, but more, the vicious antagonisms of human existence worked against of the fragile Second Republic. And for Dos Passos, the brief life of the Republic before the Civil War broke out in 1936 marked the last moments of the best times, because when Franco launched his attack against the Republic, the world was headed toward another world war. More personally for Dos Passos, political turbulence was wrenching apart friendships.

He and Katy drove south to Madrid, where Dos Passos's intention was to stay there for much of their remaining time abroad while he gathered more information and began to write his short book. They tried to get together with Hemingway, who arrived in Spain in mid-August, but he was busy with his own affairs, while Dos Passos continued to be plagued by the effects of his earlier illness so they saw much less of each other than they would have liked. They did have several lunches together at Bottin's restaurant in Madrid with an old friend, Claude Bowers, then the American ambassador to Spain. While Hemingway talked about that part of Spain which interested him—bullfights, art, and the Spanish people—Dos Passos expounded on the merits of the Second Republic. Bowers added his opinions, but Hemingway would have little or nothing to do with political conversations. "These lunches," Dos Passos recalled, "were the last time Hem and I were able to talk about things Spanish without losing our tempers."

When he was well enough, Dos Passos remained busy in Madrid collecting materials. He toured the royal palace, then the National Palace under the Republic, whose officials had appointed José Giner a curator. While Giner took Katy and Dos Passos through the palace, he told them the history of King Alfonso's abdication, which had been abrupt and almost entirely peaceful. He knew the story in detail, and as he recited each incident, he showed his friends where it had occurred. He also described to them how, when he was taking an inventory of the possessions in the palace, he had come across the Spanish crown "in a green baize bag stuffed into an old clothes closet."

Dos Passos obtained interviews with Manuel Azaña, then the Prime Minister, and with the famous philosopher Miguel Unamuno. Azaña, who was formal but courteous, spoke to Dos Passos about the stable condition of Spain. The aim of the Republican government was to distribute the country's wealth among all the people. After Azaña finished, Dos Passos asked him about Stalin, Hitler, and the Fascist movements in other European countries. Would the Pyrenees be able to block out "the murderous hatreds that were sweeping Europe?" Azaña was confident they would. Spain, after all, "had escaped the uncivilizing influence" of the World War, and he felt sure that the nation's backwardness in certain aspects would make it undesirable to the aggressive forces across the Pyrenees. "I left him feeling profoundly unhappy," Dos Passos remembered.

In some ways his talk with Unamuno was little more satisfactory. The philosopher did not speak about the Republic, but asked only, "Where are the great men?" He preferred to talk about Portuguese literature which had influenced him, and he wondered why it had not Dos Passos, whose ancestry was Portuguese.

Dos Passos's unease about the situation in Spain remained throughout his and Katy's stay, and a final incident with their Fiat shortly before they were to depart from Gibraltar for the United States seemed if not to emphasize the ineffectuality of the Republican government, then to stress the absurdity of the human predicament, which could be as humorous as it was painful. Before they were to sail aboard the *Exchorda* at the end of September, they put the Cockroach up for sale in Madrid. *"Cochecito á vender,"* ran their ad in the newspapers. Dos Passos had taken sick once more with rheumatic fever, so he lay in bed in the Hotel Alfonso, where he talked to prospective buyers while Katy served the sherry. No one would pay the asking price until an army lieutenant announced he would, but wanted to drive the car first. Dos Passos readily agreed, and the young man departed, assuring Dos Passos he would be back shortly. He did not return, however, and a day later Dos Passos called the police, who sent a plainclothes officer to get information. After another day, the policeman telephoned with the news that the car had been located and was resting in the courtyard of the home affairs office on the Puerto del Sol. Immediately thereafter another army officer came into the Dos Passoses' room. He was a captain, the brother of the erring lieutenant. The captain apologized for his brother and pleaded with Dos Passos not to bring charges. As the car was recovered and there was now another buyer for it, Dos Passos agreed not to so that he could end the whole matter before leaving. But when he requested that the police return his car, they politely declined, telling him they must have it as evidence against the lieutenant once he was located. He could not be found, however, and the Fiat remained where it was. The last Dos Passos and Katy ever saw of it, it sat safe and absurd, swathed in chickenwire so that it could not be moved from the courtyard of the government building. "The idiotic series of incidents," wrote Dos Passos, "began to seem to me . . . illustrations of the human predicament." Amused when not furious, he and Katy departed on a night train for Gibraltar.

"Summer was pretty much of a fracaso," a failure, Dos Passos told Hemingway once he had returned to Provincetown in October. He had been "sick as hell" in Gibraltar, but the voyage home had helped, and now he felt "weak but damn well." He had been given a medical exam in Boston and had been assured that no permanent damage had been done to his system. Rest and time were what he required. Once back in the United States, he sensed that life "is funny as hell under the Blue Eagle—but the chances are it wont be so funny after awhile when the boys really start to clamp down. . . . Things are certainly going to get worse," he was sure, because business was dropping off, and Congress in January 1934 would be fighting any signs of inflation. New government codes were hogtying labor, the result being that the businessmen who ran the monopolies were "in full control of the situation." Roosevelt was clever, Dos Passos conceded, but the President could not "sit on the lid indefinitely," and eventually he would "have to give up the stage to more muscular and preposterous forms of hooey."

As for himself, Dos Passos was busy. Cap Pearce wrote at the end of October inquiring how the book on Spain was progressing, as Harcourt, Brace needed to plan its spring list. Dos Passos immediately responded and apologized for not having written earlier. His illness had "considerably hampered my work in Spain," he told Pearce. "As I was laid up a good deal of the time I was not able to do half the traveling I'd intended." Because of this and because Spain was less interesting politically than he had expected, he would have to change the character of the book. He thought he might entitle it *The Republic of Honest Men*, but planned to include pieces about Russia, Mexico, Chicago, Detroit, and Washington under the National Relief Administration (NRA) as well as what he had written during the summer about Spain. The contents of the book, when it was published in April 1934, were as he had described them to Pearce. The title, however, was wisely altered to the more appropriate *In All Countries,* while the section about Spain was called "The Republic of Honest Men."

As he tried to get rid of his ill health, the best remedy was Provincetown that fall. Edmund Wilson once said to his daughter Rosalind that Cape Cod was where Dos Passos could get his feet on the ground. The house at 571 Commercial Street was what they considered home. It was the "family" house; Bill Smith, Katy's brother, also lived there until 1933, when he moved to New York. He and Katy had bought the house, which had been a ship chandler's shop, after Bill returned from Paris in 1926. With the help of a carpenter, he had added on to it substantially. The kitchen was below the main floor, which was at street level, and there was a second floor above. A spacious living room lined with bookshelves looked out over a terrace and Provincetown harbor beyond. After Dos Passos and Katy took it over, they mounted on the side facing the harbor twin nameplates which read "Delight." Dos Passos enjoyed gardening, so he planted around the terrace and even had a small garden in the narrow strip of earth between 571 and 565, the next house nearer toward the center of town. He and Katy bought 565, in fact, and Edith Foley Shay, Katy's longtime friend, lived there for many years with her husband Frank.

The house on Commercial Street could seem idyllic when Provincetown was quiet. Next door were close friends, while others lived nearby. Dos Passos and Katy, Rosalind Wilson recalled vividly, were social people who liked talk and drinks. His routine was to write from early in the morning until about 2:00 P.M., when he would emerge from the room where he worked. During the afternoon he sailed in the harbor, gardened, or took long walks, sometimes going as far as Wellfleet, more than ten miles distant, although if he journeyed that far, he might take the train part of the way. To their Provincetown friends, it was clear that Katy and Dos Passos shared intimately their lives at home. She, although not readily domestic, was so for his sake, and the result of her care was that to their friends he did not seem to be a moody artist ready to race off at a moment's notice as he had appeared to Wilson to be during the 1920s. Married to Katy and settled in Provincetown, Dos Passos was sociable, charming, polite, and just a touch distracted. Edith Foley's sisters Isabel and Pat remembered him, during one afternoon gathering of friends, talking animatedly with a cup of tea in one hand and a drink in the other.

It was during the fall of 1933 after Dos Passos's return from Spain that the novelist Robert Cantwell met him at the offices of the *New Republic* in New York. Several years later, perhaps at the time of the publication of *U.S.A.* in 1938, Cantwell described him in a sketch. Dos Passos, wrote Cantwell, "had a strange goodnatured agitated gesture when he spoke—he ducked his head sideways, grinned, stuttered a little and then said what he wanted to say. Unlike most nervous people, however, he did not seem constrained or on guard—it was just that he encountered a certain difficulty in getting his words under way." Cantwell was impressed by Dos Passos's politeness, good nature, honesty, and by the "slight importance" he placed on his own opinions. He was an attentive listener who, if he disagreed, did so tentatively and usually obliquely. When Cantwell told Dos Passos that he was having trouble writing a novel, Dos Passos stuttered a good bit, then volunteered to look at the manuscript, a gesture Cantwell took to be because of kindness rather than because Dos Passos wanted to see the work in progress. The portrait of Dos Passos at mid-career seems accurate, and to it should only be added the observation of Charles Mayo, a younger friend of Dos Passos's from Provincetown. The writer, Mayo believed, struck others—as he struck Cantwell—as being benign, almost soft because of his politeness and gentle stammer when conversation put him off. Yet underneath was a forceful, even opinionated man.

CHAPTER TWENTY-ONE

Key West, Hollywood, and Political Disagreements, 1934

Eager to be in Key West, Dos Passos and Katy departed Provincetown at the end of February 1934. They planned to remain there into May with the hope that the warm weather would cure him once and for all of rheumatic fever, vestiges of which recurred. He had had to delay a trip to Washington in January because of illness, but it was not so severe that he was not able to travel there a few weeks later to gather material for more articles about the New Deal administration. He was pressed to complete these pieces because they were also to constitute the last portions of *In All Countries,* scheduled for publication in April.

It was with relief at the prospect of getting away from the cold that they left Provincetown, stopped in New York, then about February 25 took a steamship to Savannah, from where they drove the rest of the way to Key West. By March 8 they were settled in an unglamorous, small house at 1401 Pine Street, away from the water but comfortable. "Key West is pleasant but we miss you like hell," Dos Passos wrote Hemingway that day. Ernest and Pauline were on their way to France from Africa, where they had been on safari, and Dos Passos bemoaned their absence, although "sun and salt water are proving beneficial to the elderly joints." He reported that he was "drowned in proofs" so had not yet fished, but would once that reading chore was completed. The proofs he was correcting were those for *In All Countries* and *Three Plays,* which Harcourt, Brace planned to publish in May. *Three Plays* included a revised version of *The Moon Is a Gong* (now titled *The Garbage Man*), *Airways, Inc.,* and *Fortune Heights,* an eminently forgettable play along the same thematic lines as *Airways, Inc. Fortune Heights* was produced by the Chicago Workers' Theatre in 1934 and the same year received two productions in Russia. *Three Plays,* however, was a landmark only in the sense that it signaled the end of

Dos Passos's attempts to write dramas, a decision that few challenged. The plays simply were not superior theater; caricatures and dialogue overladen with social messages hurt their dramatic impact. "However bad the American theater may be, it is not, to speak bluntly, anything like as bad as it would be if it were devoted chiefly to dramas like those which [Dos Passos] supplies," wrote Joseph Wood Krutch about them in June.

In March, after Dos Passos had mailed the proofs back to Cap Pearce, he was able to relax and enjoy the warmth of Key West. He and Katy fished, then enjoyed the company of the Hemingways, who returned in mid-April from their African journey. Ernest, delighted to be back, took his friends out in Bra Saunders's new boat, which Ernest rented every other day. What made the last half of April especially pleasant was that other mutual friends of the Dos Passoses and Hemingways were in Key West as well: the Murphys, Ada MacLeish, Dawn Powell and her husband, Esther (Andrews) and Canby Chambers, and the Charles Thompsons, who lived there. Hemingway proposed to Dos Passos that they take a trip to Havana for the May Day celebration. They did, returning to Key West "in mildly alcoholic melancholy" after two unsuccessful fishing expeditions for marlin, and after finding Ernest's Cuban friends discouraged about Fulgencio Batista's new regime.

Being in Key West gave Dos Passos enough distance to remain calm about a political imbroglio which arose that spring. On February 16, members of the Communist Party disrupted a Socialist Party rally in Madison Square Garden. He had not attended the rally but willingly endorsed a protest against the disruption when asked to do so. "An Open Letter to the Communist Party," signed by twenty-five writers and intellectuals of the non-Stalinist Left, appeared in the March 6 issue of the *New Masses*. The letter, protesting "the disruptive action of the Communist Party which led to the breaking up of the meeting called by the Socialist Party in Madison Square Garden of February 16th," was answered in the same issue by an editorial entitled "To John Dos Passos." The *New Masses* editors pleaded with him to get clear of the strange company of signers like Edmund Wilson, Lionel Trilling, John Chamberlain, Robert Morss Lovett, Clifton Fadiman, and other "vacillating intellectuals" who flitted from one political position to another. The disruption, asserted the *New Masses*, had been the natural response to Socialist vituperation. "To us," the editorial concluded, "you have been and, we hope, still are, Dos Passos the revolutionary writer, the comrade."

Edmund Wilson late in March mailed to Dos Passos in Key West some of the correspondence which had subsequently appeared in the *New Masses* concerning the protest and editorial response. Dos Passos told Wilson that he had written a short answer to the editorial, but that the editors had not seen fit to publish it yet. They soon printed it as part of a further editorial in which they declared that they had not been sufficiently discriminating about whom they embraced as allies. They had foolishly counted on vacillating literary intellectuals, persons who eventually were detrimental to the Communists because they moved from "extreme nihilism, individual anarchism, Bohemianism, skirting sometimes the edges of Communism, through Trotskyism, Lovestoneism, social-democracy to N.R.A. and thence onward to Fascism." The signers of the open letter, the *New Masses* said, were displeased with capitalism, but thought they could immediately be spokesmen for the movement they had joined. In his letter to the *New Masses* Dos Passos wrote that his reason for signing the protest letter was his "growing conviction that only a drastic change of policy and of mentality can save the radical movement in this country from the disastrous defeats suffered in Italy, Germany, Austria and Spain." He hoped for "a workers' and producers' commonwealth," but feared the "unintelligent fanaticism" that the disruption in Madison Square Garden reflected. After quoting his letter, the *New Masses* implied that apparently he had fallen into the same pattern as had the other signers. Likening him to Maxim Gorky during the early days of the Revolution in Russia, the editors hinted that Dos Passos had permitted "vestiges of liberal humanitarianism to obscure the harsh inevitability of class warfare." The editors regretted this but hoped that he would soon see his error.

To Wilson, Dos Passos remarked that his own letter responding to the *New Masses* editorial addressed to him was not to be construed as an endorsement of the Socialists, who were "bums" also. He now believed that "the whole Marxian radical movement is in a moment of intense disintegration" and all that persons like him or Wilson, who chose not to be political leaders, could do was "to sit on the sidelines and try to put a word in now and then for the underdog or for the cooperative commonwealth or whatever." Dos Passos remained convinced that the Marxists were correct in their analysis of conditions, but everything they did helped the opposition. Americans, it seemed to him, had but two choices: either "go to the stake" with the Marxists, or support a "passionate unmarxian revival of AngloSaxon democracy on an industrial basis helped by a collapse in the directors' offices." Such a movement, he believed, would differ significantly from Nazi Socialism as a reaction against Communism because the democratic revival would be toward a kind of egalitarian system that he called "old time Fourth of July democracy," while Fascism was a movement back toward feudalism. But the United States lacked a feudal tradition, so he could not believe that the nation would turn toward "feudal habits" —despotism—as the Germans had turned when they permitted Adolf Hitler to gain power.

"How you can coordinate Fourth of July democracy with the present industrial-financial setup I dont see," he concluded. "Maybe Roosevelt is already as far as we can go in that direction." Then, with an ambivalence that was typical yet odd in the light of his misgivings about the Communists, he added, "But if you dont put your money on the Communists—it's no use putting it on anybody else until they've proved something." He found himself on the horns of a dilemma that Wilson could appreciate. It was not so different from what Dos Passos had earlier thought, but the Madison Square Garden incident and his response to it marked another step back from the Communists. The movement seemed to be disintegrating, while Roosevelt had promise. So while he asserted that one ought for the moment to continue putting his money on the Communists, Dos Passos was less inclined to do it than he had been.

His political dilemma soon produced a heated discussion with Jack Lawson that was to end five years later with their friendship ruptured. During the early 1930s Lawson had appeared to be in a kind of political limbo, caught between the demands of his screenwriting in Hollywood, the "progressive" stance he had taken in the twenties, and the politics of committed Communists like Mike Gold. Although in retrospect Lawson could believe that his first years in Hollywood had contributed to his education, until 1934 he did not appear unduly dissatisfied with what he later referred to as "the ruthless and irresponsible methods of production which prevented writers from dealing honestly and creatively with their work." He had, however, labored to organize the Screen Writers Guild, of which he had been elected the first president in 1933.

Lawson faced his own dilemma: Hollywood films conveyed little or nothing of the social messages he favored. Yet his work in drama, where he hoped he could make these clear, was not well received by the left wing. After the closing of the New Playwrights Theatre in 1929, he had written a play, *Success Story*, which opened in September 1932. The drama evinced his criticism of materialistic society and implied that a person ought to make a political commitment, but left-wing critics disapproved of the play, Mike Gold asserting later that it was no more than "the mask for an overwhelming craving for money and bourgeois success." Lawson, thus, felt pressure to clarify his own political ideology, and in 1934 he attempted this clarification in correspondence with Dos Passos.

After Lawson had read the play *Fortune Heights*, he wrote Dos Passos in January, offering criticisms such as he had heard about his own work. The themes in *Fortune Heights* were murky, he protested, and the play introduced "all sorts of social ideas" while having "a very strong unresolved social content which isn't worked out ideologically." He assured Dos Passos that he did not take "a stiff Marxian Stalinist attitude," but then exploded, "Christ Almighty, it seems to me obvious that if you undertake certain revolutionary problems—evictions, the hunger march, things that are part and parcel of the whole life around us—you've got to have some revolutionary ground on which to stand." He resented Dos Passos's "inconclusiveness," reflected in "the fact that, although the play contains a revolutionary hypothesis, three quarters of it are concerned with a semi-satirical picture of middleclass break-down, that it ends up with an ironical defeatist twist, and that the Proletarian angle is ignored!" Dos Passos had shortly before criticized Lawson for his most recent plays, *The Pure in Heart* and *Gentlewoman,* which Dos Passos —rightly, Lawson conceded—thought were "removed from life." Lawson was groping toward a firmer ideological ground. "I'm not at all sure I know *how* to write the Proletarian plays which I am thinking about," he confessed, "but I feel there's got to be *something said* besides the pathos of middle-class breakdown." The pathos lent power on occasion to *Fortune Heights,* he admitted. Yet it was not enough; "the sense of groping is not enough," and "phrases (which might be interesting if developed) about 'finding the United States' are not enough." To which, Lawson acknowledged, Dos Passos might reply, "This is exactly the stage at which people find themselves." But Lawson did not believe that; he was sure that there was "a great deal more stirring."

More accurately than perhaps Lawson knew, he was defining exactly where Dos Passos found himself. Lawson, unlike his friend, was on the verge early in 1934 of making a deep commitment to Communism. He was stung once by the failures of *The Pure in Heart* and *Gentlewoman*, both of which had only brief runs on Broadway during March, and stung again by the attack of Mike Gold, who upon the appearance of the two plays immediately branded Lawson "A Bourgeois Hamlet of Our Time." The 1925 play, *Processional*, Gold wrote in the *New Masses*, had been futilitarian. Now, almost ten years later, Lawson was "still lost like Hamlet, in his inner conflict. Through all his plays wander a troop of ghosts disguised in the costumes of living men and women and repeating the same monotonous question: 'Where do I belong in this warring world of two classes?' " To the question, "What have you learned in these ten years?" Lawson, according to Gold, had to respond, "Nothing. I am still a bewildered wanderer lost between two worlds indulging myself in the same adolescent self-pity as in my first plays." Gold hammered away at his target: "To be a 'great' artist," he declared, "one must greatly believe in something," but Lawson had "no real base of emotion or philosophy," nor had he "purified his mind and heart."

One might expect Lawson to have come back fighting, but he did not. While acknowledging privately to Dos Passos that he resented "the idea of my friends that either Hollywood or 'Gentlewoman' were making inroads on my fundamental plan to use the theatre as a medium for revolutionary expression," he began issuing what amounted to mea culpas. Gold's attack had been "bitter and exceedingly dirty," he told Dos Passos and added that his answer was "what I think is a reasonable statement of my position." But instead of struggling against Gold's accusations, Lawson concluded his letter to Dos Passos by acknowledging that he felt "very strongly the necessity of a much closer contact with Communism, and much more activity in connection with it."

In the issue of the *New Masses* following that in which Gold's attack appeared, Lawson responded. He admitted the truth of 70 percent of the criticism but remarked in his defense that for persons like himself, "a genuine acceptance of the proletarian revolution is a difficult task. The majority of American fellow-travellers are struggling with the problem of their own orientation," he continued, noting that it was "strikingly evident in the work of John Dos Passos, which combines great revolutionary fervor with all sorts of liberal and individualistic tendencies." Lawson also offered in his defense that, regardless of the inadequacy of his works' political orientation, he was demonstrating an "ideological advance." *Gentlewoman*, he claimed, despite its faults, was "a play [along Marxian lines] about a dying bourgeois class."

He did not end his confessions here, however. He moved with the fervor of a religious convert, reevaluating his work, joining the party, and accepting blame for his past ideological failures. From this point on the rift between him and Dos Passos grew as the latter refrained more and more from any fellow-traveling. The seeds of the rift had already been planted by early 1934 when Lawson criticized *Fortune Heights*. Then during that spring or early summer they exchanged more correspondence. Dos Passos, in a letter that offended Lawson, blamed the failure of Lawson's plays, as well as the intolerance of the left wing, partly on what he termed "New York neo-ghetto ignorance." "The whole New York jewish theatre guild, Damrosch, Otto Kahn, Mike Gold culture (I mean jewish in the best sense)," Dos Passos asserted, "is an echo of the liberal mitteleuropa culture that has just bitten the dust with such a fearful crash in Europe." This left people only their "feudal reflexes," he believed, which took the forms of Mussolini and Hitler. The United States, on the other hand, lacked "feudal reflexes"; rather, it would fall back on a conservatism reflected by "desire under the cemetery elms, lynching bees, General Motors and the Ford car" when a political reaction such as had hit Europe set in. He felt that what was now happening in America was a retreat away from Socialism, and he preferred the retreat to occur within the framework of politics native to the U.S., rather than within a Communist structure or under the aegis of the Communist Party, whose "New York jewish leadership" was indulging in a foolish delirium of martyrdom. He told Lawson he had not seen Mike Gold's remarks, but could imagine them. What he referred to as "the whole Marxist-German socialist and Russian Jewish communist [movement]" seemed to be "frittering away into vicious and childish nonsense." Recently he had been reading the I.W.W. weekly, and he confessed that he still felt more in common with its line than with any other.

Lawson's response was an impassioned, thirteen-page, typed letter which began, "I am extremely disturbed by what you say about the Communists and the general situation. . . . I think you're terrifically wrong in this approach. . . . For Christ's sake, Dos," Lawson burst forth, "we're seeing the death-throes of Capitalism, and we're seeing it take the most brutal and bloody fascist forms in order to preserve itself a little longer." Lawson went on at length to refute his friend's views about the American scene, the Communist Party, its leadership, and its mentality. Dos Passos's views about the Jewish mind pained him; moreover, they were narrow and simplistic. To Lawson, only the Communist Party with its grounding in Marxist theory stood truly for the working class. Liberals, Socialists, and men like Edmund Wilson were nothing but "propagandists for the bloodiest reaction."

As Lawson wrote on, his passion mounted. In the full heat of his new commitment he lectured Dos Passos:

> You and myself and all the people we know, people like ourselves, are individualists, and we're soft, and we're not particularly given to accepting any kind of discipline. I feel that the Communists have the fullest justification for their distrust of the intellectuals—and the first thing for someone like myself to learn is to choose a line and then be damned humble and damned disciplined about it.

Lawson told Dos Passos that at a meeting he had attended members of the audience had accused Dos Passos of "consorting with their enemies" by writing for *Common Sense*, which they said was "directly aiming toward fascism." They were right, asserted the committed Lawson, for whom "the day of *general* revolutionary tendencies is past." And, separating himself from the majority of leftist American writers, he declared:

> The Dreisers and Sherwood Andersons and Bunny Wilsons and Archibald MacLeishes and Hemingways and Menckens and Nathans and Heywood Brouns and Calvertons and Eugene O'Neills and Roger Baldwins and Sidney Howards—The whole caboodle of 'em are lining up exactly where they belong —in the name of their aesthetic integrity, they're serving fascism and war and Jew-baiting and negro-baiting. A few of 'em will find out they made a mistake and start to scream like stuck pigs—when it's too late.

Finally he closed his letter, first reiterating his own plans to work closely with the Communists, become involved in strike activity, and accept party discipline. Then he ended with a sort of plea to his friend, whom he, like many other people, thought to be a leader of the committed, even Communist, literary Left:

> You've always (far more than myself) followed a revolutionary idea—it seems to me that now you (and all of us) are faced with a clear-cut revolutionary choice. I maintain that there is only one revolutionary line and one revolutionary party (Be as sentimental as you like about the Wobblies, but they do not represent the working class, or any portion of it, in a modern sense). And what's needed now is not sentimental adherence, but the will to fight a disciplined difficult fight.

There the matter stood. The two men saw each other infrequently during the next years and corresponded little until 1937, when after the publication of *The Big Money* Lawson discussed with Dos Passos the possibility of a movie based on the Charley Anderson narrative. The embers of their political differences, substantial by then, heated up, then simmered until 1939, when the flare-up became so intense that the friendship was burned out.

Had Lawson been in Hollywood late in the summer of 1934, he would have been able to see Dos Passos, and perhaps they could have talked through their differences. But Lawson was in the East in conjunction with the production of his plays and with his political activities, so when in July Dos Passos flew to Hollywood to work for Paramount Studios, their paths did not cross. Dos Passos's opportunity to work for films had come up suddenly. "I've just signed up to serve a term of five weeks in Hollywood teaching Spanish or something like that to Von Sternberg," he wrote Hemingway on July 27, referring to the director Joseph von Sernberg, for whom he was to work on the film *The Devil Is a Woman,* which was to star Marlene Dietrich. Dos Passos had found himself at a convenient stopping place in his work, he told Hemingway, so he had decided to try screenwriting, hoping that it might restore his finances while at the same time he could have a look at "the world's great bullshit center." His plane trip, requiring a change into an aged Ford Trimotor at Salt Lake City, took twenty-two hours. Groggy from airsickness and fatigue, he arrived in Los Angeles and went straight to the Hollywood Plaza Hotel. He was lonely; Katy planned to join him later but had remained behind in Provincetown. Nevertheless, he commented to Hemingway, he supposed the trip would be educational, and for his work he needed the sort of thing he was experiencing. But in the short time he had been in Hollywood when he wrote Ernest, he had found it less entertaining than he had expected. "People you meet out here greet you with a nasty leer like the damned in Dante's Inferno," he declared, although he could not yet see why they had such uneasy consciences.

He was amused by von Sternberg, who, Dos Passos later claimed, had been born Joe Stern in Brooklyn but in Hollywood played the role of Austrian nobility. While discussing their film project, he reminisced about a Vienna which Dos Passos asserted neither had even seen. Von Sternberg was friendly, as were Donald Ogden Stewart, who immediately paid a visit, and Francis Faragoh, Dos Passos's codirector from the New Playwrights Theatre. But these friendships were not enough to cheer him when, shortly after his arrival, he had another attack of rheumatic fever. He took to his hotel bed, where he was miserable, being attended by what he claimed to Katy were "phoney Russian waiters who bring up phoney Russian food from the restaurant downstairs." His bad spirits were not restored by the flowers Marlene Dietrich sent him, nor even very much by the Faragohs' kindness at the end of July in taking him into their home at 1644 North Orange Grove Avenue, a large, comfortable place a few blocks off Sunset Boulevard. Then to add to his misery, he heard early in August from Katy that she was on her way to Columbia, Missouri, to be with her father, who was gravely ill. She arrived in Columbia just in time on August 5; he died the next day from complications arising from a mouth infection. Before Katy could travel to Hollywood, she had to settle her father's estate; so for the next two weeks she remained in Missouri, helping her older brother Y.K. to clear up details.

Dos Passos's mood improved when Katy arrived after the middle of August and when the fever began to subside. But the brief experience of being among Hollywood's big money was a disappointment. Most of the time until Dos Passos and Katy on October 6 boarded ship for a voyage to Panama and eventually to Havana he remained bedridden at the Faragohs'. Shortly after Katy appeared he wrote Edmund Wilson to describe his various misadventures and acknowledged that, despite remaining on Paramount's payroll, "je ne suis pas heureux ici." By the time he left in October, his attitude had changed little. He had only a few chances to observe Hollywood life and the operations of the film studios, he wrote Wilson late in September, and he felt particularly useless because he had discovered at the end of his stint with von Sternberg that during the entire time another writer—he thought the man's name was Nertz—was writing the actual screenplay.

The best that could be said for his stay in Hollywood was that he had gathered some impressions of a southern California just emerging as a symbol of the new American social order which he meant to satirize in *The Big Money*. His acquaintance with von Sternberg and Marlene Dietrich became the basis of a part of the Margo Dowling narrative, while his distaste for the film industry and the glamorization of its stars caused him to pick Rudolph Valentino as the subject for a biographical sketch in which Dos Passos satirized the nation's willingness to make an idol of a vapid, if handsome, personality.*

While lying in bed at the Faragohs' he had the chance to read and to think more about the Communists' situation in the United States. As he backed off from the party line, he objected increasingly to their defining as fascistic any political position that did not conform to their orthodoxy. "Frankly," he wrote Robert Cantwell in September, "I dont see all this fatalism about fascism on the part of the communists. If you mean repressive violence, sure, we've always had that tougher than anywhere," he asserted, adding that William Randolph Hearst's demagoguery set a kind of example for "handsome Adolph." Dos Passos, however, could not envision "fascism organized into the state" because such a form of government was not in the society's background. Once more he brought forth his interpretation of history as the basis of his analysis of the situation in the United States. A pattern of feudalism had to be "in the social heritage to make it stick— and that's one thing we haven't got. What turns out in Mussolini & Hitler in semifeudal Europe (Germany & Italy only date from 1870 as pseudomodern nations) in this country turns out in Al Capone-Bilbo-Huey Long Upton Sinclair-Franklin D, the noblest Roman of them all." Such diverse types, he believed, could never be molded into a fascist state. He did not mean to imply that the monopolies would not exert power over the country, but he thought that there was "more life in the debris of democracy" than the Communists imagined. Their problem was that, involved with industry, they could see only the situations in factory towns which the industrial leadership had closed up tight. But beyond these repressive situations Dos Passos thought he saw vitality in democratic institutions, and what needed to be done was for some political movement to mobilize that vitality. At the moment both Communism and Socialism ran counter to the basic instinct of millions of Americans toward democracy. Instead of opposing all groups that did not concur with the party line, the Communists ought to respond to the desires of most Americans, create a program of broader appeal, and with popular support take control away from the monopolists.† "Americanize Marx," as he had written two years earlier, was his point, although soon he would turn away from Marxism.

He spent much of his time while an invalid reading the writings of Thorstein Veblen, whose ideas played an important part in his thinking as he moved further away from Communist orthodoxy. Veblen had been an influence since the 1920s, but during Dos Passos's illness in Hollywood, he read "a good deal of Veblen," he wrote Edmund Wilson. More and more Dos Passos admired Veblen's "delicate

*A comparison of Marlene Dietrich's background with the story his fictional film director Sam Margolies creates as part of the publicity buildup for Margo reveals how Dos Passos drew from his knowledge of Dietrich.
†Dos Passos's ambivalence, understandably frustrating to those seeking his firm political commitment, cannot be overstressed. At the same time as he discussed the futilitarian tactics of the Communists, he could assert in response to a question about his loyalties, "I'm not a communist, though I have sympathy and admiration for much they do."

surgeon's analysis," which might be the only thinking of an American economist that would have any permanent value. Dos Passos urged his friend to read widely in Veblen as Wilson worked on the series of essays that later became *To the Finland Station*. "There certainly seems to me to be more ammunition in [Veblen's] analysis than in any other for us," Dos Passos told Wilson, "because he seems to have been the only man of genius who put his mind critically to work on American capitalism." Veblen was important to Dos Passos for the reason that, as one intellectual historian has noted, "Dos Passos found Veblen's masquerade of solemnity and satire congenial, and Veblen's ability to question everything and promise nothing fascinated [Dos Passos]," who made the economist's ideas the core of what he wanted to say in *The Big Money*. It was Veblen's technicians, not party regulars, who might revitalize the United States by wresting control from the monopolies.

That October Dos Passos and Katy boarded a Fruit Line ship in Los Angeles bound for Cuba. Despite his writing to Scott Fitzgerald, once he and Katy were established in the Hotel Ambos Mundos in Havana, that he thought California was "funny" and that he had "liked it fine," they had been relieved to leave. Screenwriters were to Dos Passos a strange crowd while other Hollywood types—"racketeers, three card men etc"—were amusing oddities. So he felt relieved to be on familiar ground again, especially because when he and Katy reached Havana, Hemingway was there, in good spirits from the pleasure of having his own fishing boat, the *Pilar*. When the Dos Passoses arrived, Ernest was excited about fishing and particularly about his attempt to catch a humpbacked whale, which he had harpooned for a moment before it broke away. The friends spent a week together before Hemingway took the *Pilar* back across the Gulf Stream to Key West on October 26.

Dos Passos was interested in the Cuban political situation—"a sort of social laboratory" he called Havana—but he was still too invalided to see much of it. He and Katy remained until around November 10, when they crossed to Key West. Dos Passos's plan was to remain in Key West for a month or more while Katy traveled to Boston to enter a hospital for a series of tests, probably to seek the causes for the several miscarriages she had experienced. Then, after she had returned to Key West, they planned a trip even farther south in hopes of curing his lingering illness.

Despite Dos Passos's assertion to Gerald and Sara Murphy that Hemingway had been "in wonderful shape" and Katy's to the Murphys a month later that he "was translated when seen in Havana," Ernest was critical of Dos Passos, whose integrity he thought had been compromised by going to Hollywood to write for the films. Katy reminded the Murphys of "how irascible and truculent" Hemingway was when they had all been together in Key West the previous spring. In Havana in October, he seemed to be "a big cage of canaries, looking fine, too—and followed around all the time by a crowd of Cuban zombies who think he is Hernan Cortez. He was sweet," she added, "but had a tendency to be an Oracle I thought and needs some best pal and severe critic to tear off those long white whiskers which he is wearing." When she and Dos Passos were around him, they attempted to play that role, and there were still good times as there had been before. But, Dos Passos recalled, "things got rocky between Ernest and me more often than they used to."

Hemingway's irritability toward them, Dos Passos admitted, might have been as much their fault as Hemingway's, because they kidded him about his poses as "the famous author, the great sportsfisherman, the mighty African hunter," but he was less and less willing to accept what they meant to be gestures of friendship. He approved rather more of their playing up to him, as when he would retire to bed with a sore throat before supper, and they, Pauline, and whoever else might be visiting would take him drinks in his *lit royale,* as Dos Passos and Katy called his bedroom, where the company would eat their suppers on trays.

Such kindnesses, however, did not prevent Ernest from making snide comments about Dos Passos. "Poor Dos got rich [in Hollywood]," he complained unfairly to one friend and probably about the same time scribbled a note to himself that "Marx the whimpering bourgeois living on the bounty of Engels is exactly as valid as Dos Passos living on a yacht in the Mediterranean while he attacks the capitalist system," the reference being to Dos Passos and Katy's stay with the Murphys at Cap d'Antibes during the late spring and early summer of 1933. In addition, Hemingway had begun his tales about Harry Morgan, which became the core of *To Have and Have Not,* published in 1937. Hemingway identified with Morgan, the tough, independent Key West fisherman who was driven to crime by the economic system. But Morgan was always honest with himself, unlike one of the villains of the novel—a character who served as a contrast—the radical writer Richard Gordon, a pathetic figure whom Arnold Gingrich thought so much like Dos Passos that he warned Hemingway of the possibility of libel after reading the manuscript of the book.

Hemingway's rancor extended beyond Dos Passos, who was but one among several victims of it. In Dos Passos's case, Ernest became critical partly because he envied Dos Passos's success as a political novelist while he, Ernest, was being criticized for not abandoning his apolitical, solitary position. Moreover, Dos Passos's meek good nature irritated the bellicose Hemingway, more and more prone to bully the people around him. Dos Passos was not a special target in 1934, but he happened to be in Key West, and for Ernest, then and in the years to follow, familiarity began to breed contempt.

Yet such a suggestion makes the first cracks in their friendship seem more severe than they were in the autumn of 1934. Hemingway and Dos Passos could still enjoy each other's company. Early in December they, the painter Waldo Peirce, Bra Saunders, and Arnold Gingrich, who had just arrived, took a trip in the *Pilar* to the Dry Tortugas. Once there, Peirce set up his easel to paint in an arch of a large fort on one of the islands off which the *Pilar* lay anchored. Dos Passos had a cot with him which he set up in the shade of another part of the fort. There he reclined and wrote more of *The Big Money* in a notebook. The place was deserted, and for a couple of days they lolled around, swimming and fishing when they chose to. Hemingway, Dos Passos recalled, was manipulating Gingrich, fascinated by the Tortugas and by Ernest, who was establishing the relationship that made him a highly paid, regular contributor to *Esquire.*

On the last night in the Tortugas, Saunders cooked them a chowder from the conches he had collected to sell back in Key West. The *Pilar* was moored at a pier, and as the group ate the chowder and drank rum, two Cuban fishing boats pulled alongside, and the crews began talking and sharing the rum. Soon everyone was involved. "There were feats of strength, tales of huge blue marlin hooked and lost, of crocodiles sighted in the Gulf and rattlesnakes twenty feet long seen swimming out to sea," Dos Passos wrote. Late in the evening, the Cubans untied and anchored offshore, as did the crew of the *Pilar.*

At dawn the next day Dos Passos and the others were awakened by the Cubans, who wanted to have a farewell drink with the Americans before departing. Hung over, nevertheless the *Pilar*'s crew complied, and as they did, Hemingway came on deck with the rifle he had aboard and began a shooting exhibition. "He shot a baked-bean can floating halfway to the shore," Dos Passos remembered:

> We threw out more cans for him. He shot bits of paper the Cubans spread out on wooden chips from their skiff. He shot several terns. He shot through a pole at the end of the pier. Anything we'd point at he would hit. He shot sitting. He shot standing. He shot lying on his belly. He shot backward, with the rifle held between his legs.
>
> So far as we could see he never missed.

Only when he ran out of ammunition did he stop the remarkable performance. Then the Cubans departed, and the Americans began what was a bibulous voyage back to Key West.

Hemingway and Dos Passos could also still work together on projects of mutual interest, as they did in the case of the artist Luis Quintanilla, who had been jailed in Spain for conspiring against the Republican government. In New York the Pierre Matisse Gallery exhibited thirty-nine of Quintanilla's etchings, the program for which contained introductions by both Hemingway and Dos Passos, whose comments reflected his own strong interest in satire. In Quintanilla's etchings, Dos Passos wrote, "are the back lots, the cheap whores, the beggars and bootblacks, and the new business men greedy for power." He thought it natural that the artist should be a satirist: "most of the best Spaniards have been satirists," who had "a type of clear noontime logic." His statement about Quintanilla, aside from praising the artist's skill as an etcher, was a revealing comment about Dos Passos's own aims as a social satirist, who, he declared, "is a man who can't see filth, oppression, the complacency of the powerful, the degradation of the weak without crying out in disgust. A great satirist can turn disgust into violent explosive beauty." Quintanilla's etchings, Dos Passos believed, were strikingly similar to those of another satirist whom he admired, the German artist George Grosz. In the works of the two men Dos Passos saw a parallel because both portrayed countries which faced "a time of defeat of everything that gives men hope." Yet, Dos Passos remarked in a statement which was a blunt reflection of his own thinking, for the artist, if not for the political activist, "defeat is sometimes [more appealing to the observer's or reader's senses] than victory. A good thing, too, because there's a great deal more of it. . . . The etchings [and by extension, one might add, the harsh satire in another medium such as Dos Passos's] are the statement of a grown-up man facing a bitter world in the sun at noon."

His observation about the Spaniard's sketches illuminate much of his conception of his own work. Dos Passos was saying that defeat is the stuff of art, or at least of satiric art—a not uncommon idea, but one often neglected when considering the nature of the world of his fiction. He saw himself to be "a grown-up man facing a bitter world in the sun at noon," and as such, an artist portraying harsh realities. The defeats that abound in his best fiction have the artistic depth or, put another way, the sense of the complexity of life about them that he admired in art. Then, too, he rendered scenes of defeat because he believed the satirist's task was not to present a prescription for change or a portrait of victory. Rather, as he wrote when introducing the paintings of Grosz in 1936, the task was to be like "the doctor who comes in with his sharp and sterile instruments to lance the focusses of dead matter that continually impede the growth of intelligence." Before anyone could solve "the ugly and the savage and the uncongruous aspects of society," these had to be revealed "as brutally and nakedly as possible." Only then could the disease be cured. Dos Passos's best art is satire which, although politically slanted, is not primarily intended to uplift as a critic like Mike Gold wanted it to do. Dos Passos, like Grosz, meant to show "the horror of life."

To drum up support for Quintanilla, Dos Passos in mid-November enlisted the aid of Malcolm Cowley at the *New Republic*. He asked Cowley to have a look at the etchings, and if he liked them, to "try and get the boys to go to bat." Dos Passos's hope was that if Quintanilla's situation received enough attention, a petition might be circulated and then sent to the Spanish government with the possibility that a severe sentence could be avoided. Cowley, eager to be of help, immediately responded to Dos Passos with the suggestion that the *New Republic* print a letter about the Spaniard from Dos Passos. In fact, wrote Cowley, he had made up a letter out of the one Dos Passos had sent, and it would be run as soon as possible. Dos Passos, fearing that the wrong sort of statement might do more harm than good, cautioned Cowley that "if you print any letter from me dont put anything in about Quintanilla's needing the jack—this isn't a plea for funds . . . or particularly dont say anything about that an artistic success might influence Spanish govt or that son of a bitch [Premier Alejandro] Lerroux—that is definitely not for publication." But the warning reached Cowley too late, and the November 28 issue of the *New Republic* carried Cowley's remake of Dos Passos's letter under the title "Etcher and Revolutionist."

When Dos Passos read it, he became furious at Cowley and immediately wrote him that "publishing my confidential letter to you was a great mistake. It has just about ruined the effectiveness of what we were trying to do." Dos Passos's bitter overreaction was foolish and mean-spirited. He attacked Cowley, whom he said he had thought to be "an honest and trustworthy guy." Dos Passos told him that he could not imagine Cowley doing "anything so stupid and in its results, though not I suppose in its intent—so treacherous." Dos Passos castigated the editor for taking a risk, because Quintanilla's situation was critical, and a misstep might destroy him. "This is not a literary game played at café tables," he lectured Cowley. "If you werent willing to go to bat you should have let the matter drop. The hell of it is that there's absolutely nothing you can do to patch the situation up that wont make matters worse. I shall know better than to expect anything from you another time." To Edmund Wilson, Dos Passos exclaimed that he had "finally broken off whatever relations I can ever be said to have had with our esteemed contemporary the Neuro —the yellow bastards published a private letter I wrote Malcolm about the situation of Q. etc."

Dos Passos's ire, for which he soon apologized, could only be explained by a personal frustration at being forced because of his health to remain in Key West, by Katy's long stay away from him, or by an annoyance with the left-leaning tendencies of the *New Republic* as he pulled back. Cowley had every right to be angry in his turn, for he had tried to go to bat for Quintanilla. But he held his temper, not responding to Dos Passos for nearly two weeks, when he wrote:

> Naturally your letter of reproach—reproach is about the mildest word that could be used for it—has been bothering me ever since. After reading Hemingway's piece in the catalogue—it also mentioned the sixteen years sentence that was being demanded by the *Fiscal*—I think the only extra damage that could possibly have been done by printing the letter lay in the sentence about the possibility of getting better treatment for Quintanilla by organizing a protest in this country. On that subject you are a better judge than I am, but I don't think the Spanish government reads The New Republic. In the meantime, printing your note in the paper may help to get the signatures you want.

Underneath Dos Passos's flare-up lay a resentment against what he referred to as "the liberal weeklies," as he later admitted to Cowley. But the resentment resulted not simply from political differences; Dos Passos felt bitter because of the weeklies' literary criticism. Cowley touched on it in his letter when, after reminding Dos Passos that Hemingway had in his introduction to Quintanilla's etchings mentioned some of the points about which Dos Passos was annoyed, Cowley criticized Hemingway for being irresponsible and in the process hurting those around him. He cited a situation in which Ernest has gotten him in trouble with Marianne Moore, at the time the editor of the *Dial*. Beyond that, Cowley objected to Hemingway's blurred political vision and cited what he thought was a terrible Harry Morgan story which had appeared in *Cosmopolitan*, in which Morgan, when he became involved in a revolution, merely ended as a gangster, although that had not been Hemingway's intention.

Dos Passos's response was an interesting defense of Ernest, who, he declared, had his license as a writer because "nobody living can handle the damn language like he can." It was not only because Hemingway was a good friend that Dos Passos had gotten "thoroughly sick of every little inkshitter who can get his stuff in a pink magazine shying bricks at him." Critics, Dos Passos thought, should respect good literary craftsmen whether or not their work reflected the current political styles. Dos Passos maintained that Hemingway was neither Communist nor Fascist, and the greatest mistake of the leftists was to alienate him, or any other writer of ability, for that matter. What Dos Passos had in mind as much as Hemingway were his own differences with the Left which had been exacerbated earlier in the year by his signing the letter of protest against the disruption in Madison Square Garden. "Any man who is really trying to dope things out directly from day to day—not accepting any ready made phrases without testing them—is sure to be in wrong with the inkshitters most of the time," he asserted and concluded, "And God damn it, you've got to admire that quality—the first rate quality—in people whether you agree with them or not." His defense of Hemingway was, in fact, a defense of himself as he continued his search for a political ground on which to stand.

CHAPTER TWENTY-TWO

Politics
and *The Big Money,*
1935–1936

Dos Passos was moving faster toward new political terrain, and as he did, he wrote more to Edmund Wilson, who cautioned his friend not to jump too quickly to conclusions. Two days before Christmas, 1934, Dos Passos wrote him, first thanking Wilson for a box of books he had shipped to Key West. Dos Passos had few good words about a biography of Veblen, but reminded Wilson again to read Veblen's own writing. Dos Passos found Friedrich Engels's letters enlightening and wondered if Wilson had read William Henry Chamberlin's book, *Russia's Iron Age,* published in October 1934. Dos Passos had met Chamberlin in Moscow in 1928 and had thought him "the straightest and best informed of the foreign newspapermen" he had known there. Chamberlin's book was informative, he acknowledged, although of little permanent value because it had no clearly defined philosophic basis. But the repression and terror Chamberlin discussed at length were exactly what Dos Passos had both seen himself and heard about from Horsley Gantt and others. Now the assassination of Sergei Kirov, the leader of the Communist Party in Leningrad and a favorite of Stalin's, had resulted in Stalin's government taking revenge by dragging 103 persons from prison and shooting them. Later Kirov's murderer was captured and executed, along with thirteen other Communists. It was, Dos Passos commented to Wilson, as if after Joseph Zangara tried to shoot Franklin Roosevelt, the Secret Service had executed "a hundred miscellaneous people, some because they were wops, others because they were anarchists and others because they had stomach trouble." Such acts of terror had destroyed Dos Passos's "benefit-of-the-doubt attitude towards the Stalinists." For him, events in Russia had no further relevance—"except as a terrible example"—for the Socialist movement, if, he added, "you take socialism to mean the educative or constructive tendency rather than politics." The

Revolution in Russia had, he now believed, gone into what he termed its "Napoleonic stage," and the government was more concerned with its self-preservation than with progressivism. What he believed was "the horrid law of human affairs"—the law by which all governments eventually became "involved with power for itself, killing for the pleasure of it, self perpetuation for its own sake"—had taken hold in Russia, and the result for orthodox Communists in the United States was that any further obedience to Stalinist doctrine would merely lead up blind alleys. Dos Passos saw no point in denouncing the Communists, but he was sure that any American more interested in realities than in being on the side in popular favor should understand what was happening in Russia before citing it as proof of the merits of Stalinism or another brand of Marxism. And as people independently sought this political base, they "should be very careful not to damage any latent spores of democracy that there still may be in the local American soil. After all," he reminded Wilson, "the characteristic institutions of the Anglo-Saxon nations survived feudalism and Tudor absolutism . . . and there's no reason why they shouldn't survive monopoly capitalism." And in a postscript he added, "It would be funny if I ended up an Anglo-Saxon chauvinist—Did you ever read my father's Anglo Saxon Century? We are now getting to the age when papa's shoes yawn wide."

Wilson responded in January 1935, urging Dos Passos not to form any definite opinions about the situation in Russia because so little was known about it. He saw no reason to disbelieve Stalin's claims about a counterrevolutionary plot causing the death of Kirov, and he still thought the Russian leader was working toward Socialism. In New York Wilson found himself defending Russia against "the intelligentsia," some of whom cited the ills of that country to demonstrate the failure of Socialism. As for Socialism in the United States, Wilson agreed that Americans should not try to import the Russian brand. But he questioned whether any form of Socialism could take hold in the United States before its present institutions suffered "a general breakdown." Further, he doubted Dos Passos's claims about "Anglo-Saxon institutions." What institutions did he mean? America was, in fact, in many ways closer to other countries than to England.

Dos Passos in his turn wrote back from Jamaica, where he and Katy, after a brief stopover in Havana, were spending most of the month of January. He agreed that he still sided with "orthodox" Communists in the face of critics such as Louis Adamic and Ben Stolberg, but the terrorism of Stalin convinced him that the time had passed when a person should belong to any Marxist group. Dos Passos seemed to refuse any longer to consider Marxism distinct from Stalinism. As he had before, he was setting his mind firmly against a repressive government in power, and as Wilson soon pointed out, he was "ready to throw the baby out with the bath." But for Dos Passos none of the Marxist parties was any longer viable. The Stalinists were alienating the working classes by their repressive tactics, while the Trotskyites had "lost the popular pulse." What had to be worked out was "some entirely new attack on the problem of human freedom under monopolized industry." The steps taken by the Russians "under the iron mask of the Kremlin" were of no use to Americans, "if our aims are freedom and the minimum of oppression." As long as the Soviets were headed toward a workers' democracy, their experiments had interest, but now they had ceased moving in that direction. Dos Passos thought Americans were working toward "various forms of organization" such as labor unions and the controls of federal government within industry that were desirable, and during the struggle toward these forms he personally preferred "the despotism of Henry Ford, the United Fruit and Standard Oil" to that of Stalinists like Earl Browder and Mike Gold.

Dos Passos's enthusiasm for the U.S.S.R., he now saw, had been declining ever since the suppression of the Kronstadt rebellion in 1921. From then on the acts of repression which had discouraged his support of Russian Communism were "the massacres by Bela Kun in the Crimea, the persecution of the S.R.'s [Socialist revolutionaries], the N.E.P. [New Economic Policy], the Trotsky expulsion [from the Party in 1927], the abolition of factory committees, and last the liquidating of the Kulaks and the Workers and Peasants Inspection [after the demise of the N.E.P. in 1929], steps which left the Kremlin "absolutely supreme."

"I dont know why I should blurt all this out," Dos Passos wrote Wilson, "except that since I've been laid up I've been clarifying my ideas about what I would be willing to be shot for and frankly I dont find the Kremlin among the items." He was discouraged by what he termed "this dismal progress," because it left him back where he had begun in 1917 as he "embarked in the S.S. Chicago to see the world in the uniform of Messrs Norton & Harjes." Now in 1935 he could still read the magazine of the I.W.W., but the political situations in Germany, Austria, and Spain —which he viewed as reactions against the Left—he thought ought to "give pause to the most hardshell marxian," because "intellectual theories and hypotheses don't have to be a success, but political parties do—and I cant see any reason to induce others to engage in forlorn hopes one wouldn't go in for oneself." After urging Wilson to carry out his plan to go to Russia to see for himself, Dos Passos concluded, "Of course I've overstated the case against the Kremlin—but I'm now at last convinced that means cant be disassociated from ends and that massacre only creates more massacre and oppression more oppression and means become ends—its the sort of thing you have to grow up and look around for a number of years to see— possibly it's the beginning of adult ossification—but I dont really think so."

"Don't agitate me, comrade, I'm with you—at least on what I take to be your main contentions," Wilson answered. After reminding Dos Passos that he seemed to be ready to discard everything because of his dislike for Stalinism, Wilson noted that his friend talked as if a choice between Henry Ford and Earl Browder were realistic, while in fact no one but the Communists had ever conceived of either of these—or similar persons—as leaders of a national movement. The Communists deserved credit for their agitation and for raising essential issues, but only some intellectuals, of whom Dos Passos gave evidence of being one, ever expected political movements to meet their ideals. "I don't think you ought to let yourself be driven into Marxophobia by the present literary popularity of Marxism," counseled Wilson, who understood his literary friend's distaste for literary types—a stance, however genuine, that often amused Wilson. "It may be," he continued, "that political salvation will have to come now from outside Marxism proper," but he could not see that events in Europe were any proof. He reminded Dos Passos that the Marxist answer when Communism failed to gain power—as it had failed in Germany, Austria, or Spain—was "that the objective conditions weren't ripe, and that, as Trotsky says, no society can go till it has exhausted all its possibilities."

"But Bunny," Dos Passos wrote back immediately, "it's not the possibility of Stalinism in the U.S. that's worrying me, it's the fact that the Stalinist C.P. seems doomed to fail and to bring down with it all the humanitarian tendencies I personally believe in—all the while acting as a mould on which its obverse the fascist mentality is made—and the recent massacre is certainly a sign of Stalinism's weakness and not of its strength." This had nothing to do with Marx's own work, he admitted, and he agreed that the Communists had been effective as agitators; yet Stalinism could not help but influence his attitude toward the party. He explained that in earlier letters he had meant political groups when referring to "Marxians," not "the enor-mously valuable body of ideas aspirations, humane rebellions etc." He distrusted the psychology of "economically disinterested intellectuals" who could afford to "wal-low" in Communist prejudices. These people were exhibiting nothing more than a "middle class neurosis" such as one rarely found among the working class. "If you take Christianity, the Renaissance, the Enlightenment, the Romantic individualist revolt, the scientific spirit—a man's a man for all of that etc out of Socialism—what have you?" he asked rhetorically and answered, "Hell you might as well have Hearst-Hitler, except for the momentary pleasure of seeing those bastards bite the dust."

One might respond that to take the humane instincts out of any political movement rendered it oppressive. The gist of what Dos Passos was saying was that the Socialism of the Communists was little different in form and ideals from the National Socialism of the Nazis, a statement he would not have made had he not been backing away from the Left faster than perhaps even he was aware. The hints of where he was headed abounded in these letters to Wilson in early 1935: such phrases as "latent spores of democracy" and "institutions of the Anglo Saxon nations" reflected his growing readiness to embrace New Deal capitalism, as did his closing words in this letter to Wilson where he asserted that at present Americans had immense information and technical abilities "to carry ideas out" which ought to result in solutions to the dilemmas facing the world. "If I was a European I wouldn't think so," he concluded, "but here we still have a margin to operate on" —an assertion that foretold the "Farewell to Europe" he wrote little more than two years later.

In 1935 he began to be interested in the foundations of Anglo-Saxon demo-cratic traditions, and in this letter to Wilson expressed his desire to know more about the English Reformation. Thomas Carlyle's edition of the letters and speeches of Oliver Cromwell had not helped him, so he asked Wilson what might be good books to read about the period. Try Edward Hyde's *History of the Great Rebellion*, Wilson responded when he next wrote. Wilson had a good sense of the direction Dos Passos was heading and urged him to write something stating his present position, because "it is being rumored that you are 'rubbing your belly' and saying that 'the good old Republican Party is good enough for you.' " Wilson's suggestion was partly responsible for Dos Passos's decision in March to agree to write a paper for the first American Writers' Congress to be held in April 1935. He did it "against [his] better judgment," he told Wilson, and his aim was "to write them a little preachment about liberty of conscience or freedom of inwit or something of the sort that I hope will queer me with the world savers so thoroughly that they'll leave me alone for a while. I frankly can't see anything in this middleclass communism of the literati but a racket."

While still in Jamaica in January, Dos Passos had continued his correspondence with Robert Cantwell, who had taken umbrage at Dos Passos's slighting reference to Upton Sinclair's pamphlet *A Governor of California and How I Ended Poverty: A True Story of the Future.* Cantwell wanted to write a "project novel," about which Dos Passos had doubts, yet recognized that "the novel as natural history" was valid. Look at Defoe's work, he counseled, adding that "agitational literature" could be good. But Cantwell recognized Dos Passos's lack of enthusiasm for his undertaking and questioned it. "Naturally I was kidding about Uppie's campaign documents," Dos Passos wrote from Jamaica. He went on to explain that successful reproduction of people's past actions being so difficult in fiction, he could only imagine that to try to render the future in a novel would be practically impossible. In any case, someone trying to render "objective reality"—Dos Passos could not, he observed, "think of good writing in any other way than as reality, though I'd hate to have to define what I mean by the term"—should avoid any social preconceptions reflected in terms like "fascism." Writing under the influence of sectarian opinions was dangerous, he declared, because that meant accepting "the formulas of past events as useful for the measurement of future events and they never are, if you have high standards of accuracy." Dos Passos believed Cantwell had succeeded in conveying his ideas in his 1934 novel *Land of Plenty,* although Cantwell now wished that he had been more explicit. "But," Dos Passos reminded him, "it was certainly better to leave the strings untied than to gum them together with obsolete labels out of Daily Worker editorials," whose language he referred to as "the communist veneer of phrases that is being slicked over so many people who get their talk from New York."

Much on Dos Passos's mind was his own novel, *The Big Money,* which he was working at steadily now that his health had improved. He wanted to avoid sectarian opinion or political jargon except where he meant to satirize such, as in the narrative about Mary French, a party worker who eventually became disillusioned when she recognized that party dogma, reflected in its "veneer of phrases," caused individuals to be treated as integers rather than as humans. But life was more complex than any narrow political position could allow for, and writing from a sectarian stance, or attempting to act the proletarian when as a writer one was essentially middle class, was limiting. Striking the pose of a factory hand was as foolish as attempting that of a bank president, and this was the difficulty in finding good working class writers. "A writer as such is just that, if writing is his full time work," Dos Passos told

Cantwell, "and pretending to be something else produces all kinds of hypocrisy and mealymouthedness. . . . " Dos Passos's most forceful assertion to Cantwell was that "a man writes to be damned and not to be saved," by which he meant that the honest, independent writer goes his own way regardless of the direction of literary opinion at any given moment. He understood that he was moving against the literary Left but, as he wrote Cantwell in the spring, "it's only occasionally that you want to go in for naked ideas and formulas . . . the work in hand is always more interesting and pleasanter." Having spelled out his beliefs in the paper for the Communist-dominated Writers' Congress, he could "contentedly paddle my own canoe and to hell wid 'em." A writer could only do his best, which might be none too good, but "worrying and formularizing wont help it."

The essay Dos Passos wrote for the Congress was entitled "The Writer as Technician." It arrived in New York from Key West too late to be read at the meetings, but was included in a volume of essays from the congress published later in 1935. "In a time of confusion and rapid change like the present . . . it's not possible to write two honest paragraphs without stopping to take crossbearings on every one of the abstractions that were so well ranged in the ornate marble niches in the minds of our fathers," Dos Passos asserted, immediately taking aim at the issue of doctrinaire and sectarian phraseology. Professional writing, whatever the pressures on its authors, could nevertheless still be measured by its "discovery, originality, invention." If a writer produced something compelling and important enough, "it molds and influences ways of thinking to the point of changing and rebuilding the language, which is the mind of the group." Dos Passos went on to explain that, like a scientist, a writer by his inventions could influence subsequent thought. The writer was, in effect, a technician. But like a technician in the field of business, he had to buck "the routine and the office-worker control" that were a part of "large industrial enterprises," be they economic or social. "The main problem in the life of every technician" for Dos Passos was "to secure enough freedom from interference from the managers of society in which he lives to be able to do his work"; yet liberty, the freedom "to give rein to those doubts and unclassified impulses of curiosity that are at the root of invention and discovery and original thinking," was essential for a person's best work. As Dos Passos drew to a close, he became more explicit about his concern:

> At this particular moment in history, when machinery and institutions have so outgrown the ability of the mind to dominate them, we need bold and original thought more than ever. It is the business of writers to supply that thought, and not to make themselves figureheads in political conflicts. . . .
>
> It is easy to be carried away by the temporary effectiveness of boss rule, but it has always ended, in small things and in great, in leaving its victims stranded bloodless and rotten, with all the problems of a living society of free men unsolved. The dilemma that faces honest technicians all over the world to-day is how to combat the imperial and bureaucratic tendencies of the groups whose aims they believe in, without giving aid and comfort to the enemy. . . .

I feel that American writers who want to do the most valuable kind of work will find themselves trying to discover the deep currents of historical change under the surface of opinions, orthodoxies, heresies, gossip and the journalistic garbage of the day. . . . A writer can be a propagandist in the most limited sense of the word . . . but the living material out of which his work is built must be what used to be known as the humanities. . . .

No matter from how narrow a set of convictions you start, you will find yourself in your effort to probe deeper and deeper into men and events as you find them, less and less able to work with the minute prescriptions of doctrine; and you will find more and more that you are on the side of the men, women and children alive right now against all the contraptions and organizations, however magnificent their aims may be, that bedevil them; and that you are on the side, not with phrases and opinions, but really and truly, of liberty, fraternity, and humanity.

The piece was an eloquent statement of his belief, and one that put him at some odds with others among the contributors, Jack Lawson for one. Lawson's essay, "Technique and the Drama," discussed dramatic techniques from a Marxist perspective. Statements such as "only the theater of the left to-day can fulfill the requirements of dramatic technique: the presentation of conflict in which the conscious will is exercised toward a goal" ran counter to Dos Passos's point about remaining free from partisan politics. But while the majority of the writers embraced a Marxist—and often, Stalinist—point of view, not all did. Waldo Frank's essay, "Values of the Revolutionary Writer," argued that "the specific value, in this crisis, of the literary work of art [is] not as a chorus of revolutionary politics, not as an echo of action: but as *an autonomous kind of action.*" When Dos Passos had the opportunity to read it, he immediately sent Frank a note to say "how thoroughly I agree with and admire your statement to the Writers congress." Dos Passos wanted nothing to do with Stalinist orthodoxy. When from friends who had attended the congress he heard about such matters as the "demagogic affectations" of Earl Browder, whom Margaret De Silver denounced to Dos Passos as "far worse than stupid—he is vicious and a goddamned jesuitical liar and beast," his response was to keep his distance. Little matter that Margaret De Silver, the wife of the anarchist Carlo Tresca, was a Trotskyite; she confirmed Dos Passos's opinion that to be true to oneself the artist must remain clear of such dogmatic political partisans as Browder.

As he was preparing to leave for Russia, Edmund Wilson asked for a copy of Dos Passos's essay, which he sent. May 9, the day before Wilson was to sail, he wrote Dos Passos, first thanking him for his advice about the Soviet Union. Dos Passos had tried to arrange for his friend to use the rubles Dos Passos accumulated from publication in Russia, had told him of people to see, and had sent him four letters of introduction, with the remark that "you'll find the Russian mind, gigantic and magnificent as it is, has some very odd quirks." Wilson commented at length on Dos Passos's essay, which, he thought, might confuse "two distinct sets of considerations." He believed that writing varied between what might be termed "long-range" and "short-range writing." The former gave "a comprehensive picture of human life over an extended period of time" and tended to be written during periods of relative stability. The latter, typified by "the editorial, the public speech, the advertisement," was most pronounced during times of social upheaval. Dos Passos, because of his own aims, seemed to be denying the validity of "short-range" work, which, Wilson noted, great authors had often written when it served their purposes. "What it seems to me that you are really doing here," he continued, "is making out a case for the long-range writer. In spite of the charges of short-range propaganda which are sometimes raised against you, I never could see that you had much real taste for the kind of pamphleteering and polemics at which Upton Sinclair, for example, excels (or Lenin)." As so often, Wilson's comments offered a clear-minded and balanced perspective toward Dos Passos's ideas as he veered in a new direction. Attempting to work out social problems for himself and intent on creating "long-range" fiction, Dos Passos was ready to damn the literary Left. Use moderation, Wilson in essence was saying, and recognize all sides of the situation. It was good advice which restrained Dos Passos, at least until his experiences in Spain two years later, when what he believed he had discovered about Communist treachery brought out an instinct to label political movements as black or white. Would that he had remembered Wilson's words longer, or his own, for that matter. "One of the best things you say is about the abstractions and the human material," Wilson added in a postscript. "You can say this and ought to say it, because you have been doing this kind of work." But after Dos Passos's journey to Spain in 1937 which resulted in his making up his mind in favor of the American system of government, he tended toward polemical fiction because he was too much influenced by abstractions to maintain the complexity in his work he was intent upon protecting in 1935.

Immediately after the congress was over, Malcolm Cowley wrote Dos Passos, explaining that his paper had not been read because it had arrived in the office of the *New Masses* the Monday after the meetings. Cowley noted that those who had the chance to read the essay were bothered by a sentence about "military [militant?] Communism." He wished that Dos Passos would either drop or expand it. The main purpose of his letter, however, was to invite Dos Passos to speak at an International Congress of Writers for the Defense of Culture to be held in Paris in early June. Dos Passos thanked Cowley for the invitation, but declined it, explaining that he was still plagued by the vestiges of his illness and was also too busy working on his new novel. About his essay he commented, "as I knew the comrades would have the floor most of the time I stated the other side of the case a little more forceably than I would have if it was to have been read in an assembly of bankers say." Cowley soon had the chance to read Dos Passos's revised paper, the one that would appear in the published collection. The ideas disturbed Cowley, who argued that in a changing society a dynamic should exist between the aims of political leaders and the artistic goals of writers. The writers should fight for freedom of speech, thus forcing concessions from the politicians as they pursued their goals.

"I'm through with writing these lousy statements," Dos Passos exclaimed after receiving Cowley's letter. "I cant make myself clear. What I meant to imply was that the issue right now is the classic liberties and that the fight has got to be made on them. The reason that I see no other ground is that I dont believe the Communist movement is capable of doing anything but provoke oppression and I no longer believe the end justifies the means. . . . " He did not think that the political relationship between the leaders and the led was improving, and he objected to the party merely "parroting Russian changes of mood and opinion," an obvious reference to his distrust of the new Soviet policy of the moderate Popular Front, which the Communists had begun in the spring of 1935 to try to combat the increasing strength of Nazi Germany. "No," responded Cowley, "I think you are wrong about the Communists not being able to do anything except call down repression on themselves and others. . . . We have all got to hang together or we will hang separately." He thought liberal protest against right-wing repression had occurred only because of Communist agitation and, he assured Dos Passos, there was an encouraging activity among white-collar workers in New York that augured well. But, Cowley reminded him, one had to be there to sense it. His implication that Dos Passos was isolating himself was truer than he realized. Not that Dos Passos sought intellectual isolation, but he meant to assert his independence, as well as his deeply felt distrust of organizations and their cant.

Dos Passos could not have been in New York during the winter and spring of 1935 because of his health, but he would not have chosen to be there in any case. Key West was more satisfying to him and Katy and, once back in February from Jamaica, he could work most effectively while enjoying the usually relaxed life of the Key, where they could live economically. Even that life became stale, however, as he commented to Stewart Mitchell at the end of March. Dos Passos found Key West "pleasant enough," but was "thoroughly sick of my career as a valetudinarian." He and Katy were renting a comfortable place, he reported. They bathed every day and occasionally fished in the Gulf Stream, "a magnificent and mysterious phenomenon, always changing and always present like a range of mountains." What bothered him, though, was "the increasing difficulty and complication of the business of writing." He was finding it more and more difficult, he complained, "to get anything on paper that I can read without wanting to vomit." He had what he supposed were vain hopes that once he had finished *The Big Money* he might be able to enter "a region where simple declarative sentences, composed only of Anglo-Saxon words, will flow easily and daily from the pen." He was not exactly serious, but rather exhibiting a writer's typical frustration at the tedious hard work of writing.

Key West, he told Mitchell, was bankrupt and now in the hands of the federal Emergency Relief Administration. The result was an interesting study in microcosm of "the process of liquidation of the ordinary citizen," because on the Key "the setup of pauperism on the one hand, relief racketeering . . . with the consolidation of wealth and power in two or three hands" was highly visible. Although officials were for the most part well meaning, and the relief measures seemed on the surface "sane and necessary," the result was that what had been "a town of small owners and independent fishermen and bootleggers is rapidly becoming a poor farm." Nevertheless, the situation was revealing to him as he tried to portray the nation in his novel, while also trying to make up his mind about political philosophy.

Fretting about the progress of his novel, Dos Passos also fretted about publication plans and sales. He groused to his agent at the Brandt agency, Bernice Baumgarten, about Harcourt, Brace's plan to remainder *Nineteen Nineteen* and wondered if the publishers had given any thought to bringing it, *The 42nd Parallel,* and his new book out as a single volume. He had a hunch that they might make money that way unless sales declined further. But he could not comprehend how Harper's could keep *The 42nd Parallel* selling while Harcourt, Brace could not succeed with *Nineteen Nineteen.*

If Key West life was usually relaxed for Dos Passos, it was not always calm. An incident that involved the poet Wallace Stevens occurred sometime during the spring. Of the several versions of the episode, probably the most accurate is the one Louise Bogan wrote to Morton Zabel the following December. Bogan, a poet who disliked Dos Passos and Hemingway, relished the tale, which had been told her by Edmund Wilson, who had heard it from Dos Passos. Stevens had taken a vacation from his insurance business in Hartford, Connecticut, and traveled to Key West, where he went on a drinking spree. Thoroughly intoxicated, he barged in one day on the Hemingways and began berating Ernest, telling him he was a cad, because since all his heroes were cads, he must be one also. Hemingway on this occasion remained calm, asking Stevens if he were really that bad. "Yes," blurted out Stevens and stalked away. He then went to the Dos Passoses' place and marched in to find Dos Passos, Katy, and, apparently, other women listening to a phonograph while having cocktails before dinner. "So you're Dos Passos," Bogan reported Stevens as having said, "and here I find you, playing cheap things on the phonograph and surrounded by women in pajamas. I thought you were a cripple [radical?] and a man of culture! Women in pajamas!" With that Stevens stormed out. "Now Dos Passos's comment on all this," Bogan wrote, "is that Stevens is a disappointed man, who doens't dare to live the life of an artist, preferring the existence of an insurance broker, so that he tends to idealize men of letters. . . ." Neither Wilson nor Dos Passos admired Stevens, who was the only visitor Dos Passos ever felt like throwing out of his home, he told Wilson, but Bogan, disliking what she considered Dos Passos's literary affectations as well as his fiction, sided with Stevens. "As I see it," she wrote Morton Zabel, "Stevens was quite right: the sight of the Dos Passos menage, being O so liberated and free and emancipated and pajamaish was enough to give anyone a turn." The following spring Stevens would return to Key West and challenge Hemingway to a fight. Hemingway obliged, the result being a black eye and bruises for Stevens, who asked Ernest to keep quiet about the incident. He did, referring only obliquely to it in a letter of mid-April 1936 to Dos Passos.

A sad moment in March was the news of the death of the Murphys' son Baoth, who died of mastoiditis. Both Dos Passoses wrote Gerald and Sara, trying to console them but knowing that little could help at that moment. The Murphys had been courageous, and Katy and Dos Passos wanted them to know how much they, "living bravely and looking around at the world in spite of everything," meant to their friends. What made matters even worse for the Murphys was that because of tuberculosis their son Patrick was soon to be moved to Saranac Lake, New York, for treatment at the Trudeau Hospital.

To try to cheer up Patrick, Katy or Dos Passos wrote him on occasion, as Dos Passos did in April to describe an incident that had occurred as they headed for the island of Bimini aboard the *Pilar* with Hemingway and several other friends. Trolling for dolphins not far out from Key West, they hit a school of them and for ten minutes pulled them in before two large sharks struck Ernest's and his friend Mike Strater's lines. Hemingway muscled his shark alongside first, shot it with a rifle, and had it on the heavy gaff out of the water so that Dos Passos could photograph the catch. Ernest held a small Colt .22 automatic to kill the shark, when suddenly it convulsed and the gaff pole broke, a piece of it hitting the pistol in Hemingway's hand. The noise and commotion prevented anyone from hearing the pistol discharge, but it did, and the soft lead slug struck the brass edging along the *Pilar's* gunwale, and pieces of lead embedded themselves in Ernest's legs. He bled profusely, so although he was not severely wounded, the group decided they must return to Key West. On the way back the others cleaned Hemingway's wounds, which began to give him pain and caused him to vomit into a bucket. He was humiliated by the accident. Katy, however, had no sympathy and was furious at him because of his carelessness and bravado.

Hemingway was well enough in a week to try again for Bimini, which the group reached aboard the *Pilar* without further trouble. The island was isolated—"a few yachtsmen and sports fishermen about," wrote Dos Passos, but Bimini itself "was very much out of the world. There was a wharf and some native shacks under the coconut palms and a store that had some kind of a barroom attached, where we drank rum in the evenings, and a magnificent broad beach on the Gulf Stream side." Dos Passos and Katy enjoyed walking the beaches, bathing, and collecting shells.

In April they could not remain in Bimini for long, because Dos Passos fell ill again, and Katy had to return to the mainland to travel north to Baltimore, where she had to undergo hospitalization for the internal disorders that continued to bother her. According to Dos Passos, when Katy had returned to Key West late in May, she had been cured, but the examination and necessary treatments had "demanded very skillful handling." Both of them felt relieved after she was better; nevertheless, Dos Passos, despite nearly finishing the Charley Anderson narrative of *The Big Money* while she was gone, was lonely. Signing himself "Solitary A[pe]," he tried to cheer himself and her by writing her a story about a fox who figured in a private narrative they often shared. It was amusing, but hardly sufficed to lessen Dos Passos's disconsolate mood.

At the end of May, he and Katy left Key West to visit Havana once more before returning for a week to Bimini. There they took up their pastime of strolling on the beaches or occasionally sailing with some of the natives, who might also take them bonefishing in the mangrove shallows. Hemingway, however, was scornful of Katy and Dos Passos's puttering. He had brought some tuna rigs along on the *Pilar* and was now intent on deep-sea fishing, which he undertook with a vengeance. The day he fought his first big tuna, Dos Passos and Katy were ashore. A man named Cook, the caretaker of a defunct fishing camp on Cat Cay, Dos Passos recalled, had hooked a tuna early in the day. During the afternoon Hemingway had pulled alongside Cook's boat, and the caretaker, by this time exhausted from playing the huge fish, turned his rod over to Ernest, who instructed someone else aboard the *Pilar* to go in and pick up the Dos Passoses while he fought the tuna from the other boat. Late in the day Dos Passos and Katy arrived on the scene, where a number of craft formed a spectator circle as Ernest fought on. By dusk he had worked the tuna alongside the boat he was in, and in the light from flashlights the people aboard the *Pilar* shined into the water, they could see that the fish was immense, eight hundred to one thousand pounds, they estimated. When one man made an effort to gaff it, the tuna sounded once more, and Hemingway, cursing in a low voice, began again to work it in while a squall made up in the sky around them. Soon the tuna surfaced just ten or fifteen yards to the stern of Ernest's boat. Sharks, which were abundant in the waters around Bimini and which one of the spectators, William B. Leeds, had kept away earlier by shooting at them with a submachine gun, had not attacked the tuna yet, but as Hemingway reeled in the great fish, they hit it, tearing away its flesh until the water around the boat was cloudy with blood. When the tuna was hauled alongside, Dos Passos remembered, only its head, backbone, and tail remained. He realized years later when *The Old Man and the Sea* was published that the incident off Bimini had been the seed for the tale.

Leeds invited the Dos Passoses and Hemingway aboard his large yacht, the *Moana*, from which he had been admiring Ernest's long battle. Katy did not like Leeds and wanted to refuse, but to Hemingway's delight, he and his friends went aboard for the night as the squall became severe. Hemingway was pleased because he craved the submachine gun belonging to Leeds, who by morning had agreed to loan it to Ernest, to Dos Passos's amusement. When they left the *Moana*, Hemingway had the gun cradled under his arm.

Bimini, Katy wrote Gerald Murphy in June after she had left it, was "a fantastic place—a crazy mixture of luxury, indigence, good liquor, bad food, heat, flies, land apathy and sea magnificence, social snoot, money, sport, big fish, big fishermen, and competitive passion." The fishermen worked hard planning their strategies and were jealous of one another, while the fish were huge, "A thousand pound tuna 800 pound sharks—600 pound marlin." She mentioned Ernest's big tuna, which had been on the line eight hours. Katy then described the shark attack. Five of them rushed the fish, hitting it like a planing mill and shearing off twenty-five and thirty pounds of meat at one bite. She also told of Hemingway's shooting at sharks with Leed's submachine gun: "*rrr* . . . it's terrific to see the bullets ripping into them—the shark thrashing in blood and foam—the white bellies and fearful jaws—the pale cold eyes. I was aghast but it's very exciting," she admitted.

Upon leaving Bimini, she and Dos Passos crossed the Gulf Stream to Miami, from where they headed north around June 19 by car. Neither of them enjoyed the first part of the trip because rain poured on them each day through Florida, while the hotels boarded up along the roadside throughout the state reflected the poverty of the Depression. After a brief stay in New York, they were relieved to reach Provincetown, where Dos Passos settled down to complete *The Big Money.* Except for a visit of several days to Saranac Lake to be with the Murphys and a stop at Archibald MacLeish's farm in Conway, Massachusetts, on the way back to Cape Cod, Dos Passos remained in Provincetown through the summer. Pleased that his illness seemed to have left him, he reported to Hemingway in late July that he was "getting considerable work done." He wanted to repay Ernest some of the money he owed, but could not until he sold some work. At the moment his top priority was to complete his "lousy superannuated hypertrophied hellinvented" novel.

Although he might fret about his work, about Katy's absence when she traveled to New York in early August to try to sell her own writing, or about the poor condition of his finances, he thought the state of the nation was improving, as he reported to Edmund Wilson in Russia when he wrote on July 29. The theater Dos Passos and Katy had seen in New York on their way north had been interesting. Ethel Merman was "immense" in *Anything Goes,* although Clifford Odets's *Awake and Sing* he thought mediocre. In New York he got the feeling that the country was becoming cheerful again. "There's a sort of frivolity about everything that goes on—maybe Mr. Roosevelt's boom will really come across the counter this fall. It's a great pleasure to be able to navigate around and drink beer in bars and that sort of thing again—you get the feeling that perhaps Franklin D's frivolity is catching. . . ."

Dos Passos and Katy stayed in Provincetown until the beginning of October, when they traveled to New York, where they planned to remain for two months and live in the Village or at the Hotel Lafayette. During the summer and fall Dos Passos had written steadily, only taking time to see friends such as Jack and Sue Lawson, who visited in August, but declining to undertake diverting tasks like book reviews when Malcolm Cowley requested them for the *New Republic.* Dos Passos tried in September to humor Hemingway by praising the piece he wrote for the *New Masses* about the savage hurricane that had struck the Keys on September 2. Later in the fall he refrained from comment when Ernest wrote complaining bitterly about the adverse reception of *The Green Hills of Africa.* Even Edmund Wilson had been critical, and Hemingway wondered when his other friends might turn on him. It was a time, as Carlos Baker has noted, when Hemingway was swinging from megalomania to melancholy.

Dos Passos needed to be in New York to have access to materials such as old newspapers and song lyrics he required as he put the finishing touches on the manuscript for *The Big Money* and then began the tedious process of preparing it for publication. During the early part of 1936, he moved between the city and Provincetown while he worked impatiently. "This novel business is an awful business," he wrote Hemingway from aboard a ship of the Fall River Line on his way to the Cape. He could not at that moment understand why he had ever gotten mixed up with writing. For the first time in several years he was not bothered by rheumatic fever, but now all his energies were being drained off into his writing, and the result was "the most completely lousy feeling I've ever felt"; yet even throwing himself into his work this way, the book would not get finished. Adding to his melancholy was his constant concern about money. In mid-February he heard from Bernice Baumgarten that his income paid to Brandt and Brandt for 1935 had been the paltry sum of $684.90. Even though it was supplemented by the fees he received for short pieces in the *New Republic* and *Esquire,* his total income from writing was small most years, and he and Katy had to worry about how they were to pay for their comfortable, if not luxurious, style of life.

By March he had finished the manuscript for *The Big Money,* which Harcourt, Brace immediately began to copy-edit. The task was more demanding than usual, because to ensure accuracy in the Newsreels, for example, the copy editor, a Miss Lord, had to check the lyrics of popular songs, the precision of headlines, and the like. What Dos Passos had done, and what he suggested Miss Lord do, was to check the lyrics by reading through the index of first lines of popular songs in the New York Public Library. In some cases she might have to listen to the library's recordings to verify the words. The editing process was tedious, but on April 7, Cap Pearce wrote Dos Passos that he was sending the manuscript to the printers the next day.

With galley sheets in hand, Dos Passos, Katy, and Sara Murphy drove to Florida in late April 1936. Their ultimate destination was Havana, where they intended a week's visit with Hemingway, who had crossed to Cuba from Key West. Later Dos Passos apologized for the three of them having descended on Hemingway—the visit had its moments of acrimony because Ernest was in a mood to complain—but the rest had been good for Sara, Dos Passos was sure, although he felt as if he had not even visited because he was too busy reading galley proofs the entire time. From the Miami Colonial Hotel on May 12 he wrote Bernice Baumgarten to thank her for making some financial arrangements for him and to inform her that he was mailing galley proofs to her that night. "The proofs were a long job," he declared; "the whole thing is too damn long." He joked that he might change his name to Wolfe and call his new book "Of Time and the Sewer."

The Dos Passoses delivered Sara Murphy to the airport in Jacksonville, Florida, from where she flew to New York while they continued north by car, passing through the Smoky Mountains in North Carolina; spending a day in Washington, D.C.; and stopping in Baltimore for medical checkups at Johns Hopkins. After three or four days in New York they returned to Provincetown, where soon Dos Passos had completed reading page proofs and so could relax and begin a course of readings in American history that he had set out for himself. For a while he enjoyed having the leisure to read. He wrote Edmund Wilson at the end of June that he had just finished Wilson's new book *Travels in Two Democracies,* about Russia and the United States, and that he had gotten a feeling of "permanent pleasure" from it because of Wilson's "fine tone of eighteenth-centuryish equanimity." Thinking of his own attempts to chronicle contemporary history, Dos Passos observed that "it sure does pay to put down what happens just as it does happen—I'm not at all sure that it isnt all anybody can do that's of any permanent value in a literary way. Though actually to do that is just as difficult an imaginative process as anything else." Dos Passos had in mind the difficulty of achieving a sense of immediacy when writing reportage. He succeeded in his novels through the devices of the Newsreels and the understated reporting style of the fictional narratives. More difficult in some ways was achieving the same sense of vitality in his nonfiction, collected in volumes such as *Orient Express, In All Countries,* and *Journeys Between Wars,* the next collection that would be published in 1938. Then, also, he was thinking ahead to the techniques he would employ to try to give immediacy to early American history in the books that emerged from his program of reading.

During the summer of 1936 Provincetown was "agreeable in a goofy sort of a way," he told Wilson, although every year more tourists showed up and "the process of corruption of the country by the city is going on so fast." The freedom from the pressure of readying his novel soon made him uneasy, or at least he pretended so when he wrote Hemingway in mid-July. Dos Passos initially assumed the tough-guy pose in his banter with Ernest to ask "what the hell happened to your little chocolate friend Joey Louis?" who had lost a boxing match to Max Schmeling in June. He commented that the rough crossing from Key West to Bimini which Ernest had described in his last letter was enough to "change the shit" in Hemingway and make him "sweet as a sucking dove for a year or more." Dos Passos complained that he was "not doing a damned thing—reading Capt John Smith and Moult's Relation and stuff like that . . . weeding the garden and doing a little smalltime sailing in the harbor." He was beginning "to feel restless as hell" and wanted to travel again, but the course of reading he had set himself interfered. "When do people get time to read all that stuff?" he wondered. It took so long, and all the time he wondered if he was understanding the material. Perhaps, he wrote, he was trying to do too much at one sitting, but he felt driven to continue because he had made himself a list of books to read that was thirty pages long, and in addition he kept turning up new works. And all the while he believed he should be investigating the situations in France and Spain.*

An obvious reason for Dos Passos's restlessness during the summer was his impatience while waiting for *The Big Money* to appear. He had a sense that it would be well received. Hemingway in June had told him how fine it was after reading the page proofs, and in early July he found out from Robert Cantwell that *Time* magazine was planning to do a cover story about him to coincide with the publication of the book. After visiting the Dos Passoses, Cap Pearce wrote Bernice Baumgarten that he and his wife had visited at Provincetown, and the day they were there, "Dos had spent all the day with photographers and reporters from *Time Magazine.* Apparently Bob Cantwell has arranged to have Dos Passos' picture on the front cover of *Time* the week the book published, and that is going to have a decidedly big effect on the book's history." The same day Pearce wrote to thank the Dos Passoses for the visit and reported that the Harcourt, Brace office was "buzzing with talk about *The Big Money.*" Helen Taylor of Harcourt, Brace asked Dos Passos for

*Hemingway's earlier letter and then his response to this one from Dos Passos hinted broadly at Ernest's belligerence when they had been together in Havana. He talked in the first letter about self-destruction and trying to pull his friends down with him, then in the second mentioned contritely that he missed Dos Passos and Katy and wanted the opportunity not to mistreat them.

a two-hundred-word statement about the book for purposes of publicity, but he balked, responding that all he could say would be that *The Big Money* was intended as part of a unit of three novels, which was not a good publicity statement for the moment. Asking her to find someone else to do the task, he concluded, "Honestly I'm through with the damn book and working on something else."

As August 1, 1936, the date for the publication of *The Big Money*, drew near, Dos Passos heard from Cap Pearce the encouraging news that the book had had a good advance sale, estimated to be as many as 7,000 copies, and that it would receive major reviews in the *New York Times* and *Herald Tribune*. He was further cheered by the words of praise from friends. Jack Lawson wrote to say that the novel was "terrifically exciting . . . far more completely achieved" than the first two volumes of the trilogy. Dos Passos's most perceptive critic agreed. After Edmund Wilson had finished reading an advance copy, he wrote his friend that the novel was "a noble performance." The ending, Wilson thought, suffered by comparison with that of *1919*, in which Dos Passos's indignation against the war blazed forth. In *The Big Money* he seemed to Wilson to treat the Sacco-Vanzetti case perfunctorily, and various of the figures in the narratives might have been brought back on the scene to do "more vividly characteristic things"—Wilson applauded Dos Passos's handling of Richard Ellsworth Savage and Ben Compton—but what seemed missing sometimes were the characters' own senses of what they were achieving by their actions. Nevertheless, Wilson quickly added, what in fact occurred was admirably worked out, and the entire book was "tied up at the end with unexpected inevitableness and point." He liked best the Charley Anderson narrative, but each of the others had special qualities as well. Dos Passos's writing had become "transparent," Wilson thought, the way the Russians described Pushkin's work, by which they meant that objects showed through. In Dos Passos's case, it was experience that showed through, conveying significance without his seeming to emphasize it. Wilson could think of no other novelist doing as well what Dos Passos had done, which was to "show people in those moments when they are at loose ends or drifting or up against a blank wall." These were "moments when the social currents, taking advantage of the set of the character, will sweep the individual in." With acute perception Wilson added that "these moments and the purposive careers of your eminent men and women are the positive and negative poles of your book, between which you probably allow for more of life, cheat less on what real human experience is like (the principal exception to this is that I think you strip away too much the glamour and exhilaration of the good time which the Americans thought they were having during the Boom), than any other radical writer."

Wilson was always forthright with Dos Passos, so his remarks were high praise indeed. Other well-wishers were less clear-sighted. Upton Sinclair soon wrote to compliment Dos Passos, but he confessed that he was confused by the techniques of *The Big Money*. Someday Sinclair should read the three novels as one volume, Dos Passos responded. He hoped to bring them out that way, which he believed would lessen the confusion.

The publication of *The Big Money*—or perhaps the appearance of the three novels together as *U.S.A.* in January 1938—marked the high point of Dos Passos's reputation as a novelist. His prominent place on the front of the August 10 *Time* gave him national attention such as he had never had before. His picture conveyed the sense of a tough, proletarian writer. The article, a typical *Time* cover story, gave a biographical account before discussing *The Big Money*. The piece concluded:

> Alone among U.S. writers, Private Historian John Dos Passos has taken as his subject the whole U.S. and attempted to organize its chaotic, high-pressure life into an understandable artistic pattern. To find the equivalent of his nationalism one must look abroad, to Tolstoy's *War and Peace*, to Balzac's *Comédie Humaine*, to James Joyce's *Ulysses*.

Such high praise came as well from reviewers whose literary judgments mattered. Horace Gregory in the *New York Herald Tribune* declared in a front-page review that "only the most unresponsive reader would fail to appreciate the humor which is the force behind the keen stroke of Mr. Dos Passos's irony." Gregory believed that the author saw and understood life as it was, and his rendering of it made him "the most incisive and direct of American satirists." In a *New Republic* review of August 12, Malcolm Cowley called *The Big Money* "the best of Dos Passos' novels, the sharpest and swiftest," and admired his handling of plots and interwoven themes. Within a month, however, he wrote another piece about Dos Passos, an "afterthought," he termed it. Having read all three novels of the trilogy, Cowley now claimed to see that they were a blending of the art novel and the collective novel. In the former, he wrote, the individual is emphasized; in the latter, society as a whole. "But in both," he observed, "we get the impression that society is stupid and all-powerful and fundamentally evil." Finally, although he admired Dos Passos's "scope and richness," Cowley missed in the three novels "the will to struggle ahead, the comradeship in struggle, the consciousness of new men and new forces continually rising." Cowley's was a perceptive essay, but given his leftist stance, it is not surprising that he thought Dos Passos's satirical, bleak picture of American life to lack the upbeat proletarian statement he would have liked.

Some critics predictably were not enthusiastic. Herschel Brickell, who had written perceptively before about Dos Passos's fiction, believed that Dos Passos's figures lacked character because they were puppets of the system, and thus his America was no more than a figment of his imagination, and his reportage, valueless. A more important statement was that of Bernard DeVoto, who gave Dos Passos lukewarm praise for his novels which anatomized the time and demonstrated the author's talents for "experimentation, technical versatility, imagistic brilliance, the perfection of an advanced theoretical system of composition, and an advanced theoretical system of analysis and argument. . . ." But the books lacked warmth, emotion, and the "knowledge of life that is experienced rather than theorized about." When Louise Bogan read DeVoto's review, she gloated to Morton Zabel that DeVoto had said some good things. "If Dos Passos is a *novelist,*" she concluded, "I'm a gazelle!"

Such critics were unwilling to grant Dos Passos his satiric intention. Not that she, given her dislike of his personal style and literary techniques, would have read his statement about Luis Quintanilla which made explicit Dos Passos's intentions. Perhaps his aims would not become clear to readers until the trilogy appeared as one volume, *U.S.A.* In *The Big Money*, nevertheless, he meant to be showing characters who in the best tradition of satire scurry around but have no control of their world. The "plot" of satire, like the "plot" of the trilogy is, as the critic Alvin Kernan has written, "the mere intensification of the unpleasant situation with which satire opens." Throughout the trilogy a large number of characters—those in the biographical sketches and even those mentioned in the Newsreels as well as those in the fictional narratives—rush on and off the scene in a succession of incidents which lead nowhere in particular while demonstrating the effects of an environment of monopoly capitalism on the individual. The unpleasantness of the atmosphere increases until the trilogy ends, and that is all. Even Edmund Wilson may have missed the satiric form of the trilogy when he wrote Dos Passos that the characters needed to be brought back on stage for the sort of dénouement one might find in the classical form of the novel. Doing that would have implied a kind of order and structure to the trilogy if not to the world within it which Dos Passos did not intend to show. *The Big Money* was meant to be the final brushstroke to his satiric portrait of the United States, where change was ceaseless but progress rare. There was rather a swirl of events, the author's intention being not to condemn humans utterly along with their world, but reveal their plight and to imply that there was an alternative. And because the characters in the trilogy lack control, they are bound to appear to be puppets to some degree, flat or static if sometimes brilliantly drawn figures. Dos Passos's characters are more akin to those of the eighteenth-century British painter William Hogarth and, of course, those of George Grosz, than they are to the figures of a portraitist like Gilbert Stuart.

It is due to Dos Passos's novelistic skills that within the satiric form he was able to make his characters have a roundedness and complexity—in a word, lifelikeness. Their fullness resulted from Dos Passos's ambivalence about political systems when he was writing the three volumes of *U.S.A.*, in particular, *The Big Money.* If the truth of life is its complexity, its paradoxes, and its grays—rather than blacks or whites—then an author must render that complexity in order for his figures to be judged as characters, not caricatures, and his world as more than a hyperbolic vision. *U.S.A.*, while satire, transcends that genre. Despair is everywhere apparent, particularly in *The Big Money*, where only the narrative figures Margo Dowling and Eleanor Stoddard end well, on pain of having sacrificed human warmth to survive. J. Ward Moorehouse, if anyone the central figure of the trilogy, suffers a heart attack after collaborating with his protégé, Richard Ellsworth Savage, to bribe a U.S. Senator to protect an important advertising account. Savage, a key figure in *1919*, at the end of *The Big Money* is about to head Moorehouse's firm. He celebrates too much, gets drunk, and ends the night being knocked unconscious and robbed by two male prostitutes, who he fears will blackmail him. Charley Anderson, the central figure of *The Big Money*, has died after failing to beat a train through a railroad crossing. Eveline Hutchins Johnson has committed suicide, while Mary French and Ben Compton, dedicated radicals who try to be loyal to the Communists, have been manipulated and become disillusioned. Mary French remains working for the party as the narrative about her concludes. Ben Compton, however, has been expelled.

Despite the grimness of such conclusions and of the "Power Superpower"—symbolized by the escapades of the financier Samuel Insull—which Dos Passos decried in the final sketch of an actual American personality, there is a measure of hope at the end because the autobiographical figure of the author in the Camera Eye has gained a sense of identity. Throughout *The 42nd Parallel* and *1919* he had been moving slowly beyond his own private world of childhood, adolescence, and young manhood. In *The Big Money* he struggles further for a personal identity, a struggle which gives vitality and depth to the Camera Eyes and translates into an ambivalence toward life expressed in the other parts of the book. In Camera Eye (46) the narrator tells of walking the streets, searching "for a set of figures a formula of action an address you don't quite know" as he tries "to do to make there are more lives than walking desperate the streets hurry underdog do make." But that comes to naught, and he can only "lie abed underdog (peeling the onion of doubt) with the book unread in your hand and swing on the seesaw maybe after all maybe topdog make." The next word in the stream-of-consciousness passage is "money." He begins to understand the forces at work in a capitalist society, but still he cannot be satisfied that he has found the necessary answers. Financiers are the oppressors and yet, he reminds himself, the radicals, while being right, "are in their private lives such shits." In the next Camera Eye, he has progressed not at all, finding himself "(if self is the bellyaching malingerer so often the companion of aimless walks) . . .

> *an unidentified stranger*
> *destination unknown*
> *hat pulled down over the   has he any   face?*

By the final Camera Eye, however, after experiencing the trauma caused by the executions of Sacco and Vanzetti, he has found an identity. No longer is he an "unidentified stranger"; he has become a part of the "we" who are the striking Harlan County miners and the labor organizers, the common men with whom his sympathies have always lain who stand against "Power Superpower." Despite the individual American's failure to defeat monopoly capitalism, Dos Passos has gained a measure of hope because he can identify with this group and—at least for the moment—he has achieved a personal victory in the face of a larger defeat, the very thing of which good literature is sometimes made, as he had observed in his introduction to Luis Quintanilla's etchings. *The Big Money* becomes a statement about personal discovery and limited, private victory despite its satiric, bleak picture of an America going from boom to bust.

Beyond being satire and personal statement, *The Big Money* is also the final third of his chronicle, a vast panorama, or collage, of materials with which he meant to present the history of the first three decades of the twentieth century. He took to calling his fiction "chronicles," a term by which he meant to distinguish works like *U.S.A.* from "straight" histories in which there are not the fictional threads such as he employed. But there is another distinction between history and his "chronicles" which he did not understand. The Italian philosopher and historian Benedetto Croce, as John Diggins has pointed out, distinguished between history and chronicle thus: "The historian attempts to penetrate the core of events by entering into history and reliving in his own mind the experiences of the past; the chronicler treats his material as inert, empty of determinate content and thus devoid of self-actualizing interpretive potential. . . ." Whereas for Croce the historian sees "characters and events as alive" and their meanings "vibrat[ing] in the historian's mind," the chronicler sees those characters and events as inert relics whose ultimate meaning he does not try to comprehend. For Croce, "History is living chronicle, chronicle is dead history." To the extent that *U.S.A.* is chronicle of the sort Croce described, the trilogy is inert, if not dead. It seems merely to "record and describe . . . a kind of indeterminate determinism" to which there is "no causal order of understanding behind the disorder of events." But Diggins did not recognize that *U.S.A.* is also satire, fiction, and self-expression, and that the whole work is guided by Dos Passos's intention to show what happens to a country moving from competitive to monopoly capitalism. Undoubtedly Dos Passos had his limitations as a historian, a matter that became more apparent later when his narrative histories revealed that his mind still did not always vibrate with the meanings of characters and events. But in the case of the volumes of *U.S.A.*, both their strengths and their weaknesses stemmed from the fact that he meant them to be chronicling history and doing more besides.

In 1936 praise of *The Big Money* and a decent rate of sales encouraged Dos Passos. That September Scott Fitzgerald wrote him from Asheville, North Carolina, telling him that the book went "into everything I have ever read, felt or experienced." It was a thoughtful, affectionate letter, dictated, Scott noted on it, because he had cracked his shoulder. "Why Scott—you poor miserable bastard," answered Dos Passos, "it was damn handsome of you to write me." He sympathized with Fitzgerald about his injury, but then lectured him for writing about his "crack-up" in a series of articles for *Esquire*. "Christ man," Dos Passos scolded, "how do you find time in the middle of the general conflagration to worry about all that stuff?" Dos Passos could not sympathize with self-examinations when events were spinning the world toward another war. "We're living in one of the damnedest tragic moments in history," he asserted and told Fitzgerald that if he wanted to go to pieces, that was okay, but he ought to make it the subject of a good novel and not spill it out in "little pieces for Arnold Gingrich. . . . Forgive the locker room peptalk," he concluded. Later he recognized that *The Crack-Up* was "a remarkable piece of work."

When he heard about a fourth printing of *The Big Money* he wrote Cap Pearce to ask, "Whats all this nonsense about another printing? Are you sure you aren't binding up some lost sheets of Anthony Adverse behind that jacket. If this keeps up we'll be garnering in the mortgages with the October apples—Its probably some other book." Pearce soon answered that there had indeed been a fourth printing. In November Dos Passos learned from Bernice Baumgarten that sales had surpassed 17,000; by mid-December the figure was almost 19,000.

Buoyed by the news, he took the opportunity to bring up a matter with Pearce about which he had been brooding. To his annoyance Harcourt, Brace was remaindering *In All Countries,* and Dos Passos disagreed with their policy, because, as he spelled out in a lengthy letter, he believed that his work had some permanent value, so that instead of trying for a quick success with each volume, the publishers ought to strive for a steady sale of all of them. What bothered him was that under the present policy a reader could not obtain earlier works of an author whose most recent effort might have inspired the reader to want to see more. The book business needed stability, Dos Passos wrote, and it ought to cater less to the moods of any given moment. "Somebody's got to start bringing the bookselling and publishing business back to sanity," he continued, "and it seems to me that Harcourt, Brace is the firm to do it. . . . There are about fifty books of considerable importance published in the last fifteen years that it's absolutely impossible to buy a copy of in a bookstore." Nothing could be done overnight to change this, he realized, but a greater stability should be striven for. Pearce passed the letter on to Donald Brace, who soon responded sympathetically to Dos Passos's lament by pointing out that Harcourt, Brace attempted to backlist the works they considered most important, Dos Passos's fiction among them. Brace explained that from a business point of view a full backlisting was impossible. The matter rested there for the moment, although Dos Passos would continue to press for a fuller presentation of his work on booksellers' shelves.

The publication of *The Big Money* and all that went with it had made for what Katy called "a delirious roller-coaster kind of summer," as she wrote Pauline Hemingway in September. It had been "all very up and down, fast, yelling and out of control," but as fall approached it was calming down. Katy and Dos Passos were staying at their small farmhouse in Truro, while Edmund Wilson had the place at 571 Commercial Street in Provincetown. She reported that they had taken a trip to Maine with the Murphys and MacLeishes and would in October be going to some state fairs with Gerald and Sara. At one, the Barnstable County Fair, she planned to show a poodle and a Siamese cat, while Dos Passos intended to display some broccoli he had grown at Truro. Their lives had been full of guests, she reported. At that moment Carlo Tresca and Margaret De Silver were visiting, and the previous night a large group of people had unexpectedly dropped in for supper. Most of them she did not know, but the price of Dos Passos's fame was having to entertain them and answer questions about him and his friend Hemingway.

At about the same time as Katy wrote Pauline, Dos Passos wrote Ernest, asking about the fate of Luis Quintanilla, whom Dos Passos heard had been shot by Spanish Fascists. He feared for Spain now that General Franco had rebelled. Dos Passos commented that once the Fascists had massacred the Spaniards, they would turn on the French. The situation in Europe seemed to him about as frightful as it could be. Soon he wrote Hemingway again to report that he had heard that Quintanilla had led an attack on the Montaña Barracks in Madrid and that he was alive. And in a third letter shortly after, Dos Passos expressed his regret about not having gone to Spain to see firsthand what was happening. The course of reading that he had set for himself had stood in his way. He had had "a stagnant kind of summer," when what he should have done was to take his reading to Europe. "The wars," he noted, "is a fine place to get a lot of reading done."

More and more as 1936 drew to a close Dos Passos worried about Spain. "I dont see how the left can possibly win against Hitler Mussolini & Great Britain with France paralyzed by a temporary balance between forces. A fascist Spain will mean a fascist France and more violent reaction here & in England," he wrote Malcolm Cowley in December. During the fall he had volunteered his support to establish some sort of news service to report on events in Spain: FEEL STRONGLY ONLY USEFUL WAY PRESENT TRUE STORY SPANISH DEMOCRACY TO AMERICAN PEOPLE PROFESSIONAL NEWS BUREAU SINCERELY UNCONNECTED WITH POLITICS OR LABOR PHRASEOLOGY, he telegraphed Roger Baldwin at the American Civil Liberties Union on November 24. He had neither the time nor the experience needed to organize a bureau, he realized, but he would be glad to cooperate with those informed about Spain who might run the organization. He was eager to do something to help the cause of Republican Spain, even though its prospects for survival, he feared, were bleak.

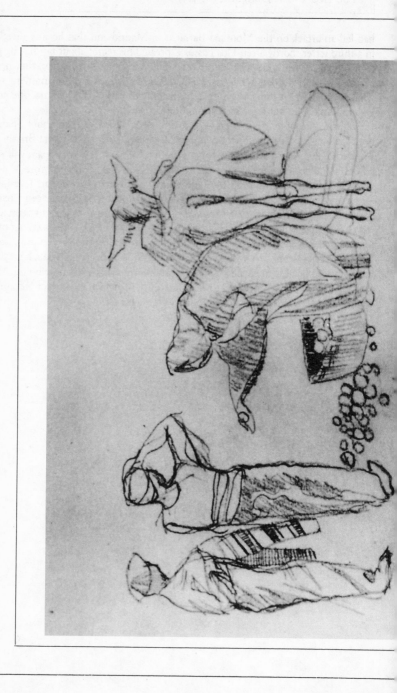

PART VI

===

Departure
from the Left,
1937–1941

CHAPTER TWENTY-THREE

Crisis in Spain, 1937

After Christmas with the Murphys at Saranac Lake, Dos Passos and Katy learned in early January 1937 that he had been elected to the Department of Literature of the National Institute of Arts and Letters. He could not spend long enjoying the award, however, because as was often the case he was preoccupied with the state of his finances. He and Katy were staying in New York, from where Dos Passos wrote Hemingway that they hoped to visit France and Spain soon to see what might remain of a Europe he feared was declining as had the Holy Roman Empire. Dos Passos felt "sore, broke, and damn sick of everything," he told Ernest, then apologized for not paying him back some of the money Hemingway had loaned him. The "lousy novel" had not made money, he wrote. What he meant, strictly speaking, was that it had sold moderately well so that he had not earned as much as he had hoped for beyond the advance Harcourt, Brace had paid him. The money he did receive, he said, went to pay off pressing debts, probably the result of his and Katy's increased expenses during the fall as well as costs incurred by her recent hospitalization and by the need to maintain their houses on Cape Cod. To tide them over, Dos Passos had to borrow money from friends such as Stewart Mitchell, whom he wrote in late January to say that he could not repay $50 he had borrowed. "Money's been gigantically tight for me this winter," he declared. Whatever Dos Passos could raise had to be fed into "the maw of several large debts that follow me like sharks." But he hoped to sell one of the Cape Cod houses soon, and that should produce some cash for a while.

Dos Passos was preoccupied as well with trying to aid the cause of the anti-Franco forces in Spain. His efforts during the fall of 1936 to help create a news service to report the facts about Spain had come to naught, so he searched for another means to present the Spanish situation to the American people. His intention after Franco's revolt against the Republic in 1936, he later wrote, was to try "to find ways to induce the Roosevelt administration to allow the republican government, which after all was the legally constituted government of Spain, to buy arms in America. The British-backed policy of nonintervention blocked every effort, and our campaign was made very difficult by the fact that we were continually embroiled with the communists, who wanted to take the campaign over for their own purposes." Frustrated by Roosevelt's policy and by the failure to develop a news service, Dos Passos while in New York conceived of the idea to make a documentary film which would depict something of the life of the common people and of their misery during the Civil War. Margaret De Silver put up a substantial amount of money at the start, and soon Archibald MacLeish, Lillian Hellman, Ernest Hemingway, and several others joined Dos Passos to form an organization they named Contemporary Historians to produce the film, for which they hired Joris Ivens as director, and John Ferno as camera man. Both men happened to be Communists.

Dos Passos met Hemingway in New York to plan the project when the latter arrived from Key West in mid-February. Disagreements between them began almost at once. Dos Passos believed the film should concentrate on the Spanish people's dilemmas; Ernest wanted it to emphasize the actual fighting. Once in Spain, they expected to settle the disagreement. Dos Passos did not realize the situation at the time, but Ernest's ill temper was exacerbated by a new love affair that had recently begun with the young journalist Martha Gellhorn. It is likely that Hemingway's feelings of guilt toward Pauline were made stronger by being around Dos Passos and Katy, two of Pauline's closest friends.

In New York the two men were able to cooperate enough to take care of some details for the production of the film. They visited the office where volunteers to fight in Spain were being recruited. The office, Dos Passos remembered, was staffed by Communists, which made him uneasy but did not bother Hemingway, whose enthusiasm for the cause outreached his limited political experience. They were given the names of Frenchmen who could tell them whom to contact for aid in Valencia, the seat of the Republican government. Next Hemingway and Dos Passos met with the Contemporary Historians group. They met the handsome, youthful-looking Ivens and agreed that Hemingway would plan the scenario, aided by Dos Passos, while MacLeish would remain in New York—where as an editor of *Fortune* he had to be anyway—and would raise funds and receive film clips when they were completed. After the meeting Katy joined Dos Passos, and the two of them had an uneasy dinner with Hemingway and Martha Gellhorn as well as others of the Contemporary Historians.

Before sailing for Europe on the *Berengaria* on March 3, Dos Passos and Katy touched base with friends and planned for the trip. In early February he had written Edmund Wilson from Provincetown to criticize Van Wyck Brooks's *The Flowering of New England*, a book he disliked as much as any he had read. More important, he wrote that he wanted to see Wilson to discuss politics, but they missed each other in New York, so the following week Wilson wrote Dos Passos, who had returned to the Cape. Wilson disagreed with his friend about Brooks's book, then turned to Russia. "What the hell?" he asked, wondering if the Russians' Popular Front stance would not lead to another war "to make the world safe for democracy," a war—as he correctly foresaw—in which the capitalists and Communists would be allied against the Fascists. Personally, Wilson had hoped to stay clear of the internecine struggles among the Marxists because he believed that little of use was left of "international socialism." Yet now he found himself on one of the committees associated with the Commission of Inquiry into the Charges Against Leon Trotsky in the Moscow Trials. The hearings were planned for April 1937, in Coyoacán, Mexico, where Trotsky lived in exile. Wilson was agitated, because both Trotskyites and Stalinists were constantly badgering him with their respective viewpoints. Dos Passos realized that he was missing something important by not traveling to Coyoacán, but he expected "that show will last longer than the European show," as he wrote Wilson next from aboard the *Berengaria.*

Katy and Dos Passos found the last several days hectic before they departed for Europe. Because a rumor had spread that Hemingway and he were going to Spain to fight, the State Department was reluctant to issue Dos Passos a passport. Hemingway had already left on February 28, so alone Dos Passos had to cope with the situation. "I'm absolutely completely and irrevocably through with all committees, protests, nonpaying magazines, relievers and uplifters whether I agree with them or not," he exploded to Wilson, while to the medical committee of the larger American Committee to Aid Spanish Democracy he wrote that "somebody in connection with one of the Spanish Committees has been using my name in ways I never authorized that have caused me grave inconvenience and threatened what little usefulness I may have as a reporter." He insisted on specific authorization in the future to use his name and asked that it be removed from "old letterheads and lists of sponsors etc."

Obtaining passports became an ordeal. More serious, although Dos Passos did not realize it at the time, was the warning he received from Carlo Tresca when they had dinner together a few nights before the Dos Passoses sailed. Tresca, an anarchist knowledgeable about European politics, warned Dos Passos, "John, they goin' make a monkey outa you . . . a beeg monkey." When Dos Passos argued that he and Hemingway had complete control over what would be filmed, Tresca laughed and pointed out that Ivens was a member of the Communist Party. In addition, all their movements and what they saw would be "for the interests of the Communist Party. If the communists don't like a man in Spain right away they shoot him," Dos Passos recalled Tresca asserting. The Italian did not use those exact words, but Dos Passos accurately presented the gist of the other man's opinions. At that moment he was dubious about them, although Tresca's warning flashed into his mind when he recognized numerous party members in the various organizations working for the Republican cause. Among the workers were some of the same people Dos Passos had seen striving for party objectives during the Sacco-Vanzetti case and the Harlan County strikes. "Rule or ruin had been their motto from the beginning. They had failed to take the Sacco-Vanzetti case away from the anarchists and liberals in Boston," he wrote. "In Harlan County they left the miners in the lurch. In Spain they were going to be successful all down the line, so successful that the republic was destroyed and the fascists won." That statement, partially true if overly simplistic, was written long after Dos Passos had suffered his final disillusionment with the Communists. Prior to that in March 1937, he expected to get "a view of Europes ruins"—as he said in a telegram to Stewart Mitchell—rather than a view of, as Dos Passos afterward interpreted it, Communist perfidy.

Once aboard the *Berengaria* he and Katy slept long hours, and he caught up on correspondence with friends whom he had not been able to contact during the press of leaving. He assured Scott Fitzgerald, who feared that Dos Passos had recently taken offense at Scott's being drunk when they had been together, that there had been no offense. He encouraged Fitzgerald to work at his fiction, then explained that he and Katy were on their way to Europe "to take a final look. I'd hate to stay away from the U.S. long these days," he added. "Things seem a darn sight more live and kicking there than anywhere else in the world—my main pleasure now is just driving around the roads and looking at the damned American continent."

Joseph Kennedy, then United States ambassador to Britain, and Bernard Baruch were traveling to Europe on the same voyage. Dos Passos had the opportunity to talk with them and hoped that he could convince them to support the cause of the Republic. Baruch appeared sympathetic to Dos Passos's ideas, yet eased him toward Kennedy, whose responses suggested that there was no chance of the United States intervening on the Republican side. Opinion about Spain was divided, he indicated. Beyond that, he wanted to avoid war, which intervention could easily precipitate. Dos Passos came away from the discussion discouraged.

He was beginning to get a sense of the fears engendered by the Spanish situation. His education continued in Paris, where he roamed about and interviewed several persons, Premier Léon Blum among them. Dos Passos's aim was to understand French political attitudes. What he found was a country very much split between conservatives, who feared Socialism while secretly admiring the strong hand of Adolf Hitler, and leftists, who feared Fascist expansion and favored support of the Spanish Republic. If the situation was not hopeless, it was not encouraging, because France was in too much of a dilemma to be able to act forcefully as Dos Passos hoped it might.

Having spent as much as three weeks in France, he parted from Katy and early in April journeyed south to Spain. The situation was that Franco's forces controlled somewhat more than a half of the country to the west. Madrid still belonged to the Loyalists but was under seige, and the Republican capital was now Valencia, Dos Passos's first objective. He took a train to Perpignan, where he was told to go to the Café Continental. There Loyalist sympathizers arranged for him to ride in a truck that was part of a small convoy going to Valencia. The trucks took a coastal route and crossed into Spain at Cerbère, from where they traveled south during that day and the next two with stops at night in Gerona and Tortosa. From the Parisian driver of the truck in which Dos Passos rode he learned of the inefficiency of the forces fighting for the Republic. The Frenchman, a member of the Communist Party, recounted how during others of his nine trips into Spain committees of anarchists in various towns had attempted to requisition his truck. The anarchists considered themselves independent of the government in Valencia, and to the driver, a Communist, the folly of such fragmentation was obvious.

Disorganization, coupled with the Communists' efforts to overcome it and at the same time gain control of the Loyalist cause, soon led Dos Passos to believe that they "fought well against the fascists but they also fought against the syndicalists, the anarchists, the socialists who made up the bulk of organized labor and against the middleclass liberals of Catalonia and the Basque country." Before the Communists had entered the conflict, the party in Spain, he claimed, was "infinitesimally small." But their drive for power soon overwhelmed the other Loyalist factions, he believed, and undermined their morale. "I'd hardly been in Valencia a day before I realized that we were licked before we started," he wrote afterward.

Given the distrust Dos Passos had for organizations and governments as well as his growing distrust of the Communist Party in the United States, it was inevitable that he break completely with the party sooner or later. The incident that made the rupture sooner was the disappearance of his longtime friend José Robles, whom he had known since his first visit to Spain in 1916–1917, and whom he had seen often in Baltimore when Robles taught Spanish at Johns Hopkins University. According to Dos Passos, Robles had been vacationing with his family in Spain during the summer of 1936 when war broke out, and he had chosen to remain to work for the Republican cause although he had been free to leave. Robles could speak Russian so was assigned to the Ministry of War, was in frequent contact with Russians who arrived with the first Soviet shipments of munitions, and was working during the fall of 1936 as English interpreter for the Russian General Goriev, who held a military command position in Madrid, although he was ostensibly serving as military attaché to the Soviet ambassador.* According to Dos Passos Robles had become an important figure with the rank of lieutenant colonel. Goriev, wrote the journalist Louis Fischer, trusted Robles, who "had a fine open face and pleasant personality, and looked the disinterested idealist." Yet late in 1936 or early in 1937 Robles had been arrested in Valencia by what Dos Passos termed "extralegal police," and when Dos Passos arrived there around April 8, Robles's whereabouts were a mystery.

Valencia in April seemed to Dos Passos little different from what it was when he had visited years earlier. The streets of the port city were crowded, its Plaza Castelar as colorful as ever, hung with "bunting and republican flags and plastered with posters," not announcing bullfights now, but civil war. But there was an air of intrigue about the Hotel International, which was crowded with men of the international brigades, "Frenchmen, Belgians, Germans, Poles, Jugoslavs, Italians; a cross section of Europe in arms."

After a lunch at the hotel, Dos Passos went to the office of the foreign press

---

*To add to the sense of intrigue surrounding the Russian involvement in Spain, Goriev was in fact a man named Berzin, and his office in Madrid happened to be only a few doors from that of General José Miaja, who was in charge of Republican forces. The question remains moot as to who did more of the planning for the defense of Madrid.

censor to present his credentials. He felt anonymous among the numerous correspondents who milled around, but was gratified to be invited to a lunch with Alvarez del Vayo, the Minister for Foreign Affairs, the next day. During the afternoon, Dos Passos paid a visit to the Robles apartment, which he located on a back street only after some difficulty. Robles's wife greeted him warmly, but her drawn, desperate look and the closed-in, dingy rooms immediately revealed that something was wrong. She informed Dos Passos that Robles had shortly before been arrested, for what she could not imagine, and now she did not know where he was nor could she get any information other than that he had been taken away for questioning because there were "certain little matters to be cleared up, wartime, no need for alarm." Yet days had passed and she had no news. She was growing desperate: "The standing in line at the policestation, the calling up of influential friends, the slowgrowing terror tearing the woman to pieces."

Dos Passos had no idea why Robles should have been arrested except that he might have been under suspicion because of his family's background, which was "of monarchical and generally reactionary sympathies in politics." A brother had been an army officer on King Alfonso's staff and now fought for Franco. But for these reasons Robles had chosen to live with his wife and son in America away from his family. Further, it was Dos Passos's opinion, as it was that of Edmund Wilson, who had known Robles when the Spaniard spent a summer in Provincetown, that no one was "less likely to have worked for the Fascists." He was distinctly a leftist of a non-Communist persuasion and "a man of excellent character." The only thing that seemed plausible was that Robles, an open person, might have been indiscreet in talking about what he knew because of his work for Goriev, or that Robles's loyalties were suspected because he had interviewed his brother, who had been captured and was imprisoned in Madrid, to press him to join the Loyalists. Beyond these reasons, Dos Passos's fears grew that Robles, because of his enthusiasms for the Republic, was a threat to the Russians' hidden objective of taking it over.

Señora Robles asked Dos Passos to find out what he could about her husband's situation. "Her idea," Dos Passos later wrote, "was that as I was known to have gone to some trouble to get the cause of the Spanish Republic fairly presented in the United States, government officials would tell me frankly why Robles was being held and what the charges were against him." With that in mind, Dos Passos after lunch the next day broached the subject to del Vayo, who "professed ignorance and chagrin" about the case and vowed to find out more. Other officials to whom Dos Passos soon talked assured him that Robles was not in any danger.

Perhaps the very day of the luncheon, however, Liston Oak, an American who had been a member of the Communist Party and who was now working for the department of propaganda in Valencia, told Robles's son, Francisco Robles Villegar —"Coco," as he was called—that his father was dead. It seemed to be only a rumor then, so Dos Passos pressed forward with his inquiries and was led while still in Valencia to believe that if Robles had been killed, it had been because "he had been kidnapped and shot by anarchist 'uncontrollables.'" Staff members of the U.S. Embassy who asked about him were told the same thing.

Now more concerned about the fate of Robles than about the filming of *The Spanish Earth*, Dos Passos headed west toward Madrid with the French journalist André Malraux in a large Hispano-Suiza. Both of them were moved by the beauty of the country and the charm of the little villages, but any romantic thoughts were dispelled as they approached Madrid, because along the roadway were trucks and soldiers marching into the city, which itself had "a grim look as if stamped out of iron." Once in Madrid, the journalists were driven to the Hotel Florida on the Plaza de Callao, where they dumped their bags out of the car, and as they did, they heard the sound of machine guns firing in the University City area seventeen blocks away.

In the lobby of the Hotel Florida the first person Dos Passos recognized was the American bullfighter and Hemingway's sometime companion Sidney Franklin, who had traveled to Madrid from Valencia with Martha Gellhorn. Franklin shared a room with Ernest, whom Dos Passos found in his room on the fourth floor. Immediately Hemingway demanded to know how much food Dos Passos had brought along, and when he answered that he had none, Hemingway reacted with scorn, which was equaled by Martha Gellhorn's when she entered Hemingway's room and was told the news. Dos Passos had been writing Ernest notes from Paris, Hemingway much later told A. E. Hotchner, in which Dos Passos expressed fervent support for the Republican cause. "Now he announced he was actually coming down to join us and we eagerly awaited his arrival because we were all starving and he had been instructed to bring food. He arrived with four chocolate bars and four oranges. We damn near killed him." Hemingway's tale for Hotchner's benefit rang with Ernest's enduring rancor after he and Dos Passos had split apart, but the fact that Dos Passos brought little or no extra food with him was true.* It was more salt in the wound in their friendship, a wound which was deepened by almost everything Dos Passos did around Hemingway that April. Ernest was aggressively ebullient because of his affair with Martha, but also because of his exhilaration about being at war and being a kind of insider, as he thought, someone who because of his prestige and courage had seen more and knew more than the other correspondents. When Hemingway was abrasive, Dos Passos's tendency was to back off, perhaps to murmur and stammer more than usual, which only increased Hemingway's scorn.

Years afterward, Ernest told apocryphal tales about Dos Passos, who, he claimed, after arriving in Madrid, had given Franklin a telegram to send to Katy in Paris. When the Madrid censor read it, he called Hemingway to find out if the message was in code. Hemingway asked what it said, and after the censor read "Baby, see you soon," Hemingway replied, "No, it isn't code. It just means Mr. Dos Passos won't be with us very long." The tale is inaccurate on several counts, not least of which is that Dos Passos would not have sent a telegram worded that way. The

---

*Lillian Hellman tells another version of the tale. When she arrived in Madrid in October 1937 she found Hemingway there, "and Martha Gellhorn, looking handsome in her well-tailored pants and good boots." Hellman recalled, "I took along two cans of sardines and two cans of pâté, and Ernest said he was glad I had brought in canned goods from Paris because John Dos Passos hadn't brought in any food but had eaten everybody else's, and he and Dos Passos had had an ugly fight about that."

story, however, is an accurate reflection of Hemingway's scorn, which mounted as the question of Dos Passos's courage, or lack of it, arose. "I couldn't believe the change in the man from the last time I had seen him in Paris!" Ernest declared to Hotchner. "The very first time his hotel was bombed, Dos packed up and hurried back to France. Of course, we were all damned scared during the war, but not over a chicken-shit thing like a few bombs on the hotel. Only a couple of rooms ever got hit anyway. I finally figured it out that Dos's problem was that he had come into some money, and for the first time his body had become valuable. Fear of death increases in exact proportion to increase in wealth: Hemingstein's Law on the Dynamics of Dying."

The accusation makes fascinating copy but lacks substance. One of Dos Passos's traits according to friends who had observed him during wartime was his calmness under fire, and the days at the Hotel Florida were no exception. Further, as Hemingway knew, when Dos Passos left abruptly from Madrid, it was not because of cowardice, but because of his dismay over what he soon discovered to be the fact of Robles's execution. In addition, Hemingway's accusation that Dos Passos feared for his skin because he had become wealthier was baseless. Ernest knew that his friend had little money in 1937. The comment reveals nothing about Dos Passos; it merely reveals Hemingway's own preoccupation with money and fame.

Life at the Hotel Florida was not as quiet as Hemingway implied to Hotchner. From Mount Garabitas Franco's artillery shelled the city daily, and the hotel received its share of hits because it was near prime targets such as the War Ministry and the Telephónica and was situated on a hill. Dos Passos wrote of one dawn when he awoke in his room on the eighth or ninth floor to a "hasty loudening shriek, the cracking roar, the rattle of tiles and a tinkling shatter of glass and granite fragments." From his window he peered out over the city, where "everything is cut out of metal in the steely brightening air." Then again there was a shriek followed by a roaring explosion, and in the silence afterward, the thin yelps of a wounded dog. Dos Passos tried to go back to sleep, but the barrage continued, so he arose, had a bath and shave, and put on his bathrobe to go downstairs. As he descended, the shelling grew heavy, and he came upon people in various stages of dress scrambling to rooms on the backside of the hotel away from the artillery barrage. On the ground floor various correspondents stirred about. An Englishman, Claude Cockburn, was attempting to make coffee, but the electric coffee pot blew a fuse and melted the plug. The American writer Josephine Herbst seized the pot from him and somehow managed to get it functioning. "Shall always remember how human you looked and acted at the old Florida that morning—amid many depressing circumstances that was one thing that made me feel good," Dos Passos wrote her two years later. Herbst herself recalled the moment vividly. While what seemed like thousands of rats scrambled in the walls of the hotel, she worked at making coffee; someone else brought stale bread; another, a toaster; and the French writer Antoine de Saint-Exupéry, who had hoarded grapefruits in his room, emerged in a blue satin robe with a basketful which he handed out, asking each woman who passed, *"Voulez vous une pamplemousse, Madame?"* and bowing courteously.

The assembled journalists talked nervously until the shelling stopped. Then they dispersed, and Dos Passos returned to his room for another hour's sleep. As Josephine Herbst remembered the morning, she sat glumly in the hotel lobby after the barrage until Hemingway came up to her to ask what her trouble was. She answered angrily that the role of Girl Scout did not suit her, at which he relaxed and asked her to his room for a drink. His intention was not to console her, however, but to urge her to tell Dos Passos to stop inquiring about José Robles, as he had been doing since arriving in Madrid. "It was going to throw suspicion on all of us and get us into trouble," he told her. "This was a war. [Pepe] Quintanilla [the brother of Luis and] the head of the Department of Justice, had assured Dos that Robles would get a fair trial. Others in authority had told him the same. He should lay off. Quintanilla was a swell guy; I ought to get to know him." But Herbst had learned in Valencia in strict confidence that Robles "had been shot as a spy." She had been told because it was known that she was an old friend of Dos Passos, and various Spaniards, worrying about his finding out the truth, somehow reasoned that by telling her they were more likely to keep it from him. Herbst felt she must honor her informant's confidentiality, but also believed that Dos Passos should be told, not to stop his inquiries, but simply to be honest with him. "The man is dead," she informed Hemingway, "Quintanilla should have told Dos." This astonished Hemingway, who immediately accepted the idea of Robles's guilt if Quintanilla said it was so. Hemingway agreed "with too cheerful a readiness" to tell Dos Passos the news, although he could tell Dos Passos no more than what Herbst had told him because he had no information beyond the little she had passed on.

Although she recalled that Hemingway had decided he would tell Dos Passos that afternoon, it is not clear that he actually did so. But the occasion, whenever it occurred, was a fiesta of the Fifteenth Brigade in a village near the castle of the Duke of Tovar among the foothills of the Guadarramas. The headquarters of the brigade were here, and foreign correspondents had been invited for luncheon to observe the ceremonies celebrating the creation of a new international brigade formed from the old Fifteenth with the addition of foreign men and officers, some of whom were Russians, or Russian trained. After speeches by the highest-ranking officers and the mayor of the village, the troops passed in review before the correspondents, General Miaja, and the staff officers. When the parade was over, the correspondents joined Miaja and the staff for a meal, where again speeches were made, most notably by the Communists Enrique Lister and Karol Swierczewski, a Pole who was known in Spain as General Walter. Both he and Lister spoke fluent Russian and had been thoroughly indoctrinated with Soviet ideology. Walter, although Polish, had lived much of his life in Russia and had served in the Red Army. After these speeches the famous Spanish singer Niña de las Peñas and the dancer Pastora Imperio came forward to perform, moved to tears by the occasion and their sadness about the Civil War.

It was during this luncheon, Josephine Herbst wrote, that Hemingway told Dos Passos about Robles. Dos Passos had a distracted air at the table but kept up his conversation with those around him. After lunch, he came up to her and "in an agitated voice asked why was it that he couldn't meet the man who had conveyed the news, why couldn't he speak to him too?" She could only think to tell Dos Passos not to ask more questions in Madrid but to wait until he returned to Valencia to talk with someone like del Vayo. Hemingway's news was not fresh; but what so distressed Dos Passos was Ernest's abrasive manner and secretiveness, which seemed to him a kind of treason.

Before the afternoon ended, there were boxing, horse racing, and soccer to be watched. Then Dos Passos, Herbst, and Hemingway drove with friends back to Madrid. It was a painful trip for Josephine because of the strain between Dos Passos and Hemingway, who leaped from the car the moment it stopped at the Hotel Florida. After the car had pulled away, Dos Passos suggested that he and Josephine walk to the Plaza Mayor, one of his favorite spots from earlier days.

Because of Herbst's account of this episode, it is believed that Hemingway broke the news of Robles's death to Dos Passos. But Dos Passos had previously learned of the probability of Robles's execution from his son Coco. In addition, it had apparently been confirmed already by a reliable source, Dos Passos's friend Carlos Posada, whom he had first met in 1916 and who in 1937 was chief of counterespionage in Madrid. When Dos Passos wrote to the *New Republic* in 1939 about the Robles case, he declared that "it was not until I reached Madrid that I got definite information from the then chief of the republican counterespionage service that Robles had been executed by a 'special section' (which I gathered was under control of the Communist Party). He added that in his opinion the execution had been a mistake and that it was too bad." Probably later in Valencia Dos Passos talked to other Spaniards "closer to the Communist Party," and these people "took the attitude that Robles had been shot as an example to other officials because he had been overheard indiscreetly discussing military plans in a café." The theory that Robles had been a "fascist spy," Dos Passos asserted, could only be the figment of someone's imagination. At least, he had never heard it from any Spaniard.

The confusion about the case and his frustration during his last days in Madrid are suggested in a letter to Dwight Macdonald of the *Partisan Review* which Dos Passos wrote two years later at the same time as he corresponded with the *New Republic.* Enclosing a copy of his letter to the latter magazine, he remarked to Macdonald about "the stupid way in which del Vayo lied to me about the manner of Robles death." To Dos Passos it seemed that "if some American wellwishers hadn't started raising a yammer about the matter in Madrid, I should have been able to get at the facts at that time, I'm sure, although Robles death had had the intended effect of making people very chary of talking about the 'Mexicans' as the Russians were familiarly known. After my American friends started to give tongue I decided that it was useless to stay longer in Spain and that my being there might be dangerous to the people I was associating with." Americans talking about the episode were part of the reason for Dos Passos's withdrawal, no doubt. But what he did not mention to Macdonald was the offensiveness of lectures about being quiet from Hemingway, Posada, and Joris Ivens, who feared that Dos Passos's questions regarding Robles would undermine the efforts to film *The Spanish Earth.* "It has always seemed to me and did then that it was a tragic mistake not to give Dos whatever evidence there was about the case and of the death," Josephine Herbst wrote to Bruce Bliven of the *New Republic* in 1939. "It should be remembered," she continued, "that Dos hated war of all kinds and suffered in Madrid not only from the fate of his friend but from the attitude of certain people on the fringe of war who appeared to be taking it as a sport. A deep revulsion followed."

One of those certain people was Hemingway, who enjoyed showing off the war and his bravado, which was another matter causing the schism between the two writers. An incident that had occurred early during Dos Passos's stay in Madrid was Ernest's shepherding Dos Passos, Martha Gellhorn, and others out to what he had nicknamed "The Old Homestead," one apartment among a row of apartment houses that faced onto the Paseo de Rosales and overlooked the Casa de Campo, a wide, open valley to the northwest beyond the city. "It used to be one of the pleasantest places in Madrid to live," Dos Passos wrote. "Now it's a noman's land." Beyond the Casa de Campo on April 9 the Loyalists began an offensive against the rebels. Hemingway had observed the attack from the apartment, and because it was such a fine observation post, brought his friends there the next day. But, as Dos Passos wrote, while one could easily observe the battle lines across the valley below, "if you step out on the paseo you're in the full view of the enemy on the hills opposite, and the Moors are uncommonly good riflemen. . . . On the top floor [of the apartment house] there's a room on that side still intact; looking carefully through the halfshattered shutters we can make out trenches and outposts at the top of the hill, a new government trench halfway up the hill and, closing the picture, as always the great snowy cloudtopped barrier of the Guadarramas. The lines are quiet; not a sound." The silence was because it was lunchtime. The rebels knew there was activity in "The Old Homestead" because the day before, and perhaps again that day, they had caught sight of the sun glinting off Hemingway's fieldglasses and the movie camera the group had with them, as well as sight of movement along the *paseo.* In the restrained reporting of *Journeys Between Wars* Dos Passos made no mention of this. In *Century's Ebb,* however, he did, portraying Ernest—George Elbert Warner—as a fool for walking along the paseo with an English correspondent in full view of the rebels despite the warning of a Loyalist corporal. "Who's chicken-shit?" Warner shouts before strutting out. When Jay Pignatelli meets him and the Englishman at the other end of the paseo, they are "puffed up like turkey gobblers." Jay points out that it was lunchtime and the rebels, "being Spaniards, would finish their *almuerzo* before they started to fire." He was correct: "as we were working our way back in the shelter of the smashed-up houses, all hell broke loose. I hate to think how many good guys lost their lives through that piece of bravado."

Soured by what he had seen and heard in Madrid—foolish bravado, secrecy, treachery, and, as he saw it, a vast waste of courage on the part of the Loyalists who were being undercut by the Communists—Dos Passos departed Madrid in mid-April for Fuentedueña, where he remained long enough to learn about the village and the irrigation project organized by the local government. The project, which was to be filmed as a part of *The Spanish Earth,* loomed larger for the local people than did the war, because irrigation would mean a better economy and would be a demonstration of the success of a Socialist government.

Dos Passos was most anxious, however, to proceed to Valencia. Once there, he inquired further about Robles, hoping that the American ambassador Claude Bowers might help him to get Alvarez del Vayo to confirm the cause of Robles's death and issue a death certificate so that his widow might at least collect the life insurance he had held in the United States. In an interview del Vayo assured Dos Passos that he would respond, but never did, and Dos Passos could never get "any record of the indictment or trials before the 'special section.'" He left Valencia discouraged, having failed to help Señora Robles in any substantial way.

Dos Passos's last stop was Barcelona, the headquarters of the POUM, the United Marxist Labor Party, where officials put a car at his disposal to take him to the French border. Before leaving Barcelona, he interviewed Andrés Nin, the head of the POUM who was soon thereafter executed by the Communists when they suppressed his party. At the hotel where Dos Passos was staying, he met the English writer George Orwell, who had been at the front with POUM troops and had been wounded. "His face had a sick drawn look," Dos Passos recalled and supposed that Orwell "was already suffering from the tuberculosis that later killed him." The two men did not talk long, but Dos Passos remembered his sense of relief to be conversing with an honest man at last. Most of the officials he had been talking to had been "gulls, . . . or self-deceivers, or else had been trying to pull the wool over my eyes," and the plight of the common people had been "heartbreaking." "There's a certain majesty in innocence in the face of death," he wrote. "This man Orwell referred without overemphasis to things we both knew to be true. He passed over them lightly"—"It's complicated . . . in Bellver our people want to know whether to move against the anarchists. In some other places they are with them. . . . You know Spain," Dos Passos quoted Orwell in *Journeys Between Wars*. Orwell seemed to understand the entire situation. "Perhaps," Dos Passos concluded, "he was still a little afraid of how much he knew."

Before Dos Passos left Barcelona for Perpignan, yet another incident occurred to convince him of Communist treachery. As he was preparing to leave, the American Liston Oak came surreptitiously to his room and pleaded for a ride into France. What was the matter? Dos Passos asked. Oak, who had come to Spain to fight for the Republic, had been working in Valencia at the Republican Press Bureau and had escaped in the nick of time after having found out that he had been reported to be politically unreliable—"questions, he guessed he'd asked too many questions." Now he feared the "special sections." Dos Passos arranged for Oak and another man, a member of the Lincoln Brigade, to accompany him, posing as his secretaries. Nervously the two followed Dos Passos when he visited San Pol on the way north to the French border, and only after they had passed the border guards at Cerbère did the "secretaries" breathe easily.

Katy may have met Dos Passos in Antibes for a few days of relaxation once he returned from Spain. By the middle of May they were both in Paris to entrain for the channel coast in order to cross to England, from where they would sail for the

United States. Hemingway also was in Paris about to return to America and unexpectedly appeared to see them off. Despite recent events Katy and Dos Passos still liked Ernest, but his grim look at the train station chilled them. Hemingway, agitated by the bustle of departure and irritated by their disagreements about the documentary film, Robles, and the general situation in Spain, demanded of Dos Passos what he intended to say about these matters. Dos Passos responded that after he had sorted out his ideas, he would tell the truth as he saw it. The Robles case, contrary to what Ernest believed, was not an isolated incident. Hemingway began to lecture Dos Passos about the necessities of war, but Katy cut him short, reminding him that Dos Passos knew about those things also. What was the use of fighting a war if you lost your liberties? Dos Passos wondered. To hell with that, Ernest snapped back. He wanted to know if Dos Passos was with the Loyalists or against them. Dos Passos shrugged his shoulders, and for an instant Hemingway cocked a fist as if to hit him. Then he let his arm drop to his side and, breathing hard, blurted out that if Dos Passos wrote about Spain as he now saw it, the New York reviewers would bury him. They would demolish him forever.

"Why, Ernest," Katy shot back, "I never heard anything so despicably opportunistic in my life!" With that the Dos Passoses stepped aboard the train while Hemingway, without a backward glance, strode away. A friendship was ended, one casualty of the political turbulence of the decade. At some point during the next year, 1938, Dos Passos met Hemingway at the Murphys' apartment in New York. The two men stepped out on the balcony to talk. After a while Dos Passos returned and remarked cryptically to Gerald Murphy, "You think for a long time you have a friend, and then you haven't." The former friends had tried to discuss Spain again, but their antagonisms quickly surfaced, and they ended farther apart than before.

CHAPTER TWENTY-FOUR

Farewell to Europe,
1937–1939

Aboard the French liner on the way back to the United States, Don Passos did not blurt out his thoughts as he tried to sort through them, but he talked about the European scene to several people, among them Margaret Tjader Harris, an associate of Theodore Dreiser. She met Dos Passos during the voyage and noticed how, like her, he was thoroughly upset by events. Once in America, Dos Passos spent a short time in New York. Then he visited Washington, D.C., briefly, in hopes of convincing government officials to alter their policies toward Spain. He recalled meeting an American diplomat, whom he did not name, at a bar in the Willard Hotel. The diplomat was to see the President and assured Dos Passos that he would demand that the Spanish Loyalists be allowed to buy arms from America. Shortly afterward, Dos Passos met the man again. Now the diplomat was docile, "no more talk of ending the blockade. No more talk of resignation. He and the President had agreed perfectly about everything." Roosevelt, the great persuader, had made the man see "the larger view," to Dos Passos's dismay.

During the summer he merely hinted at his personal anguish in letters to his friends, although within a month of his return he sent an essay, "Farewell to Europe!" to be published in *Common Sense.* To Horsley Gantt he wrote, "You had the right line from way back," referring to Gantt's distrust of the Soviets during the 1920s. "Had a very instructive trip abroad—in fact rather too instructive," he told Rumsey Marvin during the summer. "Spain is a pretty grim place right now." In August he wrote E. E. Cummings as if he were rediscovering a long-lost friend. He was, in a way, because now that Dos Passos was forswearing revolutionary politics, he felt particularly akin to his conservative—albeit largely apolitical—friend. Urging Cummings to pay a visit to Provincetown, Dos Passos commented that "as more and more old friends pass into the adult stage—singularly disagreeable among all the primates including man—they become more old and less friends." Mike Gold had recently accused Dos Passos of "remaining alas in a state of bourgeoisie unreconstructed and unliquidated adolescence," and, Dos Passos added, "I'm in my ivory tower—a damn tall one which I'm hoping to fireproof against incendiary bombs— and damn cosy there. It takes a little trip out to the firing line now and then to make you appreciate its excellence—firing line, hell, chain gang is more like it—anyway the sawdust trail is not for me." Cummings was amused by Dos Passos's retreat from political stumping and answered, "Thee can tell All That Glitters [Mike Gold] from me that, if twenty pianomovers with forty hands carried world-revolution all yee way up yee Empire State and dropped it into yee East River, yee splash wouldn't fill a pissant's vagina."

Retiring from the sawdust trail had meant for Dos Passos avoiding the opening of the Second American Writers' Congress on the evening of June 4 at Carnegie Hall. There an overflow crowd had heard Archibald MacLeish act as chairman and master of ceremonies for the session, at which Joris Ivens introduced two sequences from *The Spanish Earth*, followed by a speech by Hemingway, who was greeted with applause. He spoke of the difficulty of writing truly, and of observing "some new friends and some of long standing . . . live and fight and die." Worse than war, however, were cowardice, treachery, and "simple selfishness." He could not but have had Dos Passos in mind when he declared that finding the truth might involve risk, but was more rewarding than "disputing learnedly on points of doctrine. And there will always be new schisms," he added, "and new fallings off and marvelous exotic doctrines and romantic lost leaders, for those who do not want to work at what they profess to believe in, but only to discuss and maintain positions, skillfully chosen positions with no risk involved in holding them."

One light touch during the gloomy aftermath of Dos Passos's Spanish trip was a letter he received from his long-time friend, the writer Dawn Powell, directly after the Writers' Congress had concluded. "Dear Dos," she wrote, "I have just had a close escape from the Soviets and now I'm happy to say I'm back with the fairies (Fascists to you)." She accused him of gloating about having avoided the congress and "bragging about the way you finished off the war, you and Martha Gellhorn. . . . And then there was the writers congress with Mr. H. pumping all the way up from Bimini on water-wings." (Hemingway had flown up for the occasion.) She was amused by the opening session, "vast and impressive," she called it, with delegates who had "walked in from all over even Newport and the platform was a sea of so-called faces. Cameramen crept in and out of Don. Stewart's slacks and microphones were jammed down everybody's throat." The main event of the evening occurred when at "about ten-thirty all the foreign correspondents marched on each one with his private blonde led by Ernest and Miss Gellhorn, who had been thru hell in Spain and came shivering on in a silver fox cape chin-up." Other correspondents were less fortunate, Dawn wrote. John Gunther, for example, "could only get his [blonde] to the corner of the platform . . . [and] those who had none could take potluck on Muriel Draper or go eat a peach-pit." Powell had to admit that Hemingway's speech was good, "if that's what you like and his sum total was that war was pretty nice and a lot better than sitting around a hot hall and writers ought to all go to war and get killed and if they didn't they were a big sissy. Then he went over to the Stork Club, followed by a pack of foxes." She added that Ivens's film sequences were excellent, "particularly a soldier going home on leave part if you know what I mean."

Her letter was a kind gesture to cheer Dos Passos. She was a close enough friend to know that his recent experiences had been thoroughly depressing, and she understood that the Writers' Congress, and all the hoopla that surrounded it, were particularly difficult for Dos Passos to take. At least she could try to make him laugh at it, which she did by describing more of the proceedings. "Next day," she continued in her sardonic fashion,

> the real business of the congress began with a very splendid talk by Kenneth Burke on "The Concept of the Conceptual or the Conceptual Hypnosis of the Concept or Anyway That's Neither Here nor There but Take Like the Boss Being the Father Hypnosis or Anyway Its A Long Story." Like a flash it came over me that here was the crux of everything and nothing could have summed the whole movement up better so I shot out the door as the angry opposition to this thought got under way and I took the train to Port Jefferson and hid under a bar for two days with nothing but a bare Tom Collins between me and Trotsky's guns.

The letter produced some moments of amusement for Dos Passos during an otherwise bleak time. Not that he was utterly alone in his now complete disillusionment with the Communists. John Dewey, for one, had occasion in mid-June to write Dos Passos and affirmed that "In spite of the fact that my name appears on a good many lists of alleged liberal activities I agree with what you say about the growing futility of that sort of thing. I hope the extent to which certain CP groups and their sympathizers have carried the rounding up process will tend to bring the whole business into disrepute—the Writers Congress is a sample I imagine. . . ."

Such words of support might bolster Dos Passos's morale, but he realized that the political position he was about to take publicly would be unpopular with the vast majority of leftists. Preying on his mind was not only what he believed he had discovered about Communist scheming in Spain, but also a different understanding of the internal politics of that country. Earlier in the thirties he had argued repeatedly with Arthur McComb about its politics. McComb, who knew Spanish history well, argued that the country's plight was but a continuation of the historic pattern of military takeovers which had occurred throughout the nineteenth century. Franco, McComb pointed out, did not think of himself as a Fascist but as a conservative nationalist. His motto was "discipline and unity," and he had the enthusiastic support of many Spaniards. Before 1937 Dos Passos because of his enthusiasm for Spanish liberalism and the Republic could not accept McComb's arguments and had wanted to believe that the struggle was a straightforward one of freedom versus Fascism. But in the light of what he had seen and heard in Spain, he could understand McComb's view that the Civil War was an historically rooted, internal affair made more complex by its international implications and by the involvement of foreign nations.

Such thoughts made it impossible for him now to embrace the Loyalist cause as unquestioningly as earlier he had. And although he scorned Hemingway for having said that New York reviewers would bury him for his position, he did not believe that Ernest was entirely mistaken. Nevertheless, he intended to tell the truth as he saw it and in June sent *Common Sense* his piece "Farewell to Europe!" which appeared in the July issue. "The people of Western Europe are facing this summer a series of tragic dilemmas," his essay began, referring to the choice between Fascism and Communism that faced Europeans, a choice that to him was tragic, because futile. Americans, however, still had the opportunity to preserve their liberties, if they would not permit themselves to be infected by the "formulas for slavery that are preparing in Europe on every side." In England and France prospects for peace seemed dim because of a stalemate between the forces of the Left and the Right, while in Spain "behind the lines a struggle as violent almost as the war had been going on between the Marxist concept of the totalitarian state, and the Anarchist concept of individual liberty. More and more as the day to day needs of the army become paramount . . . the Communist Party forges ahead as the organizer of victory. The anarchists and the socialists with their ideas of individual and local freedom and self-government have given way step by step before this tremendously efficient and ruthless machine for power." Dos Passos acknowledged that the Communists had coalesced the disparate anti-Franco groups in Spain, but, he asserted, "along with their enthusiasm and their munitions," they had brought their "secret Jesuitical methods, the Trotsky witch-hunt, and all the intricate and bloody machinery of Kremlin policy." Dos Passos still hoped for a Loyalist victory, but he wondered if the price paid would not be too great a move toward "a centralized military state," which might be "somewhat modified in the direction of personal liberty by the need to conciliate the instinct against centralization of the masses and to cope with the economically cellular character of the peninsula." If, on the other hand, the Fascists won, "It would mean the final blotting out of hope for Europe."

Then, in a statement that was as clear an indication as he could make that the United States had become his "chosen country," he concluded:

> The Atlantic is a good wide ocean. An American in 1937 comes back from Europe with a feeling of happiness, the relief of coming up out into the sunlight from a stifling cellar, that some of his grandfathers must have felt coming home from Metternich's Europe after the Napoleonic wars, the feeling all the immigrants have had when they first saw the long low coast and the broad bays of the new world. At least we still have alternatives.
>
> Sure, we've got our class war, we've got our giant bureaucratic machines for antihuman power, but I can't help feeling that we are still moving on a slightly divergent track from the European world. Not all the fascist-hearted

newspaper owners in the country, nor the Chambers of Commerce, nor the armies of hired gunthugs of the great industries can change the fact that we have the Roundhead Revolution in our heritage and the Bill of Rights and the fact that the democracy in the past has been able, under Jefferson, Jackson, and Lincoln, and perhaps a fourth time (it's too soon to know yet) under Franklin Roosevelt, to curb powerful ruling groups. America has got to be in a better position to work out the problem: individual liberty vs. bureaucratic industrial organization than any other part of the world. If we don't it means the end of everything we have ever wanted since the first hard winters at Plymouth.

Delineating his position thus, Dos Passos soon received the criticism Hemingway had predicted. Mike Gold attacked his stance, and at the end of August Jack Lawson wrote to express his thorough disagreement. Lawson had been negotiating in Hollywood to write a film script of *The Big Money*. Nothing had come of the project, he informed Dos Passos, but despite Dos Passos's doubts Lawson believed there was merit in the idea of making a film; "certain vital things could come out of it," he was sure. "So you see I don't agree with you about the movies," he continued, adding, "nor about religion or politics—for that matter!" Despite their growing ideological differences during the several years prior to 1937, they had been attempting to keep their friendship alive. Dos Passos had recently written that it was a matter of "gratuitous illogical and purposeless bonds," to which Lawson responded that friendship was not just that, but "a rather serious business, and is based on a good deal of understanding—not only understanding of where people agree, but of all the vast and complicated and psychoneurotic and intellectual and emotional factors which may and do cause people to disagree. . . . As long as friends have a decent respect for themselves and their friendship, they say anything they damn well think, and I don't see why either should get angry about it."

But Lawson, in fact, was simmering about "Farewell to Europe!" and about a remark to Lawson in a letter Dos Passos had written that he had "settled down to getting my own private menagerie into my own private ark." Lawson responded,

> That's a perfectly dignified thing to do. I don't think much of ivory towers, but I can certainly respect a friend who wants to sit in one and says, "Come in and have a drink, but be courteous enough to respect my feelings and let's lay off politics"—but when you say that, and at the same time issue extremely political statements in the public prints, I say you're either kidding yourself or kidding me, and I don't respect your alleged "privacy."

Dos Passos in "Farewell" had referred to "the intricate and bloody machinery of Kremlin policy." Though distressed at the reference, Lawson wrote that he did not see why disagreement about Soviet policies should destroy their friendship. After all, the core of both their thinking processes had been "the passionate belief in human rights and liberty and dignity which we both share." But Dos Passos seemed to Lawson to be guilty of "plain ornery red-baiting," because he appeared unwilling to differentiate his hatred of Moscow's policies from "the implication that everybody who disagrees with you and approves this intricate and bloody machinery is *also, a priori* and whether they like it or not pretty damn intricate and bloody." In other words, Lawson accused Dos Passos of blaming all Communists for the violence and terror he had found in Spain.

"What I'm concerned about," Lawson wrote, "is you and myself and America." Dos Passos, he asserted, must draw a line between committed Americans and Kremlin policy. Lawson, unwilling to believe his friend would not make the distinction, was concerned to point out that not to do so was "a very real danger, and the farthest thing in the world from the free-thinking and free exchange of opinion" which Dos Passos insisted on. "It happens," Lawson noted, "that a large number of progressive and serious people *do* get together to wage what they feel is a clear-cut fight *against* something, against reaction and fascism. Communists play a large part in organizing this movement." He conceded that Dos Passos might be correct in believing that the situation was more complex than merely a struggle of good (the Left) against evil (reactionaries and fascists) and that creating "an instrument of power" (the communist machinery of government) created "a continual contradiction between the aims of the fighters for liberty and the result. All right," Lawson continued, "but in finding your way through this complexity don't cut yourself off from the whole complex of people and ideas which is the very thing you're trying to analyze." He thought that the two of them could argue constructively about how to achieve individual liberties, unless Dos Passos now believed that "the fight against communism, as an 'alien' philosophy," was more important than the beliefs that he and Lawson held in common. If that were the case, then Dos Passos was guilty of "witch-hunting and red-hating and prejudice."

Finally Lawson ended his impassioned letter to the man whom he had respected perhaps more than anyone else. After criticizing Trotskyites, for whom Dos Passos had some sympathy, Lawson concluded,

> Lots of us are dumb enough to think that [loyalty and cooperation, and faith in the honor and courage and decency of people] are the qualities that brought the anti-fascists from all over the world and especially from Russia to fight in Spain and we're pretty sick and hurt when it's described as an "intricate and bloody machinery." Think it about Russia if you want to. Say it if it makes you feel any better. But don't twist it into an unforgivable prejudice against your own sort of people, and the work they're trying to do. I assure you, friendship won't stand that.

Dos Passos responded to Lawson quickly, trying to elucidate his stance as precisely as possible while attempting as well to keep the strained friendship alive. "You must have patience with unbelievers," he urged Lawson, and declared that the real difference between their two political attitudes was that Lawson thought that ends justified means, while Dos Passos was positive that "all you have in politics is the means; ends are always illusory." And, making what was for him a significant declaration, he continued: "I think that Anglo-Saxon democracy is the best political method of which we have any and I'm for or against movements in so far as they seem to me to be consistent with its survival. To survive its got to keep on evolving. I have come to believe that the CP is fundamentally opposed to our democracy as I see it." Lawson had been correct in his previous letter: Dos Passos now saw Russian Communism, if not Marxism—exactly—as "an 'alien' philosophy," and he could no longer give the American Communist Party the benefit of his doubts. Communists were wrong, he believed, and those who did not take orders overtly from the Kremlin were nevertheless its dupes. His response once he had made up his mind was emotional at least as much as intellectual, and one which defined sharply the issues separating Communism and capitalist democracy. He found it difficult to accept any middle ground, which was what so irritated Lawson. "You cannot tell me what *my* intentions are," was Lawson's point. "You don't *know* what your intentions are," was Dos Passos's response in effect, "because they are what the Kremlin dictates, and the Kremlin reveals no secrets."

Although Dos Passos in his own mind might make some distinction between the Communism of Stalin and the theories of Marxism, he admitted little. "Marxism," he declared to Lawson, "though an important basis for the unborn sociological sciences, if held as a dogma, is a reactionary force and an impediment to progress. Fascism is nothing but marxism inside out and is of course a worse impediment." To the argument that not supporting the Communists was aiding the Fascists, Dos Passos answered, "rubbish: free thought can't possibly give aid and comfort to fascism." He defended himself against Lawson's accusation that he had not seen enough of what was going on to reach the conclusions he did. "Naturally [my] position was reached after considerable travel," Dos Passos continued, asserting:

I now think that foreign liberals and radicals were very wrong not to protest against the Russian terror all down the line. There's just a chance that continual criticism from their friends might have influenced the bolsheviks and made them realize the extreme danger to their cause of the terror machine, which has now, in my opinion, eaten up everything good in the revolution. What we have in the U.S.S.R. is a new form of society—but I dont think it shows any sign of being a superior frame for the individual human than the poor old U.S.A. And waving the fascist spook at me isn't going to make me think any different.

Knowing that he was venturing out into unpopular territory, he added, "the fact that my particular slant in thought has few adherents at present, doesn't make it any less valid in my opinion."

Lawson immediately responded, and while he agreed that they must have patience with each other, the breach widened. "You see," he admonished Dos Passos:

where my goat is gotten, and starts not only to bleat but to neigh like a horse, is that, starting from a disagreement about certain facts (what is happening in the Soviet Union, the actual functioning of the Soviets, the Russian foreign policy, etc.) you jump . . . to the *realm of theory:* that is, in order to justify your version of the facts . . . instead of proceeding to at least attempt this verification, you assume that Communists and their friends *must* have a lot of theories which fit your version of the facts; the next step: since these theories are obviously contrary to what Communists say *they* believe, they must be a bunch of the most unprincipled liars.

Lawson told Dos Passos he was "nuts" to think that Communists believed that ends justified means. Instead, not believing such was exactly what distinguished Communists from Fascists. The former, in fact, believed that "only honorable and democratic means can be used to achieve democratic ends." To Lawson it seemed clear that the war in Spain demonstrated conclusively the difference between the ends-justifying-means Fascists—who slaughtered people and destroyed property indiscriminately—and the Communist-supported Loyalists, who Lawson was convinced *"strictly,* and with no exception, employ honest, democratic means . . . for honest, democratic ends." These means Lawson enumerated as being "a People's Army, a people's education and culture, an extension of the rights of the workers and farmers and shopkeepers and professionals, observance of the most humane principles possible in war-time, open and completely frank diplomacy."

Dos Passos must have been incensed by Lawson's rhetoric, particularly when Lawson went on to say that his impression of the situation was that "there is no case, in the Soviet Union or in Spain, of people being imprisoned or executed for their beliefs." Dos Passos was thoroughly convinced of the Communists' duplicity behind the scenes; was positive of their murderous methods as in the case of his friend Robles; and was aware of their terrorism against the POUM and anarchist elements among the Loyalists whom the Communists accused of subversive Trotskyism. He knew, further, of their execution of Andrés Nin, the POUM leader, and of their forcing Largo Caballero to resign as Premier of the Loyalist government in favor of Juan Negrín.

Lawson was sure of *his* intentions as a Communist, and he could not tolerate —for that matter, could hardly comprehend—Dos Passos's conviction that being such, he, Lawson, was an unwitting victim of the Soviets. He accused Dos Passos of a "tragic isolation from activity," while Lawson and others working for the movement had learned a "deeper and richer democracy," which they were committed to protect, as were Communists in the Soviet Union and in Spain. "You don't know what you're missing," he concluded his letter, "and what you're missing is a first-rate education in actually working democratically, by democratic means, for democratic ends."

The friendship was not entirely sundered in 1937. Dos Passos in November wrote Lawson to praise a revival of the dramatist's play *Processional* while noticeably avoiding any reference to their political quarrels. Then in December Dos Passos published in *Common Sense* a piece entitled "The Communist Party and the War Spirit: A Letter to a Friend Who Is Probably a Party Member," which was as much directed toward Lawson as toward any of Dos Passos's other critics. "As I take it," he wrote to his hypothetical friend, "your argument is, in its simplest terms, that the world situation consists of war between Fascism, demagogic military dictatorship for the purposes of reaction on one side, and the principle of progressive popular rule on the other side, of which you feel the Communist Party is the spear head." Dos Passos went on to spell out the Popular Front line, but disagreed, stating that he did not think his friend's assessment was a true picture of international politics. Dos Passos could agree that "the declared aims of the Bolsheviks were admirable," but he noted, "The question is whether the dictatorship method didn't make these aims impossible to attain." He recalled that only after twenty years of totalitarian rule did the Communist Party reintroduce "at least a facade of what Marxists used sneeringly to call bourgeois democracy" to coincide with the Popular Front.

Americans wondered if the price had not been too high. Wouldn't it have been better to retain the democratic processes all along, and hadn't the result of the "human misery and repression" been "to warp the whole great enterprise in the direction of personal and bureaucratic despotism?" Clearly he thought so. American democracy had become his ideal; in fact, he now believed that "the one hope for the future of the type of western civilization which furnishes the frame of our lives is that the system of popular government based on individual liberty be not allowed to break down." Fascism, he had decided, "is a disease of sick capitalism, not a disease of democracy," and its cure was "intelligent popular government." As for Spain, liberal and Communist support had been the Loyalists' life blood, but, he wrote, "the terrible thing for Spain's confused and vigorous movement for social renovation was that the Communists entered Spain at a moment when their party was infected by the internal feud of the Trotsky heresy hunt, at the moment in its history when it was least flexible. . . . The Communists took to Spain their organizing skill, their will to rule, and their blind intolerance," and the result had been that, instead of rallying progressives to it, the party had, "as it gained in power, set itself to eliminating physically or otherwise all the men with possibilities of leadership who were not willing to put themselves under its orders."

There, apparently, the matter stood between Lawson and Dos Passos for the next year and a half. Lawson went his way in Hollywood, while Dos Passos went his, studying the origins of the American republic and emphasizing his stance to whoever would listen. When early in 1938, for example, Sherwood Anderson wrote to express his approval of the article in the December 1937 issue of *Common Sense*, Dos Passos immediately responded to thank him. "What worries me about the bastardly Communists," he added, "is that they seem to me to be spreading around (and they certainly are skillful organizers) ideas that now that they've thrown overboard all their social revolutionary aims—are purely fascist." The Communists, he noted, certainly had "the literary boys eating out of their hands. Maybe there was something in the ivory towers after all." Then from the Warm Springs Inn in Virginia he wrote Upton Sinclair late in March to express precisely the ideas he had in *Common Sense,* while adding that as for the United States, he believed increasingly that the Communists were "introducing the fascist mentality [he first wrote "methods"] that had made Europe a nightmare." "After all," he noted in an aside, "its the Bolsheviks that invented all of Hitler's and Mussolini's tricks." As a result he had come to think American Communists were "a pestiferous nuisance—Stalinist and Trotskyite alike."

Despite his scorn for European politics, in the summer of 1938 he and Katy traveled to Europe, where in July and early August they sailed in the Mediterranean with Gerald and Sara Murphy. During the cruise they landed at Paestum, Italy, where twenty years earlier Dos Passos and Lawson had traveled while on leave from their Red Cross ambulance unit. From the site Dos Passos wrote Lawson a card, reminding him that "just a little more than twenty years ago . . . you suddenly appeared here in a horse cab under the most extraordinary auspices—the temples [are] still doing well." Significantly, thirty-six years later Lawson recollected that Dos Passos's postcard had read in part, "I wonder if anything has changed since that time?" Lawson saw this as Dos Passos's attempt to reconcile their differences. He further recalled that he had never responded to the card nor had he ever written Dos Passos again until he thanked him for a copy of *The Best Times* which Dos Passos sent Lawson after it was published in 1966.

Lawson's memory in response to an interview in 1974 tricked him. The postcard did not say what he would have had it say, and he did write Dos Passos again. While in his old age Lawson wanted to believe that he and his erstwhile friend had merely drifted apart, the final break was not so smooth. Dos Passos, although firm in his convictions, was willing to overlook political differences to preserve friendship. Lawson, on the other hand, could not stay away from ideological differences, so in what was almost assuredly his last letter to Dos Passos, written the end of August 1939, he berated Dos Passos for *The Adventures of a Young Man,* his statement in fiction of his break with the left wing. The novel, Lawson declared, had so shocked him that he had not recovered. He accused Dos Passos of violating "known and available truth. The book made me angry—but anger isn't very helpful," he concluded:

> and I'd really like to be helpful—although I doubt if it's possible. In fact, I doubt if there's any common ground on which we can talk about these things. I think that's tragic. . . . I also think . . . that you're to blame—for turning so far away from the sort of agreed fundamentals of feeling and purpose, the groundwork for common thought—which is also common action—that we started with. That's not a nice thing to say—and it probably won't have any effect—but there it is. Jack.

Except for the brief interchange around *The Best Times,* the relationship cooled. Not unlike the break with Hemingway, it was a sad, if revealing, conclusion to the friendship of two American writers in the 1930s.

Dos Passos in the summer of 1937 made veiled reference to the other friendship which had already concluded, for all intents and purposes. When Stewart Mitchell wrote in mid-August asking what Dos Passos thought of a well-publicized scuffle Ernest Hemingway had with Max Eastman in the office of Scribner's editor Max Perkins, Dos Passos answered only, "Damn silly that fisticuffs for the press—in fact makes you vomit." And when in October Bernice Baumgarten wrote to suggest that Hemingway be asked to write a dust-jacket statement for the volume *U.S.A.*, which after some disagreement Harcourt, Brace had agreed to publish, Dos Passos answered only "Hemingway is out for various reasons."

It was not a matter of Dos Passos lightly dismissing his former friend from his mind. On the contrary, their clashes remained with him. But just as he had earlier kept his friendships to himself, so he kept his disagreements. Further, there were matters like finances to keep him from brooding. In September, for example, his and Katy's monies were in such disarray that he had to ask Mitchell to bail him out with a loan of $50, which he promised to repay quickly. He and Katy had suddenly found themselves overdrawn, he wrote, and apologized for not being able to organize his money more sensibly. They lived higher than they could earn, he explained, although adding that if they did not, their living "would be meagre indeed—so life is a continual race with the sheriff." They seemed always to think themselves "on the edge of a big killing of some kind," but meanwhile they were a burden to their friends.

Such worries, as well as his desire to put his troubles with Hemingway and the hurt of his disillusionment about Spain behind him, made him eager to improve the sale of his work and be on to new projects. Once he had returned to Provincetown in June, he took aim at Harcourt, Brace, who he felt had not adequately promoted his work. He asked Cap Pearce for the publishers' reaction to a "projected book of biographies," the short sketches which he had woven into the trilogy. And at the same time he broached the idea of the *U.S.A.* volume. In early July he wrote Bernice Baumgarten, first to express his dissatisfaction with the way Harcourt, Brace was handling his books, then to insist on publishing his last three novels as one, a matter for which he feared the publishers had no enthusiasm.

Pearce apparently deferred any decision about the biographies, but he, Dos Passos, and Baumgarten had an extended discussion about what Dos Passos termed "the complete novel," whose title, he informed Pearce, would be *U.S.A.* "The more I think of it the more essential it seems," he added, "both as a money making proposition and from the point of view of the work itself, to bring it out." The latest possible date for publication, he believed, ought to be the fall of 1938; he preferred the spring. Not until Donald Brace returned from Europe could a decision be reached, but once he had, the publishers accepted Dos Passos's proposition for *U.S.A.* so that by mid-August Pearce could write Dos Passos that Harcourt, Brace was "singing new tunes about the three-in-one. So! Hooray for you and Bernice." Within a month, the publishers had begun to prepare dummies of *U.S.A.*

This development, however, was not enough to satisfy Dos Passos, who wrote Pearce on Labor Day that he wanted to meet soon with him and Brace to "talk over a five year plan of publications." Further, he had some ideas about advertising and publicity that he wanted the publishers to consider, because he realized that it was "useless to pick flaws without countering with some kind of suggestion." He was beginning to conceive another book of reportage and asked Pearce what he thought about bringing out the pieces on the Spanish Civil War, or about republishing *Orient Express* with selections from *In All Countries*. He added as an afterthought the idea of pulling together all his Spanish pieces, those from *Rosinante to the Road Again, In All Countries,* and the new essays. This, in fact, was what transpired to become *Journeys Between Wars,* published in April 1938.

He kept pushing Harcourt, Brace. Writing Pearce that he would be in New York early in October to discuss *U.S.A.* and the book about Spain, Dos Passos added, "I think if we can polish off *U.S.A.* and a possible reprint of travel stuff as early as possible we'll be in a position to go ahead on a short novel which will be a completely new departure—(it may turn out to be a series) next fall." He hoped to see earlier writing which was still of interest made available in a fresh form. This he believed would set the stage for the new work. In addition, although he did not mention it to Pearce, he no doubt thought that it was a way of marking the end of one stage in his career, because in his own mind he was about to embark in a new direction, both in terms of his political stance as well as in the form of his work. The short novel he mentioned to Pearce would become *Adventures of a Young Man,* Dos Passos's statement in fiction published in 1939 about his disillusionment with the Communists in Spain. To the dismay of the Left, his politics clearly had changed, while the form of the book was thoroughly conventional, a third-person narration about a single hero, Glenn Spotswood. At the same time Dos Passos was turning to American history, so the overall form of his work would take on a new dimension as well.

In a letter written at the end of September he told Bernice Baumgarten of these plans so that she could stay abreast of his negotiations with Harcourt, Brace. "I am embarking on an almost endless series of short novels," he wrote, an indicator that with the *U.S.A.* trilogy complete, he had begun to conceive of his work as a series of what he would come to call "contemporary chronicles." He also told Baumgarten of *"The American Base* (or something like that) the set of historical pieces—[which] ought to start coming along during the winter—but I think its much better for H & B to put their minds on making a wow of U.S.A. . . . than to wait for it." *The American Base* became *The Ground We Stand On,* his first full-length study of the roots of the United States. He repeated to Bernice what he had written Pearce the day before, that he wanted Harcourt, Brace to "clear up my old stuff and have it in available form for the public, in case the public got a taste to buy it, before starting off on what are going to be a set of thoroughly new departures."

He met on October 7 in New York with Donald Brace and Pearce, who the next day wrote Dos Passos that the publishers were looking forward to a new campaign on behalf of his work. Dos Passos immediately began to organize the materials for *Journeys Between Wars* and to struggle with a prefatory note for *U.S.A.,* which would be published in January 1938. Soon he had completed both tasks. The prefatory note, Dos Passos wrote Pearce, seemed to make the best sense if it were to be printed in the same type as the "Vag" portrait which ended *The Big Money*. They were of a piece, he knew, and using the same type would enhance the reader's understanding of "the young man [who] walks fast by himself through the crowd that thins into the night streets," who is tired, lonely, and searching—who has experienced what the U.S.A. is: "the slice of a continent . . . a group of holding companies, some aggregations of trade unions . . . but mostly . . . the speech of the people." This young man is the "Vag" of the last pages who has experienced the myriad elements that constitute "U.S.A.," but has not found its promise, an ideal republic which Dos Passos, like his heroes Walt Whitman and Thomas Jefferson, dreamed about. And so at the end of *The Big Money* the young man waits, hungry and out of work, at the side of a road, while his thoughts are of the wealth and glamour which America has promised, but which he has never found. Together the two pieces made a useful frame for the trilogy and heightened Dos Passos's theme of the search for an ideal as well as his intention to present a panorama of the country the young man and thousands like him had experienced during the first three decades of the twentieth century.

While Dos Passos was pleased that Harcourt, Brace promised to work harder to sell his books, he was not content with their assurances, but instructed Bernice Baumgarten about what she should make the publishers do. "Make them get hold of Gingrich's piece that I told them about—introducing The Camera Eye things in Esquire—and read and digest it," he wrote. "Make their salesmen read it—they probably all read Esquire any way—get it into their heads that every one of the half million readers of Esquire is a potential buyer of the book." The piece he referred to was a short "Editor's Note" which headed a selection entitled "The Camera Eye" that had appeared in the April 1936 issue of *Esquire*. Labelled "semi-fiction," "The Camera Eye" was "a verbal montage" made up of bits from Camera Eyes which appeared in *The Big Money*, of other bits Dos Passos had written for the Camera Eye but had not used in *The Big Money* because they strayed from the subject of America, and of slogans and songs such as he included in the Newsreel sections. Gingrich's note, intended to clarify Dos Passos's techniques, instructed the readers of *Esquire* not to "insist upon making consecutive sense of every phrase and sentence as you go along. The effect is as cumulative as that of music or painting." The selection, Gingrich continued, "is the verbal equivalent of the inclusive technique of photography, registering apparently irrelevant and even distracting detail for the sake of achieving a complete atmospheric approximation of reality." The editor concluded his comment by summarizing the intent of "The Camera Eye," and the summary, noting the purpose of the Newsreel sort of interludes, is a substantially complete description of Dos Passos's intentions for all the Camera Eyes in *The Big Money:*

The man's approach to New York recorded both in terms of sensory impressions and of memories thus induced; (interlude: the classified ads); he recalls other positions offered and opportunities presented in the past; he "gets the job," in which he is a clumsy misfit; (interlude: our business civilization in terms of advertising, popular songs, crime and/or success stories); he goes to a Greenwich Village party, where the hostess classifies him as inhibited; he inclines toward a career as a soapbox agitator but is inhibited by honest doubt; he feels money-lust, remembers chances that might have made money, pleasures that money would have bought; he walks the tawdry streets, within the sight, the very smell of money money everywhere, nursing a growing sense of inferiority, of kinship to all the other misfits of our crowded politico-social-business set-up which leaves walking-room only for those who are diseased by doubt.

Dos Passos also suggested to Bernice that some well-known author might be induced to do a piece about the trilogy. "After all," he complained, "somebody around H & B must be able to think up selling ideas. They sell their other books all right—the trouble with them is that when they are up against my books all they can think of is the New York critics who are a bunch of dreary fatheads—or having me sign fifty copies at Lord and Taylor's—which I think is nonsense." The sales of *1919* and *The Big Money* seemed to him to prove that the company's methods were no good, and, he added bitterly, "according to Time *Mice and Men* by Mr. Steinbeck sold 187,000 copies during the period that The B.M. was selling 20,000." He was not willing—at that moment, in any case—to acknowledge that Steinbeck's short, direct novel about Lenny and George had a popular appeal his lengthy, intricately structured novels did not.

So busy was Dos Passos with these concerns as well as writing projects that during the summer and fall of 1937 he could not have taken the time for travel, even had he had the money to do so. As it was, he and Katy spent most of their time in Provincetown and only took short trips such as one early in September to visit E. E. Cummings at Silver Lake, New Hampshire. They traveled several times to New York, where they combined business with pleasure. The business was the sessions with Harcourt, Brace. The pleasure was long evenings of drinks and talk with friends such as the "Chelsea Gang," who, according to the newspaper editor William L. White, were a group of literary people so named by their critics because some of them lived at the Chelsea Hotel on Fourteenth Street. There in 1937 and subsequently the Dos Passoses, White and his wife, and others such as Susanne La Follette, Ben Stolberg, Edmund Wilson, Mary McCarthy, and later, Sinclair Lewis and his young friend Marcella Powers would meet at cocktail parties. "The subject of conversation," White recalled, "was usually the Purge Trials and this group was of the general opinion that Stalin was a tyrant—a view not shared by most New York intellectuals who called us Trotskyites, which was not an accurate description of most of us—certainly not of me."

On one occasion, in November, Dos Passos and Katy spent an afternoon visiting Edmund Wilson in Stamford, Connecticut. Dos Passos's enemy—although he may never have known she was—Louise Bogan, was there, and she made her usual comment later about the encounter to one of her allies, in this instance the poet Theodore Roethke. She wrote him that she had been subjected to Wilson's friends one afternoon. "My, how the women married to literary men hate me!" she gloated. The men for the most part knew nothing about her "more deadly qualities," but the women did, and, she added, "John Dos Passos does, too. He hates me so it is painful to watch. Thank God he does. For if ever there was a fake human being and a punk writer, J. Dos P. is that one. He is such a Harvard fake. Bunny loves him."

In December Dos Passos was in New York again, and during the stay he visited Theodore Dreiser at his apartment. The two authors had a conversation which was recorded and later published by Margaret Tjader Harris in the journal *Direction*, which she had just started. Dreiser and Dos Passos rambled on not very clearly about labor, economics, the press, and politics. Little of the conversation was of note, except that Dos Passos mentioned his idea of reinstilling a sort of participatory democracy which he was settling on and which would become the basis of his later politics. "Basic industries and monopolies," he believed, should be gotten under public control. "You have got to find some kind of spirit for that," he insisted to Dreiser. "Get the New England town meeting into bureaucratic industry in some form." The idea was the germ of what he would put forward as an ideal for America in *The Prospect Before Us,* a volume published in 1950.

Toward the end of the conversation he made plain to Dreiser his new acceptance of the United States when he remarked that "America is probably the country where the average guy has got the better break." When Dos Passos had returned from Europe the last time, he noted, "It seemed to me . . . that there was more chance for people in America, and the people looked livelier, better."

With this attitude, he was, as he told Dreiser, anxious to see more of the country, in particular, to learn more about the Midwest. But before Dos Passos and Katy could travel again, he had to check proof for *Journeys Between Wars,* which was to be published in April 1938. Not until late February or early March did they set off on what she told Sara Murphy was "a fine high-speed trip through Alabama down to New Orleans, slogging upon the Mississippi delta through seas of mud—visited all the old River Towns, Natchez, Vicksburg, Memphis, Cairo, saw the Norris Dam and T.V.A.—towns—Cumberland Resettlement." When she wrote Sara, they had returned far enough north and east to be staying at the Warm Springs Inn in Virginia, where they spent the last part of March.

At Warm Springs Dos Passos caught up with his correspondence. He told Stewart Mitchell about spending a fine early morning roaming around Andrew Jackson's Hermitage near Nashville, Tennessee. It is not inferring too much to read in this Dos Passos's renewed interest in American history. "There's life in the old continent yet," he thought, as long as one did not "spend too much time in the pestilencial fever of the eastern seaboard."

He also took the time to answer William Bond, a graduate student at Harvard who was then working on a paper for a course in literary criticism. Bond had asked about the possible influence on Dos Passos of Walt Whitman. Dos Passos responded that as a child he had read a lot of Whitman and imagined that "a great deal of the original slant of my work comes from that vein in the American tradition." He was positive that the "slant" to his work was more likely to come from Whitman

—"and perhaps Veblen," he noted—than it was from Marx, whom he had read incompletely and late. "The Marxist critics are just finding out, with considerable chagrin, that my stuff isn't Marxist," he observed. The assertion made sense to Dos Passos because he had turned away from the Communists, but reading *U.S.A.* one would not think Dos Passos's claim so apparent. Individuals like Ben Compton could be portrayed as victims of the Communists; yet reading in *U.S.A.* of the swirl of forces that led to economic collapse in 1929, one might be hard-pressed not to read a Marxist historical imperative into *U.S.A.*, despite Dos Passos's claim to the contrary.

The remark was part of his continuing retreat from the Communists and the Spanish situation, an unpleasant reminder of which he received from Hemingway sometime during the spring or summer. Ernest sent Dos Passos a mean-spirited cable before sailing for France on one of his trips back to Spain that summer. In a letter afterward he apologized for the cable, which had seemed funny at the time, but later seemed merely obnoxious, he admitted. What caused him to write, however, was a piece by Dos Passos in which he wrote of the Communists' manipulation, and Hemingway was furious about this. He told Dos Passos that he was wrong about the people he called Russians. They were not, Hemingway insisted, and either over-looked or refused to recognize that Russian-born or not, someone like General Walter was a Communist, trained in Russia. Dos Passos, Hemingway supposed, wanted to tell the truth, but how could he when he had been such a short time in Spain? Moreover, if he wanted to tell the truth, why didn't he, instead of writing of things he could not know about.

Hemingway believed he knew about the makeup of the Loyalist army because he had been with them in battle. They were not, he asserted, Communist-dominated. To which Dos Passos would have responded that of course many soldiers might not be Communists, but that was irrelevant, because that was not the level on which political conniving happened. Hemingway termed vicious Dos Passos's attempt to paint the Loyalist struggle as he had. He saved his barbs for last, accusing Dos Passos of writing crookedly for money and then, in a gesture that clearly was meant to mark the end of their friendship, he bid Dos Passos "so long." Hemingway accused his former friend of knifing him in the back, and to make the charge hurt more, he reminded Dos Passos of the money he, Hemingway, had loaned him. Had there been any hope of reconciling their differences, this letter ended it.*

---

*Hemingway could not accept the possibility that Dos Passos's views were valid. He was positive that Dos Passos had spent too little time in Spain to discover the truth, and he blamed what he saw as the loss of Dos Passos's hunger to report—write—truthfully and well on his marriage to Katy. Somewhat after this Hemingway wrote Malcolm Cowley and in the course of the letter asked what Dos Passos was doing. The last Ernest had heard, Dos Passos was going to expose them all, but, Hemingway observed, unfortunately Dos Passos no longer knew anything. Just like Rudyard Kipling's, his ability to write had been ruined by domestic life. Hemingway proceeded to tell Cowley the tale which he later related to A. E. Hotchner with embellishments about Dos Passos's wiring Katy as soon as he had arrived in Madrid.

It may have been some satisfaction to Dos Passos late in his life to read—if he did—a book such as The Spanish Civil War by Hugh Thomas. This is perhaps the definitive history of the war, and with impressive documentation Thomas authenticates Dos Passos's views of what went on in Spain, although not always drawing the same conclusions.

Such painful reminders of the emotions engendered by the Civil War had the effect of making Dos Passos desire all the more to tell his side of the situation. In Provincetown by April, after the trip south and west, he worked steadily until the end of June, when he and Katy departed for Europe to cruise in the Mediterranean with the Murphys. The voyage took them along the coast of Sicily before they left the Murphys' schooner. Katy and Dos Passos in early August stopped in Rome, Pisa, and Florence before taking the train to Paris, where they were by midmonth.

Late in August they returned to Provincetown, from where in September Dos Passos described in a letter to Robert Hillyer his reaction to the trip. "It would have been dandy," he declared, "if it hadn't been that instead of Italy you now have Mussoliniland—I don't see how our fascist friends can like it so much there—why should you like to live among people that make you despise the human race?" He thought that "the miserable wops" appeared poorer than they were twenty years earlier; they fawned more and were "thievish and beggary—their bread is adulterated, their spaghetti is bad and their clothes are ragged and they look scared to death." In comparison, France, "that decadent democracy, seemed full of life and vigor; people actually laugh there."

Closing, Dos Passos assured Hillyer that he and Katy were "in fine shape except for a pestiferous lack of money." The problem seemed to be becoming chronic. "God damn it," he exclaimed, "I'm sick of being always broke." That fall, due to the expense of their trip with the Murphys and due to the modest sales of *U.S.A.* and *Journeys Between Wars*, Katy and Dos Passos were more pressed for money than usual. Although he disliked making public appearances, he seriously considered signing up for a lecture tour to enhance their income, but soon discarded the idea because he doubted his ability and, more important, desired to work steadily at *Adventures of a Young Man* and the historical narratives. But at the end of September he sent a hurried note to Stewart Mitchell asking for a loan of $100. "We suddenly find ourselves in a terrific jam—overdrafts mortgage etc.," he wrote. Mitchell complied immediately, and a week later Dos Passos wrote to thank him. The Bass River Savings Bank was "once more appeased," Dos Passos commented, and he and Katy hoped soon to be able to walk around Provincetown without trying to avoid the garageman, the grocer, and Mr. Horton the milkman.

Despite staying close to home, Dos Passos and Katy continued to have difficulty with their finances. Just after the New Year, they had to borrow from Rumsey Marvin in order to make a payment on their home loan. Dos Passos could hope that *Adventures of a Young Man*—the first draft of which, he noted on the manuscript, he completed "Jan 27 '39 3:30 P.M."—would improve his situation when it was published. But he was concerned about the book, which portrayed Communist perfidy, because, as he wrote Bernice Baumgarten in March, "I'm very afraid they [Harcourt, Brace] are going to muff this novel, because it wont please the orthodox leftists who will try to quietly stifle it, and it probably wont please any other group of reviewers." He asked Bernice to talk to either Harcourt or Brace, whom he felt would be more sensible about the problem than younger people in the publishers' offices, who would be too inclined to damn the book. He wondered if Henry Wallace or Harold Ickes might be induced to review it, since he believed they would find the subject matter interesting. But getting attention for the book was "a hell of a job to hand anybody," he admitted, due to "the power of ideological intrigue at the moment."

Dos Passos knew whereof he spoke. The leftist critics had already attacked him for his pieces in *Common Sense;* for his ambivalence toward—if not opposition to —the Communists expressed in his pieces about the Spanish Civil War published in *Esquire* and then in *Journeys Between Wars;* and for his doubts expressed in *U.S.A.* What had caused the attacks was that party writers like Mike Gold and Granville Hicks had read Dos Passos's work in the light of "Farewell to Europe!" and "The Communist Party and the War Spirit." Both Gold and Hicks felt compelled to reassess *U.S.A.*, for example, after it had been published in January 1938. Gold admitted that formerly he had praised the volumes of the trilogy and had "ignored the merde and looked for every gleam of . . . proletarian hope." But rereading the triology, Gold could now see that Dos Passos was going nowhere. The *merde* was important to Dos Passos's psychology, wrote Gold, and "after a brief, futile effort, he has sunk back into it, as into a native element." Hicks was no less insulting when he reviewed *U.S.A.* in April 1938. Dos Passos, whom he had praised in 1934 as "the revolutionary writer, the comrade," he now accused of "irresponsibility, banality, naiveté, and sheer stupidity." Because of Dos Passos's remarks subsequent to his disillusionment in Spain, Hicks declared that Dos Passos was "as unreliable as a man can be and . . . capable of any kind of preposterous vagary."

Dos Passos, therefore, had good reason to worry about the reception *Adventures of a Young Man* would receive when it was published on June 1, 1939, as he knew that its contents would infuriate the leftists and offend the liberals. In the novel Dos Passos took a single hero, Glenn Spotswood, and put him through experiences like Dos Passos's own during the 1920s and 1930s. His earliest notes for the book suggest how nearly autobiographical parts of the story would be. One page of notes begins:

Prep Schooling and Youthful Errors
Look up—outline events
   1924—1929
Harlan Miners Speak
Account of the Sacramento Trial

and continues to list matters like "Brooklyn—lodging house," "Drunken parties— Village," and "Melancholia Villa," all of which are obvious references to Dos Passos's experiences in the twenties. And from the moment he first conceived the novel he had in mind the end as it was published. Glenn, disillusioned with Communism but still an idealist, fights for the Loyalists in Spain. Yet because he has been found politically unreliable, the Communists send him on a mission at the front lines which he and his Communist companions know will lead to his death. "The little house," Dos Passos jotted down in his first notes about the final scene:

> The smell of shit
> The screaming children
> Artillery fire getting closer and closer
> The G.P.U. guys—two send
> him out with the pails of water

Dos Passos's point in the scene was to portray the kind of Communist treachery he believed had killed José Robles.

He made clear his intention for the novel in a statement which he wrote before completing the manuscript. "Adventures of a Young Man," he declared, "is the first of a series of contemporary portraits in the shape of stories," and he described briefly the point he was trying to make through his central character, Glenn Spotswood, who "has been raised in the tradition of American idealism. He suffers from a congenital sense of right and wrong. He grows up alone in the world of the twenties and thirties. He has a tough time." Thinking that this might somehow be incorporated into an introductory statement or perhaps even a dust-jacket comment, Dos Passos next wrote, "Not to be typed in my own words," and continued to describe his projected book:

> The novel will probably run a little more than 200 pp. Takes place mostly in the East. Glenn Spotswood's adventures take him into a number of different kinds of ways to make a living. He's exposed to a variety of movements and worldsaving devices. He's a counselor at a boy's camp, sells bonds, works in a bank, in a chocolate factory, in an ice cream plant, as a labor organizer and as a Washington lobbyist. Generally, like Sinbad in the old song he gets
> > in bad in Tokyo and Rome
> > In bad in Trinidad
> > And twice as bad at home.

He stuck to his intentions, although the novel was longer than he had predicted. And as he expected, he, like Sinbad, got in bad with many reviewers. The novel, wrote Samuel Sillen in the *New Masses*, was "almost inconceivably rotten" and "a crude piece of Trotskyist agit-prop" that suffered from "sloppy writing, hollow characters, machine-made dialogue, editorial rubber stamps." Sillen believed that the book failed because "Dos Passos has gone sour. It is not merely that he is bitterly and stupidly opposed to the Soviet Union. It is not merely that he misrepresents the battlers for freedom in Spain. He finds nothing that is good anywhere. Ultimately it is not the Soviet Union that he libels, but humanity everywhere."

The critical responses to *Adventures of a Young Man* were as significant as the novel, for they reflected the political controversies still rife in the late 1930s. Malcolm Cowley, sympathetic with the Communists, criticized Dos Passos as severely as had Sillen, if with less vitriol. Cowley's review, which inspired Dos Passos's letter to the *New Republic* to explain the circumstances surrounding José Robles's death, was entitled "Disillusionment." Dos Passos's disillusionment, Cowley wrote, had resulted in "the weakest novel [he] has written since 'One Man's Initiation.'" Cowley admitted that disagreement with the author's politics affected this judgment, but, he continued, take away politics and there was little left to the novel, because it lacked the technical innovations of *U.S.A.* and because its hero, Glenn Spotswood, was "simply not interesting or strong enough to carry the burden of the story." While expressing his dislike for the book, Cowley declared that Dos Passos, disillusioned, might become utterly cynical.

In August 1939, the anti-Stalinist author James T. Farrell took on other critics of *Adventures* in the *American Mercury.* Thoroughly familiar with the political battles of the 1930s because he had been through them himself as a fiercely independent leftist, Farrell recognized that Dos Passos's portrayal of Communist power politics had offended reviewers, but, Farrell wrote, "the fundamental meaning to be drawn from this novel" was like that in *Bread and Wine* by Ignazio Silone. Both writers were "concerned with integrity," something that Glenn Spotswood strove to maintain and, as a result, died for. *Adventures,* asserted Farrell, asked the question, "how is integrity to be maintained in revolutionary politics?" Such questions were impossible to avoid once one sensed that "the revolutionary party of Lenin has become the counter-revolutionary party of Stalin," and Dos Passos in Farrell's opinion was correct to raise the problem despite the critics' "political reasons" for disliking the novel. "The reception given 'The Adventures of a Young Man,'" Farrell concluded, "reads like a warning to writers not to stray off the reservations of the Stalinist controlled League of American Writers to which more than one of the critics belong."

Perhaps the most balanced response to *Adventures* was that of John Chamberlain, who in the *Saturday Review of Literature* considered the entire range of Dos Passos's work and decided that *Adventures of a Young Man* was important because "it clearly shows the trend of [Dos Passos's] mind," although as a novel it was slight by comparison with *U.S.A. Adventures,* Chamberlain recognized, was "a satire on the American radical movement . . ." and as such would be criticized. It was, nevertheless, "a reasonably good story, and a true one" about the abuses of power which American proletarian fiction had largely ignored. But more than simply portraying abuses of power, *Adventures* treated the "psychological turmoil" of an idealist. "In reporting the private war of Glenn Spotswood," Chamberlain wrote, "Dos Passos investigates all phases of the old dilemma: how to keep the political struggle for power from conquering or corrupting the humanity to which all reformers and revolutionists should aspire." Chamberlain saw that Dos Passos did not know how to solve the problem and could portray the state only "as something inherently vicious unless checked by 'limited' government."

Did this mean that Dos Passos would no longer fight for a better world? Chamberlain asked rhetorically. He did not think so, because, as Chamberlain had noted earlier in his essay, Dos Passos was close to what, thirteen years before, he had described as the stance of Bartolomeo Vanzetti. "Of Vanzetti," Chamberlain observed, "Dos Passos wrote in 1926":

His anarchism . . . is less a matter of labels than of feeling, of gentle philosophic brooding. He shares the hope that has grown up in Latin countries of the Mediterranean basin that somehow men's predatory instincts, incarnate in the capitalist system, can be canalized into other channels, leaving free communities of artisans and farmers and fishermen and cattle breeders who would work for their livelihood with pleasure, because the work was itself enjoyable in the serene white light of a reasonable world.

Chamberlain, who like Edmund Wilson knew Dos Passos as a friend, was acutely perceptive to pick this quotation out from his earlier writings. It explained Vanzetti as Dos Passos saw him, but more, it explained the author and was, in fact, an intellectual self-portrait which would be as accurate a statement about Dos Passos's stance at the end of his life as it had been about him in 1926 or 1939.

Neither Chamberlain nor Farrell believed that *The Adventures of a Young Man* was one of Dos Passos's major novels, but they correctly recognized its importance as a statement of its author's position and as an indicator of the political climate despite its condemnation by numerous critics. Its problem as a novel stemmed from the method Dos Passos elected to recount the story of Glenn, a difficulty suggested by the title.

Characters were always of primary importance in Dos Passos's fiction because through them he conveyed his view of history and his own attitudes toward contemporary society. When he attempted to have a single character bear the weight of his intentions to chronicle, satirize, and protest, he was less successful than he had been in *U.S.A.*, with its sweeping portrayal of American society. Dos Passos relied in *Adventures* on what Edmund Wilson called "systematic descriptions" of settings and on an external treatment of Glenn, although Dos Passos meant to convey the workings of his hero's mind. Wilson wrote his friend in early May after reading a reviewer's copy of the novel. "The theme is fine," he told Dos Passos, "but I don't think it's one of your best things artistically." He complained that the "systematic descriptions" which Dos Passos had eliminated in *U.S.A.* had reappeared. There should have been more about how Glenn felt—"his hopes for society and himself" —and fewer set pieces. Wilson advised Dos Passos to "correct your extraversion" because the themes of *Adventures* were not suited to "the old rationalistic method." Some parts of the novel were good, however, and Wilson concluded that he hoped it would "jolt people in some quarters."

Dos Passos considered Wilson's comments before answering later in May that he was not sure if he agreed. "The inadequacy of the straight naturalistic method" might be true, but he had seen no other way to do what he intended. The critical controversy surrounding the novel after its publication caused Dos Passos to think more about Wilson's comments, so late in June he wrote again about *Adventures* being "too extraverted." "What I'm wondering is whether you are giving the behavioristic method the credit of being a method," Dos Passos asked. He explained that "by behavioristic method I mean the method of generating the insides of the characters by external description—Defoe does it supremely." Whether he had succeeded in *Adventures* was another matter, he recognized, but to ask him to be "less extraverted" was "like asking Joyce to be less 'intraverted' and less pedantic —Pedantry and introversion are the materials he builds his work out of."

Wilson's response in mid-July was one of those long, instructive letters of wide-ranging criticism that he would occasionally send to his friends. "To begin with," he wrote, "I don't think your account of what you are doing in your books is accurate. You don't merely 'generate the insides of your characters by external description.' Actually, you do tell a good deal about what they think and feel." He pointed out that no novelist could remain entirely "behavioristic," and his criticism of *Adventures* was simply that it did not adequately convey the "insides" of Glenn. "The sour picture of his experiences in New York is like *Manhattan Transfer* but off the track," he explained, "because the object of *M.T.* was to give a special kind of impression of New York, whereas in *Y.M.* you are concerned with the youthful years of an idealistic young man. You make all the ideas seem phony, all the women obvious bitches, etc.—you don't make the reader understand what people could ever have gotten out of those ideas and women." Wilson expressed something that had always puzzled him about Dos Passos: "I've never understood why you give so grim a picture of life as it seems in the living," he declared. Dos Passos seemed "to enjoy life more than most people and [was] by way of being a brilliant talker," but to Wilson he seemed always to have his characters speak in clichés, and "they always get a bad egg for breakfast." Wilson sometimes thought Dos Passos's literary bleakness was a kind of obligation. But, he admitted, having thought more about *Adventures,* it now seemed better "from the point of view of the idea itself." Dos Passos, however, had not quite written it, Wilson concluded, and Glenn remained banal, although what he stood for was important.

Wilson's comments were generous, but he recognized that the novel was a substantial falling off from Dos Passos's best work. In fact, with the publication of *The Adventures of a Young Man,* his reputation began to decline. It would be easy, but unfair, to blame this falling off on the critics who disapproved of what Dos Passos had to say. The decline resulted from Dos Passos too frequently not quite carrying his ideas out, as Wilson had remarked about *Adventures.* In lieu of working through in a narrative to what he meant to convey, he might allow slabs of description to stand, slabs sometimes hardly altered from some reportage he had previously written.

It was as if Dos Passos's literary passion had lessened after his experiences in Spain in 1937. He held firmly to certain ideas; he had control of the techniques of writing he had employed with excellent effect in *U.S.A.,* but he seemed no longer inspired to create unique fiction of the very highest order. The change was subtle, for he still had immense energy, but it did not result in more books as significant as *Three Soldiers, Manhattan Transfer,* and *U.S.A.* That he had become interested in history is certainly one reason for the lesser scope and importance of the fiction he wrote during the remainder of his life.

More important, however, to explain whatever falling off there was in the importance of his fiction was the fact that he decided once and for all about the merits of Communism. After 1937, he scorned it as a political philosophy and despised the machinations of the American Communist Party and of the Kremlin. Yet perhaps it is more accurate to say not that he had lost any of the passion evinced in his best work, but rather that instead of emerging in his later fiction in portrayals of the complexities of human existence, the passion tended to pour forth in books which in places read as much like treatises as like a novel. Instead of "showing" in his fiction, as Hemingway urged him to be sure to do after the publication of *1919*, Dos Passos became intent on "telling" because he felt adamantly the need to convince others of the rightness of the political ground on which he stood.

He was accurate, despite the critics' vituperation, about many of the machinations he portrayed, but any political struggle had more to it than simple good and bad. What he had missed about the struggle against Franco's rebels because he was not present during the early days of the Civil War, and because when he did reach Spain in April 1937 he immediately became engrossed in the Robles incident, was a spirit among the Loyalists which the wife of the Spanish writer, Arturo Barea, described when she wrote Dos Passos in 1939 to thank him for sending a copy of *Adventures*. She agreed, "I am afraid that the end [of the novel] is only too possible; but it is a pity," she continued, "that your young man could not have that great impression of a simple mass solidarity which I had in Madrid of the very first months —that experience which has helped me to resist the deep bitterness I felt, of course, when they began to hunt me down." Such a solidarity was what Dos Passos had imagined he sensed among those protesting the sentences of Sacco and Vanzetti in 1927. A decade later, he had lost much of his uncritical enthusiasm for the Left. The death of José Robles completed the disillusionment.

Before *Adventures* appeared in June 1939 to create a critical furor, Dos Passos and Katy left Provincetown and drove to Baltimore in early March, where they remained for much of the month, staying with Horsley Gantt while Katy underwent tests at the Johns Hopkins hospital. Whatever her illness, she was well enough to be able to take a trip to the Southwest. "We've been cruising around West Texas," Dos Passos wrote Stewart Mitchell from Santa Fe at the end of April. "Very blood heating country hot as hinges of hell in fact but damn fine place to live—nothing is more encouraging than travelling round the U.S.," he added, reflecting his new sense of America as his "chosen country." Despite this feeling of having discovered his homeland, he felt restless, as he remarked to Wilson shortly after he and Katy had returned to Provincetown in May. "I'm a little reluctant to settle down any-where," he admitted, showing his distaste for what the East represented by commenting that "I seem to have a better time away from the eastern seaboard at present"—one immediately thinks particularly of New York, its literary critics and political imbroglios.

This remark was of a piece with what he wrote in response to a questionnaire sent him by the editors of *Partisan Review*. His sympathies, he said, were with the common man—the people he had been discovering in his travels away from the eastern seaboard—and his allegiance was with what he considered "the good side of what's been going on among people on this continent since 1620 or thereabouts." He praised the "real democracy in the very mixed American tradition," a democracy which he hoped would enable the country to maintain its liberties and humaneness despite the social transformations taking place. He also spoke out against "the total bankruptcy of Europe." He had come to think "that in politics the means tend to turn out to be more important than the ends"; hence he now believed "the more our latent pragmatism and our cynicism in regard to ideas is stimulated the safer we will be."

These comments were a direct response to the Golds, Sillens, Cowleys, and Lawsons whose politics now clashed with his. The remarks were also an expression of his disgust with the New York intelligentsia and in a less obvious way with his New York publishers, who he felt once again had mishandled his work. *The Adventures of a Young Man* was selling at a modest rate: in mid-June fewer than 9,000 copies had been sold, and by late September, only 10,000, by which time its sales were essentially ended. As a result, his income continued to be small, as it had been during the previous two years.*

Finances continued to worry him and Katy, and he could see no obvious way free of their problems, although admittedly they did not cut back on their life style, which was comfortable, if not luxurious. He was now committed to his historical studies, but common sense told him that these would not produce a large income. Katy continued to have medical expenses during the summer, while their bills in Provincetown mounted. When she was in Baltimore in early August for another medical checkup, Dos Passos wrote her in a glum mood to complain of the bills that were pouring in. He reported that Rumsey Marvin had loaned them $200 which would tide them over for a short while, but hardly solve their problems. Dos Passos told her that they had a summons to appear in court about nonpayment of a coal bill. "Oh Katy," he begged her, "let's not run up any more bills or buy any more houses. I've always lived successfully from hand to mouth without the slightest worry, but I cant combine that with unpaid bills and financial operations," a plea to himself as much as to her to curtail some of their unbusinesslike ways.

With help from friends like Marvin and Stewart Mitchell they managed, but could afford few if any jaunts away from Provincetown during the remainder of 1939, while he worked ahead on the projected historical narratives. The first fruit of his lengthy studies was an edition of the works of Tom Paine, for which Dos Passos wrote an introduction. During his and Katy's trip to the Southwest in the spring of 1939, he had mentioned the edition in a letter to his Provincetown friends Hutchins and Neith Hapgood, explaining that it was "all part of a project for a series of historical essays about the American tradition of individual liberty, where it comes from and what it amounts to." The edition, published in February 1940, was a modest one, but Dos Passos's fifty-two page introduction evinced how much historical study he had put into the period of Paine's life. This material he used more fully in *The Ground We Stand On,* published the following year.

A letter dated June 9, 1939, from Harcourt, Brace to Bernice Baumgarten listed sales of Adventures *to be 8,347; one dated September 28, 1939, listed 10,051. Dos Passos's agents Brandt and Brandt wrote him on September 27, 1939, that his income from them during 1937 and 1938 had been $4291.05 and $2557.39, respectively.*

Considering Dos Passos's stance by 1939, it is not surprising that he was attracted to Paine and made him the subject of his first published work in what was for Dos Passos a new field of writing, colonial American history. He saw the era as very like the present, and Paine akin to himself. Of Paine he wrote:

> He was to go on, with complete disregard of the consequences to himself, fervently explaining his doctrines and checking them with complete candor to meet transforming events. He had the best nose of any man who ever lived for the political happenings of the moment. . . . His journalistic pieces and letters urging this or that cause form one of the most acute critical descriptions we have of the great changes in the life of western Europe he lived through. The extraordinary courage and steadfastness with which he held to his basic conceptions, in favor or out of favor, makes his career of the greatest interest to generations like our own who are living through a similar period of changing institutions.

As what was perhaps the most creative decade of Dos Passos's life ended, he set off in new political and literary directions. The author whom American Communists had considered their best and brightest figure they now damned. The same man, whom Jean-Paul Sartre in 1938 had acclaimed "the greatest writer of our time" for his fiction, had now turned to historical narratives. His reputation, fairly or unfairly, had already begun to decline after the appearance of his novel about Glenn Spotswood's adventures. Thus it must have been with considerable wonder about the future that Dos Passos looked toward a new decade. One cannot help but read as some sort of omen the fact that, two days before the thirties ended, Dos Passos, age forty-three, wired Rumsey Marvin New Year's greetings but also asked to borrow $100.

CHAPTER TWENTY-FIVE

A New Ground
to Stand On,
1940–1941

Something had left Dos Passos. To Hemingway, angered by his former friend's disagreements about Spain, the loss was of talent and the courage to write truly, a loss engendered, as he wrote Malcolm Cowley, by Dos Passos's marriage to Katy. But Ernest's assessment was off the mark, motivated as much as anything by his idiosyncratic code of honor and his own marital difficulties.

He was, however, not the only one to believe that a degree of vitality or a touch of passion had been drained from Dos Passos. The unsympathetic critics of *Adventures of a Young Man* asserted as much. Their declarations might be partly discounted as the angry retorts from leftists and liberals who felt betrayed. Yet such sympathetic people as Howard Phillips noted a loss as well during the next years. Katy and Dos Passos's good friend in Mexico City wrote Carleton Beals in July 1943 about a visit they had paid some weeks earlier. They had been "roaming about the Southwest and suddenly decided to drive down to Mexico. I found both of them as likeable as ever, though in some way changed," Phillips declared. "Particularly so Dos," he added, noting that his friend had not "aged much physically, but he seems to be burdened with an inner weariness which defines itself in unrest (After the long trek from Texas and the months they had spent travelling all over the States, they spent most of their time here in driving about the tourist byways)." Phillips wondered if Dos Passos's mood might stem from disappointment about "the modest success of his latest book," *Number One*.

But it was due as well to something else. It was a kind of world weariness that Phillips noticed in 1943, and it was a fatigue not isolated to Dos Passos, but one that settled upon many among his generation of writers who had experienced World

War I, had then lived through two quite different decades, each with its own frenetic pace, and had endured first the trauma of the ill-comprehended Spanish Civil War toward the end of the second decade and then the increasing certainty and finally the actuality of a second world war. The excitement and hopes generated by events between 1917 and 1939 had brought the world to another massive conflict, and the result was a disillusionment such as Phillips observed. Dos Passos had always been a satirist, of course, so a bleak literary vision was nothing new to him. But Phillips noticed an inner weariness about the man himself, a fatigue that could not be discarded even by embracing American democracy or making heroes of its founding fathers such as Tom Paine, or most particularly, Thomas Jefferson.

Dos Passos was less aware than others of any inner fatigue when the 1940s began, since he was as busy as ever with writing projects and with trying to keep his and Katy's heads above the financial waters. He would not have seen anything symbolic about his request for a loan from Rumsey Marvin. It was hardly unusual. Still for the author of *U.S.A.* to have to borrow from friends in order to cover "bad checks . . . flitting around the house like bats," as he wrote Rumsey Marvin, seems inauspicious, at least. Even the trilogy was not going to produce the capital to put Dos Passos's finances in order, so he was asking for money to tide him and Katy over while he made new arrangements. He hoped to refinance a federal housing mortgage by paying off some of it and rearranging the rest at a lower interest rate. Like many people in debt, he was convinced that he could set his affairs on a sounder footing if only he had more capital to work with.

Within days of his request of Marvin, he wrote Stewart Mitchell to ask for a loan of $300. He explained that he and Katy could borrow no more from their bank but that he owed the Gotham Book Mart $200 which Edmund Wilson had arranged sometime earlier for Frances Steloff, the Mart's owner, to loan Dos Passos, using the original manuscript of two versions of *Manhattan Transfer* as collateral. The loan had been to pay an insurance premium. Now unless Dos Passos repaid the principal, the Mart would sell the holograph of *Manhattan Transfer* for less than he believed it was worth. Slightly embarrassed, in February he pushed further the idea of selling the manuscript once he had repaid Frances Steloff. He wrote Clarence Walton of the Widener Library at Harvard to tell him of the manuscript and inquire about its value. When Walton suggested that the best thing was for Miss Steloff to investigate the market, Dos Passos thanked him and decided to let the matter drop.

"So far the year has been full of financial alarums and excursions but the general tone of our finances is surprising firm," he wrote Mitchell with more hope than assurance when he asked for the $300. He could always request an advance on the Guggenheim Fellowship which had been his main support, he assured Mitchell. But his best hope for solvency lay with his war risk insurance, which came due in January 1941, and against which he could now borrow. His Aunt Mamie Gordon had been "keeping" the policy for him, he told Mitchell, and only recently had he recovered it from her.

Behind the hint that Mrs. Gordon had not released the policy willingly lay a major reason that Dos Passos and Katy's finances had been as precarious as they were. He became aware that his aunt and her husband had withheld monies owed him when, after his disillusionment in Spain, he took a greater interest in the United States and particularly in Virginia, "home" to him and the birthplace of numerous colonial Americans about whom he was now writing. In 1917, just prior to sailing for Europe with the ambulance service, Dos Passos had authorized his aunt to collect all money and property that might become payable to him. A year and a half later, before returning to Europe with the Medical Corps in November 1918, he gave to her in trust his power of attorney and deed over his interest in John R.'s estate, which in Dos Passos's case meant the co-ownership with his half-brother Louis of their father's land in Westmoreland County. During the next two decades Mr. Gordon and his son-in-law collected income for the land amounting to approximately $100,000, only $15,000 of which was ever turned over to Dos Passos by 1940 under the terms of the trust. During the twenties and early thirties he had paid no attention to what the Gordons were doing and assumed that his aunt was forwarding whatever was due him. But when in the late thirties he took a renewed interest in the Virginia land at the same time as he was attempting to improve his finances, he discovered the Gordons' dishonesty. In 1940 he traveled to Virginia to investigate the situation; then in 1941 through his lawyer C. D. Williams he brought civil suit against his aunt. Finally, the case was settled in April 1944. He obtained clear title to the land and money from the proceeds of the sale of properties in Pelham, New York, that belonged to Mrs. Gordon and members of her family. The money awarded Dos Passos was not a large sum, but enough that when Katy deposited the check in their bank in Provincetown, the teller remarked that it would take her and Dos Passos quite some time to overdraw that one.

With the Virginia land on his mind in late January 1940, Dos Passos traveled to Washington before Katy joined him in February. They moved to Alexandria, Virginia, while he worked at the Library of Congress in connection with his historical narrative and fitted in trips to Westmoreland to look into the status of his property. Then in April he traveled to Ecuador on behalf of the New World Resettlement Fund to arrange for the settlement of Spanish Republican refugees. He took the job seriously, staying in Ecuador for a month before returning to Virginia and thence in early June to Provincetown, where Katy and he remained through the summer as he strove to complete *The Ground We Stand On*.

In a further effort to improve his finances, he decided against having a literary agent and in June wrote Bernice Baumgarten that, although she had done a fine job, he was going to have to manage without her because an agent was "a luxury I just cant afford." Alfred Harcourt, sympathizing with her a few days after Dos Passos had written, commented that "Dos is a fine person, but too much inclined to try to force the facts to conform to his wishes. When they dont, either his agent or publisher or both gets the blame—and learns to be philosophical." Harcourt's tone suggested his own uneasiness about Dos Passos's situation with Harcourt, Brace. He knew the writer was unhappy about the sales of his books, and Harcourt probably suspected that a change of publishers was on Dos Passos's mind, which it was. When late in 1940 he wrote Edmund Wilson, he complained about Harcourt, Brace's inadequate handling of Wilson's book, *To the Finland Station*. Sue them, Dos Passos suggested, then backed off, complaining about "their bloody complacency" and deceitfulness. After Harcourt, Brace ran a small first printing of *The Ground We Stand On* in 1941 and did not promote it as he would have liked, he left them to move to Houghton Mifflin.

Despite their worries about money and the need to complete the historical narrative, Dos Passos and Katy ventured south late in the summer. Shortly after he had returned to Provincetown in September, Dos Passos wrote Rumsey Marvin that he had just returned "from Virginia where we are trying to establish for ourselves a small self liquidating project; the trouble is its still liquidating us." Soon he went to Virginia again, in part to examine the architecture of Thomas Jefferson—"I'd never understood how original he was as an architect," he wrote Stewart Mitchell —and in part to look after the Virginia land. With some regularity he visited Westmoreland until he moved there for good in 1949, and it seems clear that he and Katy intended to make it their home during at least several months each year. But he found it difficult to be an efficient absentee landlord, so during the forties the land did not produce the income from timber, crops, and cattle he had hoped it would.

It was hard to look after the land because, for all his good intentions, he was distracted by his other projects and by the specter of another world war. He continued to work for the New World Resettlement Fund and traveled to Haiti at the end of 1940 to see about placing refugees there. He also served as treasurer of the Joint Campaign for Political Refugees in which the Resettlement Fund and the International Relief Association were cooperating. In addition to traveling on behalf of the fund, he wrote open letters asking for contributions to enable refugees to be brought out of Europe.

Most of his time, however, went toward the completion of his history. Checking historical detail he found a tedious business that required a meticulousness of a different sort than he needed for his fiction. Again and again he asked one or another of his friends for help and turned especially to Stewart Mitchell and Edmund Wilson, who offered corrections to Dos Passos's manuscript. Thanking Wilson for his comments, Dos Passos wrote that the new book "will probably be called *The Ground We Stand On*, with some sort of substitute such as The Establishment of an American Bent." As Wilson had expected, the book would "deal . . . with the divergence of an American from a late English tradition, both branching from the main stem of English thought and culture, according to this thesis, definitely shattered by the ruin of the Commonwealth." Its spirit, Dos Passos believed, carried on in New England in an "ossified form," whereas "the country gentleman republicanism of the seventeenth century," extremely important for the Commonwealth, remained in Low Church Virginia. There two strains out of the

Commonwealth merged in the American Revolution, while in England an "oli-garchic empire" emerged, "encysting" what was left of the Commonwealth tradi-tion but from which came men as varied as Tom Paine and Samuel Insull who fled to America, carrying the tradition with them. Dos Passos's central thesis was that, despite being obscured during the nineteenth and twentieth centuries, "the great Anglo-Saxon tradition" of the Commonwealth had taken root in the United States, still endured, and was the foundation on which the nation should build its defenses against the European ideologies he had inveighed against since his disillusionment in Spain.

When a number of years later Dos Passos prepared a speech about Thomas Jefferson, he began by trying to answer the question why a novelist was "meddling in history." The process had been "a fairly logical one," he believed, because although he had started out as a novelist, he had been a "certain kind" who, like Stendhal and Thackeray, told stories that entailed "the presentation of the particular slice of history the novelist has seen enacted before his own eyes." His fiction, he supposed, had "more than most this sort of origin," and it seemed a logical step from it to history. What he said was true; his eye for details and fragments of history had been with him from the beginning and was the basis for his chronicle fiction.

Yet he overlooked, or did not state in his speech, the ideological significance of his turn to history. He searched in United States history for a justification of what had come to be his belief that the American democratic tradition was superior to European ideologies. As contemporary society became ever more complex, he sought for alternative models—some would say simplistic ones—to the intricate bureau-cratic structures he saw being built. And he sought figures who might act as models for contemporary man in his struggle to free himself from the fetters of mass society. Jefferson was the figure Dos Passos most admired because he respected the Virgin-ian's eighteenth-century liberality and concern for smallness in government. It did not matter to him that Jefferson's liberalism and agrarian democracy became con-servatism in the twentieth century. That they did clarifies why Dos Passos, still liberal if no longer radical when he began his studies of the historical roots of American democracy, could become a conservative Republican, an arch-opponent of New Deal politics, and a proponent, in his last years, of the ideology surrounding Senator Barry Goldwater of Arizona. Add to Dos Passos's belief in conservative Jeffersonianism his profound distrust of Communism after 1937, and one has pre-cisely the reasons for his political shift. *The Theme Is Freedom* he entitled a collection of his essays in 1956 to demonstrate the consistency of his ideals. His point was that he adhered to the political point of view which seemed to him most promising of personal freedom at a given moment in history. He was consistent about that; nevertheless, his change from the Left to the Right was a drastic one, whether or not he wanted to admit it.

Although the change would not find full expression until years later, its seeds were apparent in *The Ground We Stand On,* published in August 1941. In an epigraph, Dos Passos quoted from the preface to Joel Barlow's *Columbiad,*

> My object is altogether of a moral and political nature. I wish to encourage
> and strengthen, in the rising generation, a sense of the importance of republi-
> can institutions; as being the great foundation of public and private happiness,
> the necessary aliment of future and permanent ameliorations in the condition
> of human nature . . .

"This is the moment in America," Barlow continued, "that true and useful ideas
of glory may be implanted in the minds of men here, to take the place of the false
and destructive ones that have degraded the species in other countries. . . ." And
in another epigraph, this one to a chapter entitled "The Use of the Past," Dos Passos
quoted from a letter written in 1787 by Thomas Jefferson, in which he asserted, "If
any of our countrymen wish for a King, give them Aesop's fable of the frogs who
asked a King; if this does not cure them, send them to Europe. They will come back
good republicans." Dos Passos's paean to the republic contained an opening chapter
about the use of the past and then a lengthy section about Roger Williams and
chapters about Jefferson, Barlow, Benjamin Franklin, Samuel Adams, Hugh Henry
Brackenridge and, as a kind of backdrop, chapters about England before and during
the period in which these men lived.

The book was an important document to understand the author's stance during
the remainder of his life. He had come to appreciate history as the means to a
"continuity with generations gone before." "In times like ours," he wrote, "when
old institutions are caving in and being replaced by new institutions not necessarily
in accord with most men's preconceived hopes, political thought has to look backwards as well as forwards." Dos Passos included himself when he noted that "Americans as a people notably lack a sense of history" and that only after "a lot of callow
debunking" had the intellectuals of his generation come to "understand the actuality of the American past," because "the stale murk of massacre and plague and
famine" of World War I and its aftermath had blurred their vision. In the twenties,
"the millennial gospel of Marx" seemed the answer to those of his generation
opposed to the normalcy of Harding and Coolidge, but the problem with Marxism
was that "its principles had to be carried out on earth." To the dismay of the
disillusioned intellectuals the Russian experiment proved a failure; in fact, Dos
Passos contended, "The history of the political notions of American intellectuals
during the past twenty years is largely a record of how far the fervor of their hopes
for a better world could blind them to the realities under their noses." These realities
were that "from 1917 on, the gulf between Europe and America, that had seemed
so narrow and bridgeable then, widened and widened." The political history of
Europe in the intervening years was tragic:

> In Europe the police state the Bolsheviks had called into being under the
> delusion that they could use it to force men into the mold of a good society,
> ran its normal course 'toward tyranny bloodshed and despair. In Italy and
> Germany the fascist and nazi regimes, after dumping the humanitarian baggage

overboard, took over and improved the efficient machinery for driving the mass which the Bolsheviks had invented in their one party system. The businessmen and politicians of the oligarchic and even of the approximately selfgoverning states of Europe proved helpless to hold their divided nations together in the face of an incomparable industrial machine so skillfully rigged for the purposes of destruction.

The United States, meanwhile, had seemed to stand up "fairly well," and those who thought democracy to be rotten at its core, Dos Passos believed, should turn not to European alternatives, but to an understanding of the roots of democracy, to the "heritage of the habits and traditions and skills of selfgovernment," the last term the key to what he thought was essential. Rampant industrialization had threatened the fact of "selfgovernment," he wrote, but not its validity. "If we can counter the deathdealing illusions of Europe with practical schemes for applying the selfgoverning habit more fully to our disorganized social structure, to the factories, unions, employers' associations, chains of stores, armies that are imposed upon us by today's methods of production and destruction, then the . . . doubts will be quiet," he asserted. And, he added revealingly, "Even if it means reversing the trend of our whole society in order to make it continually more selfgoverning instead of less so, the trend will have to be reversed. The alternative is destruction." Such a reversal was what Dos Passos sought for the rest of his life. He wrote about the need for it; he sided with the political party most empathetic with the idea; he tried, after the end of World War II, to create an agrarian life in Virginia that realized his goal of individual freedom within the framework of the limited rural politics of Westmoreland County; and he turned for a model to Thomas Jefferson, who more than anyone else among the founders of American democracy "had this worldpicture [of selfgovernment] so clearly in his mind that the imprint of it was sharp on everything he did." The absence of "primary selfgovernment," Dos Passos credited Jefferson with believing, "would be the ruin of . . . democracy."

When it was published, *The Ground We Stand On* was favorably received for the vitality of the individual chapters about Williams, Barlow, and the others, and for its appreciation of American democracy. But it was seen as a partial history at best. "The general object of the work is admirable; the execution has grave flaws," wrote historian Allan Nevins, who believed that the volume was "a valuable contribution to true Americanism" although Dos Passos did not do justice "to the great complex of institutions and ideas that went into the making of Anglo-American principles and institutions in the political field; his view is too narrow."

Nevins's assessment was accurate. Dos Passos's view was too narrow because he sought to separate "the American bent" from European—even from English—political institutions. He did not intend it, but in his effort to clarify his thesis he simplified, and in his effort to emphasize the particularity of the American tradition, he appeared to be an isolationist, fearful of foreign influences. "If we can keep the fabric of a selfgoverning republic unbroken at home, we are in no danger from the attacks of the slave states of Europe and Asia," he concluded *The Ground We Stand On.* "If we can't, everything we as Americans have stood for from the beginning will have been in vain."

One of his longtime friends, Gilbert Seldes, cautioned him about what Seldes was sure was an unintentional hint of bigotry. He wrote Dos Passos that he had almost set aside *The Ground We Stand On* because in the opening chapter Dos Passos had implied that "the selfgoverning tradition had been diluted by the diverse habits of the stream of newcomers from Europe." This was "the most poisonous kind of doctrine," Seldes warned. There was no evidence to support it, he added, and Dos Passos needed to recognize that "Americans are not Anglo-Saxons and that the 'bedrock habits' of Americans were not formed by Anglo-Saxons but by Jews and Portuguese, Bulgars and Italians and Germans and twenty-one other races." The meaning of the term *American*, Seldes continued, "is that it was formed by the action upon one group of all the other groups and vice versa."

Dos Passos deserved Seldes's strictures because, while he scorned bigotry, he was coming close to it with his blend of nationalism and Anglo-Saxon pride. He did distrust the influence of outsiders; he had said as much to Jack Lawson in the 1930s when he criticized "the whole New York jewish theatre guild, Damrosch, Otto Kahn, Mike Gold culture" which he accused of being "an echo of the liberal mitteleuropa culture . . . in Europe." As long as he remained skeptical of the American system, he remained open-minded. After he had embraced the United States, however, too often he sounded intolerant, although his harsh tone reflected less his complete conviction or a bigot's complacency than the fervor of his concern about American "selfgovernment." But hyperbole on the written page was nothing new for the man who was in person shy and diffident.

His interest in Jefferson as the forties began led him to contract to write a biography of the man. The book, *The Head and Heart of Thomas Jefferson,* was not published until 1954, because other writing projects intervened, because he was distracted by momentous events such as the war and, very simply, because the biography was more of a task than he had imagined. Doing the research for it kept his mind on history so that, despite his other writing, he frequently thought as a historian; and some of his later fiction has a perfunctory quality, as if he were writing it out of habit.

The historical projects engaged him in 1941, but he kept up his usual activities of other writing and travel. After Scott Fitzgerald's death in December 1940, which saddened Dos Passos, he contributed a short piece for the *New Republic* that appeared in February 1941, in which he castigated critics who had written about Fitzgerald's work as nothing more than period pieces and had ignored *The Great Gatsby.* "Many people consider 'The Great Gatsby' one of the few classic American works," Dos Passos declared; "I do myself."

The land problems with Aunt Mamie Gordon and her family occupied him and Katy as well. Bringing suit entailed trips to New York and to Virginia, where they stopped while traveling to or from St. Augustine for a vacation during the month of April. The lawsuit created uncertainty in their lives, as Katy mentioned in July to Rumsey Marvin and his wife while explaining why it would not work for the Marvins to visit Provincetown. "Law-suits, and all kinds of nasty blockades" had complicated their lives, and now, she reported, Dos Passos would be away for a month in England. Don Passos and Katy visited Wiscasset, Maine, in August before he left on his journey, during which he meant to investigate conditions and to try to determine what sort of society was developing in Britain as a result of the war.

He arrived in London in mid-September in "the most beautiful autumn weather of the century." The days and nights were clear, and, as the Germans were not bombing the city during that period, there was "a holiday air" about London in the late afternoons because of the silver barrage of balloons poised in the air above. Dos Passos attended the congress of the P.E.N. Club his first morning, then spent his next days examining the various sectors of the city and talking to firefighters and civilians from numerous walks of life. Later during the month he remained abroad, he traveled south to a channel port and north to Scotland. Throughout Scotland and England he was impressed by the pluck of the people as demonstrated by Winston Churchill, about whom he wrote, "Nobody else embodies the stolid resistance which is the rocky base of English patriotism, the fellow-feeling as islanders under seige which the toffs and underdogs share." He was not impressed by the members of the House of Commons, who seemed to him to represent "the stodgiest conservative machines and the stodgiest of labor bureaucracy," but he believed that despite the Commons, the war had created conditions whereby there had been "a great deal of stimulating interpenetration of classes." Britons had learned that survival demanded "a new kind of social efficiency," although he was uncertain about what direction the society would take.

One person who impressed him particularly was H. G. Wells, whom he met at the P.E.N. Club congress. Wells, a "spruce figure . . . [with] his sharp-clipped white mustache and the liquid alertness of glaze-blue eyes," invited Dos Passos to talk in his home at the edge of Regents Park. The American was impressed by the pessimism of Wells, who had come to believe in the likelihood that "the human race was incapable of adapting itself to its own invented world." He told Dos Passos that planning the future lay with Americans, and he had little confidence in them. "All we can do," he concluded, "is to go on telling the truth whenever we can," a statement that appealed greatly to Dos Passos, who could imagine himself the iconoclastic voice of truth speaking in a wilderness. "In my opinion," he ended his second of two articles about England,

> We English-speaking peoples are facing, all of us singly and collectively, the
> *aut Caesar aut nullus* dilemma. To survive at all we have to reconquer the world
> the tories have lost. To win the war, and more especially to win the dangerous
> peace that will follow it, we must have, as well as supremacy in aviation and
> industrial brains, a fresh formula for the application of our traditional selfgov-
> ernment and all the social habits it implies, to the modern industrial setup.

These articles sounded the same theme as had *The Ground We Stand On*. The "fresh formula" Dos Passos hoped for was Jeffersonian democracy. The foundation for the political stance he took after World War II was in place: he was prepared to believe that the "dangerous peace" was going to be lost because the Western world would not embrace the formula he believed essential.

PART VII

Years of
War and Grief,
1941–1947

CHAPTER TWENTY-SIX

World War II:
The Domestic Scene,
1941–1944

The month-long trip to England ended October 15, when Dos Passos traveled to Spain and from there flew by Clipper to the United States, arriving on the eighteenth. He immediately plunged into the projects that had kept him busy during the summer. "Ever since I got back from England I've been fighting a number of engagements on various fronts—law suit in Va., magazine business in New York and now the South Americans [a reference to more work for the New World Resettlement Fund]," he told the Marvins early in December.

Amid this work he was shocked by the news of the Japanese attack on Pearl Harbor, despite his sense that war was imminent. "No way of forgetting that December afternoon," he wrote later. "Driving into New York from Long Island I went into a Second Avenue ginmill to make a phone call and heard disaster pouring out over the radio." Regardless of his disagreement with Roosevelt's foreign policy as in the case of Spain, he recognized that a commitment to war meant support for the government.

"Damn the Japs, and the wops and the squareheads: gosh it's a big order," he wrote Robert Hillyer on December 10. Despite sounding like an isolationist in articles and books such as "Farewell to Europe!" and *The Ground We Stand On*, he believed that fighting the Japanese, Italians, and Germans was the only way by the end of 1941 to regain what, as he wrote in his pieces about England, the old-guard Tories had lost. In fact, Dos Passos had not been an isolationist in the usual sense. Although he did not make it clear in what he published, he believed that during the thirties the United States should have interceded with the governments of France and England to try to force them to be sterner with Hitler and Mussolini. This might have kept the country out of war, which had been his ultimate hope.

But intercession would have demanded an internationalism of the United States to achieve isolationist ends. He did not acknowledge or admit that in the 1930s there was strong public sentiment against American involvement in Europe's squabbles.

At the time of Pearl Harbor he was in New York to discuss with the editors of *Harper's* articles he planned to write about his visit to England and about the social conditions in wartime America, the "state of the nation," as the series of pieces was entitled when they were published together in book form. His work for the next months was demanding because he had to travel around the country gathering information for the articles when he was not in Provincetown writing.

But the essays about England and the condition of the United States were not his only literary projects. On his mind since completing *Adventures of a Young Man* had been another novel in what would become his next trilogy, *District of Columbia*. He thought the new volume would again be about a Spotswood, this time Tyler, the older brother of Glenn, who had died in Spain. As it evolved, it focused as much on a political demagogue for whom Tyler was a secretary, the politician being a thinly fictionalized version of Huey Long, who had fascinated Dos Passos ever since he had first observed the Louisiana politician at the Democratic presidential convention in 1932. The character Dos Passos created was Homer T. "Chuck" Crawford, about whose source he later admitted that "the nearest I ever came to a character completely from life was Huey Long in 'Number One,' " as the novel was entitled. As Dos Passos wrote about "selfgovernment" in *The Ground We Stand On*, he thought more about the demagogue and quoted Long, whom he considered "one of the smartest aspirants" ever to strive to be an American dictator, as saying, "When fascism comes to America, it will come as antifascism." Dos Passos's point was that in the guise of a populist Long had striven to control the people by taking as much power to himself as he could. The more Dos Passos grew concerned about the imperative of "selfgovernment," the more he believed it timely to write a novel about a would-be American dictator, particularly because, as the nation's involvement in World War II became greater, he saw signs that the administration in its desire to combat foreign despotism might choke off freedom and "selfgovernment" at home. A novel then about the likes of Huey Long would be a reminder of the danger before the nation, a danger of which Dos Passos was reminded when he agreed during the summer of 1941 to serve with Carlo Tresca as a vice-chairman of the Civil Rights Defense Committee, organized to aid in the defense of twenty-nine truckers and union members in Minneapolis, Minnesota. The twenty-nine, some of them also members of the Trotskyist Socialist Workers' Party, had been indicted at the instigation of the Justice Department on charges of conspiracy to overthrow the government by force and violence. Dos Passos helped with an appeal for funds, and in late August before departing for England he composed an open letter to the *Nation* in which he expressed his concern about the repressiveness of the government's action in the "Minneapolis Case."

"Dear _____: No matter how good the intentions of a man in public service are when he starts out, I think you'll agree that it's exceedingly difficult for him to avoid leading a double life," Dos Passos began his piece in the *Nation*. "Only too often the members of the aggregations of men that make up a government lose all contact with the public needs they were got together to serve," and in the process, the politicians undermined "the self-governing system and the liberties" they were supposed to uphold. With war practically upon the country, Roosevelt's administration, Dos Passos believed, citing the Minneapolis Case, had "committed a number of acts that tend to put the bases of self-government in jeopardy." The indictment against the truckers and union members had "the peculiar twist of Stalin's famous frame-ups in Moscow," and convictions would be "a severe moral blow to the American cause." The best way to fight despotism, he argued, was not to repress fringe groups such as these Trotskyites, but to support freedom "wholeheartedly, even recklessly."

The tendency Dos Passos thought he saw in the New Deal toward bureaucratic centralization and hence a sort of despotism instead of toward individual freedoms soon caused him to turn against Roosevelt. "Under Roosevelt," he wrote later about the early years of the New Deal, "the poorest immigrant, the most neglected sharecropper in the eroded hills came to feel that he was a citizen again." But power corrupts, Dos Passos believed, and as the government had become "a storehouse of power," there developed "a situation that would have alarmed even the most authoritarian statesmen of our early history." No one was capable of handling the "immense political power" that had accrued to the New Deal; yet "the fear of the loss of power" engendered the despotism Dos Passos scorned. "Consciously or unconsciously, Roosevelt could find no other way of consolidating the vast power . . . that the success of the New Deal brought him," Dos Passos declared, "than by leading the country into war." His retrospective accusation, made in the 1950s during the height of the Cold War when many believed that a dying Roosevelt had given away peace, was extreme, while at the same time Dos Passos acknowledged that war might have been inevitable. What was extreme was not that he accused Roosevelt of having led the nation into war—in this view he was hardly alone—but rather the motive he assigned him. This idiosyncratic reading of history reveals more about Dos Passos's sometimes paranoid distrust of bureaucracy and power than it illuminates about the Machiavellian tactics of the thirty-fifth President.

The New Deal's dangerous tendency to misuse its power, which Dos Passos was convinced he was witnessing in 1941, was the impetus he needed to write *Number One*. It was his conviction that the fictionalized tale of Huey Long would be a parable of warning. Dos Passos began to work on the novel when he could, collecting data about Long and his supporters. Among his notes, for example, are a copy of a printed letter Long sent his admirers concerning the establishment of a weekly newspaper to be entitled the *American Progress*, and clippings from Louisiana papers about former Louisiana governor James A. Noe, whose trial for corrupt dealings with the Win or Lose Oil Corporation was in the news early in 1942. Among other matters, the case brought out that Noe and the corporation had concealed Long and his wife's involvement in the dishonestly run organization.

To make as clear as he could the relationship between politicans and the masses of people, Dos Passos included prose-poem interchapters. *"When you try to find the people, / always in the end it comes down to somebody,"* the first of them began, and each one described a different sort of "typical American," about whom, Dos Passos concluded the book,

> *weak as the weakest, strong as the strongest,*
> *the people are the republic,*
> *the people are you.*

When he first considered the prose poems, he jotted down a version and some notes about them that clarified his intentions. "A man is himself and he's also the people —anybody," Dos Passos wrote,

> and he's also part of an organization—Catholic Church—Communist party— Chamber of Commerce—political machine interspersed with Chuck's adventures should be pieces giving a feeling of the lives of the masses of the people —with as many million focuses as there are people. . . . Also occasionally a flashback a comment from some guy on the street, in a lunch wagon, in a bar in a drugstore—to keep Chuck's history in focus with the life around him.

Dos Passos's early jottings reveal where he thought the heart of the story was:

> climax where Tyler whose wife has been building him up to make a great citizen of him—discovers that he knows and she knows what kind of a business [Crawford's oil corporation] is.
>   The point where a man gets to be a thorough scoundrel—up to then it had been possible to pretend to themselves there was something to Duke [Chuck] other than personal greed for women, power, money.

As Dos Passos composed the novel, he discarded the idea of Tyler Spotswood being married. Rather, he is depicted as loving Crawford's wife Sue Ann, a pretty, honest woman who feels affection for Spotswood but is too loyal ever to consider leaving her husband, even though she comes to realize who Crawford has become. If it was Dos Passos's intention to make Crawford his subject, it is Spotswood's point of view that becomes the moral perspective from which the reader observes the demagogue's dishonesty. A weak man, Tyler finally acknowledges to himself the politician's true colors after Tyler reads a letter from his deceased brother Glenn, who wrote, "It's what you do that counts, not what you say. . . . Tyler, what I'd started to write you about was not letting them sell out too much of the for the people and by the people part of the oldtime United States way." Reading this, Tyler realizes that by acquiescing to Crawford's entreaties to conceal the dishonest oil dealings, he is betraying Glenn. As the novel ends, Tyler is frozen into inaction, uncertain of what he will do except that he will no longer conspire to protect Senator Crawford.

Dos Passos completed a preliminary version of the novel without the interchapters by October 1942, and it was published in early March 1943. Dos Passos's friend

Howard Phillips may have been correct that Dos Passos was disappointed by its sales, and thus its impact, but sales of more than 17,000 copies by mid-June were far better than the total sales of his previous novel and roughly as successful as any volume of *U.S.A.* *

Despite the novel's didactic tone and such stylistic quirks as Dos Passos's irritating habits of linking words—"selfrespect," "sorryforhimself," "deepcarpeted" —and having his women characters "titter," "giggle," "shriek," "chirp," and "whine," he had written a strong book whose momentum rose effectively toward its conclusion when Tyler realized that he had betrayed not only himself, but Glenn and Crawford's constituents. Dos Passos must have been pleased by the critics' reception, especially after their generally negative response to *Adventures of a Young Man.* They recognized his intention to explore demagoguery in *Number One* and judged the book in that light. Stephen Vincent Benét called the novel "a brilliant portrait" of political life, while Horace Gregory in his front-page review for the *New York Times* thought the novel "one of the best . . . I have read in the past two years" and a book "that should be read by every intelligent man and woman in the United States." If *Number One* was a well-done documentary about a demagogic Senator, it did not sufficiently explain his motivations. Nor were the characters of Tyler and Sue Ann fully convincing. But reviewers perceived that these points about the art of the novel were of less concern to Dos Passos than was the political question. "What can be done in the republic to prevent another 'Number One'?" asked Howard Mumford Jones. "If enough readers ask this question," he concluded, "I suspect Mr. Dos Passos will be satisfied."

Dos Passos's work on *Number One* during 1942 was interspersed with several trips to Virginia about the lawsuit and newly begun work on the colonial house at Spence's Point—part of John R.'s estate—that Dos Passos and Katy hoped eventually to make their home for a part of each year. Then, too, he traveled to Arkansas, Texas, and in December to Maine as he gathered material about "the state of the nation." Once the work on *Number One* had been completed, early in 1943 he began to travel more extensively to complete his researches for the series of articles that would appear in *Harper's* under the title "The People at War."

Before one trip to investigate war work in the Detroit automobile plants, Dos Passos met Carlo Tresca for lunch in New York City. They talked about the situation in Italy, and Tresca told Dos Passos that the Italian organizations in New York were bickering about who would control what in the wake of Mussolini's impending defeat. Tresca was deeply involved in the political machinations. In fact, Dos Passos knew that there were "tentative plans in Washington" for Tresca to return to Italy and organize a political group to oppose the Communists. But these plans never materialized. The night of the day they lunched together, January 11, 1943, Tresca was shot to death as he emerged from the lower Fifth Avenue office of the newspaper he edited, *Il Martello.*

Dos Passos was shocked; the murder appeared to him more proof of Commu-

*As of June 15, 1943, Number One *had sold 17,197 copies in the United States and 350 in Canada.*

nist perfidy. He recalled that a few days after the shooting a representative of the district attorney's office spoke to him, hoping to learn more about who might have slain Tresca. Neither of them had any clues, and all they could agree on was that the murder had been committed by a hired gunman. Years later when asked about Tresca, Dos Passos responded that he was probably killed by a gunman "at the instigation of the same gang that killed Trotski in Mexico." He admitted there was no certain proof, but contended that, as "the Communists were planning to take over Italy after Mussolini's collapse," they would have wanted Tresca out of the way. "During the last ten years," Dos Passos wrote in an appreciation of Tresca for the *Nation,* "in his last great fight against the Fascists and Communists, he became in the best sense of the word a conservative. His last campaigns were all aimed at protecting the Italian population he loved against a new influx of brutal European logic."

Depressed both by the loss of a respected friend and by the realization that the murder was a gruesome reminder of a covert political war with the Communists which Dos Passos feared Americans naïvely ignored, he traveled to Detroit in mid-January for a visit of several days. His goal there and around the country during the rest of 1943 was to answer the now-familiar questions, what effect was the war having on Americans and what would be the effect on the tradition of "selfgovernment" of the new industrialization and technology created by the war. He believed, as he wrote in an introductory chapter to *State of the Nation* after he had completed the series of essays about "The People at War," that "It will be the methods we use in industry and in the services to cope with the things that are happening to us now that will determine the shape of our society in the years to come." Dos Passos was convinced that the nation had been remarkably successful in its methods of production, with the result that the lives of Americans were improving while social distinctions lessened. The people were greatly adaptable, but in their fluidity lay "possibilities for good and evil." Material prosperity was not in question. "The question is whether we have the will and the brains to use the opportunities which the new skills and the new knowledge and the new frontiers are opening up to perfect and develop the institutions of selfgovernment. . . ." That question remained unanswered.

After Detroit he traveled to Washington, D.C., with a visit to Virginia before he headed farther south in February. He visited Birmingham and Mobile, Alabama, and New Orleans late in the month, from where he wrote Robert Hillyer about enthusiasm for this "big untidy soulstirring country we live in. I feel myself continually tortured by curiosity about it," although he confessed to being "tired of trying to pick the brains of the local inhabitants—who have it must be admitted—very small oyster like cerebral cortexes." His mood improved when shortly thereafter Katy joined him, and together they traveled through Texas before driving down into Mexico during March and April, then back to Provincetown in May. In June Dos Passos returned alone to Washington. There, as during other trips, he stayed part of the time at the home of Gardner Jackson, the brother of his Harvard classmate Roland Jackson. Gardner, whom Dos Passos had first met during his part in the

defense of Sacco and Vanzetti, now worked in the New Deal administration and
was Dos Passos's entrée into that world. As Dos Passos talked to administrators,
politicians, and members of the armed forces, he sensed an overwhelming frustration
that colored even more his picture of the administration. Functionaries at any level
would not work for the public interest, and much of a person's energy was spent
fighting one or another power bloc. Washington seemed a case of too many people
with conflicting aims working for a government that had lost its reformist instincts
by being entrenched too long in power. "There are too many people in this man's
country, too many all in one place," Dos Passos wrote Katy unhappily late in June.
He told her that he had just been at the Pentagon and had come away "immensely
depressed. How are we going to run the world," he asked, "if we cant do any better
with the Pentagon."

The bureaucratic procedures that frustrated the administrators he interviewed
were only part of his portrait of the capital in wartime. Dos Passos observed Franklin
Roosevelt at a White House press conference and was bothered by the President's
unwillingness to talk openly about issues such as "rationing, the coal strike, price
control." He looked haggard and soon cut off the conference. This fatigue and
secretiveness Dos Passos noticed when he interviewed Harry Hopkins, one of the
men closest to Roosevelt. "Some time ago," Dos Passos wrote after the interview,
Hopkins had "made up his mind and closed its windows on the world. He starts
talking about how the running of the war is necessarily in the hands of a few men.
Only they know the facts." Hopkins kept talking about "only a handful of men"
as if these were the people who controlled the nation's destiny. Bored with domestic
issues, Hopkins to Dos Passos seemed unconcerned about the internal life of the
nation, thus about what was evolving as the war continued. It was Dos Passos's
conviction that the Roosevelt administration had lost touch with the people, and
the nation was in danger of losing the advantages of power it was gaining during
the war through its immense productivity.

After spending July and August in Provincetown while he crystallized his
thinking in his writing, Dos Passos began traveling again, in September first to the
mining regions of Pennsylvania, then during the latter half of October and early
November to the Midwest and West. "Oh dear—at it again—broadening interests,
acquaintance, trying to stretch comprehension around a lot of new indigestable
situations. Why cant I stay home? And read the classics," he wrote Katy from
Pittsburgh. But he admitted that the city was interesting, and he had just been
drinking whiskey for three hours in a "flophouse for bums" with a Catholic priest.
Except for missing Katy, he enjoyed the travel, which familiarized him with people
and parts of the country he had not known before, such as the region of southern
Ohio and Iowa, where he was eager to learn about farming methods that produced
a high crop yield. Especially because he hoped to turn his Virginia land to productive
farming, he was pleased to find out how such farmers as Roswell Garst in Coon
Rapids, Iowa, achieved the results he did with hybrid corn of a hundred bushels to
an acre. Successes bred an optimism about the country—as distinct from the administration—that Dos Passos repeatedly found during his investigations which

ended in Spokane, Washington. People were producing goods, and the country had enormous potential, he recognized. The problem was to make production benefit the people under a government that loomed bureaucratically in Washington, D.C. The West, he wrote Katy, appeared strongly Republican because of people's discontent with Roosevelt's administration. "It looks as if the only people who could re-elect Franklin D [are] the old guard republicans," he cracked, but admitted that Roosevelt still had "a fifty-fifty chance" in 1944.

It had been fun "barging around," he told Katy, but he missed her and felt "uneasy about creditors, the situation on the [Virginia] farm etc." They had to stabilize their situation there, he wrote, by selling what land they deemed necessary before the land boom was halted. Once again his concern reflected their financial strain. In 1943, although they sold their house in Truro, matters hardly seemed to improve. So when there was a delay in receiving payment for the articles he was writing, Dos Passos again had to contact a friend, Robert Hillyer, in this case, just before Christmas, to ask for a loan of $100. When a check for the articles appeared, Dos Passos held off borrowing Hillyer's money, but a month later he asked for it again. *State of the Nation* held him chained to his desk, he wrote, and he found himself in "a can't get any money till I finish the book, cant finish the book until I get some money dilemma." He was able to return the loan in March, and early in April 1944 he reported to Hillyer that "the great Virginia lawsuit came to a head last week in the Federal Court with a victory for our side—but like military victories it leaves the mopping up to be done—The question is whether we can get any money back." Eventually he and Katy received a sum from the settlement, but until it arrived their income was as precarious as ever—when Max Eastman wrote to solicit an article for the *Nation,* Dos Passos responded that, although he was honored by the request, during the past few years he had been "too damn broke, to be brutally frank, to do unpaid articles."

CHAPTER TWENTY-SEVEN

World War II:
The Pacific and the Wreckage
of Europe, 1944–1945

The romance of being a professional writer was a luxury that Dos Passos infrequently enjoyed as he worked to earn an income. Houghton Mifflin had published *State of the Nation* in July. By November he was complaining to Lovell Thompson, his editor at Houghton Mifflin, that the company had done "an excellent routine job," but that the results with *Number One* and *State of the Nation* were little better than had been those when Harcourt, Brace was his publisher. As authors are wont to do, Dos Passos thought that his books were neither sufficiently displayed in bookstores nor even adequately stocked. Consequently they were inaccessible to anyone who might want to read them. His publishers, he suspected, did not consider his books —particularly his reportage—"of permanent value and interest to the inhabitants of these states," a mistake because he found people who admired such works as *State of the Nation* more than his fiction. Moreover, the publisher Jonathan Cape in England was still selling *Orient Express* "to a lot of bloody limejuicers" after almost twenty years. His frustration mounted as he had no concrete suggestions for another selling approach, "But hell Lovell," he closed his letter, "that's what you are sitting in that office looking out at those starlings all day for."

With *State of the Nation* completed he turned to planning his next short-term project, another book of reportage, this one about the theaters of war. The book, to be entitled *Tour of Duty,* would be about American operations in the Pacific and about Germany after her defeat. He planned to leave for the first part of his tour late in the fall of 1944. In the meantime, he and Katy remained in Provincetown while he labored at the biography of Jefferson and at a shortened version of *State of the Nation* which appeared in September in *Life.*

Before he left for the Pacific he and Robert Hillyer had a not altogether pleasant exchange, because Hillyer, after reading *Nineteen Nineteen*, was affronted to discover that Dos Passos had used him in creating the character Richard Ellsworth Savage. "I dont think there's much Hillyer in Savage," wrote Dos Passos to Hillyer in response to his complaint, "except for the story of the late General Hillyer that you probably noticed I cribbed from your career and some peace conference courier stories." Explaining his technique, he continued, "when you start making up people for a book you cant help taking incidents and traits from the lives of your friends and your own." But that was not at all the same as producing a portrait, something he would not know how to do. Yet people, not recognizing the process of fictionalizing, wrote him claiming to be the models for his characters. "It's a hell of a business," he concluded. Hillyer, however, was not placated and complained again. "Really you've got it all wrong," Dos Passos responded. Savage, like all of his fictional characters, was "a synthetic character" and neither a portrait nor a caricature of Hillyer. "You've written novels yourself," he reminded his friend, "and you know how you start out with a few notions and anecdotes about somebody you know and then other scraps of the lives of other people get in and a large slice of your own life and then if you are lucky the mash begins to ferment and becomes something quite different."

It had never occurred to Dos Passos that Hillyer, if he read *Nineteen Nineteen*, would be other than amused. Dos Passos assured his friend he had "always liked and admired" him and meant no harm. "You live in a dimension so different, so much ampler, so much uglier and so much lovelier than any character in any book," he reminded Hillyer, "that even if someone tried to make up a portrait of you I dont see why you should be affected by it because it simply would not be you." He asked Hillyer to "forgive the friend for the transgressions of the novelist," which he soon did, recognizing the truth of Dos Passos's reminder that "our novels and schoolrooms aren't all of our lives." Their friendship of thirty years was on a different and more important plane. Dos Passos's was a good letter, reflecting his concern for friendship as well as an understanding of the art—and limitations—of fiction.

During the fall he had arranged with *Life* magazine to do a series of articles from the materials that would afterward become *Tour of Duty*. The pressure to write would be severe, but he was pleased by the prospect of the income and a wide readership. In a good frame of mind, thus, he left for the West Coast and the Pacific theater at the beginning of December. From San Francisco he flew to Hawaii, where he arrived on December 9. Soon he was in the Pacific theater of war. He spent Christmas on Kwajalein, one of the Marshall Islands, then the navy transported him to several of the atolls in the Marianas. "Hawaii / Marshalls / Marianas / Ulithi / Guerrillas / Manila / Guadacanal / Bypassed areas / New Caledonia / Air Force New Guinea / Australia" ran a note he jotted down about his tour in the Pacific.

On the last day of 1944 he wrote Katy from Majuro, in the Marshalls, and told her that he had traveled as far south as Apamama, one of the Gilbert Islands almost on the equator. He had been to Tarawa, another of the Gilberts and now a backwater a little more than a year after it had been the scene of brutal combat. As he visited these atolls he attempted to absorb some sense of the adequacy of the military's logistical procedures and to get a feel for the mood of the servicemen behind the front lines. He was tremendously impressed. "You cant imagine the transportation by air and boat there is in these parts," he wrote Katy and described the efficiency of American operations on the islands:

> The minute we land on an atoll it begins to look like LaGuardia Field. We bring in distillators to distill seawater. We attack the flies and the rats. We oil for mosquitos. We level everything off and establish a city dump. The result isnt picturesque but it's eminently practical so that in the central Pacific at least the islands become extraordinarily healthy. Meanwhile in the places where we are not life goes on as it did a long time ago. The brown Micronesians fish and sail their magnificent outrigger canoes and fatten somewhat on the overflow of our canned goods. I havent had time to go fishing yet or to get a sail in a canoe, but I still have hopes.

After the New Year he visited Enewetok, a small "way station" in the series of bases built as the battles moved toward Iwo Jima. In mid-January he was on Saipan, where one evening he observed the impressive spectacle of eighty-one B29 bombers returning from a mission. As the planes landed, the people on the ground were tense, waiting to find out if any bombers had been lost. That night none was, and only one man suffered a minor injury. Shortly thereafter Dos Passos from Ultihi boarded a battleship on a mission to bombard Iwo Jima. "At sea on a battleship," he wrote Katy on January 23. "It's wonderful aboard here," he told her. "Excellent company. Good food. Clean towels. Hot showers. The only trouble is . . . it is too much machinery. The whole great mammoth is so packed with machinery and men in blue dungarees curled up in every crevice that I cant find my way around. When there is an alert I am supposed to get to my battle station or lookout, a place called Sky Control." But he invariably found himself climbing to the wrong spot. "Then you are given earplugs a helmet a May West life belt asbestos gloves, mask hood and God knows what all into which you are supposed to climb. It's very confusing. I fumble and stumble around like a centipede in skiboots."

His spirits and health were "splendid," he reported, and although he told Katy that they "mustn't do too much of this kind of thing separately," he declared that he would not have missed the trip to the Pacific for anything in the world. The operations aboard the battleship fascinated him because of their intricacy as well as the skill with which they were carried out. He observed a destroyer in his formation down a Japanese torpedo plane as the ships neared Iwo Jima, which from the close-in range of 6,000 yards the battleship shelled with salvos from her sixteen-inch guns. With binoculars Dos Passos could see the Japanese airfields on Iwo Jima, could observe the destruction caused by the bombardment ashore, and could see the hulks of two transport ships burning at the water's edge where they had been beached. The raw power of the battleship and the proximity to the enemy made the voyage an exhilarating one.

After this episode Dos Passos immediately headed for the Philippines, and as luck would have it he arrived in Tacloban on Leyte with the aim of going on to Manila only two days after American troops had reached the city. He entered Manila on February 5 and spent the next weeks in the surrounding region while he investigated army operations and the conditions of life the natives had endured under Japanese rule. He observed action when the Japanese struck back, and he heard firsthand details about the combat and the brutality of their occupation. Before leaving the area of Manila he interviewed General Douglas MacArthur, whose poise and awareness of an audience Dos Passos noted without passing judgment. From near Manila he wrote Gerald and Sara Murphy that he had been kept "most amazingly busy," especially as now he was cabling material to *Life* instead of merely making notes for future use. The day he wrote the Murphys he was resting "in a ruined sugar plantation set among big trees draped with Bougainvillea and an immense growth of philodendron." Around him were "immense wallowing caraboo with big black buffalo horns." He was distressed by the sight of "the tiny dusty underfed people" he saw and whose plight he was reporting. "The burning and pillaging and murdering of the retreating Nips," he wrote, "has left the civilians in a heartbreaking plight. Popeyed correspondents keep sending off horrible atrocity stories. The surprising thing about them is that they tend to be understated rather than exaggerated." The situation, he added, was "the grimmest I've seen since South Russia way back in '21."

A few days later he was shuttled back to Leyte, where as at Santo Tómas earlier he interviewed people—some of them Americans—who had conducted guerrilla warfare against the Japanese. He flew to the island of Mindanao, still occupied by the Japanese, where near an airstrip controlled by Philippine guerrillas he talked with them and their American commander, Colonel James Grimstead. Then he returned to Leyte before proceeding by plane to Dutch New Guinea—across its Granje Range and low over villages so remote that the natives in alarm brandished and even threw their spears at the C47 transport—and southward to McKay and finally to civilization in Brisbane, Australia. There on March 12 he was, he wrote Katy, finally able to take his ease "in a large hotel room with bath and hot and cold running water —and streetcars go by outside and there's not a trace of burning and bombing. . . ." He confessed to feeling "a little dizzy and fearfully sleepy" after the 3,800-mile flight from the Philippines, but he was pleased to be in Australia, where he could take some rest and recreation before the trip back to the United States.

It was either in Brisbane or Sydney, his next stops before heading home, that Dos Passos was miraculously fortunate to survive a freak accident. Strolling along a beach where American officers took their R and R, he was struck on the head by the wing-tip of a Curtis-Robin airplane which buzzed the beach. He was knocked unconscious, but the injury was not severe, and he said little about it to anyone. Fortunate to be alive, he departed Australia late in March and finally arrived on April 9 in San Francisco, where he telegraphed Katy of his return, and within days he was in Provincetown for the spring and summer to write up his Pacific experiences.

The memory of them continued to exhilarate him as few things had in recent years. Despite fatigue from the travel, he was "very much cheered and stimulated," he wrote Edmund Wilson, who was in Europe in mid-May. He had seen "more attractive and interesting people in the space of a few months than I'd seen in years and came back with considerable confidence in the ability of younger and less important Americans to cope with the terrific problems that face us everywhere." The technical things which Americans could do, they did "so damn well." But back in the United States and looking at "the overall political picture," he felt "appalled again," despite the optimism that should have been engendered by V-E Day on May 8, 1945. World War II was fast becoming World War III while America betrayed its Allies and fed enemies such as the Russians, he fretted, thinking of the Yalta agreements of the previous February and of the inexperience of the new President, Harry Truman.

From Rome Wilson responded that he had seen only England and Italy to date. Europe was "pulverized and the atmosphere is suffocating," he thought, while the people were "more provincial and more nationalistic" than ever. Yet the only thing that could save them was "a European federation," and that could be achieved only through "international socialism." It was the Socialists who Wilson thought had the best chance of standing up to the Stalinists, and he could not understand what he gathered was Dos Passos's "loss of faith in late years in [his] old more or less socialist ideals." To Wilson anything other than a revival of Socialism in Europe seemed "decadent, disgusting, and hopeless."

"I dont quite understand your remark about 'faith' in socialism," Dos Passos wrote back. "Socialism is something we've got, so it looks to me, like railroads and air conditioning and cancer." Being a fact, it was not a matter of "faith," Dos Passos contended. Faith, "the unreasoned fringe of belief," was what he retained in "individual liberty," which needed to be applied somehow to "the various forms of socialism the world suffers from." But the Socialists did not appear to Dos Passos to have moved beyond "the bureaucratic state of mind" that he despised in whatever form. In the United States the bureaucracy was evident in organizations like the OPA; in England, in the mentality of the Labourites. "We seem to be heading towards monolithic bureaucratic social systems whether they are based on force as in Russia or on persuasion and apathy as in England and the United States," he declared. This depressed him, but "spilt liberties" were gone for good, he supposed. Nevertheless, he thought that the United States might still produce "some livable variation of the deadly pattern." No other nation had "the surplus energy or wealth" to succeed. If Americans managed their affairs well enough at home, they might produce "something analagous to the British reform bill" after the Napoleonic wars, but he saw little sign of it at the moment. Closing, Dos Passos complimented Wilson on his edition of Scott Fitzgerald's *The Crack-Up*, which now seemed to Dos Passos "quite admirable." Then as an afterthought he added, "I dont think people have explored enough in recent years the possibilities of our banal American arbiter-government notion," which he described as "government as the referee among warring monopolies, cartels, trade unions etc.," and which he began to think he would prefer to even the "most benign" sort of "monopolistic socialism."

In such a mood Dos Passos was prepared for the worst when he journeyed to

Europe for *Life* in October, November, and early December 1945. This trip took him via the Azores to Paris, south to Biarritz, back to Paris, and on to Germany and Austria, where he visited among other places Frankfurt, Bad Wiessee in Bavaria, and Vienna before going to Nuremberg and finally Berlin, from where he returned to Paris, soon to depart from Le Havre aboard the small aircraft carrier *Croatan* on December 5.

What he found in Europe was as depressing to him as the situations in the Pacific had been exhilarating. It was hardly the Europe he remembered. From the moment he arrived in Paris, the Continent appeared bleak—not France as much as Germany, however—and he craved to be gone. Even in Biarritz, where he drove by Jeep in clear autumn weather, he felt depressed. Although he observed that France had not been devastated, he confessed to Katy, "I havent much appetite for Europe at present. I want to be home—that's about the size of it." And as he moved on into Germany, his gloom deepened. Writing her at the end of October from Wiesbaden, he noted that "Here is all the brutality of war and army life without the enlivening element of danger that gives it what poetry it has." He missed Katy more and more and was counting the days until he might leave, which would be soon after the opening of the Nuremberg trials of the Nazi leaders scheduled for November 20. Letter after letter to her during November reiterated his near-despair, helped not at all by the cold, damp weather of late autumn and the destruction he observed. "I dont like it over here. Not us nor the squareheads nor nobody," he added in a postscript to one letter, as if Katy did not already understand that. "I wish I could shake off the gloom"; "I have had about as much of the ETO [European Theater of Operations] as I can absorb already"; "The cold and stagnant sky of Northern Europe presses down on you [in Berlin] from above cutting out all light and warmth—[while] the miserable inhabitants with blue lips and hollow eyes drag their little boats of wood or slog about under shapeless bundles of things. . . . A cold dank hell"—such were his sentiments as he attempted to gather information.

While in Paris in October he attended a press conference for Charles De Gaulle and was more impressed by the general than he had expected to be. De Gaulle spoke well and seemed to have some of the "sly and old fashioned French" about him, Dos Passos wrote Katy. De Gaulle was intent on building up the army; at the same time he was concerned about reconstruction and was adeptly drawing in American dollars at a ridiculously low rate of exchange. Ten days later, after driving south to Biarritz, Dos Passos had decided that "the French are pulling themselves together in their own peculiar way. Everything is on the verge of collapse, but things dont collapse."

Not surprisingly, *Tour of Duty* reflected his gloom. "Frankfurt resembles a city as much as a pile of bones and a smashed skull on the prairies resembles a prize Hereford steer," he declared. The Germans scurried around the ruins like ants around a crumbled anthill. "Vienna is heartbreaking," he wrote after visiting that city. There the presence of the Russians was an added irritant. Tales of their repression and brutality abounded, adding fuel to the fire of Dos Passos's dislike, hatred, in fact, of their officialdom. Finding out about the Russians, he wrote, was an almost insurmountable task, because added to the language barrier was "the fact that for nearly thirty years now the only view of the world outside the Soviet Union its citizens have had has been through the distorting prism of Marxist propaganda." Thus, the Russians believed that a deep-seated hostility worked between the two sides when in fact, Dos Passos observed, Americans in Vienna had "an almost pathetic desire to lean over backwards to understand Russian needs and Russian prejudices," a desire that led in his opinion to the Western leaders during the conferences at Teheran, Yalta, and Potsdam "dealing out all the trumps to the Russians." This Cold War attitude had not yet entirely taken hold in the United States, but Dos Passos found it prevalent among Americans in Europe disgusted with the "quadripartite governments of Berlin and Vienna."

The opening of the war-crimes trials at Nuremberg on November 20 did little to alleviate his pessimism. "The Nazis are a strange crew," he wrote Katy on the twenty-second. Hess appeared to have "some disease of the brain"; Streicher and Funk were "monstrosities," but the others seemed "men of considerable intellectual brilliance." Goering appeared to see himself as a kind of "master of ceremonies," plump, spoiled, and outgoing. When the American Robert Jackson opened the case for the prosecution on the twenty-first, Dos Passos was impressed. "A few more speeches like that," he told Katy, "and the poor old ship of state that has been wallowing rudderless in the trough of the sea will be back on its course." Jackson seemed to be making sense out of what might otherwise be construed as nothing more than an act of vengeance. Dos Passos would never forget "the look of horror and terror" that came over the Nazis when Jackson presented as evidence the orders to massacre the Jews. "Jackson represented the USA as I like to see it represented," Dos Passos wrote.

But for all that he was not sure that the trials could achieve their purpose. That evening an Eastern European, perhaps a lawyer or a college professor, asked him if the trials would reestablish justice. Had the Allies not committed crimes as great as those of the Nazis? the European asked. Dos Passos was not able to answer more than that justice was the Allies' intention. "Intentions aren't enough," the man responded, and Dos Passos had no retort. He could only say goodnight and go "gloomily to bed."

From Nuremberg he traveled by automobile to Berlin, the "cold dank hell" he described to Katy. He remained there four days before taking a train toward Paris. In the other berth in his compartment aboard the train was an American, a Professor Zucker, with whom he soon began to talk about the Russians. The professor spoke of "concessions" and "appeasement." Americans "were collectively just like Chamberlain with his umbrella: 'Peace in our Time.'" The professor spoke German and had talked with German Communists. These people thought Americans effective industrially, but with the war over, they were convinced the United States was finished. "War production had been American capitalism's last great effort," Dos Passos's acquaintance quoted the Germans as saying. "Our way of life and our prattle about liberty were obsolete hypocrisies. . . . Capitalism would split on its own contradictions. As a nation we were already dead and didn't know it." Americans, the Communists thought, did not understand "the world of manipulated political power." "We should never," Dos Passos quoted the professor, "underestimate the Russians." The feeling that Dos Passos took away with him on the train out of Berlin, he wrote, was one of "nightmare." Then or during the previous days in Berlin he scribbled in a notebook marked "Berlin 1945":

> Who sups with the devil must need a long spoon—it is time Americans got it through their heads that Democracy & Dictatorship cant cooperate—not that democracy is perfect or that Russian dictatorship is perfect

and later he added: "The great mistakes in our history

1. not abolishing negro slavery in 1776
2. the way reconstruction was carried out
3. The policy toward Mussolini & Hitler
4. The policy towards Russian dictatorship

In Paris he was interviewed by a young reporter for the military newspaper *Stars and Stripes,* and the two argued about Russia. Recording the episode in *Tour of Duty,* Dos Passos no doubt rendered it so as to present his stance as best he could. It was, nevertheless, a useful device to set forth his ideas. The reporter asked him if he would deny the Soviet Union was a success. "I certainly would," responded Dos Passos. "It's produced a different social setup, but instead of wage slavery you've got real slavery to the State. . . . The untrammeled power of the ruling class in the Soviet Union makes you wonder whether the profit motive is as bad as it has been painted."

The young man asked what Dos Passos thought the Versailles treaty after World War I had produced. "Fascism," was Dos Passos's answer. And the new peace? "Fascism multiplied by Fascism, I suppose." Dos Passos went on to argue for capitalism and democracy as the best means toward liberty, to which the reporter asked if Dos Passos ever wondered what his young self would think of what he was now saying in defense of "the monopoly interests." "You mean I'd think I was an old reactionary," answered Dos Passos. "No, I don't think so," he continued. "I have changed and so have the times. . . . In those days the Soviet Union was a dream. Now it's a reality." He told the reporter that it was persons like him who were the reactionaries. A free society did not emerge from statism, but from "selfgovernment. The individual man has got to be strong enough socially and economically to stand on his own hindlegs and to talk back to his Government if he has to." No one could be trusted to have absolute power. But it was security, not freedom, people wanted, Dos Passos had the younger man retort, to which Dos Passos answered in turn, "It's only in a free society that life is secure. I don't understand why you boys won't see that. . . . It seems so axiomatic."

Having had more than his fill, as he saw it, of such defeatism, Dos Passos sailed December 5 for the United States aboard the *Croatan* and during the week-long voyage made notes about his journeyings of the last month and a half. "Vienna piece," he wrote the last day aboard the carrier, "When you think of the things we've done so well in this war—the brilliant planning of supply—the Philippines campaign the Normandy landings it does seem that somebody could work out a plan of action in Europe and Asia—all we need to do to have the whole world with us is practice what we preach we have the force to back it up."

He was relieved to be able to take his mind off such matters, if but briefly, when Katy met him in New York, where they remained a short while before returning to Provincetown. Dos Passos planned to spend the next weeks writing the last three articles of his series for *Life* and to expand and revise them and the Pacific materials for *Tour of Duty*. He did not forget his political concerns for long. In Provincetown a letter from Upton Sinclair had been awaiting his return. Two days before the end of 1945 Dos Passos responded to Sinclair's questions about literary matters, then concluded:

Never felt so much sadder and wiser in my life as after this trip to Europe. Maybe the Russians are right and man is vile and can only be ruled by terror —but I still refuse to believe that everything the West has stood for since the first of our Forefathers tumbled out of their leaky boats to do their washing on this beach I'm looking out at as I write must go on the ash heap. My god the tide runs strong against us.

CHAPTER TWENTY-EIGHT

"My Sweet My Lost Love,"
1946–1947

The tenets implicit in Dos Passos's articles that appeared in *Life* and subsequently in *Tour of Duty* when it was published in August 1946, were those he would maintain until his death. They were not starkly different from those he had held since 1937, when he had turned against the Communist movement of which the Russians were a major part. During World War II he had concentrated his attention upon American traditions, upon, that is, creating a new nationalistic sense. But with the end of the war, with the Axis powers defeated and the Cold War about to commence and with what he had been predisposed to see among the ruins of Europe, he turned full force on Russia as the incarnation of Communism. Always prepared to see those things which he despised as threats, Dos Passos now gave what he hated—Communism—nationhood and military power which menaced the nationalism that he had painstakingly propounded.

Not that his position appeared unusual or conservative then as far as international politics were concerned. Intellectuals such as Sumner Welles, until recently Undersecretary of State, Walter Lippmann, and Hamilton Fish Armstrong, the editor of the journal *Foreign Affairs,* had been propounding in their writings an internationalism whose aim was to further specific United States interests throughout the world. These interests were defined as democratic and were bound up in the term "free world," but, said their proponents, they ought to be enforced by power. "We need . . . to practice what we preach we have the force to back it up," Dos Passos had written to himself in 1945 and sounded little different from Armstrong, who had spoken of "the unlimited range of our national interests." Where Dos Passos parted company drastically with these thinkers was in his distrust of American bureaucracy—the later Roosevelt and then the Truman administrations—which

429

became for him an evil contiguous to the bureaucracy of big labor and together with it created a villainy almost as menacing, in Dos Passos's view, as the Russian conspiracy.

Could as intelligent, successful, and personally amiable a man as Dos Passos really believe in the existence of conspiracy and banal, bureaucratic repression as profoundly as he seemed to? The evidence confirms that he did. Urbane and knowledgeable, he was withal shy and introverted, always distrustful of dominating or intimidating power, be it in the form of aggressive capitalism or a nameless bureaucracy. He was skeptical about people en masse, who, if not by nature entirely evil, nevertheless had a propensity for allowing their instincts toward order to become repression. Further, his responses were emotional as much as they were intellectual. Affronted by the Communists in Spain, for example, he could never forgive them nor separate his personal loathing for their execution of José Robles from his interpretation of their motives. Spain had been a chaotic chapter in which many bizarre, murderous episodes had occurred. He accepted the chaos, but could not finally take it into account when evaluating politics as means. And, utterly committed to individual freedoms, he interpreted conspiracy when society impinged upon the rights of the individual. He understood that an increasingly complex society was bound to put strains on libertarianism; yet he could only decry those pressures. But instead of seeking a way out for the individual in new alternatives, he sought it in the lessons of the past. Though history can indeed instruct, Dos Passos became too wedded to what lay behind our present civilization. To be sure, in so doing he was like many another satirist, a disappointed idealist who, sickened by the present, harkened to a past that he believed deserved rehabilitation.

"Where Do We Go From Here?" was the question Dos Passos posed in his next article to appear after he had finished *Tour of Duty*. In 1946 he and Katy had once more toured parts of the United States—in March they were in Florida on their way as far west as Mexico, where in April they drove through the Rio Grande valley, "a pure busman's holiday" he called it—and from his observations he wrote another "state of the nation" piece for *Life* to report what he believed was the confusion between labor and business. "Where do we go from here?" one of the persons he spoke to had asked. Dos Passos did not know; his piece presented the confusion. The drift and uncertainty was a natural outgrowth from what he had portrayed in the latter half of *Tour of Duty*, "the lapse and the loss of faith in our purposes and in ourselves" that Jonathan Daniels in a laudatory review of the book noted was Dos Passos's aim to reveal.

Dos Passos and Katy, however, were sure about their own purpose to farm their land and to restore the house at Spence's Point, so during 1946 they visited Westmoreland several times. By October the restoration was far enough along that he wrote Sara Murphy on the sixteenth that he and Katy were "actually sleeping in the house." He was busy with writing, as usual. In addition to preparing an essay for *Life*, he worked at the Jefferson biography and on one of his trips to Virginia spent some days in Charlottesville for research among Jefferson's papers. The press of other affairs occupied him too. He and Katy had been made the godparents of one of two sons of a Provincetown painter, Charles Kaeselau. After the boys' mother died, both of them lived with the Dos Passoses at 571 Commercial Street sporadically during the early 1940s, and Dos Passos and Katy helped to put them through school. Having no children of their own, they took pleasure in having the boys there, and Katy found the company agreeable when Dos Passos was away on his trips, despite the responsibility and additional financial drain.

There were other personal commitments. In 1946 Dos Passos busied himself also trying to arrange for a scholarship for Coco Robles to Johns Hopkins. Coco, in Europe, was having obvious difficulty because of his and his father's political backgrounds. And in correspondence Dos Passos kept up his attacks against the Communists, as in a letter to an acquaintance, Gene McNerney, who had queried Dos Passos as to his thoughts about criticism of Dos Passos and the columnist George Sukolski. The criticism, Dos Passos responded, was "the state of mind that is causing liberal thought in this country to settle into a set [of] blind prejudices that are only useful to the Communists, who are, in my opinion, rigging up the neatest and most unbeatable machine for the exploitation of man by man that has ever been devised." Just because the belligerent nationalism of the American Legion was usually wrong did not, he added, "mean that the Commies are right."

Dos Passos set aside his work on the biography of Jefferson during the early months of 1947 to work on *The Grand Design* that was to follow *Adventures of a Young Man* and *Number One* in the *District of Columbia* trilogy. He could write while he and Katy were traveling, as they did in February and March to Key West and then in May to Spence's Point. After returning to Provincetown, they planned the trip to England they would take in July and August to gather material for more *Life* articles. "Britain's Dim Dictatorship," published late in September 1947, was a follow-up on the pieces he had written about England in the fall of 1941 for *Harper's*. He and Katy traveled around Great Britain investigating the conditions of business and labor under Clement Attlee's Labour Party regime. Dos Passos found both sides discontented and his article was slanted against Britain's "planned economy," but it was by no means as severe as the subtitle provided by the editors of *Life* would suggest: "Under a government of their own creation, British working people are gradually being strangled to death in a morass of poverty and ineptitude," ran the subtitle. The piece was more restrained, more a work of reportage than a polemic, although Dos Passos clearly was not pleased with the direction the English government had taken since 1941, and when he and Katy boarded the *Queen Mary* on August 21 to return to the United States, he exclaimed in a letter to Marion Cummings, "Westbound thank God!"

Once back, he and Katy did not remain in Provincetown long before they were on the move. On the afternoon of September 12 they left Provincetown by car, headed for Old Lyme, Connecticut, where they planned to stay the night at the Bee and Thistle Inn, a spot they enjoyed on their drives to and from the Cape. From there they planned to motor the next day to Norfolk, Connecticut, to visit C. D. Williams and his wife. It was late in the day that tragedy struck. Just before sunset they were driving along Route 28 on the outskirts of Wareham, a short distance off the Cape. Katy had fallen asleep on her side of the front seat, and Dos Passos was having difficulty seeing as he squinted to avoid the sun, which hung like a bright orange ball in the road ahead. Suddenly there was a ripping crash, and he was struck unconscious. Moments later he came to, to the sound of the car's horn blaring without end, and he turned, dazed, to see Katy's lifeless body, practically decapitated, lying next to him. The realization came slowly. They had rammed into the back of a truck with its tailgate down that was parked at a slight angle out into the road. The top of their car had nearly sheared off, and the same blow that had killed Katy had severely lacerated Dos Passos's face and destroyed his right eye.

By the time aid arrived it was dark. Two policemen lifted Dos Passos from the car, and only then did he realize the extent of his injuries and how much he was bleeding. Nevertheless, cupping his gouged-out right eye in one hand, he walked to a pay telephone at Suddard's Garage nearby and called Edie Shay in Provincetown. "Look, Edie," he blurted out, "Katy's dead." He told her what few details he could, then let himself be placed in an ambulance to be taken to a doctor in Wareham who treated him before sending him on to Massachusetts General Hospital in Boston. The doctor had called ahead to Dr. Abraham Pollen, an eye specialist who had never seen Dos Passos but had met Katy a short while before. Pollen met Dos Passos at the hospital, examined the right eye and told him it was irreparable, and at 12:30 A.M. on the thirteenth proceeded to operate for about four hours. Afterward, his face covered with bandages, Dos Passos was placed in a room where he would recuperate for several days before being released. Pollen recalled newsmen clustering about him on that day at the hospital. He told them all he could of Katy's death and Dos Passos's injuries, from which, except for the right eye, he expected Dos Passos to recover completely. Pollen's overriding memory of the episode was of Dos Passos's remarkable courage.

Eben Given visited Dos Passos in the hospital on the thirteenth and found him still groggy from the operation but able to talk. Given offered a grave site for Katy in his family's plot in the Truro cemetery, and it was there that she was buried after a service. that Dos Passos could not attend because of his injuries. Edmund Wilson found the service poignant. Katy had been at the center of the life he knew on the Cape, and now she was dead, and a long phase of that life was gone, he later told Dos Passos. The cemetery had seemed "light, clean, and dry and yet human up there among the old four-square churches," and from it that afternoon he had a beautiful view of the bay off Truro and of the marshes and sandy beaches in the late sun. As Wilson stood near her grave, what she had been "and the little hilltop cemetery" gave the memory of the years gone by "a kind of dignity such as I did not ordinarily grant it."

Other friends visited Dos Passos in the hospital also, among them Marion and Bill Smith, who saw him the evening before Katy's funeral on the Cape. They found him propped up in bed, learning to read with his good eye. They were moved by his emotional strength, for instead of dwelling on Katy, he talked about books and mutual friends and of what might be done with the house in Provincetown. He soon thanked friends who had written him. "This is so much the worst thing thats ever happened to me," he told Robert Hillyer, "that its hard not just to sit in a chair and snivel. Fortunately I have a great deal of work on hand and the good old sheriff right around the corner so I'll have to stir my stumps." He claimed that "the eye business is nothing" and added that Dr. Pollen was already preparing him an ornate artificial eye.

Former friends were quick to respond. Hemingway cabled as soon as he heard of Katy's death, and Dos Passos, Ernest told Malcolm Cowley, wrote back a letter that was sad but affectionate. Cowley had commented that, while feeling sorry for Dos Passos, he could not forgive his illiberal ideology in the years since the Spanish Civil War. Hemingway admitted he had thought that too, but had tried to put it out of his mind and think only that Dos Passos ought not to have been allowed to drive because of his poor eyesight. When something as bad as the accident occurred, one ought not to place blame anywhere. Ernest felt sorrow and fondness for the Dos Passos he had once known, if only sorry for the new man whose politics seemed somehow the result of his investments. At least the new Dos Passos was not testifying before Congress, and it was horrible that Katy had been killed after he had sacrificed his honor for her, Ernest wrote.

Dos Passos kept up a brave front, but it was hard. "Strange what a labor it seems to write a letter," he told Edie Shay five days after the accident. His grief sometimes rolled over him in waves, but only time could lessen that, and meanwhile memories of Katy were an important part of the process of learning to cope with her death. When he was released from the hospital, Phyllis Given drove him out the Cape to the cemetery in Truro. She parked the car, and he walked alone to where Katy had been buried in the Givens' secluded plot. He spent a good while there before returning quietly to Phyllis's automobile. Later, he arranged for a plain slate headstone that read:

KATHARINE SMITH,
BELOVED WIFE OF JOHN DOS PASSOS
MY SWEET MY LOST LOVE

In September he could not remain on the Cape for long because he had to return to Boston for further treatment for his injuries. He stayed with Stewart Mitchell in Cambridge much of the time until October 2, when he departed for Snedens Landing, New York, where he stayed with Lloyd and Marion Lowndes before they drove to Virginia and Spence's Point. He remained for a week or more in Virginia because he had in mind moving there for, as he wrote Edie Shay, "If I tried to avoid all the places I'd been happy with Katy I'd have to get off the earth because there's nothing lovely in life that doesn't make me think of her, but I find it perhaps a little less painful to be down here than in P'town. I'm not going to try to live there for the present." Everything he tried was harder without Katy than he could have imagined, although he enjoyed the company of Mr. and Mrs. Walter Griffith, who managed his farmlands. Learning more about this gave him plenty to do, and in addition he was taking up his writing projects again.

He did return to Provincetown in October, however, before taking the train with Walter Griffith to visit the farmlands of the Midwest. There he meant to gather information for another *Life* article. In Provincetown he needed to pack what he would require for the trip and for living the next months, although he left the closing up of 571 Commercial Street and the shipping to Virginia of some possessions to Marion and William Smith.

The time back on the Cape was almost more than he could bear. From Provincetown before leaving he thanked Max Eastman for his letter of condolence. "My physical mishap, beside the other loss, seems a very trivial thing," he wrote. "I'm already tottering about a weirdly empty world." A letter he received from Canby Chambers at about that time was a poignant reminder of what Dos Passos had lost. Katy, Chambers wrote, "always seemed to me so *alive*. Once, when I saw her angry; but usually when you were being playful and were calling each other names like 'Kingfish' and 'Possum.' . . . After your marriage you brought her to see me in the American Hospital of Paris. She gave me pussy-willows. These were just right, like so many things about Katy." One afternoon Charles Mayo and his father took Dos Passos for a boat ride along the beautiful shoreline around Truro, and he talked wistfully of the places they passed where he and Katy had walked or picnicked. But the experience was too saddening, Mayo sensed, and he could tell that Dos Passos was through with Provincetown.

Before he left he sorted through some of Katy's things, not to throw them away, but simply to have, once more, a sense of her, of that vitality Canby Chambers felt and Edmund Wilson mentioned when he wrote Dos Passos about her death. "Katy must have been a wonderful companion," he was certain. "I had the impression that you were never bored with her, and that—rather shy with most other people—she must have been inexhaustibly entertaining with you and inexhaustible in her gift of investing life with something that the statistics don't add up to but that is one of the only reasons why one would like to see life continue on this planet." Wilson had put it exactly. They had a private world between them which was theirs alone, a world where they entertained each other with stories, where she had been "possum" and he "ape." "What a charming story about the Keeper of the Alligators," she had written him once from Provincetown while he was in Nuremberg in 1945, and she elaborated upon the tale he had made up in a letter. "M. Fish, I love you so much. Darling, I would give anything to hear the Chinaman sing in the night—sometimes he would, you know." The weather in Provincetown then had been beautiful, "the fairest of the year, sweet as summer but so sharp and winey," and she would awaken during the night and look at the ships' lights in the Provincetown harbor and watch the flash of the Truro light and long for him. She amused him with tales of their friends and then closed, asking him not to forget his "Passionately devoted / Eternally faithful / Bookkeeping / Bookwriting / Painting / Cleaning Working / in the garden furbrushing / architectural agricultural / monetary Katy Dos Possum."

As he went through her papers in October 1947, he picked up a notebook on which he had written for her, "This is the Opossum's Other Book." In it he had begun a tale about a fox, two dogs named Mutt and Jeff, and a black man named

Jake. But he had not finished it, and now as he looked through the notebook he thought of Katy and wrote on a piece of paper,

> *My sweet lost love*
> *you laugh downstairs in*
> *the morning*
>   *and the sun on the harbor*

The "archipelagos of remorse and boundless continents of grief" that he felt for her pressed in, and he had to get away and find some solace among friends and in his work, "the only thing," he later told Robert Hillyer, "that gives life any plausibility at the moment."

PART VIII

A New Life,
1948–1960

CHAPTER TWENTY-NINE

Travels to New Lands and Marriage, 1948–1949

After the middle of October Dos Passos and Walter Griffith took a train to Iowa, where they stayed with Roswell Garst and his family in Coon Rapids. Dos Passos convalesced and learned about agricultural processes from his host, whom he had first met in Washington, D.C., at Gardner Jackson's home in the early 1940s and had soon thereafter visited while he was writing his "state of the nation" articles. When Garst had heard of Katy's death, he telephoned Dos Passos and invited him to come out to Iowa. Dos Passos accepted, knowing that the change would be good for him and planning to use the visit to gather information for yet another piece for *Life*, this one to be about the new methods of farming which had revolutionized agricultural production.

Each morning at the Garsts, Dos Passos wrote in his room until noontime, then after lunch he walked about the nearby farms. He was influenced by what he saw and by Garst's enthusiastic reporting of the freedom and success an energetic farmer might have. "Nobody talks about anything but corn and hogs and oats and fertilizers and its a liberal education in the art of farming," he wrote Sara Murphy from Coon Rapids. On Dos Passos's mind also was an essay he was writing for *Life* entitled "The Failure of Marxism." As he wrote it he thought of Garst's description of what American agriculture had achieved, which made him all the more certain that the planned economics of Socialism were a danger to mankind. One morning from his room at the Garsts he wrote Edmund Wilson his thoughts, inspired by the entrepreneurial success he was observing in Iowa and by the last of several articles about Socialism by Jean-Paul Sartre, of whom Dos Passos wrote, "The weakness underlying his political thinking as I see it is this: he has not confronted the basic verity (at least so it is coming to seem to me) that socialism is a new system of exploitation of man by man very much more total and without any of the loopholes that capitalism allows—through which the individual can escape and lead a life of comparative freedom and dignity." Without such loopholes, "all socialist thinking," he concluded, treaded "on the quicksand of later day liberalism" which, because it had embraced bureaucratic organization, was not what citizens of a self-governing community needed. As far as "the well-being of men and women" was concerned, he wrote in "The Failure of Marxism," the issue was not between capitalism and Socialism but between "the sort of organization that stimulates growth and the sort that fastens on society the dead hand of bureaucratic routine or the suckers of sterile vested interests." He believed that much of the world was becoming "a museum of socialist failures" and that the United States had first "to understand clearly the needs of our own society and its relationship to the regime of the law of the club that centers in the Soviet Union." Failure to do so on the part of Roosevelt and his advisers had cost America its wartime victory. Only "where new avenues for men's ingenuity and enterprise are constantly opening up"—as on the Iowa farms—"and where the areas of individual liberty are expanding" could a self-governing community survive. "We had forgotten," he wrote, "that the only sensible foreign policy for the U.S. was to encourage liberty and oppose oppression." In the *Life* essay he concluded by condemning Russia and finally criticizing "British socialism," whose "ultimate implications" were not far different from the Russian sort in that socialism wherever it existed contracted rather than expanded personal liberties.

It is easy to understand Dos Passos's convictions, enhanced as they were by the example of the Iowa farmers, although in his enthusiasm for their productivity he overlooked the fact that Garst's operation was itself big business. Dos Passos distrusted bigness in all forms; small, independent communities such as Jefferson had idealized and Coon Rapids seemed to be were his goal. "Our chance of working our way through to a better society would be moderately good," he had a character say when he incorporated the essay about the farms into a book, "if we could find some way of initiating a powerful movement towards decentralization in industry and in government. I say give industry and government back to the people, where they live, in the small and mediumsized towns." The character then expressed his fear that trade unions were leading to "overcentralization" as well. But the problem facing anyone striving for decentralization was that American society had grown complex and its elements interdependent during the twentieth century. The United States by 1947 was primarily urban and industrial, and to say that the answer to enhancing individual liberties was to give "industry and government back to the people" was simplistic and hardly an answer at all. Yet Dos Passos had nothing more detailed to offer.

There was, too, the vagueness of his assertion that American foreign policy ought "to encourage liberty and oppose oppression." These were general aims commonly accepted—"I believe that it must be the policy of the United States to support free peoples who are resisting attempted subjugation by armed minorities or by outside pressures. I believe that we must assist free peoples to work out their destinies in their own way," President Harry Truman asserted while defining what

became the Truman Doctrine early in 1947. But what did these noble generalizations mean as they were applicable to Dos Passos's thought then: war against the
Soviet Union, or economic support for those peoples who opposed Russia's expansionist designs? Dos Passos detested war. Economic support, however, which was the
essential nature of the Truman Doctrine and the Marshall Plan, did not stifle the
Communists as he would have wished. He did not approve of the United States's
international policy, which seemed one of appeasement, but neither did he support
belligerent conservatives who thought war should be waged against the Communists. Yet so adamant was his opposition to Communism that, while not openly
advocating conflict, he more than once flirted with the "solution" of fighting the
"law of the club" with a club. The result was a sometimes querulous illiberalism
which condoned the Communist witchhunting of Congressman Parnell Thomas,
Chairman of the House Un-American Activities Committee for a time in the 1940s,
or that of Senator Joseph McCarthy afterward. Vigilance at home coupled with
limited government, Dos Passos reasoned, could save American institutions. In the
hands of a McCarthy vigilance paradoxically became blind vengeance resulting from
fear and worked against the very liberties and decentralization Dos Passos espoused.
He could not, however, separate from his ideal of "selfgovernment" his belief in an
imminent Communist threat and thus was willing to support antilibertarian measures.

Dos Passos's mind was occupied with these problems as he and Walter Griffith
ended their visit to the model farms of Iowa on November 10, when they traveled
east by train. Griffith returned to Warsaw, Virginia, while Dos Passos went to
Lowndes's home at Snedens Landing, which became his main base for the next two
years. Being busy and having the company of the Lowndeses and their daughter
Susan cheered him. "Life only seems bearable when I'm working or talking to small
children," he wrote Edie Shay after he had been at Snedens Landing for several
weeks, and a month and a half later he confessed that he felt "pathetically dependent on seeing friends just at present."

A satisfaction that also gave life meaning came late in November when he
heard of his election to the American Academy of Arts and Letters. Van Wyck
Brooks, who informed him, Sinclair Lewis, Deems Taylor, Edna St. Vincent Millay,
Carl Sandburg, and Eugene O'Neill had all nominated Dos Passos, and his selection
was announced November 25. He became the fifth occupant of Chair 14, previously
held by Willa Cather.

Rarely at ease in public, Dos Passos would have found the ceremony distressing
because he was still unused to his artificial eye, his other injuries were still healing,
and he would have felt particularly uncomfortable around strangers. As he told Edie
Shay, he remained dependent on friends. He visited the Gantts in Baltimore and
his cousin, Lois Hazell, in Washington during the Christmas season, then returned
to Snedens Landing, where he remained until February 1948, when he traveled first
to Virginia, then journeyed to Nassau to visit the John Marquands, and to Haiti,
where he, the Givens, Esther Chambers, and for a part of the time, Dawn Powell,
stayed at the Hotel Oloffson in Port-au-Prince for a vacation until mid-March.

He enjoyed himself with these old friends and took an interest in Haiti, "the oddest damn place I ever saw," he wrote Edmund Wilson as he thought about the local architecture, the craze for primitive art, and the tourism he had observed. But familiar faces turned up. The night before he wrote Wilson he had had dinner with Selden Rodman and his wife—Rodman had been one of the editors of the journal *Common Sense*—a Haitian businessman and his wife, and a "tall young American who seemed to have had some connections with Princeton and said he'd won an Atlantic Monthly prize." Dos Passos was amused at the young American's and Rodman's apparel—they both wore "sooty batik shorts," and the younger man had a gold button in one ear. "The only party who made much sense was the Haitian" who seemed "quite a sound fellow." Dos Passos was not being a crank; he was simply amused by the fads of dress in Haiti. Primitive art had caught on, "fomented by a man named DeWitt Peters and the local boys seem to enjoy hugely selling to American tourists." Some of the paintings, he admitted, were quite striking. Yet another fad was the island's religious cults: "Nobody ever stops talking about voodoo, zombies, possessions, Baron Samedi, etc," he commented. It was all unbelievable, and he looked forward to the arrival of Dawn Powell, whose wry wit would balance off the foolishness.

Wilson in a letter to Dos Passos had criticized "The Failure of Marxism," which had appeared in *Life* in mid-January. "It's too hot to take up your political arguments," Dos Passos responded, admitting that the article had irritated a good many people. The only support he had received was from a local paper in Saskatchewan. But he could not understand why people were irritated anew each time he spoke out as he had in the article, "because its the same line I've been pursuing since The Ground We Stand On to the effect that it's political methods and not political aims that count." People like Wilson, he joked, were "just blinded by prejudice," but he was serious when he added, "whoever's to blame its obvious that the international picture is going from worse to worser."

That spring he and Louis Dos Passos made a final settlement of the Virginia land between themselves, for which Dos Passos stopped off in Warsaw on his way north before returning to Snedens Landing. In the division he took 2,100 acres of land that included the more valuable waterfront acreage. To pay for it, he mortgaged it for $21,500 to a local doctor, an arrangement which concerned him until the debt was paid off several years later. In 1948 he was willing enough to assume the burden of debt, however, because he was eager to start new roots away from Provincetown. The fact is that Dos Passos desperately wanted to build a life for himself where the memories of Katy were not overpowering. Provincetown haunted him. After a brief visit in 1949 he wrote Sara Murphy that "it was sweet seeing old friends on the Cape but its still too painful there." There was more possibility in Virginia, where he had spent a part of the summer of 1948 after having divided the land with Louis. The Lowndeses and he late that June drove there and enjoyed looking about the land around Spence's Point, swimming in the Potomac, and considering the problems of the farm with Walter Griffith. Dos Passos remained in Warsaw after the Lowndeses departed, and he threw himself with enthusiasm into the business of finding tenants for the main house, talking with a resident about a land swap, and coping alongside Griffith with some of the idiosyncrasies of country life. When he described these to the Lowndeses, he sounded more cheerful and less dependent than he had at almost any time since Katy's death almost a year before.

Even so, he did not remain in Virginia long, because during the summer of 1948 he was pressed to finish the novel *The Grand Design.* As well as to meet a publishing deadline, he wanted to finish the book because at the end of the summer he had scheduled a lengthy trip to South America on an assignment for *Life.* Central to his purpose also was to put his concern for the nation before the public.

The Grand Design, published in January 1949, drew upon several sources: his experience with government administrators in Washington, his travels while writing the essays for *State of the Nation,* his visits to Roswell Garst in Iowa, and obviously his belief that Communism and the deadening hand of bureaucracy were threatening the nation's existence. Herbert Spotswood, the father of Glenn and Tyler, is an influential radio commentator in this novel. His story, important to its scheme but by no means at the novel's center, reflects the point Dos Passos intended to make: the American people too often were duped by words instead of acting for themselves to protect "selfgovernment." As Glenn had written to Tyler before his death, "It's what you do that counts, not what you say." Spotswood is a hollow man, pleased with his authority as a commentator but not truly knowledgeable about what he says nor attuned to others—he is so self-centered as neither to have understood Glenn nor to care to help Tyler when he is desperate after his break with Chuck Crawford.

> *The republic's foundations are not in the*
> sound *of words,*
> *they are in the shape of our lives, fellowcitizens.*
> *They trace the outlines of a grand design. To*
> achieve
> *greatness a people must have a design before them*
> *too great for accomplishment. Some things we*
> have learned, *but not enough; there is more to learn.*
> Today
> *we must learn*
> *to found again*
> *in freedom*
> *our republic*

concluded the trilogy and the last of the prose poems which interspersed the narratives about various characters in *The Grand Design.* Dos Passos's theme was his familiar one that "the grand design" of the United States lay in the deeds of Americans who should seek a Jeffersonian freedom. For all its good intentions at the start, the New Deal had been bankrupted by a proliferation of bureaucratic power, and a Franklin Roosevelt of 1933, a

*smooth broadshouldered figure confident and tall . . . the President newly elected
who strode out on the arm of his son erect almost jaunty in his legbraces*

and who could speak of "a leadership of frankness and vigor and support of the
people themselves which is essential to victory," was by his fourth term in 1945,

*an aging man, an ill man, a cripple who had no time to ponder history or to find
the Danube or the Baltic or Vienna on the map: so many documents to sign,
so many interviews with Very Important Personages, such gloss on the young
men: "Yes Mr. President," "No Mr. President." The decisions were his. He
could play on a man like on a violin. Virtuoso. By the modulations of his voice
into the microphone he played on the American People. We danced to his tune.
Third term. Fourth term. Indispensable.*

War is a time of Caesars.

"In essence," wrote the critic Linda Wagner, *"The Grand Design* is a story
of ruin, the price in 'great people' necessary to fuel Roosevelt's plans." To tell his
story Dos Passos, as his notes reveal, extended the narratives from the beginning of
the New Deal until 1943, the prose poems carrying on to 1945. His major figures
in addition to Herbert Spotswood were a businessman, Millard Carroll, and a
farming expert, Paul Graves, who came to Washington believing in the promise of
agricultural reform. But gradually their ideals were frustrated by the bureaucratic
operations of the Agriculture Department headed by Walker Watson. In creating
his characters Dos Passos drew closely from life. Millard Carroll was based on Milo
Perkins, a New Dealer who worked under Henry Wallace, Secretary of Agriculture
during the early days of Roosevelt's administrations and Vice President from 1941
to 1945. Graves emerged from the people Dos Passos met in Iowa, with a touch of
Walter Griffith added, perhaps. "Paul and Peggy Graves in Wilmington, N.C. /
oldest boy Paul—Pauline—scientific agriculture / gets job with Bob Garst & Henry
Wallace / Department of Agriculture—Scotch-irish look—goes to Horton, Texas"
ran some of Dos Passos's earliest notes as he detailed his characters. Walker Watson
was a composite of Harry Hopkins—whom Dos Passos had met in Washington
during World War II and disliked for his talk about "only a handful of men"
knowing enough to run the country during the war—and Henry Wallace, whom Dos
Passos had come to scorn for what seemed to him Wallace's ambition for power.
But more, he scorned Wallace because of his desire to accommodate the Russians
after the war and his consequent creation of the Progressive Party of America, whose
candidate he was for the presidency in 1948. Wallace was manipulated by the
Communists, and to Dos Passos he seemed part fool, part villain.

Numerous other characters—including Georgia Washburn, another of Dos
Passos's women figures victimized by circumstance—played significant roles in the
novel which was intended to bring to a close Dos Passos's somber vision of the era
of the New Deal and of Washington, D.C. Although not as populated as *U.S.A.*,
the *District of Columbia* trilogy—particularly *The Grand Design*—had a large cast

of characters to serve his purpose of chronicling an era and a city, whose inhabitants, because it was the national capital, represented the various political currents and countercurrents in the country.

His purpose was also, as usual, to satirize the people and their ideologies. Because of the tone of moral urgency about *The Grand Design*, few critics recognized Dos Passos's satire when the book was published. It was missed also because "it . . . shocked people as blasphemy against the Great White Father," as Edmund Wilson wrote, offering praise for the book that most critics did not. More common than praise was condemnation because it was "an angry, embittered book, . . . primarily a provocative political tract"; "a temporary lapse of energy"; "dull and mechanical as fiction." For these reviewers missing Dos Passos's satiric intent mattered little since, having faith in the liberal vision of the New Deal, they disagreed with his point of view. Nevertheless, this novel—and nearly all of his fiction, in fact —has a place too few readers granted it because, as Arthur Mizener asserted in an introduction to *District of Columbia*, each character (caricature is a better term) "contributes in his way to our understanding of the drift of the community's life, and if [the author] sees them thus with passion and intelligence, then he will produce neither romance nor tragedy but the most serious kind of satiric comedy." Yet another reason for the disdain accorded *The Grand Design* was that Dos Passos continued to be a political, not infrequently polemical novelist in a period when writers and the public were withdrawing from political activism, when intricate, even precious, styles became fashionable in novels whose subject was the private, inward terrain of a complex character's mind.

Overlook Dos Passos's satiric intention and *The Grand Design* lacks substance and is hardly more than his statement of a condition without an explanation, as the historian John Diggins saw it. "Dos Passos," he wrote, "offered only a moral perception of a real danger; unable to provide a convincing historical analysis of the causes of that danger, he could not offer a political solution to it." Diggins believed that Dos Passos had enough understanding "to realize that capital is the calculus of growth and consolidation, but he could not follow that logic to its frightful conclusion: The curse of big business means the curse of big government." This is an astute observation that neglects, however, Dos Passos's satire, which even Wilson, who liked the novel, appeared to overlook: "I enjoyed *The Grand Design*—I think it much the best of the three," he told his friend. He thought the book "enormously skillful in the writing . . . and in the swift and subtle presentation of social-political processes." But Dos Passos's characters seemed "less convincing as human beings." Wilson considered them mediocrities and complained that "everybody connected with the New Deal was not as mediocre as that." How about some Jeffersons, Barlows, and Paines in the fiction, he asked, and how about not "making everybody talk in clichés?" But mediocrity and trite language are part of the satirist's vision, and that was the fictive vision of Dos Passos.

Working through the summer, he was able to complete *The Grand Design* before he left for South America on September 6, 1948. He had made contact with Hemingway, who was living in Cuba and who was feeling kindlier toward his former friend not only because of his sadness at Katy's death but because, as he had told Archibald MacLeish as far back as 1943, Dos Passos was traveling and learning again. He missed the Dos Passos he had known earlier more than the man of the days in Madrid in 1937. Hemingway feared, however, that Dos Passos would never forgive him because of the Robles incident. But Dos Passos was pleased to try to renew the friendship and generously stopped to visit in Havana. He arrived in time for a farewell party for Hemingway, who was departing by ship for Europe. "The old Monster . . . had his weight down and seemed in splendid fettle," Dos Passos wrote Sara Murphy shortly afterward. The party aboard ship dragged on, and Dos Passos, although enjoying himself, left after six hours of drinking champagne. It was the last time they saw each other.

From Cuba Dos Passos flew to Bogotá, Colombia, his first stop in South America on an extended trip to study "the competition between government by dictation and government by consent." Latin America, because of the poverty of its peoples, was a prime target for the Communists; yet they had not succeeded in taking over. But a fierce struggle was going on, he believed, and he declared that "If we are to win in the contest it is up to us to study more carefully and more dispassionately than [the Communists] do the social situations we have to deal with."

Bogotá, a city that had recently experienced tremendous growth, exemplified the volatile state created by the new conditions. The spring before Dos Passos's visit, a popular uprising had broken out during a Pan-American conference, and the Colombians' confusion about the causes of the unrest and its solutions was for Dos Passos a matter of great concern. He did not remain long in Colombia, however, before flying to Rio de Janeiro, where he learned at the *Time-Life* news service bureau that William White, the bureau chief, and his wife, Constance, were about to drive into the raw country inland. He joined them, and on their way north they stopped in villages where food and lodgings were rudimentary. Large towns like Ouro Prêto and Juiz de Fora provided comfortable hotels, making the trip for Dos Passos a thoroughly enjoyable introduction to Brazil. Fifteen years later he wrote, "When people ask me why I keep wanting to go to Brazil, part of the answer is that it's because the country is so vast and so raw and sometimes so monstrously beautiful; but it's mostly because I find it easy to get along with the people."

He flew next to Vitória on the coast several hundred miles northwest of Rio. In Vitória he found out about Brazil's public health service and its problems—a matter that revealed a lot about the country's development—before traveling by railroad to Colatina, Aimorés, and Governador Valadares, towns inland along the Rio Doce. There and later at the mining town of Itabira Dos Passos got a sense of Brazil's mineral wealth, but also of the difficulties in mining it. The country, he repeatedly declared, appealed to him as much for what he felt were its people's pioneering instincts as for its natural beauty. Traveling as far north and west as Goiânia, seven hours by plane from Rio, he was moved by the patriotism of two intellectuals whom he met. They had come to distrust Communism and wished that the United States would provide leadership to counter the Communists. To learn more about the development of the interior, Dos Passos flew from Goiânia farther inland into wilderness to meet Dr. Bernardo Sayão, an engineer in charge of building roads for the government. Dos Passos, when he met Sayão, was immediately taken with the man's independence and enthusiasm for his work. He had, Dos Passos wrote later, "the greatest quality of leadership of any man I ever met."

No such praise did Dos Passos have for anyone in Buenos Aires, where he journeyed after stopping in Montevideo, Uruguay, across the estuary of the River Plate. In Montevideo people expressed their concern about the Argentinian strong-man Juan Perón and his wife Evita. In Buenos Aires, despite a general air of contentment on the part of the public, Dos Passos soon had little respect for the rule of the *peronistas*. Perón's assurances of plenty had coopted the labor unions, which backed him. Among union members Dos Passos found satisfaction when he visited the resort hotel of the Retail Workers' Union near Mendoza, a western town in the foothills of the Andes. "Before the *peronista* revolution," one worker told him, "only the oligarchs, only the very rich could enjoy this. Now any member of our union can come and spend his vacation here."

Dos Passos did not ignore the relative prosperity he saw, but what concerned him was that the Argentinian public had chosen security instead of freedom. In Buenos Aires he found the press censored, the political opposition ineffectual, and everywhere posters, portraits, and other reminders of Juan and Evita Perón. Dos Passos attended a *peronista* meeting where to the crowd's chants of "Ev-ita, Ev-ita, Per-ón, Per-ón," the President and his wife entered the auditorium. It was not just the cold air outside that chilled Dos Passos when after some time Evita spoke. "A shrill scolding voice starts in long breathless sequences," he wrote. She denounced "the oligarchy and the American imperialists who are opposing the new constitution so much needed to establish the rights of labor, social security for the aged and the sick, the firm foundation for a new powerful democratic Argentina." Her voice sent a shiver down his spine because her shrill scolding reminded him of "another shrill voice, scolding over the air not so many years ago: Hitler's." Dos Passos admitted to being impressed by the energies of the two Peróns, both of whom he met during his stay. They were attractive physically, but they had a "slickness" he despised, no matter how they might try to cloak their methods.

As he began his return trip to the United States, he crossed the Andes by narrow-gauge railway into Santiago, Chile. There he interviewed among others President Gonzales Videla, who described to him the economic difficulties facing Chile and told of the pressures against a democratic regime from the Communists. From Videla and soon after from acquaintances in Lima, Peru, Dos Passos received the same message: the United States was ignoring Latin America; it was not offering enough economic aid, and it was not supporting democracy against Communism.

From all the material he gathered during his trip of nearly three months in South America, only two articles appeared in *Life*, one about the Brazilian Bernardo Sayão, and the second about a visit of Evita Perón to a home for indigents. The rest of the material he began putting together once he had returned to the United States in December 1948, and it appeared in his next book of reportage, *The Prospect*

Before Us, where, although excellent, the material was almost entirely neglected because when the book was published late in the fall of 1950, critics scorned it for its political slant.

Such a reception in 1950 was no worse than *The Grand Design* received when it appeared immediately after the New Year in 1949. Although Dos Passos kept busy writing about his South American trip and planning for a series of articles about the wheat business which the General Mills Corporation had hired him to do, he was distressed by the treatment accorded his latest novel. Negative responses to his political statements now were commonplace. Believing himself misunderstood, he recognized that, as Hemingway had warned him in 1937 could be the case, he was being treated as a back number by the critics.

But his depression was not only due to the treatment the critics accorded his ideas. He was lonely as he set about trying to create a new life for himself. Living with friends like the Lowndeses or the Griffiths, while pleasant, was no substitute for life in a place of his own. Without Katy, he could not bear to remain long at the partly refurbished house at Spence's Point, while Provincetown was too full of memories to enjoy even in the company of good friends. The winter of 1949 was as bleak a time as he ever experienced, a period when his busyness could not offset an accumulation of defeats: Katy's death, works that were critical as well as financial failures, and national and international politics that seemed to him to betray the ideal of personal freedoms while accommodating—even succumbing to—the Communists whom he despised.

Hoping that somehow at least he might improve his personal life, Dos Passos invited a woman a good deal younger than himself, Helen Parker, to go with him to Havana in February. She was a tall, attractive divorcee he had met in New York, who was articulate and had a great interest in literature—and literary figures. To Dos Passos it seemed as if they might have enough in common to consider marriage. They stayed at the Hotel Ambos Mundos, but before long their affair soured. It was not that they came to dislike each other, exactly, but their ages became a barrier; her interests were not his, and he could not keep up with her impetuosity, while he was living too much in his past, which she could stand for only so long. The trip that had begun with optimism soon ended with her leaving alone for New York while he remained in Cuba and tried to fill his time with work, but became more despondent than ever.

Lonely, distracted, even disoriented in some ways was how Elizabeth Holdridge found Dos Passos when she saw him at the Lowndeses in the spring of 1949. She had herself been widowed when her husband Desmond was killed along with Marion Lowndes's brother Emerson in an automobile accident in 1946. She and her son, Christopher, lived in Mount Kisco, New York, and she worked in New York City for the *Reader's Digest* art department. When she saw Dos Passos he was in the midst of trying to organize his articles for the General Mills series for which he traveled to western New York, Alabama, Kansas, Iowa, Michigan, Minnesota, and California during April and May as he sought a sense of the company's operations. The story, he had written Abbott Washburn, who was his contact with General

Mills and the manager of its Department of Public Services, was shaping into something like:

1. Buying the wheat
2. The Flour Business
3. By products, present and future and incorporated in there somewhere will be a sort of social analysis . . .

He had collected masses of material and faced what he told Washburn was "a horribly difficult job of selection."

After several lunch dates, Elizabeth offered to help Dos Passos organize his articles over the long Memorial Day weekend. He eagerly accepted, so in New York they worked for three days in a sitting room of the Fifth Avenue Hotel where he was staying while he wrote. Each evening she returned to Mount Kisco. The day they completed the work, he invited her to have dinner with him before he put her on a train home. As they sat conversing, she recalled, she reached to pick up something on the table and Dos Passos leaned over and put his hand on hers. "Well," he asked, "is it one for all and all for one?" He was asking her to marry him, she realized, and she accepted. They made plans to be married early in August at her brother-in-law's farm north of Baltimore, but before that they had to put their affairs in some order. Dos Passos during the latter part of July journeyed briefly to Provincetown to take care of several matters, then traveled to Wiscasset, Maine, where he stayed with the Lowndeses, who were vacationing there. Elizabeth began arrangements to sell her house in Mount Kisco, and on August 6 she and Dos Passos were married "privately in a cornfield," as he told Sara Murphy. They had then to drive immediately to Spence's Point "to go to work on the farming and house organization," matters about which they felt pressed because in September Dos Passos was to travel to Italy for a P.E.N. conference.

With his second marriage Dos Passos began a new life at the age of fifty-three. Elizabeth Holdridge, thirteen years younger than he, was a tall, attractive woman with a reserved manner and a quiet humor. She appreciated Dos Passos's intelligence and love of travel and offered him the solidity and affection he had needed from the moment of Katy's death. Yet she was very different from Katy, with a different sort of beauty and little of Katy's sometimes acerbic wit that could startle friends. Elizabeth had in addition physical strength and an organizational touch that Katy lacked, qualities that would be useful as Elizabeth and Dos Passos operated the Virginia farm. This was no case of either of them trying to relive what had gone before. They made a fresh start for themselves, and their twenty-one years together would be happy and eventful.

CHAPTER THIRTY

Virginia,
the Chosen Country,
1949–1950

At Spence's Point the Dos Passoses worked hard to make the house as they wanted it before leaving for Europe in September. It was livable but in disorder. Elizabeth found it with books piled on the floors. She worked there and between trips returned to Mount Kisco to make final arrangements to sell her house.

It was with relief that they left for Italy, with a stopover in Paris, in September. Elizabeth recalled Dos Passos's popularity with the Italian people. His works were well known to them, and they paid him much attention, even to following him sometimes a hundred or more strong down the streets. The trip was a kind of honeymoon before they established a routine in Virginia, where the first years of farming were not easy financially. Although she invested the proceeds from the sale of her house, their collective income was not large. The land was saddled with a mortgage, and Dos Passos received no more substantial royalties from his books than before, necessitating tasks like writing the series for General Mills, for which he was paid $5,000, or writing the text for Time-Life's *Picture History of World War II* which appeared in 1950. The task demanded more research, thus more time, than he had thought it would, but he accomplished it, and the income permitted them to complete an addition to the house.

The addition was needed because Elizabeth soon became pregnant and the house lacked the space for another child besides Christopher. When construction began, the dust and clatter of the building created a general commotion not eased by inconveniences such as the lack of a telephone, which was installed only after they had been married a year. But for all that they enjoyed their existence and most of the rigors of country life. "The weather continues springlike with wintry interludes—cherry and plum in bloom—doves coo in the pines in the early morning,

449

peepers peep round the edges of the marshes," Dos Passos wrote the Lowndeses late in February 1950. He reported that six calves, all bulls, had been born, and one cow died calving. Despite being away from friends like the Lowndeses, he had decided that "Spence's Point stands up very well as a winter habitation." He, Elizabeth, and Christopher had driven to Williamsburg the day before to celebrate her birthday. Trips like that, a child to deal with, and the foibles of the house—in this case "some remarkable mice"—were small matters, the tone of his letter implied, on which he thrived

On May 15, 1950, in Baltimore, Elizabeth gave birth to "a tiny squalling leaky little character" whom the parents named Lucy Hamlin Dos Passos, the father, fifty-four and obviously proud, wrote Stewart Mitchell several days later. Her name combined Dos Passos's mother's given name Lucy and Elizabeth's family name Hamlin. Dos Passos could not have been more pleased. He had wanted children, but Katy had suffered several miscarriages. Now with a daughter and stepson, he and Elizabeth had a real family which gave him a comfortable, settled feeling to enhance his sense of rootedness that came from having the farm.

The family remained in Baltimore several weeks before returning to Westmoreland to resume a life that was rarely tranquil. "Our summer has been rendered nightmarish by building operations that drag on and on becoming daily more expensive," he told Edmund Wilson in early August. A month and a half later he was sorry to have missed Wilson in New York, but reported that he had had to return quickly to Westmoreland because of being tied up with his writing "and with all the exasperating complications of trying to build a wing . . . on the house and with the resulting pillage of the farm and woodlands to find the cash to pay the bills."

He missed literary friends and discussion, he told Wilson repeatedly. "Life down here is interesting and highly exacting but it is sadly lacking in conversation," he wrote in 1951. Yet living in Virginia was not a case of retiring from what was going on. He traveled often to New York for literary business and kept up with authors he knew and admired: for example, Wilson's play *The Little Blue Light* entertained him when he read it on the train back to Baltimore in July 1950. He had high praise for William Faulkner and his latest novel at that moment, *Intruder in the Dust,* which, Dos Passos had told Edie Shay, had carried him away so that "in spite of the clap trap plot I read Go Down Moses and Light in August." "The Bear" seemed "pretty wonderful" too, although that much Faulkner at one time could produce "a glut of horrors." "You can say everything in the world against Faulkner," he had declared to her, "but I think he's still our greatest living novelist in the flamboyant Dickens-Dostoevsky line (with a touch of pure pulp of a Wilkie Collins sort)."

Other contemporary writers disappointed him. He was discouraged by T. S. Eliot's *The Cocktail Party,* he told Wilson, while Hemingway's novel *Across the River and Into the Trees* was a travesty. "How can a man in his senses leave such bullshit on the page?" he asked. He recognized that every author wrote "acres of bullshit but people usually cross it out." Reading Hemingway's novel made Dos Passos wonder if he had gotten all his own bad writing "into the wastebasket in time." Two years later he was more approving of *The Old Man and the Sea,* parts of which were "the old master at his best," although "an envious competitor might complain that the whole operation is a little too shrewdly calculated." Hemingway was "betting on a sure thing," but Dos Passos wished him well. Thinking back on *Across the River and Into the Trees* he liked it better than the sea story despite its faults. "It may be," Dos Passos admitted to Wilson, "that my recollections of his Cuban-fishermen-with-marlin stories, as told in the old days, a little took the edge off it. I liked it better the way he used to tell it."

Wilson was his intimate literary friend, the one Dos Passos turned to for stimulation and with whom he kept up a lively discussion by letter about his wide reading, which at that time in addition to Faulkner, Eliot, and Hemingway included Steinbeck and Moravia and French writers such as Sartre, Malraux, and Genêt, contemporary "topical" writers like Thor Heyerdahl—whose *Kon Tiki* expedition intrigued him—and a wide range of writers whose works touched on one or another aspect of the eighteenth century, the age of Jefferson.

Because of work at the farm, the addition to the house which dragged on, and Lucy's arrival, the Dos Passoses remained at Spence's Point throughout the summer of 1950, although the following year they began what was to be a custom for them of taking a month away from the farm during July and August. But staying at home in 1950 did not leave them lonely. Lucy was christened at the Yeocomico Church on August 17, and for the occasion the Murphys and the Lowndeses visited Spence's Point. During succeeding years they returned a number of times to be a part of an almost steady stream of visitors—friends like them, literary people, or occasionally journalists who wanted to interview Dos Passos. He made sure to keep up friendships of long-standing. The Marvins, Williamses, Hillyers, and Cummingses visited, for example, and even Edmund and Elena Wilson traveled down from Cape Cod early in the 1950s. A Mr. Peck, the local taxi driver in Wellfleet, drove them to Virginia, so was part of the household for the three nights of the visit. Elizabeth did the cooking and kept an informal household, but Wilson did not think it appropriate for Mr. Peck to eat with the Dos Passoses and Wilsons, so she had to feed him separately. The occasion was hectic from her point of view: there were the Wilsons to entertain as well as Mr. Peck to be looked after; Wilson held forth as dogmatically as he berated Dos Passos for doing; and all the while the children had to be cared for. The friendship survived the visit, although the Wilsons did not return to Virginia.

Elizabeth tried to make certain that the children did not lack for friendship. For Lucy's first Halloween she organized a large party which involved nine children, nine adults, noise, extensive decorations, and a lot of work. "But it *was* fun," she wrote the Lowndeses afterward, and exactly the sort of thing that gave her and Dos Passos pleasure. For holidays they were likely to gather local friends at Spence's Point with sometimes tumultuous results, as at Christmas, 1950, when the Walter and Fairfax Griffiths and the Robert Cardens came for a midday feast. First Christopher injured his hand when he and the Carden boys were playing with a newly installed dumbwaiter. Dos Passos and Robert Carden rushed Christopher to the home of the local doctor, where they received word that the field behind the Cardens' was on fire. Christopher proved to be no more than bruised, and the fire was soon subdued by firemen who arrived on the scene from the nearby village of Kinsale. "By nightfall," Dos Passos wrote the Lowndeses, "everybody was eating rather over done turkey." What he forgot to mention was that amid the confusion Lucy had managed to stand up by holding onto a coffee table and had drunk what was left in cocktail glasses on it. When the confusion subsided, the others found her curled up asleep in a corner of one room.

Despite the demands of life in Virginia, Dos Passos wrote steadily. Once he had completed "The General" during the summer of 1949, he turned to another novel and to adapting into book form his essays for *Harper's* and *Life* about England and about South America as well as those about business and agriculture in the United States along with the just completed series for General Mills. The book of reportage, *The Prospect Before Us*, was published in the fall of 1950. Dos Passos revised and reordered his materials more completely than he usually did for his collections of reportage because he meant the essays to be of a piece. He considered *Prospects* his "politics book," the one in which more than he had before he spelled out specifically his ideas. The format he chose was to have a "Mr. Lecturer" discuss these ideas, for which Dos Passos drew heavily from his essay "The Failure of Marxism," and to have members of his audience represent various political and social attitudes—those of business, agriculture, labor, and so forth. In his introductory remarks the lecturer discussed his ideas; his creator's essays about England, South America, and the United States served as examples of the lecturer's points.

Dos Passos put great stock in *The Prospect Before Us*. It was not well received, however, because critics thought it a minor effort and more, an ineffective one. As Norman Thomas wrote, "it is a disservice rather than a service when a man of Dos Passos' stature as a writer and as an observer concentrates on one issue and the formulation of one proposition concerning self-government and calls the result 'The Prospect Before Us.' "

Thomas rightly admired Dos Passos's essays about South America and recognized that the author was no convert to Toryism, as his critics had accused him of becoming after they had read "Britain's Dim Dictatorship" and "The Failure of Marxism." Thomas faulted Dos Passos, nevertheless, for not recognizing the achievements of Clement Attlee's Labour government during the years between the appearance of the articles in *Life* and 1950. And reflecting the opinion of numerous critics, Thomas declared that "the answer to our difficulties is not a rejection of planning because it can easily become bureaucratic, political and inefficient." What was needed, rather, was "to work out the conditions of ownership and control the techniques of planning which will best permit the participation of self-respecting individuals all over the world." He understood that such an idea might be in Dos Passos's mind, but it received "no adequate treatment" in the book. Dos Passos had thought much about new forms of planning, but always he returned to generalizing about the need for Jeffersonian democracy. Hence his plan for the future seemed hardly a plan at all. And in *Prospect* the puppet figures of the lecturer and his audience seemed merely simplistic, unredeemed by any satiric intent as were the caricatures in his fiction.

One can understand why Dos Passos's "politics book" was not well received, but that made the fact no less discouraging for him. When in 1954 he wrote an early draft of the novel *The Great Days*, he rendered a fictionalized version of the discouragement he had felt. Roland Lancaster, his autobiographical hero, recalled his depression about the critics' reception of *Blueprint for the Future:*

> They found words enough to jump down his throat with when the book was published. Every vested sentimentality, every selfserving citadel of illusion in the country was outraged. Author meets the critics. Ro remembered himself sitting in a row of men in front of microphones in some bright hall. Lord they had roasted him for daring to intimate that we had allowed our successful war to end in one of history's most crushing defeats. The fury of their rejection had thrown him off balance. They thought him something very low indeed. A man who found fault with the way the United Nations had been set up, who pointed out the strategic advantage we had given the Communist armies was a reactionary as bad as a nazi. He remembered the self-satisfied look on their faces as they mouthed their epithets. They were having themselves a time pouring out scorn on his head. . . . And the little squirts in the audience who yammered their puny echoes of the party line. . . .
>
> But there had been more to it than that. It was his fault too that he had failed to put it in a way that people could understand. . . . And so the years of failure had begun.

The passage compressed into one moment the critical response to several works beginning with *Adventures of a Young Man*, but the nadir of Dos Passos's literary reputation might well be placed around 1950, when after more than a decade of attempts to explain his postradical politics he labored to sum them up in *The Prospect Before Us*. It was meant to be his blueprint for the future, and it was scorned.

If the years of failure had begun for Roland Lancaster with *Blueprint for the Future* and had thrown him off balance, his real-life counterpart had learned already to live with literary defeat by the time *The Prospect Before Us* was published, and he continued writing. Even more important for his equilibrium, he had a sense of security that resulted from the presence of Elizabeth and the children and the constant activity on the farm. This newfound security was what he needed to write his next novel, *Chosen Country*, which was his statement in fiction about embracing the United States—"O My America My New Found Land" he entitled the final chapter—and about his marriage to Katy, something of which he could not write until it was part of a life behind him. Jay Pignatelli was the autobiographical hero whose experiences approximated Dos Passos's, and Lulie Harrington, a second major figure whose experiences were drawn from what Katy had told Dos Passos about herself. Other characters were based on members of her family and on the young

Ernest Hemingway, whom she had known during their youths in the lake country of northern Michigan and subsequently in Chicago after World War I. Writing about the novel later, Dos Passos declared that "In Chosen Country I tried to make the current of the narrative even more dense, in a somewhat elegiac mood, very different from the continual present tense of Manhattan Transfer and U.S.A." Whether or not the narrative is as dense as he would have had it be, the mood of the novel is elegiac, less acidly satiric than earlier novels and a loving portrait of Katy as well as a usually good-spirited picture of those around her.

In 1952 Dos Passos wrote Bernice Baumgarten, whom he had asked to be his literary agent again, and during the course of a letter concerning problems he was having with Houghton Mifflin, he explained that "My work so far has more or less fallen into two periods, the first from *Three Soldiers* through *U.S.A.* and the second from *Adventures of a Young Man* through *Grand Design.*" The latter novels he thought to have been "ably characterized" by Arthur Mizener in his introduction to *District of Columbia.* "Chosen Country," he continued, "starts a third period. I have a series of several novels planned out to hang on the careers of some of the characters in *Chosen Country* which is conceived as a sort of prologue to the series."

The books in the third series—*Chosen Country, Most Likely to Succeed,* and *The Great Days*—are autobiographical to a greater degree than the others. They make more of a unit than first they appear to because not only are they linked by their autobiographical nature and by the reappearance of certain characters but also by their political themes. In *Chosen Country* Jay Pignatelli chose America. In *Most Likely to Succeed,* a novel based on Dos Passos's experiences with the New Playwrights Theatre, Jed Morris—partly a caricature of Jack Lawson—supported the Communists, thus undermining the United States. In *The Great Days* we learn from Roland Lancaster how the nation won the war but lost the peace, and we see a powerful government figure, Roger Thurloe—drawn from James Forrestal—driven to suicide by his inability to strengthen the country's defenses against the Communist threat. The three novels trace a path from personal acceptance and hope to subversion and defeat, the very thing, of course, which Dos Passos himself felt.

His comment to Bernice Baumgarten revealed the overall plan he had for his fiction. In addition to this third series, he wrote two more chronicles using the techniques of *U.S.A.* These books, *Midcentury* and *Century's Ebb,* carry the reader to 1969—the last piece in *Century's Ebb* is about the Apollo 8 and 11 moon shots of December 1968 and July 1969, so in effect he had in his technically innovative chronicles spanned the years of the twentieth century he knew. In sum, the novels of what he considered his first period are innovative treatments of the army, New York City, and the United States—time period, 1900–1929. Those of the second are technically conventional treatments of national and international politics—time period, 1933–1945. Those of the third are also technically conventional and retrace the time already covered, but concentrate on the life the author knew best, his own. The two other novels—*Midcentury* and *Century's Ebb*—written while he was also composing those of the third period, show less of his personal world, although Dos Passos included a Jay Pignatelli narrative in *Century's Ebb,* the last novel he wrote.

The result is a series of thirteen chronicles which examine the life of the twentieth century from a variety of perspectives. He was the inquisitive artist, peering in, questioning, mocking, criticizing, and—just occasionally—praising. What is remarkable about Dos Passos's fiction is not its uniformly high quality. The novels are uneven, some mediocre. Rather his achievement is how much of American society he encompassed in them as he probed the national scene.

Chosen Country is one of his better-done portraits of a segment of American life. As well as narratives about Lulie and Jay, Dos Passos included biographical sketches of figures who represented the world he meant to portray in the novel. These portraits are fictionalized treatments of his mother and father, Katy's father, Richard Norton of the Norton-Harjes ambulance group, Mary Heaton Vorse, whom Dos Passos had met in Paris in 1919 and knew later in Provincetown, and Clarence Darrow, the famous lawyer. Dos Passos's intention was not to render these figures exactly while changing only their names, but to extract from their lives what seemed representative of the era the novel was about. And for all his similarity to Dos Passos, Pignatelli is not strictly autobiographical but draws upon the career of John R. Dos Passos as well, the author's point being to make Jay more representative. The character has a good deal of Glenn Spotswood in him as well. He is an idealist whose efforts only alienate him from the radical groups he tries to aid. Jay, however, unlike Glenn, does not end badly but finds personal satisfaction in marriage and a country. As the novel concludes, he and Lulie, just married, stand together looking out at a cove along the New England coast—the actual setting for Katy and Dos Passos was the mouth of the Sheepscot River near Wiscasset, Maine—and Jay says to Lulie, "Together we begin to make . . ." and she concludes, "This wilderness our home."

When it was published in 1951, the book was better received than had been any of his works since *Number One*. It was considered a major novel, Arthur Mizener even acclaiming it perhaps the best Dos Passos had written. Dos Passos's friends admired the novel as well. After Archibald MacLeish had finished it, he wrote Dos Passos that he thought *Chosen Country* "not only your best but one of THE BEST." He could not, however, comprehend Dos Passos's politics. Senator Robert Taft, whom Dos Passos supported, seemed to MacLeish an "unspeakable hypocrite and the symbol of everything Jay Pignatelli hated." But MacLeish understood what Dos Passos was saying about "the institutions of the Republic" and blessed him for it. "They do indeed have to be saved from those who would save them to destroy them," MacLeish remarked.

Edmund Wilson liked *Chosen Country* almost as much as did MacLeish. It "fascinated" him, but he confessed that he found it hard to judge the book because he kept seeing before him the real people from whom the characters came. He thought the title "colorless" and objected to the sometimes cliché-ridden dialogue, although Dos Passos was less guilty of that than he had been in previous novels. The particular strengths of *Chosen Country*, Wilson believed, were Dos Passos's skill in "evoking sensations and places" and in conveying the nature of the lives of his characters. Wilson was not as pleased with the treatment of what appeared to be the Sacco-Vanzetti case, and he thought that Dos Passos was portraying the Communists' cynical exploitation of events as occurring earlier than was the case.

Dos Passos responded that he had not intended the Sabatini case in the book to resemble that of Sacco and Vanzetti—nevertheless it is hard not to make the connection—and he believed that he was correct that the Communists by 1927 were already manipulating matters for their own ulterior motives. Looking back at his experience in Boston, he was sure that "the complete pattern of communist behavior was already there," although he "was too full of adolescent hoopla to pay attention to it." He appreciated Wilson's comments, but found "the concomitanta of publication more and more depressing" as "the ego damnation" spelled itself out more forcefully in each volume he wrote.

If he saw the novel as an ego damnation, it was less apparent to others. Perhaps when he made the remark he had in mind his next novels, which would be somber portraits of defeat. *Chosen Country* seemed a damnation of Ernest Hemingway, if of anyone. Or at least so it appeared to Hemingway, whom the book enraged. He and Dos Passos had exchanged friendly letters recently. He had congratulated Dos Passos after his marriage to Elizabeth and then in October 1951 had thanked Dos Passos for a kind letter about the death of Pauline, Ernest's second wife. Hemingway recalled fondly the good times in Pamplona, Austria, Key West, and at sea and mentioned his love for both Pauline and Hadley. But within months he read *Chosen Country* and erupted to William Smith, also the model for a character in the book, that in Cuba he kept "a pack of fierce dogs and cats trained to attack one-eyed Portuguese bastards who wrote lies about their friends." Hemingway was portrayed as George Elbert Warner, a likable enough boy who was a younger companion of Lulie Harrington. He was something of a bully, although a good woodsman. But what incensed Ernest and made him think the portrait "loathsome" was that Dos Passos had Warner, back in Chicago as a reporter after World War I, capitalize on a scandal that occurred to Lulie's brother Zeke and his wife Mugsie, who were modeled after Katy's older brother Y.K. and his wife Doodles. "Honest" John Dos Passos, Hemingway wrote in 1952, had taken ill-recalled stories he had heard from Katy and while the two of them were Ernest's guests in Key West and had fouled them up more. But the fact was that, while Dos Passos embellished stories he had heard by having Mugsie accidentally wound someone with a pistol and having Warner capitalize on the episode in the papers, Ernest had betrayed the confidences of Doodles during the summer of 1921 to the point where Y.K. had been furious enough to break off their friendship. To Y.K. Ernest had seemed loathsome. Dos Passos's motivation for including partially biographical tales in *Chosen Country* was a mixture of amusement and scorn; yet had Hemingway not been so sensitive, he would not have reacted as he did, because the incident with Y.K. and Doodles had not happened as Dos Passos told it, nor for that matter was George Elbert Warner any more a precise portrait of Ernest than was Pignatelli of Dos Passos. But any hint of friendship on Hemingway's part vanished, and the last of the groundwork for his scathing portrait of Dos Passos in *A Moveable Feast* was laid. There Dos Passos became a pilot fish who led the rich Gerald and Sara Murphy to the true artist,

Ernest, whose idyllic life with Hadley they managed to ruin during March 1926 in Schruns. The description of Dos Passos was no fictionalized rendering but the direct statement of Hemingway at his most mean-spirited, the saddest of final words about a friendship that had been important for them both.

CHAPTER THIRTY-ONE

A Question of Loyalties,

1951–1956

When toward the end of the summer of 1951 Dos Passos finished preparing *Chosen Country* for publication, he announced to Edmund Wilson that he was "now entirely committed to the termination of this Jefferson operation and I'm finding it a hell of a lot of work, with only the prospect of another goddamn book to shove down the goddamn rathole." Partly his depressed mood stemmed from the mediocre sales of his books, partly from the fact that he found himself continually stymied by problems about Jefferson's life such as evaluating reports that he had mulatto children. Dos Passos believed the evidence pointed against it, but the matter was confused and typical of the sort of blocks that slowed his work. "There are situations I can imagine quite easily but others I haven't collected enough data to be able to visualize," he wrote. He complained that historians merely obscured what would be useful to him. The difficulties of historiography did not lessen, so the Jefferson biography progressed slowly until it was finally completed in 1953.

He took little time off. The family visited Wiscasset and made a brief stop on Cape Cod during July and August 1951, but other than that they remained in Westmoreland. The next year they repeated the schedule until September, when they began what became a pattern for most of the years while the children were in primary and secondary schools. They rented a place in Baltimore where they lived during the week while the children attended school. Then on weekends they drove to Westmoreland. Baltimore appealed to them because they could be near friends such as Horsley Gantt, because the schools for the children were good, and because Dos Passos could work at the Enoch Pratt or the Peabody libraries. Once that routine began, he did his research at one or the other library until shortly before 4:00 P.M. each weekday, when he put away his materials and sat by a window looking out for the arrival of Elizabeth. She usually drove up in front of the building after she had picked up the children, Christopher from Gilman and Lucy from the Homewood School once she began attending in 1953, and later, from the Bryn Mawr School. Dos Passos was one of the favorite readers of the director of the Peabody Library, where Dos Passos had a desk and did the major portion of his research. Modest and unassuming, he was unobtrusive about using the library and sat at his desk holding a book close to his face in order to read it. He seemed concerned not to annoy Elizabeth by being slow to meet her, as she might get peevish about having to double-park her car in front of the library while she came inside. To the director, Elizabeth seemed to have Dos Passos well in tow.

The director was misreading contentment for docility and obedience. Disturbed by politics, Dos Passos was satisfied with his personal life, and even when financial worries loomed, he was relaxed with his family. In Baltimore he enjoyed pleasures like concerts, movies, and occasional lunches at the 14 West Hamilton Street Club, a men's club where he could talk with Horsley Gantt and Hamilton Owens, editor of the *Baltimore Sun* and a close friend once the Dos Passoses began to spend their winters in Baltimore. Sometimes he and Elizabeth bowled in the late afternoons, a diversion which he found rested his eyes. Dos Passos took pleasure in other small amusements, finding it "a truly delicate attention," for example, to be favored with a box of pickles from the Heinz Company on his fifty-seventh birthday, as he told Stewart Mitchell. This was a side of him that rarely showed in public or in his writing. But with close friends or with his family he laughed easily at little absurdities like the box of pickles, or some years later, a note he received from the Anti-Nicotine League scolding him by asking if he wanted to go down in history as a human chimney after they saw a picture of him puffing a large cigar. He could laugh with Elizabeth as well about their financial straits, which might sometimes threaten but which he was usually confident about weathering and which, in truth, seemed less severe to observers and as much the result of a comfortable standard of life as of impoverishment. He could always, he joked to Elizabeth, set up a food stand out in the Potomac River on the Maryland side and advertize it as "Dos and Betty's Eats and Gambling" if their finances slipped too far.

In 1952 he was even pleased with politics when Dwight Eisenhower was elected President. It was not "the complete change of air" he would have preferred, but he felt relief. "The country," he noted, "had been too long on the Roosevelt tack," and it was good to see it change direction. He hoped that under Eisenhower the nation might strengthen its will to fight the Communists, and particularly he hoped that a new administration might combat internal subversion, for despite the work of the House Un-American Activities Committee and that of Senator Joseph McCarthy, Dos Passos continued to believe that the nation was being subverted. When Whittaker Chambers's book *Witness* was published in the spring of 1952, the *Saturday Review* asked several people, among them Dos Passos, to respond. He took the occasion to excoriate those who in his opinion were conducting a slander campaign against Chambers. The slurs seemed to Dos Passos the mark of "a society dedicated to its own destruction." He could not understand how the nation could become so flaccid. "A living organism that fails to react to danger is sick or dying," he warned. "Can it be that the 'liberals' who control communications in the press and the radio and the schools and the colleges in this country have already crawled under the yoke of the Communist Party? I mean in spirit. We know they are not dues-paying members. Or has an immensely clever propaganda machine been able to make them dupes of a sinister hoax?"

For him the danger of internal subversion was entirely real, and for that reason he defended McCarthy and his ilk to the considerable irritation of friends like Edmund Wilson. "Dos spent a night with us a few days ago," Wilson wrote his and Dos Passos's mutual friend Chauncey Hackett in December 1952. "We always begin with a super-animated conversation, then I become exasperated with him and begin to tax him with his absurdities. . . ." A year and a half later in June 1954, just two days after Joseph Welch, the lawyer for the army in the McCarthy-Army Hearings, had in effect destroyed the Senator's demagogic witchhunt by demanding of McCarthy, "Have you no sense of decency?" Dos Passos decried to Wilson how liberals had made McCarthy their whipping boy. He allowed, nonetheless, that he would like to spend an evening with Wilson "even at the risk of being beaten about the head and ears with the 'raw head and bloody bones' of that dreadful senator from Wisconsin. Don't you think maybe somebody might start thinking of something else?" he asked.

McCarthy, soon to be censured, now embarrassed Dos Passos, but it was more than a bit unwarranted for him then to ask that people start to think of something else. Dos Passos had approved of McCarthy's goals, and it was the Senator who had sought and created publicity about the hunt for supposed Communists. Further, the nation was still watching the televised Army-McCarthy Hearings, which were in full swing. It was the Senator, too, who had smeared the reputations of a number of people, something that Dos Passos did not acknowledge. McCarthy might seem "dreadful," but that was hardly adequate repudiation of a political figure who threatened as much as anyone in the United States the liberties Dos Passos claimed to cherish.

He never repudiated McCarthy, in fact. Instead, in an impassioned—and inaccurate—biographical sketch in *Century's Ebb*, he portrayed McCarthy as a patriotic country boy vilified by politicians and liberals soft on the Communists. "Investigating Communists was a dangerous business," wrote Dos Passos. "They fought back in devious ways." He went on to claim that one HUAC Chairman, Martin Dies, had been driven out of politics, and he cited the fact that another, Parnell Thomas, had been jailed for accepting salary kickbacks, Dos Passos's implication being that these men had been done in by the Communists. McCarthyism became a bogey, he asserted, and for fear of it only a brave man "dares think straight about the dangers this country faces in a Communist-dominated world." This was an instance when Dos Passos could maintain an emotional commitment to something—in this case McCarthy's hunt for Communists—which ran directly counter to his intellectual conviction about personal liberty. He could overlook the similarities between the bullying tactics of McCarthy and those of Huey Long, whom he had castigated in *Number One*. Ends did not justify means, Dos Passos declared; yet because of his hatred of Communism he was willing to tolerate dubious means to achieve the end of scouring alleged Communists out of government.

Except when it became a personal matter. In 1953, as part of the government's loyalty program, Horsley Gantt's case came to the attention of a government investigator because Gantt had lived and worked in Soviet Russia and because he was a government employee by virtue of his work at the Pavlovian laboratory he had established at the Veterans' Administration Hospital in Perry Point, Maryland. Further, during America's alliance with the Soviets in World War II, Gantt had supported war relief to Russia and had spoken to "organizations for Soviet American friendship." Of such material were loyalty cases made. In January Dos Passos signed a sworn statement attesting to the loyalty of Gantt, about whom he declared, "the idea of Dr. Gantt's being a party to or a dupe of the Communist conspiracy in this country is absolutely ludicrous." Subsequently, Gantt was served a notice of investigation by the local government agent, which meant that until he was cleared, he could not work.

As Gantt recalled the episode, the night before he received the notice he had talked with Dos Passos, who said that he believed McCarthy was doing good and necessary work. But as soon as Dos Passos heard of Gantt's plight, he conferred with Hamilton Owens, who advised that Gantt get a conservative lawyer to represent him. His friends contacted Frank B. Ober, who had been responsible for the establishement of a loyalty oath law in Baltimore. Ober took Gantt's case, and in May Horsley received his clearance, which he celebrated by giving a party that included his friends, Ober, and the government investigator. Dos Passos was correct that to link Gantt with any Communist conspiracy would have been ludicrous. Gantt was basically apolitical and had made his doubts about Communist ideology known to Dos Passos when they had been together in Russia in 1928. In addition he had written about Russian medicine in a way no sympathizer with the Soviet government would have done. But what Dos Passos did not care to recognize was that although his close friend had been cleared through the efforts of influential people like him and Hamilton Owens, other persons just as innocent as Gantt had not been so fortunate and in the wide swath cut by various investigators had been found guilty by association and hearsay. Dos Passos was unalterably convinced of a massive Communist conspiracy, and the more it was denied—and the more America's strength relative to Russia seemed to decline—the more adamantly he asserted its existence. Never did the stubborn and opinionated part of him that lay beneath the shy exterior appear more clearly.

Dos Passos's statements about himself in the affidavit for Gantt reflect his absolute assurance that he had seen the truth and that he could identify a Communist. After explaining how he had become interested in "the Soviet experiment," he told of traveling to Spain in 1937 to assist the Republic. There, he continued,

My observations in Spain brought about my complete disillusionment with Communism and the Soviet Union. The Soviet Government operated in Spain a series of "extra legal tribunals," more accurately described as murder gangs, who put to death without mercy all whom they could reach and who stood in the way of the Communists. Subsequently they smeared their victims' reputations. I became satisfied that a victory for the Republic would mean a triumph for Communism and withdrew from Spain. Subsequently I described this situation in fictional form in a novel entitled "The Adventures of a Young Man." By this time I was thoroughly convinced that foreign ideologies were no substitute for the American system. I set forth this view in a series of essays entitled "The Ground We Stand On." Making frequent trips to Washington, I also became aware of the Communist infiltration of agencies of the United States Government and of our media of communication and expression (such as the radio). I described this infiltration in fictional form in a novel entitled "The Grand Design." This novel may have made some contribution to preparing public opinion for the loyalty program. My reflections on the subject of government have persuaded me that decentralization of power, i.e., the opposite of the Soviet system, is highly important. I express this view in a book on Jefferson entitled "The Head and Heart of Thomas Jefferson," about to be published.

As I am a writer the evolution of my thinking is well known in literary circles and has been frequently mentioned in print by book reviewers and other critics. I have paid a certain penalty for my change in attitude because a leftist approach is rather predominant among leading book reviewers; the comment on my books tends to be distinctly less enthusiastic than in my earlier days, and characteristics formerly hailed as virtues have become faults.

My experience has however enabled me to determine with confidence whether or not a given person or a given point of view shows Communist sympathy. I know very well the turns in the party line for thirty years, and I know what talk and action during that period has denoted the party member, the fellow-traveler, the Communist sympathizer, the deluded but innocent liberal, and the non-political patriotic American, respectively.

Dos Passos's career stands up well under close scrutiny. His enthusiastic support of anti-Communist zealots was perhaps the single sorry aspect of a life noteworthy for its integrity. His conservatism was not questionable, but rather his willingness to support people such as Parnell Thomas and Joseph McCarthy who toyed recklessly with the freedom of others. He was not alone, of course, in acting as he did. Numerous politicians embraced McCarthy as he rose in power; many more remained quiet. That citadel of conservative integrity, Senator Robert Taft, supported the Wisconsin Senator's modus operandi and had advised him in 1950, "If one case doesn't work, try another." Dos Passos's anti-Communism was even in accord with the liberal mentality to the extent that it, too, accepted as fact the threat of international Communism, and he was in accord with the consensus mood of the 1950s, at least as described by the journalist and historian Godfrey Hodgson:

Confident to the verge of complacency about the perfectibility of American society, anxious to the point of paranoia about the threat of communism —those were the two faces of the consensus mood. Each grew from one aspect of the experience of the 1940s: confidence from economic success, anxiety from the fear of Stalin and the frustrations of power.

Dos Passos, however, had the reputation of a man of letters, an intellectual who would not permit emotional biases to contradict intellectual precepts. But he was not the objective observer. He was always as much emotionally as intellectually involved in the causes he took up, and his virulent anti-Communism was a venting of his pent-up frustrations against those who had killed José Robles, against Franklin Roosevelt and the New Dealers who in his mind came to epitomize what he always despised about governments, and against the critics who never seemed to appreciate his work, be it radical or conservative. The question inevitably arises: how could this advocate of McCarthy in the early 1950s be reconciled with the man who had written *U.S.A.* or who had declared in defense of the indicted Minneapolis truck drivers in 1941 that despotism "can be routed by a democracy that is wholeheartedly, even recklessly, for freedom. Can't we be as reckless on the right side as they are on the wrong?" To the despair of his earlier advocates, it was hard to believe the two writers were the same.

His mood at the end of 1953 was one of some depression, although certainly not of despair. As he told Rumsey Marvin in the fall, "This has been a hellish year. Drouth, crop failures, financial setbacks of all kinds, but were all alive and kicking and in good health." Despite having sold off Cherry Grove Farm, a portion of land in Westmoreland, and with the proceeds having paid off the mortgage on the rest, Dos Passos and Elizabeth did not feel financially secure because of the problems he mentioned to Marvin. These, plus his concern about politics and the sense that he was being scorned by critics for his political stance sustained the bitter concern he had expressed in his piece about Whittaker Chambers's descent into hell. As a result he was pessimistic about the reception to be accorded the Jefferson biography on which he had labored for more than a decade. He felt sometimes as if he "were working down at the bottom of a well," he wrote Max Eastman on Christmas Day, 1953. The solitude that came from his position and from aging and drifting away from friends hedged him about; "the growing sense of isolation blues me up at times," he concluded. And, although he was pleased that Eastman had appreciated what he had been trying to do in the biography, he expected when he went to New York in mid-January 1954 to face "obsequies" for the book instead of a celebration about its publication.

The Head and Heart of Thomas Jefferson was not received as poorly as Dos Passos had feared it might be, although its sales, he told Robert Hillyer in the spring, were flaccid. The book reflected the "hell of a lot of irreplacable time and money" he had used to write it. It contained a remarkable amount of detail and demonstrated his thorough knowledge of Jefferson's career up through his departure from Philadelphia in 1793. Dos Passos's intention, as the title suggests, was to explain Jefferson by examining his cultural milieu as well as the national and international forces at work at the time. He meant to portray "the system of things in which we are placed," to quote the title of section II of the biography. The result was on the whole impressive and was recognized as such, despite the fact Jefferson was more than once lost in the "maze of local detail," a complaint of the critic Irving Howe. Howe suggested also that Dos Passos had not probed "very far into Jefferson's thought," and this was a distinct weakness in what purported to be an intellectual biography. In retrospect, Howe's criticisms seem fair. One would not turn first to *The Head and Heart* to learn about Jefferson nor to read at a sitting a narrative about the period. The biography was conceived and written in fits and starts, and the myriad details make the narrative line difficult to follow. Yet from it a reader can gain a sense of the era and Jefferson's relation to it, while frequently Dos Passos with his direct style brought alive one episode or another. The book was no failure, despite the author's doubts.

The same concerns that had caused his worry about the success of the biography produced the mood of his next novel, *Most Likely to Succeed*, published in September 1954. Few of the characters were warmly portrayed, although they were amusing caricatures. The book's subject is the gradual subjugation to the will of the Communists of a talented, facile playwright turned Hollywood scriptwriter. Given Dos Passos's attitudes toward the Communists by the 1950s, it is no wonder that he mocked their intrigues and the foolishness of liberals whom he thought they were duping. Jack Lawson was deeply hurt when he read the novel, because Jed Morris, the playwright, and Felicia Hardestie, his mistress and later common-law wife, were partly based on him and his second wife, Sue Edmond. He had more reason to be offended than had Hemingway about *Chosen Country;* yet Lawson need not have taken *Most Likely to Succeed* as an entirely personal attack. Dos Passos included episodes from his own life in the portrait of Jed because he was satirizing the ultimately unhappy experiences of the New Playwrights Theatre and his brief stay in Hollywood. Thus, as well as Lawson and Sue Edmond, Mike Gold, the Faragohs, Em Jo Basshe, Otto Kahn, and Joseph von Sternberg were the subjects of satire. Dos Passos in addition caricatured Hutchins Hapgood and his wife, "old time liberals" whose eccentric, impractical ways had amused him in Provincetown, and through all these characters' lives were woven his experiences as well as some of Katy's.

He had problems closing the novel. A first draft ended with the suicide of Jane Marlowe, a beautiful, rich woman whom Jed met at the beginning of the book and had an affair with aboard ship as he returned from Morocco to begin the theater experiment. But because Dos Passos wanted to satirize the Communists and the harsh discipline of the party, he altered the ending to have Marlowe die as a result of Jed's involvement with the Communists. Finally, however, her death never occurred, and *Most Likely to Succeed* closed not with any sort of tragic climax to Jed's love affair but with his weak acquiescence to party orders, a conclusion more consistent with Dos Passos's attitude toward the characters and the subject, although an unsatisfactory ending for the needs of fiction because the reader has no idea what is to become of Jed.

Taken as satire the book succeeds. The caricatures are humorous as are the arguments and the failures of the left-wing dramatists and the political figures among the Hollywood film colony. Edmund Wilson wrote that he had enjoyed the novel, which he thought Dos Passos's "most *amusing*," particularly the caricature of Hutchins Hapgood, whose major role in life might well be that of a model for a minor figure in some work of fiction. Wilson was not satisfied with the inconclusive ending, and he criticized Dos Passos for having a cast of characters almost entirely Jewish, the implication of that being that the world of the theater and film was Jewish. Dos Passos answered that he appreciated Wilson's finding something to laugh at in the novel. As for the characters, "they all went Jewish as fast as I got them down on the page."

Many reviewers, however, read the book "with depressing seriousness," as Dos Passos acknowledged to Wilson. Such a response was understandable, given the touchiness of the subject during the 1950s and critics' sometimes personal involvement with the politics, if not the theater and film, which were the materials of the novel. Granville Hicks faulted it for its "cold, detached, unhappy boredom," the result, he believed, of Dos Passos having completely severed himself from his earlier radicalism. The novel, Hicks concluded, was no better than "the work of a not very promising beginner," which coming from Dos Passos marked "a literary debacle" and "one of the saddest things that happened in recent literary history." No more laudatory was Harold Clurman—an admirer of Jack Lawson's work during the twenties and thirties—who wrote that although the character Jed Morris was "a phony, a mental incompetent, and a moral castrate, 'Most Likely to Succeed' cannot even be called venomous. It is merely libelous."

The novel is not libelous, however, because the characters are not the portraits Clurman thought them, nor is it as cold and detached as Hicks believed it, for Dos Passos's emotion was wrapped up in his scorn for aspects of the theatrical and movie world he recalled, and he expressed that scorn through satire. Rather than being detached from what he had been, he was deeply involved with his past. He thought his own participation naïve in retrospect, and he judged himself and those around him harshly. Lawson was an important component of Jed Morris, but so was Dos Passos, and he directed the acerbic humor of the book not only against Lawson and the others, but against himself.

That, nevertheless, was something his publishers, like the reviewers, did not perceive. When in late 1952 he first presented a part of the manuscript for the book to Houghton Mifflin, they balked at contracting for it. Dos Passos became thoroughly irritated because at the same time that he and Lovell Thompson discussed the manuscript, Thompson explained that the company had made an error of accounting, crediting Dos Passos with sales of 2,300 more copies of *Chosen Country* than had in fact been sold during the first half of the year. Dos Passos contacted Bernice Baumgarten and asked her to represent him once again, and he told her that the error made it imperative, he thought, to find another publisher. Beyond the accounting error, another reason to leave Houghton Mifflin was that they seemed to "have gone stale on the whole proposition" of publishing his work.

Their enthusiasm for *Chosen Country* had been, he believed, for that book alone, while their handling of *District of Columbia* had been "execrable." Now they did not want to consider *Shall Be the Human Race*, as he first titled *Most Likely to Succeed*. "I suspect that Lovell's real objection came to the surface in something he blurted out while we were talking," Dos Passos wrote Bernice. He thought Houghton Mifflin feared that the book might be considered anti-Semitic "because the main character, who turns out to be a pretty unpleasant fellow is of Jewish origin." But, he asserted, "such an attitude is so far from my way of thinking and feeling that I can't help resenting the imputation rather hotly." In any case, he was looking over the manuscript with that issue in mind and thought that "building up some of the other characters" might give the story a "broader base."

Dos Passos was irritated enough with Houghton Mifflin that he wanted to sever all relations with them. "Don't be too impressed by Lovell's crepehanging finale," he cautioned Bernice. "My foreign stuff holds up remarkably well. My English sales . . . are even improving. In this country my stuff has always been resented by some and admired by others." He was so agitated that the same day he wrote her a second letter to accompany an early draft of *Most Likely to Succeed*. He would be in New York in ten days, he said, and he hoped she could have looked into other publishing possibilities by then. "Of course I wont get my ideal publisher or responsible employee in a publishing firm," he acknowledged, but he wanted to describe such a person for her benefit: "In politics (which is all important these days), he must be progressive conservative. A touch of Henry Regnery with more money behind him and perhaps less of 'now it can be told.' He needn't admire U.S.A. but must show some interest in my later work. Even Lovell thinks The Grand Design was my best book. He must think about distribution and marketing twenty four hours a day." Discussion between author, agent, and Houghton Mifflin continued for more than a month before Lovell Thompson convinced Dos Passos not to abandon Houghton Mifflin altogether. Instead, they held a contract for a "Jasper Milliron" novel—eventually published as *Midcentury*—while Prentice-Hall was pleased to accept *Most Likely to Succeed*.

Dos Passos had hopes that Prentice-Hall would be able to sell more books than had Houghton Mifflin. His new publishers worked hard, but had only "indifferent success," not a new story for him. In 1954 and until he was able to complete his next historical narrative, *The Men Who Made the Nation*, his finances were of particular concern. He and Elizabeth laid out some lots on their shoreline land. But these did not sell rapidly, and with no large income from his fiction, with the farm under cultivation but not yet producing a substantial return from crops or timber, with the cost of a place in Baltimore and schooling for the children, and with the historical narrative taking much longer than Dos Passos had planned, he had to borrow from a bank in Hague, near Westmoreland. Before *The Men Who Made the Nation* was published in 1957, he and Elizabeth borrowed four times. To try to reduce expenses, they gave up their place in Baltimore in 1956. Christopher boarded for a time at the Gilman School, while Lucy went to public school in Hague. But always, it seemed, other problems cropped up, such as severe erosion along their beach fronting the Potomac. After attempting to stem the erosion for several years, they had a sea wall erected in 1957 at considerable expense.

To help the financial situation in 1954, he undertook a lecture tour, the result, he told the Murphys, "of three unfortunate years in farming and other reverses." His trip during October and the first half of November took him through the Midwest and as far as Oregon, where in November he wrote Edmund Wilson that he found lecturing "a highly depressing occupation [which] almost, but not quite, takes away the pleasure of travelling round the country." He vowed not to lecture again unless he had to, which might be the case, because "making a living seems to get harder every year." After he had finished the tour, he complained to Edie Shay that the "spell of lecturing took up an awful lot of time but I had to do something to bring in some dough."

Although he did not like lecturing, he felt he learned something about the country, and the trip provided him with an insight into the minds of students. Whereas in his day colleges had produced people interested in business, then the vested interest, now he believed the vested interest was government, and it was that with which students identified. " 'Directive,' " wrote Dos Passos after he had returned from the tour, "is the sacred word. . . . The man who values the good opinion of his fellows today is pained by any pert remark that questions the eternal rightness of the men who make it their duty to run the lives of the rest of us." College students were identifying with "institutional authority," that is, government, and because colleges and universities seemed to Dos Passos traditionally to "form the sacred ark in which the ruling dogmas of any particular era are protected from the criticisms of the profane," he distrusted them. They were the spawning grounds for a new ruling class, the bureaucrats. "The institutional mind drifts naturally into concepts of socialism," he asserted, since that, "after all, only means a society run from one central office," and to the bureaucrat, this seems more efficient. "The odd tenderness toward communism and communist causes that seems to be felt by a good many men of the foundations and colleges," he wrote, "might be explained along the same lines. Communism is the most vigorous form of control from a central office that exists in the world today." The bureaucrats' and academicians' touchiness to criticism and their tenderness toward Socialism, he had found, made it difficult to speak out as he chose: "Just try to get up in a college lecture hall and say you are in favor of the Bricker amendment, or whisper the word Yalta, or speak with respect of the late Senator Taft." Students had challenged his conservatism, even derided it, and as a result the best he could say for the tour was that it had been instructive.

With the lecture tour finished, he concentrated on completing what he told Stewart Mitchell was "a sort of rapid (I hope) narrative history of the period from Yorktown to 1808," the last year of Jefferson's second administration. To Edie Shay he described his book in more detail. "I'm off again into the Jeffersonian period," he wrote late in January 1955. "It's a kind of narrative history from Yorktown to Jefferson's second administration. I think I'll call it 'The World Turned Upside Down.' You know that was the tune their band played when Cornwallis' troops marched out to surrender. I'm trying to get the other characters Washington,

Lafayette, Madison, Burr, John Adams Hamilton Robert Morris etc in so T. J. will be seen *mostly* from the outside. Like everything, it's turning out much more work than I had bargained for."

Except for three weeks in August on Cape Cod and a few days in Wiscasset, Dos Passos followed closely a routine of weekday work in Baltimore and weekends and the summer in Westmoreland during 1955 and the first part of 1956. Although his major project was the historical narrative, he also completed a draft of a novel, *The Great Days,* in 1955 and arranged for publication in March 1956 of a collection of essays strung together with a narrative to demonstrate, as the title indicated, that in all his work *The Theme Is Freedom.* Going back as far as essays he had written for the *New Masses* in 1926, he meant to show that he had consistently espoused individual freedoms against whatever was the vested interest of the moment.

He avoided any such theme in *The Men Who Made the Nation,* which concentrated on the historical figures of Revolutionary America whom Dos Passos admired. He labored to complete the book—"I'm almost dead from working round the clock to finish a gigantic historical narrative," he wrote Robert Hillyer in late April 1956. The final draft spanned the years from 1781 until Alexander Hamilton's death in July 1804, a period four years shorter than he had first intended. Then except for a trip in August with the family to Wyoming, Utah, and Colorado, he wrote, revised, and then proofread the long manuscript until autumn. When the volume was published in February 1957, it was well received. Dos Passos was at his best; the book has a brisk style and is constantly interesting, incorporating a wide range of detail and numerous historical figures. If it has a fault, it is, as the historian Dumas Malone commented in his review, that Dos Passos made "no attempt to show what [the] doings [of Washington, John Adams, and others] really added up to. . . . One misses in these pages any deep consciousness of the meaning of historic events." Dos Passos, of course, had written about historical meanings elsewhere. His aim here was a readable narrative about events and the men he regarded as heroes and villains in the drama of the founding of the United States. He succeeded, using to good effect something of the techniques that had enabled him to incorporate numerous characters and events in his chronicle fiction.

He could be satisfied with the narrative, because if it was not an intellectual exercise, it read well and demonstrated that his talents as a stylist were undiminished. But despite this and other literary projects, he had, he wrote Edmund Wilson in October 1956, "almost ceased to think of myself as a literary gent." He missed having anyone to talk to "in the old republic of letters sort of way" and often saw in his mirror "an unsuccessful farm operator or mismanager of timber deals." Although he was writing as much as ever, he had reason to feel distracted. Farm operations took an inordinate amount of time, and he was frustrated when they produced little or no financial gain. Yet his statement to Wilson was an exaggeration. He continued to be involved in literary matters. In 1956 he seriously considered an invitation from the University of Virginia to serve as a writer-in-residence for a period. "I'm tempted by anything that looks like a meal ticket these days," he admitted to Robert Hillyer. He did not take the position, but his literary and political interests led him to Mexico during the early fall to attend a meeting of the Congress for Cultural Freedom, and soon after returning to Westmoreland he responded at length to William Faulkner, who had invited his ideas about a conference of writers to win support for the United States from foreign intellectuals. Having just been among Latin Americans, Dos Passos found himself appalled by the "violence and virulence" of their attacks against the United States. "The liberal intellectuals down there," he wrote Faulkner, "talk as if they were ready to let the Commies take over any day." Dos Passos believed that officials in Washington did not comprehend how foreigners viewed the nation, and he thought that Faulkner's proposed conference would be a success if somehow it could alert the officials to foreign views. American prestige during World War II had been based on "massive military and political strength," he wrote, but this had been "succeeded by massive military and political weakness."

He corresponded further with Faulkner and in response to a questionnaire indicated that he doubted the efficacy of a conference, but believed that free expression and extensive cultural exchanges were the best things that could happen. Little came of Faulkner's efforts; what was interesting about Dos Passos's responses was that, despite his virulent anti-Communism, he opposed official organizations of writers and supported statements in Faulkner's questionnaire such as "Writers shouldn't be organized—must be free," and "Have our works properly translated and distributed abroad, without special frills or official commentary."

CHAPTER THIRTY-TWO

New Ventures and
Reflections on Past Defeats,
1956–1960

In 1956, during the Cold War, the presidential election was of more concern to Dos Passos than was Faulkner's proposed conference. Although a confirmed Republican and supporter of Dwight Eisenhower, he found Adlai Stevenson, he told Stewart Mitchell, "not at all an unattractive figure." After following Stevenson for two days of campaigning in New York and New Jersey, Dos Passos had an overwhelming sense of "the futility of the process." Stevenson was hardly a great statesman, Dos Passos thought, but even if he were, nothing would be accomplished. It hardly mattered who won the election, for little would change in government because "the gears of selfgovernment just dont mesh into the machinery of government." He thought the mesh might be achieved, although it was a miracle which he did not know how to accomplish. He was not ready to despair, but he had no answers. He was, however, more satisfied with Eisenhower than with Stevenson, and the Republican victory in November pleased him because he had confidence that under Eisenhower and Secretary of State John Foster Dulles the United States would oppose Communism more enthusiastically than it might under a Democratic administration.

But the Republicans were little if any better about curbing the vested interests of government and of big labor, which in the mid-fifties was just coming to Dos Passos's attention. He had long known of the struggles between unions and management. As he became more conservative, he observed with a hardly critical eye the operation of such corporations as General Mills, and his distrust of labor organizations grew. Then, too, he followed with interest after it was formed the Senate Select Committee on Improper Activities in the Labor and Management Fields, a committee known as the McClellan Committee after its chairman, Senator John McClellan of Arkansas. Because of Dos Passos's interest and because, as he wrote Robert Hillyer in the spring of 1958, he was "trying to pay the bills with articles," he agreed to write a piece about what the McClellan Committee had been hearing from union members. Like so many others of Dos Passos's projects, he expected this one to serve several purposes. He was interested in the situation of the American working man who he believed was caught, as he expressed it to one of the persons who had contacted the Senate committee, "between the millstones of predatory management and predatory labor." Dos Passos wrote the article for *Reader's Digest.* In addition he proposed to Dodd, Mead, the publishers of *The Theme Is Freedom,* that he write a history of labor in the United States, a project that was abandoned after he and the publishers realized how much research would be required to complete the book. But he made further use of his extensive research for the *Reader's Digest* article, which required him to read several thousand letters to McClellan's committee and to interview a number of the correspondents. Union members, he found, were not opposed to unions, but to bigness, corrupt leadership, and compulsory membership. The material Dos Passos gathered as well as these ideas became the basis for two of the narratives of *Midcentury,* published in 1961.

Before Dos Passos could undertake his investigation of the labor unions, he had to complete the revisions to his novel *The Great Days,* a task that during 1957 was interrupted by trips to New York in February at the time of the publication of *The Men Who Made the Nation* and again in May to accept the Gold Medal for Eminence in Fiction from the National Institute of Arts and Letters. At a dinner before the award Elizabeth Dos Passos sat next to William Faulkner, who was to present the medal to Dos Passos. The meal and various talks dragged on, agitating Faulkner more and more. He appreciated Elizabeth's willingness to pass him her wine, which she did not care for, but by the time he was to make the presentation to Dos Passos, Faulkner was in no mood to give a speech and thrust aside the one he had prepared. He shoved the medal at Dos Passos and declared, "Nobody deserved it more or had to wait for it longer."

Dos Passos's acceptance speech was less curt. Commenting on his writing, he talked about himself as a satirist. He acknowledged the unpopularity of some of his work and for the benefit of those people who might find it embittered he responded:

> I wonder if any of you have ever noticed that it is sometimes those who find most pleasure and amusement in their fellow man, and have most hope in his goodness, who get the reputation of being his most carping critics. Maybe it is that the satirist is so full of the possibilities of humankind in general, that he tends to draw a dark and garish picture when he tries to depict people as they are at any particular movement. The satirist is usually a pretty unpopular fellow. The only time he attains even fleeting popularity is when his works can be used by some political faction as a stick to beat out the brains of their opponents. Satirical writing is by definition unpopular writing. Its aim is to prod people into thinking. Thinking hurts.

More than because it said anything new, the statement was noteworthy because Dos Passos reaffirmed his intention to satirize, although to blame the satiric content of his work for its unpopularity—with the critics or with the public—was oversimplifying matters.

It was only after a two-week trip in September to Japan to participate in a P.E.N. Club literary conference—where to the amusement of another participant, John Steinbeck, Dos Passos was fawned over and begged for autographs—that he was able to settle down in Westmoreland to complete *The Great Days,* the novel in which he juxtaposed a fictionalized account of his depressing trip to Cuba in 1949 with "the great days" of his and Katy's lives before and during World War II, the moments of the nation's greatest power. He had difficulty finding a publisher. Monroe Stearns, the editor of trade books at Prentice-Hall, which had published *Most Likely to Succeed,* declined *The Great Days* after he had read an early version of it in 1955. The novel seemed to him incomplete, offensive in some places, and fragmented because of flashbacks Dos Passos too frequently employed without integrating them into the present time of the novel. Stearns feared that the book if published as it stood would seriously hurt Dos Passos's reputation, and he urged the author to write the entire story of the central character, Roland Lancaster, in much greater detail.

Dos Passos took back the manuscript to rework it. The early version had told the story of the autobiographical character, Lancaster, and his dismal affair in Cuba with a younger woman, Elsa, whom he thought he might marry. In the course of the several days he was with Elsa in Cuba, he thought back to the time when the United States was winning the war by exerting its industrial and technological expertise, a time of victory for the country rather than of the defeat that hung in the air during the years afterward, when the nation appeared oblivious to its declining influence in Latin America and elsewhere. In Cuba Lancaster uncovered information about a revolution, but no one wanted to publish his story. "Ro's plans for his story," Dos Passos scribbled in an early note for *The Great Days,* were "to express the precarious state of American influence in Latin America." Elsewhere he jotted down about Roland, "What he wanted to do with himself. His one last chance to get a sense of urgency into American thinking . . . American affairs." Lancaster's unhappy episode with Elsa was equated with America's "defeat" after its wartime victory, but a problem in the early version was that their affair had little to play off against in Roland's past except the remembered scenes of his wartime experiences, some presented almost exactly as Dos Passos had rendered them in *Tour of Duty.* The flashbacks, as Monroe Stearns had written Bernice Baumgarten, merely fragmented the story of Elsa and Roland. Before reworking the manuscript, Dos Passos sent it to Doubleday for their consideration, but their editor, LeBaron Barker, did not think it should be published as it stood, although he acknowledged that it had "a haunting, nostalgic quality" as well as "considerable force." The flashbacks, however, did not come alive for him and seemed irrelevant padding. Barker liked the tale of Elsa and Roland and suggested that it could be made into a short story if the flashbacks were deleted and a conclusion added, because as the manuscript stood the reader did not know what would happen to Lancaster, disillusioned and without money after Elsa left him in Miami.

Rebuffed by the publishers, Dos Passos in 1957 revised the manuscript, the major change being to give more substance to the flashbacks by introducing another character, Roger Thurloe, for whom Dos Passos drew upon his knowledge of James Forrestal, the Secretary of Defense from 1947 to 1949. Lancaster knew Thurloe, at whose behest he reported on the war. In addition, Roland's wife Grace worked for Thurloe and became emotionally tied to him. The result was that the flashbacks to the war include Thurloe and Grace and seem to have a more immediate relationship to Lancaster and his present circumstances. Further, by having Thurloe speak about the political situation, Dos Passos made clearer his purpose in including the reportage about the war. Among notes about Thurloe which Dos Passos wrote as he developed the character are quotations that express what he meant to convey. "Our problem," goes one, "to achieve accommodation between the power we now possess, our reluctance to use it positively, the realistic necessity for such use, and our national ideals." Another note about Thurloe reads, "What he keeps saying is what could I have done [effectively] We had the moment of greatest power we let it slip through our fingers." Other notes reflect Dos Passos's anti-Communism: "Thurloe says the real reactionaries are those who call themselves revolutionists: communism will result in the exploiting of the common man by his state"; or again, "Thurloe's 2 problems: 1. How to meet the Russians 2. How to get some policy into the disintegrated government that had been held together only by Franklin Roosevelt's demagogery." Thurloe, like Forrestal, was overwhelmed by the onus of his position and committed suicide, yet another act signaling the defeat Lancaster sensed in his own as well as the nation's life at the end of the novel. It was a defeat Dos Passos had himself felt deeply when in early 1949 he had invited the real life counterpart of Elsa to Cuba with him.* More than half a decade later, the memory of the incident, but more, of the great days, Katy, and his now dwindling fame weighed him down momentarily. To the notes he copied out for the revision of *The Great Days* he appended a sad conclusion:

> *When he shall hear*
> *His loved ones story whispered in his ear,*
>   *woe woe will be the cry*
> *No quiet murmur like the tremulous wail*
> *of the love bird the querulous nightingale*
>   *Finished copying*
> *Three in the morning—went into*
> *[quiet] kitchen and jumped out of the window*
> *to his death*

---

*In his notes for Thurloe, Dos Passos occasionally referred to him as Forrestal, and in other notes he listed a proposed section of the novel as "Conversation with a sleeping girl" and added "thoughts about Helen. . . ."

After he had rewritten the novel, Sagamore Press accepted it, and it was published in the spring of 1958.

To anyone familiar with its autobiographical nature, the novel was poignant, but to those who were not, it seemed a poor effort, didactic at times when Roger Thurloe spoke and disjointed because of the flashbacks. Edmund Wilson recognized immediately that Lancaster was an autobiographical figure, and from Dawn Powell —who knew of Helen Parker and whose own trip to Haiti when Dos Passos was there in 1948 was part of the source for the Elsa-Roland episode in Cuba—he learned of the background to the tale. He praised the portrait of Lancaster and Dos Passos's handling of landscapes and the characters in Cuba. But he thought Dos Passos had failed to make clear why Lancaster and Roger Thurloe turned against the New Deal, or what happened after Lancaster recognized that the United States was declining in influence.

"Perhaps I should have expatiated on Ro Lancaster's opinions," Dos Passos responded to Wilson, "but it seemed so corny that I cut it all out. By the way," he added, "I dont think I ever did go along with Franklin Roosevelt's Dr Win-the-War as I did with his Dr New Deal in its early stages." He noted that he had voted for Roosevelt in 1940 "as the lesser of the two evils." Of more appeal to him had been "the results of wartime organization" which he had recorded in *State of the Nation*, while *The Great Days* represented "something of the inevitable disillusionment with that enthusiasm for airfields and labor-management committees and floating bases and amphibious landings." He still believed, he told Wilson, that "we have something better to teach the world than the Russians have. The essential thing is the politics of balance and moderation," which, he could have gone on to say, were what the Russians lacked, so that when in Hungary in 1956 they crushed a nationalistic outburst but the United States dared not intervene, he grieved.

Wilson was correct; the book left too many questions unanswered, and Dos Passos's other critics faulted that while failing even to praise what Wilson thought was good. "I wish he had not published this tired book," wrote William Hogan, the reviewer for the *San Francisco Chronicle*. "His reputation rests with his own great days." Malcolm Cowley was equally disappointed, asserting that *The Great Days* "does not belong on the same shelf with 'Manhattan Transfer' or 'U.S.A.,' or even with the fine historical study . . . 'The Men Who Made the Nation.' " Cowley thought that the novel was "written smoothly, with sharp details, and the war passages are vivid," but he believed that "the two stories, of past and present, are not intertwined in such a way that they reinforce each other or lead to a joint climax." What had happened to Dos Passos? Cowley wondered. Dos Passos had always "been a lonely person, of the utmost personal integrity, and there is nothing in his career that explains or depends upon literary fashions," so Cowley found it difficult to believe that some drastic change had occurred to produce the "aversion and repulsion" which he thought to be "dominant moods" in the novel, where nothing was "enjoyed or enjoyable." The problem, Cowley concluded, was that Dos Passos had not taken the time to write well now that he had lost the "vigor and spontaneity" of youth. Cowley's theory was intriguing. Perhaps Dos Passos had not spent enough time working out his story; certainly he had lifted slabs of reportage from an earlier nonfiction work. But there was much that was poignant in the tale of Elsa and Roland in Cuba, and the bleakness of mood was hardly a rare thing in modern fiction. Cowley seemed to be confusing faulty structure and the novel's mood, an entirely separate matter. Even, perhaps especially, in Dos Passos's best fiction, the mood was bleak.

Dos Passos was not pleased with the poor reviews the book received, but, he remarked to Wilson, the novel was "water over the dam," and besides, as he told an interviewer several years later, "I don't think I've lost very much sleep by what you would call the critical reception of my work. I've been very fortunate in a way. If a thing is knocked in one place, somebody else may like it somewhere else. *The Great Days* was very much ignored in this country, but it went quite well in England and Germany. I wouldn't have been able to make a living without the international market."

The poor reception of *The Great Days* in America bothered him less than it might have because he had not considered the book a major work and was quickly busy with other projects and with travel. He immediately began another novel, *Midcentury,* and worked at the same time on a book of pictures with an accompanying narrative for Prentice-Hall about his now familiar band of American leaders during the years before the Revolution until 1810. The volume, *Prospects of a Golden Age,* was published in 1959. In addition, he contracted with Doubleday to write another volume in the same series as that of *The Men Who Made the Nation,* this book to be about the twenty-year period from President McKinley's assassination in 1901 until the inauguration of Warren G. Harding in 1921. The history, entitled *Mr. Wilson's War,* was published in November 1962. And, with Lucy now old enough to travel comfortably, trips were easier, which buoyed his spirits because he had lost none of his interest in traveling. After he, Elizabeth, and Lucy had been to Mexico during November 1957, he remarked to Robert Hillyer that "I still find travel—any kind of travel—invigorating."

By the time *The Great Days* was published in March 1958, the Dos Passoses had taken a house once again in Baltimore, where he could more easily do the research for his *Reader's Digest* article about labor, for *Midcentury*—which because of its inclusion of Newsreel-like documentaries and biographies required the sort of research *U.S.A.* had—and for both *Prospects of a Golden Age* and *Mr. Wilson's War.* He could hardly have been busier with his writing, and in addition, he was already anticipating the six-week trip he, Elizabeth, and Lucy were to take to Brazil the next summer.

From mid-July until the end of August they traveled in Brazil, where one of their major ventures was into the interior to visit the site of the city Brasília, which was then being constructed in the wilderness. Particularly Dos Passos was intrigued by the architecture of the city's chief designer, Oscar Niemeyer. Guided by his new friend Dr. Israél Pinheiro, who headed the government corporation responsible for the building of Brasília, the Dos Passoses received a detailed tour of the site and the land surrounding it. Pinheiro ensured that they met people working at Brasília who might give them a sense of the excitement of the project, and before the Dos Passoses left Brazil, Pinheiro had seen to it that they talked with President Juscelino Kubitschek, a major force behind the new city, and with Niemeyer. To get a better sense of how an inland city like Brasília might fare, the three Americans traveled inland from the site to Goiania, also an "invented city," and to other spots in the states of Goiás and Mato Grosso. Dos Passos was impressed with the prosperity of these regions and with the enthusiasm of the people he met. The new settlements, he noted, had little of the poverty he had observed elsewhere.

After returning to Rio, they flew to Curitiba, inland to the south, where he lectured at one of the binational centers supported partly by the U.S. State Department. From Curitiba they were driven northwest to Monte Alegre and then flown in a small plane to Maringá, a fresh city in the midst of a fertile region ideal for growing coffee. By the end of the journey, Dos Passos's enthusiasm for Brazil was even greater than it had been in 1948.

The trip was the sort he enjoyed most. He and Elizabeth were constantly on the move and in the process met a wide variety of people. It provided him with material for an article about Brasília and assuaged his urge to travel so that, once back in the United States, he could settle into his writing tasks. The family maintained the routine of Baltimore during the week and Westmoreland on weekends until the following spring of 1959, when Dos Passos, Elizabeth, Lucy and Christopher, Eben and Phyllis Given, Charles and Inga Mayo, their son and a friend of Christopher's all cruised aboard a chartered boat in the Bahamas for two weeks. It was a relaxing, enjoyable voyage during which, on April 1, Dos Passos called Edmund Wilson in Wellfleet on the ship-to-shore radio and pretended to be a Cuban revolutionary. Wilson was not amused by the joke and hung up. Dos Passos called again to clear the air, but Wilson hung up on him once more.

Such good spirits—as well as the trip itself—partly reflected Dos Passos and Elizabeth's easier financial circumstances. With a series of books contracted for, articles for which he was paid well, and occasional lectures, he had a steady income that relieved the uncertainties they had felt during the earlier years of their marriage. In addition, as he wrote Robert Hillyer in November 1959, "I've more or less retired from farming, thank God, having sold my interest in the cattle—but lumbering and 'forest practices' take up, and delightfully, a good deal of time." They no longer faced the losses they had previously incurred, as the land had begun to provide an income from lumber and other crops. The arrangement was better than before, because Dos Passos was too preoccupied with his writing and away too much in Baltimore to cope with the constant demands of farming full time.

Relieved of worries about the cattle, he still felt pressed by other tasks. Once he completed *Prospects of a Golden Age*, he concentrated on the manuscript for *Midcentury*, "a long documentary narrative in the (modified) manner of U.S.A.," he described it to Hillyer. He remarked that at that moment he was "distracted by a stage version—or at least a 'theatre in the round' version—of some of the U.S.A. material that is now running in the Hotel Martinique—of all places—in New York." The dramatic version of *U.S.A.*, adapted for the stage with the help of Paul Shyre, opened at the Martinique Theatre on October 28 and had a successful run of slightly more than seven months. The play, drawing from figures such as Richard Savage, from the Newsreels and Camera Eye sections, and from the biographies, was acted —or rather, spoken with some accompanying action—on a bare stage, but achieved a powerful effect because of the pace and broad sweep of the four narrative devices.

The adaptation was the result of an agreement which Dos Passos had signed in 1958 with Shyre and two other men, Nick Spanos and Howard Gottfried, whose interest was to promote film and dramatic versions of *U.S.A.* Dos Passos was encouraged by the production at the Martinique and for several years afterward fretted about other productions of the play and about possible film versions. The whole matter was complicated by an earlier agreement Dos Passos, Spanos, and another person, Gene Towne, had signed "to organize a venture with respect to 'U.S.A.' for motion picture and related purposes." As more people entered the scene, more wanted a share of whatever profits might accrue. And as more people became involved, Dos Passos became more anxious that something occur. When, except for the stage adaptation, nothing did, he became frustrated, and before the last of the initial agreements lapsed in 1961, considerable acrimony arose between him, Spanos, Towne, and Gottfried. What seemed to Dos Passos lethargy on their parts particularly annoyed him in the early 1960s, because after the production of *U.S.A.* in 1959, he had received offers for the use of the adaptation as well as offers of cash advances from Hollywood agents interested in promoting a film. But the prior agreement with Spanos, Towne, and Gottfried prevented his acceptance. Dos Passos repeatedly sought help from his lawyer, C. D. Williams, who could do little until the agreements expired except to keep Dos Passos from complicating matters further. The entire affair cost more in time and money than it should have, but was a good example of Dos Passos's way of dealing with people. Too often, as he admitted to Williams at one point during the lengthy disagreements between him, Spanos, Towne, and Gottfried, he had "lean[ed] over backward to give the other fellow a break" against Williams's advice. Basically generous and shy, Dos Passos's inclination was to be pliant; then he became angered by the consequences. It was part of the same approach that had caused other fallings out. He would acquiesce more than he inwardly meant to, and the consequences might be irksome.

At the time of the opening of the play Dos Passos had written a piece, "Looking Back on 'U.S.A.,'" which appeared in the *New York Times.* He discussed his involvement with the New Playwrights Theatre in the 1920s, but more important was what he wrote about his politics, because it was a clear, if brief, explanation of why he had moved away from "liberalism" and of what he meant to convey in all his work. The political terms of the 1920s did not apply in the 1950s, he asserted: "All the concepts have been stood on their heads. 'Liberalism,' for example, used to be equated with enthusiasm for individual rights; now it tends to mean identification with central governing power." Yet, whatever the changes in where he stood politically, he affirmed that "the basic tragedy my work tries to express seems to remain monotonously the same: man's struggle for life against the strangling institutions he himself creates."

PART IX

═══

Century's Ebb,
1960–1970

CHAPTER THIRTY-THREE

Midcentury and Embracing the Republican Right, 1960–1962

The enduring struggle for life against "strangling institutions" that seemed to Dos Passos to loom ever larger as the 1960s began was what he sought to express in *Midcentury,* on which he worked while completing the research for and writing *Mr. Wilson's War.* Both books were demanding. He had some hope that *Midcentury* might be published in 1960, but he could not finish it soon enough, so it appeared early in 1961, making 1960 the first year since 1955 that a book of his had not been published. The only break he took from the task of writing until he finished *Midcentury* was a customary vacation during August, when he, Elizabeth, and Lucy sailed aboard the *Vulcania* to Naples; from there they traveled to Venice, then through Switzerland and west to some of the World War I battlefields in France which he wanted to see in connection with the history about the years surrounding the war. From Château-Thierry they drove south to Avignon and Nice, then flew to Portugal, where they traveled through the country after visiting Madeira aboard a small, crowded steamer, whose officers turned over their wardroom to the three Dos Passoses. Mattresses were spread on the deck to accommodate the Americans and, Elizabeth recalled, they slept fitfully to the sound of music that came from the bar over a loudspeaker throughout the night.

In the spring of 1960 Dos Passos had written Lovell Thompson at Houghton Mifflin about the possibility of fall publication for *Midcentury.* He thought he might be able to produce a final typescript by April, but even then to try for the fall might rush production, because the manuscript was the sort that would require careful attention. Dos Passos eventually mailed the manuscript to Houghton Mifflin later in the spring, taking time to revise carefully because of the criticisms he had received from Thompson. Dos Passos, in fact, was irritated at some of the suggestions which had come from a committee of young readers who had balked occasionally at a draft version. To Thompson's suggestion that Dos Passos rewrite the manuscript according to the recommendations of the committee, Dos Passos retorted, "The final rewriting of a book is a much too hazardous enterprise to entrust to a committee. There's not much sense in making recommendations at this stage of the game, because the things your editorial people liked or disliked may appear in a totally different light or may not appear at all in the final version." He had hoped, he declared, that Houghton Mifflin would be intrigued enough to make a commitment on the basis of the draft. "Your final typescript wont be exactly what a publisher would want," he reminded Thompson. "It probably wont even be what I would want. It will only be the best I can do at the time. That is my responsibility." Knowing that the book, as he told Thompson, was a "delicately cantilevered" operation not "susceptible of much change," and thinking back to Houghton Mifflin's lack of interest in his previous two novels, Dos Passos wondered if it would "be simpler, and saving of headaches, hypertension and cholesterol if Houghton Mifflin said No right now." But Thompson, who continually championed Dos Passos's work, persevered, and Houghton Mifflin published *Midcentury*, which for fifteen weeks the *New York Times* listed as a best seller.

The "delicately cantilevered" novel was a somber chronicle of the United States at midcentury in which Dos Passos returned to the techniques of *U.S.A.* Prose poems, similar to the Camera Eye, began each of three sections, and a final poem concluded the book. Documentary sections appeared throughout as did the Newsreels, a difference being that the Documentaries emphasized less the chronology of the period and aimed to convey the nature of American culture, which was materialistic, self-indulgent, and engrossed in industrialization achieved at the cost of satisfying human relations. Fourteen biographical sections portrayed contemporary figures who represented the various forces at work in American society: heroism and discipline—qualities little regarded in a flabby society—were present in Generals Douglas MacArthur and William Dean, the latter the leader captured in the Korean War who withstood wounds and torture by his captors and did not collaborate with them. The ills of big labor—bossism, corruption, and alienation from the common laborer—were reflected especially in a sketch of three Teamsters' Union presidents, Dan Tobin, Dave Beck, and Jimmy Hoffa, while the threat of Communism in the unions was revealed in Dos Passos's sketch of the leader of the West Coast longshoremen, Harry Bridges; the unions' growth to power, in the sketch of John L. Lewis, which ended:

> *weighed down by the years he retired,*
> *his miners,*
> *from being serfs of the mineowners forever in hock to the*
> *company store,*
> *had become the top aristocracy*
> *of the best paid working class in history.*

And what seemed to Dos Passos the ruthless drive of unions to organize was clear in a biography of Walter Reuther, who in 1946 had become president of the UAW and vice-president of the CIO. The other figures whom Dos Passos sketched were the film magnate Samuel Goldwyn, Senators John McClellan and Robert La Follette, Jr., Eleanor Roosevelt, Robert Oppenheimer, an unnamed psychoanalyst, and finally, the film actor James Dean, whose appearance of resentment and bitter scorn symbolized to Dos Passos the mood of contemporary American youth, whom he called "The Sinister Adolescents."

In addition to the Documentaries, prose poems, and biographies, Dos Passos included seven sections of Investigator's Notes which he drew from the information he had obtained to write the article about the McClellan Committee. And, as in *U.S.A.*, he included narratives about fictionalized characters whose stories were meant to typify some aspect of American society. Of these there were five major figures, and a sixth, an adolescent named Stan Goodspeed, who appeared in a last, short narrative. One of the figures was Blackie Bowman, a sort of composite drawn from people like Gladwin Bland, the model for Mac in *The 42nd Parallel,* and Slim Martin, a sailor, sometime contributor to the *New Masses,* and friend of Greenwich Village writers with whom Dos Passos had maintained a correspondence. In the novel Bowman was an old man reminiscing in a veterans' hospital—Martin in 1956 was confined to a hospital—about the struggles of radical labor movements during the earlier decades of the century. The narrative about the industrialist Jasper Milliron had its basis in Dos Passos's experiences while writing the series, "The General," for the General Mills Corporation. Milliron sought to make the production of flour more efficient, but was thwarted by the corporate bureaucracy. Big capitalism, Dos Passos was saying, was every bit as bad as big government and big labor.

Dos Passos's materials for *Midcentury* reveal from where he drew three other narrative figures, Terry Bryant, Frank Worthington, and Will Jenks. Bryant, a strong-minded man, opposed union corruption and eventually died in a fight with thugs from another union. Dos Passos's idea for Terry came from a man named Edward Grant Taylor, with whom he had corresponded at the time he was writing his article about the McClellan Committee. Taylor, too, was strong-minded and honest and as a result ran afoul of his union hierarchy. A difference between him and Bryant, however, was that Taylor did not die. The death Dos Passos drew from an incident he read about in a newspaper which recounted the death of a man named Henry Bujalski after a fight with one Armand Carlomagno, president of Taxi Drivers' Union Number 128 in Pittsburgh.

Dos Passos had found out about this incident because another of the situations he had learned of while reading through the files of the McClellan Committee was what in *Midcentury* he termed "The Great Taxicab War." A veteran of World War II, Adolph Fram, had started his own taxicab company to fight the monopoly of the Yellow Cab Company in Pittsburgh. Dos Passos gathered letters and pamphlets concerning Fram's fight and from them created the narrative of Will Jenks, for whose independent Redtop Cab organization Terry Bryant worked after he lost his previous job through the conniving of his union bosses, company management, and government arbitrators.

The story lines of the narratives about labor and management figures—except for Blackie Bowman's reminiscences—cross. Jasper Milliron was Will Jenk's father-in-law and became involved in the taxi operation. Another labor figure, Frank Worthington, was head of the rubber workers' union of which Bryant was a member until he quit. Terry wrote Worthington about local problems but received no adequate response, Dos Passos's point in the portrait of the union leader being that he was ineffective about handling the problems of his union. The leadership, that is, had lost control of its large organization. Worthington was modeled after Leland Sanford Buckmaster, who in 1945 had become head of the United Rubber, Cork, Linoleum, and Plastic Workers of America, and who for an article for *Life* in the late 1940s Dos Passos had interviewed. In the *Life* piece he did not mention the loss of control; this was called to his attention by a remark in one of Edward Taylor's letters that Leland Buckmaster was ineffective in the local unions. With this in mind, Dos Passos had only to use Buckmaster's biography, which he already knew, to create Frank Worthington, whose career followed almost precisely that of Buckmaster.

A final brief narrative was about Stan Goodspeed, a relative of Milliron's wife and an adolescent who went on a spending spree using his father's credit cards. Dos Passos got the idea for Goodspeed from a newspaper story about Joseph R. Miraglia, a nineteen-year-old clerk making $55 a week. Dos Passos's intention is apparent from the title of the section, "Tomorrow the Moon," which juxtaposed the nation's technological brilliance with the shallow and corrupt self-indulgence of the young man:

> . . . A pad for indoor-outdoor living, airconditioned, soundconditioned with builtin appliances and luminous ceilings; an easy to operate aerodynamically advanced private plane for fast cool clean direct nonstop travel, a cosmic butterfly powered by parabolic mirrors, a spin out beyond the stratosphere in a supersonic spaceliner. Why not? And much more . . . Stan Goodspeed's throwing a ball . . . Yeah man,

thought the young American as his monologue concluded and was followed by a closing prose poem in which the narrator, walking his dog at night, mused about the condition of modern man:

> *The dog trots eager, sniffing the night, proud of*
> *her man's steps behind. The man,*
> > *shamed drags beaten strides, drained of every thought but*
> *hatred*
> > > *of the tinpot pharoahs whose coarse imprecations*
> > > *the impartial transistors have been dinning in his ears.*
> *Evil is indivisible. By hate they rose to flashbulb glory*
> *and the roar of cowed multitudes, police sirens shrieking*
> *how great the leader, how little the led: the abject mike*

ever waiting to receive
     the foul discharge of their power to kill. The lie
squared, the lie cubed, the lie to the power of x deals
death like a tornado. By hate they live. By hate we'll
see them die. We've seen them die before. The hate remains
     to choke out good, to strangle the still small private voice
that is God's spark in man. Man drowns in his own scum.
These nights are dark.

This prose poem ending *Midcentury* was perhaps his harshest indictment of man, that "paragon of animals" as he seemed to the dog who looked up at her master, the narrator. But the dark mood of the last satiric chronicle to be published during Dos Passos's lifetime was inevitable, for, as he declared in a speech he had given at Carleton College in 1960, "Satire is the state of mind of a disappointed moralist. It was in the cards that the writing of a would-be chronicler like myself should become more and more satirical as the years went by." For "more satirical" one might read "more protesting," but whichever, Dos Passos's point was that increasingly American society offended his moral vision, which compelled him to be an ever fiercer critic.

Discussing *Midcentury* some years later, the historian John Diggins posed the question, "What accounts for the night of despair that overcame Dos Passos at midcentury?" The answer, Diggins believed, lay "in the demise of three historical possibilities that at one time or another had given him hope in the future: the failure of the labor movement to achieve genuine trade union democracy; the failure of capitalism to free itself of external controls on the one hand and inner cupidity on the other; and the failure of science and technology to fulfill Veblen's dream of liberating modern culture from all that was irrational, wasteful, stupid, and oppressive." Man, as Dos Passos had written for the *New York Times* in 1959, was constantly struggling for life against "the strangling institutions he himself creates," and to Dos Passos it seemed that each new *ism*—corporate capitalism, Marxism, Freudianism, scientism—entrapped man more and prevented him further from making a reality of the social values that had been the goal of Washington, Jefferson, and the other founders of the nation. His view in *Midcentury* was not new; it was only bleaker, and nothing in the remaining years of his life would alter his vision. His final chronicle, *Century's Ebb*, on which he worked sporadically until his death and which was published posthumously, he called "a last forlorn Chronicle of Despair." The tumultuous antiwar protests of the late 1960s so infuriated him that to friends he wrote, "The rank criminal idiocy of the younger generation in this country is more than I can swallow."

Despite its somber tone, *Midcentury* was less intemperate than would be *Century's Ebb*, and it was as well received by the critics as had been any of his fiction since *U.S.A.* Before *Midcentury* was published, several magazines sent members of their staffs to interview him, and he confided to Lovell Thompson that "from my examination of the NY interviewers, I'd say we'd have to prepare for a mixed reception, but this time it will be mixed, rather than universal repudiation." Dos Passos had been "appalled" by the person from *Newsweek*, who had not read *Midcentury* and "was still looking for McCarthyites under the bed."

Dos Passos's assessment of the book's reception was accurate; important reviews such as those of Granville Hicks in the *Saturday Review* and Harry T. Moore in the *New York Times* considered it Dos Passos's most ambitious work since the first trilogy. Hicks, however, never an admirer of Dos Passos's work since the late 1930s, could only muster faint praise for *Midcentury*—it sounded "tired and fretful," he wrote, even if parts like the Blackie Bowman narrative had the vitality of *U.S.A.* Yet Hicks could admire Dos Passos's personal integrity and determination to speak out. Moore, however, was much freer with his praise and declared that *Midcentury* was on a par with *U.S.A.* and written in a masterful style. It was, he concluded, "one of the few genuinely good American novels of recent years," praise which helped the book to have a commercial success Dos Passos had infrequently enjoyed.

Midcentury was vintage Dos Passos, the satire no less scathing than that in earlier novels which had been severely criticized. It was, if anything, more scathing in passages such as the prose poems. But the broad sweep of the chronicle novel prevented Dos Passos's harsh critique of American society from seeming to have a relentlessness such as had offended reviewers of *Adventures of a Young Man* or *The Grand Design*, for example. The "documentaries" could be humorous, while the movement from one narrative technique to another gave the book a rapid pace.

Dos Passos had reason to be pleased, and despite what he described to Robert Hillyer in July as "a desperate flurry to finish" *Mr. Wilson's War*, he, Elizabeth, and Lucy took a relaxed trip to Spain during August and early September. They drove from Madrid north to Santander, where they met Christopher and a friend of his and in their rented Fiat drove west and southward along a portion of the border with Portugal, then eventually as far south as Granada before flying home by way of Lisbon. The two boys left them in Madrid after a trip made memorable by the fact that they had to get out of the Fiat at steep hills and back the car up them because it lacked power.

Although this was not the first time that Dos Passos had returned to Spain since 1937, it was his first extended visit. He was moved by some of the places which he had loved and which had figured prominently in his life, and the trip was made more poignant after he read in July of the circumstances of Ernest Hemingway's death by suicide. From the small town of Bailén in the south of Spain he wrote Sara Murphy in August that "until I read of his poor death I didn't realize how fond I'd been of the old Monster of Mount Kisco. In Madrid I found myself in places I'd been with him. Hélas."

The intense memories sparked by the trip would produce no more work about Spain, but they, as well as inquiries from scholars and friends about earlier days, made Dos Passos consider writing some kind of memoir. He had toyed with the idea as far back as 1957 when Lee Barker at Doubleday had suggested that he write an autobiography. He had asked for time to think about the proposal; then his arduous schedule of writing had prevented him from doing anything more about a memoir, but when Robert Elias, a professor of American literature, invited Dos Passos to speak at Cornell in the spring of 1959 and at the time of the lecture brought up the idea of publishing a new edition of *One Man's Initiation: 1917*, Dos Passos began to think more about his early career—"the best times," his memoir, published in 1966, called it. The Cornell edition of *One Man's Initiation: 1917* did not appear until 1969, but as Dos Passos worked with Elias on the new edition, for which he wrote an introduction, he delved into his notebooks from the period of World War I, and these sharpened his interest in a memoir. He also reexamined his letters to Arthur McComb, who had sold them to the American Academy of Arts and Letters. Dos Passos may have first become aware of these when Daniel Aaron wrote him about them while preparing his study, *Writers on the Left*.

In 1961 Dos Passos responded to Robert Elias's questions about the publishing history of *One Man's Initiation: 1917* that he had no idea what was in the letters to McComb but that Elias had his permission to look at them. Eventually Dos Passos read them himself and drew upon them for his introduction to the Cornell edition. Trying to help Elias, in 1961 he had found in an old trunk at Spence's Point the manuscript for "Seven Times Round the Walls of Jericho," the unpublished novel which he and Robert Hillyer had partly written together during their time as ambulance drivers near Verdun. Although he recognized that he should not publish the novel, it enhanced his interest in a part of his life he had thought little about for a long time. Also in 1961 Robert Hillyer asked about using the letters Dos Passos had written him. Dos Passos gave permission, and Hillyer sent him copies, which Dos Passos used as he had the McComb letters, when he wrote *The Best Times*.

As he answered questions about his life for Aaron, Elias, Hillyer, and others, he realized how full a life his had been and how much he enjoyed his recollections, so when he could he pored over his papers, journals, and the collections of letters which he had saved to and from his father and mother and from his friends and acquaintances. If he did not use them soon, literary scholars were going to, but an obvious place for them was in a memoir.

Dos Passos did not begin in earnest to write the memoir until *Mr. Wilson's War* and several other projects were completed. Like *The Men Who Made the Nation*, the Wilson volume was a broad, general picture of the era it was about, 1901–1921. Its reception after it was published in November was favorable, although the historian and biographer of Woodrow Wilson, Arthur S. Link, found *Mr. Wilson's War* "filled with errors in nomenclature, and, even more, in errors of fact." He suggested that Dos Passos "should have read more widely," but he praised the descriptions of World War I in France as "excitingly and vividly" written. The British military historian S.L.A. Marshall was less reserved, declaring that "Dos Passos has never written with a lighter, more whimsical touch. . . . In its pace, scope, and style, the narrative is reminiscent of [Frederick Lewis Allen's] 'Only Yesterday.'" The errors Link noted were a fault and reflected the speed at which Dos Passos worked, but the book was meant to be a popular history, and as that it succeeded.

One brief respite from his work occurred early in March 1962, when before an audience of some 18,000 conservatives in Madison Square Garden he received a second annual award certificate from the Young Americans for Freedom, Inc. Amid patriotic banners, the sounds of the "Battle Hymn of the Republic," and excited protestations against President Kennedy, Dos Passos accepted his award in the company of Senator Strom Thurmond of South Carolina, the economist Ludwig von Mises, the actor John Wayne, and, as John Diggins wrote, "other messiahs of the new American Right." To old-time left-wingers it was painful to find Dos Passos at the same rally where these other men were presented awards and where the audience paid vociferous tribute to the African leader Moise Tshombe, former New Jersey governor Charles Edison, and Herbert Hoover, the bête-noir of the Left during the early years of the Great Depression.

No matter how often Dos Passos might declare that his theme had always been freedom, the extreme shift in his political affiliations to which this rally was a testimonial was difficult to comprehend. Age, disillusionment, a certain complacency about the status quo in rural Virginia, and a loss of contact with the mood of elements other than the new Right in the nation all contributed to the change as Dos Passos manifested it in the 1960s, and in addition there was his enduring need to set himself against whatever he saw to be a dominating force. It was more a matter of personality than he believed. His stubborn defiance was that which had turned him against the Rover Boys of Choate, the Harvard aristocracy, the governments of the nations fighting in World War I, capitalism, and Communism. As Herman Melville said of Nathaniel Hawthorne, Dos Passos declared "No, in thunder" and took satisfaction in his stubborn isolation from the literary norms. Whatever group Dos Passos might passionately ally himself with was one that saw itself as a defiant minority struggling for liberty against a self-satisfied majority. Just so the anarchists in Spain, the Communists before Stalinism engulfed them, the early New Dealers, the advocates like James Forrestal of a strong defense after World War II, and later, the Young Americans for Freedom and their allies the Goldwater Republicans. Little matter to Dos Passos that the rest of the nation considered these last to be apologists for wealth and privilege. To Dos Passos in the early 1960s the new Republican Right stood defiantly *against* . . . against much of what a complex, technological society is, and the stance satisfied him.

He took time off for little else than the rally in 1962 until *Mr. Wilson's War* was ready for publication. Then in August he, Elizabeth, and Lucy visited Peru and Brazil, where he remained during September to travel into the northeastern region of the country after the other two had returned to the United States so Lucy could begin her school. While the three of them were together, they first spent two weeks in Peru—seeing Lima and the ruins of Andean civilizations along the Urubamba River inland before flying eastward to Equitos, a town in Peru at the head of the navigable waters of the Amazon. From there they took the single weekly flight to Manaus, a city on the banks of the Amazon in Brazil. The slow airplaine, a battered "Catalina" amphibian, landed along the way at the town of Leticia in Colombia on the borders of Peru and Brazil. The next stop was at Benjamin Constant, then Tefé, and only after four more uncomfortable hours by plane did they arrive at Manaus as the sun set. After spending a short time there learning from their guides about the agriculture in the region and taking a fishing trip on the Amazon, they flew by jet to Brasília to visit Israél Pinheiro and observe the development of the city since they had last seen it in 1958. The city had progressed, but was still new and raw. The resulting inconveniences were not especially distracting, however, so the Dos Passoses enjoyed their stay before they rented a car and drove to Goiânia, and then flew to Rio de Janeiro. There Dos Passos investigated the political situation, which was enlivened by the fact that elections were to be held in the fall of 1962. An important figure whom Dos Passos had first met in Washington ten years earlier was Carlos Lacerda, a journalist, political activist, and in 1962 the governor of the state of Guanabara. The Dos Passoses and some Brazilian friends took Lacerda to lunch near Petrópolis, and a few days later Dos Passos visited him again at his apartment in Rio, where Dos Passos was able to find out more about this energetic man whose anti-Communist politics attracted him.

Before Elizabeth and Lucy departed, Dos Passos lectured at the Brazilian-American Institute in Rio. Elizabeth recalled their utter fatigue afterward because their ability to speak Portuguese had been taxed while they attended a three-hour reception in Dos Passos's honor after the lecture. He also spoke with law students at the University in São Paulo, where the anti-American attitude worried him. In September he traveled by himself to Recife on the northeast coast. He stayed with friends, the Douglas Ellebys, with whom he shared his gloom that the United States–Latin America Alliance for Progress had stalled and that Communism—in Brazil he thought it was the sort of "modern Communism" which Fidel Castro had instituted in Cuba—was threatening whatever leadership the United States could provide. To have a better sense of what he termed "the uneasy northeast," he drove with Douglas Elleby north along the coast to Natal, the capital of the state of Rio Grande do Norte, a region where poverty created political unrest. But Dos Passos was encouraged by the administrative abilities of the young governor, Aluísio Alves, whom he met and followed briefly as the governor campaigned for reelection. He interviewed the bishop of the region, whose Christian labor movement the religious leader hoped would be independent of politicians, Communists, and businessmen. His aim was to create strong labor unions. Dos Passos returned from his talk with the bishop feeling relieved by the man's determination.

After Dos Passos had returned to the United States in early October 1962 from Buenos Aires, where he had flown to give a talk at a P.E.N. conference, he began to put together a book of reportage about Brazil from the notes he had made during his trip and from the materials he had gathered during his earlier journeys there in 1948 and 1958. *Brazil on the Move* appeared in 1963; although it recounted his fears about Communism, it concluded with a description of the merriment which accompanied a campaign appearance by Aluísio Alves in the town of Mossoró. Dos Passos meant to convey not only his hope for a democratic Brazil but his fondness for the people, a fondness which drew him back in 1966 and again in 1969 and which as much as his own ancestry was the impetus for *The Portugal Story,* a historical narrative he wrote in the last years of his life.

CHAPTER THIRTY-FOUR

An Unflagging Desire to Write, 1963–1967

Throughout Dos Passos's career he had fulminated against academics; yet he was pleased early in 1963 to serve for three weeks as writer-in-residence at the University of Virginia. He had been asked about the position in 1956, but it had not worked out for him to take it. Then from 1957 until his death in the summer of 1962, William Faulkner had held the position. During February Dos Passos lived at the Colonnade Club, a building whose cornerstone Jefferson had laid, on the old campus of "Mr. Jefferson's University." In addition to working with students, Dos Passos was able to do research toward his next Jefferson books, a children's biography entitled *Thomas Jefferson: The Making of a President,* which would be published in 1964, and a third volume for the "Mainstream of America" series to be entitled *The Shackles of Power: Three Jeffersonian Decades,* covering the period 1807–1831.

To continue publishing as much as he did, his routine of writing had to remain constant. The children's biography of Jefferson required little new research, but the book covering the three decades was more involved. Further, as if to coincide with the Goldwater presidential candidacy, Dos Passos planned to collect his later political essays into a book, *Occasions and Protests,* which was published in October 1964. Thus during 1963 he worked diligently until the end of July, when he, Elizabeth, and Lucy began a driving trip that took them to Stratford, Ontario, then Minnesota, Wyoming—where they hunted and fished for nine days on the Boyer Ranch in Savery—New Mexico, Colorado, and home. Despite a hernia operation in mid-July, Dos Passos was able to enjoy the trip and by late September was feeling well enough to fly to Rome on a four-day visit at the invitation of the anti-Communist Centro di Vita Italiana. Then he returned once again to his work routine, which he interrupted long enough in the late fall to review Edmund Wilson's protest, *The Cold*

War and the Income Tax. "Your Protest aroused my patriotic gore to the point of causing me to sound off in the pages of National Review," he wrote Wilson the day before Christmas. He hoped that his friend would not find the article offensive, but believed that he had confronted Edmund "on some rather important points."

A lively political argument developed between them. Wilson could not stand Goldwater—"surely one of the biggest asses in our asinine country," he called him —and had twitted Dos Passos the previous spring about his award from the Young Americans for Freedom. At that time Wilson had mentioned that he was writing the protest, which he hoped would be "the hottest thing since Tom Paine." Wilson had neglected to pay his income tax for a number of years, and the imbroglio in which he became involved with the Internal Revenue Service embittered him, especially because a substantial portion of his tax money was going to support the Cold War. Dos Passos, although agreeing with his friend about the repressiveness of the tax, took exception to Wilson's denunciation of the Cold War and asked in the *National Review,* "Please Mr. Rip Van Winkle, Wake Up Some More." Wilson, who had likened himself to the figure of legend for being asleep while life passed him by, was guilty of losing himself "in the group obsessions of the Liberal intellectuals," Dos Passos claimed. Ethel and Julius Rosenberg had been executed and Alger Hiss jailed on dubious evidence, Wilson asserted. This and Wilson's belief that there was no Communist scheme for world conquest sounded to Dos Passos like "another robot of the ventriloquists of Communist propaganda.

"For better or worse the uselessness of war has been basic in my political thinking all my life," Dos Passos declared, adding that he had "always had fellow feeling for the isolationists. I should like to have seen the United States develop into a great neutral nation, like Sweden or Switzerland." Nevertheless he argued that military spending was necessary in the face of Communist expansionism. Atomic warfare was a reality, he declared, and denunciation of it would serve no purpose as long as the other side remained belligerent. Our best protection was more arms and a thorough civilian defense system. Wilson, Dos Passos wrote, "slurs over the realities, upon which useful analysis must be based, of the disasters for the cause of civilization which have resulted from American fumbling and American folly." To blame as Wilson did "all the 'cold war tensions' which have been the journalistic commonplaces of the last few years on 'American encirclement of the Soviet Union' " was according to Dos Passos "to fall into a trap set by the Communist propagandists and to do their work for them." Despite his dismay about the attitudes of Wilson and other "liberals," Dos Passos did not feel as "unnecessarily helpless" as did Wilson. "If tendencies toward the good didn't survive interwoven with the forces of destruction in the flow of events we wouldn't have had any civilization to lament the passing of," he believed.

When Wilson read Dos Passos's review article late in January 1964, he responded, trying to pick apart various of his friend's points. "You've been railing against 'the liberals' all your life," he remonstrated with Dos Passos, "and my impression is that your conception of them is a projection of some suppressed alter ego that you perpetually feel you have to discredit." First Dos Passos had attacked from the radical perspective, now from the conservative. Wilson accused Dos Passos of being "as gullible as you ever were in the twenties" and guilty of "meaningless banalities."

Wilson's point about Dos Passos suppressing his liberalism was telling. His opposition to the liberals was as if he had to oppose the majority among the circles in which he moved. The only time he had admitted to being liberal was during the thirties as he swung from the Left toward the Right, and after he felt betrayed in 1937, his vehemence against liberal intellectuals was in a way a cry against that part of himself which had permitted the betrayal.

"I dont agree with a word of it," Dos Passos responded to Wilson's criticism, and he asked for a moratorium: "Pax." But Wilson would have none of it and wrote back protesting more of Dos Passos's declamations. "I really don't think you are well equipped for this moral political editorializing," he told Dos Passos and suggested that he should stick to writing such as *Brazil on the Move*. Dos Passos in his turn expressed his frustration with trying to continue the argument because Wilson was in an "in between world—between for and against." Wilson complained about Dos Passos's "use of 'right' and 'wrong.'" Dos Passos had come to decide—"with Jefferson and the eighteenth century people—that these terms represent something definite in the human makeup. . . . We really aren't talking the same language." Wilson then asserted he believed that traditional Socialism and capitalism were outdated and that the real problem for people in America as in Europe was "to prevent the apparently inevitable tendency toward centralization and nationalization from crushing individual initiative and any leeway for minority groups," a position scarcely different from Dos Passos's, except that Dos Passos believed in an overwhelming threat from the Communists. Dos Passos felt that their discussion had reached an impasse: the two of them had arrived at "diametrically opposite conclusions from the same set of facts." There the matter rested, although Wilson continued to grumble about his friend's enthusiasm for Goldwater. Wilson told Dos Passos when he saw him that he was like a kid in front of the Beatles, and to Dawn Powell he complained that Dos Passos's ecstatics over Goldwater in the *National Review* were "too girlish for words."

Wilson's irritation stemmed from a piece Dos Passos had written after he had returned from the Republican Convention in San Francisco in July, 1964. There he had watched with pleasure as the conservatives denied the presidential nomination to the likes of Nelson Rockefeller, George Romney, and William Scranton. Goldwater was their candidate, and to Dos Passos's satisfaction he won. "Behind Goldwater are the new groupings," Dos Passos concluded his article, "people who look to the American tradition as the source of victories for individual opportunity [the struggle for which was] the mightiest conflict in a generation."

He was back in Virginia from San Francisco only a short time before heading west with his family for an August vacation. They spent some time at the Boyer Ranch in Wyoming again, drove north and west to Seattle, and journeyed by train, bus, and sternwheeler ship as far as Anchorage, Alaska, from where they flew back to New York at the beginning of September. Before the November elections Dos

Passos wrote another piece for the *National Review*. Recognizing that Goldwater was unlikely to win, Dos Passos chose to stress the importance of maintaining a conservative opposition which could alter the present trend toward bigger bureaucracies and "practical collaboration, under a smokescreen of anti-Communist palaver, with the Communists to destroy civilization in a large part of the world." The essay, full of the sort of generalizations which exasperated Wilson, suggested no practical programs for conservative reform but pleaded for a continued effort from the Republican Right, whose emergence had excited Dos Passos during the campaign for the presidency.

Even after the Goldwater candidacy had ended, Wilson fretted if Dos Passos commented about public affairs, as in 1966, when he criticized the New Left in the *National Review*. "Your pronouncements on current events continue to give me the creeps," Wilson wrote. To him the article seemed nothing more than Dos Passos's "latest piece of idiocy." Dos Passos's trouble, Wilson admonished him, was that he had been born a liberal but was ashamed of the fact and hid it by creating a fictional character, which prevented Dos Passos from learning what others were thinking.

Although Lyndon Johnson's resounding victory and the notable lack of success of conservative candidates for Congress in November distressed Dos Passos, he did not dwell long on his disappointment. His writing projects continued to be demanding. In fact, he was publishing at a frenetic pace: two books in 1964, none the next year, but three in 1966. Hence during 1965 he was occupied with completing *The Shackles of Power*, which appeared in March of the following year, and once that historical narrative was finished, he turned his attention to his memoir, *The Best Times*, and to a collection of excerpts from his work which Houghton Mifflin planned to publish in November 1966, under the title *World in a Glass*.

In May 1965, he journeyed to New Haven, Connecticut, where he worked for several days at the Yale University Library reading the letters and papers of Alexis de Tocqueville for *The Shackles of Power*. The Frenchman's work, especially *Democracy in America*, excited him. He commented later that it "should . . . be read in French because translation slows the pace and makes the style seem heavy when it is actually effervescent."

His trip to New Haven coincided with a visit he was to pay to the Choate School in nearby Wallingford on May 8. Choate had invited him back to receive its Alumni Seal Prize Award, which it had previously awarded to John Kennedy and Adlai Stevenson, among others. Dos Passos had long since forgotten any animosity toward the school; now he thought that as an adolescent he had been something of an eccentric and Choate, a school in a New England setting that was frequently idyllic. "Having been raised partly in Europe and partly in Washington and the Northern Neck of Virginia," he declared, "[Choate] was my first experience with New Englanders. I might add that it was the New Englanders' first experience with me." He recalled some of his most pleasant memories: hitching long rides during the winter on the baker's and milkman's sleighs; floating on ice cakes in the pond near the school in the early spring; canoeing on the Quinnipiac River, which even in those days "seemed to others a pretty sordid little stream smelling of whale oil soap from the silver factories up around Meriden but for us it was the Amazon." Although he did not mention the difficulties he had faced at Choate, he intimated that he had been out of place: "I was a skinny little creature," he recollected, "nearsighted, timid about personal encounters, hating competitive sports but mad about the outdoors." Boys then, as in any era, had a difficult time finding "a foothold on the slippery globe," he knew. But he suspected the process was harder in 1965, when "every avenue of the senses is continually assailed not only by the siren voices of hucksters singing 'Cigars, cigarettes, tiparillos' but by the subtly deluding propaganda of all the groups of men that seek power. In the search for truth there are no secret formulae that can be handed down from one generation to another."

Dos Passos's remarks were well suited to the occasion and largely free of the prattle that annoyed Wilson. But Dos Passos could not avoid asserting when he concluded that "Truth, I believe, is absolute. Some things are true and some false. You have to find it." To him the absoluteness of truth had come to mean that "right" and "wrong" could be clearly defined and further by a leap in logic had come to mean that human beings, the very ones whose nature contained elements of right and wrong, could ascertain absolutely which forms of government were best. For Dos Passos it was a case that "the best government is the least government." But he would not acknowledge the oversimplicity of that idea. What was "least" for one segment of society was not necessarily "best" for another, and when he became absolutely convinced of his version of the truth, he lost touch with the complexity of modern society. Wilson had tried to tell him this, but Dos Passos's stubborn nature resisted, and in addition the tumultuousness of the late 1960s in America made him more positive than ever that there was a "right" and a "wrong" and that the "wrong" was in the ascendancy.

Two months before the ceremony at Choate Dos Passos had been stricken with viral pneumonia which had gotten into the pericardium. The result had been "irregularities and malfunctions" of the heart, he explained to Rumsey Marvin later in the year. The illness had not lasted long, and although he planned to work at a slower pace, he found that he could proceed quite normally. But in June when he and Elizabeth had been visiting the Givens at Truro he had had "a seizure of gasping and heaves." A local doctor had given him an injection which halted the seizure, and since then he had been taking medicines and felt fine, he assured Marvin in February 1966. "I suspect that some damage done by the old rheumatic fever may be catching up with me," he remarked, but as he was now seventy, "everything is gravy."

The illnesses in March and June 1965 did not prevent his traveling as much as ever. He and Elizabeth took Lucy to the West Coast in July and August to see colleges—she settled eventually on Occidental College in Los Angeles and began her schooling there in 1967. The three of them not only looked at schools but traveled along the coast as far south as Ensenada and north to Gold Beach, Oregon, before driving east through Idaho to the Boyer Ranch in Wyoming. The whole trip, he wrote his cousins the Camerons, had been "very therapeutic."

Dos Passos's schedule of work and trips during the remainder of his life does not suggest that he had slowed down his pace, despite his protestations to Rumsey Marvin. If anything, it suggests that he was attempting to do as much as he could fit in. With *The Shackles of Power* he completed the work he would do on Jefferson and his era. The book, like the others in the "Mainstream" series, was praised as a swift-moving narrative but not as an important history, criticism to which Dos Passos was by now inured. Organizing the selections for *World in a Glass* was relatively easy, but writing *The Best Times* was not. He discovered how many details he had forgotten, and before he finished he had to consult extensively his old journals, notes, and letters to be sure of his facts. Even then he made mistakes, as Edmund Wilson informed him after the book was published in the fall of 1966. But they were small errors—in the spellings of foreign words and in memories about their friendship. Wilson had never been, as Dos Passos had it, "an honorary member of The Society of American Magicians," nor had he ever ridden between New York and Red Bank on a motorcycle. Wilson mentioned other episodes about which he differed with Dos Passos, but he had enjoyed the book, especially those parts about John R. and about Dos Passos's travels in Persia. "Why didn't you tell about your experiences during the Spanish War and the reasons—execution of Robles, etc.— for the coolness between you and Hemingway?" Wilson asked, because to him the episodes "seemed so characteristic both of him and of you." But it was characteristic of Dos Passos not to mention these experiences. Not only were they not a part of "the best times," but telling them would have soured the tone of the memoir, when Dos Passos meant to write with affection and good humor about his family, friends, and experiences.

The book was appreciated for that by the reviewers as well as by former friends. Dos Passos sent Jack Lawson a copy after asking Lawson's sister Adelaide if she thought he would like one. Lawson appreciated the gesture and in a somewhat formal response called the memoir "engaging and generous." While some critics were puzzled why Dos Passos had stopped his memoir in the early thirties, they praised it, most particularly for its style and its generous portraits of the author's generation of writers. Dos Passos received his best press in a long time, better than that for *Midcentury. Time* magazine even suggested that his work was enjoying a revival.

For Dos Passos the reception of *The Best Times* marked the end of a personally happy year. His health, while wavering, was not yet precarious. During 1966 he had been able to enjoy trips to the Yucatán for two weeks in March during Lucy's spring vacation, and to Brazil during the last of July and all of August. "We've just completed one of the best trips ever—really getting into the dry and dusty hinter-land," he wrote Edmund Wilson from Rio just before they left Brazil. They had visited friends in Rio and had traveled to Goiânia, from where they flew farther north into the interior to be deposited on the banks of the Araguaia River, a tributary of the Tocantins. There they boarded a *botel* aboard which they cruised north along the river, tying up each night to a sandbank and hunting for turtle eggs and fishing in the evening light. Near where their voyage began they visited the village of the Tapirapé tribe. At the village the Dos Passoses were amused when an old hunter came up to them, pounded his chest, and declared, "I John." Dos Passos pounded his chest in return and responded, "I John." It was just such direct friendliness that appealed to Dos Passos. When he concluded *The Portugal Story*, he told of another chance meeting with a Brazilian couple who lived along the banks of the Araguaia while they fished and then smoked their catches, which eventually they took upriver to the settlement of Mato Verde. Elizabeth and he were struck by the few possessions of the couple, whose simple life and openness the Americans found appealing. "There was such serenity about this man and this woman alone and at home in the enormous wilderness that it was a wrench to leave them," Dos Passos wrote. When he recollected them, they came to symbolize the self-reliant individualism that was his ideal and what he had discovered in Brazilians such as the road builder Sayão, Carlos Lacerda, Israél Pinheiro, and numerous others.

On this trip they had also visited their friends Ellen and Carson Geld near São Paulo and had driven to, among other places, the colonial town of Paratí on the coast near Angra dos Reis. The entire journey had filled Dos Passos with an enthusiasm which he expressed in little more writing about the country except that in connection with *The Portugal Story*, but conveyed in a lecture in January 1967 at Ohio State University while visiting Rumsey Marvin in Columbus.

Amid the researches for the book about Portugal, he gave readings from his work from time to time and labored at the manuscript for *Century's Ebb*, which he referred to as his "thirteenth chronicle." When Lovell Thompson asked what it would consist of, Dos Passos responded, "Well the central story seems to be still 'The Later Life and Deplorable Opinions of Jay Pignatelli.' Interwoven with that are several stories; a young Greek business man; a character who turns out to be a cross between Eddy Gilbert and Bobby Baker who ends up in Brazil; an Iowa seed corn magnate. The final part will be about the building of one of these new from the ground up cities—like Columbia, Md." Dos Passos realized tht the volume might be quite different by the time it was complete, but that was how it looked in 1967 "from the notes and scattered semicompleted bits." He could not do much more on the book, he told Thompson, until he had gotten the Portuguese off his chest, which he hoped would be by the end of the year.

As usual, completion of the historical narrative took longer than he anticipated. To check materials he, Elizabeth, and Lucy took a trip in July and August 1967 to Portugal, where for almost a month and a half they traveled extensively while he looked at historic locations and excavations and studied documents in the national archives. Dos Passos combined these firsthand observations with material drawn primarily from secondary sources to recount the history of the growth of the Portuguese nation, its "peak of empire" and its abrupt decline as a major European power during the sixteenth and early seventeenth centuries. When the book was published in April 1969, it received praise as had his other histories for its lively narrative pace and for his ability to portray characters and scenes vividly. Further, because comparatively few general histories of Portugal had been written in English, the volume was commended as a worthwhile addition.

But histories to suit contemporary critics must be more than narrative; the books must tell why as well as what; they are expected to struggle with the meanings of what happened, and this *The Portugal Story* did not do. The historian J. H. Plumb in his generous review summarized the strengths and weaknesses of the book, and his remarks seem equally applicable to Dos Passos's other histories as well. "Dos Passos," wrote Plumb, "brings to his material a novelist's acute eye for human character and a narrative skill that any historian might envy; and he has produced one of the most readable books on the subject that I know. He is particularly adept at the brief dramatic profile." Plumb believed that Dos Passos was "a brilliant narrator"; yet "one realizes the great distance that . . . lies between the professional historian and—without using the word in any perjorative sense—the amateur." It was not that Dos Passos had not read widely nor even that he had not assimilated his materials. Rather, he was accustomed to writing reportage, to recounting what happened, and not to interpreting it as the professional historian would.*

*In fairness to Dos Passos, it should be noted that Doubleday's "Mainstream of America" and "Mainstream of the World" series, the latter of which The Portugal Story was part, were intended to be narrative, popular histories.

CHAPTER THIRTY-FIVE

The Last Years,
1967–1970

The last decade of Dos Passos's life was satisfying because he received recognition as he had not since the 1930s and, because of more literary income and profits from the Virginia land, he did not have to worry about finances as before. A particularly satisfying trip, thus, was the one he and Elizabeth took in November 1967 to Italy, where in Rome at the National Academy of Lynxes he received the Antonio Feltrinelli prize for fiction, which included a cash award of 20 million lira, roughly $32,000. Edmund Wilson had written Dos Passos about the prize in early April, and at that time Dos Passos was prepared to refuse it because he miscalculated the amount in lira to be $3,200, little more than the cost of a trip for him and Elizabeth to receive the award. But she and Lucy, aware that he was not good with figures, recalculated and quickly realized that the amount was far more substantial. At that Dos Passos was only too happy to make the trip. He and Elizabeth flew to Lisbon, Madrid, and then to Rome, where at the award ceremony in the Corsini Palace he delivered a speech about "what makes a novelist." He described the gestation of his chronicle fiction and discussed the aims and qualities of narrative writing in a thoughtful essay that revealed much about his own development and about the kind of "objectivity" he sought in his work. Afterward, but before leaving for the United States, he and Elizabeth were fêted repeatedly; they still managed a short train trip to Trieste.

Perhaps Dos Passos by 1968 had a sense that his weakening heart would not permit him to travel easily for long, so that although the work on *The Portugal Story* dragged on, he and Elizabeth soon traveled again, this time in February and March 1968 to Florida, California—where Lucy joined them for a trip to Arizona and down into Mexico—and then from California back to Florida before returning to Virginia.

They visited friends wherever possible; for some it was the last time they saw Dos Passos. Dudley Poore was one of those. Dos Passos and Elizabeth visited him at Summerland Key, near Key West, and Poore afterward vividly remembered his friend cheerfully striding up to Poore's cottage carrying a basket in which he had the makings for cocktails. The moment seemed to Poore typical of Dos Passos, who was in private a warm, generous, good-humored person, quite different from the image created by his satiric fiction and his polemics.

After Dos Passos had finally completed *The Portugal Story* in the summer of 1968, he and Elizabeth in July and August traveled again to visit friends: the Garsts in Coon Rapids, Iowa, and the Marvins, who were spending their summer at Walloon Lake in upper Michigan. While there the four of them attended a church service during which a memorial for Ernest Hemingway was read. Quietly but firmly Dos Passos stood up and left the church in a gesture of distaste more severe than anything he had written about Ernest in *The Best Times*. Ernest's remarks in *A Moveable Feast* no doubt were still galling. Before returning to Westmoreland, Elizabeth and he flew to Boston to visit Lovell Thompson at Gambit, Incorporated, the publishing house he had recently founded after his retirement from Houghton Mifflin, then drove north into Canada and back to Maine, where they stayed with the Givens on Bare Island, near Stonington, and with the Lowndeses in Wiscasset.

The trip was not the last of his travels for the year, however. In October he and Elizabeth flew north so he could give a talk at Union College in Schenectady, New York. Renting a car in Albany, they drove to Conway, Massachusetts, to spend a night with Archibald MacLeish and his wife; then after the session at Union they took a bus to New York, where Dos Passos conducted business with Doubleday and during the following two days met the Harold Westons and at another time Adelaide Gaylor, with whom the Dos Passoses saw an exhibition of Italian frescoes at the Metropolitan Museum of Art, dined, and finished their day with the W. C. Fields movie, *My Little Chickadee*.

Dos Passos's talk at Union College had been in the form of an informal discussion with students and faculty members, one of whom, Frank Gado, began the session by quoting from Dos Passos's 1916 essay, "A Humble Protest," written for the *Harvard Monthly*. "Has not the world today somehow got itself enslaved by this immense machine, the Industrial system?" Gado began reading and quoted several paragraphs of the piece. "Where was that? I haven't seen it," Dos Passos asked, and when Gado identified the essay and its author, Dos Passos remarked, "I didn't recognize it at all. It's really pretty good."

Gado used the piece as a way to have Dos Passos comment on the similarities between college students of his own generation and those in 1968 whose increasing protests against the Vietnam war irritated and confounded him. He believed there were many similarities, yet felt an important difference was that the ideas of his generation "were really more constructive than those of the current generation." He recognized that both were reacting against the same forces, "but now the reaction is one on a larger scale and more virulent." The present rebellion was "a tantrum of spoiled children who really have had too much done for them." He recounted his shock at the events of World War I and his dismay that in this country "people's minds became imprinted with slogans," which was what he thought had happened to contemporary protest movements like Students for a Democratic Society (SDS). They seemed fanatical and amid all their protest could offer no solutions.

Later he was asked what similarities he might perceive between the agitation in support of Sacco and Vanzetti and that of the Vietnam war and civil rights. The Sacco-Vanzetti case seemed to him more understandable. "I had great sympathy for the Anarchist movement at the time," he recalled, adding that the attitudes of the anarchists "served to freshen people's minds." But with age, he continued, he had come to discover "the way the human race works: in simple terms, top dog always gets to the top, no matter what the system is. . . . No change in ideology changes that basic fact."

Dos Passos could not quite understand why the distinctions he made between his Old Left and the New Left he despised were not clear to the students to whom he spoke. But what most disturbed him was the force of the protest against the Establishment in 1968. By the time he visited Union College, he had observed on television the violence at the Democratic National Convention in Chicago the summer before, and he knew of the protests which had gone on outside the tightly regulated Republican Convention in Miami Beach where Richard Nixon was nominated for the presidency.

Dos Passos had begun to harangue the New Left in the essay that infuriated Wilson, which after publication in the *National Review* became the foreword to *The American Cause,* by Russell Kirk. In it, Dos Passos lashed out at what he considered "the delusions of the New Left . . . the last sour exhalations of the decaying liberal creed." It was the cry of a man who had felt himself betrayed by liberalism, which now seemed to him always ready to open its doors to international Communism. Dos Passos might hear it asserted, but could never accept that many, in fact the majority of the students protesting against the war and for civil rights sought exactly what he desired: a less technologized, less bureaucratic government. Certainly they did not seek the Communism he feared. He could not separate their protest from his belief that if the United States did not wage war in Vietnam, the Communists—whom he did not differentiate from one nation to another—would gain.

"We are suffering from a disease of prosperity," he told the journalist John Davenport when he interviewed Dos Passos in the spring of 1968. It was the "rich kids" who were espousing the New Left, he believed, while the "children of the working people" tended to be conservative. "I kind of sympathize with their bewilderment in today's complex society and its corporate mentality," he conceded, "but why should they fall for the biggest corporation of all—the Communist Party? Furthermore, a corporation like General Motors doesn't have the power of life and death." The observation was too simplified; "rich kids" and the "children of working people" did not fit into the neat categories he implied, nor did many fall for "the biggest corporation of all."

Somewhat less pat and more moderate—the private as compared to the public

Dos Passos—were his responses to Lucy in 1968 when she asked him to "comment on the new college generation." " 'Better educated' is a positive good," he wrote. " 'Sophisticated' I dont think much of. Discoverers and inventors are usually unsophisticated people. . . . 'Liberal' as you know has become a term of abuse with me. All of the phrases that had meaning fifty years ago and are now decayed and rotten are going out with the tide. I sincerely hope that Mr. George Wallace isn't going to lead the reaction. People are going to face up to the fact that there is a great deal more evil than good in the human character and that the monster has to be kept under control."

Part of Dos Passos's distaste for the New Left stemmed from his romanticization, as was the case throughout his life, of the working class. The spring before he died he wrote Lucy complaining about "the poor palefaced WASP's" who spent "those countless hours staring at TV." He had seen the documentary film *Woodstock,* which he found intriguing as a sociological statement. The "half naked people" who swarmed around at the rock concert repelled him, and it was his observation that "Nobody, except the construction workers who put up the stand, looked as if they had done a decent days work, plain physical labor, in their lives. . . . Instead of sobbing about how bad the system is," he added, "the people of your generation should be trying to develop themselves, physically and mentally and morally into decent human beings." He assured Lucy that he agreed with more of her ideas than she imagined, but, he added, "still I feel it is tragic that the young people have allowed themselves to be led by their elders into this hysteria about Cambodia." He acknowledged that there was "room for rational differences of opinion on the whole subject," and he reminded her that he had "always wanted the United States to be a neutral country like Switzerland." Yet the American incursion into Cambodia of May 1970, seemed to him "the first rational military step taken in the whole war, and whether you agree with him or not President Nixon deserves acclaim instead of obloquy for having had the courage to try it in the face of [an] overwhelming Communist-inspired propaganda campaign. . . . If Nixon fails it is just this generation that is raising such cain that will have to bear the brunt of the results."

He meant to be moderate, but the issue came back to Communism, and any political power play by groups like the SDS seemed to him the design of the Communists. Just so did he view the civil rights struggle. He was not a racial bigot and expressed great sympathy for the plight of blacks in America late in his life. But he thoroughly distrusted anything like the Black Power movement, suspecting that it was part and parcel of what he believed had inspired the SDS. "I am making my usual annual contribution of $350.00," he wrote to the vestry of Cople Parish in Westmoreland in 1969, but it was "with the understanding that none of the money will go out of Cople Parish to be spent directly or indirectly on the black power movement." And the previous spring, in reference to disturbances at Cornell University, he had commented bitterly to Marion Lowndes that he had been "glad to see that the students and faculty at Cornell at least are reacting against being bullied by the black hoodlums they allowed into the college. The S.D.S. are much more dangerous because they are intentional wreckers very much under Communist influence and with a great deal of money . . . to spend," money he surmised might have come to the movement from the "liberals" of the Ford Foundation. "Who benefits by [S.D.S.'s] 'boyish pranks'?" he asked, and answered, "Ho Chi Minh of course."

As did many other white Americans, Dos Passos favored what he considered gradualism. Civil disobedience had become anathema to him despite his own assertions about the need for protest during World War I and after, despite his stance during the 1930s, and despite his admiration for the founders of the nation who had practiced massive civil disobedience. He could agree with protesters that the United States needed reform, but so fearful of Communism was he that he believed reforms should only take place within the guidelines of the system. Yet he also believed that the system had become too ponderous to be responsive to individuals. The dilemma of how to produce a responsive government he had pondered throughout his life. When he died, he was no closer to solving it than he had been in 1917, when he had declared to Arthur McComb that his only hope lay in revolution and "wholesale assassination of all statesmen, capitalists, war-mongers, jingoists, inventors, scientists —in the destruction of all the machinery of the industrial world, equally barren in destruction and construction."

More rewarding than ruminations on the unsolvable problems of politics was Dos Passos's trip to Easter Island in January and February 1969. He and Elizabeth departed from New York on January 11, flew to Miami and then to Santiago, Chile, from where after a day's delay they flew to the island. There they spent nearly a week learning about the island's people, its rock carvings, and stone statues while Dos Passos took notes for a short piece he wrote that became the introduction and conclusion to several narratives about Easter Island. Before he died he was able to complete a book, *Easter Island: Island of Enigmas,* which Doubleday published the year after his death. He and Elizabeth had a fine time, and shortly after they had returned from the island to Chile, he wrote Marion Lowndes that they were "suffering a great nostalgia for the great statues, the rock carvings the mysteries such as how did tutora reed (which only grows on Lake Titicaca) get there—and the people," of whom he and Elizabeth felt they had seen too little. The gigantic statues and their history moved him: "The whole strange prehistory unrolls as you ride around—in bumpy pickups over rocky roads of stony dust—first the fantastic efforts to carve out and move the statues to their locations on the great megalithic platforms —then after some social upheaval the equally strenuous efforts to knock them all down," he wrote to Lucy from Santiago.

In Chile his health worsened when he contracted what he later described as "a violent throat infection," which brought on a crisis when he nearly strangled while eating at the U.S. Embassy in Santiago. Soon, however, he was well enough to travel again, and before he and Elizabeth returned to Westmoreland early in March they journeyed to Argentina and to Brazil, where in Porto Alegre they stayed with the noted writer Erico Verissimo; then near São Paulo they visited the Gelds.

During the spring Dos Passos's health improved enough that he was able to work on the essay about Easter Island and in May to travel with Elizabeth to Cape Kennedy to observe the Apollo 10 rocket launch. The event stirred him, and in a piece which he wrote for the United States Information Service and which later appeared in modified form as the final segment of *Century's Ebb*, he declared that with the success of the Apollo 8 flight "Mankind was on the threshhold of a new beginning." In the face of the horrors of the twentieth century the Apollo program reasserted man's spirit and satisfied his search for knowledge. The moon shots, which demonstrated man's technological skills, might also arouse his spirit of adventure. To a nostalgic Dos Passos they seemed possibly to be symbols of a nation reawakened from the flaccid materialism he scorned and to mark the beginning of "a period when the most fruitful human effort converges on space exploration." He hoped that from the technology of the Apollo program might come "the solution of a hundred different problems."

The tone of his last pieces like that about the Apollo program reflected a basic optimism that lay beneath his scorn for man's opportunism. It was as if, knowing he did not have long to live, he meant to round out his literary canon on a hopeful, not a pessimistic, note. He was reminded of his mortality during the summer of 1969 when, visiting the Givens on Bare Island in Maine, he had a minor heart attack one night. Elizabeth sat him up in his bed until morning, when he felt well enough to leave, but his condition remained poor. Soon after he returned to Virginia he and Elizabeth moved to the small apartment they kept in Cross Keys Village in Baltimore, where they stayed while he underwent tests and then treatment at Johns Hopkins.

Although he was able during the fall of 1969 to return to Westmoreland, his health was precarious. He was losing weight as the doctor had instructed him to, but the result was that he was weak and had to return periodically to the hospital for further care. After a stay there in January 1970, he and Elizabeth traveled in March to Tucson, Arizona. On his arrival he was so weak that he required a wheelchair in the airport, but his strength increased so that by the time they returned to Westmoreland, he was well enough to do light work in the garden at Spence's Point. The winter, however, had been "damned unpleasant," he told Edmund Wilson, and he remained frail.

During these last months of his life he kept busy, corresponding with friends, working at *Century's Ebb* once the Easter Island book had been completed, and doing such small chores as offering criticism to Horsley Gantt of an editorial he wrote about the psychologist B. F. Skinner and sponsoring William F. Buckley for membership in the Century Club in New York. These were the sorts of things that even while invalided he could do, which was fortunate because in early June his sickness, diagnosed as congestive heart failure, flared up and grew more serious in July. He had to go to Baltimore again for treatment, then was able to return to Westmoreland before he and Elizabeth began a drive to Maine, where they spent the month of August in a small cottage at Head Tide.

Their trip back at the end of the month was long and painful for Dos Passos. His health had worsened, necessitating another medical visit to Baltimore. He was weaker than ever, and it seemed best for him to stay in a convalescent hospital, the Good Samaritan, where he had occasionally been before. He was lonely and wistful, sensing that he was near the end of his life. On September 21, Horsley Gantt visited him for the last time after Dos Passos telephoned and asked him to come. Gantt in his diary noted that now his friend saw hardly anyone and often felt too weak to continue a visit for more than fifteen minutes. But on this occasion Gantt remained for a half-hour while the two of them had an intimate conversation and Dos Passos talked about the philosophy of the unknown. He had been reading about the ideas of Hume and Berkeley from a book which he had borrowed from Horsley, who noted Dos Passos's wistfulness when he said he was going to the Virginia mountains the next weekend. "He is so weak," Gantt ended his entry about Dos Passos on the twenty-first. "He talks so slowly, can hardly totter. I shall miss him terribly—my best friend."

Dos Passos seemed well enough to move to the small apartment at Cross Keys Village later in the week and on the twenty-seventh to visit the Brodnax Camerons for dinner in nearby Bel Air. But he was quiet and appeared to the Camerons to be in serious discomfort. The next morning after helping Dos Passos to get comfortable in their apartment, Elizabeth left for a short time to buy a newspaper. When she returned, she found him sprawled on the floor with a gash on his head. She telephoned Horsley Gantt and asked him to come at once. He arrived in fifteen minutes and immediately attempted artificial respiration, but to no avail. At about 9:00 A.M. on September 28, 1970, Dos Passos died of congestive heart failure.

On October 1 a service was held in the Trinity Episcopal Church in Baltimore. As Dos Passos had requested, the service was in the prayer-book language he had admired. On October 7, after another service at the Yeocomico Church near Spence's Point, his remains were buried next to the grave of his mother, and later Elizabeth had a stone placed at her husband's grave which reads simply:

JOHN DOS PASSOS
1896–1970

"A Last Forlorn Chronicle of Despair"

Dos Passos's death did not mark the end of his publications. *Easter Island* appeared in 1971, and in 1975 Lovell Thompson published *Century's Ebb* over the Gambit imprint. The chronicle novel was unfinished; Elizabeth and the editors had to determine the order of some of its parts and to guess in several places about how Dos Passos meant to add to the panorama he had previously presented in *U.S.A.* and *Midcentury.* In *Century's Ebb* he included pieces entitled "1937," "1939," and "1948," which like the Newsreels in *U.S.A.* served as background and revealed his belief that Franklin Roosevelt's New Deal was becoming a ponderous bureaucracy. Dos Passos turned to one of his heroes, Walt Whitman, to express his fears about the United States as it became a supernation. Four of the five parts into which *Century's Ebb* was divided include lyric pieces by or about Whitman. But Dos Passos's Whitman was not the exuberant poet of "Song of Myself" who celebrated pre-Civil War America. Rather he was the author of *Democratic Vistas,* the pained nationalist who feared that the "fervid and tremendous *Idea*" which had been our story-book democracy was mired in "solid things . . . science, ships, politics, cities, factories," during the years of "unprecedented material advancement."

To his own question, "are we indeed men worthy of the name, Walt Whitman, in these 'years of the modern, years of the unperformed'?" Dos Passos's answer was both "yes" and "no." No, because he believed that America had failed to meet the international challenge of Communism and the domestic challenge of materialism and violence, a failure he rendered through biographical sketches of people like George Orwell; the philosopher John Dewey; politicians such as Joseph McCarthy, Wendell Willkie, and Henry Wallace; Secretary of State John Foster Dulles; the scientists Robert Goddard and James Watson; the founder of the Kodak Company George Eastman; the assassin Lee Harvey Oswald; and the Black Muslim Malcolm X. Dos Passos also included several longer narratives about characters like Danny De Long, a composite of Lyndon Johnson's protégé Bobby Baker and of Eddie Gilbert, a financial sharpie who embezzled money during the 1960s and took refuge in Brazil, where Dos Passos had met him. Another narrative was about the autobiographical figure Jay Pignatelli, through whose career Dos Passos conveyed his disillusionment with the left wing, and particularly his sense of the Communists' betrayal because of their secret involvement in the death of José Robles.

But Dos Passos could also respond, "Yes, something about us is indeed worthy of the name." The Apollo rocket flights had demonstrated man's "mastery of matter," and the moon landing in July 1969 marked man's ability to perform for once as Dos Passos believed Whitman would have his countrymen perform.

Although some of the sections of *Century's Ebb* such as "1948," the narrative about Jay Pignatelli, and several of the biographical sketches—little more than an accounting of facts—were unfinished, Dos Passos's intentions were not obscure. There was no mistaking his conviction about the direction—the ebb—of this century's tide. His fears were clearest where his hatred of Communism was apparent: when he provocatively protrayed Joseph McCarthy as little more than a country boy bewildered by the intrigues of a liberal bureaucracy; when he sympathized so entirely with John Foster Dulles's brinksmanship that he ignored the complexities of international diplomacy; or when, detailing the career of Lee Harvey Oswald, he described General Edwin A. Walker—one of Oswald's targets—as "a plainspoken man who had resigned from the Army to defend the American cause." The description had some truth, but ignored the fact that the general was a wild-eyed radical of the Far Right, as much within the lunatic fringe as some of the radicals on the Left whom Dos Passos had come to despise.

He did not have time before he died to polish *Century's Ebb*. But neither the incompleteness nor the bias in what he told Harold Weston was his "last forlorn Chronicle of Despair" is what matters about the book. What matters is that it is the final work of a major American writer of the twentieth century who had struggled throughout his literary career to convey a panorama of twentieth-century society. Although his work, especially books like *Adventures of a Young Man, The Grand Design, The Prospect Before Us,* and *The Great Days,* may strike readers as too polemical, anyone wanting to dismiss Dos Passos should remember that he was not a crank, but an intelligent, thoughtful man who agonized about politics. He was not alone when he shifted from Left to Right, and his sorrow about his chosen country was akin to that of literally millions of his countrymen who despaired—as he never did—about their nation. *Century's Ebb* is not so much a diatribe from the Right as a final statement in which Dos Passos, who had devoted his career to observing America, hoped to awaken other Americans with his words. If, like his earlier chronicles, it often paints a dark, even a savage picture, it also reflects his pleasure and amusement in his fellow men, who might scurry about foolishly and self-importantly, but who have as well their moments of tragedy, of compassion, and of greatness. The book rounded out his vision of American life and marked the end of his lover's quarrel with the world.

Like Whitman, Bartolomeo Vanzetti was one of Dos Passos's heroes. What Dos Passos had said about the Italian anarchist in 1926—what John Chamberlain in his 1939 review of *Adventures of a Young Man* reminded his readers was the author's own stance—was still true of Dos Passos when he died. Vanzetti's politics, Dos Passos had written, were "less a matter of labels than of feeling, of gentle philosophic brooding." Vanzetti hoped, Dos Passos believed, that "somehow men's predatory instincts, incarnate in the capitalist system, can be canalized into other channels, leaving free communities of artisans and farmers and fishermen and cattle breeders who would work for their livelihood with pleasure, because the work was itself enjoyable in the serene white light of a reasonable world." All that need be added to this to be an intellectual portrait of Dos Passos at the conclusion of his life was that he had come to believe that the capitalist system might function for the good of everyone; yet we should remember that even in later works like *Midcentury* he portrayed corruption and greed under capitalism. He thought it the best possible system, but it was constantly being abused because, as he had told Lucy, "there is a great deal more evil than good in the human character." In fact, it may be that the substantial difference in Dos Passos early and late was his final conviction that evil was not a part of some of us, but of us all. He had become, as he himself claimed, a disillusioned moralist and as a result a more complete—and ever harsher —satirist of the American scene.

Notes and Sources

The notes are keyed to the text by page number and lead-in phrase. Sources identified in the text are not repeated in the notes.

Abbreviations of books by Dos Passos referred to in the notes:

BOM   *Brazil on the Move*. Garden City, 1963.
CC   *Chosen Country*. Boston, 1951.
CE   *Century's Ebb*. Boston, 1975.
DC   *District of Columbia*. Boston, 1952.
FC   *Facing the Chair: Story of the Americanization of Two Foreignborn Workmen*. Boston, 1927.
14C   *The Fourteenth Chronicle: Letters and Diaries of John Dos Passos*, ed. Townsend Ludington. Boston, 1973.
GWSO   *The Ground We Stand On*. New York, 1941.
IAC   *In All Countries*. New York, 1934.
JBW   *Journeys Between Wars*. New York, 1938.
LTTP   *The Living Thoughts of Tom Paine: Presented by John Dos Passos*. New York, 1940.
MC   *Midcentury*. Boston, 1961.
MT   *Manhattan Transfer*. New York, 1925.
NO   *Number One*. Boston, 1943. Volume two of *District of Columbia*.
OE   *Orient Express*. New York, 1927.
OMI   *One Man's Initiation: 1917*. Ithaca, 1969. First published in 1920.
PBU   *The Prospect Before Us*. Boston, 1950.
PC   *A Pushcart at the Curb*. New York, 1922.
PS   *The Portugal Story: Three Centuries of Exploration and Discovery*. Garden City, 1969.

RRA	*Rosinante to the Road Again.* New York, 1922.
SN	*State of the Nation.* Boston, 1944.
SON	*Streets of Night.* New York, 1923.
SP	*The Shackles of Power: Three Jeffersonian Decades.* Garden City, 1966.
TBT	*The Best Times: An Informal Memoir.* New York, 1966.
TGD	*The Great Days.* New York, 1958.
TIF	*The Theme Is Freedom.* New York, 1956.
TOD	*Tour of Duty.* Boston, 1946.
TS	*Three Soldiers.* New York, 1921.
USA	*U.S.A.* New York, 1938. Includes *The 42nd Parallel, Nineteen Nineteen,* and *The Big Money.* References in the text are to the readily available Houghton Mifflin Sentry edition (Boston, 1963).

People, books, and collections frequently cited:

AAALC	Collection of American Academy and Institute of Arts and Letters (Dos Passos to Arthur McComb)
AM	Arthur McComb
Baker	Carlos Baker, *Ernest Hemingway: A Life Story.* New York, 1969.
BB	Bernice Baumgarten
CAP	Charles A. ("Cap") Pearce
Diggins	John P. Diggins, *Up From Communism: Conservative Odysseys in American Intellectual History.* New York, 1975.
DP	Dudley Poore
DPC	Collection of Dudley Poore
EEC	E. E. Cummings
EECL	*Selected Letters of E. E. Cummings,* F. W. Dupee and George Stade, eds. New York, 1969.
EH	Ernest Hemingway
EDP	Elizabeth Dos Passos
EDPC	Collection of Elizabeth Dos Passos
EW	Edmund Wilson
EWC	Collection of Edmund Wilson, Beinecke Library, Yale University
EWL	*Edmund Wilson: Letters on Literature and Politics, 1912–1972,* Elena Wilson, ed. New York, 1977.
EWTT	Edmund Wilson, *The Twenties,* ed. and with an introduction by Leon Edel. New York, 1975.
FSF	F. Scott Fitzgerald
GLC	Germaine Lucas-Championnière
GLCC	Collection of Germaine Lucas-Championnière
GM	Gerald Murphy
HBJ	Collection of Harcourt Brace Jovanovich
HDC	Collection of Honoria Donnelly, daughter of Gerald and Sara Murphy
HG	Horsley Gantt
JDP	John Dos Passos
JHL	John Howard Lawson
JHLC	Collection of John Howard Lawson, Morris Library, University of Southern Illinois at Carbondale
JRDP	John Randolph Dos Passos
KDP	Katharine Dos Passos
LASM	Lucy Addison Sprigg Madison
LDP	Lucy Hamlin Dos Passos

LSH   Lois Sprigg Hazell
MC   Malcolm Cowley
ML   Marion Lowndes
RH   Robert Hillyer
RM   Rumsey Marvin
RSM   R. Stewart Mitchell
SM   Sara Murphy
TL   Townsend Ludington
UVA   Collection of the papers of John Dos Passos, Alderman Library, University of
        Virginia, Charlottesville.

CHAPTER ONE

PAGE

2   "I want you . . . ": JRDP to Ida L. Pifer, April 24, 1912, UVA.
3   "You are sure . . . ": JRDP to Ida L. Pifer, June 13, 1902, UVA.
     Born February 9, 1854 . . . : Julia Duryea Sprigg Cameron to TL, Sept. 21, 1975.
4   "I dreamt Thee . . . ": 14 C, p. 5.
     Her sister-in-law . . . : LSH to TL, Oct. 13, 1975.
     "My dear Mother . . . ": James Madison to LASM, Feb. 13, 1885, UVA.
5   "I wonder in my heart . . . ": JRDP to LASM, Aug. 21, 1892, UVA.
6   "You cannot . . . ": UVA.
8   "A slim . . . ": From a statement about JRDP by J.I.C. Clarke, EDPC.
     Dos Passos remembered . . . : TBT, pp. 2–5.
     "Fought at Antietam . . . ": Howard Knott, "John Randolph Dos Passos," *Dictionary
     of American Biography,* Vol. III, New York, 1930, p. 388.
     But, "So far . . . ": TBT, p. 5.
9   He distrusted . . . : *The Inter-State Commerce Act: An Analysis of Its Provisions* (New
     York, 1887), p. xiii.
10   The Anti-Trust law, he argued . . . : *Commercial Trusts: The Growth and Rights of
     Aggregated Capital* (New York, 1901), p. 9.
     The same year . . . : William Lawrence, "The Relation of Wealth to Morals," *World's
     Work,* I (1901), pp. 286–292.
     "The American Beauty Rose . . . ": W. J. Ghent, *Our Benevolent Feudalism,* (New
     York, 1902), p. 29.
     He asserted . . . : *Commercial Trusts,* p. 89.
     "Individuals do suffer . . . ": *Commercial Trusts,* p. 94.
     To conclude . . . : *Commercial Trusts,* pp. 134–137.
12   John R. called . . . : *The Anglo-Saxon Century and the Unification of the English-
     Speaking People* (New York, 1903), p. xi.
     Never could he . . . : TBT, pp. 6–7.
     "Dear Ida . . . ": JRDP to Ida Pifer, undated, UVA.
13   But for all his concerns . . . : TBT, pp. 7, 3–4.
     Not surprisingly . . . : TBT, pp. 7, 10.
     He scorned . . . : LSH to TL, Oct. 13, 1975.

CHAPTER TWO

14 He felt like . . . . : CC, p. 26.

Although Dos Passos . . . : "Les Lauriers Sont Coupés," *Harvard Monthly*, 62 (April 1916), pp. 48–51.

19 "The glare of its huge staring eye . . . ": "Les Lauriers Sont Coupés," p. 49.

In the first Camera Eye sequence . . . : USA *(The 42nd Parallel)*, pp. 5–6.

21 When many years later . . . : TBT, p. 11.

The same scene appears . . . : CC, pp. 21–22.

John R. wanted . . . : TBT, p. 11.

22 Dos Passos remembered . . .: TBT, pp. 8–9.

When he arrived "home" . . . : LSH to TL, undated memoir about JDP.

23 "For every privilege . . . ": Quoted in Harold L. Tinker, "Memorial Address," *Choate Alumni Bulletin—Memorial Issue*, 29 (n.d.), p. 26.

24 "I hated boardingschool . . . ": TBT, p. 15.

He saw himself cut off . . . : USA *(The 42nd Parallel)*, p. 73.

"Was it the bar sinister . . . ": CC, p. 26.

"You sat . . . ": USA *(The 42nd Parallel)*, p. 77.

25 More than seven years later . . . : 14C, p. 220.

But boarding-school life . . . : TBT, p. 12.

By 1908–1909 Dos Passos . . . : 14C, p. 56. Information about JDP at Choate is from Choate School files.

26 When Dos Passos was away at Choate . . . : TBT, pp. 13–14.

27 "I am so thankful . . . ": LASM to JDP, Nov. 16, 1909, UVA.

"Your mother dictated . . . ": LASM to JDP, Jan. 31, 1910, UVA.

28 "Don't forget . . . ": JRDP to LASM, Dec. 11, 1910, UVA.

"I know him . . . ": JRDP to JDP, Jan. 25, 1910, UVA.

"I am very sorry to say . . . ": 14C, pp. 12–13.

29 Although he and his parents . . . : LSH, undated memoir about JDP.

30 Although it is not clear . . . : JRDP to JDP, Oct. 12, 1910, UVA.

When he returned to school . . . : 14C, pp. 13–14.

31 "I so wish . . . ": Diary, UVA.

32 George St. John took the occasion . . . : 14C, p. 15.

33 "Today I spent . . . ": 14C, p. 16.

CHAPTER THREE

34 "It's hard . . . ": TBT, p. 19.

John R's holdings . . . : Information about JRDP and Sandy Point: Mr. and Mrs. Fairfax Griffith, Mrs. Walter Griffith, interview with TL, May 12, 1976.

37 These leisurely trips . . . : TBT, pp. 19–20.

Once he was old enough . . . : 14C, p. 21.

38 (Footnote) James Madison remained . . . : Fairfax Griffith, interview with TL, May 12, 1976.

In a Camera Eye passage . . . : USA *(The 42nd Parallel)*, pp. 85–86.

Or another time . . . : USA *(The 42nd Parallel)*, pp. 119–120.

39   May 3 had been . . . : Wright, p. 10.
     The youth feels . . . : "July," *transatlantic review*, 2 (Sept. 1924), p. 155.
     As a kind of refrain during much of the story . . . : "July," p. 170.
40   Herf's dream of passion . . . : "July," pp. 178–179.
     He even repeated . . . : USA *(The 42nd Parallel)*, p. 215.
     Yet a third time . . . : CC, pp. 36–37.
41   So after passing . . . : TBT, p. 15.
     "The time is very short now . . . ": JDP to LASM, April 14, 1912, UVA.
     In his imperfect French . . . : JRDP to JDP, Dec. 1, 1911, UVA.
42   The invalided Lucy . . . : LASM to JDP, March 29, 1912, UVA.
     He could sound stuffy . . . : TBT, p. 16.
     "Nous sommes arrivés . . . ": 14C, p. 16.
43   When he wrote *The Best Times* . . . : TBT, p. 15.
     His concern . . . : 14C, p. 8.
44   He wrote that night . . . : Diary, UVA.
45   "My dear Mother . . . ": JDP to LASM, March 22, 1912, UVA.
     "The stream of sensation flows by . . .": 14C, p. 89.
46   "Have I the faculty . . . ": 14C, p. 107.
     "A double foreigner . . . ": CC, p. 26.
     "You ask me . . . ": 14C, pp. 19–20.
     In stilted prose . . . : 14C, pp. 17–18.
47   By May 5 . . . : JDP to LASM, May 5, 1912, UVA.

CHAPTER FOUR

50   On one occasion . . . : TBT, p. 17.
51   "It was a wise . . . ": JRDP to LASM, June 12, 1912, UVA.
     "Psychology as I said yesterday . . . ": JRDP to LASM, Aug. 23, 1912, UVA.
     "Our real happiness . . . ": JRDP to LASM, July 13, 1912, UVA.
53   "All sorts of strange characters . . .": *New Republic*, 86 (April 29, 1936), pp. 332–33.
54   Writing about Dos Passos . . . : MC, "Dos Passos: The Learned Poggius," *Southern
     Review*, 9 (Jan. 1977), p. 6.
55   One afternoon was spent . . . : JDP and JRDP to LASM, Sept. 21, 1912, UVA.
     On the morning of the twenty-second . . . : TBT, p. 22.
     Early in October . . . : 14C, pp. 20–21.
     Under the headline . . . : *Boston Evening Transcript* (Monday, April 28, 1913), p. 12.
56   "The Aesthetes . . . ": MC, *Exile's Return* (New York, 1959), p. 35.
     Dos Passos, who for a while . . . : TBT, pp. 23–25.
57   "No jarring note . . . ": "An Aesthete's Nightmare," *Harvard Monthly*, 60 (May 1915),
     pp. 77–78.
58   "Lay sermons . . . ": JRDP, UVA.
59   They visited . . . : 14C, pp. 25, 31.
     Thus in June . . . : Quoted with punctuation changes in TBT, p. 3.
60   His loneliness was . . . : TBT, p. 22.

Nevertheless, during these years . . . : Articles listed in unpublished *Writings of John Dos Passos, Sr.*, UVA.

His reaction . . . : Diary, UVA.

61 While feigning . . . : Information from Registrar's Office, Harvard University.

"Trains . . . ": UVA.

62 During the month . . . : Diary, UVA. Quoted in part in 14C, pp. 21–23.

64 Two months later . . . : Review of Louis Couperus, *Small Souls*, *Harvard Monthly*, 59 (Feb. 1915), p. 169.

CHAPTER FIVE

68 Dos Passos had reconciled himself . . . : 14C, pp. 24–25.

69 He jotted down . . . : 14C, p. 34.

70 As the novel ends . . . : SON, pp. 309–311.

A close friend, Dudley Poore . . . : DP, numerous interviews with TL.

71 "We sat up . . . ": Charles Norman, *E. E. Cummings: The Magic-Maker* (Indianapolis, 1972), p. 33.

72 "How do you write . . . ": Norman, *E. E. Cummings*, pp. 47–48; Samuel Eliot Morison, *Three Centuries of Harvard* (Cambridge, 1936), pp. 437–438.

73 Still, he wrote . . . : 14C, p. 25.

76 In the same issue . . . : Cuthbert Wright, "A Note on Pagan Morals," *Harvard Monthly*, 62 (March 1916), pp. 1–7; JDP, "Salvation Army," ibid., p. 12.

77 In his correspondence . . . : 14C, pp. 26–27.

He passed on . . . : JDP to RM, undated, UVA.

78 To widen his own experience . . . : 14C, p. 31.

But as close . . . : JDP to RM, undated, UVA.

He wrote that walking . . . : JDP to RM, Jan. 24, 1916, UVA.

Marvin was slow to answer . . . : 14C, pp. 32–33.

79 Dos Passos explained . . . : 14C, pp. 34–35.

80 Five weeks later . . . : 14C, pp. 36–38.

During the exam period . . . : 14C, pp. 39–40.

81 During these last days . . . : 14C, p. 37.

Once his exams were over . . . : 14C, p. 42.

82 The Cape Codders were . . . : JDP to RM, undated, UVA.

83 The next day he walked . . . : JDP to RM, undated, UVA.

An inquisitive visitor . . . : KDP and Edith Shay, *Down Cape Cod*, rev. ed. (New York, 1947), p. 187.

Dos Passos found . . . : JDP to RM, undated, UVA.

He scoffed to Marvin . . . : 14C, pp. 40–41.

CHAPTER SIX

86 Soon after, Dos Passos . . . : JDP to RM, undated, UVA.

She was an occultist, . . . : 14C, p. 43.

"Car il me faut . . . ": JDP to RM, undated, UVA.

On July 5 . . . : 14C, p. 43.

87 By mid-July . . . : JDP to DP, July 15, 1916, DPC.

88 So he implored . . . : 14C, p. 44.
    "This is a clam . . . ": JDP to DP, Aug. 8, 1916, DPC.
    He described McComb . . . : TBT, p. 25.

89 "The poor must learn . . .": AM, "Art and Industry," *Harvard Monthly*, 62 (June 1916), pp. 122–123.
    "No one had . . . ": JDP to AM, Aug. 7, 1916, AAALC. Quoted in part in TBT, p. 25.
    Chafing at his isolation . . . : 14C, pp. 45–46.

90 Poore took the comments to heart, revised . . . : JDP to DP, Aug. 26, 1916, DPC.
    "We want a new Enlightenment—new Byrons . . . ": JDP to AM, Aug. 26, 1916, AAALC. Quoted in part in TBT, p. 25.
    He told Poore . . . : JDP to DP, Sept. 15, 1916, DPC.

91 He read even more . . . : JDP to RM, Sept. 20, 1916, UVA.
    In another letter . . . : 14C, p. 47.
    Dudley Poore wrote . . . : DP to JDP, Sept. 20, 1916, UVA.
    Dos Passos rejoined . . . : JDP to DP, undated, DPC.

92 Marvin was told . . . : 14C, p. 48.
    APPEARING BACK BAY . . . : JDP to DP, Sept. 29, 1916, DPC.
    Dos Passos carped . . . : JDP to AM, undated, AAALC. Quoted in part in TBT, p. 26.

93 He wrote Marvin . . . : JDP to RM, undated, UVA.
    Dos Passos's "sea of modern life" was akin . . . : *America's Coming of Age* (New York, 1958), p. 78.
    He tried to impart . . . : JDP to RM, Oct. 14, 1916, UVA.
    That evening John R . . . : JRDP to Mrs. Harris, undated, UVA.

CHAPTER SEVEN

95 In a letter of thanks . . . ; JDP to Mrs. Marvin, undated, UVA.
    Although the shadow . . . : 14C, pp. 49–50.
    "I always feel . . ." : JDP to DP, Oct. 30, 1916, DPC.

96 "Yah Dudley . . . ": JDP to DP, Oct. 30, 1916, DPC.

97 He wrote Marvin . . . : 14C, pp. 50–51.
    In one letter . . . : JDP to DP, Oct. 30, 1916, DPC.

98 As if to illustrate . . . : JDP to DP, Oct. 30, 1916, DPC.
    The carved chair, he decided, was . . . : JDP to DP, Nov. 18, 1916, DPC.

99 His room . . . : 14C, p. 52.
    The mountains . . . : Diary, UVA.
    "A wonderful sight . . . ": JDP to DP, Nov. 18, 1916, DPC.
    On this trip . . . : 14C, pp. 55–56.

100 All the hiking . . . : 14C, pp. 51–52.
     "I have so much to tell . . . ": 14C, pp. 52–53.

101 The night he returned . . . : Diary, UVA.

When Marvin wrote . . . : 14C, pp. 53–54.

102 He became friends . . . : TBT, pp. 30–33.

By the middle of November . . . : JDP to AM, Nov. 16, 1916, AAALC.

Within every American, said Dos Passos . . . : JDP to AM, Nov. 16, 1916, AAALC.

103 As he huddled in his room . . . : 14C, pp. 56–60.

105 In mid-December . . . : 14C, pp. 60–61.

106 A gypsy strummed . . . : RRA, pp. 14–16.

He wrote Marvin later . . . : 14C, pp. 63–64; TBT, pp. 33–34.

107 Just before the New Year . . . : JDP to RM, Dec. 30, 1916, UVA.

The city, he wrote . . . : JDP to AM, Jan. 4, 1917, AAALC.

108 As he was about to leave Denia . . . : JDP to RM, Jan. 9, 1917, UVA.

109 The next morning . . . : 14C, pp. 64–65.

As he rested . . . : JDP to DP, Jan. 11, 1917, DPC.

CHAPTER EIGHT

115 Death followed immediately . . . : TBT, p. 40. Some of the quotations from JRDP's letters at UVA are found in TBT, pp. 29–40.

His plans . . . : 14C, p. 66.

Few ships were sailing . . . : 14C, pp. 66–68.

116 Then he settled in with his Aunt Mamie . . . : 14C, p. 69.

"It is less than a month ago . . .": George St. John to JDP, undated, Choate School files.

117 A year before his death . . . : UVA.

He told Dudley Poore on May 8 . . . : JDP to DP, May 8, 1917, DPC.

As spring approached . . . : 14C, p. 69.

Correspondence between Dos Passos, Gomme . . . : For a full discussion of the publication history of *Eight Harvard Poets*, see Norman, *E. E. Cummings*, pp. 50–64.

Dos Passos, now more eager . . . : 14C, pp. 70–71.

118 The spirit of Greenwich Village life . . . : *The Day in Bohemia or, Life Among the Artists* (New York, 1913), pp. 11, 14. For much of my information about New York I am indebted to Allen Churchill, *The Improper Bohemians* (New York, 1959); and to Susan Edmiston and Linda D. Cirino, *Literary New York* (Boston, 1976).

120 In April he assailed . . . : JDP to RM, April 22, 1917, UVA.

Early in May . . . : 14C, p. 72.

121 Dos Passos should have been pleased . . . : "Young Spain," *Seven Arts*, 2 (Aug. 1917), pp. 476–477.

122 He wrote Marvin . . . : 14C, pp. 73–75.

The Brevoort . . . : Edmiston and Cirino, *Literary New York*, pp. 60–61.

"We were the outer circle . . .": 14C, p. 75.

In an only slightly less . . . : JDP to AM, these sections quoted in Daniel Aaron, *Writers on the Left* (New York, 1961), pp. 358–359.

123 On June 20 . . . : JDP to AM, these sections quoted in the introduction to OMI, pp. 6–7; 14C, pp. 75–76.

CHAPTER NINE

124 They kept singing . . . : 14C, p. 85.

125 The numbers might even be higher . . . : Alistair Horne, *The Price of Glory: Verdun 1916* (New York, 1963), pp. 327–328.
It reads in part . . . : 14C, p. 86.

126 There was only . . . : JDP to AM, June 28, 1917, AAALC.

127 Dos Passos, speaking the best French . . . : TBT, p. 48.
At Poitiers . . . : 14C, p. 87.
The next morning . . . : TBT, pp. 49–50.
On July 31 . . . : 14C, p. 89.
Earlier in the month . . . : JDP to AM, July 20, 1917, AAALC.

128 When he recalled . . . : 14C, p. 89.
"It's a perfectly . . . ": JDP to DP, July 9, 1917, DPC.
"One swears . . . ": TBT, p. 50.
Once when he . . . : JDP to DP, undated, DPC.
While at Sandricourt . . . : RSM to JDP, June 27, 1917, UVA.

129 At Châlons . . . : 14C, p. 90.
While his unit . . . : JDP to AM, July 31, 1917, AAALC.
What he scribbled . . . : JDP to DP, July 31, 1917, DPC.

130 They disgusted him now . . . : 14C, pp. 89–91.

131 August 2 . . . : OMI, pp. 10–11.
Ideas for the new fiction . . . : OMI, pp. 10–16.

132 He wrote them out in letters . . . : 14C, p. 97.

133 While he was still . . . : OMI, pp. 16–18.

134 The Verdun that . . . : Horne, *The Price of Glory*, pp. 173–174; 186–187; 240.
Apprehensive about . . . : 14C, p. 91.
That same day . . . : JDP to DP, Aug. 15, 1917, DPC.

135 In a typical *abri* . . . : Edward Weeks, *My Green Age* (Boston, 1973), p. 53.
Huddled in the *abri* . . . : 14C, p. 92; TBT, pp. 53–54.
He wrote Poore . . . : JDP to DP, Aug. 22 and 23, 1917, DPC.
"It's queer how . . .": 14C, pp. 91–93.

136 He wrote Poore that the ambulance . . . : JDP to DP, undated, DPC.
During the offensive . . . : 14C, pp. 93–96.

137 Three days later . . . : 14C, pp. 96–98.

138 Having been under fire . . . : JDP to DP, Sept. 1 and 6, 1917, DPC.
From Remicourt . . . : 14C, p. 99; OMI, pp. 24–25; TBT, pp. 55–56.

CHAPTER TEN

139 In the meantime . . . : 14C, p. 99; OMI, pp. 27–28.
Dos Passos found the time . . . : JDP to DP, Sept. 14 and 30, 1917, DPC.

140 When he was first there . . . : 14C, p. 100.
Van den Arend often went . . . : TBT, p. 57.
For the most part . . . : 14C, p. 102.

141   One evening . . . : CC, pp. 209–212.
      The war had made him . . . : 14C, p. 134.
      "It was a time of sudden . . . ": TBT, pp. 57–58.
142   "In that part . . . ": 14C, pp. 102–105; JDP to DP, Nov. 29, 1917, DPC; *The Best Times*, p. 59.
143   That evening Lawson . . . : 14C, pp. 106–107.
144   If in Paris . . . : 14C, pp. 103, 107–108.
      He grew excited by the writings . . . : JDP, "What Makes a Novelist," *National Review*, 20 (Jan. 16, 1968), p. 29.
145   "Futurism," wrote the art critic . . . : "The Art World: Futurism et Seq.," *New Yorker* (Dec. 17, 1973), p. 103.
      Stuck in Milan . . . : JDP to DP, Dec. 16, 1917, DPC.
      Four days later . . . : 14C, pp. 109–110.
146   Their quarters were . . . : 14C, pp. 112–113.
      "The Italian Government . . . ": TBT, p. 62.
      As 1917 drew . . . : 14C, pp. 114–115.
147   (Footnote) Fairbanks . . . : Sydney Fairbanks to TL, June 23, 1975.
      With time heavy . . . : 14C, pp. 118–121.
148   The next day . . . : 14C, pp. 124–125.
149   Instead he ended . . . : PC, p. 77.
      "Venice achieved . . . ": 14C, pp. 125–127.
150   The ambulance runs . . . : 14C, pp. 132–135. Sydney Fairbanks identified the German DP referred to as "Heyne" (14C, p. 135), interview with TL, June 13, 1975.
151   In March rumors . . . : Diary, UVA.
      "We get spurts . . . ": 14C, p. 145.
152   "One stands shivering . . . ": 14C, pp. 137, 141.
      "I'll say she . . .": Sydney Fairbanks, interview with TL, June 13, 1975.
      Their humor extended . . . : 14C, pp. 143–149.
153   Several nights later . . . : 14C, p. 153.
154   "The hounds are on the scent . . . ": Diary, UVA.
      Dos Passos recalled . . . : TBT, p. 65.
      All of them headed south to Naples . . . : 14C, p. 162.
155   They arrived late in the afternoon . . . : 14C, p. 163.
      The meal . . . : 14C, p. 166.
      The next morning . . . : 14C, pp. 163, 165–166.
      The afternoon walk . . . : 14C, pp. 163–164; DP interviews with TL.
156   Cummings, released from . . . : EECL, pp. 45–46.
157   "Of course people . . . ": 14C, pp. 171–172.
      The world had become . . . : 14C, p. 173.
      By mid-April . . . : 14C, pp. 177–178.
158   "I suddenly became . . . ": 14C, pp. 179–180.
      What Dos Passos wrote Giner . . . : 14C, pp. 150–153.
159   (Footnote) When Dos Passos . . . : JHL interview with TL, Oct. 17, 1974.
      He continued to evacuate wounded . . . : 14C, pp. 182–184.

Fairbanks remembered the meeting . . . : Sydney Fairbanks, interview with TL, June 13, 1975.

(Footnote) That this meeting . . . : TBT, p. 141; Baker, pp. 40–43.

160   At Vicenza, the others left . . . : 14C, pp. 187–188.

When Dos Passos reached Rome . . . : TBT, pp. 68–69; 14C, p. 188.

161   When Marvin made . . . : 14C, p. 189.

Parisians died, but . . . : TBT, p. 69.

162   In the summer of 1918 . . . : Kate Drain Lawson, interview with TL, Oct. 16, 1974.

(Footnote) Kate Drain soon fell in love . . . : DP, interview with TL, April 4, 1979; Kate Drain Lawson, interview with TL, October 16, 1974.

Dos Passos took time . . . : 14C, p. 192.

At the same time . . . : 14C, p. 193.

163   He particularly remembered a night . . . : TBT, p. 70.

Writing Marvin a short time later . . . : 14C, p. 193.

In August he traveled . . . : 14C, pp. 196–197.

Amused by some of the people . . . : TBT, p. 71; OMI, pp. 31–33.

164   Well intentioned though St. John was . . . : George St. John to JDP, Aug. 14, 1918, Choate School files.

CHAPTER ELEVEN

165   The incongruity between Bay Head . . . : 14C, p. 207.

Sitting on the beach . . . : Diary, UVA.

166   "In a hall on Olympus . . . ": PC, p. 106.

Scott, Dos Passos recalled, was . . . : TBT, p. 72.

After talking with him . . . : 14C, p. 208.

167   The incidents he listed . . . : Diary, UVA. See also 14C, pp. 209–211, and Chapter 7 of OMI, pp. 127–150; also, Chapters 8, 9, 10, and 11, pp. 151–174.

Marvin recalled . . . : RM, interview with TL, June 3, 1971.

A short time later . . . : Diary, UVA.

169   In the published novel the lines remained . . . : OMI, p. 166.

The draft board . . . : TBT, pp. 71–72; 14C, p. 211.

Queen Ennui seized him . . . : 14C, p. 215.

The first Sunday . . . : 14C, p. 212.

170   "You can't imagine . . . ": 14C, p. 213–217.

He wrote Arthur McComb . . . : TBT, p. 73.

Every letter to his friends . . . : 14C, p. 224.

He was nevertheless absorbing impressions [and material about Camp Crane, Camp Merritt, and voyage on Cedric] . . . : 14C, pp. 219–232.

173   He caught the flu also . . . : 14C, p. 232; TBT, p. 79.

From among "crumbling cusps" . . . : 14C, p. 235.

He welcomed work . . . : 14C, pp. 234–237.

174   Dos Passos claimed . . . : TBT, p. 75.

With little work to do . . . : 14C, pp. 237–239.

175   Before he was free . . . : JDP to RM, undated, UVA; 14C, p. 244.

In fact, as soon as he arrived . . . : 14C, p. 244.

Paris that spring . . . : JDP, Foreword to Blaise Cendrars, *Panama or the Adventures of My Seven Uncles* (New York, 1931), p. vii; JDP, "What Makes a Novelist," p. 30.

176   In a Camera Eye section . . . : USA *(Nineteen Nineteen)*, pp. 345–346.

When Rumsey Marvin dared . . . : JDP to RM, undated, UVA.

177   A friend of Lawson's . . . : JDP to DP, April 6, 1919, DPC.

Much later . . . : TBT, p. 77.

"Part Two of Fibbie . . . ": JDP to DP, April 29, 1919 DPC; 14C, p. 251.

178   On one rainy morning . . . : JDP to RM, April 10, 1919, UVA.

So he continued . . . : 14C, p. 247; JDP to RM, May 4, 1919, UVA.

179   "Have written three chapters . . . ": JDP to DP, May 21, 1919, DPC.

In what Dos Passos later labeled . . . : UVA.

180   Around the time . . . : 14C, pp. 253–254.

"I've been for the second time . . . ": JDP to DP, May 21, 1919, DPC.

"Pelleas for the third time . . . ": JDP to DP, undated, DPC.

She was, she recalled, *fou* . . . : GLC, interview with TL, June 9, 1974.

181   After hearing a concert . . . : JDP to GLC, June 18, 1919, GLCC.

He was a little in love . . . : For a fictionalized description of his relationship with GLC, see CC, pp. 348–351.

The army had difficulty . . . : JDP to RM, July 17–22, 1919, UVA.

Free at last . . . : TBT, p. 78; 14C, p. 254.

CHAPTER TWELVE

182   In London Dos Passos hoped to confirm . . . : TBT, p. 77.

He talked about himself . . . : JDP to RM, undated, UVA.

183   "My desires . . . ": 14C, p. 259; Diary, UVA.

London seemed . . . : JDP to RM, July 25, 1919, UVA.

His contemplative mood . . . : 14C, p. 257.

184   As Dos Passos recounted . . . : TBT, p. 79.

Years later . . . : TBT, p. 81.

What filled his mind . . . : Diary, UVA.

185   "To lose the habit . . . ": 14C, p. 259.

186   Early in August . . . : Reader's report, Aug. 8, 1919, Allen and Unwin files.

He telegraphed the publishers . . . : 14C, p. 261.

"*I wonder* . . . ": PC, pp. 123–124.

187   The two men traveled . . . : TBT, p. 80; RRA, p. 146.

To Germaine Lucas-Championnière . . . : JDP to GLC, Sept. 1, 1919, GLCC.

Early one evening . . . : DP, interviews with TL.

188   On his way south . . . : Diary, UVA.

In the province of Málaga . . . : 14C, p. 260.

Set behind a garden . . . : Diary, UVA.

So to the amusement . . . : DP, interviews with TL.

189   When late in September . . . : RRA, pp. 104–114.

In Elvas . . . : Diary, UVA.

"How can you stay . . .": 14C, p. 264.

"The damned army . . . ": Diary, UVA.

190 For several weeks . . . : DP, interviews with TL.

In mid-October . . . : 14C, pp. 265–266.

191 Two and a half months later . . . : 14C, p. 276.

They set themselves up . . . : 14C, p. 270.

"Some music exists . . .": JDP to GLC, Dec. 16, 1919, GLCC.

He and McComb argued . . . : 14C, p. 270.

192 When Allen and Unwin . . . : 14C, p. 284.

He deleted one offending passage . . . : 14C, pp. 288–289.

193 "Delectable, preposterous . . . ": 14C, p. 277.

The January issue, however . . . : 14C, pp. 278–281.

194 His advice to Mitchell . . . : JDP to GLC, March 16, 1920, GLCC.

"At the topmost tower . . . ": 14C, p. 288.

It was a gateway to the east . . . : 14C, pp. 290–291.

He thought *Three Soldiers* . . . : Reader's report, June 12, 1920, Allen and Unwin files.

195 And then told him . . . : Allen and Unwin to JDP, June 21, 1920, Allen and Unwin files.

"Seven Times" was essentially . . . : Reader's report, June 27, 1920, Allen and Unwin files.

Despite their reader's enthusiasms . . . : Allen and Unwin to JDP, July 12, 1920, Allen and Unwin files.

"Rainy day—leaden sky . . . ": JDP to GLC, June 17, 1920, GLCC.

196 Life there no longer . . . : JDP to GLC, July 27, 1920, GLCC.

CHAPTER THIRTEEN

200 From the moment . . . : 14C, p. 299.

"New York—after all . . . ": JDP to GLC, Sept. 23, 1920, GLCC.

201 One such theater experience . . . : 14C, p. 301.

November 1 he went . . . : 14C, p. 304.

To add to his pleasure . . . : TBT, p. 82.

202 "Ball bearings bolts and hinges . . . ": Diary, UVA.

Late in the afternoon . . . : TBT, pp. 83–84.

"There's no escaping drinks . . . ": 14C, p. 305; JDP to GLC, Nov. 20, 1920, GLCC.

203 He wrote Hillyer . . . : 14C, pp. 302, 307–308.

She remembered . . . : Elaine (Orr) MacDermot, interview with TL, March 7, 1972.

204 "I have just finished . . . ": JDP to GLC, Dec. 6, 1920, GLCC.

Three weeks later . . . : JDP to GLC, Dec. 27, 1920, GLCC.

Dos Passos insisted . . . : 14C, p. 307.

205 They had a relaxed . . . : TBT, p. 88.

"Such wearing of white mantillas . . . ": 14C, p. 311.

Cummings, also enthusiastic . . . : EECL, pp. 74–78.

To Edmund Wilson, Cummings related . . . : EWTT, p. 207.

206   From there they ascended . . . : EECL, pp. 77–78.
       In May he mailed off . . . : 14C, p. 310.
       In Paris that spring . . . : TBT, p. 90.
207   It was a "fine jolly place" . . . : 14C, p. 311.
       Adelaide had paid . . . : Adelaide Lawson Gaylor, interview with TL, Aug. 8, 1974.
       If *Three Soldiers* sold well . . . : 14C, p. 314.
       Before he left Venice . . . : OE, p. 5.
       Dos Passos told Jack Lawson . . . : 14C, p. 315.
       When the American naval commander . . . : TBT, pp. 91–92.
208   August 7 he sat aboard . . . : 14C, pp. 316–317.
       The trip to Tiflis . . . : OE, pp. 38–42.
       He had, he said . . . : 14C, p. 321.
       At Tiflis the N.E.R. party . . . : OE, p. 42; TBT, p. 93.
209   When Dos Passos spoke . . . : OE, pp. 45–46.
       Before he left Tiflis . . . : TBT, p. 94.
       The sights along the way . . . : JDP to AM, quoted in part in Melvin Landsberg, *Dos Passos' Path to U.S.A.* (Boulder, 1972), p. 95.
       Dr. Tabataba procured their "phaeton" . . . : TBT, p. 98.
210   That city, he found . . . : 14C, p. 320.
       He was able to wander . . . : 14C, pp. 322, 320.
       He was, he decided, . . . : 14C, pp. 319–320.
       An overnight train ride joggled him [and details of the desert crossing] . . . : TBT, pp. 106–125; OE, pp. 114–150.

CHAPTER FOURTEEN

213   "You are as famous as Wrigley's . . . ": JHL to JDP, Dec. 7, 1921, UVA.
       Heywood Brown . . . : "A Group of Books Worth Reading," *Bookman,* 54 (Dec. 1921), p. 393.
214   Seated in the luxurious Hotel Bassoul . . . : 14C, pp. 344–346.
       He saw much of Cummings . . . : EECL, pp. 82–83.
215   "I've never had . . . ": JDP to GLC, Feb. 27, 1922, GLCC.
       A month later Cummings thanked . . . : EEC to JDP, March 26, 1922, Houghton Library, Harvard University.
       TO WHOM IT MAY CONCERN . . . : TBT, p. 89.
216   "New York too hectic . . . ": JDP to RM, March 13, 1922, UVA; 14C, p. 349.
       "We are passing by New Haven . . . ": JDP to GLC, undated, GLCC.
       He quickly settled . . . : TBT, pp. 127, 139.
       By late in May . . . : EWL, p. 85.
       "Je suis très bien . . . ": JDP to GLC, May 15, 1922, GLCC.
217   Dudley Poore recalled that Dos Passos . . . : DP, interviews with TL.
       Trying to write . . . : 14C, pp. 305–306.
218   Marvin delighted in Dos Passos's amusement . . . : RM, interview with TL, June 3, 1971.

The wedding, at least . . . : EWL, p. 87.

His friend Wilson, later characterizing . . . : EW, *I Thought of Daisy* (New York, 1967), pp. 101, 73.

Later in the twenties . . . : EWTT, p. 323.

219   Dos Passos was not quite so detached . . . : EWTT, p. 360.

He recalled them "as big-bodied and dressed" . . . : Matthew Josephson, *Life Among the Surrealists* (New York, 1962), p. 44.

Such a person was Esther Andrews . . . : TBT, pp. 135–136.

Dos Passos "was rather" . . . : EW, *I Thought*, p. 100.

220   The little town, he wrote, owned . . . : TBT, p. 137.

(Footnote) One of the Dudley sisters . . .: Correspondence; Caroline Dudley to JDP, UVA.

221   He had met them before . . . : TBT, pp. 127–130.

222   His eyes, he informed Germaine Lucas-Championnière . . . : JDP to GLC, Oct. 13, 1922, GLCC.

"Talk about stale flat and . . . ": JDP to AM, undated, AAALC.

Never, he asserted, had he tried . . . : JDP to AM, Oct. 23, 1922, AAALC.

"Moderately luminous . . . ": 14C, p. 352.

"Lost articles . . . ": 14C, pp. 353–354.

223   "At certain times styles and methods . . . ": 14C, p. 637.

Now he was completing it . . . : JDP to AM, undated, AAALC.

Both these interests emerged . . . : Foreword to JHL. *Roger Bloomer* (New York, 1923), pp. v-viii.

224   "As soon as everything is sufficiently . . . ": JDP to AM, undated, AAALC.

"He was a dandified dresser . . .": TBT, p. 145.

He hiked the fifteen or twenty . . . : For the information about JDP's visit to Plessis, I am indebted to Pierre Lostanlen, a friend of Germaine Lucas-Championnière, with whom I corresponded until his death in 1977.

225   Dos Passos and Murphy had lunch . . . : TBT, p. 146.

"I'm not sure . . . ": GM to JDP, Dec. 10, 1959, UVA.

The premiere was to be . . . : Calvin Tomkins, *Living Well Is the Best Revenge* (New York, 1972), pp. 33–36.

226   "I cultivated the pose of sidewalk . . . ": TBT, pp. 146–147.

That spring, in fact . . . : William Rubin, *The Paintings of Gerald Murphy*, Catalogue of the Museum of Modern Art (New York, 1977), p. 28. For information about *Within the Quota*, see also Tomkins, pp. 40–41.

227   "I can understand that . . . ": Tomkins, p. 34.

Sometime in early July the three . . . : Norman, *E. E. Cummings*, pp. 180–181; EECL, p. 74.

"The tale," observed Dos Passos, "lost nothing . . . ": TBT, p. 133.

228   The small town, he wrote Saxton, was "one of . . . ": 14C, p. 355.

He asked Saxton to mail Scott Fitzgerald . . . : Andrew Turnbull, ed., *The Letters of F. Scott Fitzgerald* (New York, 1963), p. 196.

"A novel," he wrote . . . : JDP to GLC, undated, GLCC.

Dos Passos resumed his . . . : JDP to GLC, undated, GLCC.

229　The early notes . . . : Notebooks, UVA.

"Jesus I am broke . . . ": JDP to RM, undated, UVA.

He tried to alleviate . . . : 14C, p. 355.

230　He took a room . . . : 14C, pp. 356–357.

Dos Passos also saw something of Sherwood Anderson . . . : 14C, p. 636.

The levees along the Mississippi were good . . . : 14C, p. 357.

231　He made his way north . . . : JDP to GLC, April 3, 1924, GLCC.

Subsequently, he enjoyed the train ride . . . : JDP to GLC, April 23, 1924, GLCC.

She often stayed . . . : Crystal Ross Dabney, interview with TL, May 11, 1976.

232　"In those days," remarked Dos Passos . . . : TBT, pp. 142–145.

Dos Passos and Crystal Ross . . . : Crystal Ross Dabney, interview with TL, May 11, 1976.

233　"I found myself . . . ": 14C, p. 358.

"It was fun and we ate well . . . ": TBT, pp. 154–156. See in addition Baker, pp. 128–130; and Robert McAlmon and Kay Boyle, *Being Geniuses Together: 1920–1930* (New York, 1968), pp. 273–277.

234　Finding an inn still open, they took . . . : TBT, pp. 156–157; McAlmon and Boyle, *Geniuses*, pp. 277–279.

"Working in a red plush room . . . ": 14C, p. 358; for accounts of Antibes, see TBT, pp. 148–150; Tomkins, *Living*, pp. 39–44; and Nancy Milford, *Zelda: A Biography* (New York, 1970), pp. 122–125.

CHAPTER FIFTEEN

236　"I'm living in extreme calm . . . ": JDP to RM, Oct. 27, 1924, UVA.

He so testified, whereupon the judge . . . : Kate Drain Lawson, interview with TL, Oct. 16, 1974.

About it Lawson wrote . . . : JHL, *Processional: A Jazz Symphony of American Life in Four Acts* (New York, 1925), pp. v, vii-viii.

237　The "futuristic settings . . . ": "A Tall Feather for the Cap of Harvard Players," *Boston Evening Transcript*, May 13, 1925, section 1, p. 10.

To understand themselves in the context . . . : *Vanity Fair*, 24 (May 1925), pp. 64, 114.

Dos Passos's interest in the *New Masses* . . . : TBT, p. 165.

"Just received . . . ": 14C, p. 338.

238　He admired her "unexpected combinations of things . . . ": MS entitled "Pictures to Look At: A Manhattan Primitive," UVA.

During the early months of 1925 he labored . . . : 14C, p. 360.

In Provincetown Dos Passos secluded . . . : JDP to RM, undated, UVA.

He would return to Columbia Heights, . . . : *The Letters of Hart Crane, 1916–1932*. Ed. Brom Weber (Berkeley, 1965), p. 213; "The Art of Fiction XLIV," *Paris Review*, no. 46 (Spring, 1969), p. 164.

239　"I never understood exactly why people . . . ": 14C, p. 364.

Hemingway could not believe this, remembering . . . : EH to JDP, April 22, 1925, UVA.

240　Dos Passos was disgusted . . . : 14C, p. 361.

The Murphys had acquired . . . : TBT, pp. 150–151.

Now it was . . . : 14C, pp. 362–363.

241   With that mailed to the United States . . . : EH to his parents, Sept. 25, 1925, Lot 151, Sotheby Parke Bernet catalogue, *Important Modern First Editions*, auction of March 29, 1977; Baker, p. 160.

Ernest did not have enough money . . . : Baker, p. 158.

Soon, he had written enough . . . : TBT, pp. 157–158; Baker, pp. 158–160; Scott Donaldson, *By Force of Will: The Life and Art of Ernest Hemingway* (New York, 1977), pp. 38–41; Fitzgerald, *Letters*, p. 195.

"Wasn't Dos Passos' book astonishly good? . . . ": Fitzgerald, *Letters*, p. 196.

The reviewer for the *New York Times* . . . : *New York Times*, Nov. 29, 1925, p. 5; *Literary Review*, Nov. 28, 1925, p. 5.

242   But most pleasing of all . . . : *Saturday Review of Literature*, 2 (Dec. 5, 1925), p. 361.

"A little halfdeserted town . . . ": JDP to Eugene Saxton, Dec. 25, 1925, Houghton Library, Harvard University.

He complained of . . . : TBT, p. 162.

243   The food, drink, and general festival . . . : TBT, pp. 158–159; Baker, p. 166.

He thought *The Moon Is a Gong* "more interesting . . . ": *New Republic*, 46 (March 31, 1926), p. 174; for a full discussion of *The Moon* and of the New Playwrights Theatre, see George A. Knox and Herbert M. Stahl, *Dos Passos and "The Revolting Playwrights," Essays and Studies on American Language and Literature*, 15, Uppsala and Copenhagen, 1964.

244   "The idea as I remember was to revive . . . ": 14C, p. 619.

Many years later, responding to John P. Diggins . . . : JDP to John P. Diggins, April 3, 1966, UVA.

"As mechanical power grows . . . ": "The New Masses I'd Like," *New Masses*, 1 (June 1926), p. 20.

245   Gold's thrust at Dos Passos . . . : "Let It Be Really New!" *New Masses*, 1 (June 1926), pp. 20, 26.

Gold's review of *Manhattan Transfer* . . . : "A Barbaric Poem of New York," *New Masses*, 1 (Aug. 1926), pp. 25–26.

"I dunno," answers Jimmy, "pretty far . . . ": MT, p. 404.

As if to show . . . : "300 N.Y. Agitators Reach Passaic," *New Masses*, 1 (June 1926), p. 8. For an account of the Passaic strike, see Landsberg, *Dos Passos' Path to U.S.A.*, pp. 127–131.

246   He met Aldino Felicani . . . : TBT, pp. 166–168; "The Pit and the Pendulum," *New Masses*, 1 (Aug. 1926), pp. 10–11, 30; FC, pp. 58–71.

He and Rumsey Marvin had finally . . . : 14C, pp. 340–341.

247   After a morning's writing he could swim . . . : JDP to GLC, July 16, 1926, GLCC.

Given recalled . . . : Eben Given, interview with TL, July 18, 1974.

248   If this generation . . . : "A Lost Generation," *New Masses*, 2 (Dec. 1926), p. 26.

Referring to the months before the execution . . . : TBT, p. 169.

"Harried heckled and harassed by various . . . ": 14C, p. 364.

He covered nearly twenty-five miles . . . : TBT, pp. 169–170; 14C, p. 364.

249   "A grey sprawling redbrick . . . ": 14C, p. 365.

But he had enjoyed himself there . . . : JDP to EW, Dec. 9, 1926, EWC.

CHAPTER SIXTEEN

250 Also, there were several people to whom . . . : JDP to Carleton Beals, Dec. 13, 1926, Collection of Carleton Beals.

"Sunshine and beer and cigarettes and flowers . . . ": JDP to RSM, Dec. 15, 1926, Boston Athenaeum.

"One eats spicy meals . . . ": JDP to GLC, Dec. 30, 1926, GLCC.

251 The huge murals of Diego Rivera . . . : "Paint the Revolution!" *New Masses*, 2 (March 1927), p. 15; TBT, pp. 170–171.

An American whose tales . . . : TBT, p. 170; Gladwin Bland to JDP, Aug. 3, 1932, UVA; Carleton Beals to TL, July 10, 1974.

252 Beals was sometimes amused . . . : Carleton Beals, *Glass Houses: Ten Years of Free Lancing* (Philadelphia, 1938), pp. 245–249; Carleton Beals to TL, Feb. 24, 1974.

"Everything," he wrote Rumsey Marvin . . . : 14C, pp. 365–366.

253 "When the Carranzistas killed Zapata . . . ": "Zapata's Ghost Walks," *New Masses*, 3 (Sept. 1927), p. 12.

"Which side are you on, . . . ": "Relief Map of Mexico," *New Masses*, 2 (April 1927), p. 24.

He could repeatedly join political . . . : Joseph Freeman, *An American Testament* (New York, 1936), pp. 372–373.

"The cardinal impulse . . . ": John Carter, *Man Is War* (Indianapolis, 1926), pp. 2–6; 8–12.

254 "Until the end of time . . . ": Carter, p. 351.

But Mexico diverted him . . . : 14C, p. 366.

Ernest answered in mid-February . . . : EH to JDP, Feb. 16, 1927, UVA.

255 He obliged Hemingway by writing . . . : 14C, p. 368.

Hinting to Robert Hillyer . . . : JDP to RH, March 27, 1927, UVA.

Cummings, who was amused . . . : EWTT, pp. 205, 536.

In April 1927, he wrote . . . : 14C, p. 369.

256 Dos Passos's designing included sets . . . : Knox and Stahl, pp. 114, 121.

These he described . . . : "Toward a Revolutionary Theatre," *New Masses*, 3 (Dec. 1927), p. 20.

Differences in taste and politics aside, . . . : "They Want Ritzy Art," *New Masses*, 4 (June 1928), p. 8.

Even after the last staging—his own . . . : "Did the New Playwrights Theatre Fail?" *New Masses*, 5 (Aug. 1929), p. 13.

That, however, was in 1929; in the spring of 1927 . . . : "the Art of Fiction XLIV," p. 164.

On his mind . . . : "The Art of Fiction XLIV," pp. 162–163.

The series . . . : "What Makes a Novelist," p. 31.

257 "A long narrative . . . ": "Introductory Note," UVA. Published in the Modern Library edition of *The 42nd Parallel* (New York, 1937), pp. vii-ix.

"The only excuse . . . ": "Statement of Belief," *Bookman*, 68 (Sept. 1924), p. 26.

"Songs and slogans, political aspirations . . . ": "What Makes a Novelist," *National Review*, p. 31.

As he set about the task . . . : Notebooks, UVA.

260 Such friendly reviewers as Paxton Hibben— . . . : "Letter to John Dos Passos," *New Masses*, 3 (June 1927), p. 28.

From Mount Sinai, where he was again . . . : JDP to GLC, May 10, 1927, GLCC.

261   He immediately wrote . . . : *Nation*, 125 (Aug. 24, 1927), p. 176.

The marchers were diverse, including . . . : Michael Gold, "Lynchers in Frockcoats," *New Masses*, 3 (Sept. 1927), p. 6.

"You cant imagine how queerly your wire . . . ": 14C, p. 371.

262   To Dos Passos, despite the growing sense . . . : EWL, p. 154.

Dos Passos was among those arrested . . . : TBT, pp. 172–173.

"It was a moment of strange heartbreak . . . ": "The Never Ending Wrong," *Atlantic*, 139 (June 1977), pp. 37–64.

"What about this goddamn human race anyway? . . . ": 14C, pp. 371–372.

263   *This isn't a poem* . . . ": "They Are Dead Now," *New Masses*, 3 (Oct. 1927), p. 7.

"We are two nations," he continued . . . : USA *(The Big Money)*, pp. 413–414.

264   *The Belt* was "vigorous" . . . : "Troubles in the Crank Case," *New York Times* Oct. 20, 1927, sect. 1, p. 33.

His only breaks . . . : Milford, *Zelda*, p. 150.

He designed the sets for Lawson's . . . : Knox and Stahl, p. 121.

Him seemed to Dos Passos . . . : "Mr. Dos Passos on 'Him,' " *New York Times*, April 22, 1928, sect. 9, p. 2.

Still bitter about the Sacco . . . : EWL, p. 145.

To friends such as Hemingway . . . : UVA.

265   But that did not materialize, so he had . . . : TBT, p. 173.

By mid-April he was exhausted, driven . . . : 14C, p. 385.

"The past year has been . . . ": JDP to GLC, April 16, 1929, GLCC.

Katy, in fact, may have even been engaged . . . : Rosalind Wilson interview with TL, Aug. 20, 1975.

Perhaps they had carried on a short affair . . . : "Summer People," *The Nick Adams Stories* (New York, 1972), pp. 217–228; Philip Young, " 'Big World Out There': The Nick Adams Stories," *Novel*, 6 (Fall, 1972), pp. 15–16.

When Dos Passos arrived in Key West . . . : Notes for TBT, UVA.

266   (Footnote) A tale about him goes . . . : For information about Smith, see Warren Browne, *Titan vs. Taboo: The Life of William Benjamin Smith* (Tucson, 1961); for the tale about Y.K. and his father, Marion (Mrs. William) Smith to TL, Oct. 2, 1976.

Whatever, she and he were deeply attracted . . . : This sketch of Katy is based on TL interviews with Marion Smith, June 14, 1975; Rosalind Wilson, Aug. 20, 1975; Mrs. Robert Wheland and Mr. and Mrs. Edwin Dickinson, July 30, 1975; Mr. and Mrs. John Howard Lawson, Oct. 17, 1974; and DP, numerous times.

"Pleased to have met you . . . ": KDP to JDP, June 22, 1928, UVA.

CHAPTER SEVENTEEN

267   From there, after a few days . . . : JDP to EH, June 1, 1928, UVA.

They saw the city's night life, Dos Passos . . . : TBT, p. 174.

Dos Passos was attracted . . . : For this and the following material about Leningrad, see "Rainy Days in Leningrad," *New Masses*, 4 (Feb. 1929), pp. 3–5; TBT, pp. 174–178.

268   Dos Passos declined . . . : 14C, pp. 386–387; HG, interview with TL, June 3, 1978.

269   Dos Passos's recollections of Lee, who talked . . . : "The Art of Fiction," p. 157; TBT, p. 178.

An editorial in the *New York World* . . . : July 4, 1928, p. 10; *New York World,* Aug. 31, 1928, p. 10.

In Moscow, he quickly established a routine . . . : TBT, p. 179.

The "most interesting and lively people" . . . : 14C, p. 386; TBT, p. 180.

270   The films that he admired . . . : JDP to GLC, undated, GLCC.

271   Dos Passos shared a cabin with two other men . . . : IAC, p. 41.

The expedition he was to join . . . : TBT, pp. 183–186.

"Then there's a great deal of food— . . . ": 14C, p. 387.

Early in September . . . : TBT, pp. 187–192; IAC, pp. 47–52; HG, interview with TL, June 3, 1978.

272   He was, he wrote later . . . : IAC, pp. 52–54.

He had stayed . . . : TBT, pp. 193–194; IAC, pp. 58–59.

273   "Now I am established . . . ": JDP to GLC, Oct. 9, 1928, GLCC.

"Will it be prejudice or popery?" he asked . . . : 14C, p. 388.

When Dos Passos wrote . . . : *New Republic,* 62 (April 16, 1930), pp. 236–240.

He had glimpses of the fear . . . : IAC, pp. 66–69.

274   At the train station . . . : IAC, pp. 4–6.

In the U.S.S.R. things were both so good . . . : JDP to GLC, Dec. 8, 1929, GLCC.

In late February 1929 . . . : Valia Gerasimova to JDP, Feb. 25, 1929, UVA.

275   Jack Lawson half tempted him . . . : JHL to JDP, Dec. 28, 1928, UVA.

"Dont you ever write any plays . . . ": 14C, pp. 389–390.

Even though during the following summer . . . : "Did the New Playwrights Theatre Fail?" *New Masses,* 5 (Aug. 1929), p. 13.

276   "The battle," he assured her . . . : JDP to GLC, April 8, 1929, GLCC.

In March, he resigned . . . : 14C, pp. 390–391.

277   "Dos," he wrote back . . . : JHL to JDP, undated, UVA; Knox and Stahl, pp. 89–90.

Yet, Lawson later believed . . . : JHL, interview with TL, Oct. 17, 1974.

Ernest and several other friends . . . : TBT, p. 199.

He wrote Edmund Wilson . . . : 14C, p. 391.

278   "Great walking round here and working like . . . ": JDP to RM, April 29, 1929, UVA.

There was a kind of twenties decadence . . . : EWTT, pp. 429–430 (Wilson dated the wedding in 1927).

Dos Passos saw a good bit of Wilson . . . : EWL, p. 167.

From there he wrote Poore to thank him . . . : 14C, p. 392.

279   She hoped Dos Passos . . . : KDP to JDP, June 28, 1929, UVA.

They found the farm . . . : KDP to JDP, July 9, 1929; July 25, 1929; and undated, UVA.

Late in August . . . : 14C, pp. 393–394.

To add to the gaiety . . . : Marion Smith to TL, January 2, 1979.

280   He was genuinely pleased . . . : EH to JDP, Sept. 4, 1928, UVA; quoted in part in TBT, p. 202.

Hidden from the main road . . . : EWL, p. 202.

281   Dos Passos reviewed three books . . . : "Edison and Steinmetz: Medicine Men," *New Republic,* 61 (Dec. 18, 1929), pp. 103–104.

The other significant piece . . . : "Books," *New Masses,* 5 (Dec. 1929), p. 16.

CHAPTER EIGHTEEN

284 "My books could hardly have sold less . . . ": TBT, p. 205.
"I've always lived . . . ": 14C, p. 523.

285 "Camera Eye," he headed a page . . . : Notebook, UVA.
The second volume, he told Malcolm Cowley when . . . : 14C, p. 404.

286 Four months later . . . : TBT, p. 203; Milford, pp. 169–170.
Before Dos Passos and Katy arrived, Hemingway . . . : Baker, pp. 206–207.

287 Katy and Dos Passos, in January . . . : TBT, pp. 203–204; 14C, pp. 377–378; for information about Cendrars, I am indebted to Jay Bochner, *Blaise Cendrars: Discovery and Re-Creation* (Toronto, 1978).
The sections would be retained. . . . : Patience Ross to Brandt and Brandt, undated, UVA.
He painted watercolors and worked . . . : TBT, p. 204.
"*I've seen the silent trains . . .* ": *Panama or the Adventures of My Seven Uncles* (New York, 1931), p. 30.

288 "The poetry of Blaise Cendrars . . . ": *Panama,* "Translator's Foreword," pp. vii–viii.
Before they left, Dos Passos and Katy may have . . . : Baker, p. 210.
"Pleasant weather, Columbus! . . . ": EECL, p. 116.

289 She noted that *The 42nd Parallel* was twice as rich . . . : *Books,* (Feb. 23, 1930), p. 30.
Henry Hazlitt commenting . . . : "Kaleidoscope," *Nation,* 130 (March 12, 1930), p. 298; Wilson, "Dahlberg, Dos Passos and Wilder," *New Republic,* 62 (March 26, 1930), pp. 157–158.

290 One of the most perceptive reviews . . . : "John Dos Passos Satirizes an America 'On the Make,' " *New York Times Book Review* (March 2, 1930), p. 5.
"Frankly," noted Patience Ross of A. M. Heath, "Mr. Dos Passos . . . ": Patience Ross to Brandt and Brandt, June 6, 1930, UVA.
During the summer he assured . . . : 14C, p. 394.
"Dos Passos is up here . . . ": EWL, pp. 199, 202.

291 In a piece in the *New Republic* . . . : "Back to Red Hysteria," *New Republic,* 63 (July 2, 1930), p. 169; "Wanted: An Ivy Lee for Liberals," *New Republic,* 63 (Aug. 13, 1930), p. 372.
His cry to the Left in 1926 . . . : "The *New Masses* I'd Like," p. 20.
He distrusted dogmas, and . . . : 14C, p. 398.

292 The particular incident he cited was . . . : "Back to Red Hysteria," p. 168; "For Southern Political Prisoners," Letter to the editor, *New Republic,* 64 (Sept. 3, 1930), p. 75.
And in the spring of 1931 . . . : "The American Theatre: 1930–31, Is the Whole Show on the Skids?" *New Republic,* 66 (April 1, 1931), pp. 174–175.
With Floyd Allington . . . : Baker, pp. 215–217; 14C, p. 379.

293 While objecting that he could not "swallow . . . ": 14C, p. 398.
"I keep piling up written typewritten pencil-written . . . ": JDP to Eugene Saxton, undated, Houghton Library, Harvard University.
In the published edition, only the first sentence . . . : manuscript, UVA; USA *(Nineteen Nineteen),* p. 105.
Dos Passos wrote Wilson . . . : 14C, p. 399.

Beals recalled their visit . . . : *Glass Houses,* pp. 248–249.

294 The piece Dos Passos wrote to conclude *1919* . . . : USA *(Nineteen Nineteen),* pp. 407–412; for an account of the ceremony, see Francis Russell, *The Shadow of Blooming Grove: Warren G. Harding in His Times* (New York, 1968), pp. 476–483.

295 An episode that reflected . . . : Patience Ross to Brandt and Brandt, Dec. 22, 1931, UVA; 14C, p. 400.

296 Harper's had no wish to attack Morgan . . . : 14C, p. 380.

297 In August, as chairman of the National Committee . . . : *New Republic,* 67 (Aug. 5, 1931), p. 318.

In addition to Dos Passos, Lester Cohen . . . : W. A. Swanberg, *Dreiser* (New York, 1965), p. 384.

Harlan County was, as Dos Passos later reported . . . : "Harlan: Working Under the Gun," *New Republic,* 69 (Dec. 2, 1931), p. 62.

Dos Passos, like the others, was surprised that . . . : TBT, p. 206.

As the committee talked over . . . : "Harlan: Working Under the Gun," pp. 62–67; JDP, ed., *Harlan Miners Speak: Report on the terrorism in the Kentucky coal fields* (New York, 1932).

298 " 'We're not afraid of the wind,' " he quoted . . . : "Harlan: Working Under the Gun," p. 66; 14C, p. 401. Information about the Dreiser Committee visit is taken primarily from Swanberg, pp. 384–387, and from Dos Passos's essay about Harlan.

"All we accomplished . . . ": TBT, p. 207.

299 The two receipts for Joe Busa ran the same . . . : UVA.

Dreiser sent a lawyer to Kentucky to look . . . : Swanberg, p. 388.

Dos Passos, nevertheless, was asked . . . : TBT, p. 208; Adelaide Walker commented on Dos Passos's anger in Harlan in an interview with TL, July 31, 1975.

In December he tried . . . : Harold Weston interview with TL, June 14, 1971.

He also traveled to Washington to report . . . : *New Republic,* 69 (Dec. 16, 1931), pp. 153–155.

CHAPTER NINETEEN

301 The sea voyage of a little over a week . . . : "Atlantic Fisheries," *Fortune,* 11 (March, 1935), pp. 69–73.

302 On the whole Dos Passos thought . . . : 14C, p. 402.

After landing in El Progreso . . . : 14C, pp. 404–406.

But the trip was also instructive; Dos Passos . . . : 14C, pp. 407–408.

Malcolm Cowley, having clarified for himself . . . : "Poet and the World," *New Republic,* 70 (April 27, 1932), p. 303; Henry Hazlitt, "Panorama," *Nation,* 134 (March 23, 1932), p. 344.

303 Most pleasing of all . . . : EH to JDP, March 26, 1932, UVA.

304 In any event, what he had read . . . : 14C, pp. 409–410.

"To hell with your swingers.": *Important Modern First Editions,* part one, catalogue of Sotheby Parke Bernet, Inc., Lot 155, auction held March 29, 1977.

One scanty page reflects . . . : Notes, UVA.

306 Henry Ford stood for something similar . . . : USA *(The Big Money),* p. 466.

He studied each figure carefully . . . : Among JDP's papers at UVA are call slips for the two books, checked out to him from the New York Public Library on Feb. 10, 1933.

307 Dos Passos wrote that despite . . . : USA *(The Big Money)*, pp. 254, 387.
    In a draft of the biography . . . : Manuscript, UVA.
    He emphasized the irony of life, and more, the . . . : USA *(The Big Money)*, p. 338.
308 Among his papers . . . : UVA.
    Dos Passos's piece . . . : "Washington and Chicago. Part I: The Veterans Come Home
    to Roost. Part II: Spotlights and Microphone," *New Republic*, 71 (June 29, 1932),
    pp. 177–179; 14C, pp. 410–412; "Detroit: City of Leisure," *New Republic*, 71 (July
    27, 1932), pp. 280–282.
309 Roosevelt, of course, did receive the nomination . . . : "Out of the Red with Roosevelt,"
    New Republic, 71 (July 13, 1932), pp. 230–232.
    He eventually voted for the Communist candidates . . . : TIF, p. 103.
    "Is the forgotten man trying to remember? . . . ": "Four Nights in a Garden: A
    Campaign Yarn," *Common Sense*, 1 (Dec. 5, 1932) p. 22.
310 When Dos Passos wrote the piece for *Common Sense*, . . . : "The Radio Voice,"
    Common Sense, 3 (Feb., 1934), p. 17; the piece was slightly altered when it was
    republished in IAC, where JDP indicated that he wrote it at Provincetown in March,
    1933 (p. 253).
    After his first essay there . . . : "Doves in the Bull Ring," *New Masses*, 10 (Jan. 2,
    1934), p. 13; "The Unemployment Report," *New Masses*, 10 (Feb. 13, 1934), pp.
    11–12; "Grandfather and Grandson," *New Masses*, 21 (Dec. 15, 1936), p. 19.
311 Yet Bingham . . . : Frank A. Warren, III, *Liberals and Communism: The "Red
    Decade" Revisited* (Bloomington, 1966), p. 35.
    "Who today in any camp . . . ": "What Do the Liberals Hope For?" *New Republic*,
    69 (Feb. 10, 1932), p. 348.
312 In April he sent a draft . . . : EWL, pp. 222–224; 14C, pp. 382, 409.
313 A writer could not avoid . . . : "Whither the American Writer," *Modern Quarterly*,
    6 (Summer, 1932), pp. 11–12.
    Later, when his remark . . . : 14C, p. 413.

CHAPTER TWENTY

315 Also, Hemingway during the spring of 1933 . . . : Baker, p. 239.
316 The attack was severe [and information about early 1933] . . . : 14C, pp. 425–432.
317 They took short trips to spots along the French coast . . . : JDP to CAP, undated, HBJ.
    The townspeople set them off with no apparent . . . : TBT, pp. 226–227.
318 There was a Socialist . . . : TBT, p. 227; IAC, pp. 123–127.
319 "These lunches," Dos Passos recalled . . . : TBT, pp. 219–220.
    He also described to them how, when he . . . : IAC, pp. 128–130; TBT, pp. 222–224.
    Dos Passos obtained interviews . . . : TBT, pp. 224–225.
    Dos Passos's unease . . . : TBT, pp. 228–229.
320 "Summer was pretty much a fracaso . . . ": 14C, pp. 433–434.
    Dos Passos immediately responded . . . : CAP to JDP, Oct. 27, 1933; JDP to CAP,
    undated, HBJ.
321 As he tried to get rid of his ill health . . . : TL interviews with Rosalind Wilson, Aug.
    10, 1975; Isabel Whelan and Patricia Dickinson, July 30, 1975; Mrs. Marion Smith,
    June 14, 1975; Mr. and Mrs. Eben Given, July 14, 1974.
    Dos Passos, wrote Cantwell, . . . : Robert Cantwell, typescript of a sketch about JDP,
    University of Oregon Library.

Yet underneath was a forceful, even . . . : Charles Mayo, interview with TL, July 30, 1975.

CHAPTER TWENTY-ONE

323   "Key West is pleasant . . . ": JDP to EH, March 8, 1934, UVA.

324   "However bad the American theater may be . . . ": "Hissing the Villain," *Nation*, 138 (June 27, 1934), p. 735.

They did, returning to Key West "in mildly . . . ": Baker, pp. 259–260.

"To us," the editorial concluded, "you have been and, . . . ": *New Masses*, 10 (March 6, 1934), pp. 8–9.

They soon printed it as part . . . : "Unintelligent Fanaticism," *New Masses*, 10 (March 27, 1934), pp. 6–7.

325   To Wilson, Dos Passos remarked . . . : 14C, pp. 435–436.

326   Although in retrospect Lawson could believe . . . : JHL, "Biographical Note," *Zeitschrift für Anglistik und Amerikanistik*, 4, no. 1 (1956), p. 73.

The drama evinced his criticism of materialistic . . . : Mike Gold, "A Bourgeois Hamlet of Our Time," *New Masses*, 11 (April 10, 1934), p. 29.

The themes in *Fortune Heights* were murky . . . : JHL to JDP, Jan. 24, 1934, UVA.

327   Gold hammered away at his target: "To be a . . . ": "A Bourgeois Hamlet," pp. 28–29.

But instead of struggling against Gold's . . . : JHL to JDP, April 9, 1934, UVA.

In the issue of *New Masses* . . . : "Inner Conflict and Proletarian Art: A Reply to Michael Gold," *New Masses*, 11 (April 17, 1934), pp. 29–30; I am indebted to Gerald Rabkin, who discusses Lawson's career in *Drama and Commitment: Politics in the American Theatre of the Thirties* (Bloomington, 1964), pp. 127–165.

328   Dos Passos, in a letter that offended . . . : 14C, pp. 446–447.

Lawson's response was an impassioned . . . : JHL to JDP, no date, UVA.

329   "I've just signed up . . . ": 14C, pp. 437–438; TBT, p. 215.

330   He had only a few chances to observe Hollywood . . . : 14C, p. 443.

331   "Frankly," he wrote Robert Cantwell . . . : 14C, pp. 441–442.

(Footnote): At the same time as he discussed the futilitarian . . . : JDP to BB of Brandt and Brandt, Nov. 14, 1934, UVA.

"Americanize Marx," as he had written . . . : "Whither the American Writer," p. 12.

332   Dos Passos urged his friend . . . : 14C, p. 443.

Veblen was important to Dos Passos . . . : Diggins, pp. 84–85.

When the Dos Passoses arrived, Ernest was excited . . . : 14C, p. 445.

Dos Passos was interested in the Cuban . . . : 14C, p. 451.

Then, after she had returned to Key West . . . : 14C, p. 448.

"He was sweet," she added . . . : 14C, p. 421.

But, Dos Passos recalled . . . : TBT, p. 219.

333   "Poor Dos got rich [in Hollywood]," he complained . . . : Baker, pp. 266, 612.

But Morgan was always honest with himself . . . : Baker, p. 298.

Hemingway and Dos Passos could still . . . : TBT, pp. 215–218. Dos Passos dates the trip in the spring of 1935, but Baker indicates that Gingrich was in Key West in December, 1934 (Baker, p. 269).

334 In Quintanilla's etchings . . . : "Facing a Bitter World. A Portfolio of Etchings," *Esquire*, 3 (Feb. 1935), p. 25.

335 Rather, as he wrote . . . : "Grosz Comes to America," *Esquire*, 6 (Sept. 1936), p. 128. The essay in practically the same form became the introduction to *Interregnum* (New York, 1936).

He asked Cowley . . . : 14C, pp. 450, 453–455.

336 "Naturally your letter of reproach . . . ": 14C, p. 421.

Underneath Dos Passos's flare-up lay a resentment . . . : 14C, p. 457.

Dos Passos's response . . . : 14C, p. 456.

CHAPTER TWENTY-TWO

338 Two days before Christmas . . . : 14C, pp. 458–460.

339 Wilson responded in January . . . : EWL, pp. 255–257.

Dos Passos in his turn . . . : 14C, pp. 460–462.

340 "Don't agitate me, comrade . . . ": EWL, pp. 257–259.

341 "But Bunny . . . ": 14C, pp. 465–466.

Try Edward Hyde's . . . : EWL, pp. 259–260.

342 He did it "against . . . ": 14C, p. 468.

Look at Defoe's work, he counseled . . . : 14C, p. 452.

"A writer as such is just that . . . ": 14C, pp. 463–464.

343 "It's only occasionally that you want . . .": 14C, p. 476.

The essay Dos Passos wrote . . . : "The Writer as Technician," *American Writers' Congress*, ed. Henry Hart (New York, 1935), pp. 78–82.

344 Statements such as "only the theater of the left . . . ": *American Writers' Congress*, p. 128.

Waldo Frank's essay . . . : *American Writers' Congress*, p. 71.

When Dos Passos had the opportunity to read it . . . : JDP to Waldo Frank, undated, Van Pelt Library, University of Pennsylvania.

When from friends who had attended the congress . . . : Margaret De Silver to JDP, undated, UVA.

Dos Passos had tried to arrange for his friend . . . : JDP to EW, undated, EWC.

Wilson commented at length . . . : EWL, pp. 263–267.

345 Cowley noted that those . . . : MC to JDP, April 30, 1935, Library of the State University of New York at Buffalo.

About his essay he commented, "as I knew . . . ": 14C, p. 473.

The writers should fight for freedom . . . : MC to JDP, May 16, 1935, Library of the State University of New York at Buffalo.

"I'm through with writing these . . . ": 14C, p. 477.

346 "No," responded Cowley . . . : quoted in part in 14C, p. 422; MC to JDP June 3, 1935, Library of the State University of New York at Buffalo.

Even that life became stale . . . : 14C, pp. 468–469.

347 He groused to his agent . . . : JDP to BB, received Aug. 30, 1935, UVA.

If Key West life . . . : *What the Woman Lived: Selected Letters of Louise Bogan, 1920–1970*. Ed. Ruth Limmer (New York, 1973), p. 121; EW mentions the incident in a 1969 letter (EWL, pp. 701–702); and Baker discusses the 1936 fight in his biography of Hemingway, p. 285.

The Murphys had been courageous . . . : 14C, p. 467.

348   Trolling for dolphins . . . : 14C, p. 472; TBT, p. 210; Baker, pp. 271–272.

According to Dos Passos, when Katy had returned . . . : 14C, p. 475.

The day he fought . . . : TBT, pp. 210–214.

349   Bimini, Katy wrote Gerald Murphy . . . : KDP to GM, June 20, 1935, HDC; published in part in 14C, p. 423.

350   Pleased that his illness . . . : 14C, p. 479.

There's a sort of frivolity . . . ": 14C, p. 480.

Dos Passos tried in September to humor Hemingway . . . : 14C, p. 482; Ernest Hemingway, "Who Murdered the Vets?" *New Masses*, 16 (Sept. 17, 1935), p. 9.

It was a time, as Carlos Baker has noted, when . . . : Baker, p. 291.

"This novel business is . . . ": 14C, p. 483.

351   In mid-February he heard from . . . : BB to JDP, Feb. 17, 1936, UVA.

By March he had finished . . . : CAP to JDP, April 7, 1936; JDP to CAP, undated, HBJ.

Later Dos Passos apologized for the three . . . : 14C, p. 484; JDP to EH, June 3, 1936, UVA.

He joked that he might change his name . . . : JDP to BB, May 12, 1936, UVA.

The Dos Passoses delivered Sara Murphy . . . : JDP to EH, June 3, 1936, UVA.

He wrote Edmund Wilson at the end of June . . . : 14C, p. 485.

352   Dos Passos initially assumed . . . : 14C, pp. 485–486.

(Footnote) He talked in the first letter about self-destruction . . . : EH to JDP, June 10, 1936, and July 18, 1936, UVA.

Hemingway in June had told him . . . : EH to JDP, June 10, 1936, UVA.

"Dos had spent all day . . . ": CAP to BB, July 15, 1936, UVA.

The same day Pearce wrote to thank . . . : CAP to JDP, July 15, 1936, HBJ.

353   Asking her to find someone else to do the task . . . : JDP to Helen Taylor, July 7, 1936, HBJ.

As August 1, 1936, the date for the publication . . . : CAP to JDP, July 27, 1936, HBJ.

Jack Lawson wrote to say that the novel . . . : JHL to JDP, undated, UVA.

After Edmund Wilson had finished . . . : EWL, pp. 278–279.

354   "Alone among U.S. writers . . . ": "Private Historian," *Time*, 28 (Aug. 10, 1936), p. 53.

Gregory believed that the author saw . . . : "The Big Money," *New York Herald Tribune Books* (Aug. 9, 1936), p. 1.

In a *New Republic* review . . . : "The End of a Trilogy," *New Republic*, 88 (Aug. 12, 1936), p. 23; "Afterthoughts on Dos Passos," *New Republic*, 88 (Sept. 9, 1936), p. 134.

Herschel Brickell, who had written . . . : "The Big Money," *Review of Reviews*, 94 (Sept. 1936), p. 12.

A more important statement . . . : "Anatomist of Our Time," *Saturday Review of Literature*, 14 (Aug. 8, 1936), p. 13.

"If Dos Passos is a *novelist*," she concluded . . . : *Letters*, p. 137.

355   The "plot" of satire, like the "plot" of the trilogy . . . : *The Cankered Muse: Satire of the English Renaissance* (New Haven, 1959), p. 31.

356   *The Big Money* becomes a statement . . . : For a fuller discussion of *U.S.A.* as satire and as a tentative statement of hope, see TL, "The Neglected Satires of John Dos Passos," *Satire Newsletter*, 7 (Spring, 1970), pp. 127–136; and "The Ordering of the Camera Eye in *U.S.A.*," *American Literature*, 49 (Nov. 1977), pp. 443–446.

357   He took to calling his fiction "chronicles" . . . : See "Contemporary Chronicles," *Carleton Miscellany*, 2 (Spring, 1961), pp. 25–29.

      The Italian philosopher . . . : Diggins, pp. 102–103.

      It was a thoughtful, affectionate letter . . . : FSF to JDP, Sept. 21, 1936, UVA.

      He sympathized with Fitzgerald . . . : 14C, p. 488; "An Interview with John Dos Passos," special issue of *Idol*, the literary quarterly of Union College, 14 (1969), p. 20.

      When he heard about a fourth printing . . . : 14C, p. 487; CAP to JDP, Oct. 4, 1936, HBJ; BB to JDP, Nov. 9, 1936; CAP to BB, Dec. 17, 1936, UVA.

358   "Somebody's got to start . . . ": 14C, pp. 489–490.

      It had been "all very up . . . ": KDP to Pauline Hemingway, Sept. 15, 1936, UVA.

      He feared for Spain . . . : 14C, pp. 486–487, 492; JDP to EH, undated, UVA.

359   More and more as 1936 . . . : JDP to MC, undated, Library of the State University of New York at Buffalo; JDP to Roger Baldwin, Nov. 24, 1936, Columbia University Library.

CHAPTER TWENTY-THREE

362   Dos Passos felt . . . : 14C, pp. 503–504.

363   His intention after Franco's revolt . . . : TIF, p. 115.

      In New York . . . : Baker, p. 300; Archibald MacLeish to TL, July 28, 1976; in reconstructing these events I have relied also on Dos Passos's thinly fictionalized account in CE, pp. 35–44.

      In early February . . . : 14C, p. 505; EWL, p. 286.

364   "I'm absolutely completely . . . ": 14C, pp. 506–507.

      Tresca, an anarchist . . . : TIF, pp. 116–117.

365   Prior to that in March 1937 . . . : JDP to RSM, March 2, 1937, Boston Athenaeum.

      He assured Scott Fitzgerald . . . : 14C, p. 507.

      Dos Passos came away from the discussion . . . : Notes for CE, UVA; CE, pp. 50–53.

      What he found was a country very much . . . : JBW, pp. 330–344.

366   Disorganization, coupled . . . : TIF, p. 118.

      According to Dos Passos . . . : 14C, p. 527; Louis Fischer, *Men and Politics* (New York, 1946), p. 429. I am indebted to Stanley Weintraub's excellent study *The Last Great Cause: The Intellectuals and the Spanish Civil War* (New York, 1968), pp. 270–271, for pointing out Fischer's comments and for discussion of "Goriev."

      But there was an air . . . : JBW, pp. 356–357.

      After a lunch at the hotel . . . : JBW, pp. 357, 359; 14C, pp. 527–528; EWL, pp. 356–357; to get a further sense of the situation, I have drawn on Dos Passos's rendering of it in CE, pp. 77–78.

367   Señora Robles asked . . . : 14C, p. 528.

368   Immediately Hemingway demanded to know . . . : JBW, pp. 361–363; CE, pp. 81–82.

      (Footnote) Lillian Hellman tells . . . : *An Unfinished Woman* (Boston, 1969), p. 103.

Years afterward, Ernest told . . . : A.E. Hotchner, *Papa Hemingway* (New York, 1966), pp. 132–133.

369   Dos Passos wrote of one dawn . . . : JBW, pp. 364–365; Josephine Herbst, "The Starched Blue Sky of Spain," *Noble Savage*, 1 (Feb. 1960), p. 95; Baker, p. 309.

"Shall always remember . . . ": 14C, p. 524.

370   Walter, although Polish, had lived . . . : Baker, pp. 306, 310.

It was during . . . : Herbst, "Starched Blue Sky," pp. 96–99; JBW, pp. 375–381.

371   Hemingway's news was not fresh . . . : CE, pp. 90–92.

When Dos Passos wrote . . . : 14C, p. 528.

Enclosing a copy . . . : 14C, p. 526.

"It has always seemed . . . ": Josephine Herbst to Bruce Bliven, June 30, 1939, Beinecke Library, Yale University.

372   "It used to be . . . ": Baker, pp. 308–309; JBW, pp. 368–369; CE, pp. 89–90.

The project, which was to be filmed . . . : JBW, pp. 385–388.

373   In an interview del Vayo assured . . . : 14C, p. 529.

"It's complicated . . . ": JBW, p. 392.

"Perhaps," Dos Passos concluded . . . ": TIF, p. 145.

Before Dos Passos left . . . : TIF, p. 146; CE, p. 96.

374   Hemingway, agitated in the bustle . . . : This account is based on Dos Passos's rendering of it in CE, pp. 98–99, and a nearly identical account, William L. White to TL, Dec. 30, 1970.

At some point . . . : 14C, p. 498.

CHAPTER TWENTY-FOUR

375   She met Dos Passos during the voyage . . . : Margaret Tjader Harris to TL, June 20, 1971.

Roosevelt, the great persuader, had made . . . : TIF, p. 149.

To Horsley Gantt he wrote . . . : HG, interview with TL, June 3, 1978.

"Spain is a pretty grim place . . . ": 14C, p. 498.

376   "It takes a little trip . . . ": 14C, p. 509.

Cummings was amused . . . : Richard S. Kennedy, *Dreams in the Mirror: A Biography of E. E. Cummings* (New York, 1980), pp. 386–387.

He spoke of the difficulty . . . : Weintraub, pp. 197–198.

One light touch . . . : Dawn Powell to JDP, undated, UVA.

377   "I hope the extent to which certain CP groups . . . ": John Dewey to JDP, June 12, 1937, UVA.

378   But in the light . . . : DP, interview with TL, April 4, 1979.

"The people of Western Europe . . . ": *Common Sense*, 4 (July 1937), pp. 9–11.

379   Lawson had been negotiating . . . : JHL to JDP, Aug. 29, 1937, UVA.

380   Dos Passos responded . . . : 14C, p. 514.

382   He knew, further, of their execution . . . : For a discussion of these maneuverings in 1937, see Frank A. Warren, III, *Liberals and Communism*, pp. 133–137.

He accused Dos Passos . . . : JHL to JDP, Sept. 14, 1937, UVA.

Dos Passos in November wrote Lawson . . . : 14C, pp. 512–513.

Then in December . . . : "The Communist Party and the War Spirit," *Common Sense*, 6 (Dec., 1937), pp. 11–14.

383 When early in 1938 . . . : 14C, pp. 515–517.

384 From the site . . . : JDP to JHL, Aug. 8, 1938, JHLC.

He further recalled . . . : JHL, interview with TL, Oct. 17, 1974.

The novel, Lawson declared . . . : JHL to JDP, Aug. 30, 1939, UVA.

385 When Steward Mitchell wrote . . . : 14C, p. 497.

And when in October . . . : JDP to BB, letter received Oct. 26, 1937, UVA.

They seemed always . . . : 14C, p. 511.

He asked Cap Pearce . . . : JDP to CAP, undated, HBJ.

In early July he wrote . . . : JDP to BB, July 3, 1937, UVA.

Not until Donald Brace . . . : CAP to JDP, Aug. 10, 1937, HBJ.

386 He added . . . : 14C, p. 510.

Writing Pearce . . . : JDP to CAP, Sept. 28, 1937, HBJ.

In a letter . . . : JDP to BB, Sept. 29, 1937, UVA.

He met on October 7 . . . : CAP to JDP, Oct. 8, 1937; JDP to CAP, undated; JDP to CAP, undated, HBJ; USA, pp. v–vi, and in *The Big Money*, pp. 492–494.

387 The piece he referred to . . . : "The Camera Eye," *Esquire*, 5 (April 1936), pp. 51, 112.

388 Dos Passos also suggested . . . : JDP to BB, Oct. 26, 1937, UVA.

"The subject of conversation," White recalled . . . : William L. White to TL, Dec. 30, 1970.

She wrote him . . . : *Letters*, p. 167.

389 The two authors . . . : "A Conversation. Theodore Dreiser and John Dos Passos," *Direction*, 1 (Jan. 1938), pp. 2–3, 28.

Not until late February . . . : KDP to SM, March 20, 1938, HDC.

At Warm Springs . . . : JDP to RSM, March, 1938, Boston Athenaeum.

Dos Passos responded . . . : 14C, p. 516.

390 In a letter afterward . . . : EH to JDP, undated, UVA.

(Footnote) Hemingway could not . . . : EH to MC, undated. For the opportunity to see this letter I am indebted to Maurice F. Neville; Hugh Thomas, *The Spanish Civil War* (New York, 1961).

391 Late in August . . . : 14C, p. 520.

"We suddenly find . . .": JDP to RSM, Sept. 30 and Oct. 6, 1938, Boston Athenaeum.

Just after the New Year . . . : JDP to RM, Jan. 30, 1939, UVA.

But he was concerned . . . : JDP to BB, received March 24, 1939, UVA.

392 Both Gold and Hicks . . . : Mike Gold, "Change the World," *Daily Worker*, Feb. 26, 1938, p. 7; Granville Hicks, "To John Dos Passos," *New Masses*, 27 (April 26, 1938), pp. 22–23.

His earliest notes . . . : UVA.

393 The novel, wrote Samuel Sillen . . . : "Misadventures of John Dos Passos," *New Masses*, 32 (July 4, 1939), pp. 21–22.

Cowley's review . . . : "Disillusionment," *New Republic*, 99 (June 14, 1939), p. 163.

394 Thoroughly familiar . . . : "Dos Passos and the Critics," *American Mercury*, 47 (Aug. 1939), pp. 489–494.

Perhaps the most balanced . . . : "John Dos Passos," *Saturday Review of Literature,* 20 (June 3, 1939), pp. 3–4, 15–16.

395   Wilson wrote his friend . . . : EWL, pp. 317–320; 14C, p. 522.

397   She agreed . . . : Ilsa Barea to DP, July 15, 1939, UVA.

"We've been cruising . . . ": JDP to RSM, April 29, 1939, Boston Athenaeum.

"I'm a little reluctant . . . ": 14C, p. 522.

This remark was . . . : "The Situation in American Writing," *Partisan Review,* 6 (Summer, 1939), pp. 26–27.

398   (Footnote) A letter dated . . . : UVA.

"Oh Katy . . . ": 14C, p. 523.

During his and Katy's trip to the Southwest . . . : JDP to Neith Hapgood, undated, Beinecke Library, Yale University.

399   Of Paine he wrote . . . : LTTP, p. 12.

The same man, whom Jean-Paul Sarte in 1938 . . . : "John Dos Passos and 1919," *Literary and Philosophical Essays,* trans. Annette Michelson (New York, 1955), p. 96.

One cannot help but read . . . : JDP to RM, Dec. 29, 1939, UVA.

CHAPTER TWENTY-FIVE

400   Katy and Dos Passos's good friend . . . : Howard Phillips to Carleton Beals, July 18, 1943, Collection of Carleton Beals.

401   Still for the author . . . : JDP to RM, Jan. 4, 1940, UVA.

He wrote Clarence Walton . . . : JDP to Clarence Walton, Feb. 2 and Feb. 22, 1940, Houghton Library, Harvard University.

"So far the year . . . ": 14C, p. 530.

402   During the next two decades . . . : "Amended Complaint" of Dos Passos against Mary Lamar Gordon and Others, Nov. 14, 1941; C. D. Williams interview with TL, June 14, 1971; EDP to TL, Feb. 3, 1973; 14C, p. 501.

In a further effort . . . : JDP to BB, June 15, 1940; Alfred Harcourt to BB, June 18, 1940, UVA.

403   Sue them, Dos Passos suggested . . . : 14C, pp. 532–533.

Shortly after . . . : JDP to RM, Sept. 9, 1940, UVA; JDP to RSM, Oct. 25, 1940, Boston Athenaeum.

Thanking Wilson . . . : 14C, pp. 531–532.

404   When a number . . . : UVA.

405   "My object is altogether . . . ": GWSO, pp. v, 2.

406   "The general object of the work . . . ": Allan Nevins, "Roots of Democracy," *Saturday Review,* 24 (Sept. 13, 1941), p. 6.

407   "If we can't, everything . . . ": GWSO, p. 401.

One of his longtime friends . . . : Gilbert Seldes to JDP, Oct. 7, 1941, UVA.

"Many people consider 'The Great Gatsby' . . . ": "Fitzgerald and the Press," *New Republic,* 104 (Feb. 17, 1941), p. 213.

The lawsuit created . . . : KDP to RM, July 30, 1941, UVA.

408   He arrived in London . . . : "England in the Great Lull," *Harper's,* 184 (Feb. 1942), pp. 235–244; "Some Glasgow People," *Harper's,* 184 (April 1942), pp. 474–480.

CHAPTER TWENTY-SIX

412   "Ever since . . . ": JDP to RM, Dec. 10, 1941, UVA.
     "No way of forgetting . . . ": TIF, p. 163.
     "Damn the Japs . . . ": JDP to RH, Dec. 10, 1941, UVA.

413   The character Dos Passos created . . . : John K. Hutchens, "On the Books," *New York Herald Tribune Weekly Book Review,* Jan. 30, 1949, p. 10.
     As Dos Passos wrote . . . : GWSO, p. 7.
     Dos Passos helped . . . : Alan M. Wald, *James T. Farrell: The Revolutionary Socialist Years* (New York, 1978) pp. 93–96; JDP, "To a Liberal in Office," *Nation,* 153 (Sept. 6, 1941), pp. 195–197.

414   "Under Roosevelt . . . " : TIF, p. 162.
     "When you try to find . . . ": NO, pp. 1, 304.

415   Dos Passos's early jottings . . . : UVA.
     "It's what you do . . . ": NO, p. 282.

416   They recognized his intention . . . : Benet, "He gets to the Senate with a Hillbilly Band," *New York Herald Tribune Weekly Book Review,* March 7, 1943, p. 3; Gregory, "Dos Passos and the Demagogue," *New York Times Book Review,* March 7, 1943, pp. 1, 18.
     "If enough readers ask this question . . . ": Jones, "Sound-Truck Caesar," *Saturday Review,* 26 (March 6, 1943), p. 8.
     They talked . . . : TIF, p. 174; JDP to John Diggins, April 21, 1966, UVA.

417   "During the last ten years . . . ": "Carlo Tresca," *Nation,* 156 (Jan. 23, 1943), p. 124.
     He believed . . . : SN, pp. 1, 5.
     "I feel myself . . . ": 14C, p. 536.

418   "There are too many . . . ": 14C, p. 537.
     "The bureaucratic procedures . . . ": SN, pp. 218–226.
     "Oh dear . . . ": JDP to KDP, Sept. 4, 1943, UVA.

419   "It looks as if . . . ": 14C, p. 541.
     State of the Nation held him . . . : 14C, p. 542.
     He was able to return the loan . . . : 14C, p. 501.
     Eventually he and Katy . . . : 14C, p. 543.

CHAPTER TWENTY-SEVEN

420   His publishers . . . : 14C, p. 546.
     Before he left . . . : 14C, pp. 543–545.

421   "Hawaii/Marshalls/Marianas . . . ": UVA.
     On the last day . . . : 14C, p. 547.

422   "At sea . . . " : 14C, p. 548.
     He observed . . . : TOD, pp. 81–92.
     After this episode . . . : TOD, pp. 169–171.

423   From near Manila . . . : 14C, p. 549.
     There on March 12 . . . : 14C, pp. 550–551.
     It was either . . . : EDP, interview with TL, Oct. 28, 1979.
     Despite fatigue . . . : 14C, p. 552.

424   From Rome Wilson . . . : EWL, pp. 424–425.
        "I dont quite understand . . .": 14C, pp. 553–554.
425   What he found . . . : 14C, pp. 554–562.
        While in Paris . . . : 14C, pp. 555–556.
        Not surprisingly . . . : TOD, pp. 244, 279, 282–283, 286.
426   "The Nazis are . . .": 14C, p. 561; TOD, p. 301.
        "Jackson represented the USA . . .": 14C, p. 560.
        Had the Allies not . . . : TOD, pp. 307–310.
        The professor spoke . . . : TOD, pp. 312–314, 324.
427   Then or during the previous days in Berlin . . . : UVA.
        In Paris he was interviewed . . . : TOD, pp. 326–330.
428   "Vienna piece," he wrote . . . : 14C, p. 502.
        "Never felt . . .": 14C, p. 563.

CHAPTER TWENTY-EIGHT

429   "We need . . . to practice what . . .": For a discussion of the internationalism/national-
        ism issue, see Geoffrey Perrett, *Days of Sadness, Years of Triumph: The American
        People, 1939–1945* (Baltimore, 1974), pp. 279–286.
430   "A pure . . .": JDP to EW, March 18, 1946, EWC. Dos Passos did not know;
        his piece . . . : "Where Do We Go From Here?" *Life*, 22 (Jan. 27, 1947), pp.
        95–96.
        The drift and uncertainty . . . : "The American War Procession," Jonathan Daniels,
        Saturday Review, 29 (Aug. 3, 1946), p. 7.
        Dos Passos and Katy, however . . . : 14C, p. 503.
431   The criticism, Dos Passos responded . . . : JDP to Gene McNerney, March 24, 1946.
        Quoted in part in Catalogue no. 78 (1978) of Paul C. Richards.
        The piece was more restrained . . . : "Britain's Dim Dictatorship," *Life*, 23 (Sept. 29,
        1947), pp. 120–122; JDP to Marion Cummings, Aug. 21, 1947, Houghton Library,
        Harvard University.
        On the afternoon of September 12 . . . : The account of the accident and its immediate
        aftermath is put together from Dos Passos's rendering of it in CE, p. 221; Mr. and
        Mrs. Eben Given, interview with TL, July 18, 1974; Mr. and Mrs. Edwin Dickinson
        and Mrs. Robert Whelan, interview with TL, July 30, 1975; Capt. and Mrs. Charles
        Mayo, interview with TL, July 30, 1975; and Dr. Abraham Pollen, interview with TL,
        Oct. 28, 1977.
432   Katy had been . . . : EWL, p. 449.
        They were moved by his emotional . . . : Marion Smith, interview with TL, June 14,
        1975.
        "This is so much . . .": 14C, p. 578.
433   Hemingway admitted . . . : EH to MC, Oct. 30, 1947, collection of Maurice Neville.
        "Strange what a labor . . .": JDP to Edith Shay, Sept. 17, 1947, collection of Mrs.
        Robert Whelan.
        He remained for a week or more . . . : JDP to Edith Shay, Oct. 8, 1947, collection
        of Mrs. Robert Whelan.
434   "My physical mishap . . .": JDP to Max Eastman, Oct. 19, 1947, Lilly Library, Indiana
        University, Bloomington, Indiana.

Katy, Chambers wrote . . . : Canby Chambers to JDP, Oct. 18, 1947, UVA. Quoted in part in 14C, p. 375.

But the experience . . . : Charles Mayo, interview with TL, July 30, 1975.

"Katy must have been . . . ": EWL, p. 449.

"What a charming story . . . ": KDP to JDP, Nov. 3, 1945, UVA.

As he went through . . . : EDPC.

435 The "archipelagos of remorse . . . ": 14C, pp. 581–582.

CHAPTER TWENTY-NINE

438 "Nobody talks about anything but corn . . . ": JDP to SM, Nov. 5, 1947, HDC; Roswell Garst, to TL, June 14, 1971.

One morning . . . : 14C, p. 579.

439 As far as "the well-being . . . ": "Failure of Marxism," Life, 24 (Jan. 19, 1948), pp. 96–98.

"Our chance of working . . . ": PBU, p. 294.

These were general aims . . . : The Truman quotation as well as a full discussion of America's foreign policy dilemmas in the 1940s are found in Chapter 2 of Godfrey Hodgson, America in Our Time (New York, 1978).

440 "Life only seems bearable . . . ": JDP to Edith Shay, Dec. 4, 1947 and Jan. 22, 1948, collection of Mrs. Robert Whelan.

He became the fifth occupant of Chair 14 . . . : 14C, pp. 568, 579–580.

441 He enjoyed himself . . . : 14C, p. 583.

After a brief visit in 1949 . . . : 14C, p. 589.

442 When he described these to the Lowndeses . . . : 14C, p. 584.

Spotswood is a hollow man . . . : DC (The Grand Design), p. 446.

For all its good intentions . . . : DC (The Grand Design), pp. 4, 417.

443 "In essence," wrote the critic Linda Wagner . . . : Dos Passos: Artist as American (Austin, 1979), p. 124.

"Paul and Peggy Graves in Wilmington, N.C. . . . ": UVA.

444 It was missed also because . . . : EWL, p. 453.

More common than praise . . . : Lloyd Morris, "Dos Passos Offers Political Tract in Fiction," New York Herald Tribune Weekly Book Review, Jan. 2, 1949, p. 3; H. M. Robinson, "Socio-Economic Surface," Saturday Review of Literature, 32 (Jan. 8, 1949), p. 8: Orville Prescott, "Outstanding Novels," Yale Review, 38 (Spring, 1949), p. 573.

Nevertheless, this novel—and nearly . . . : Arthur Mizener, Introduction to DC, p. ix.

"Dos Passos," he wrote . . . : Diggins, p. 242.

"I enjoyed The Grand Design . . . ": EWL, p. 453.

445 Hemingway feared, however, that Dos Passos . . . : Carlos Baker to JDP, April 5, 1966, describing EH letters to MacLeish of June 30, 1943, and Dec. 26, 1943, UVA.

The party aboard ship dragged on . . . : 14C, p. 585.

From Cuba Dos Passos flew . . . : PBU, p. 133.

But a fierce struggle . . . : PBU, p. 137.

Fifteen years later he wrote . . . : BOM, p. 14.

He flew next . . . : PBU, pp. 138–175.

446 No such praise . . . : PBU, p. 191.

Dos Passos did not ignore . . . : PBU, pp. 198–213.

447 She was a tall . . . : Louise Thomas, interview with TL, Nov. 13, 1979

448 He had collected masses of material . . . : JDP to Abbott Washburn, May 3, 1947, UVA; 14C, p. 587.

After several lunch dates . . . : EDP interview with TL, Sept. 6, 1973, and letter, July 28, 1979.

They had then to drive . . . : 14C, p. 589.

CHAPTER THIRTY

449 At Spence's Point . . . : EDP, interview with TL, Sept. 6, 1973.

The task demanded more research . . . : EDP to TL, Feb. 3, 1973.

"The weather continues . . . ": 14C, p. 590.

450 On May 15, 1950, in Baltimore . . . : 14C, p. 590.

A month and a half later . . . : 14C, pp. 592–593.

451 Two years later . . . : 14C, p. 599.

Wilson was . . . : 14C, pp. 590–596; JDP to Edith Shay, May 21, 1949, collection of Mrs. Robert Whelan; EWL, pp. 487–491.

A Mr. Peck . . . : EDP, interview with TL, May 12, 1976.

"But it *was* fun," she wrote . . . : EDP to the Lowndeses, Nov. 4, 1950, UVA.

452 "By nightfall . . . ": 14C, p. 595; W. Fairfax Griffith, interview with TL, May 12, 1976; EDP to TL, Aug. 6, 1979.

As Norman Thomas wrote . . . : "Casual Reflections of a Random Rover," *New York Herald Tribune Book Review,* Nov. 5, 1950, p. 4.

453 "They found words . . . ": UVA. None of this appears in the published version. See TGD, pp. 296–297.

454 Writing about the novel later . . . : UVA. From an early version of "Contemporary Chronicles," *Charleton Miscellany,* 2 (Spring, 1961), pp. 25, 29.

"My work so far . . . ": JDP to BB, Nov. 9, 1952, UVA.

455 As the novel concludes, he and Lulie . . . : CC, p. 485.

It was considered a major novel . . . : Milton Rugoff, "Rich Ore Mined From a Familiar Vein," *New York Herald Tribune Book Review,* Dec. 2, 1951, p. 5; Arthur Mizener, "Dos Passos' Story of the Yearning that Makes Americans," *New York Times Book Review,* Dec. 2, 1951, p. 7.

After Archibald MacLeish . . . : Archibald MacLeish to JDP, undated, UVA.

Edmund Wilson liked . . . : EWL, p. 503.

456 Dos Passos responded . . . : 14C, p. 598.

He had congratulated . . . : EH to JDP, Sept. 17, 1949, and Oct. 30, 1951; 14C, p. 597; Baker, pp. 495, 654, 81–82; EH to Charles Fenton, July 29, 1952, collection of Maurice Neville.

But any hint . . . : EH, *A Moveable Feast* (New York, 1964), pp. 207–209.

CHAPTER THIRTY-ONE

458 When toward the end . . . : 14C, pp. 593–594, 596.

459 Dos Passos was one . . . : William Filby, interview with TL, June 11, 1977.

Sometimes he and Elizabeth . . . : EDP to TL, Oct. 15, 1979.

Dos Passos took pleasure . . . : 14C, p. 604.

He could always, he joked . . . : EDP, interview with TL, Sept. 6, 1973.

"The country," he noted, "had been . . . ": JDP to RSM, Dec. 12, 1952, Boston Athenaeum.

When Whittaker Chambers's . . . : "Mr. Chambers's Descent Into Hell," *Saturday Review,* 35, (May 24, 1952), p. 11.

460 "Dos spent a night . . . ": EWL, p. 509.

He allowed, nonetheless . . . : 14C, p. 606.

He never repudiated . . . : CE, pp. 151–165.

461 In 1953 . . . : 14C, p. 603; HG, interview with TL, June 3, 1978.

"My observations in Spain . . . ": 14C, pp. 600–601.

462 That citadel of conservative . . . : William Manchester, *The Glory and the Dream* (Boston, 1974), p. 527.

463 "Confident to the verge . . . ": *America in Our Time,* p. 75.

"Can't we be . . . ": "To a Liberal in Office," *Nation,* 153 (Sept. 6, 1941), p. 197.

"This has been . . . ": 14C, pp. 570–571.

He felt sometimes . . . : 14C, p. 605.

The book reflected . . . : JDP to RH, undated, UVA.

464 Howe suggested . . . : "The Perils of Americana," *New Republic,* 130 (Jan. 25, 1954), p. 16.

Jack Lawson was deeply hurt . . . : JHL interview with TL, Oct. 17, 1974.

Dos Passos in addition caricatured . . . : JDP interview with TL, July 5, 1968.

A first draft . . . : UVA.

465 Edmund Wilson wrote . . . : EW to JDP, Nov. 1, 1954, UVA.

As for the characters . . . : 14C, p. 607.

Many reviewers . . . : Granville Hicks, "Dos Passos—The Fruits of Disillusionment," *New Republic,* 131 (Sept. 27, 1954), p. 18; Harold Clurman, "Communists by Dos Passos," *Nation,* 179 (Oct. 9, 1954), p. 310.

Dos Passos contacted . . . : JDP to BB, Nov. 9, 1952, UVA.

466 He was so agitated . . . : JDP to BB, Nov. 9, 1952, UVA.

His new publishers worked hard . . . : Monroe Stearns to BB, Jan. 19, 1955, UVA.

467 After attempting to stem . . . : EDP to TL, Feb. 3, 1973; EDP, interview with TL, Sept. 6, 1973.

His trip during October . . . : JDP to Murphys, Sept. 30, 1954, HDC; 14C, p. 607; JDP to Edith Shay, Jan. 1, 1955, collection of Mrs. Robert Whelan.

" 'Directive,' " wrote Dos Passos . . . : "It's All for Our Own Good," press release from the Spadea Syndicate, Inc., Feb. 4, 1955, UVA; this piece was incorporated with changes into TIF, pp. 245–248.

With the lecture tour . . . : JDP to RSM, Jan. 18, 1955, Boston Athenaeum; JDP to Edith Shay, Jan. 25, 1955, collection of Mrs. Robert Whelan.

468 He labored to complete . . . : 14C, p. 608.

If it has a fault . . . : Dumas Malone, "While American History Was Marching On," *New York Times Book Review* (Feb. 10, 1957), p. 4.

But despite this . . . : 14C, p. 609.

"I'm tempted . . . ": 14C, p. 608.

469   Having just been among . . . : JDP to William Faulkner, Oct. 9; Oct. 31; Nov. 27, 1956, UVA.

CHAPTER THIRTY-TWO

470   Although a confirmed Republican . . . : 14C, p. 610.

471   Because of Dos Passos's interest . . . : JDP to RH, April 18, 1958, UVA.
      He was interested in the situation . . . : 14C, p. 614.
      In addition he proposed . . . : Allen Klots to TL, April 4, 1970.
      Union members, he found . . . : "What Union Members Have Been Writing Senator McClellan," *Reader's Digest*, 73 (Sept. 1958), pp. 25–32.
      At a dinner . . . : 14C, p. 572.
      "I wonder if . . . ": "Acceptance by John Dos Passos," *Proceedings of the American Academy of Arts and Letters and the National Institute of Arts and Letters*, Second Series, No. 8 (New York, 1958), p. 193.

472   It was only after . . . : Mr. and Mrs. Brodnax Cameron, interview with TL, July 9, 1971.
      Stearns feared that the book . . . : Monroe Stearns to BB, Jan. 19, 1955, UVA.
      "Ro's plans . . . " : UVA.
      Barker liked . . . : LeBaron Barker to JDP, July 30, 1956, UVA.

473   "*When he shall hear . . .* ": UVA.

474   Edmund Wilson recognized . . . : EW to JDP, April 13, 1958, EWC.
      "Perhaps I should . . . ": 14C, p. 617.
      "His reputation rests with his own . . . ": "Study of a Has-Been by John Dos Passos," *San Francisco Chronicle*, March 18, 1958, p. 27.
      Malcolm Cowley was . . . : "Success that Somehow Led to Failure," *New York Times Book Review*, April 13, 1958, pp. 4, 5, 45.

475   Dos Passos was not pleased . . . : 14C, p. 617; "The Art of Fiction," p. 158. Although published in 1969, the *Paris Review* interview with David Saunders took place in the early 1960s.
      After he, Elizabeth, and Lucy . . . : JDP to RH, Jan. 3, 1958, UVA.
      From mid-July . . . : BOM, pp. 62–100.

476   It provided him with material . . . : "Dream City in the Wilderness," *Reader's Digest*, 74 (April 1959), pp. 181–186.
      It was a relaxing . . . : Charles Mayo, interview with TL, July 30, 1975.
      In addition, as he wrote Robert Hillyer . . . :" 14C, p. 621.

477   The dramatic version of *U.S.A.* . . . : Information about the adaptation of *U.S.A.* and the disagreements surrounding it comes from: "The Complete Text of: 'USA' by John Dos Passos and Paul Shyre," *Theatre Arts*, 44 (June 1960), pp. 24–49; C. D. Williams, folder of papers dated from 1956–1963 relating to the episode.
      He discussed his involvement . . . : "Looking Back on 'U.S.A.,' " *New York Times*, Oct. 25, 1959, sec. 2, p. 5.

CHAPTER THIRTY-THREE

480   Mattresses were spread . . . : EDP to TL, Jan. 18, 1979.
      Dos Passos, in fact, was irritated . . . : 14C, p. 622.

481   *"Weighed down . . ."*: MC, p. 116.

482   Slim Martin . . . : Correspondence with DP is at UVA.

Dos Passos's material   . . . : Letters from Edwards Grant Taylor, the newspaper clipping about the death of Henry Bujalski, and materials about Adolph Fram's taxicab war are at UVA; JDP's earlier piece about Buckmaster is "Where Do We Go From Here?" *Life*, 22 (Jan. 27, 1947), pp. 95–96, for further information about Buckmaster's biography, see *Who's Who in America*, 30 (Chicago, 1958), p. 383.

483   Dos Passos got the idea . . . : UVA.

". . . A pad for indoor-outdoor . . . ": MC, pp. 494–496.

484   But the dark mood . . . : UVA; the speech was revised and published as "Contemporary Chronicles," *Carleton Miscellany*, 2 (Spring, 1961), pp. 25–29.

Discussing *Midcentury* . . . : Diggins, p. 248.

The tumultuous antiwar . . . : 14C, p. 643.

Before *Midcentury* was published . . . : 14C, p. 623.

485   Dos Passos's assessment . . . : Granville Hicks, "Of Radicals and Racketeers," *Saturday Review*, 44 (Feb. 25, 1961), pp. 25–26; Harry T. Moore, "Proud Men in an Age of Conformity," *New York Times Book Review*, Feb. 26, 1961, pp. 1, 51.

The two boys left them in Madrid . . . : EDP to TL, Oct. 15, 1979.

From the small town . . . : 14C, p. 623.

He had toyed with the idea . . . : JDP to BB, March 1, 1957, UVA.

486   The Cornell edition . . . : JDP to Robert Elias, letters between 1958 and 1961, Cornell University Libraries.

Also in 1961 . . . : JDP to RH, Oct. 21, 1961, UVA.

Its reception . . . : Arthur S. Link, "Mr. Wilson's War," *New York Times Book Review*, April 7, 1963, p. 41; S.L.A. Marshall," "What Happened Over Here," *Saturday Review*, 45 (Dec. 29, 1962), p. 42.

487   Amid patriotic banners . . . : Diggins, p. 8.

Then in August . . . : The description of the 1962 Brazilian trip is in BOM, pp. 101–205.

CHAPTER THIRTY-FOUR

491   "Your Protest . . . ": 14C, p. 624.

At that time Wilson had mentioned . . . : EWL, pp. 639, 642.

"For better or worse . . . ": "Please Mr. Rip Van Winkle, Wake Up Some More," *National Review*, 16 (Jan. 28, 1964), pp. 71–74.

When Wilson read . . . : EWL, pp. 643–644.

492   "I dont agree . . . ": 14C, p. 625; EWL, p. 645.

Dos Passos in his turn . . . : 14C, p. 626; EWL, p. 649.

Wilson told Dos Passos . . . : Dawn Powell to the Murphys, Aug. 9, 1964, HDC.

"Behind Goldwater are the new . . . ": "The Battle of San Francisco," *National Review*, 16 (July 28, 1964), pp. 640, 652.

Before the November elections . . . : "What Hope for Maintaining a Conservative Opposition?" *National Review*, 16 (Oct. 20, 1964), pp. 907–909.

493   "Your pronouncements . . .": EWL, p. 666; EW to JDP, Dec. 7, 1966, UVA.

He commented later that it . . . : SP, p. 412.

"Having been raised . . . ": MS in Choate School files; quoted in part in 14C, pp. 574–575.

494   Two months before . . . : JDP to RM, Nov. 21, 1965 and Feb. 2, 1966, UVA.

The whole trip, he wrote . . . : JDP to Mr. and Mrs. Broadnax Cameron, Aug. 8, 1965, collection of Broadnax Cameron.

495   Wilson had never been . . . : EWL, p. 665.

Lawson appreciated the gesture . . . : JHL to JDP, Jan. 19, 1967, JHLC.

While some critics . . . : "The Hidden Artist," *Time*, 88 (Nov. 18, 1966), p. 127; see also, for example, Granville Hicks, "John Dos Passos Reminisces," *Saturday Review*, 49 (Nov. 26, 1966), pp. 33–34.

"We've just completed one of the . . . ": JDP to EW, Aug. 30, 1966, EWC.

496   It was just such . . . : PS, pp. 380–381.

When Lovell Thompson asked . . . : 14C, p. 629.

497   The historian J. H. Plumb . . . : "Perspective," *Saturday Review*, 52 (May 31, 1969), p. 22.

CHAPTER THIRTY-FIVE

498   He described the gestation . . . : "What Makes a Novelist," *National Review*, 20 (Jan. 16, 1968), pp. 29–32.

499   The moment seemed to Poore typical . . . : DP, interview with TL, Aug. 25, 1971.

Renting a car in Albany . . . : JDP to LDP, Oct. 20, 1968.

"Where was that? . . . ": Frank Gado, ed., "An Interview with John Dos Passos," a special issue of *Idol*, the literary quarterly of Union College, vol. 45, 1969, pp. 5, 23.

500   In it, Dos Passos . . . : Foreword to Russell Kirk, *The American Cause* (Chicago, 1966), pp. 5–15.

"We are suffering . . . ": John Davenport, "Four Decades After Three Soldiers," *Washington Post Potomac Magazine*, May 5, 1968, p. 26.

Somewhat less pat . . . : 14C, pp. 631–632; 638–640.

501   He was not a racial bigot . . . : JDP, interview with TL, July 5, 1968; JDP to the Vestry of Cople Parish, Dec. 10, 1969, UVA.

And the previous spring . . . : JDP to ML, April 23, 1969, UVA.

502   When he died, he was no closer . . . : Aaron, *Writers on the Left*, p. 359.

The gigantic statues and their . . . : 14C, pp. 632–633.

In Chile his health worsened . . . : 14C, p. 637.

503   The event stirred him . . . : "On the Way to a Moon Landing," publication of the United States Information Service, undated.

The winter, however, had been . . . : 14C, p. 637.

During these last months . . . : 14C, pp. 640–641, 644.

504   On September 21 . . . ; Diary of HG, entries of Sept. 21 and Oct. 7, 1970.

EPILOGUE

506   But Dos Passos could also . . . : CE, pp. 13, 467, 434.

Acknowledgments
and Credits

To the many people whose friendship and aid were essential for the preparation of *The Fourteenth Chronicle*, I restate my thanks. That help was again crucial as I wrote this biography. I am indebted, further, to all those who provided me with information, materials, and on occasion room and board while I was preparing *A Twentieth Century Odyssey*.

I offer long overdue thanks to Professor Christopher Armitage and thank for their help Alice Auerbach, Edward B. Ayres, Mrs. Anne Taliaferro Bauer, Carleton Beals, Marion C. Belliveau, Professor John Britton, Peter and Donna Burr, Julia Sprigg Cameron, Dr. Dwight Cavanaugh, John Chamberlain, Joan Colebrook, Malcolm Cowley, Robert Coonrod, Mr. and Mrs. Lewis Dabney, Vera Dickey, Mr. and Mrs. Edwin Dickinson, Honoria Donnelly, Dr. Kenneth W. Duckett, Bertha Fairbanks, Mr. and Mrs. William Filby, Mrs. Horsley Gantt, Adelaide Lawson Gaylor, Eben and Phyllis Given, Dr. Peter Griffin, Mr. and Mrs. W. Fairfax Griffith, and Mrs. Walter Griffith.

Thanks are due as well to Lois Hazell, Professor Richard Kennedy, Elinor Langer, Kate Drain Lawson, Mandy Lawson, Sue Lawson, Professor James Leutze, Pierre Lostanlen, Germaine Lucas-Championnière, Archibald MacLeish, Captain and Mrs. Charles Mayo, Maurice Neville, Dr. Abraham Pollen, Reynolds Price, Donna Rhein, Donald Ogden Stewart, Professor Alan Wald, Adelaide Walker, Edward Weeks, William W. Whalen, Mrs. Robert Whelan, Elena Wilson, Rosalind Wilson, and Ella Winter.

I should like to express my appreciation for his encouragement to Professor Louis Rubin, and to Professors Lewis Leary and Arlin Turner for theirs.

Likewise, my thanks go to Lovell Thompson, without whose sage advice my work on John Dos Passos would not have gone far, and to Elisa Petrini, without whose editorial wisdom it would not have been satisfactorily completed. The research skills of Judith Brazinsky, Mark Lucas, and Gail St. John were extremely important, as were the typing—and sometimes editorial—skills of Joyce Bradshaw, Carol Griffith, and Joan Swann. I appreciate their intelligent help.

As always, it was a great pleasure to work in the Manuscripts Division of the Alderman Library of the University of Virginia at Charlottesville. To Ned Berkeley, Anne Freudenberg, Greg Johnson, and Mike Plunkett, my special thanks.

I am indebted, further, to the American Philosophical Society for a travel grant awarded me during 1974–1975, and to the University of North Carolina at Chapel Hill for a travel grant during 1975 and for a Kenan research leave during the fall of 1976.

Portions of this book appeared in somewhat different form in the following publications: *American Literature, Lost Generation Journal, New Republic,* and *Virginia Quarterly Review.*

Letters and other documents of John Dos Passos are quoted by permission of Elizabeth H. Dos Passos and by permission of those individuals or libraries whose collections are cited in the notes to the text. Letters written to me are quoted by permission of their authors. A piece by Robert Cantwell is quoted by permission of Mary Nelson and the University of Oregon Library; an unpublished letter of E. E. Cummings is quoted by permission of © Nancy T. Andrews, and Houghton Library, Harvard University; one of F. Scott Fitzgerald, by Frances Scott Fitzgerald Smith; one of Josephine Herbst, by Hilton Kramer and the Collection of American Literature, Beinecke Rare Book and Manuscript Library, Yale University; several of John Howard Lawson, by Mandy Lawson; one of Archibald MacLeish, by himself; one of Gerald Murphy, by Honoria Donnelly; ones of Charles A. Pearce and Bernice Baumgarten, by Harcourt Brace Jovanovich; and one of Gilbert Seldes, by Marion Seldes.

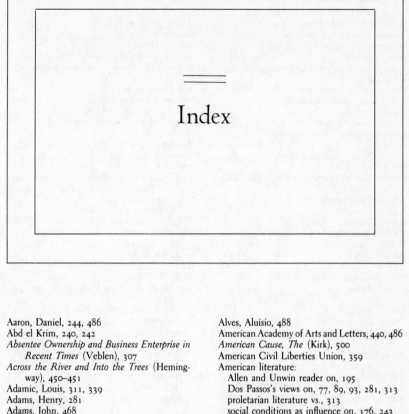

Index